# Direct Psychotherapy

**28 AMERICAN ORIGINALS**

VOLUME ONE

# Direct Psychotherapy

## 28 AMERICAN ORIGINALS

Edited by
**Ratibor-Ray M. Jurjevich**

 **University of Miami Press**
Coral Gables, Florida

We acknowledge permission to reprint copyright material for the following
chapters in these volumes. Chapter 20, "Reality Therapy," condensed and
modified from *Reality Therapy* by William Glasser, M.D. Copyright © 1965 by
William Glasser, M.D. Reprinted by permission of Harper & Row, Publishers,
Inc. Chapter 26, "Synanon," reprinted with permission of The Macmillan
Company from *The Tunnel Back: Synanon* by Lewis Yablonsky. Copyright ©
by Lewis Yablonsky, 1965. Chapter 28, "Recovery, Incorporated: Mental Health
Through Will Training," reprinted with permission of The Christopher Publishing
House from *Mental Health Through Will Training* by Abraham A. Low. Copy-
right © 1960.

# Contents

## VOLUME ONE

# Foreword

The treatment of neurotic disorders in the thirties, the forties, and the fifties has been characterized by a monolithic dependence on unverified "dynamic" principles, a complete dependence on the belief in, rather than the proof of, the efficacy of psychoanalytic methods of one kind or another, and a refusal to countenance the claims of any other kind of approach, whether symptom-oriented or not. Among the favorite shibboleths of that period were the denial of any kind of spontaneous remission, the insistence on the "return of the symptom" when purely symptom-oriented therapy was attempted, and the rigid adherence to some form of "symptom substitution" hypothesis for all nonanalytic forms of therapy. Most notable of all was that not only was there no proof for any of these beliefs, but no proof seemed to be required; all these beliefs were considered self-evident and taught in university departments of psychology and psychiatry without regard to the gradually accumulating evidence suggesting that in fact very little truth was attached to any of them.

Cremerius (1) demonstrated that many different types of treatment gave results equally as good as psychoanalysis and that recipients of all these types of treatment relapsed in about half of the cases within the next eight or ten years, almost regardless of type of treatment. Eysenck (2) and Levitt (5) demonstrated that spontaneous remission was the rule, rather than the exception, and that psychotherapy, whether analytic or not, did not produce better results than no treatment. Wolpe (6) showed that symptomatic therapy could produce strikingly good results in a very short time and that relapse or symptom-substitution did not follow. Followers of Skinner showed the promise of operant conditioning, even in areas where most psychiatrists had thrown in their hand (3). Behavior therapy, i.e., the application of the principles of modern learning theory to the treatment of neurotic conditions, suggested numerous new methods which are being widely investigated by psychiatrists and psychologists impatient with the all-too-frequent failures of orthodox methods (4). There has clearly been a thaw in the ideological freeze; the log jam that has been holding up progress for over thirty years is breaking up, and new and hitherto neglected ideas and methods are being looked at again from a less prejudiced point of view. It may be suggested that this development is all to the good; the substitution of competition for monopoly has obvious advantages that only those who benefit from the protection afforded by the monopoly would deny.

I would not claim that all the methods seeking recognition are good and useful, nor would I say that any of them are necessarily superior to those we have become accustomed to seeing practiced in hospitals and clinics. Some of these approaches are extremely unlikely to disprove the null hypothesis when compared with placebo treatment or no treatment at all.

This opinion, however, does not affect my welcome to the book as a whole. The existence of many warring theories and methods is a good thing in that it demonstrates both that the truth, the whole truth, is not yet known to us, and the even more important fact that where a choice has to be made it must be made on the basis of factual, experimental evidence. The reader may be bewildered by the plethora of views, ideas, methods, suggestions, claims, and counter-claims, but this bewilderment is a good thing if it leads him to ask for experimental proof and empirical support for any statements made. We may with advantage recall Hume's wise statement: "If we take in our hand any volume, let us ask, does it contain any abstract reasoning concerning quantity or number? No. Does it contain any experimental reasoning concerning matter of fact and existence? No. Commit it then to the flames; for it can contain nothing but sophistry and illusion." If there is much sophistry and illusion in this book, at least they will be apparent by comparison of one chapter with another; the monolithic climate of the past thirty years has successfully managed to obfuscate this important truth and hidden our ignorance under a veil of universal verbal agreement. The virtue of this book is to have given voice to the diversity of approaches; this very diversity makes it all the more difficult to overlook the need for empirical proof and quantitative evidence.

The importance of books like this one may be illustrated by reference to the well-known experimental studies of Ash, who showed that experimental subjects, when quizzed regarding matters of fact, such as whether one line was longer or shorter than another, would often fall in with the unanimous majority of experimenter's accomplices who gave the wrong answer. If even one other person could be found to break this unanimity, the spell was gone, and subjects would testify according to their actual beliefs. So also in respect to psychotherapy: the very fact that students of the subject become aware of the lack of agreement, the absence of unanimity, on the question of the virtue of "insight"-oriented "uncovering" types of therapy and learn about the facts regarding symptom-oriented types of treatment will make them more able to form their own independent opinions based on fact and experiment rather than on belief and supposition. Even the best teacher is only too likely to be a propagandist in his own cause; books like this one destroy the basis of such propaganda by informing the reader of the wide variety of different approaches, and also of the lack of factual information which would help him to come to a rational opinion. If the reader comes away from reading this book with the firm resolve never to believe another assertion in this field which is not backed by hard evidence, the editor will have earned our everlasting gratitude!

HANS J. EYSENCK, PH.D., D.SC.
*Professor of Psychology*
*(Institute of Psychiatry)*
*University of London*

## REFERENCES

1. Cremerius, J. *Die Beurteilung des Behandlungserfolges in der Psychotherapie.* Berlin: Springer-Verlag, 1962.
2. Eysenck, H.J. The effects of psychotherapy. In H. J. Eysenck (Ed.) *Handbook of abnormal psychology.* New York: Basic Books, 1960.
3. Eysenck, H.J. (Ed.) *Experiments in behaviour therapy.* New York: Pergamon Press, 1964.
4. Eysenck, H.J., & S. Rachman. *The causes and cures of neurosis.* San Diego: R.R. Knapp, 1965.
5. Levitt, E.E. Psychotherapy with children: a further evaluation. *Behav. Res. Ther.,* 1963, 1, 45–51.
6. Wolpe, J. *Psychotherapy by reciprocal inhibition.* Stanford University Press, 1958.

# Acknowledgments

I am obligated to many friends and co-workers, without whose aid I would hardly have been able to complete *Direct Psychotherapy: 28 American Originals*. My appreciation concerns participants and helpers on both the present two volumes of the *28 American Originals* and a forthcoming volume, *Developments on Four Continents*.

My gratitude goes first to the contributors or their representatives for their cooperativeness.

The work on *Direct Psychotherapy: 28 American Originals* was carried out and practically finished while I served as the Chief Psychologist, Psychiatric Clinic, Lowry Air Force Base. Colonel Sidney M. Bashore, M.D., Commander of the 3415 Dispensary, Lowry Air Force Base, Denver, Colorado, and my immediate chiefs, Major Yale L. Klugman, M.D., and later Captain James K. Medelman, M.D., the chiefs of the Psychiatric Clinic, showed ample understanding and provided administrative and moral support for the undertaking.

Mrs. Evelyn Ferber, Secretary of the Psychiatric Clinic, displayed a willingness to work beyond the call of duty and played an essential role in the preparatory and later stages of the book. Mrs. Annabelle Torre continued her helpful support of the project after resuming her duties as secretary of the clinic. Airmen Terry "Kim" Marriner and George DePeyster were faithful and willing helpers in the first stages of the enterprise, and Darrel D. Naasz, James E. Sidey, James Soethe, and William Watson were helpful in the final labors of the *Direct Psychotherapy*. My wife, Vera, helped on many occasions in various chores. Her greatest help, of course, was in relinquishing her husband's company during the many hours required by *Direct Psychotherapy*.

I was very fortunate in being able to utilize the wisdom, experience, and support of Professors O. H. Mowrer, Frederick C. Thorne, John Vayhinger, and Bernard Spilka at various stages of the work. Any shortcomings in its plan and execution must necessarily be considered my own.

Mr. Donald F. Krill, M.S.W., assisted in anglicizing an earlier draft of the introduction and has contributed many valuable points, though without wishing to be identified with all the ideas I have expressed here.

The articles written by authors of foreign background have been improved greatly in their style through the capable editing of Mrs. Marlene Chambers, who has taught writing and published articles in various fields.

I acknowledge the kind permission of the following publishers and authors to quote from the books and articles under their copyrights: Academy of Religion and Mental Health; *American Journal of Psychiatry;* Aldine; George Braziller, Inc.; Professor Rudolph Dreikurs, M.D.; Professor Henri F. Ellenberger, M.D.; Free Press of Glencoe; Grune and Stratton; *Journal of Clinical Psychology; Journal of Nervous and Mental Disease;* J. B. Lippincott Co.; Professor Jules Masserman, M.D.; J. A. M. Meerloo, M.D.; Professor Martin Orne, Ph.D.; Philosophical Library; *Psychoanalytic Review; Science;* and the University of Chicago Press.

# Introduction

Critics of the United States have spoken badly of many an American trait, institution, and cultural attitude, but none of them has ever disparaged the pioneering spirit of Americans. A contemporary Spanish philosopher has even spoken reverently of Americans as a new and superior cultural breed, able to improvise and to dare adventures of which tradition-bound people are incapable.

The early American pioneers abandoned security and struck out upon new paths apart from established society. They suffered isolation and deprivation, entered new territories, and in the long run enriched a society which often considered them inferior.

The psychotherapists presenting their methods in this volume showed genuine pioneering spirit in their profession. Despite the disdain of a psychoanalytic Establishment that considered their efforts "superficial," these psychotherapists sought to open new frontiers in helping patients stabilize their personalities and free themselves from disturbances of emotion and character. Some of them had personal contact with Freudian psychoanalysis and found it either useless or harmful. Mowrer (44) had three analyses with three different analysts, and none did him any good; his experience only delayed the discovery

1

of a more potent cure which he finally embodied in Integrity Therapy. In this respect Mowrer was preceded by the grand old man of American psychology, Boring (7), who found psychoanalysis to be an exercise in futility.

Ellis (17) entered the field of psychotherapy with the assurance proper to a trained psychoanalyst, only to learn that it was an ineffective way of helping patients. He next tried "psychoanalytically oriented" therapy and found it more beneficial to patients than the orthodox Freudian method. By engaging patients in an active struggle with their handicapping emotions and directing them away from compulsive dwelling on past events, Ellis finally evolved Rational-Emotive psychotherapy. With it he has been achieving far more significant improvements than with the passive methods, allegedly deepest therapy, in which he was trained. Ellis' experience is paralleled by Campbell's (9) disillusionment with Freudian psychoanalysis. After undergoing vigorous indoctrination under the guise of personal and control analyses, Campbell treated more than thirty patients and found no improvement in them. Two of them showed even definite signs of having been harmed by the procedure that was acclaimed as the most effective psychotherapeutic method. His realization that he had been indoctrinated in a subtle fashion is summed up in the title of his book, *Induced Delusions: The Psychopathy of Freudism.*

Anderson (4), similarly trained in two psychoanalytic agencies, found the method theoretically misleading and therapeutically unproductive and developed better approaches by going "beyond Freud" (3) to Assumption-Centered Psychotherapy. With the temerity worthy of a pioneer, Glasser (24) realized early in his training that the Freudian method which was solemnly delivered to him as *the* psychotherapy was hindering instead of promoting the recovery of patients in his charge. Together with his teacher, Dr. G. L. Harrington, he developed Reality Therapy.

Early in his career as a psychologist, Salter (56) found Freud's method inefficient and evolved a direct method of treatment along Pavlovian lines, his Conditioned Reflex Therapy (57). E. Lakin Phillips (48) was incensed at the harm done patients in clinics by slavish regard for psychoanalytic precepts. His search for a better psychotherapy finally resulted in the Assertion-Structured Therapy. Storrow (65) observed that the ritual of insight gathering and the assumed causation real or fantasied traumas have in psychological abnormalities were used as resistance by patients. As a psychiatrist, he considered it his task to get his patients to cope better with life problems rather than to provide excuses for them for their current malfunctioning, and he evolved the Verbal Behavior Therapy.

Many other physicians, psychologists, and intelligent laymen have written about the deleterious effects of the Freudian method, of the threat it offers to the psyche and to the capacity for coping with the world. Some titles may indicate the kind of criticism of psychoanalytic concepts and treatment provided in the books, and a partial list may also suggest the massiveness of opposition to the Establishment: K. Dunlap, *Mysticism, Freudianism and Scientific Psychology* (15); H. Egyedi, *Die Irrtümer der Psychoanalyse. Eine Irrlehre mit einem genialen Kern* (*The Blunders of Psychoanalysis: A Mistaken Theory with a Superb Core*) (16); A. Wohlgemuth, *Critical Examination of Psychoanalysis* (69); M. Harrington, *Wish Hunting in the Unconscious* (27); E. Ludwig, *Doctor Freud: An Analysis and a Warning* (39); R. Allers, *The Successful Error: A Critical Study of Freudian Psychoanalysis* (2); C. H. Campbell, *Induced Delusions: The Psychopathy of Freudism* (9); A. Salter, *The Case Against Psychoanalysis* (56); R. T. La Pierre, *The Freudian Ethic* (35); H. K. Wells, *The Failure of Psychoanalysis: From Freud to Fromm* (68); M. Natenberg, *Freudian Psycho-Antics: Fact and Fraud in Psychoanalysis* (47); P. Bailey, *Sigmund the Unserene: A Tragedy in Three Acts* (5); S. Rachman (Ed.), *Critical Essays on Psychoanalysis* (52); E. R. Pinckney and C. Pinckney, *The Fallacy of Freud and Psychoanalysis* (49); H. K. Johnson, *Psychoanalysis—A Critique* (31); and many writings of Jung, Adler, Horney, Eysenck, and others.

Impressed by the riches of incisive observations and negative evaluations, I gathered them into a four volume "Integrated Anthology of Criticism: The Hoax of Freudism; Freud's Non-Science; The Pseudo-religion of Freudism; Freudism and Christianity: Irreconcilable Adversaries." I hope they will soon be in the hands of readers.

It is amazing that in spite of such extensive criticism the theory and practice of psychoanalysis could still remain dominant in a scientific community. The American pioneers described in the two volumes of this book had difficulty gaining a hearing and maintaining their professional self-respect in the face of opposition by many recognized leaders in psychiatry and clinical psychology.

The blunt approach of this introduction is intended to point to psychoanalytic inadequacies and distortions and to contribute to the readiness in the psychotherapeutic community to consider the newer methods of psychological treatment offered in these volumes. For viewing respectfully and with interest other psychological and psychotherapeutic systems, some mental health professionals need to throw off their Freudian blinders and inspect without bias the theoretical and technical approaches of non-Freudian thinkers. "We find no new tools," Bacon warned us, "because we take some venerable but questionable proposition as an indubitable starting point." The physicians did not start scrubbing their hands after dissecting cadavers, in spite of numerous deaths of women at childbirth, until Semmelweis demonstrated a new way of looking at obstetric practices. The psychotherapy field is replete with superstitions and unvalidated assumptions. It needs demythologizing at this time. In the States, this amounts to de-Freudianizing it. Bindra, writing in the *Canadian Journal of Psychology* in 1970 and quoted in *Medical World News,* Sept. 24, 1971, expresses well the verdict on the Freudian system which is implied by most of the papers in this book: "available research suggests that the psychodynamic approach, like many other ideas in the history of science, has turned out to be a 'wrong lead.'"


## PSYCHOANALYSIS AS A THERAPEUTIC FAILURE

The most damaging criticism of Freudism, as far as psychotherapists are concerned, is that it often fails as psychotherapy. Low (38) surveys the poor showing in some of the earlier studies. Eysenck (19) provides evidence that psychoanalysis does not prove in statistical evaluations any better than the remission rates of spontaneous recovery, in spite of hundreds of hours invested by the patients and thousands of dollars spent. This fact is one of the problems of psychoanalysis: the Freudian treatment, eighty years after its launching, is still being sold to patients on the basis of the analyst's faith in it. An expensive remedy seems hardly worthwhile if its objective benefits are not easily recognizable.

Of course, there is no shortage of Freudian self-praise. The psychoanalysts have established their brand of treatment as most "profound," "radical," "deep-going," "reconstructive." Other treatments are "superficial," "symptomatic" (an offensive term), only "reparative," "supportive." Many members of the medical and allied professions have accepted such claims uncritically. I disagree with the superiority implied by Freudians for their therapy and their disparagement of other psychotherapeutic approaches as less beneficial to the patient. I am convinced that if the non-Freudian approaches offered in this text are not more effective than psychoanalysis they are at least less likely to lead to the vast expenditures of time and money.

The empirical validation of psychoanalysis, when we discard the statements of Freudians themselves and some of their patients, does not offer much more hopeful a picture than statistical consideration. Beside the failures of the analyses of Wortis (70) with Freud, of Campbell (9) and Natenberg (47) with recognized psychoanalysts, of Mowrer (44) with Freud's pupil Sachs and two other well-trained analysts, and of Boring (7) with a renowned teacher of psychoanalysis, the professional literature contains records of futile treatment and corrosion of families and individuals (39,45,49).

These disappointments as to the psychotherapeutic value of psychoanalysis are not surprising. Freud himself did not benefit by it. He carried out for more than two years a self-analysis that his disciples hailed as equivalent to the analysis with an analyst. Yet, after it, Freud was as prone to neurotic weakness as before. The main benefit he derived from his analysis was literary: he wrote of his findings in several of his early books. His self-analysis only strengthened his confidence in his theories and enabled him to be more assertive in recommending his suggestions to his patients and readers.

The preceding paragraph touches upon what is perhaps one of the crucial considerations in understanding psychoanalysis as a failure in psychotherapy. Neither before nor after his analysis was Freud primarily interested in psychotherapy. By his intimate motivations he was no physician at all. His deep needs were not philanthropically oriented as they are in good physicians. His ambitions led him toward research, writing, and scientific recognition rather than service to sick human beings. In one of his letters to Fliess, Freud speaks of his patients as his victims and his tormentors. In another, he writes of his painful disinterest in a treatise on a children's disease which he was obligated to write, and which prevented him from continuing work on his favorite psychological speculations. In the Thirties, Freud told Wortis that he much preferred students to neurotics in analysis.

## TRADITIONAL SUPERSTITIONS REGARDING PSYCHOTHERAPY

Skinner (60) relates an incident with pigeons which has definite analogical implications for understanding the current misperceptions about psychotherapy. The pigeons were left overnight with Skinner's reinforcement machine, which delivered food pellets intermittently, irrespective of the pigeon's actions. When the experimenter entered the room in the morning, he found the pigeons in all sorts of postures. Some held one wing down, others twisted their necks, some stood on one leg. Apparently they were thus attempting to force the machine to yield food as it had done at some earlier moments during the night when they happened to exhibit this particular behavior. Dumb birds, we might say. But we should be in no haste to laugh at them. Supposedly intelligent men show similar superstitions. Psychoanalysis is a case in point.

Freud was working with disturbances for which medical treatment was unknown. Some disturbances yielded to hypnosis, some did not; some were cured by suggestions, others were not; some grew better spontaneously, others grew worse. Some doctors used Burq's "esthesiogénie," applying metals to the hysterically paralyzed tissues, with satisfying results; other doctors read only the influence of suggestion in the procedure. Freud used the much vaunted Erb's apparatus for electrical stimulation and eventually discarded it, interpreting its sporadic success as based on suggestion. Initiating what he imagined to be a suggestion-free procedure, Freud obtained some good results and evolved a routine according to what seemed to be the conditions for success: the couch; the anonymity of the therapist; "free" association; hours upon hours of outpourings in practically interminable therapy; exhaustive search for sexual and other childhood traumas to obtain "insights"; manipulating transference; casting the patient's statements in the molds of theoretical fancies the suggestiveness of which Freud had tried on himself and other subjects previously. The routine grew more complex by the day, and the disciples were overwhelmed by the intricacies of the procedures. They remained oblivious to anything but the field circumscribed by the doctrine. The invisible reinforcing machine of spontaneous remission and suggestion continued to yield cures intermittently, and the Freudians ascribed them to their ritual. They kept stubbornly to it. The pigeons could not come to the simple conclusion that their particular tricks were illusory even though they saw other pigeons obtaining the pellets by different tricks. They held to the belief in the superiority of their own procedure.

Other therapists obtained good results without the couch. Some faced the patient and conversed with him, and some improvements were evident as well as failures. Some therapists discarded the interminable diggings into the past; some stopped searching for insights regarding early traumas and concentrated on a better functioning in the present and a more hopeful outlook to the future as principal curative procedures, and they obtained results no worse than those brought about by the orthodox Freudian method. Some deliberately disregarded the Freudian doctrines of transference and resistance and concentrated on immediate feelings, and still some patients improved while others did not. Some therapists used quite different interpretations from those believed true by Freudians, and the patient did not seem to find these less true and less helpful than "deep" psychoanalytic readings into the psyche. The libido and the Oedipus complex, castration fears and latent homosexuality, anal and oral fixations, and all the peculiar paraphernalia of Freudism were thrown out by some therapists, and still patients found their way to recovery and thanked the therapist's wisdom for it. Some therapists charged their patients nothing, and the patients benefited from therapy no less than those paying thousands of dollars for Freudian treatments.

In spite of these contradictions to their "psychodynamic" assertions, the Freudians remained steadfast by their formulas. They were unshaken even when, a few years ago, an officially appointed committee of the American Psychoanalytic Association organized a wide-scale research project on the benefits of psychoanalysis only to suppress the report when it was found that the results were meager and damaging. Yet many adherents went on teaching Freudian precepts as "psychoanalytic science" in medical schools, universities, and institutes. They stifled other potentially more efficacious approaches by their assertions that psychoanalysis and the "psychodynamic" psychotherapies are treatment par excellence, everything else being almost inconsequential.

## A MASSIVE DOMINANCE OF PROFESSIONALS AND HARM TO PATIENTS

It is impossible at this stage of our relative ignorance about psychotherapy to document the damage done by the dominance of Freudian precepts in what is ambiguously called the field of mental health. One can only speak on the basis of personal convictions and insights gained from clinical experience. The therapists contributing to these volumes testify indirectly to the futility of Freudian therapy by having developed treatments apart from the prevalent model in the States at this period. I would merely offer two of my own experiences with misleading Freudian presuppositions. These experiences represent some of the stepping stones toward my definitive identification with non-Freudian, direct, and behavior psychotherapies. The cases also exemplify some of the orientations to psychotherapy which have led to innovations described by the contributors in this book.

A foreign-born woman in her thirties was referred to me after the psychiatrist whom she had been seeing for a year left the city. He was a kind, quiet, conscientious man. She related to me in a friendly uninhibited way, and the transition from one therapist to another seemed accomplished successfully, partly because the new therapist was also a "foreigner." I felt as if she were continuing, without appreciable interruption, the healing process which, I imagined, was initiated in so many interviews with the previous therapist. She spoke of her depressions, of pains in her abdomen, of headaches, of long-standing emotional coldness between her and her husband. She seemed worried about her inability to live with him in an unfriendly relationship or move toward a divorce. I mostly listened in the first session, though I had understood her situation sufficiently to say at the end of the interview, "I imagine that you are coming to see that the unpleasant relationship with your husband is one of the sources of your unhappy feelings. Once you make the decision either to break up the marriage or work toward improving it, you might get to feel less uneasy." She suddenly straightened up in the chair, became agitated and flushed in the face, and shot back angrily and fearfully: "How do you expect me to get hold of this situation so quickly? That's impossible. I can't decide on things so quickly." Her voice trailed off and angry tears appeared as she struggled with the imagined threat from her "unsympathetic" therapist. I was taken aback by my misjudgment of what this woman wanted from therapy. With other patients, I usually handled therapy as a collaborative problem-solving, but apparently the woman before me wished to maintain her painful situation, extracting an additional benefit in the sympathetic attention of a male therapist.

I reassured her only partially: "I am sorry that I gave you the wrong impression. I did not say that you have to reach a solution next week or next month: I implied only that you will decide when you want to start getting yourself off the hook which you feel is hurting you." She gave me a reproachful glance upon leaving. Apparently she was disappointed, comparing me unfavorably with her former therapist whose interviews made her "feel better afterwards."

In the following interviews, what she called her "hypochondriacal complaints" became worse. There was an almost permanent headache on one side, and she feared a brain tumor. I agreed with her idea of obtaining a medical checkup; when she did, no organic cause was found. "This might make it easier for you, for you will be less worried about health and freer to look for the emotions which are leading to your uneasiness," I told her, only to discover I had said the wrong thing again. She gazed at me sideways and sighed. Taking the warning light into account, I let her talk of innocuous matters.

Some of her history was obtained in the next two or three interviews. She was the younger of two siblings. Her mother preferred her to the older sister, for the patient was quiet and compliant. Her mother used the patient's good manners and good marks when scolding the older daughter. The patient played with dolls, alone, did not make friends in school, spent time reading. Once, however, she got in such a rage with her sister that she chased her with a knife. That was the worst thing she remembered doing in her childhood. Then at fourteen came the big shock of her life: her parents were divorced. She lived alternately with her mother and father, both of whom had remarried shortly after the divorce. She left school, worked as a seamstress, joined a military organization from which she was later discharged for anxiety reaction. A romance with an older man broke up over religious differences, and later she married her present husband "for security." Things went wrong from the beginning: although married for the second time, he was sexually clumsy and began the first intercourse without preparation, leaving her frustrated when he turned his back to her and fell asleep. Her hatred and contempt of him had remained at a constant level throughout ten years of marriage. She complained of his limited interest, his self-centeredness, and his lack of warmth.

If I had seen her a few years earlier, the two of us would have had a royal time hunting all possible insights about how her past was determining her present. She was intelligent, literate, and sensitive; such a hunt would have been quite a lot of fun, "delightful brainpicking," as Ellis (18, p. 5) calls it. At that earlier time I was awed by so-called mental illness as an insidious process of early traumas leading to inevitable personality "sickness." In the course of time, though, I had largely liberated myself from the medical model of psychopathology and had begun to see the "illness" essentially as a refusal to take responsibility for oneself and others.

In the sixth interview, I tried again to lead her toward finding her role in her troubles. I consistently led her to "objective reviewing" of her stress, as Alexander (1) calls it. I asked how she was responding to her husband. She told how she avoided any physical contact with him, condescending to intercourse with him every few weeks at his insistence. There was nothing interesting she could talk to him about, nor did she think it would do any good to bring him to talk with the therapist. I rejoined with calculated tactlessness, "I guess he is as discouraged by your rejection as you are by his." She appeared pained by such brashness. After a pause of about two minutes, she said, "I do not know what to do." She seemed to say this more in compliance with the demands implied by me than because she wished to do anything. "As we go along," I continued, "you might consider what you might do to make things less unpleasant for the two of you. You might also want to join the group of married couples with whom I am working. They can help you, and you can help them."

The patient did not appear for the next interview. One hour later, she called to tell the secretary that she had not slept well the night before, that she had taken a nap at noon and overslept. She felt, anyway, that the doctor was not helping her, and she would not see him any more. She inquired about whether she could see some other therapist.

If this case had occurred while I was under the influence of psychoanalytic precepts in therapy, I would have felt guilty of a technical mistake, of mismanaging the situation, of hurting the patient's interests. Expecting such an unpleasant reaction in myself, I would not have dared displease the patient. But having discarded the accumulation of "insights," even emotional ones, as the primary method of psychotherapy and considering the frank confrontation of the patient with the implications of the present situation as the main therapeutic agent, I felt only slightly uneasy about the situation. A probable source of my assurance lay in my having tested my psychotherapeutic approach and found it efficacious in a controlled study with fourteen severely maladapted adolescent girls (33). I felt that, in the long run, the patient had been brought closer to an efficient response to her situation, though she currently rejected it, than if she had spent months musing over her troubles as if she had nothing to do with their occurrence. Like her previous therapist, who had thoroughly absorbed his psychoanalytically oriented training and never departed from it in his subsequent practice, I could have kept the patient by passively sympathizing with her. (After all, priests have for centuries heard futile, basically insincere confessions but have never made a pronouncement that such pretenses of repentance are an efficient method for the care of souls.) Such practice seems to me to be an abuse of the professional role and a reinforcement of the dependency and masochistic pathology out of which the therapist is supposed to lead the patient; it is a failure of therapeutic responsibility and an unethical practice, even though it might not be listed as such in official codes. If a physician did not warn a patient about the harmful effects of smoking, a poorly balanced diet, or loss of sleep, he would be failing in his duty. No lesser failure is committed by a psychotherapist who sees the effects of emotional misdevelopments but only continues to listen to the patient instead of actively offering help in the struggle against such pathogenic habits. And yet this failure is what can be expected to happen in "permissive," nondirective, or interminable therapies and psychoanalyses.[1]

No wonder then that a woman psychologist, perplexed with anxiety over a program she had set up in a company, would tell Ellis (18, p. 167), "I think I've learned more in these three sessions with you than I did in my whole four years of analysis." in his article (see Ellis, Vol. One, p. 295) Ellis described another case successfully treated in twenty-nine sessions, after four and a half years of time spent in psychoanalysis.

Lazarus (36) reports the treatment of a claustrophobic 17-year-old girl who had been treated by psychoanalysis for two and a half years without any benefit in her condition. Treated by desensitization therapy in thirty-eight sessions over two months, she obtained enough mastery over her emotional reactions that therapy could be discontinued.

I remember the futility of "treating" one of my early patients, a case in which my inactivity led to definite therapeutic failure. I let this rigid, repressed, middle-aged man ramble along with phobic complaints and innocuous material. I assumed a "permissive" role, letting him use the therapy and myself in his own way. After about twenty-five interviews of struggling against his repression of anything that happened

---

[1] One of the psychoanalytic reformers, Alexander, expresses a similar view: "In general, of course, the present is always determined by the past; still, many contemporary analysts believe that there is an unwarranted neglect of actual life circumstances. The patient comes to the therapist when he is at the end of his rope, so entangled in emotional problems that he feels he must have help; the analyst should never allow the patient to forget that he came to him to resolve these problems. The interest in the past history at the expense of the present is a residue of the historical period when research in personality dynamics was of necessity a prerequisite for developing a rational treatment method." Alexander and Selesnick quote Sandor Rado's comments: " 'The patient must learn to view life, himself, and others in terms of opportunities and responsibilities. . . . Even when the biological material on hand reaches far into the past, interpretation must always begin and end with the patient's present life performance, his present adaptive task. The significance of this rule cannot be overstated. . . . The goal of both Rado and Alexander is the same: to minimize the danger of encouraging undue regression and evasion of the current adaptive tasks.' " (1, pp. 326–329)

before his twelfth year, he described his early fear that his grandmother would not be at home when he returned from grade school. He told of running to check whether she had disappeared as his mother and father had when he was three years old. At last, I thought, we had reached an insight about his agoraphobia and generalized anxiety. In the next interview, he appeared unusually jubilant about something. He hit the desk with his hand and beamed: "I've licked it, by golly!" I looked up, thrilled by the miraculous effects of insight that I imagined had been obtained in the previous session. The patient continued: "I can now take tranquilizers without feeling guilty and inferior about it." I sagged in my chair, and so did my respect for therapeutic effects of insights.

When I asked this patient how things were at home, he would deny any unpleasantness there. The therapy was discontinued after forty interviews, and I believed I had helped him toward being less neurotic. Then, six months later, the patient's wife called. She sounded very upset on the telephone. She described her husband as a regular household tyrant. His older son had grown into a disturbed young man under his father's rejection and criticism and was failing in school. The wife was close to a breakdown, unable to tolerate her husband's moods and irritations any longer. She wanted a divorce. His tensions had made him practically impotent, but he blamed her "loose" vagina for his failures.

Obviously, in my permissiveness and passivity I had failed to help this patient in the matters important to him. Were I to meet such a patient again, having since discarded the dominant views of American Freudianized therapy, I would attempt to overcome his evasiveness through contacts with the wife and possibly the son, by confronting him with his self-deceptions, by suggesting that he might want to discontinue therapy since he avoids grappling with any significant issues, or by any other method suitable to induce him either to struggle with his problems or to quit wasting his own time and mine.

Other therapists participating in this book express similar disagreement with the psychoanalytic routine. The examples of the little boy Aaron, of the Veterans Administration hospital patient Roy, and others described by Dr. Glasser in his paper (see Glasser, Vol. Two, p. 562) amply illustrate the failures of a passive, psychoanalytically based, uninvolved role for the therapist.

Anderson (Vol. One, p. 257) points out to the colleague who consulted her on the case of the passive-aggressive, if not paranoid, nun, that he was not treating her, i.e., moving her toward the solution of her problems, but was merely being used to gratify an immature woman's need for attention. Cain (Vol. Two, p. 611), in reaction to the prevalent emasculation, softness, and self-seeking of our culture, opposes the Freudian position about what is therapeutic: "We are concerned with solving problems, not learning how to live with them."

Mowrer (46) and Mainord (Vol. One, p. 129) recommend a de-emphasis on emotions in therapy and a stress on actual behavior. They warn against making the patient comfortable instead of leading him to better behavior. Several other writers in *Morality and Mental Health* (45) reveal a similar emphasis. Storrow (Vol. One, p. 67) tries to turn his patient's fixations on self-pity toward an active struggle with the problems, toward the realization that his own behavior is bringing about his difficulties, just as I did with the patient who sought to avoid the responsibility for her own life. Menninger has noted "the accusations of unsympathetic outsiders who allege that what certain patients want is not cure but treatment and that what some psychoanalysts want to do is to treat rather than to cure" (42, p. 110).

I experienced another instance of the subtle influence of psychoanalytic views upon clinical practice when I took part in a staff meeting of a large mental health clinic. Psychologists, psychiatrists, and social workers were about equally represented among the eight staff members. A psychologist reported the case of an 11-year-old boy who had been referred to the clinic for evaluation and help because of persistent fighting with other children on the school playground and in the neighborhood. He had tried to join the games of older boys but was involved in many fights with them, too. He settled into the role of a sullen loner and a bully. The psychologist, who had worked with delinquent youngsters in the past, reported that the behavioral and verbal expressions of the boy in the testing period left no doubt that a serious character disorder was in the making. The social worker who had interviewed the parents described them as a suburban couple, both working full time, social climbers with only superficial contact with the boy. They were annoyed that their son cast a shadow on their social image. The mother, was, as is often the case in such circumstances, domineering, demanding, efficient, and cold. The father was withdrawn, taking a back seat and failing to assume the role of a supportive male adult to the boy. The parents had expressed some interest in doing something about their son.

In view of the chronic shortage of time at the clinic, the psychologist, who was not a Freudian enthusiast, recommended that a few interviews be held with the father. The plan would be to bring him around to see that he was letting the boy down, that his son could develop into a juvenile delinquent unless he were drawn into a closer and more active relationship with his father. Even as the psychologist outlined this plan, some staff members expressed dismay. After a short discussion, it was decided not to go further into the case except to send a report to the school principal and to see if the boy would get into worse troubles.

Why did such a negligent decision come about? In the same meeting, less serious cases were assigned continuing professional attention; the lack of staff time was not the explanation. The recommendations of the psychologist were generally accepted as guidelines for other cases, so rejection of the psychologist could not have been the explanation either. The most feasible explanation was that the clinical thinking of the dominant staff members was too deeply steeped in Freudian concepts. They "knew" without deliberation that any common-sense intervention would be useless in the case of a predelinquent boy. They were certain that the emotional forces were so formidable that only long, deep therapy would be of any use. The psychologist, not sharing the belief in Freudian lore, had hoped that there might be enough power of reason left in this disturbed family to overcome its sickness. But Freud has said "it is common sense which produces all the ills we have to cure" (70, p. 18).

Ellis has observed that the "depth-centered prejudices" keep the psychoanalytically trained professionals blind to what is "under their noses" (18, p. 174). Anderson (Vol. One, p. 257) gives examples to show how therapists become blinded by their training. Phillips (48, pp. 24–28) provides several illustrations of how psychoanalytically trained workers in mental health clinics harm both children and parents by wearing the Freudian blinders provided by their instructors: they disregard everyday problems and reactions, discard the patient's reality concerns as "superficial," transpose everything into some mystical "deep" pathology, refuse to give advice which the troubled parents seek in order to start correcting their blunders. They ask the question why, which can be answered only indecisively, and do not ask more practically important questions: How (the patient produces his troubles) and what (attitudes and situations bring about the troublesome symptoms). Smith (61, p. 122) describes how "Freudian-oriented colleagues advised strongly against the patient revealing her transgression to her husband" in Integrity Therapy—a procedure which had a dramatic improvement effect in the treatment of his hysterical patient. His colleagues were therapeutically wrong exactly because they were in theoretical accord with dominant Freudian beliefs.

Post (51) proposes a useful countertherapy for patients who have been overtreated in Freudian therapies: to put a lid on the id. This is done by deliberate neglect of the pathological and concentration on the healthy interests, goals, and tasks presently facing the patient.

Post describes a 34-year-old woman who had been "treated" for 8 years by five therapists (three of whom were in training at the time). Trying to be admitted to the hospital on an emergency basis, she revealed that she had been well indoctrinated by the prevalent "psychoanalytically oriented" trends. She reported: "I have no sense of identity because my mother has always considered me an extension of herself. . . . Because of crucial events at the age of three I want to go to bed with my father and kill my mother." She had difficulty "establishing meaningful heterosexual relationships." "I have discovered that my sexuality has been transferred from the appropriate place to my mouth. I learned that when I developed positive feelings for my therapist and told him 'I could eat you up' " (51, p. 475).

In spite of this enlightening treatment, she could not concentrate on current difficulties and always reverted to some similar experience in her childhood, such as "sibling rivalry." Post helped her deal with current problems, but continued to act the "village idiot" when she reverted to her Freudian jargon.

Another patient whom Post tried to extricate from the cobwebs of "psychodynamic" practices was a 23-year-old man who had spent 6 years in a psychoanalytically oriented private hospital. The referral note said that he felt very worried about his homosexual tendencies and about his sexual desires for his mother. Apparently he had been made into the proper model of psychopathology so that he could presumably be cured of it. He, too, had been steeped in the Freudian psychomythological categories. As with other patients, part of the Freudian cure was to imbue him with the notions of his "therapist." "It was implicit and the patient later confirmed this, that the therapist not only had not attempted to help the patient suppress these feelings but had encouraged their elaboration. The patient later complained that the doctor seemed only interested in sex and didn't seem very interested when he spoke about work" (51, p. 478).

The patient spoke blandly of masturbation as one of his recreational pursuits and talked of various colors and shapes of breasts. When the new therapist asked him why he spoke this way, he explained: "Aren't you supposed to say everything that comes to your mind?"

The therapist countered the patient's Freudian indoctrination and instructed the nurses in the day room not to respond to his talk about homosexuality but to show an interest in his future plans for employment and outside adjustment.

Post points to the ego deterioration in these patients, the "hypochondria of the mind" as Schmideberg called it, which had passed for therapy. They were "so caught up in the free association that they were unable to consider current difficulties, speaking and behaving as if the normal censorship processes were no longer effective" (51, p. 480). He notes that with Freudian therapists, "an overtreated patient can be extremely seductive in leading a therapist down the garden path of primary process" (51, p. 480).

It should be of concern to the medical profession as well as to the public to ask whether it makes sense to allow the Freudians to supplement the patient's real maladaptive pattern by building in him their own pathological model. Their masking of the actual psychopathology, resulting in distracting the patient, might produce some changes, even some improvement, but the question remains whether the induced change is preferable to the original condition.

## THE DIRECT METHODS OF PSYCHOTHERAPY

Once we see the Freudian superstitions about psychotherapy for the shibboleths that they are, we are free to conceptualize the whole process in a more sensible and realistic fashion. I start by asking: What is curative in psychotherapy?

The basic change in the newer conceptualizations of psychotherapy is in a direction away from an exaggerated veneration of the therapist's operations toward a greater appreciation of the innate recuperative powers of the mentally disturbed. Some professional psychotherapists tend to ascribe magic powers to their particular methods, pronouncing them to be peculiarly curative. Freudians are especially prone to this self-delusion. They are led to it through their training, compulsive stress upon minutiae, and the mystical "depths" of interpretations. New trainees get caught up in the promotional persuasiveness of the established psychoanalysts. The trainees are mystified from the beginning by the esoteric knowledge they are led to believe they will acquire if they undergo a personal Freudian conditioning. When they enter practice, they faithfully apply this training to their patients. When their patients turn for the better, the faith of analysts is reinforced. Yet, like the rest of us psychotherapists, psychoanalysts cash in on the patient's inherent capacities for recovery. Many studies have shown that a large number of patients, even up to two-thirds of them, achieve without treatment a recovery statistically comparable to that of patients exposed to various psychotherapeutic methods. About one-third, or at least about one-sixth of neurotic or psychotic patients, do not improve, with or without psychotherapy. Apparently they have their reasons for not wanting to move out of what impresses the professionals as a maladaptive state.

Of course, the knowledge that healers only cooperate with and aid the natural powers of recovery is as old as medicine. Such was the view of Hippocrates. The ancient physicians spoke of *vis medicatrix naturae* (the healing power of nature). Freud (23, p. 121) quotes one of the old French doctors: *"Je le pensai, Dieu le guerit"* (I thought of it, God cured it). The atheistic Freud and his followers could not, however, maintain the modest attitude of religious doctors. They tended to put themselves in God's place, pointing to their skill as the source of cure.

The manifold psychotherapeutic methods described in this book demonstrate the falsity of the claim that there is some peculiar healing virtue in the elaborate "psychodynamic" handling. Little of Freudian concepts is employed in these direct methods of therapy; yet, they are no less successful in practice. The inevitable conclusion from this observation is that our conceptualizations are practically irrelevant to psychotherapeutic processes. What appear essential to the patient are not the intellectual formulations of the therapist (although these might be esssential crutches for the therapist), but the experience of support, interest, friendliness, relationship, "the therapeutic eros" of Seguin (59). Dreyfus (14) postulates "humanness" as a variable underlying the successful treatments by disparate psychotherapeutic methods. Such essential human relatedness in therapy can be achieved through many theoretical and technical approaches. Meares (40) ascribes the trusting relaxation into prelogical modes of experiencing, the atavistic regression, as the common factor to all psychotherapeutic help. None of the many methods of therapy devised so far has a monopoly on curativeness, in spite of the very intricate theory of which some boast; none has been able to establish a superiority on the basis of verified results. All draw their successes from mobilizing the homeostatic powers through awakening hopes, lending the ego strength for better reality awareness, strengthening moral and religious motivations, building better habits of inward and outward reacting, particularly relaxing. Reviewing the poor results of psychoanalysis, Colby ironically suggests that therapists might be doing an injustice to the patient by depriving him of the benefits of spontaneous remission by their "treatment" (11, p. 356).

Trying to find a way out of the maze of Freudian presuppositions, which were imposed upon them by training, reading, and prevalent professional preconceptions, the authors represented in this book evolved their concepts of psychotherapy. The common feature of these psychotherapies is that they deal with the psychopathological manifestations directly. These methods do not seek primarily to lead the patient to "insights" by exhaustive reviews of the past. They are not strongly interested in etiological investigations but concentrate on modifying the current pathological expressions. The psychotherapists handle the symptoms directly. If a patient suffers from an anxiety reaction, they do not go into the "unconscious" roots of it, but show him the irrational concepts to which he is holding (see Ellis, Vol. One, p. 295) or the prideful assumptions which are misleading him (see Anderson, Vol. One, p. 257). They might attempt to lessen conflicts with conscience in order to calm emotions (see Mowrer, Vol. Two, p. 515). A patient with a character disorder is not induced to dig into traumas and unwholesome influences of the past but is helped to obey his consciously held values (see Glasser, Vol. Two, p. 562) or led to role-enacting of a more mature personality (see Kelly, Vol. One, p. 394), to religious identifications and practices, to restitution and openness with the wronged and others (Integrity Therapy; see Mowrer, Vol. Two, p. 515), or to scientific, objective analysis of the disturbed behavior (see Ligon, Vol. One, p. 433). The homosexual or addict is not further confused by Freudian permissiveness and moral ambiguity but is treated kindly as a wrongdoer who needs to give up his malpractices through disciplined training and jostling his feelings, as in Synanon (see Yablonsky, Vol. Two, p. 747); through confessing and undertaking socially positive roles, as in Alcoholics Anonymous (see Bellwood, Vol. Two, p. 795); by constraining his actions from following the symbolic representation, as in Dr. Low's methods (see Low, Vol. Two, p. 818); or by evolving an inspiring meaning of life, as in Cain's methods (see Cain, Vol. Two, p. 611) and in Rev. Burroughs' approach (see Burroughs, Vol. Two, p. 717). In other cultures methods of direct therapy have been evolved which could also be used with benefit for emotional stabilization in our circumstances. The sitting exercises of Zen (58) and Yoga (67), coupled with the religious-mystical views of these traditions, could lead to a reduction of agitation and tension as primary disturbances of our civilization. Morita therapy (43) has certain common features with the religious practices of Christian asceticism, which have often led to tightening the self-organization and binding disintegrating trends (see Burroughs, Vol. Two, p. 717).

There are many therapeutic innovations developing outside the Freudian orthodoxy which have shown some features of direct therapy. By way of example, we can consider psychotherapies by hypnosis before and after Freud, the persuasion therapy of Dubois, various educational therapies, Ferenczi's active therapy, Stekel's emphasis on current conflicts and moral problems, Jung's and Rank's leading of patients to goals as all precursors of the direct therapies. Even Dollard and associates (12, p. 109), working within the Freudian theoretical categories, criticizes his student-therapist for considering childhood experiences instead of labeling clearly the patient's experiences and concentrating on her current conflict. Some Freudian ego therapists give the impression of emphasizing conscious conflicts and considerations of reality. However, their expositions are so lacking in clear methodology and theory that even writers tolerant of Freudism, as Ford and Urban (21), consider them inadequate. Janet (30, p. 858) considered excitation of the patient as the main general method of psychotherapy. He commends Vittoz for training patients in maintaining attention. The "moral treatment" of Pinel and his followers in this country was in many ways a "direct" therapy. What Janet said of his compatriots, alluding to Freudism, applies quite well to American psychotherapists: "French psychiatry has unfortunately forgotten its traditions and is inclined to tow in the wake of foreign metaphysics."

However, the realistic and pragmatic American psychotherapists have never fully abandoned the active approaches for Freudian metaphysics, to mention only two examples. Cameron (8) sees the "improved behavioral responses" as the chief task of therapy. Stevenson (63) noticed that patients recovered after successfully mastering some challenge and directed their attention not to the relationship with the therapist but with others. His patients were occasionally assigned therapeutically useful tasks. He did not hesitate to guide them to be more assertive or affiliative and to reward or punish them by raising or lowering his fees according to the patient's utilization of interview counseling in his life situation (64).

In one respect every psychotherapy is direct: all deal with the immediate expression of the patient's memories, thoughts, feelings, or intentions as presented in the interview. Robbins, a psychoanalytically oriented therapist points out:

> What we analyze is not a historical event, a dream, a current episode or a future ambition. We cannot analyze, as we were once so fond of thinking, the id, the super-ego, and the ego. We never ob-

serve these phenomena as isolated entities, existing as independent, detached categories. *We never analyze anything but the patient in action*—in the act of recalling, in the act of dreaming, in the act of a transference relationship or in the act of projecting into the future. . . . So that we never observe nor do we even analyze anything but this present activity, this present character structure, in motion. . . . The only resistance we ever analyze, regardless of its immediate context, is the patient's resistance to becoming something other than he is, his resistance to change. (55, p. 107)

The difference, then, between the direct and Freudian therapies is in the type of content on which the therapist induces the patient to focus. The direct therapists concentrate mainly on the symptoms and topics concerned with the present and the future, the Freudian therapists on the past primarily and on the current issues only secondarily.

## CONCLUSIONS

The contributions of the authors in this book appear to justify several conclusions regarding theories and practices of psychotherapy.

1. Insight demoted. Gathering of insights about past traumas is not essential for the patient's improvement in psychotherapy. This overemphasis on insights is one of the durable Freudian fallacies. The extraordinary amount of time wasted in Freudian therapies upon uncovering etiological connections between past experiences and present symptoms is due not to a therapeutic need but to a colossal misunderstanding. Freud was not interested in healing the patients especially; he cared more for investigations of his theoretical hunches and testing the patient's susceptibility to surreptitious or overt suggestion as the alleged confirmation of his psychologizing notions. Grinker (26) describes the stultifying effects which Freud's investigational model has on psychotherapists in training. Discarding of the Freudian paradigm leads to direct confrontation with maladjustments, with symptoms, making for a shorter and more economical, but no less effective, psychotherapy. Moderate delving into the past and more extensive attention to current reactions and the goals of the future seem to be more therapeutic.

Meehl (41), a prominent psychologist sympathetic to Freudian suppositions, gives a simple explanation of why "psychodynamic" therapists cannot achieve marked results by chasing insights. Speaking as a former "rat psychologist," he points to the illusory expectation that understanding the sources of traumas should lead to abolition of their consequences.

> Recognizing that habits and reinforcement schedules are just as important in understanding learned behavior as drives and affects, suggests the modification of psychotherapeutic procedures along lines of response strengthening and shaping through positive reinforcement. Specifically, we ought not to assume that whenever the anxiety sign is sufficiently extinguished and the defensive system had been sufficiently worked through by interpretative methods, the drive system of the organism will somehow automatically do the rest. (41, p. 67)

The behavior therapists are doing just that: extinguishing the learned behaviors and reinforcing the new desired responses. Herzberg (29) had followed these considerations in setting psychotherapeutic tasks for his patients besides talking of their past traumas. "On learning principles, one would expect task setting to be an extremely powerful auxiliary procedure at certain stages in therapy: and under some circumstances with some patients, it might even be a necessary condition of getting a patient over the hump" (41, p. 68).

2. Emphasis on the past and the unconscious is deleterious to treatment. Instead of concentrating on the guesses about the unconscious roots of maladjustment, treatment appears more beneficial to the patient when it leads his attention to the current and overt psychopathological manifestations. The abundant conjectures about the hypothesized unconscious motivations are potentially more a means to resistance than to recovery. The hunting for the mysterious workings of the unconscious enables the patient to divert his attention from his responsibility in maintaining the symptoms; it leads to a psychotherapeutic impasse in which the patient and the therapist go on commiserating about the abuses and inadvertent self-abuses in the patient's life, regarding which nothing can be done, instead of actively struggling to change the patient's maladapted reactions. It might serve the ends of the Freudian analyst to keep the patient in the sphere of the unconscious and of the past: it makes the therapy longer and more mystifying; it gives the analyst a chance to interpose Freudian assumptions into the patient; it is conducive to the infantilization of the patient and the supposedly curative transference phenomena. But it certainly does not serve the therapeutic needs of the patient to lead him to abandon himself to the peripheral issues instead of dealing with his central problem of better performance in his situation. Glasser (24) deliberately avoids this pitfall of Freudian disservice to patients; Mowrer (Vol. Two, p. 515) holds his patients' attention upon the responsible dis-

charge of their social responsibilities; Adler (13) had parted ways with Freud largely because of the unhealthy disregard of the social roles of the patients in psychoanalytic "therapy"; Morita therapists (43) appear to train the patients to concentrate upon the given task instead of their past or even present woes. Rather than spending hours in developing the details of how his patient became neurotically timid, Lazarus (37) helps him by directing him toward assertive responses; a similar straightforward method was employed by Salter in his Conditioned Reflex Therapy (56). It is for this same reason of holding the patient to the therapeutic task that direct therapists neglect or discourage the discussion of dreams or do not invite free associations as methods by which the patient can sabotage the recovery.

3. Stressing healthy rather than sick aspects. Freudian concentration upon the imagined or real genetic aspects of psychopathology tends to reinforce in the patient the role of a sick person, a role which he plays explicitly anyway, as Grinker and others have pointed out. This deepening of the sick role might be useful to the analyst, for it leads to feelings of guilt and inadequacy in the patient and makes him more pliable to the demands of the psychoanalytic ritual; it certainly does not help the patient to lead him to structure his role in terms of a victim of developmental circumstances, a hopelessly damaged individual incapable of repairing himself, dependent upon the analyst's wits for straightening out his emotional tangles. Many writers have been reporting lately the pernicious influences upon the patient's behavior when his doctors structure him as a sick individual. Even Neo-Freudians sounded an alarm at the neuroticizing of patients by therapists attuned only to the sick functions of persons in treatment. Speaking at a symposium on "Emphasis on the Healthy Aspects of the Patient in Psychoanalysis," Weiss sees "a kind of professional neurosis in many psychiatrists and psychoanalysts which causes them to fix their attention upon the morbid and pathological and to disregard or underestimate the health potential, the constructive aspect of the patient" (6, p. 194). He recognizes that "psychoanalysis still lacks clear concepts of healthy growth, healthy self-acceptance, healthy assertion, healthy relationships and healthy sexuality" (6, p. 196). Other members of that round-table discussion support Weiss' criticisms.

The direct therapists avoid this snare of unwittingly reinforcing psychopathological developments; they all seem to pay attention to the healthy potentials in patients rather than to their sick aspects. The therapist's concentration upon the healthy possibilities for the patient is conducive to a more hopeful and more active patient role in overcoming maldevelopments. "Whoever can increase the patient's courage and self-confidence, can exert a corrective influence," Dreikurs (13) recognizes plainly and humbly. This concept was held by Dr. Morita (43), too.

4. The canard of substitution of symptoms. The clinical experiences of the direct and behavior therapists demonstrate the falseness of another Freudian prejudice: that these methods, dealing with symptoms, are superficial therapy and that they lead inevitably to substitution of symptoms. Eysenck (20) and Lazarus (37) deal with this fallacy.

Spiegel (62) demonstrates that symptom substitution is likely to occur as a function of therapist's expectations. On clinical examples he shows that pain or seizure are or are not reported according to the implicit or explicit attitude of the doctor in charge of the patient. A pessimistic or morose therapist may unwittingly induce appearance of symptoms in his patients, just like a hopeful therapist may dispel them.

5. Discarding the medical model of mental disturbance. Most of the methods described in this book do not seem to subscribe to the medical model of "mental illness." Psychological disturbance is seen as a perceptual misstructuring, the result of illogical assumptions, violation of the conscience, or retention of infantile emotional patterns. The "myth of mental illness" does not seem to be a part of these therapists' conceptualization regarding what is wrong with their patients. Their approach is accordingly more rational, more educational, more hopeful, and it places more reliance upon the patient's power of recovery. Mainord (Vol. One, p. 129) frankly dispenses with the role of "healer" for the therapist and "sick" person for the mental patient. A number of contributors do not belong to what is conventionally considered the mental health professions. They are ministers and priests, philosophers and educators. Their interest in the contributions to the recovery from emotional disturbances widens the concept of psychotherapy beyond the limits currently imposed by the monopolists.

6. For many, values are basic to mental health. Many of the contributors imply or state their belief in the role of values in emotional disturbance—a role that increases the personality disintegration when disregarded by patients and reduces it when the values are taken seriously as guides in life. This belief is not only the case with writers who are serving in professional religious capacities but with a number of others too: Mowrer considers a religiously guided conscience as the best aid to mental health; Tweedie (Vol. Two, p. 641) develops an integration of Christian views with psychotherapeutic effectiveness; Frankl (22) finds that a religious philosophical meaning of life helps to over-

come the inner disease of the modern man; Morita therapists imbue their patients with the feeling of oneness with nature, of obedience to nature and acceptance of hardships as part of life. Other writers, discussing religious influence more specifically, point to the sources of mental health which emanate from religious traditions. Herr (Vol. Two, p. 696) describes the potentials for emotional stability which can be drawn from Christian sacraments and mystical practices; Vayhinger (Vol. Two, p. 678) describes the role of the pastoral counselor in stabilizing people with emotional troubles. To those who object that these sources of mental health have only limited value because they are predicated on faith, we might well reply that professional psychotherapies are also limited to those who have faith in the therapist and are willing to take seriously his recommendations. Mental patients without faith in the therapist and in the professional presuppositions he represents are "untreatable."

My understanding of the psychotherapeutic potency of a practiced religion is based on my appreciation of the role of symbols [the "Word" of Pivnicki, (50)] and emotions in human life. Religions contain some of the most emotionally energizing symbols: Love, Law, Father, Heaven, Hell, Cross, Wisdom, Death, Eternity, Soul, Sacrifice, Redemption, Resurrection, Righteousness, Peace, etc. A revival of feelings connected with these symbols is likely to strengthen self-controls, to uplift the sagging spirit, to renew hope and inspiration, and in that way to provide a means of overcoming the weakness of a personality organization.

7. Wide applicability of direct psychotherapy methods. There is a decided advantage in many of the methods described in this book: they are relatively simpler, more easily learned and practiced than the elaborate, needlessly complex treatments of psychoanalysis. They can be practiced by educated and sensitive individuals without these individuals having to undergo the esoteric and rigorous indoctrination training required of the psychoanalytic therapist. Ministers and priests, teachers and lay counselors may fruitfully use some of these methods and techniques in work with people whom they are trying to help out of quandaries. These statements do not deny the therapeutic usefulness of the refined sensitivities and comprehension of the more specifically trained clinicians, but they are directed to the practical need for psychotherapeutic personnel which cannot be filled by the limited numbers of Ph.D.'s and M.D.'s.

Various experiments have demonstrated the therapeutic usefulness of psychotherapists with modest training levels. Heine (28) has described the therapeutic effects of a group of medical students who were not at ease in their temporary role as psychotherapists, but who achieved results comparable to trained therapists. We can expect that many pastoral counselors and teachers, already oriented to considerate dealing with human beings, could do a better job than the hurried and relatively immature medical students. Rioch (54) has shown that mature, middle-aged, college-trained women can become effective psychotherapists after a moderate amount of training. Carkhuff and Truax (10) have demonstrated that individuals with even less formal education than Rioch's counselors can be trained to do satisfactory psychotherapy. One of the conclusions drawn from these experiments with "nonprofessional" therapists is that trained psychotherapists should give up their direct work with patients and should concentrate on training and supervising the work of lay therapists. These could undoubtedly find the approaches of these volumes more accessible than the prevalent "psychodynamic" methods.

8. Theoretical complexity is not equal to therapeutic effectiveness. Some psychotherapists, conditioned to the complicated Freudian theory, might miss theoretical complexity in the methods described in this work. The articles in this collection are at different levels of elaboration and theoretical sophistication. But even when less accomplished technically, these approaches represent the growing edges of the exploding field of psychotherapy. The relatively simple theoretical structure might be misinterpreted by some as lack of scientific validity and clinical effectiveness with patients. We need to remember in this connection that the medieval exorcists had an extremely involved theory and procedures and that they did "heal" quite a number of patients, but we do not judge their healing methods by the complexity of the notions they considered correct and authoritatively taught to their students. In any case, Gottesman (25) has shown that the complexity of constructs of the therapist is not related to his ability to be effective psychotherapeutically.

The over-all impression from the methods represented here leads to a different concept of psychotherapy than that built on the scholastic pedantry and spurious psychodynamics of Freudian schools. The latter are top-heavy with theoretical fantasies and forbidding with esoteric secrets about psyche. These American originals depict psychotherapy as a human rather than an overly elaborated technical process. Psychotherapy is presented in this book as a broadly educational experience, a corrective and supportive influence of one person on another, a help toward better integration of personal and social functioning by infusing rational, moral, and religious guidelines into dis-

ordered reactions. Psychotherapies described in this collection eliminate the superstructure of Freudian models and show that much simpler theoretical frameworks are sufficient conditions for therapeutic work, the theoretical principles and verbal superstructure being more essential for the security of the therapist than for the benefit of the "patient." The criterion of the worth of these approaches is not the ability to talk learnedly about what is supposedly taking place in the patient, but a pragmatic effect in the lives of those who need help. These approaches worked in varied therapeutic situations and they enabled many practitioners to render the help needed by patients, subjects, or counselees; no further validation can appropriately be demanded at this stage. The educators employ many methods and non-theoretical improvisations with their students, the main educational tool being the person of the educator, his humanness, devotion, interest, and capacity to inspire and convey his intentions and ideas in a clear fashion. The student's learning is the vindication of the educator's method. The architects of Hagia Sophia in Constantinople built daring dome spans fourteen centuries ago using relatively primitive principles of stress dynamics, and their marvelous work still stands. The religious and moral leaders of the distant past as well as of the present led to pacification and transformation of many persons without ever taking recourse to the ratiocinations typical of some modern "mental health professionals."

9. The subscientific level of psychotherapy. The critical and scientifically trained reader will notice that many methods described have not reached the stage of experimental validation. Many of them, including religious methods, have been empirically and clinically validated, but this is the level of prescience, that is, of the art and skill and intuition. At the scientifically primitive level of development on which we find much of the current psychotherapy, these ingenious methods are acceptable and beneficial. Thorne (Vol. Two, p. 847) takes a stricter view of the subscientific level of contemporary psychotherapists. He proposes a valuable concept of "case handling" for the unvalidated psychotherapies, which pretty well encompasses all the current psychotherapeutic practices. Thorne takes a number of the present writers to task for not providing scientifically acceptable evidence for the effectiveness of the methods proposed.[2] This is certainly desirable though not feasible

---

[2] Incidentally, some readers may find it useful to read Thorne's conclusion first (Vol. 2, p. 847) to get an overview of the entire two volumes and a summary of some of the methods proposed by various therapists. The index entries can be used for the same purpose.

at this stage. After all, the Freudian psychotherapy has been practiced for more than seventy years, and its validity has not yet been scientifically demonstrated. The direct methods, particularly those based on learning theories, are definitely superior to Freudian methods regarding their amenability to scientific evaluation since their operations can be readily tested and verified. The psychoanalytic postulates are so vague and inclusive, "rubber theories" as Kelly (34) called them, that little scientific procedure can be carried out with them.

Those of us who doubt the value of scientizing human personality and relationships and see in the unavoidable scientific reductionism an essentially distorting mirror for the most important aspects of human nature might welcome the lack of scientific efficiency in some of the American Originals. Every scientism carries the danger of dehumanization. A systematic scientist is bound to use rational, rationalistic, and naturalistic approaches, whereas human nature is at its best beyond these confines and in the realm of spiritual and intuitive behavior.

10. Psychotherapy not limited to medical or "psychodynamic" models. The varied approaches developed by the psychotherapists show the richness of personal styles in helping the mentally disturbed. Instead of thinking in Freudian formulas, these therapists evolved methods of functioning which were appropriate to their own persons and, we would say, to the therapeutic needs of their clients. By their multitude and variety, these methods demonstrate that psychotherapy is a human process of great complexity, which can be carried out through many techniques and by various professions. Neither medical nor even less "psychodynamic" auspices are essential to give psychotherapeutic help.

11. Direct methods not equivalent to directive method. The direct methods described should not be confused with directive versus non-directive designations. The direct therapist may be permissive, moderately "client-centered," or quite directive and temporarily controlling. More probably, there would be a sensible mixture of the two approaches, partly depending on the phase of the therapeutic process. In any case, the dichotomy directive–nondirective is a false one. I believe all psychotherapy is directive. Nondirectiveness exists only in the degree of covertness and in the therapist's theoretical notions. Truax (66) has shown that even Rogers in his classical client-centered phase reinforced some of the client's behaviors inadvertently by his "nondirective" behavior.

12. Avoidance of disguised indoctrination. Unlike Freudian approaches, direct therapies, being more technical than "ideological"

[Rank (53)] are less likely to interfere with the patient's values and with his moral and religious attitudes. This consideration may be a decided advantage for those who suspect and resent the injection of irreligious Freudian prejudices into patients during the protracted and infantilizing "psychodynamic" therapies. In "The Hoax of Freudism" (32), I have reviewed many published experiences with Freudian therapy, revealing it unmistakably as imposition of therapist's views of life and psyche upon the patients. In its essential effects there was little to distinguish Freudwashing from other forms of brainwashing: a specific *Weltanschauung* was transmitted to the patient under the guise of mental health.

## REFERENCES

1. Alexander, F., & Selesnick, S. T. *The history of psychiatry*. New York: Harper and Row, 1966.
2. Allers, R. *The successful error: a critical study of Freudian psychoanalysis*. New York: Sheed and Ward, 1940.
3. Anderson, C. M. *Beyond Freud: a creative approach to mental health*. New York: Harper, 1957.
4. Anderson, C. M. The pot and the kettle. *J. Amer. Med. Women's Assoc.*, 1963, **18**, 293–298.
5. Bailey, P. *Sigmund the unserene: a tragedy in three acts*. Springfield, Ill.: Thomas, 1965.
6. Boigon, M. Emphasis on healthy aspects of the patient in psychoanalysis: a round table discussion. *Amer. J. Psychoanal.*, 1966, **26,** 193–212.
7. Boring, E. G. Was this analysis a success? *J. Abnorm. Soc. Psychol.*, 1940, **35**, 3–10.
8. Cameron, D. E. The conversion of passivity into normal self-assertion. *Amer. J. Psychiat.*, 1951, **108**, 98–102.
9. Campbell, C. H. *Induced delusions: the psychopathy of Freudism*. Chicago: Regent House, 1957.
10. Carkhuff, R. R., & Truax, C. B. Lay mental health counseling: the effects of lay group counseling. *J. Consult. Psychol.*, 1965, **29**, 26–31.
11. Colby, K. M. Psychotherapeutic processes. In P. R. Farnsworth (Ed.), *Annual review of psychology*. Palo Alto, Calif., 1964.
12. Dollard, J., Ault, F., Jr., & White, A. M. *Steps in psychotherapy: study of a case of sex–fear conflict*. New York: Macmillan, 1953.
13. Dreikurs, R. Disclosure technique in Adlerian psychotherapy. In R. M. Jurjevich (Ed.), *Direct psychotherapy: Developments on four continents*. Coral Gables., Fla.: University of Miami Press, in preparation.
14. Dreyfus, E. A. Humanness: a therapeutic variable. *Personnel and Guidance Journal*, 1967, **45**, 573–578.
15. Dunlap, K. *Mysticism, Freudianism and scientific psychology*. New York: Mosby, 1920.

16. Egyedi, H. *Die Irrtümer der Psychoanalysie: Eine Irrlehre mit einem genialen Kern.* Vienna: Braumüller, 1933.
17. Ellis, A. Outcome of employing three techniques of psychotherapy. *J. Clin. Psychol.*, 1957, **13**, 334–350.
18. Ellis, A. *Reason and emotion in psychotherapy.* New York: Stuart, 1962.
19. Eysenck, H. J. The effects of psychotherapy. In H. J. Eysenck (Ed.), *Handbook of abnormal psychology.* New York: Basic Books, 1960.
20. Eysenck, H. J. Foreword. In R. M. Jurjevich (Ed.), *Direct psychotherapy: 28 American originals.* Coral Gables, Fla.: University of Miami Press, 1972.
21. Ford, D. H., & Urban, H. B. *Systems of psychotherapy: a comparative study.* New York: Wiley, 1963.
22. Frankl, V. E. Logotherapy and existential analysis. A review. *Amer. J. Psychother.*, 1966, **20**, 252–260.
23. Freud, S. *Therapy and technique.* New York: Collier, 1963.
24. Glasser, W. *Reality Therapy: a new approach to psychiatry.* New York: Harper & Row, 1965.
25. Gottesman, L. W. The relationship of cognitive variables to therapeutic ability and training of client-centered therapists. *J. Consult. Psychol.*, 1962, **26**, 119–125.
26. Grinker, R. R. A transactional model for psychotherapy. *Arch. Gen. Psychiat.*, 1959, **1**, 132–148.
27. Harrington, M. *Wish hunting in the unconscious.* New York: Macmillan, 1934.
28. Heine, R. W. (Ed.) *The student physician as psychotherapist.* Chicago: University of Chicago Press, 1962.
29. Herzberg, A. Active psychotherapy. In R. M. Jurjevich (Ed.), *Direct psychotherapy: Developments on four continents.* Coral Gables, Fla.: University of Miami Press, in preparation.
30. Janet, P. *Psychological healing: a historical and clinical study.* New York: Macmillan, 1925.
31. Johnson, H. K. Psychoanalysis—a critique. *Psychiat. Quart.*, 1948, **22**, 321–338.
32. Jurjevich, R. M. The hoax of Freudism: an integrated anthology of criticism. Unpublished manuscript.
33. Jurjevich, R. M. *No water in my cup: experiences and a controlled study of psychotherapy with delinquent girls.* New York: Libra, 1968.
34. Kelly, G. A. *The psychology of personal constructs.* Vols. 1 and 2. New York: Norton, 1955.
35. La Pierre, R. T. *The Freudian ethic.* Des Moines, Iowa: Duell, Sloan and Pearce, 1959.
36. Lazarus, A. A. Behavior therapy with identical twins. *Behav. Res. Ther.*, 1964, **1**, 313–319.
37. Lazarus, A. A., & Davison, G. C. Reciprocal inhibition concept and desensitization therapy. In R. M. Jurjevich (Ed.), *Direct psychother-*

*apy: Developments on four continents.* Coral Gables, Fla.: University of Miami Press, in preparation.

38. Low, A. A. *Mental health through will training: a system of self-help as practiced by Recovery Incorporated.* (12th ed.) Boston: Christopher, 1965.

39. Ludwig, E. *Doctor Freud: an analysis and a warning.* New York: Hellman, Williams and Co., 1948.

40. Meares, A. Psychotherapy based on atavistic regression. In R. M. Jurjevich (Ed.), *Direct psychotherapy: Developments on four continents.* Coral Gables, Fla.: University of Miami Press, in preparation.

41. Meehl, P. E. Psychopathology and purpose. In P. H. Hoch & J. Zubin (Eds.), *The future of psychiatry.* New York: Grune and Stratton, 1962.

42. Menninger, K. *The theory of psychoanalytic technique.* New York: Basic Books, 1958.

43. Momoshige, M., & Shin-ichi, U. Morita therapy. In R. M. Jurjevich (Ed.), *Direct psychotherapy: Developments on four continents.* Coral Gables, Fla.: University of Miami Press, in preparation.

44. Mowrer, O. H. *Abnormal reactions or actions? An autobiographical answer.* Dubuque, Iowa: Brown, 1966.

45. Mowrer, O. H. (Ed.) *Morality and mental health.* Chicago: Rand McNally, 1967.

46. Mowrer, O. H. Conscience and the unconscious aspects of Integrity Therapy, *J. Communic. Disord.,* 1968, **1,** 109–135.

47. Natenberg, M. *Freudian psycho-antics: fact and fraud in psychoanalysis.* Chicago, Ill.: Regent House, 1952.

48. Phillips, E. L. Newer approaches. In D. Brown & E. L. Abt (Eds.), *Progress in clinical psychology.* Vol. 3. New York: Grune and Stratton, 1958.

49. Pinckney, E. R., & Pinckney, C. *The fallacy of Freud and psychoanalysis.* Englewood Cliffs, N.J.: Prentice Hall, 1965.

50. Pivnicki, D. The beginnings of psychotherapy. In R. M. Jurjevich (Ed.), *Direct psychotherapy: Developments on four continents.* Coral Gables, Fla.: University of Miami Press, in preparation.

51. Post, J. Putting a lid on the id. *Psychiat. Quart.,* 1956, **40,** 472–481.

52. Rachman, S. (Ed.) *Critical essays on psychoanalysis.* New York: Macmillan, 1963.

53. Rank, O. A departure from Freudian psychoanalysis. In R. M. Jurjevich (Ed.), *Direct psychotherapy: Developments on four continents.* Coral Gables, Fla.: University of Miami Press, in preparation.

54. Rioch, M. J., Elkes, C., Flint, A.A., Udansky, B. S., Newman, R. G., & Dilber, E. National Institute of Mental Health pilot study in training mental health counselors. *Amer. J. Orthopsychiat.,* 1963, **33,** 678–689.

55. Robbins, B. S. The process of cure in psychotherapy. In P. H. Hoch & J. Zubin (Eds.), *Current approaches to psychoanalysis.* New York: Grune and Stratton, 1960.

56. Salter, A. *The case against psychoanalysis.* New York: Holt, 1952.
57. Salter, A. *Conditioned reflex therapy.* New York: Capricorn, 1961.
58. Sato, K. Zen training and its psychotherapeutic implications. In R. M. Jurjevich (Ed.), *Direct psychotherapy: Developments on four continents.* Coral Gables, Fla.: University of Miami Press, in preparation.
59. Seguin, C. A. *Love and psychotherapy: the psychotherapeutic eros.* New York: Libra, 1965.
60. Skinner, B. F. Superstition in the pigeon. *J. Exper. Psychol.,* 1948, **38,** 168–172.
61. Smith, V. H. Identity crises in conversion hysteria with implications for Integrity Therapy. *Psychotherapy: Theory, Res., Prac.,* 1966, **3,** 120–124.
62. Spiegel, H. Is symptom removal dangerous? *Amer. J. Psychiat.,* 1967, **123,** 1279–1281.
63. Stevenson, I. Direct instigation of behavioral changes in psychotherapy. *A.M.A. Arch. Gen. Psychiat.,* 1959, **1,** 99–117.
64. Stevenson, I. The use of rewards and punishments in psychotherapy. *Compar. Psychiat.,* 1962, **3,** 20–28.
65. Storrow, H. A. *Introduction to scientific psychiatry: a behavioristic approach to diagnosis and treatment.* New York: Appleton-Century-Crofts, 1967.
66. Truax, C. B. Reinforcements and non-reinforcements in Rogerian psychotherapy. *J. Abnorm. Psychol.,* 1966, **71,** 1–9.
67. Vinekar, S. L., & Vahia, N. S. Psychophysiological therapy based on ancient Indian concepts. In R. M. Jurjevich (Ed.), *Direct psychotherapy: Developments on four continents.* Coral Gables, Fla.: University of Miami Press, in preparation.
68. Wells, H. K. *The failure of psychoanalysis: from Freud to Fromm.* New York: International Publishers, 1963.
69. Wohlgemuth, A. *Critical examination of psychoanalysis.* London: Allen and Unwin, 1923.
70. Wortis, J. *Fragments of an analysis with Freud.* New York: Simon and Schuster, 1954.

Part One

# PHYSIOLOGICAL
# AND BEHAVIOR THERAPY
# APPROACHES

In this section we meet some of the most sophisticated modern developments in the theory of psychotherapy which grew out of the psychology of learning. One of the advantages of these developments is that, in contrast to the vague and mostly untestable propositions of psychoanalysis, they offer clear and simplified conceptualizations of what is being done with the patient and why. They approach the ideal of the experimental and scientific psychologist, the operational grace.

Like all simplifications regarding man and his situation, they may run the danger of missing the higher and finer aspects which are grasped more sensitively and represented with less distortion in humanistic, phenomenological, and existential approaches, as well as in some philosophical considerations and in the deepest of artistic creations. This danger can be avoided if the therapists working with these schematizations of human beings retain their sanity and see their practical operations in the widely embracing perspective of humanness, which, in the ultimate analysis, escapes all scientifying attempts. Otherwise, the exclusively scientific approach, without a profound respect for individual human beings, brings in its wake the inhumanity that this century witnessed in the Nazi and Communist regimes alike. We can only hope that clinical sensitivity would prevent scientific practices with human beings from sinking to the level of those with laboratory animals and that men would not be treated as mere organisms to be reconditioned. That this possibility is neither idle fear nor idle hope might be glimpsed from the fact that one of the most prominent representatives of Behavior Therapy (in fact, the man who first proposed the name), Professor Arnold A. Lazarus, has proposed the system of Personalistic Psychotherapy[1] to counter the mechanistic temptations of less sensitive practitioners.

Phillips demonstrates a systematized way of helping patients reach a clearer understanding of their presuppositions, assertions, and the sometimes misleading outcomes of their personality reactions. In an analogous attempt, Storrow helps his patients reach a better integration of their behavior by unlearning unadaptive verbal patterns and learning more-effective verbal behavior operations. Stampfl and Levis practice what seems to be the most direct therapy in desensitizing troubled patients by presenting them with troublesome stimuli. Salter, through the successes of his simplified Pavlovian approach, belies the current psychoanalytic superstition that therapy must always, or usually, be long, "deep," and laden with esoteric interpretations. Mainord illustrates a straightforward approach of operant group psychotherapy with hospitalized psychotics. Taulbee and Folsom show another successful treatment method to reeducate hospital inmates into nonpsychotic reactions. O'Flaherty proposes a treatment of scrupulosity which is inaccessible to the conventional psychotherapeutic methods; his technique has features reminiscent of the paradoxical intention and dereflection of Frankl's Logotherapy, although O'Flaherty based his therapy on the insights of a spiritual leader of the Anti-Reformation. Haugen utilizes a method of treating anxious patients which is opposite to the customary approach of the psychotherapist: instead of detensing the patient's organism by reducing the conflicts of his mind, Haugen starts by relaxing the muscles through Jacobson's technique and succeeds in reducing the patient's mental unrest by untensing his body. An additional feature of Haugen's method will appeal to the busy medical practitioner: Haugen found that he could use the auxiliary nursing personnel to help the patient psychotherapeutically.

---

[1] Lazarus, A. A. *Behavior therapy and beyond.* New York: McGraw-Hill. 1971. An outline of his position is provided in C. M. Abramovitz. Personalistic psychotherapy and the role of technical eclecticism. *Psychol. Rep.,* 1970, **26,** 255–263.

Chapter 1

# Assertion-Structured Therapy: A Behavioral Position

## E. LAKIN PHILLIPS

E. Lakin Phillips: b. 1915, Higginsville, Missouri.
B.S., in music, history, education, Missouri State College, 1937. M.A. in educational psychology, University of Missouri, 1940. Ph.D., in child psychology, University of Minnesota, 1949.
Professor and Director, Psychological Clinic, George Washington University, 1962-date. Chief Clinical Psychologist, National Orthopaedic and Rehabilitation Hospital, Arlington, Virginia, 1952-1962. Chief Clinical Psychologist, Arlington Guidance Center, 1949-1956.
Books: *Psychotherapy: A Modern Theory and Practice* (1956). (Co-author) *Short-Term Psychotherapy and Structured Behavior Change* (1966); *Educating Emotionally Disturbed Children* (1962); *Discipline, Achievement and Mental Health* (1960); *Psychology and Personality* (1957).

The psychotherapeutic persuasion displayed in this paper had its origins in my work[1] in a child guidance center. The emphasis on "assertion" was originally meant to convey the idea that people assert, display, or simply state, with their behavior, what is fundamental or important in their behavioral economy at a given time or under given circumstances. One might broaden this term to include expressed attitudes, verbalization, and stated feelings (9).

It was important to me to develop a method of psychotherapy and consultation about mental health problems which steered clear of traditional "depth" concepts, thereby avoiding reliance on such notions as unconscious motivation, repression, and defense. Although these and other concepts found in traditional views of psychotherapy have some literary and imaginative appeal, they have shown themselves relatively barren in a scientific sense.

It will be shown later in this paper that some changes were sug-

---

[1] The author is indebted to Mrs. Jane Burkhardt for helpful suggestions in the preparation of this paper. The author takes full responsibility, however, for the content of this paper.

gested by developments in operant behavior and in cybernetics. These two sets of influences have caused some shift in the therapeutic locus, which will be detailed in the following discussions.

## ASSERTIONS

We start, then, with behavior: What one asserts. In today's terms, this position is a "behavior change" or "behavior modification" therapy (6, 20). It is also ahistorical. It further emphasizes short-term therapy and the working out of problems in the matrix of social interaction, not in terms of intrapsychic forces or mental content.

In working with children, we could take advantage of observations of child behavior, which is easier to observe than adult behavior. In extending the work with children to therapeutic contacts with parents and teachers, we could place the child's observed behavior in the context of adult behavior. It was further advantageous to see that adults often misinterpreted or misread the behavior of children. They imputed motives, causes, historical conditions, etc., which were often untrue or irrelevant. One might say that all a child has to deal with in his world of people and things is his behavior. Adults, on the other hand, can confound their behavior by reporting on themselves differently from the way they otherwise behave or by "theorizing" in misleading or confusing ways.

Given the behavior that is open to observation, we next become involved in stating what variables are important in changing behavior and in understanding it.

If someone asserts something with his behavior, that behavior has a consequence in the environment. It may be punished; it may be ignored; or it may be reinforced (rewarded, approved). We have, now, two variables: the behavior occurs (is observed), and it has some consequence in the environment.

Frequently behavior is more complicated than this. The behavior observed may be opposed by other behavior by the same individual, or it may be in conflict with behavior by other persons, or it may be in conflict with some kind of standard or norm. The assertion implied by the behavior is then said to be disconfirmed. The world is complex, and very few events have a simple history or a simple consequence. For the most part, behavior is woven into a web of interaction with other people and with new and old events within the person's own behavior repertoire.

If behavior had a simple outcome, we would not need the notion of conflict. Or, if conflict (or opposition, or lack of reinforcement) ended an assertion, we would not need to talk about the repetitiveness, or the redundancy in behavior. An astonishing thing about some behavior is its repetitiveness or redundancy—it continues to occur despite opposition and lack of (obvious) reinforcement, and it may continue even when it is destructive or detrimental to the over-all behavioral economy.

Earlier, the theory posited under the name "assertion-structured therapy" dealt with these four concepts: assertion, consequence (confirmation or disconfirmation of assertion), conflict (producing tension and symptom), and redundancy. It was stated that these four concepts, which refer, in turn, to empirically observable events, were sufficient to account for observed abnormality and for psychotherapeutic change and that they could cover conceptually the content of psychotherapeutic exchange.

## CONFLICT

Certainly people in psychotherapy are manifestly in conflict. It is not too difficult to show that they assert propositions about themselves, about others, and about the world which gain credence or reinforcement in some cases and not in other cases and that the latter instances often cause these persons the overt difficulties in living, as well as contributing to subjective distress. It is also true that if problems were once posed, then solved or dismissed, few if any individuals would seek help; it is only when the problem situations become intense and persistent and when the individual faces the same hopeless enigmas over and over (redundancy) that he feels he has to call upon others for help.

Within the notion of conflict there are empirically describable dimensions that are also instructive to the student of human behavior and to the practicing therapist. Conflict (1, 7–9) may be broken down into approach and avoidance variables; and, these variables show certain characteristics in the sense of steepness of gradients (toward or away from a goal area). It is often possible in psychotherapy to see how persons approach a conflict situation with some initial assurance, but when caught in the throes of the avoidance and approach dimensions, they become entangled, constricted, even paralyzed.

In the development of the assertion-structured position, we considered overcoming conflict to be the primary goal of psychotherapy. This goal might consist in reducing the avoidance gradient conditions (reducing fear, anxiety) and in increasing the approach gradient, or both. While these somewhat abstract notions were not always amenable to detailed clinical specification, the conceptual ordering afforded by the approach-avoidance gradients was instructive to the therapist and also to the patient. The value of instruction found in the gradient notions was especially valuable in the case of the double approach-avoidance gradient, that is, where each goal area was complicated by both positive and negative tendencies. The human case would appear to be most often an example of double approach-avoidance gradients or continua.

## TRADITIONAL CONCEPTS OMITTED

As part of the assertion-structured position in therapy, it was held that life histories, unconscious motivation, etc., were not viable concepts. What appeared to be needed, as a growing number of people were saying, was a set of theoretical notions and working principles that would deal with the environment of the patient in ways that would facilitate change and not remove the problem to a distant time or place. Assertions were manifest, open; perhaps they were not always reported verbally or properly conceptualized by the patient, but they were in principle nonetheless open to observation and verification. The therapeutic task, then, became one of delineating different channels available to the individual, either specifying those openly present in his behavioral economy or in his environment, or those potentially under known or knowable circumstances. These solutions involved changing one's assumptions, or assertions; changing some aspects of relationships with others (which was an assertion); and changing other environmental factors (altering the effects of assertions).

## INTERFERENCE AS THERAPEUTIC MODE

The therapeutic maneuver termed "interference" was also important. If one were to see the therapeutic task as lying on a social plane before one, so to speak, then there were many ways to interfere with the ongoing, disturbed or unwanted behavior of the patient. One might interfere therapeutically, by altering the environment directly in some crucial ways (10, 11, 13–15, 17), or the interference might consist of challenging the assumptions or assertions of the patient himself ("You really want people to believe anything you say, and you get awfully mad if they disagree or fail to follow your lead"); which is, in effect, an environmental change since the therapist is now part of the patient's environment. Or the interference may consist of other environmental changes in interpersonal relations in some important ways, such as to alter a given parent–child relationship, a given teacher–child relationship, or a relationship with any person whom the patient considered important.

Interference, then, rather than exploring the past in search of some important nuclei of experience, became the therapeutic mode. Although the term interference is subject to misunderstanding, there is no implication here that the interference notion is an authoritarian one, or that solutions are imposed without regard to the individual's behavioral economy. Synonyms of interference would be interposition, interrupting, perhaps confrontation, and the like.

Closely related to interference as a therapeutic mode is the term structure. Conflict has been considered to abound in unstructured or unclear situations where the participant does not know what is expected (or required) of him, where the alternatives are not delineated, where the consequences are perhaps unclear or unreliable, or where they are remote. To restructure a situation is to make the limits or boundaries clearer; it is to set up definite expectations or requirements, with consequences clearly tied to alternatives in differential ways and with remote events juxtaposed to current ones.

In parent–child relationships where problems arise often, there is much evidence of unclear structure, conflictful conditions, or weak structure. The same may be said of educational problems among children. If children daily face a clear classroom structure with demands on behavior and achievement clearly defined, and equitable steps provided for achieving them, there is little likelihood that children will become serious behavior problems (5, 16) or serious educational problems.

Structure implies a firmness, a set of rules or regulations serving as guidelines, and implies that these guidelines have a functional relation to the goals sought; structure does not imply aversive control. By definition, an individual who is badly disturbed lacks structure. A situation that does not produce the desired results can be shown to lack suitable structure. The lack of structure may, in turn, house conflicts between persons or "within" a person from time to time, so that solving or reducing conflicts implies a restructuring; or, conversely, firming up structure would entail conflict resolution or amelioration.

The therapeutic application of structuring may work as illustrated in the following example. Parents of a nine-year-old boy seek help for the lad's disturbed behavior, emotional outbursts, disciplinary problems, and failure in school work. The therapist first seeks a definition or description of the circumstances under which these complaints are observed. In our real case, the following data on problems were gathered:

    1. Stubborn, refuses discipline. Ex.: Fails to get dressed on time in morning; will not eat meals; refuses to come in when called; wastes time at school. These events occur daily or several times per week.

    2. Causes disciplinary problems at school. Ex.: Interrupts other children; taunts others or invites their attention to his antics in class; wants to control games, choosing of partners in games. Teacher reports these events in one form or another, almost daily.

    3. Sasses parents. Ex.: Says, "I won't—you can't make me." This event occurs often in embarrassing situations among others.

    4. Problems with peers. Ex.: Feels others don't like him; thinks he gets an unfair shake in games; feels left out when peers decide on activities. Complains of these feelings to parents at least a time or two per week.

In gaining further information about the lad in question, we determined that the parents take a "soft" attitude toward him, let him get by without conforming to their stated requirements, admonish or warn him constantly but fail to follow through on stated objectives, let the boy talk them out of their positions with regard to routine activities, such as eating, free time, play activities, and so on, through a large number of unclear, unreliable, and undependable relationships.

To help parents in conflict with children, we help the parents set fewer goals but set them unmistakably clear; this is an important therapeutic step. With his behavior, the child asserts propositions about himself (wanting his way against all odds and all reason) and comes into conflict with parents and peers where the conflict is sometimes resolved in his favor (others "give in" in order to maintain peace), and at other times not (which may occasion his display of temper or hatred toward others), and he shows a remarkably redundant tendency to the same behavior day after day at home and at school.

Thus the problems presented by this child—highly typical of many children with troubles at home and at school—illustrate our four variables: assertion, confirmation or disconfirmation of assertion, conflict (producing tension and symptoms), redundancy. As a result of all this display, a number of so-called symptoms or complaints or signs of unhappiness and unproductivity occur. Entering this matrix of activity has to be done with some hopefully intelligent guidelines. Thus therapeutic interference or interposition begins with helping the parents set clear expectations or requirements, helping them specify the limits or boundaries within which the behavior is to occur (time and space boundaries, such as time for eating, taking turns in games or sports; and responsibilities, such as hanging up clothes, taking baths, and so forth). The interference is a simple one of prohibiting the ongoing but unwanted or disturbed behavior of the child in question and interfering with the unwitting or confused parental participation in the same behavior, to the end that alternative behaviors begin to occur and are progressively encouraged (reinforced) and extended.

One could apply these notions to all kinds of clinical problems or therapeutic interventions. It is simply a matter of arranging data, or getting data, appropriate to the major concepts guiding the therapeutic procedures. What is distracting, however, in most clinical cases is the endless descriptions of complaints, symptoms, problems, without any very satisfactory organization of these occurrences in a way that permits systematic and economical intervention. Actually, the myriad of so-called symptoms and complaints that characterize different ways of reacting to conflicts are legion, and little is gained by trying to describe and pigeonhole these behavioral occurrences. Some decisive action is called for if we are to know what description means and if we are to test behavior change potentialities.

It seems productive to apply these concepts (assertion, etc.) to problems found among the seriously disturbed, to problems of adolescents, to college and young adult populations, as well as to specific classifications, such as phobic cases, study habits problems, bed-wetting and other behavior disorders among children, and so on. The presenting problem itself, although a necessary starting point, is not the major consideration; rather, it is how the stated or observable problem(s) are interfered with (and their conceptualization) that makes the present position a behavioral therapy.

## NEWER DEVELOPMENTS

Despite the apparent usefulness of the concepts previously stated, over several years I came to feel that the conflict paradigm was a bit too cumbersome in some situations and, also, that it placed too much emphasis on descriptions of pathology and not enough on the solution.

Two sets of influences which have affected me over the past few years have caused a shift in the therapeutic locus and some revision of the concepts. These influences derive from operant behavior and from cybernetics. How these influences operate will constitute the remaining considerations of this paper.

The notion of assertion-put forth in the first section matches well the current stress on behavior as it is understood in behavior therapies of all kinds. The disconfirmation concept (or confirmation, if this is the case) is also behavioral, but it refers more closely to whether the behavior in question meets a positive consequence (that is, whether it is reinforced) or a negative consequence (that is, whether it is punished, or whether reinforcement is delayed or withheld). The cardinal concept of reinforcement, so important in operant behavior, although not as well specified, was built into interference (or assertion structured) therapy from the beginning.

In the newer version of these ideas, the importance of conflict is minimized. Of course, conflict occurs in the environment between an organism and another organism, or between an organism and parts of its environment, or between various behaviors in the organism's repertoire. However, in a therapeutic or behavior change context, the dwelling on conflict, its dimensions, its approach and avoidance and double-approach-avoidance characteristics appear to be less heuristic than former ideas indicated. It is much more important in interfering with unwanted behavior to ask questions about what maintains the unwanted behavior (that is, what reinforcement occurs which may escape ready notice) and to ask questions about how new behavior may be developed, encouraged, reinforced. Shaping and fading procedures assume a much greater role; and the dropping of the avoidance behavior becomes far less important.

Being self-critical here, I would say that the original intent of interference theory to avoid the common pitfalls of "depth" psychology and psychotherapy was reduced somewhat by an emphasis on the concept of conflict and thereby too great a focus on the pathology itself. Conceptually, it is not only possible, but it appears to be productive, to leave out the notion of conflict and to focus instead on the degrees of freedom available in the organism's repertoire (which is to say in the environment) to overcome the unwanted behavior and to instill more desirable behavior. We do not need to know all about the conflict, only the degrees of freedom to overcome it.

By the same reasoning, the notion of consequences (confirmation or disconfirmation) takes the major role in the newer formulation of interference. What one does, in fact, in an operant behavior therapy is to account for the conditions under which the unwanted behavior occurs and to ask questions about what maintains this behavior (noting, usually, that reinforcement "sneaks in" early following the unwanted behavior and thus makes change more difficult and obscures the importance of later punishment to intended correction). All this is by way of saying that behavior is maintained by its consequences; hence, a careful and detailed study of the consequences is mandatory.

Although the older formulation of interference theory and assertion-structured therapy never meant to consider symptoms in a medical-model sense, this misapprehension nonetheless occurred. The earlier writing emphasized "tension—symptoms," intending to show that out of the tension created through conflict, the so-called symptoms occurred; but it was never intended that symptoms were other than inefficient behaviors with respect to the solving of problems. By abandoning the notion of conflict, we reduce the chances that the allied concepts of symptoms and tension will be misunderstood, and we also gain the advantage of not being as much concerned with describing pathology.

The notion of redundancy still appears to be useful, if for no other reason than to point to the fact that some set of conditions is keeping the unwanted or inefficient or disturbed behavior in force. The notion of redundancy also keeps us away from medical-model notions of pathology, which tend to imply, if not to state explicitly, that the observed behavior is an artifact of a "more basic pathological process." Redundancy has its own legitimate reason for being, and its study is important in behavior change and in psychotherapy.

Schedules of reinforcement are very important in operant analysis of behavior (3). These schedules not only point to the importance of reinforcement, per se, but to nature's ways of maintaining integrity, some of them remarkably resistant to change, others surprisingly susceptible to change.

While the interference theory position never analyzed schedules of reinforcement in the precise, experimental manner afforded by a pigeon in a pecking apparatus, the implications of early or immediate reinforcement vs. delayed or improbable reinforcement and various regimens of reinforcement were qualitatively recognized.

The therapeutic practice in assertion-structured therapy of putting individuals on schedules (the adult management of the child being the most cogent and illustrative case) was built into the system from the beginning, and most therapeutic change was attributed to this "change in structure" or "firming up structure" concept. Actually, the notion of "structure" carried the implication of scheduling, controlling reinforcement, juxtaposing later consequences earlier in the behavioral series, and relating observable behavior to definitive outcome.

Thus, operant methods of analysis have had a salutary influence on my interference or assertion-structure position. The operant influence has raised the importance of the concept of consequences to a considerably higher degree, played down the value of analyzing conflict, per se, and reemphasized the behavioral implications of assertions. What we have left as a result of operant influence on assertion-structured therapy is simply behavior, its context, and its consequences. When we act as therapists and wish to change behavior, we study the consequences more finely and expect to find reinforcements that show how the unwanted behavior is maintained. We look further into the environment to see how these unwanted or pathological behaviors are maintained, whereas cursory attention to them suggests only that perhaps some "powerful inner forces" or "drives" are operating to keep the disturbance current.

An illustrative case will cover the previously mentioned points. A sixteen-year-old adolescent male given to late hours, some experimental drinking, and some deceptive behavior directed toward parents (taking the car without permission, stealing money from parents' purses) was referred for therapy. There was obviously conflict between parents and son, although this varied with the behavior in question, and it varied with father vs. mother vis-à-vis the child.

These data will help us to get started. In the original version of interference theory, a considerable amount of time might be spent in saying that as the child approached the time of decision and action (whether to take the car, whether to take money for some later spending, etc.), he would be harder to control; and guilt would have been explained on the basis that when the conflict lessened and the adolescent was less active in pursuing his unilateral goals he had more time to think about this behavior and to note remorse. There were many issues that are currently viewed as "side issues" or as by-products of subtle reinforcements that originally were discussed mainly around the notion of conflict and its resolution.

Originally, the consequences coming to the adolescent via the parents would have emphasized the aftereffects and to a lesser extent would have attempted to influence the facts before the case. Today the emphasis would move on a general stepwise planning of the adolescent's time and recreation and less on consequences for untoward action. It is more important now to preclude or control the developing problems through changed regimens and altered parent–child interactions.

Factors permitting the maintenance of the adolescent's unwanted behavior would be such practices as his using the car for pleasure, gaining prestige from peers by having the car, factors operating long before parental detection caught up with him. His persistence in carrying out his unwanted behavior could be seen to revolve about the social reinforcers available to him, despite the later parental admonitions, threats, punishments, and attempted corrections.

The natural reinforcers in the environment available to the youth and to his parents for altering his unwanted behavior can be such things as a legitimate use of the car, or specific opportunities to earn money by setting up specific contingencies. Setting up these contingencies has always been part of the interference position, but the importance of contingencies comes into therapeutic consideration earlier, and perhaps more forcefully, as a result of influence from operant analysis of behavior.

## THE INFLUENCE OF CYBERNETICS

Cybernetics has also had a profound influence on the interference model. Cybernetics, like operant analysis, emphasizes consequences, or what some (2, 4, 12) have called "controlling the effects." Cybernetics also emphasizes the steering or controlling or guiding properties in explaining or in understanding behavior. Controlling the effects and steering behavior are highly prepotent concepts, and one may get along with them very well without adding many other notions.

Behavior is steered or guided by knowledge of results, or by what is known as feedback (2, 16, 18). Feedback has the property of feeding back to some controlling or regulating center the consequences of its actions. The compelling thing about this concept is that it applies across nature—from simple regulatory processes in machines (such as the thermostat regulating temperature) to variable homeostatic processes in complex living systems. Feedback tells the system where it is going, provides a basis for goal directedness, and supplies the basis for the notion of integrity or organization.

Moreover, feedback links one element of behavior to another. A long series of behaviors are linked together, gain integrity and purpose, by and through feedback. A child sharpens his pencil, sits down to work, makes marks on paper that solve problems, gets approval from his teacher, carries his behavior on to more complex problems, gains approval again, etc. Feedback may be shown to illustrate and possibly to explain how unwanted behaviors gain in strength, in that each element of behavior forms a loop, and the characteristics of the loop are such that some original condition is strengthened (made more likely) through the operation of interim elements in the loop.

Loops have properties that permit and encourage analysis of the behavior of elements in the loop, and they prove heuristic just as operant analysis of the schedules of reinforcement prove heuristic. A loop composed of several elements is open to alteration, and some "rules" exist whereby the change may be effected. Some rules are:

1. Each element has a positive (amplifying) effect on the outcome of the loop or a negative (counteracting) effect on the outcome of the loop.

2. Elements in the loop lying closest to a given outcome can be changed and may have the most important effect on the outcome.

3. Elements in a loop have no priority or causal properties; they simply continue (amplify) or negate (counteract) the over-all direction of the loop.

4. One may make a functional analysis of a segment of behavior in this manner and show how the loop can be conceptualized as "starting" or "stopping" at one of several arbitrarily chosen points or junctures.

Suppose we take the case of a child who is having trouble with school work, although the child is able to perform the work. We begin our hypothetical loop with the fact that when he comes home from school he engages in play activities away from home (instead of doing his homework); when he comes in at dinner time, study is not possible; after dinner he has his "favorite television shows" to watch; by the time the television shows are over, it is too late to study, and another set of opportunities is lost. We may even extend this loop into the night: he goes to bed too late, sleeps less well due to the accumulation of exciting television shows, is drowsy and unable to attend well in class the next day, and is ill-prepared to assemble his work at school in preparation for study at home.

The point of the loop is that, starting with "poor school work," we find each element, each juncture, contributing to this poor showing by augmenting or amplifying the conditions that keep him from study effort. We could begin the loop with "exciting television shows," or we could start with "play after school." Where we begin the analysis does not really matter as long as we recognize that each element plays into the next one and that there are no "deviation counteracting" or corrective elements present. Everything that happens tends to worsen his academic plight.

The loop is illustrated in Figure 1.

Even though we may begin the analysis of the component elements in a loop at any arbitrary point, something more is to be said about how to change the loop. As per our previous points, changing the loop

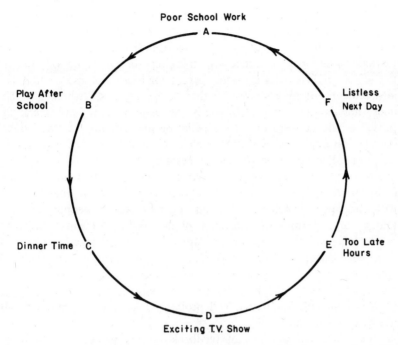

Figure 1. Illustrating how factors or elements (A,B,C . . .) feed into one another and how the series of factors feeds back to point A, in the sense of amplifying A. Theoretically, one can enter the loop at any point or select any point as a crucial one for purposes of therapeutic change.

is best accomplished by entering at some point closest to the point of desired change: In this case, we want to change "poor school work." We may also want to change a number of elements in the loop, for the more we control, the better we can direct or steer the child's behavior.

Also, some factors or elements in a loop do not have much influence on the outcome; we will want to eschew such factors and place our emphasis on factors that have a differential effect. In overcoming the poor study effort, we will not want to analyze the nature of the child's restlessness or whether he has nightmares as separate issues. As we take care of known elements in the loop, the nighttime problems would abate very quickly.

Obviously, there is great economy and considerable value in looking at behavior in terms of a feedback loop. We obviate the need for variables other than those referring to observable behavior, and we do not really need "reinforcement" except in the special case of saying that each element in a loop augments (reinforces?) or counteracts (fails to reinforce?) the previous element. There is, however, a remarkable similarity in cybernetic thinking—in the sense of studying the effects (consequences)—to operant analysis of consequences (reinforcement). It may simply be that "consequences," whether in animals, man, nature, or machines, is the generic term, and social approval or the delivery of a food pellet or the signaling of "well done" are specific instances of this over-all directional aspect of complex interactions between elements in a system. The way we change behavior is to alter some interim course (change an element in a loop from one direction to another direction), and all we are really dealing with are specific behaviors linked together via a feedback process that, in turn, permits the alteration of the course of events (or, as we say in behavior change psychotherapy, permits a change-in-behavior).

Other concepts from cybernetics, such as entropy (and negative entropy), could be discussed, but space does not permit. The general conceptual power of cybernetic thinking is so great and so useful in the study of behavior that it will probably take decades for us to utilize its potentialities.

The functional analysis of feedback in this manner suggests that the whole matter of changing behavior can be looked at in terms of "change agents" and a "change plan." The patient (the "change object") may be his own change agent, or someone else (parent, teacher, spouse) may serve in this manner. The whole therapeutic enterprise can be looked at as a change plan of narrow or wide scope, depending upon the problem. The therapist can be viewed as an "architect of change," or as one who plans change on as limited a basis as the consulting room with one patient or on as broad a basis as a whole school system, institution, or segment of society. To act advisedly and economically in these cases, the therapist or architect of change will employ cybernetic principles, or perhaps those of operant conditioning. The therapist acts in a much broader way than he is conventionally inclined to act when in a one-to-one relationship in a therapy office.

## INTRODUCTION OF CASE

The following case—of a 22-year-old female, a college senior, illustrates a number of facets of the present therapeutic persuasion. The continuously active, interfering manner of the therapist is readily apparent; both patient (P) and therapist (T) are active. There is also a continuous search for, and explication of, what the patient is asserting; with some semifinal notion that she is asserting mainly anger and resentment at being asked an unfair question. This assertion, in turn, relates to other problems she has posed, and the conceptualization of her difficulty—or most of it—in terms of her anger is well under way in this, the fifth, interview. She had a total of fifteen interviews and appeared to have emerged considerably more mature, less emotionally volatile, more able to regulate her daily life with some satisfaction and some degree of freedom from the debilitating attitudes and behavior previously displayed.

T: What has been happening lately?

P: Something happened the other night that was not very good. I was taking this test and all of a sudden my mind turned off. It was not that I hadn't prepared; I just couldn't prepare; I just got to the point where I could not do anything. And the night before I had thought I would just sit down and write down what I knew. I just thought this would be a way to study since my mind was not absorbing. I thought that I would see what I knew. I thought it would be a method of studying and getting the information together if I could write down what I knew. So I wrote it in the form of a letter, because that is an easy way for me to write, and I just got even more confused writing, and I have what I wrote there. When I got to the test, my mind was blank and I could not think of anything, so I just handed in the letter, but I am afraid that I flunked this test.

Comment: This 22-year-old college senior had acted impulsively on many occasions and had run away from home more than once. We can say she was asserting behavior (or being immediately reinforced) that was pretty likely to get her into later difficulty. The episode related here in regard to an examination seemed to trigger off thoughts of the same kind of reaction (running away from something unpleasant). She also shows in the following pages considerable inability to talk intelligently and clearly about how she felt on the examination.

T: What test was this?

P: This was my English course.

T: That is the one that you had trouble with before.

P: And really I had an exact recurrence of that time I ran away; I felt the same. It was exactly the same feeling. I just went back to the dorm, and then I cut my next class. And I had to talk to somebody, and I went back and talked to my roommate. I just had to be with people, just so that I would not let myself run away.

T: That was a week ago today.

P: Yes.

T: Right after I had seen you on Monday?

P: Yes.

T: But you were preparing all right for the test when I saw you on Monday.

P: I know. I had done all the reading and I was preparing and everything. But my mind just panicked. I wrote something when I was in class. I have written stuff like that before when I felt that way. It is sort of like I am not writing it, almost as though somebody else is writing it.

T: May I keep this? (an example of writing under tension)

P: Yes. And then I wrote this. I wrote this when I started writing about the way I felt about the course.

T: Now that is when you were studying the night before?

P: And it was just that the test was so subjective and so. . . . (passes a second exam paper to the therapist)

T: This looks pretty good; what is the matter with this? (referring to the exam she passed over to therapist)

P: Well, that is the way I felt about the course. He gave us these quotes that I suspected he was going to give us. That is what I sort of expressed in that letter I wrote. He wanted us to analyze these quotes; and, my thoughts were so confused because the quotes seemed so all inclusive, and I knew that I just was not capable of analyzing the man. So I got a mental block and I could not even begin to analyze this.

T: Can you give me an example of a quote?

Comment: Here is an example of trying to get very specific information about what was upsetting her. She was sputtering her disapproval of the examination to such an extent—like a crying child trying to tell you that someone did something to him but being unable to articulate it due to his upset—that it took a considerable amount of discourse to identify just what the test required and just how she felt she performed inadequately (and why). We are trying to identify what she was asserting here. Later we learn that she disapproved of the type of question asked, but take note of the circuitous ways in which she circles about this problem.

P: One of them was—just in general because he would not let us keep the test—the one that I started writing on was one of Jonathan Edwards'—when he was in college he read Locke and Descartes, and he understood that there was a whole new concept of man's universe and men were going to have to adjust themselves to it. This idea was "cosmic principles" and like that, which is directly opposed to Edwardian theology. But I was supposed to discuss Edwardian theology in light of this quote. This was only half the test. Well, from the last test when I saw how much he expected, I knew that I could sit there and write, and it would not be good enough. Jonathan Edwards' theology is like a circle—it is a nice compact thing to intuitively understand, but to sit down and to write it out point by point—it is like a circle—where do you begin? At what point can you begin to describe it or analyze it and yet have it come out in a circle? I could not do it.

T: One place is as good as another to start on a circle, isn't it?

P: Yes, but there is so much interrelation that it would be hard to put it in writing; it would have taken me an hour to begin to write about the man. All that I could think was that it was an impossible task.

T: All you saw was this circle spinning in front of you and you couldn't get on. How many quotations did you have?

P: Well, I had two questions or quotes for 75 minutes in the examination.

T: Each question was based on a quotation, is that it?

P: Right.

T: You don't remember the quotation? What was, in general, the nature of the quotation? I was not sure I understood you a while ago.

P: About Descartes and Locke, and their new concept of the universe, where the universe was only ruled by cosmic principles and, of course, Edwardian theology says that maybe this is true but you have religion of the heart, which is part of the heart, part of the man. And then there is this whole system of theology that is worked out. And we have only read 20 pages of the man.

T: But you are answering it right now.

Comment: Here is an excellent example of her apparent ability to answer the question and calls for some confirmatory or reinforcing behavior on the part of the therapist. The problem is less with her actual knowledge of the stated material and more with her approaching the question in a reasonably intelligent way. She is dominated by her feeling (assertion) that the professor has asked an unreasonable question and so prone to react to this condition and not to the intent of the question itself. There is a continuing grappling with this problem throughout the interview—almost to the end.

P: Yes, but I didn't think—the trouble was I had never studied before where I really thought about something with limited time and space and that I could only learn limited factors. But I had been thinking about this man for a period of three or four weeks, and the more I thought about him, the more complicated I realized he was and the more intricate the man was. And it just seemed that there was so much to say.

T: You were overwhelmed, and you did not know how to select. But this was a matter of getting started selectively, wasn't it? Because you are telling me a lot of things about him now which undoubtedly would have been related to the examination.

Comment: In this statement by the therapist there is a clear movement toward describing what the problem is: The problem is, in part, that she did not select correctly from among the many things she knew in answer to the question. So much feeling and emotion and fluster had been generated by her dislike for the question posed that she did not avail herself of her own knowledge. This is just becoming apparent.

P: I know, and this was the problem, there is so much to the man.
T: But you can't cover everything, can you?
P: But this was the problem. I told you about the last quiz I had with this teacher, and this is what scared me. The last time he seemed to want everything of significance, so I felt like he wants everything about the man; plus he wanted quotes to support everything. I knew enough without even putting quotes in and finding appropriate quotes to support it. And it was an open book test, which even floored me worse.
T: What was the second question?
P: The second question was about Ben Franklin; there was a choice among three quotations.
T: And you were to take one and elaborate?
P: I took one which was something like—it was trying to say that Franklin's motives were pure in gaining his wealth; that his virtue came first and his wealth came second. I knew what I could have written if I wanted to just answer it regularly, but I disagreed totally with the quote, because I don't think that anybody has a pure motive. And I started to react that way on the test, but by this time it was pretty late and I was so scared and everything that I wrote some to this effect, but it was very short; and I realize now that if my mind had been in thinking order I could have reworded it and logically seen it through.
T: Again, it was not lack of information; it was an inability to coordinate your own thoughts. And what did you end up doing with this second question? Did you throw in the towel on that too?
P: I had thrown in the towel before I realized. You see, there were all these quotes that were sort of nonspecific, sort of general quotes that took a lot of reading and understanding. They were not just direct quotes; they had lots of shape and meaning and it took a lot to understand the quotes. The quotes were so general, and it was difficult to pick out specifically what they meant, and so I wrote a paragraph and then about a page. I told the professor that I thought that the person who had written the quote was off base; you can't say that anyone has a pure motive, and that his gaining wealth would be not pure virtue because it would be selfish in effect. I said that a man like Franklin defies pinpointing and categorization and that somehow I could not categorize the man.

Comment: To tie up one piece of behavior with another is often a constructive therapeutic tactic. She was saying, in effect, she could not encompass either Edwards or Franklin within the confines of the question. She was asserting again that the expectation was unfair. We see a trend here. We see also, falling back on the previous interviews, that she has tended to "throw in the towel" when she felt she could not meet a situation (answer a question, reply to someone who differed from her, handle a situation in which her ideas were considerably different from others). We could say that these behaviors represented disconfirmation of her long-range attitudes and practices when she was unsuccessful or when she had to operate at a disadvantage. However, perhaps as a result of the previous therapeutic interviews, and as a result of her own decisions about what she wants to change, she is challenging her own narrow conception of her behavior in the past and is currently grappling with it in new ways. She is finding new reinforcers to replace escape from unpleasant situations and to appreciate her own strengths.

> T: So what was the upshot of all this? Did you flunk the exam? Or did your professor say that he would not accept the way that you had answered the question?
> P: I have no idea because he had only corrected five last Thursday, and I have the class right after this, but he has 100 exams to correct, so I am not expecting it for a while. I was so scared—and I had another test coming up Thursday and I had one yesterday too—and so for the one on Thursday I had to relax myself and not study too much, which was bad. But it was just so that I would not panic. I tried to relax myself and just study in general and take it easy with my studying just so that I at least would be able to get through the hour and 15 minutes, although I would not do as good a job as I wanted to.
> T: What was Thursday's exam?
> P: It was in history and was more specific, which made me feel better.
> T: But you did not feel disorganized like you did before, after the literature exam.
> P: I felt that if I had studied more or if I had studied better, I would have less trouble.

Comment: Here she is showing some evidence of calming down, of accepting the examination and trying to make a reasonable showing on it through practical measures. The tensions and symptoms, generated from the conflict situation (not wanting to answer the professor's question, yet having to do so) are now beginning to moderate some, as she gives evidence of asserting more liberal propositions about herself and her course.

P: But once in the test, I decided that I would rather stay with the test. I stayed with the test for the full hour and 15 minutes and I thought about the questions and I did not try to magnify everything or begin to feel like I was a total failure because I could not do it. I just wanted to make myself stick it out. And yesterday I had another test. And my roommate and I studied together, and we talked about the test and the ideas. The test was the kind of test I expected. In any kind of theory test like that, I have no idea how I will do or what the professor wants, because that is so subjective, but I felt fairly good about the test. I felt better about yesterday's test than the other two tests.

T: But you can't tell if your judgment is correct or not.

P: I got a "B" on my Latin test.

T: The one that you told me about last week when you were here? (Pause) What do you think sets up this panicky reaction? Do you think that it is lack of preparation, or do you think it is because you don't approach the answer correctly in the situation?

Comment: Now that she is calmer, we can pose the question again: Is it that she actually does not know the material, or is it that she refuses to roll with the punches? The latter seems more likely. At first she seems to dodge the question, but her thoughtfulness is not really a dodge; it brings us up to another consideration, namely, that she is learning to regard exams and other things in her life differently. She is trying to throw off a yoke, but she is indiscriminate in doing it. Her skill level is low, her efforts to throw off what she considers pressure are faulty, and her aim is unclear. But she is working on the problem, and something will come of it. Some would say she was acting "defensively," but it seems more clearly in relation to the facts to say that she is haltingly learning new behaviors; she is learning new assertions which will be more confirmable—if we have understood her situation correctly.

P: The thing of it is that I don't know why these tests have become such big barriers with me because always before I was able to study less than a lot of kids. I knew kids who would study hours more than I would, and we would come out with the same grade because I knew how to select my information. I could figure out what the teacher was going to ask and be very selective in what I learned, and I always got good grades. Tests were really no major problem with me.

T: You are talking about a different school though.

P: But there were three different schools that I attended before coming here.

T: And in all three of them you did better? Is it that you have a contrary set of professors or very difficult courses now?

P: Yes. (Pause) Yesterday I did manage to pick out the important things, and I felt better because I talked to other kids and they did not know what he was going to ask, and it turned out that I had figured out what he was going to ask. We had previously discussed everything that was on the test. I don't know how well I wrote and how much more information I could or should have given, but I successfully predicted what type of question the man would ask.

T: In other words, you picked the right topics for study among those possible ones. So was this a lucky guess, or do you think you really discerned something in the professor's evaluation during the lectures?

P: I think I discerned something; I think I had it figured out.

Comment: Here she is finding in her own behavior on other occasions the strength and self-direction she needs. She is finding an example in her own repertoire, which is better than any I can give her, of how to solve her problems. Confirmation is now following her assertions rather than disconfirmation. The chance of her behavior "paying off" is increasing, and new and more stable behaviors are open for reinforcement.

T: But you can't do this in the literature course that you were talking about a while ago?

P: But again, I think I have this course more in perspective than my writing would indicate. I was studying with my roommate, and we talked with two or three other kids who had the same test, so I was able to relate my preparation to theirs. I was able to relate myself to other members of the class.

T: You had more foreknowledge in the case of some exams than in others; and when you lack foreknowledge, of course, it is more difficult to prepare. But now that you have experienced this difficulty, do you think the next time you have an exam you will be better prepared?

P: In this course I am going to see if I can get an interview with the professor because I have such a mental block about the course that I don't know what to do.

T: Have you had any exams in English literature other than the one you just described?

P: I had an earlier quiz in that class in which I got a "C", which did not set me up too well.

T: That is a "C" in a quiz and an exam that we don't know the results of but still feel discouraged about it. Will there be another hour exam before the final?

P: There will be another quiz before the final and an optional paper.

Comment: We are referring now to upcoming events. Will there be an opportunity to prepare better for future exams? And will she see that preparation is one important thing but actually selecting her answers is an equally important matter? She seems to be zeroing in a bit better on the target of how she takes the examination itself. Assertions are improving; confirmation (reinforcement) of them is more likely.

> T: An optional paper—what does that mean?
> P: That you don't have to do it.
> T: If you do it, does it enhance your grade?
> P: Yes, it can.
> T: Have you given consideration to doing that so that you are bolstered in case you fall down on this hour exam?
> P: I have given sort of consideration to it.
> T: What would you write on?
> P: Well, the thing is, I should have picked someone. You pick some author, and you write on some aspect of his work.
> T: What interests you along that line?
> P: I sort of rejected the idea of doing the paper because of my other work.
> T: But if you are in arrears in this course, gradewise, would it not be worthwhile to consider writing this paper?

Comment: Here is a suggestion that she might consider writing the paper for extra credit. Is this not permissible? Yes, from the present therapeutic standpoint. She has begun to loosen up some, she is considering alternatives to her former behavior which has gotten her into difficulty, and she is seeing the test behavior as part and parcel of larger problems she has had in the past. To miss the cue she is giving the therapist in regard to encouraging her to tackle the extra credit paper is to miss a constructive opportunity. There is some risk in encouraging her to undertake this work, but she is basically a good student (a "B" average for three years of college), and there is need for her to learn to accept and be challenged by reasonable assignments (by existing assignments, even if she does not always regard them as reasonable). There is potentially powerful reinforcement value in her doing the extra paper and getting a good mark on it.

> P: I guess it would be.
> T: When do you have to make a decision and tell the professor your topic?
> P: By the end of November we have to have a topic handed in.
> T: In other words, that is about two weeks from now?
> P: Yes, and then on another date we have to have an outline of the paper turned in, and then we hand the paper in later at the end of the semester.
> T: The paper is not due until the end of the semester, but the outline is due before the end of the month. Well, suppose you think about this some and see what kind of provisional topic or outline you might come up with, because it occurs to me that if you are in a deficit

condition here and you know that there are certain prescribed things that you can do to get out of it, it might follow that you try to do these things. Does that make sense to you?

P: Yes. I was thinking about my studying and why I am having such a difficult time with the test and I sort of figured it out. I sort of figured that I used to use study for an escape. No matter what was going wrong elsewhere, I would stop everything; I would stop anything else that was going on, and I would concentrate totally on what I was studying or writing a paper on. I would escape from everything, and so on, no matter what other kinds of problems I had, I could always study.

Comment: Now we have the most important part of the interview—her own theory about why she has behaved as she has and how it ties in with larger issues having great meaning to her. Is this insight? I do not really care, but I do want to point out that the assisting and germinating attitudes and comments of the therapist, the emphasis on her behavior and not so much on what she feels (we have to know how what she feels is a function of her behavior in some situations—we have to see how the feeling is, itself, a stamp of approval or disapproval on what she has actually done), have apparently gone a long way in a short while to encourage her self-corrective comments and her larger grasp of the issues at hand. Her repertoire is increasing in resourcefulness; there is less conflict. Cybernetically speaking, she is not caught up in deviation-amplifying loops, and there is less redundancy in her behavior.

P: I could put in a concentrated effort on the studying and block everything else out. I don't know if this has any relation, but I am not really up for escaping anymore.

T: You don't have to "escape" now. It is a case of integration or adjustment in one area having a slightly adverse effect on another until you rebalance them. Is that right?

P: Yes. It seems to me that I always used the total concentration that I was able to muster up. I could use it for an escape. I find some even now when I am studying for a test that I can't study and prepare for a social situation. If I am to go to dinner on a date, then I get nervous. I get nervous just at dinner, because I keep wanting dinner to be over so that I can get back to my studying, and I don't want to talk to anybody or listen to anybody. It becomes the "be all; end all" of my existence until the test is over.

T: But this is not so much the case now as it used to be?

P: Right. I would like to be able to integrate both and get a positive outlook on studying, so that I am not so emotionally tied up in it.

T: Maybe you are in the throes of a change here in your attitude and in your practices from a more tense type of application to a more relaxed one, but you have not quite made the transition and until you make the transition, exams will be a little bit upsetting to you.

Comment: This is a therapeutic recap of what she has just said, but in different terms, and with the implied meaning that the still lingering confusion or lack of total self-direction is part of a larger change effort and not to be considered as discouraging. This comment of the therapist is by way of reinforcing her own efforts and is to assist her in continuing to try to overcome the problem more completely.

> P: And for this test yesterday, I threw myself back into what I am used to.
> T: To the old method?
> P: To the old method because I had to. I wanted to get through this exam and feel that at least I had done something about it. And in order to do it, I sort of had to put in the concentrated effort again.

Comment: Here is an example of the typical vacillation of one unsure of his own behavior. In learning new skills, we are aware of the fact that old habits often interfere, and there may be a plateau reached, or there may be a return to earlier, less skillful behavior. However, the trend is clear here with her, but it is important to say this to her and to look to future opportunities to further improve matters.

> T: But on the other hand, you should think of studying as something that you do as you go along, rather than a last ditch stand a day or two before the exam.
> P: But see, that is what scares me because I sit there and study, yet am not able to relate to these theories and what I was reading about. It was like I could learn all kinds of concepts and theories and like that, but I did not relate to them. It is like playing word games for me and nothing more. I never began to relate to any of them.
> T: Maybe you related too much to Jonathan Edwards in a negative way, because you kept saying, "I can't look at him this way." You were negating the value of the question in a sense; weren't you? Maybe you were too emotional, then, rather than impartial.

Comment: Here is another effort to clarify what her confused behavior means. It means mostly that she is still grappling with the problem of concentration and accepting the question on an exam (or an assignment) more or less at face value and separating this requirement from the ones where she is not obliged to follow another's lead or submit herself to someone's pressure. This could be called a problem on discrimination learning.

> P: I should be able to objectively understand what I read, and particularly understand the workings of philosophies or the theories of

people, and compare them and contrast them without getting at all involved in the people. But it has been more like a crossword puzzle.
T: So, if you get involved emotionally, you lose perspective, or lose your skill in coping with the questions. I hope I understand what you mean, and I think we need to talk about this some more because when you become better related to what you are learning or involved in it, you really ought to know it better and ought to have a greater facility because you like it.
P: I enjoyed playing the games with the theories as long as I did not relate to them.
T: How did you relate to Edwards, do you think, since you disagreed with him so much?
P: Well, there I was trying to understand this man as a man; he was not just a lot of theories, he was a person to me.
T: Well, why were you studying him to learn about him this way rather than to learn about his theories? What appeal did he have, or what dis-appeal did he have that made this an emotional kind of connection rather than an intellectual one, if we can use this distinction momentarily?
P: I don't know what there was about him, except that he was a mystic.
T: Do you agree with his mysticism?
P: Yes, in a sense. It seemed to me that I hit upon this man, he was a man of terrific intellect and he wanted to relate to his religion, and he had to turn to his heart rather than turn to his head. I just think that he realized that the heart was more than the head.
T: This was not a theology; it was more of a personal, from-the-heart religion that he was espousing.
P: Right, and it was the only way he could.
T: But where do you come into this picture? This appeals to you, but when you received this question from the professor it seemed to do violence to this emotive aspect of his religion, and the emotive aspect of your interest in the man. In other words, you were asked by the examiner to switch off from this religion-of-the-heart and intuitive understanding, etc., to pull this apart in a piecemeal fashion and evaluate it.

Comment: Back to her again, and back to her problems in the context of the course. Actually, Jonathan Edwards, or Benjamin Franklin, or anyone could be the topic, and any kind of intellectual or so-called emotional content could be under discussion, and we might have the same problem from her. It is important to again focus on her and not on Edwards or Franklin. Coming back to this general point time and time again seems to be a necessary aspect of the therapy. She doesn't learn the solution from one exposure.

P: It made me mad—because he was a man and you could say that he was this, this, this, and this, but it does not describe the man. It does not make him a person. It just makes him a lot of ideas. He is an individual. I could not sit down and write about Jonathan Edwards in total. I would be doing him a disservice by writing about him.

Comment: I can risk a conceptual or deductive leap here and say that her anger is really the heart of the problem of her feeling, her discussion, her performance on the test. She is just plain angry that she is asked to do something she prefers not to do. But, of course, she is caught in the trap of commitment to the course, wanting to do well, needing to succeed in her own eyes, etc. In a sense we could have collapsed the entire discussion found in this protocol and have simply said she was mad at having to take the exam in the manner described. If the therapist does this too readily, however, he risks losing the patient's understanding and perhaps losing the patient altogether. But now that the fat is in the fire—namely, her anger—we have a lot more to work on, and we have a very cogent way of conceptualizing and describing her behavior in a multitude of situations. The main assertion is anger.

T: But this is the peculiar part of your relationship with what you know about Jonathan Edwards that is causing you to get "hung-up" on the exam.
P: But I felt the same way about Ben Franklin too. I felt like saying, "You are asking me to read 20 pages of a man and analyze him." If he had asked me specific questions or specific points about what he believed—(pause)—but on the exam I was supposed to describe this man in toto in a sense, and I could not do it.
T: I understand what you are saying, and the same attitude was felt with regard to Ben Franklin. So what we are really down to is your emotional objection to the question or the examination. You said yourself if this had been brought to you in terms of specific questions, such as, did he do this or was he so and so, you could have answered these. But to produce a synthesis of this sort was a violation of emotional integrity you considered important, on the basis of your study and understanding of each of these people.
P: And I began to realize that I did not really know anything about the man.
T: Why don't you convey this to your professor?
P: This is what I conveyed in that letter.
T: In other words, the letter was your apology and also your reply to this question, which you did not like. Do you think that in your letter you revealed your knowledge and understanding of both Edwards and Franklin?
P: I tried to; I wrote a page describing his theology and said that this does not begin to describe it because it is easy to say all this, but it does not give you a picture of the man. I said that I am supposed

to relate to this man in so many ways and said that it was impossible in the short time that I was given.

T: You were telling the professor in a sense that he was asking the wrong questions. All right, let's see what happens with this, but let's also be prepared to answer the wrong question, as you see it, on subsequent examinations, particularly in this course and with this professor, and be forewarned and forearmed in the event that you may face this again.

Comment: Here is some tidying up the loose ends: On the one hand, you have your objections; but, on the other hand, you have to make your way through the course. Let's be practical and sensible, the therapist is saying.

P: It is just lately that I've had this trouble with exams. I used to always be able to write exams because I could sense what a teacher would ask and be sure I could sit down and write about it. But now I get to the point that when they ask me a question that I do not like I tell them that I don't like it, and why, because I don't want to answer it if I think it is a bad question. I have gotten to a point where I can't. . . . (began crying, visibly upset)

Comment: And now here she is doing some of her own tidying up of the issues, relating her past behavior on exams to her present behavior, but observing that even though the present trend has some objectionable aspects to it, and some problems she must yet overcome, she is still better off now than before when she was using her studying to escape other responsibilities and opportunities. This is real growth!

T: I understand. This could represent some kind of growth and integrity and independence on your part, particularly in the light of our seeing that you have been too ready to submit to anyone before. But it may be that you chose your battleground at the wrong time, as far as this professor and this course are concerned. I am not saying this critically; I am just saying it tactically. This might not have been the best time or place to assert yourself and your independence.

P: I guess after doing it so long, I just got mad. After a point, I just get mad when the question seems to me to miss what real knowledge is about, and, as a result, I am not conveying what I really know or what I really feel about something.

T: And you have a right to your ideas, but on the other hand, we have to look at the consequences of your exam writing, and we have to study the problem in terms of what you are here for. Well, let's leave off at this point today, and we will pick it up next week.

## CASE OF AN ADULT MALE

A brief resume of a 39-year-old married male professional case is as follows. This man, with a brilliant scholastic record, has never come to fruition in his professional life. He has changed jobs frequently, has many "nasty encounters with peers and superiors over the years" in his words, and always felt he never got the opportunity his ability merited. He displayed a good deal of chagrin about being considered "a veritable child prodigy who never made good" on the one hand and an individual who said he never got the kind of professional opportunity he felt he could handle. His problems covered many areas of work, personal life, marital life, and so on. One difficulty that bothered him considerably at the time I am writing about was that of fruitless days on the job. While there were many details not encompassed in the following conceptualization of one aspect of his problem, the points made in the cybernetic loop analysis seemed to "make sense" to him in an intellectual way and provided an entry point for his own more concerted effort to change, rather than simply complain about his plight or feel depressed because he had not lived up to his promise.

Specifically our present analysis hinges on his complaints that he seldom ever had a good workday. Characteristically, he slept poorly, got up late, dragged off to work relying on the benefit of his wife's prodding and supplications, slumped in his chair at work (in a scientific and research organization), had frequent abrasive encounters with peers owing to his poor and irregular work habits, and returned home at night even more defeated but excessively ruminating about what had occurred during the workday. He had equally discouraging encounters with his wife and, on occasion, with friends in social gatherings.

A loop describing his day is pictured in Figure 2.

As indicated in the analysis in Figure 1, referring to the inefficient student, the loop can be entered in a conceptual way at any point whatsoever. In a practical way, the point of entry should be one that is easiest to enter, one that is closest to the desired point of critical change, and a point where the proficiency in changing the whole loop is likely to be highest. Some effort to tackle the "poor sleep problem" through relaxation methods and through handling wakeful periods of the night did not prove useful, owing in part to the patient's great resentment at the time of waking and his highly ruminative way of dealing with tension at that time. I was never sanguine about handling the actual wakeful period at night but felt from the beginning that another part of the loop should be tackled; however, the patient felt most depressed by the sleeplessness and desired to do something at that juncture first—without success.

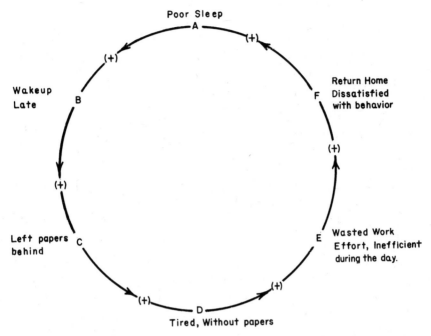

Figure 2. Showing how a series of steps or junctures in a loop serves to augment the problem of a 29-year-old male with respect to daily work.

Later, after much discussion and exploration of how he handled his sleeplessness during the night, it became evident that the getting up time was really crucial. If he got up on time, he got off to work without additional complications, even though he remained tired and sleepy. Also, leaving for work on time was one small item of success that was really under his control, and this morale booster seemed to work effectively for most of the rest of the day (save for unexpected abrasive encounters with others related to specific and somewhat unpredictable aspects of the day's work).

In addition to getting up on time, he prepared his papers and other details the night before and placed them in his valise near the door, ready for the following day's exit at 8:15 A.M. Of course, attention was given to the nature of his work assignments, their size, how well they could be broken down into manageable units, how priorities could be established and followed, how time could be saved for emergencies, and so on. But the practical steps that really cracked the problem of his day's work evolved from this simple loop analysis of his actual behavior (which he described exceptionally well, but with an abundance of minutia similar to the introspections of one reporting on a drug-stimulated "trip"). He had taught himself to think in ruminative ways about his problems and their many facets and was more adept at speculative inquiry than at decisive action.

It is interesting to report that he at first rejected the idea of the loop as "nothing but a superficial base-touching without knowing the nature of the game you are playing." Receiving this kind of criticism commonly from patients—and from professional peers, also!—did not deter me in encouraging him to try it out and report back in empirical ways what he observed. He was gradually persuaded that there was some merit in his paying attention to his actual behavior, as contrasted with what "all this behavior, these minutia of events, *really* mean." Although he was rigorously trained in the physical sciences and capable of brilliant exchanges in conversation, as well as illuminating chains of complicated reasoning, he applied these rigors hardly at all to himself. Moreover, I almost had to "sell" him on the advantages of even starting an analysis of one small bit of his problem in the way delineated here.

Suffice it to say in this brief example that the prototype of his daily work offered in cybernetic loop terms allowed him to take a giant step forward in respect to his job. He was able to better his relationships with peers and superiors, and soon he began to get down to productivity he could be proud of. At this writing he is in the process of applying similar analyses of his difficulties outside the confines of his job.

## SUMMARY

In summary, assertion-structured therapy (or, more generically, an interference position) has always had a strong behavioral bias, but through the influence of operant analysis of behavior and cybernetics, it is felt that the original position has gained in precision, in objectivity, and in parsimonious use of variables. At all points, subjective or mental states are eschewed. An earnest effort is continually being made to relate behavior change theory to the general area of behavior study and to larger systems of analysis (such as cybernetics).

The cumulative effect of this kind of theorizing and practicing has been to pose two broad questions that I think are fundamental to behavior change wherever it is found. The first question is

What (how much) behavior must be controlled or changed in order to produce a general effect?

This question not only stresses the importance of theory as it may give direction and regulation to behavior change efforts, but it also holds up the value of parsimonious solutions to problems. When we can begin to answer this question broadly across many specific problems of change, and accurately in the sense of avoiding wasted or inefficient effort, we will to this extent have not only an important technology of behavior change but will have contributed materially to truly masterful theorizing.

The other question, implied by the very term "behavior change," asserts a proposition (rather than asking a question), to wit:

> If you can explain, control, or understand behavior, this knowledge will provide a basis for change.

Or, stated more challengingly, if one truly understands behavior, he can bring it under control or change it. If one cannot state how to control or change behavior, his knowledge is correspondingly weak.

In summing up, the use of any behavioral model, although it may seem to some to neglect important phenomenological variables, actually appears to be more economical at the conceptual level and more effective in producing behavior change over a wide assortment of cases and disturbances at a practical, clinical level. There are, of course, many possible behavioral models, as this volume clearly shows, and the bases for choice among behavioral models may not yet be clear to us. It is most likely that new behavioral models related to psychotherapy (or behavior change) will be promulgated. This makes the future interesting and exciting and helps today's student of behavior change to realize he is contributing to a scientific enterprise that may have wide implications and importance.

## REFERENCES

1. Brown, J. S. The generalization of approach response as a function of stimulus intensity and strength of motivation. *J. Comp. Psychol.*, 1942, **33**, 209–226.
2. DeLatil, P. *Thinking by machine.* Boston: Houghton Mifflin, 1957.
3. Ferster, C. B., & Skinner, B. F. *Schedules of reinforcement.* New York: Appleton, 1957.
4. Greniewski, H. *Cybernetics without mathematics.* London: Pergamon Press, 1960.

5. Haring, N. G., & Phillips, E. Lakin. *Educating emotionally disturbed children.* New York: McGraw-Hill, 1962.
6. Krasner, L., & Ullmann, L. P. *Research in behavior modification.* New York: Holt, Rinehart & Winston, 1965.
7. Miller, N. E. Experimental studies of conflict. In J. McV. Hunt (Ed.), *Personality and the behavior disorders.* Vol. 1. New York: Ronald Press, 1944.
8. Miller, N. E. Comments on theoretical models illustrated by the development of a theory of conflict. *J. Personality,* 1951, **20,** 82–100.
9. Phillips, E. Lakin. *Psychotherapy: A modern theory and practice.* New York: Prentice-Hall, 1956.
10. Phillips, E. Lakin. Contributions to a learning theory account of childhood autism. *J. Psychol.,* 1957, **43,** 117–124.
11. Phillips, E. Lakin. The use of the teacher as an adjunct therapist in child guidance. *Psychiatry,* 1957, **4,** 407–410.
12. Phillips, E. Lakin. Diagnosis in terms of effects. *Amer. Psychol.,* 1958, **13,** 344. (Abstract)
13. Phillips, E. Lakin. Parent-child psychotherapy: A follow-up study comparing two techniques. *J. Psychol.,* 1960, **49,** 195–202.
14. Phillips, E. Lakin. Interference vs. extinction as learning models for psychotherapy. *J. Psychol.,* 1961, **51,** 399–403.
15. Phillips, E. Lakin. Logical analysis of childhood behavior problems and their treatment. *Psychol. Reports,* 1961, **9,** 705–712.
16. Phillips, E. Lakin, & El-Batrawi, S. Learning theory and psychotherapy revisited: With notes on illustrative cases. *Psychotherapy: Theory, Res. & Practice,* 1964, **1,** 145–150.
17. Phillips, E. Lakin, & Haring, N. G. Results from special techniques for teaching emotionally disturbed children. *Exceptional Children,* 1959, **26,** 64–67.
18. Phillips, E. Lakin, & Wiener, D. N. *Short-term psychotherapy and structured behavior change.* New York: McGraw-Hill, 1966.
19. Phillips, E. Lakin, Wiener, D. N., & Haring, N. G. *Discipline, achievement, and mental health.* New York: Prentice-Hall, 1960.
20. Ullmann, L. P., & Krasner, L. *Case studies in behavior modification.* New York: Holt, Rinehart & Winston, 1965.

Chapter 2

# Verbal Behavior Therapy

## H. A. STORROW

H. A. Storrow: b. 1926, Long Beach, California.
A.B., University of Southern California, Los Angeles, 1946. M.D., University
of Southern California School of Medicine, 1950. Residency Training
at the Sheppard and Enoch Pratt Hospital, USPHS Hospital, Lex-
ington, Kentucky, and Brentwood V.A. Hospital, Los Angeles, 1950–
1955.
Professor of Psychiatry, University of Kentucky College of Medicine, 1966–
date. Professor of Psychiatry, University of Minnesota School of Medi-
cine, 1965–1966. Associate Professor of Psychiatry, University of
Kentucky School of Medicine, 1960–1965. Assistant Professor of
Psychiatry, University of California School of Medicine, Los Angeles,
1956–1960. Private psychiatric practice, 1956–1960, 1965–date.
Fellow, American Psychiatric Association. Chairman, Medical Education
Committee, Kentucky Psychiatric Association.
Books: *Outline of Clinical Psychiatry* (1969). *Introduction to Scientific
Psychiatry: A Behavioristic Approach to Diagnosis and Treatment*
(1967).
Articles: About 20 in professional journals.
Psychotherapy as interpersonal conditioning. In J. H. Masserman (Ed.).
*Current psychiatric therapies.* Vol. 5. New York: Grune & Stratton,
1965. Pp. 76-86. Learning, labeling, general semantics, and psycho-
therapy. *General Semantics Bulletin,* 1963–1964, **30** and **31,** 84–86.
Depression masquerading as apathy. *J. Ky. St. Med. Assn.,* 1964, **62,**
292-293. Operational classification of the varieties of psychotherapy.
*Dis. Nerv. Syst.,* 1963, **24,** 463–471. Is psychotherapy effective?
*Southern Med. J.,* 1962, **55,** 368–373.

**W**hat is verbal behavior therapy? How does it differ from other
forms of psychiatric treatment? What's new about it anyway? These
are fair questions that deserve careful answers.[1]

---

[1] This paper has been condensed, with permission of the publishers, from
Storrow, H. A. *Introduction to Scientific Psychiatry: A behavioristic approach to
diagnosis and treatment.* New York: Appleton-Century-Crofts, 1967.
For details concerning these methods, please consult this reference.

Since verbal behavior therapy is a form of psychotherapy, our first task is to define psychotherapy. Although this sounds simple, it is not. Definitions of psychotherapy differ because supporters of specific approaches like to deny the label to their opponents' methods.

Taking a broad-minded point of view, William Schofield (3) calls psychotherapy a conversation with therapeutic intent.

My own definition may raise some hackles, but here it is: The term psychotherapy covers all those methods for the psychological modification of disturbed human behavior that depend primarily upon a relationship established for this purpose between a professionally trained therapist and a patient. This definition obviously requires clarification.

What is behavior? I like Hilgard's definition: "Those activities of an organism that can be observed by another organism or by an experimenter's instruments." (2, p. 614) I expand this definition with an additional phrase: "Or can be inferred from such observation." Subjective processes, such as thoughts and feelings, are behavior, too; they differ from finger twitches, eye blinks, and galvanic skin responses only in their inaccessibility to direct observation.

What is disturbed behavior? Disturbed behavior is behavior that causes trouble, enough trouble to warrant treatment.

How can behavior be modified? There are two major ways: (1) somatic methods and (2) psychological methods. Somatic techniques aim at changing behavior by directly altering underlying biological functions. Drugs and electroshock treatment are examples. Physicians, of course, have a legal monopoly in this area. Although somatic methods often supplement psychotherapy, or vice versa, they are separate forms of treatment.

I reserve the term psychotherapy for psychological treatment techniques. These techniques depend upon manipulating environmental stimuli that influence behavior. Stimuli may be manipulated during treatment sessions, between sessions, or both. Although psychological methods may modify biological processes, they do so indirectly. They impinge upon the intact organism rather than upon cells, organs, and organ systems.

Psychotherapists are persons with professional training in at least one system of behavior modification techniques. Acceptable professional training for psychotherapy is a matter for acrimonious arguments at interdisciplinary cocktail parties and committee meetings. All psychotherapists consider their own backgrounds excellent. Most are willing to admit psychiatrists, clinical psychologists, and at least some social workers to the fraternity. (Social workers are more acceptable if they call themselves "counselors" and their patients "clients.") Beyond this point the questions become too fuzzy for me to settle.

## THE VARIETIES OF PSYCHOTHERAPY

A few years ago Robert Harper (1) described 36 "systems" of psychotherapy. Some new ones have appeared since then. If we content ourselves with an oversimplified picture, however, we can distinguish two major classes of approaches: the dynamic psychotherapies and the behavior psychotherapies. These have sprung from different theoretical views of the relations between environmental stimuli and human behavior.

The dynamic psychotherapies are based upon a "three step" model of environment–behavior relations. Environmental stimuli control a complex set of hypothetical interacting "forces" within the personality, and these forces control behavior. The term "dynamic" refers to this network of forces and counterforces. They are inferred from behavior alone and bear no specified relationship to central nervous system structure or function.

A further assumption also guides the efforts of dynamic psychotherapists: understanding or "insight" is necessary for behavior change. When patients understand the forces responsible for their behavior and the reasons the forces have come to act as they do, behavior becomes more adaptive. When behavior fails to change, this fact means that insight is inadequate in some way. Behavior changes that occur without insight are allegedly superficial and temporary.

This emphasis on understanding guides dynamic psychotherapy technique. Therapists shun anything they feel may influence their patients. They limit their activity to questions, brief comments, and interpretations of what patients "really mean." They refuse to answer questions, offer advice, or see relatives. These techniques are often labeled "nondirective." Although it is impossible to avoid influencing patients, dynamic psychotherapists make heroic attempts to keep this influence to a minimum.

We must keep one caution in mind as we conclude this brief discussion of dynamic psychotherapy. The picture I have given is seriously oversimplified; there are many variations in practice. Many dynamic psychotherapists give advice and indulge in more directiveness than are called for by their theories. Other therapists use nondirective techniques exclusively but would be shocked to hear their theories labeled "dynamic."

The behavior psychotherapies or behavior therapies reject the "three step" behavior model previously discussed. Although the behavior therapist accepts the idea that human beings have a central nervous system and that events at biological levels correlate with behavior, he feels that inferences about internal events from behavior alone are nonproductive. He prefers to look directly at relationships between environmental stimuli and his patient's responses. He feels that, within limits, behavior is learned and that the laws of learning provide the most fruitful means for understanding stimulus–response relationships.

The behavior therapist uses techniques explicitly derived from learning theory. As he gathers information from his patient, he asks the following questions of his data:

1. What are the behavior patterns that need changing?
2. What current situational stimuli maintain these patterns?
3. How can the current stimulus situation be altered to help the patient learn more adaptive behavior?

Although behavior therapy as yet runs a poor second in the popularity race with the dynamic therapies, it is a vigorously growing infant. There are potentially as many behavior therapy techniques as there are methods for administering stimuli to human beings. Many of these fit the experimental laboratory better than the psychotherapist's consulting room. Although a rapidly expanding literature describes methods and applications, few attempts have yet been made to formulate an organized approach to clinical problems.

Verbal behavior therapy is a first approximation of such an approach. It grew out of years of trying to apply learning theory principles to psychiatric office practice. Verbal behavior therapy claims descent from both of the two major "houses" of modern psychotherapy. It draws its theory, its goals, and many of its methods from behavior therapy; it uses the tools and some of the techniques of dynamic therapy. Many of its elements are as old as psychotherapy itself; what's new is the collection of these into an integrated whole on the basis of the principles of learning theory.

Verbal behavior therapy also rests upon one further assumption. "Assumption" is perhaps too weak a term; the idea has been amply validated both in the laboratory and in the consulting room. Words can be effective conditioned stimuli and reinforcers. They can serve as vehicles for reward and punishment. For therapeutic use they have many advantages over other stimuli: they are always available and require no special equipment. Skillfully used, they are potent treatment tools.

In summary: Verbal behavior therapy uses the basic principles of learning theory and the traditional verbal tools of the psychotherapist. No equipment is required beyond a room, two chairs, and two people, both of whom can talk and listen. Even the room and the chairs could perhaps be eliminated, a modification I have not yet tried. Although most of my personal experience has been with individual treatment, I have found verbal behavior therapy effective for group work as well.

## GENERAL PRINCIPLES OF VERBAL BEHAVIOR THERAPY

Verbal behavior therapy differs from "standard" psychotherapeutic approaches in a number of ways.[2] Chief among these are its focus on observable or reportable behavior rather than upon hypothetical inner dynamics and its focus upon the present rather than upon the past. In this approach the therapist characteristically directs attention to current behavior difficulties and to the settings in which they occur. Since new adaptive behavior can be more easily displayed with the therapist than with important figures in the environment, behavior between interviews must be as much an object of attention as that which occurs during the sessions.

## THE OPENING PHASE OF TREATMENT

The beginning phase of treatment sets the therapeutic stage. It usually lasts at least three or four interviews and may take as many as nine or ten. During these early sessions the verbal behavior therapist devotes his time to the following tasks: Adaptation, diagnosis, specifying goals, negotiating the therapeutic contract, establishing the therapist as a source of reinforcement, and teaching the patient how to learn.

Let us take a closer look at each of these.

### Adaptation

In conditioning studies the experimenter always allows time for his subject to "adapt" to the experimental situation. Before beginning the

---

[2] Portions of the remainder of this paper have been modified, with permission of the publishers, from Storrow, H. A. Psychotherapy as interpersonal conditioning, in J. H. Massermann, (Ed.), *Current psychiatric therapies.* Vol. 5. New York: Grune and Stratton, 1965. Pp. 76–86.

experiment he waits until preliminary fear and exploratory responses have subsided. Psychotherapy is certainly a novel situation, and all patients probably find it mildly aversive at first. I handle problems of adaptation in a number of ways. I avoid probing into sensitive areas until the patient has become reasonably comfortable. I examine the circumstances that led to treatment and discuss the patient's reactions. I clarify the purpose of treatment and broadly outline how it will proceed.

*Diagnosis*

This word has a special meaning for the verbal behavior therapist. It includes formulating each patient's case by specifying positive symptoms, negative symptoms, and central symptoms. Treatment then proceeds directly from this formulation. Let us take a quick look at each of these classes of symptoms.

We use the word "repertoire" to designate all the learned responses a person is capable of performing. The responses he is capable of performing in a given situation is the repertoire for that setting.

The responses in any repertoire have different probabilities of occurrence. Preferred responses have a high probability; less-preferred responses have a low probability and therefore occur only if preferred behavior patterns are blocked for some reason.

The patient with a positive symptom suffers because a maladaptive response ranks high in his repertoire, i.e., has a high probability of occurrence. The response may be maladaptive in itself, i.e., a strong tendency to attempt suicide, or it may be maladaptive because of the setting in which it occurs or because of its intensity. Submissiveness is adaptive in certain situations but causes trouble when it is expressed toward everyone.

Negative symptoms occur when an adaptive response is absent or almost absent from a patient's repertoire, when the behavior pattern has a very low or zero probability. Delinquents, for example, characteristically lack conditioned anxiety and guilt responses to situations involving "temptation"; they also usually lack the conditioned patterns of persistence that characterize normal persons. These are negative symptoms.

What are central symptoms? When an emotional illness develops, the central symptoms are the root problems that appear first. The troubles they cause nurture the secondary disturbances that complicate the clinical picture in most patients we see.

Central symptoms relate to these secondary disturbances much as false assumptions can relate to systematized delusional patterns. When a set of delusions is well organized, the whole thing becomes logical if we buy one or two crazy ideas. Suppose that a paranoid patient claims he's a Federal courier and that a wrinkled old envelope he carries bulging with smudged papers is a diplomatic pouch full of state secrets. If we accept these assumptions, his delusion that the noise of a backfiring automobile comes from sniper shots aimed at him by a bearded man in a trenchcoat suddenly seems logical.

Central symptoms may be positive or negative. They may be classically conditioned emotional responses or instrumentally conditioned voluntary responses or both.

Central symptoms, in theory at least, can be the only symptoms presented by a patient. Such cases are simple psychiatric disturbances, and they represent the bulk of the cases described in the behavior therapy literature to date. Examples are anxiety reactions, and phobias without other maladaptive behavior patterns. I say "in theory" because such patients seem to shun my office and those of most psychiatrists I know. Furthermore, I suspect that most such "simple" problems would turn out to be complicated were they intensively studied. Most "everyday" psychiatric problems are complex. They consist of central symptoms plus elaborate patterns of secondary disturbances.

How do central symptoms produce complex disturbances? Maladaptive behavior leads either to relief of discomfort or to positive reward of some kind. Otherwise it would extinguish. But it also has delayed consequences. Through its impact on the environment or on the patient's view of his environment, problem behavior produces painful or aversive stimulation. The patient reacts to these new aversive stimuli in his customary fashion, with new distressing emotional responses and new avoidance or escape behavior. Patients usually arrive in our offices only after self-administered "first aid" has failed and the process of symptom development has continued for some time. By then the "present illness" is a chaotically complicated network of interlocking maladaptive responses. But the central symptoms still provide the key.

*Specifying goals*

Since verbal behavior therapy focuses upon definite response patterns, its goals can and should be stated precisely. I describe what I expect to happen to the central symptoms and to the other major symptoms that make up the presenting clinical picture.

*Negotiating the therapeutic contract*

When I have completed my diagnosis and decided upon appropriate treatment goals, I share my findings and recommendations with my patient. If he accepts my proposals, treatment can proceed on the foundation of a free and open agreement about what the problems are and what can be done about them. Edward Sulzer (5) calls this mutual acceptance of goals and methods the therapeutic contract. If my patient rejects the contract, I have two choices: offer a new contract with modified goals or refuse treatment.

*Establishing the therapist as a source of reinforcement*

This important task usually requires several interviews; sometimes it takes months. In fact, it continues throughout treatment as a secondary goal.

A potent source of reinforcement can be recognized by its marked impact on behavior. I know my reinforcing value has risen to a useful level when I note certain changes in the patient's behavior: He begins to express positive feelings for me and begins to look forward to the sessions. He begins to demonstrate respect for me as a competent professional person. He begins to value my opinions. He tries to act upon suggestions. He begins to value and to seek my approval and to be at least mildly upset at signs of disapproval.

We establish and strengthen secondary or conditioned reinforcers by linking them with rewards. I try to become a rewarding figure for the patient, for example, by giving him my undivided attention and avoiding disapproval in the early sessions. There are also a number of other techniques for accomplishing this important task, but they cannot be covered in this brief discussion.

*Teaching the patient how to learn*

Learning new behavior is work, hard, uncomfortable work. It requires abandoning well-trodden paths for strange and unfamiliar ones. In a sense, it requires giving up a bird in the hand in the hope of finding two in the bush. The patient must forego the small but certain rewards that maintain his present behavior in the hope of gaining large but uncertain rewards in the future. Usually this process requires a temporary increase in his level of discomfort.

To accomplish these tasks the patient must learn how to learn; he must acquire an expectation that new responses will yield new and greater rewards. This expectation comes partly from small initial successes. It comes also from the "therapeutic climate" created by the therapist. Let us look at this facet of verbal behavior therapy.

The therapeutic climate communicates to the patient what is perhaps the most important message he will ever hear. In general terms this message says:

> Stop feeling sorry for yourself. Self-pity is self-defeating. It is a certain way to block all constructive solutions to your difficulties. You may have had the worst childhood on record and you may even now be surrounded by troublesome, irritating people and problems. No matter. *You* are responsible for your own future. Your own behavior is causing your present difficulties. Stop asking yourself what you have to be bitter about and start asking what you are doing to make trouble for yourself. Then ask what you can do to improve the situation.

I transmit this message by words and actions. I tell it to my patients over and over in different ways, illustrating the points with incidents from his life. I may even use illustrations from my own life, although this can be overdone. Furthermore, I communicate the message by consistently acting as an ethical, responsible person in all my dealings with the patient.

When the patient receives this message and, more important, when he begins to act on it, the technical work of the middle phase of treatment can get under way.

## THE MIDDLE PHASE OF TREATMENT

Therapeutic efforts focus on the central symptoms. If these have been correctly identified, favorable changes in them should lead to improvement in the entire symptom pattern.

Treatment techniques vary according to whether the central symptoms are positive or negative and according to the reasons for their persistence. Many central symptoms include both positive and negative elements and are maintained by more than one mechanism. Combinations of techniques are therefore often needed.

I use a large number of treatment procedures during the middle stage of therapy. Most of these have been suggested by others in the past. The contribution of verbal behavior therapy lies in that these techniques are here integrated into an organized approach with a broad range of application.

In this brief introduction I can simply present these techniques without describing them. They are covered in detail in the book from which this chapter has been condensed (4).

TREATMENT TECHNIQUES FOR POSITIVE SYMPTOMS

*Extinction Techniques*

I. Reinforcement reduction
   A. Withholding positive reinforcement
   B. Withholding aversive stimuli
      1. Permissiveness
      2. Fantasy
      3. Hypnotically induced sensory deprivation
II. Reducing patient responsivity
   A. Relaxation training
      1. Standard
      2. Verbal self-stimulation
   B. Drugs

*Counter-Conditioning Techniques*

I. Encouraging the initial emission of new responses
   A. Passive techniques
      1. Expectations
      2. Successive approximations
      3. Cognitive mediation
   B. Active techniques
      1. Providing a pattern
      2. Instruction and encouragement
      3. Homework
      4. Role playing
         a. Standard
         b. Fixed
      5. Posthypnotic suggestions
      6. Drugs
II. Coupling weakened aversive stimuli with incompatible voluntary responses
   A. Relaxation responses
      1. With fantasy
      2. With homework
   B. Assertive responses
   C. Sexual responses
   D. Verbal self-stimulation
   E. Self-disclosure
   F. Emotive imagery
III. Reinforcement techniques
   A. Differential reinforcement
      1. Social approval
      2. Tangible reinforcers
      3. Tokens
   B. Successive approximations
   C. Shift from continuous to intermittent reinforcement

IV. Punishment techniques
    A. Social disapproval
    B. Tangible punishments
    C. Aversive self-stimulation
        1. Massed practice
        2. Fantasy
    D. Drugs

### TREATMENT TECHNIQUES FOR NEGATIVE SYMPTOMS

  I. Encouraging the initial emission of new responses
    A. Passive techniques
        1. Expectations
        2. Successive approximations
        3. Cognitive mediation
    B. Active techniques
        1. Providing a pattern
        2. Instruction and encouragement
        3. Homework
        4. Role playing
            a. Standard
            b. Fixed
        5. Posthypnotic suggestions
        6. Drugs
 II. Positive reinforcement techniques
    A. Differential reinforcement
        1. Social approval
        2. Tangible reinforcers
        3. Tokens
    B. Successive approximations
    C. Shift from continuous to intermittent reinforcement
III. Negative reinforcement techniques
    A. Social disapproval
    B. Tangible negative reinforcers

## THE CLOSING PHASE OF TREATMENT

During the closing phase of verbal behavior therapy, the therapist takes steps to shift the therapeutic focus from the treatment hours to the much greater number of hours that lie between them. The patient must substitute social reinforcements available in his daily life for the rewards he has been receiving during the sessions.

We can distinguish four stages for closing, each with slightly different tactics: the pre-closing stage, the confrontation, the closing, and the post-closing stage. Let us look at each in turn.

The pre-closing stage begins during the middle phase of therapy and continues throughout treatment. I begin to plan for termination almost as soon as I start work. Although I know that my patient must become somewhat dependent upon me to permit progress, I also realize that too much of a good thing can make termination a problem. I try to block the idea that treatment consists of the interviews alone by consistently focusing on what goes on between them. As environmental rewards increase, I point this out and offer approval for my patient's increasing independence. It is much easier to prevent treatment from developing into a way of life than it is to reverse the process.

The confrontation usually takes one interview. It comes when I have decided that termination should be seriously considered. I present this idea for discussion, give my reasons, and offer my patient plenty of opportunity to give his reactions. The confrontation interview rarely comes as a surprise. The immediately preceding sessions have usually offered abundant cues that it is in the offing. If my patient accepts the idea of closing, we set a period of time for the closing process. If he objects, we devote one or more sessions to discussing what our goals might be should we continue to work together. If the goals seem worthwhile and attainable, we may even negotiate a new therapeutic contract.

The closing stage lasts for about a month after the confrontation. Although the patient may have accepted the idea of closing, he almost always has second thoughts. "Can I really get along without treatment?" "Have I actually improved as much as I thought?" "Do you really think I'm ready to get along alone, or do you just want to get rid of me?" I answer all these questions and any others that arise. I accept and respect my patient's feelings of insecurity. I point out that they are to be expected under the circumstances. But I also point out that he has adequately managed worse problems in the past.

I also respect the possibility that my patient's objections may be valid and that termination may indeed be premature. If he convinces me, we may agree to continue treatment with revised goals.

Then we come to the post-closing stage. During the confrontation or during the closing stage, an almost inevitable question is, "What will happen to me if I begin to have problems again?" I answer by pointing out that the patient's ability to cope with stress has greatly increased but that a money-back guarantee against future emotional problems is impossible. I further indicate that I am always available to discuss any new difficulties that may arise: by telephone, by letter, or in person.

## A CASE STUDY IN VERBAL BEHAVIOR THERAPY

Mary Winters[3] came to see me complaining of depression and of fear amounting almost to terror that she might give in to impulses toward suicide. Her anxiety was at least partially justified; she had made a serious suicide attempt several years before.

Mary was having trouble going to sleep at night and even worse difficulty in awakening in time to get the children off to school. Since she had lost all her zest for almost any activity, household chores were piling up alarmingly. Apparently she was spending most of her time thinking about how frightened and depressed she was.

Although Mary initially appeared to want to know what she was doing to cause herself all these difficulties, it soon became clear that she already had an explanation: her problems were other peoples' fault. She was married to an ineffectual and unsuccessful lawyer who failed to provide enough money for the "gracious life" she felt she deserved. The two bickered constantly; both had been considering divorce. Mary's mother-in-law criticized her at every opportunity for both real and fancied deficiencies. Her husband vacillated between defending Mary and siding with his mother.

The central symptoms began to clarify themselves by the second or third interview. Mary had convinced herself—almost convinced herself, that is—that she was the prisoner of a fickle fate. Who could possibly deal with both a critical, dominating mother-in-law and an ineffectual, unappreciative husband at the same time? Why should one even try? Her depression was her response to this view of the situation. It permitted her to express her resentment without taking responsibility for it, and it conveyed the message, "I'm sick. Don't expect anything from me." Since even Mary could not fully believe in this view of the circumstances and since she could see that her abandonment of a responsible role was beginning to harm the children, feelings of guilt were compounding the problems.

This view of the central symptoms determined the course of treatment. Stated briefly, my goal was to help Mary stop blaming and start living. The persons closest to her might very well have severe emotional problems of their own. Mary's task, however, was to take personal responsibility for her own decisions and for her own life. In the

---

[3] Although this patient is a real person, her name and the details of her problems and of the situation in which they arose have been altered to prevent identification.

early interview, therefore, I paid even more attention than usual to the therapeutic climate. I hammered home, again and again, the message that people cause most of their own problems and that they must solve them by effective personal action.

Early in treatment I also prescribed small doses of an antidepressant drug. When depression is an important part of the presenting clinical picture, this complex set of emotional responses makes effective coping behavior difficult. The medication had the expected effect; it helped clear the way for further work.

As the depression cleared somewhat and as Mary "got the message" that she must change her situation by changing her own behavior, the stage was set for the middle phase of treatment. In this case the opening phase took about 12 therapy sessions, a bit more than usual. I had to be very careful to clarify the difference between my attitudes and those expressed for so long by husband and mother-in-law. My interest was not in fixing the blame for the trouble—I could not be less interested in that—but in helping Mary find ways of responding that would help her find a happier and more effective life.

## MIDDLE PHASE OF TREATMENT

At this point a number of treatment techniques are open to the verbal behavior therapist. I chose to use the "fixed role" method suggested by Kelly, Vol. One, p. 394. I composed and wrote down a description of an imaginary woman who was much like Mary in many ways but who behaved differently in certain critical areas. I described this hypothetical person as generally optimistic about the future and devoted to the welfare of her loved ones regardless of their appreciation or lack of it. This devotion was rewarding in itself. I further described my "character" as firm in her own conviction and willing to stand up for her own views on both major and minor issues regardless of who expressed contrary opinions. I emphasized that this person presented her views without resentment because she said what she thought before anger had much chance to arise.

I presented this "role" to Mary and asked her to "play" it for two weeks as if she were a character in a play. She was to try to play the role as convincingly as possible regardless of her own convictions concerning appropriate behavior in any given situation. She was not to tell any one what she was trying to do.

Mary expressed reservations about her ability to act out this role. I gave her a good deal of encouragement, instructed her to keep track of the details of any difficulties and report them to me, and stated that we would use role playing in the interviews to help with any problems.

Mary's success was unexpectedly complete. During the two week period she "faced up" to both her mother-in-law and husband on several occasions and learned that her new patterns of behavior produced favorable changes in their responses to her. An important feature of this technique is that the patient is told that he will be released from his obligations at the end of a fixed, relatively short period. This makes it easier for him to accept the therapeutic instructions. When I released Mary from her obligations, however, she continued most of the new behavior patterns because of their proven effectiveness. As the central symptoms improved, the depression lifted and remained so as drug dosage was gradually reduced to zero.

Termination in this case was easy. Because of the techniques employed, Mary was convinced she could handle her problems on her own, and she was eager to try.

This case has now been closed for slightly more than three years, although I hear from Mary from time to time and have seen her for one follow-up interview. Although she reports occasional brief episodes of mild depression usually after a spat with the mother-in-law, she has thus far been able to control all of them. She does this by doing the things she learned in therapy. She refuses to blame her mother-in-law for being the kind of person she is or to blame herself for handling a given situation poorly. She simply looks for her "mistake" and tries to make sure she does not repeat it in the future.

## A FINAL NOTE

Since verbal behavior therapy is a complete system of psychiatric diagnosis and treatment, a therapist using this method must work somewhat differently from most psychotherapists, starting with the first interview with a patient. The details of these methods cannot possibly be dealt with in a short article such as this. If this paper has stimulated your interest sufficiently to make you want to try the approach yourself, I suggest you consult my book (4).

## REFERENCES

1. Harper, R. A. *Psychoanalysis and psychotherapy: 36 systems.* Englewood Cliffs: Prentice-Hall, 1959.

2. Hilgard, E. R. *Introduction to psychology.* (3rd ed.) New York: Harcourt, 1962.
3. Schofield, W. *Psychotherapy: The purchase of friendship.* Englewood Cliffs: Prentice-Hall, 1964.
4. Storrow, H. A. *Introduction to scientific psychiatry: A behavioristic approach to diagnosis and treatment.* New York: Appleton-Century-Crofts, 1967.
5. Sulzer, E. S. Research frontier: reinforcements and the therapeutic contract. *J. Consult. Psychol.,* 1962, **9**, 271.

Chapter 3

# Implosive Therapy

## THOMAS G. STAMPFL and DONALD J. LEVIS

Thomas G. Stampfl: b. 1923, Cleveland, Ohio.
B.S.S., in sociology, John Carroll University, 1949. M.A., 1953, Ph.D., 1958, in psychology, Loyola University.
Professor of Psychology, University of Wisconsin-Milwaukee, 1968–date and Visiting Associate Professor, 1966–1967. Associate Professor of Psychology, John Carroll University, 1954–1967. Chief Psychologist, Catholic Child Guidance Center, Cleveland, Ohio, 1954–1960. Director, Neumann School for Retarded Children, Chicago, Illinois, 1952–1954. Consultant, Hawthornden State Hospital, 1965–1966.

Donald J. Levis: b. 1936, Cleveland, Ohio.
B.S.S., in sociology and psychology, John Carroll University, 1958. M.A., in clinical psychology, Kent State University, 1960. Ph.D., in learning theory, Emory University, 1964. National Institutes of Mental Health Postdoctoral Fellowship in Clinical Psychology, Lafayette Clinic, 1965.
Associate Professor of Psychology and Director of Psychology Research and Training Clinic, University of Iowa, 1966–date. Laboratory of Psychobiology, Lafayette Clinic, 1965–1966. Lecturer, Emory University, 1963–1964.
Books: Learning Approaches to Therapeutic Behavior Change (1970).

The theory and techniques of treatment presented in this paper had their inception in the attempts of the first author (37) to develop a learning-based approach to psychotherapy which would integrate in a consistent manner learning principles with traditional psychodynamic personality theory. The techniques were originally developed in 1957 to treat patients suffering from relatively mild neurotic reactions.[1] Subsequently, the techniques were extended and applied to patients who displayed increasingly severe patterns of symptomatic behavior and personality disorganization. Marked changes in symptomatology usually

---

[1] The first author expresses his gratitude to Dr. George Golias of Hawthornden State Hospital and Dr. Robert Hogan of Illinois State University for their participation in extending the techniques of treatment used in implosive therapy.

occurred within one to fifteen implosive sessions, although treatment time has been extended in relatively severe cases of neurotic reactions, in psychotic reactions, and in cases of character disorders.

The plan of the present paper is to develop the theory and technique underlying implosive therapy (IT) in conjunction with three clinical cases. The final sections of this paper will then deal with an extended presentation of the IT procedure and theoretical model, along with an account of the experimental evidence supporting the position. Unfortunately, limitation of space does not permit a completely detailed presentation of the system (see 17, 18, 20, 22, 37–43).

## THE RADIO COMPULSION CASE

The basic theory of IT may be illustrated by a relatively simple case taken from the first author's files early in the development of the implosive procedure. A college student suffered from a mild case of compulsive behavior. Upon retiring at night he felt the urge to check to see if he had left the radio on. Reassuring himself that the radio was off by getting up to check it, he would experience uneasiness that somehow it might still be on. For several years (each night with few exceptions) he had checked it from several to fifty times. Pulling out the plug or carefully checking the radio seemed to help, but the relief experienced was temporary. Furthermore, the behavior was getting worse. The increasingly frequent checking of the radio prompted the student to seek help. He reported that any failure on his part to engage in radio checking was attended by much apprehension and anxiety. Subjectively, he felt that something "terrible or catastrophic" might happen.

Since the authors are committed to a learning model, the patient's behavior described above is assumed to be acquired. Symptoms, in the present case the compulsive behavior of checking the radio to be sure it is turned off, are viewed as avoidance responses carried out by the patient in an attempt to prevent and remove himself from anxiety-eliciting stimulation. Checking the radio reduced the immediate anxiety. The anxiety-eliciting stimulation that provides the motivation for learning the avoidance response (symptom) is assumed to be acquired through a simple classical conditioning paradigm frequently employed in laboratory studies. Basically, the conditions necessary for the conditioning of anxiety occur when a "neutral" stimulus immediately precedes an inherently aversive unconditioned stimulus (UCS), such as intense punishment or pain. With sufficient pairings of the "neutral" stimulus with the unconditioned stimulus, the "neutral" stimulus becomes a conditioned stimulus (CS) that elicits anxiety upon presentation. Thus, the conditioned anxiety can be viewed as a response in anticipation of strong aversive stimuli.

When dealing with human psychopathological problems, we find that the reoccurrence of UCSs (traumatic situations) is highly improbable because of the historical nature of the original conditioning trials. Thus, the motivation sustaining adult human pathology is believed to be primarily a result of exposure to anxiety-eliciting CSs that have not as yet lost their aversive properties.

If such is the case, one may well ask what are the CSs producing the anxiety in our patient which are reduced by his compulsion (avoidance response) and what stimulus or stimulus pattern could be said to be responsible for his feeling that something "terrible or catastrophic" would happen? Furthermore, why do the CSs continue to elicit anxiety in the absence of any real danger, and what are the conditions needed to decondition the anxiety-eliciting stimuli?

To answer the question of what CSs are producing the anxiety in our patient, it appears that the thought or image of the radio on is the immediate cue that is highly correlated with the occurrence of the patient's symptom. However, if the patient fails to check the radio, a more pronounced negative affective reaction occurs. Most likely the thought "radio on" is only one aversive stimulus of many present which make up the total stimulus complex responsible for the emotional reactions reported by the patient. That is to say, a stimulus pattern or patterns stored within the patient's memory, but apparently below the level of verbal report, are believed to be responsible for the subjective experience that something "terrible or catastrophic" will happen. These avoided patterns are assumed to be ordered sequentially in terms of their accessibility to the patient and in terms of the amount of anxiety they elicit. The more aversive the cues, the greater their inaccessibility to the patient's immediate awareness. In psychodynamic theory, the compulsion "binds" anxiety by preventing anxiety-eliciting dangerous associations from surfacing to awareness.

The learning literature has been quite consistent in specifying the operational conditions sufficient to decondition or extinguish conditioned anxiety. The complete exposure or presentation of the CS in the absence of the UCS will lead to extinction. Failure of complete or substantial extinction in the present case occurs because the patient's symptom is designed to avoid as quickly as possible the stimulus "radio on." This, in turn, prevents those stimulus patterns functioning below the level of verbal report from being experienced vividly with their accompanying emotional reaction. In other words, those cues with the greatest emotional loading never get exposed long enough to undergo a substantial extinction effect.

Theoretically, it would follow that if one could circumvent or block the patient's symptom, greater length of exposure and a subsequent extinction effect to the avoided CSs would occur. Furthermore, if those sequentially avoided cues with higher anxiety-eliciting properties could be vividly reexperienced with their accompanying intense emotional reactions, a marked diminution in anxiety should result. Complete accuracy in presentation of the avoided stimulus patterns would not be essential since a good approximation of the stimulus complex would produce considerable deconditioning of the emotional response by a generalization of extinction effect.

When the patient was asked what might happen if the radio were left on, he replied after a time that perhaps a short circuit would occur and a fire would result. The patient was told to go to bed and either imagine that the radio was on or to turn it on. He was then asked to imagine a tiny spark occurring as a result of a short circuit. The spark would produce a tiny flame that would get bigger and bigger and finally result in a general conflagration in which the room, the house, and he would burn up. He was told to experience the scene as vividly as possible and to tolerate as much anxiety as possible.

The patient reported at the next session that he had tried to do this and had experienced much anxiety. Interestingly, he reported that in the middle of the fire he clearly heard his father's voice calling his name. (No mention had been made of his father in the initial interview.) The patient was living apart from his family at the time, and the patient's father was not present when the father's voice was heard calling him. Shortly after this episode, the patient's compulsive symptom was reported to have disappeared, and it had not returned months later when he graduated from school. Other improvement in his behavior also was noted which consisted in a general reduction of tension in other formerly anxiety-producing situations.

Subsequent analysis revealed that the patient's father had been severely critical of the patient throughout his childhood as well as an extremely severe taskmaster. His father was a fanatic on such things as lights being left on and faucets running. He also was severely reproving and punitive when the patient committed one of these acts. Considerable lecturing of the catastrophic consequences of such behavior was a prominent feature of the father's behavior at these times.

In summary, our analysis is simply that the cue "radio on" initiated a redintegrative process for the patient in which cues (stimulus patterns) were elicited representing past situations in which punishment (primary or secondary) had occurred. These conditioned patterns produced relatively strong anxiety reactions, and the symptomatic radio checking compulsion served to avert temporarily the activation of these patterns or to terminate them if already activated. This response, then, prevented subsequent extinction of the anxiety associated with the cues from occurring. It is not intended to imply that the dynamic conditioned motivation of the patient was as simple as this. Clinically, it was clear that considerable latent hostility was experienced toward the father. Whether additional dynamic patterns, such as repressed (avoided) sexual CSs or other motives, were present must be determined. Redintegrative cues are pervasive and include external stimulus objects as well as behavior that violates the value system to which the individual has been conditioned, e.g., sexual or aggressive thoughts or acts, drinking alcoholic beverages, or even card playing, dancing, or smoking. If present, these additional stimulus patterns also will need to be extinguished.

## THE "HYSTERICAL BLIND" CASE

The second case chosen for presentation is one taken from Brady and Lind (5) in which an operant conditioning technique of treatment was applied. Although this case has generated some controversy (4, 10), it was selected because it provides a vehicle for illustrating some of the key principles of implosive therapy as noted in the preceding case and because it further helps in the understanding of how the theory relates to practice.

A male patient, 40 years of age, had been functionally blind for a period of two years. Psychiatric treatment including psychotherapy had been unsuccessful in changing his condition. An operant conditioning procedure was introduced in which the patient was required to press a button between 18 and 21 seconds after his previous response. A correct response caused a buzzer to sound. In a half-hour testing session, the score of the patient was tabulated. High scores were reinforced by praise, approval, and increased hospital privileges; low scores by criticism, disapproval, and a reduction of hospital privileges. A baseline level of performance was calculated for the first six sessions. In the seventh session, without telling the patient, a barely perceptible light was introduced which coincided with the 18 to 21 second interval, thus providing a discrete discriminative stimulus for correct responding. Since the light could facilitate correct responding, a visual discrimination on the part of the "blind" patient should lead to his achieving higher scores.

The following results of this experiment are of interest from the viewpoint of the theory underlying IT. Contrary to expectation, the introduction of the barely perceptible light markedly depressed rather than increased the patient's score. A disproportionate number of responses were then emitted prior to the onset of the light which in effect prevented the light from going on. This deterioration in the patient's performance occurred without his giving any indication of being consciously aware of the light. Furthermore, the patient reported being very anxious during the session in which the light was introduced. Following the session, manifest signs of intense emotionality were present as indicated by trembling, perspiration, and the verbal report of the patient of feeling "very frightened." At this time the patient also spontaneously made comments concerning incidents in which he had become extremely angry with his wife.

With subsequent trials the patient's performance then continued to improve to the previous baseline level but not beyond. By observing the patient directly through a peephole, observers noted that the patient had covered his eyes with his forearm, thus preventing any possibility of seeing the light. To counteract the patient's new strategy, Brady and Lind introduced a 100-watt bulb placed directly in front of the patient and told him of its presence. The patient's reponse rate again deteriorated and then recovered and exceeded the previously established baseline level. The patient accounted for his superior performance without implying a visual response on his part by maintaining he used the heat of the bulb as his cue for responding, although Brady and Lind stated that the temperature changes actually were too small to be detectable.

In the following sessions, Brady and Lind gradually reduced the intensity of the light. They told the patient that at some point the temperature change would be too small to detect and that the patient would have to make use of vision. The patient's scores continued to improve although he reported seeing nothing. Improvement in the patient's behavior on the ward was noted also as indicated by his increased cooperation with hospital personnel and less defensiveness about his blindness. Coinciding with his improvement in adjustment, the patient spontaneously again expressed angry feelings toward his wife and mother-in-law. He commented that he did not see "eye to eye" with his wife, and he reported being so angry toward her that he "couldn't see straight."

At the 43rd session, the patient's operant level of performance suddenly deteriorated. Following this session the patient reported that during the 43rd session he could see again and that he was "paralyzed" when this happened. A combination of anxiety and exhilaration accompanied the regaining of his sight. At this point Brady and Lind introduced patterns of visual stimuli as the discriminative stimulus. The patient's operant responding improved to a virtually perfect performance. Coinciding with this stage, the patient was able to use vision on the ward increasingly, and his clinical condition continued to improve. Thirteen months later the patient had still retained his vision and had made other significant gains in his adjustment.

It is noteworthy that Brady and Lind interpreted the changes in the patient in terms of dynamic theory. They say, "Modern psychoanalytic theory would regard the patient's blindness as a manifestation of repression and his relative freedom from overt anxiety an indication of the 'success' of this repression . . . anxiety maintains the repression, and any threat to this repressive defense would be accompanied by an increase of anxiety" (5, p. 300). Brady and Lind are mystified, however, why psychotherapy had not been successful originally.

From the viewpoint of implosive therapy, being able to see may well have functioned as a redintegrative cue that, in turn, activated anxiety-eliciting stimulus patterns (angry feelings) that provided the motivation for not seeing. Elicitation of these patterns in the absence of negative reinforcement led to a reduction in the anxiety-producing value of these patterns and made seeing acceptable again. Since the patient's poor adjustment was in part based on the anxiety potential of these patterns, a general improvement in adjustment was effected.

In our view, the advantages of the type of operant procedure employed in this case in contrast to psychotherapy resulted from the following points:

1. The motivational value of the procedure forced the patient to experience the redintegrative cue.
2. The persistence inherent to the procedure employed did not allow the defensive maneuvers of the patient to terminate the experiment. Nor did Brady and Lind terminate the procedure because the patient "got worse," (experienced intense anxiety) when the light was first introduced.
3. The use of an actual light introduced perceptual clarity to the

stimulus conditions which the patient was motivated to attend. Note the authors' use of the procedure of introducing patterned visual stimuli as the discriminative stimulus. The patient had to look intently in order to make use of the stimulus for responding. This procedure is analogous to the IT technique of achieving perceptual clarity, although IT emphasizes both the redintegrating stimuli and the redintegrated stimulus patterns.

Of course, there are undoubtedly other avoided stimulus patterns present in this patient which would be worthwhile to investigate.

## THE WASTEPAPER BASKET CASE

In the preceding two case presentations, an attempt has been made to emphasize the role of the redintegrative stimulus pattern and the need for such avoided cues to be exposed with perceptual clarity to facilitate the extinction of their anxiety-eliciting properties. The last case chosen for presentation was selected primarily to illustrate in greater detail the method by which the implosive therapist determines those redintegrative cues from which the patient is protecting himself, and the technique and manner in which the avoided cues are represented to the patient.

The patient, a thirty-five-year-old male, seen by the first author, complained of strong obsessive tendencies mostly concerning dirt and numerous compulsive behavioral patterns including frequent handwashing. Other complaints included somatic symptoms (e.g., itching, stomach pains, heart pains, lump in the throat, difficulty in swallowing) and phobiclike anxiety experienced in relation to specific events or objects (e.g., driving a car, walking close to a machine at work). In addition, intense anxiety was experienced in the absence of any recognizable stimulus, coupled with a generally depressed mood, including feelings of isolation, loneliness, and suicidal thoughts. Pervasive characterological attitudes directed toward others also were noted. Many of these symptoms were reported to have started in childhood and continued to the present time.

The first task of the implosive therapist prior to actual treatment is to determine the symptom contingent cues that are responsible for initiating a particular symptom, for example, the compulsive behavior of handwashing. An analysis of the situation surrounding this symptom indicated that one of the main surface cues triggering off the compulsion was the sight of a wastepaper basket. The patient reported that when he found himself close to a wastepaper basket he would leave quickly to wash his hands. The wastepaper basket itself did not appear to be the primary motivator but most likely precipitated other redintegrative stimuli that were more completely avoided from verbal (conscious) awareness.

The therapist's second task prior to treatment is to attempt to determine as many of the avoided cues comprising the rest of the total stimulus complex as possible. Since the conditioning trials with the UCS present occurred historically, the task of accurately establishing the original conditioning cues through interview and case history techniques is difficult and time consuming. However, after a few diagnostic interviews, a trained therapist can usually speculate upon the etiology of the patient's present pathology. That is to say, a "good guess" about the significant personal, environmental, and dynamic interactions shaping the patient's behavior can be made usually within a short period of time. Essentially, the IT therapist follows this same strategy. On the basis of information obtained in the initial interview, he simply develops hypotheses about the significant avoided cues.

As stated earlier, from our learning theory position all that is necessary for effective extinction of the motivating source driving the symptoms is simply to re-present the avoided cues in the absence of primary reinforcement. Because of lack of direct knowledge about many of the actual conditioned cues involved, both the *symptom contingent cues,* which are based on an analysis of the environmental cues associated with the performance of the patient's symptoms, and the *hypothesized avoided cues,* which are based upon clinical knowledge and information obtained from the patient, are presented in the most vivid or realistic manner possible. Since many of the cues conditioned are believed originally to involve predominantly a combination of auditory and visual modalities, an attempt is made to produce the cues in the patient's imagery, rather than by simply reproducing them verbally. The IT therapist usually starts with the suspected lower anxiety-provoking cues and upon their extinction gradually introduces the more intense anxiety-provoking stimuli.

After analyzing the contingencies surrounding the patient's hand-washing compulsion, the therapist decided it seemed reasonable to suppose that stimulus patterns associated with dirt were aroused by the sight of the basket. The patient himself admitted that the basket reminded him of dirt. In an attempt to extinguish the anxiety to these cues, the therapist asked the patient to close his eyes and imagine as clearly and vividly as possible the following sequence. The therapist described a scene where the patient sees himself going closer and closer to the basket until he finds himself reaching into the basket. As his hand dips into the basket and is retracted he finds that he has placed his hand into an exceedingly dirty basket.

To determine whether or not the above presented scene includes any of the avoided CSs, the therapist can employ an operational measure. If the hypothesized cues elicit anxiety upon presentation, the assumption is made that these or similar cues have been conditioned previously. The greater the degree of anxiety elicited, the greater the support for continuing the presentation of the hypothesized cues. To define the anxiety response, either psychophysiological techniques (e.g., GSR, heart rate, skin potential) or behavioral observations (e.g., sweating, flushing of the face, increased motor behavior) can be used as a measure. For clinical purposes, the latter method usually is both quite adequate and easily observable. If the hypothesis presented is not confirmed by the patient's reactions, a new hypothesis is selected.

In the present case, a discernible emotional reaction was quite evident in the patient, although, as yet, the qualities of the dirt had not been described to him. According to our learning theory position, each repetition of such a scene should result in some extinction effect for the anxiety associated with the stimulus value of the scene. The scene itself may be considered to represent a stimulus pattern. Continual repetition of this pattern did produce a marked decrease in the observable anxiety reactions of the patient.

Implosive therapy assumes, however, that there is an interrelated sequence of stimulus patterns which are reactivated by the initial reaching into the dirty basket. Since the patient's symptom depends, to a large extent, on the anxiety-arousing capacity of these patterns, an attempt is made to approximate these patterns through the presentations of the hypothesized avoided cues. In the present case, the IT therapist puts into the basket those objects whose stimulus value corresponds to the stimulus patterns (avoided, repressed, dangerous associations) that are thought to comprise more of the anxiety-eliciting total stimulus complex, actual and potential, which motivates the hand-washing symptom.

Experience has indicated that many of the clinical hypotheses generated by psychoanalytic theory have proved useful in the selection of hypothesized avoided cues. The therapist in this case hypothesized, for example, that the patient's obsessive concern about dirt was related to severe cleanliness training during the anal period. To decondition anxiety-eliciting cues in this area, the therapist's function is to expose as many of these cues as possible without allowing the patient to avoid or terminate them.

To illustrate the above point, a description of the wastebasket scene continues. The patient is instructed to pull out his hand and look at it. The IT therapist, as vividly and in as rich detail as possible, describes to the patient a combination of spit, mucous, vomit, and fecal material dripping from the patient's hand. The greenish and yellowish shimmering grain of mucous and spit and the soft, chocolate, mushy and moist quality of the fecal material as it drips off of the patient's hand is described. The patient now is displaying considerable anxiety as evidence not only by facial grimacing and muscular twitching, but also by beads of perspiration that are appearing on his skin. At this point, the therapist may dwell for several minutes on the stimulus qualities of the dirt, upon the patient's urge to wash his hands, and upon the fact that he is unable to do so. As the anxiety of the patient appears to stabilize and starts to decline in intensity with repetitions of this scene, the therapist describes additional scenes based upon the inferred dynamics of the patient.

Ordinarily, anal material and other more anxiety-arousing CS patterns are introduced late in time in the therapy. This patient was not exposed to anal scenes until the 11th implosive session. Previous to this, the scenes introduced involved primarily cues with less anxiety-eliciting value which were lower down on the therapist's list of hypothesized sequentially avoided stimulus patterns. Once these cues are extinguished, the deeper, more intensive cues are more accessible. Periodic interviewing throughout the implosive sessions usually reveals considerable additional information that the patient is unable to verbalize previously. This information can then be incorporated into new scenes.

The following descriptions of additional hypothesized cues will give the reader a better understanding of the type of cues that are thought to be more completely avoided and how these cues are incorporated into implosive scenes. Assuming that oral incorporative tendencies were present as would be consistent with psychoanalytic principles, the therapist asked the patient to visually imagine eating the material from his hand. An attempt again is made to achieve as much clarity and vividness as possible. The grittiness of the feces and sliminess of the saliva, part of which spills off of the mouth and drips out over the lips (like a very small child eating a chocolate ice cream cone), is described. All of the sensations are dwelled upon, including the "lump" in the throat and then in the stomach. Like acid this abhorrent material eats out the stomach lining, heart, and other internal organs. The initiation of this sequence produced a very marked emotional reaction in the patient. He uttered soft gurgling sounds, and a strained, fixated glassy gaze, and paralytic-appearing posture spread over his body and face. The therapist continues to dwell upon this sequence (5 to 10 minutes) until there is a discernible drop in overt signs of emotionality.

The anxiety temporarily experienced by the patient, which can be noted from the previous description of the patient's reaction, appeared to be quite intense. As mentioned earlier, our learning theory model explicitly states that one way to substantially weaken previously conditioned associations is to experience completely the anxiety conditioned to these cues. Interestingly enough, thirteen years of experience with this technique have indicated that IT patients, including a number of the so-called low ego strength patients are quite capable of experiencing these high states of anxiety without detrimental effects. Perhaps this is related to the procedure of introducing with clarity intense anxiety cues for a sufficient duration to permit considerable deconditioning.

The CSs comprising the stimulus complex which surrounds the original conditioning trials are believed to comprise both exteroceptive and interoceptive cues. Many of the interoceptive cues which preceded punishment may have included hostile, aggressive, fearful, or sexual thoughts similar to the magical and primary process thinking emphasized by psychoanalytic theory. The implosive therapist has discovered through experience that the introduction of primary process material that fits the dynamics of the patient does indeed elicit considerable anxiety, which suggests previous fear conditioning to these cues. Some of this material already has been described; but, to illustrate primary process material in greater detail, we will continue with this case.

After the oral incorporative material was presented, a series of outhouse scenes was introduced. Numerous details of toilet-training scenes were enacted where the patient was asked to see himself as a child being trained to sit on the outhouse seat. Parental punishment accompanies these scenes. The patient slips through the seat (a common fear of children) and falls with a splash into the broad brownish mass of fecal material. He flails around in the smelly darkness, and he is hit from time to time by those using the seat above. He visually fixates the bare anus above as it prepares to release a bowel movement that hits him in the eye. Finally, the patient leaves society and makes a septic tank his home. In detail, he eats, sleeps, cooks, bathes, swims, and gives cocktail parties in his septic tank home. He keeps jars and pails of especially selected fecal material from his abundant supply, and he prepares all of his meals from a selection of this material. A great variety of other anal expulsive and retentive scenes also were incorporated into this septic tank sequence.

In an attempt to interrelate the primary process type cues involving dirt with those involving aggression, the therapist asked the patient to visualize himself expeling anal darts, baseballs, or bombs (in the position of a football center) at an anally shaped target or at targets representing his parents. He also retains anal material until he balloons ten times his usual size, and then he releases it in one shattering expulsive blast upon his enemies, devastating them totally.

The scene presented especially in this last sequence might appear to the reader to be too harsh and unsympathetic to the patient, despite the fact that the theoretical model calls for such "drastic" measures. It should be kept in mind, however, that the IT therapist is simply dealing with words and imagery, which in and by themselves hardly can be considered inherently aversive.

As a result of these and other IT sessions, the patient's handwashing compulsion disappeared along with most of the somatic symptoms, depressed moods, and suicidal thoughts. Wastepaper baskets and dirt were no longer excessively avoided by the patient.

Let us now turn to a more extensive and systematic presentation of the procedure and theory of IT.


## PROCEDURE

Two standard clinical interviews with the patient usually provide sufficient information to begin IT. The number of clinical interviews is optional. Additional information concerning the dynamic motivation of the patient is easily obtained during the implosive process.

The interviews provide the therapist with the opportunity to construct a general outline of the main symptoms and their interrelationship to other individuals and events as they fit into the history of the patient. Frequently, the therapist requests the patient to list on paper as many of the difficulties that he is experiencing as he can recall. Ordinarily, nothing is explained to the patient concerning the technique or theory of IT before the patient undergoes an implosive session. The therapist may explain in simple language some of the principles underlying the procedure after the first implosive session. Near the end of the second interview the therapist asks the patient to close his eyes, and 10 to 20 minutes of imagery involving essentially neutral scenes are introduced. The patient may be asked to imagine any of a variety of objects (e.g., picture hanging on a wall, house, mother, father, himself, automobile). No attempt is made to emphasize potentially anxiety-arousing stimuli. Emphasis is placed on obtaining clarity and detail in the imagery. The patient is asked to see the object clearly and to describe it to the therapist. Some patients will report imagery that is essentially static (stationary), and in such cases the therapist encourages movement (e.g., walking down the street) in whatever setting the patient is imagining. In general, the therapist establishes a baseline for the patient's ability to imagine various scenes. Auditory as well as visual imagery is encouraged.

The neutral imagery also enables the therapist to clarify his role in the following implosive sessions. For example, he is established as the basic director of the scenes and as an interrogator of what is happening. Frequently, the patient may visualize at this time imagery that is mildly anxiety arousing. The therapist does not encourage anxiety aroused at this time, and he may suggest other more neutral scenes.

The first implosive session is initiated after a few minutes of conversation during the third session by having the patient close his eyes and review the imagery pictured in the second session. On the basis of an analysis of the information secured concerning the patient, the therapist has planned the stimulus patterns that he wishes to present during this session. The initial scene is relatively unimportant since the therapist directs the imagery and can take almost any scene however far removed from the aversive stimulus patterns (dynamics) and change them to correspond to the avoided anxiety-producing case. Scenes are introduced in proportion to their hypothesized anxiety-provoking value. For example, if a depressed patient's behavior indicates that "death wishes" toward his father are close to awareness (relative failure of avoidance), the therapist may introduce scenes incorporating aggression that initially involves verbal expressions of aggression toward a father figure (actual or symbolic). Then physical expressions of aggression will be sought (e.g., slapping, punching, kicking) and then "primary process" aggression (e.g., killing, mutilating). The procedure is relatively rapid—scenes frequently change every several minutes. Of course, any scene presented is constantly changing. There are changes within scenes and changes between scenes. Many variations within a single scene are possible.

Belief or acceptance, in a cognitive sense, of the themes introduced is not asked for, and no attempt is made to secure any admission from the patient that material introduced actually applies to him. This procedure appears to facilitate the introduction of cues analogous to "depth" interpretations of dynamically oriented therapies.

It is convenient to begin by using some past punishing or traumatic incident reported by the patient. In other cases, therapy might begin by "replaying" a frequently recurring dream. Sometimes the therapist uses animals (wolves, bears, spiders, etc.) for their symbolic (generalization) value. The therapist is not simply attempting to arouse anxiety, but to arouse anxiety to stimulus patterns presumed to underlie the symptom picture of the patient. In those cases, where there are clear-cut situational cues (symptom contingent cues), as in phobic reactions or compulsive behavior, the therapist may start or move quickly to scenes incorporating these cues. The patient is asked to talk to people seen in imagery. The words are usually supplied by the therapist. The patient is asked to say the words out loud.

The therapist's goal is to expose the patient to more and more of the avoided stimulus patterns that provide the motive force for his symptoms. The arousal of anxiety to these patterns would be expected to produce resistance on the part of the patient to the procedure. The IT therapist is extremely persistent. The profound relief experienced by many patients following a single session of IT is such that they are motivated to return for further IT sessions. Thus, every attempt is made to circumvent initial resistance to the procedure. Especially in the initial session some patients will say: "It's not true." The therapist's response is, "Whether it's true or not, just do it." Patient: "I wouldn't do that." Therapist: "I don't care whether you would really do that, just do it now." Patient: "I can't do it." Therapist: "Yes, you can."

If the patient does not progress with the sequence after several minutes of therapist pressure, the therapist changes the scene to a less anxiety-arousing one temporarily. However, within minutes the therapist returns to the rejected scene and urges the patient to continue with it. Usually the patient is able to complete the previously rejected scene or at least complete a greater part of it than before. Patients may occasionally threaten to leave the office, but only one patient of the first author in thirteen years of experience with the method ever actually left. This patient returned and eventually completed the therapy. Neither author can recall premature termination by a patient because of the nature or intensity of the stimulus material introduced.

Certain types of patients resist the procedure more than others. Neurotic patients are almost always cooperative, except in cases of scrupulosity when almost anything can be defended against by designating the IT procedure as sinful. Some patients with characterological disorders are especially resistant; they appear unable or unwilling to tolerate discomfort of any type. Psychotic patients are sometimes difficult because of their general disorientation, which makes it hard to secure their cooperation.

## THEORY

The theory underlying IT is heavily dependent on the analyses proposed by Dollard and Miller (9), Mowrer (28, 29, 30, 31), and Shoben (33), although it differs in some essential details from them and extends certain critical features of the analyses these psychologists have proposed. In addition, extensive use was made of the phenomena, concepts, and data of the experimental animal laboratory in implementing certain features of the IT technique and theory. Laboratory studies indicate that fear states can be conditioned in the organism leading to behavior that is labeled as neurotic, psychosomatic, or even psychotic (e.g., 6, 7, 21, 24, 25, 46). The basic theoretical orientation is that of two-factor learning theory. Two-factor theory (28–30, 34) states that an organism can be made to respond emotionally to an originally "neutral" stimulus (CS) by the presentation of the "neutral" stimulus with a noxious stimulus. If a tone is paired with electric shock, the organism will respond to the tone with objectively verifiable changes in his physiological state, such as changes in blood sugar and heart rate. The emotional state may be described as fear or anxiety. The stimulus which produced the fear can be construed to function as a danger signal or warning stimulus. The fear or anxiety produced by the warning stimulus functions as a motivator of behavior, and the reduction or elimination of the fear state serves as a reinforcer of behavior. If the tone is conditioned to produce fear, then any action taken which terminates the tone will be automatically strengthened (or guided more accurately). A danger signal paired with another "neutral" stimulus will transfer some of its fear-eliciting properties to the new "neutral" stimulus (higher-order conditioning). Since all conditioning takes place in context with other stimuli, it is more accurate to state that a stimulus pattern ("neutral" stimulus plus context of stimuli) precedes noxious stimulation. Further, since the "neutral" stimulus is presented over time, the stimulus pattern is temporally organized. Finally, the conditioning process ordinarily involves multiple stimulus patterns sequentially organized in time. In a sense it is misleading to say that a single discrete stimulus elicits the fear. (For a further discussion and elaboration of the role of contextual and sequential cues see 16, 17, 35, 36). Laboratory studies indicate that subjects can learn a wide variety of responses in order to terminate feared stimuli.

It is assumed that many, if not all, of the anxiety states experienced in the human are a product of many conditioning experiences in the life of the individual which can be understood in terms of the conditioning model of the laboratory. Past specific experiences of punishment and pain confer strong anxiety reactions to initially "neutral" stimuli. These experiences are believed to be represented neurally, and the neural engram (memory, image) may be considered as possessing the potential to function as a stimulus pattern.

The stimulus patterns correlated with the past experience of pain need not be represented ideationally (level of verbal awareness) to elicit the anxiety state. Thus, a subliminal area (an area below the level of verbal report) of neural functioning is necessary to account for all of the phenomena associated with psychopathological behavior.

The maladaptive behavior of neurotic and functionally psychotic patients, and possibly including patients with personality disorders may be viewed within the context of three main categories:

1. Involving the establishment of well-learned avoidance responses where symptoms and defense mechanisms "bind" anxiety. Behavior is relatively successful in minimizing or eliminating affectively charged stimulus patterns. Patients with "successful" symptoms or defenses experience relatively little anxiety. Clinically, "unconscious anxiety" is seen in conversion reactions, some phobic and obsessive-compulsive reactions, and some cases of chronic schizophrenia.

2. Involving a relative failure of avoidance behavior where symptoms and defensive maneuvers are relatively unsuccessful in preventing affectively laden stimulus patterns from being activated. Considerable manifest emotionality is present in such patients. Examples are patients with neurotic or psychotic depressions, those patients described as suffering from "free-floating anxiety" or the experiencing of acute anxiety attacks, and many acute schizophrenic reactions.

3. Involving a deficit in the learning of positive affectively charged stimulus patterns. There is a lack of positive emotional response in these patients. Meehl (26) refers to this pattern (state) as anhedonia. Emotionally deprived children, some cases of chronic schizophrenia, and some cases of personality disorders are examples of this deficit.

The IT therapist attempts to re-present, reinstate, or symbolically reproduce as close an approximation as possible of the cues (stimulus patterns) which are presumed to underly the symptoms of the patient

(patient symptomatology). Interoceptive as well as exteroceptive cues are thought to make up the total stimulus pattern. Where anxiety is bound, that is, where some symptom is relatively effective in preventing avoided cues from being activated as specified in the first category in the preceding list, the goal of the therapist is to reexpose the patient to approximations of these cues. Avoidance learning is relevant since it can be said that the patient, by his behavior, is avoiding these cues. Miller (27) and Solomon and Wynne (34) have stated that extinction (deconditioning) should be most rapid when a full-blown emotional reaction is made to occur. A number of experimental studies corroborate this interpretation (see 8, 15, 45). A corollary to this principle is reflected in experimental studies of Lowenfeld, Rubenfeld, and Guthrie (23) and Wall and Guthrie (44) which indicate that the more clearly a subject perceives anxiety-eliciting stimuli when followed by nonreinforcement, the more rapid the extinction of the emotional response.

Where a relative failure of avoidance has occurred, as, for example, in cases of depression, anxiety reactions, and acute schizophrenia, a partial basis for extinction is present. Thus, these patients tend to have a high percentage of spontaneous remissions (recoveries). The assumption here, however, is that a partial avoidance of dangerous stimulus patterns is still operative. The depressed patient may experience much guilt, but still he tends to avoid a complete acknowledgment of the past and present behavior which is partly responsible for redintegrating the stimulus patterns eliciting the guilt feeling. This is simply to say that patients with a relative failure of avoidance are still not experiencing as completely as possible the stimuli, actual and potential, seen as important agents in their depression. Since partial extinction tends to occur, responses are resumed or new ones learned which maintain avoidance and lead to spontaneous recovery. Nevertheless, these patients tend to relapse since relatively complete extinction for these stimulus patterns has not occurred. The IT therapist proceeds on this assumption in the treatment of depressed patients. In imagery, he attempts to attain perceptual clarity for those stimulus patterns actively producing the guilt (depression) as well as to include stimulus patterns still relatively avoided. Our usual finding is that there are many events in the past life of the depressed patient for which he maintains almost complete avoidance (repression). The IT therapist motivates the patient to experience approximations of these events. The effect is to temporarily make the patient even more depressed while these patterns are being experienced. Some relief from the depression is commonly observed following a single session. Additional sessions are necessary for a more lasting recovery. A major part of the IT approach to depression is consistent with Mowrer's guilt theory (32) of abnormal behavior reinterpreted in terms of conditioning principles.

In addition to symptom contingent cues (situational cues), the areas which usually incorporate hypothesized dynamic cues can be categorized under the following ten major headings: (1) aggression; (2) punishment; (3) oral material; (4) anal material; (5) sexual material; (6) rejection; (7) bodily injury; (8) loss of control; (9) acceptance of conscience and (10) autonomic and central nervous system reactivity. (For a more detailed presentation of the various cues and scenes represented by these categories see Reference 40).

A number of other stimulus patterns are commonly encountered or emphasized in addition to those stated above.

## EXPERIMENTAL STUDIES

As noted earlier, the IT technique has been applied to a wide variety of psychopathological problems with apparent success. However, history cautions us concerning the advisability of placing too much emphasis on clinical impression. The efficacy of any technique must in the last analysis be determined on the basis of sound experimental data. The final section of this paper deals with the published data presently available. Three studies involving patient populations have been reported so far.

Hogan (11) compared two groups of hospitalized mental patients; 26 were treated by the implosive method, and 24 patients were treated by conventional therapeutic techniques (insight and supportive therapy). Cases were classified as successful if their status one year following treatment were that of released or discharged from the hospital. Eighteen of the 26 implosively treated patients were designated as successful by this criterion whereas only eight of the 24 nonimplosive patients were successful. This difference was statistically significant. Hogan also reported that the implosive group shifted significantly away from pathology on five Minnesota Multiphasic Personality Inventory (MMPI) scales, although the conventional group showed little or no change. A separate comparison involving only the MMPI $T$ scores indicating pathology (70 and above) was also made. The implosive group shifted away from pathology an average of $-11.5$ $T$-score points, whereas the conventional treatment group displayed a mean shift of only $-0.6$.

The second patient study to be reviewed was reported by Levis and

Carrera (19). These investigators studied the effectiveness of IT with outpatients. One experimental and three control groups with ten subjects per group were studied. The experimental group received ten one-hour implosive therapy sessions. One of the control groups received conventional-type treatment for essentially the same number of sessions as the IT group. This group was employed as a control for both the number of therapy sessions and duration of treatment. Another control group received conventional-type treatment for an average of 37 sessions. These patients were treated by one of the IT therapists prior to his having any knowledge about implosive therapy. This group was employed as a control for possible skills and personal qualities of the therapist which might be operating independently of the treatment technique, and because it was thought desirable to compare the implosive group with a group in which treatment was terminated. The final control group consisted of a waiting therapy control group in which no formal treatment was given. This group was employed as a control for the possible therapeutic effects resulting from commitment to and expectation of professional treatment rather than from formal treatment. Pretreatment and posttreatment MMPI's were administered to each subject. Scores on the MMPI $T$ above 70 showed significant decreases following treatment for the implosive group when compared to the control groups which showed little or no change. The mean $T$-score decrease for the IT group was $-8.3$; the mean drop for the combined control groups was only $-1.1$. Furthermore, the mean difference score across all clinical scales for the IT group ($M = -53.1$) was significantly different from the mean of the combined control groups ($M = -8.0$).

The final study to be reviewed was carried out by Boudewyns and Wilson (3). These investigators compared the effectiveness of implosive therapy, nonsystematic desensitization, and milieu therapy. Eleven hospitalized patients who showed a significant elevation on either Depression (scale 2) or Psychasthenia (scale 7) of the MMPI were treated in each of the behavior therapy groups with ten patients being treated by milieu therapy. Patients were seen for fifteen sessions or less. Therapists were counterbalanced across treatments. Of the $T$ scores above 70, 45.3% treated with IT, 34.5% treated with desensitization, and 14.6% treated with milieu therapy, fell within normal limits following therapy. The mean difference score across all clinical scales was $-59$ for the IT group, $-34$ for the desensitization group, and $-5$ for the milieu group. Other measures were provided which also showed the IT treatment to be superior. The authors concluded from the available six-month follow-up data that the gains made in the IT group were still holding up, while the gains reported for the desensitization *S*s were not. It is of interest to note the similarity in MMPI changes among the IT conditions for these three studies.

Implosive therapy has also been reported effective in removing fears of small animals with college students serving as subjects (1, 2, 12–14). Levis (18) noted, however, caution should be exercised in generalizing from nonpatient to patient populations.

Although the above results are encouraging, considerably more systematic experimental work is needed before any definite conclusions about IT effectiveness can be made.

## REFERENCES

1. Barrett, C. L. Systematic desensitization versus implosive therapy. *J. Abnorm. Psychol.,* 1969, **74,** 587–592.
2. Borkovec, T. D. The comparative effectiveness of systematic desensitization and implosive therapy and the effect of expectancy manipulation on the elimination of fear. Unpublished doctoral dissertation, University of Illinois, Champaign, 1970.
3. Boudewyns, P. A., & Wilson, A. E. An experimental comparison of the effects of implosive therapy, desensitization therapy, and milieu therapy on an inpatient population. Paper presented at the American Psychological Association, Miami, September 1970.
4. Brady, J. P. Hysteria versus malingering: A response to Grosz and Zimmerman. *Behav., Res., Ther.,* 1966, **4,** 321–322.
5. Brady, J. P., & Lind, D. L. Experimental analysis of hysterical blindness. *Arch. Gen. Psychiat.,* 1961, **4,** 331–339. Reprinted in C. M. Franks (Ed.), *Conditioning techniques in clinical practice and research.* New York: Springer, 1964.
6. Brady, J. V., Porter, R. W., Conrad, D. G., & Mason, J. W. Avoidance behavior and the development of gastroduodenal ulcers. *J. Exper. Anal. Behav.,* 1958, **1,** 69–73.
7. Cook, S. W. The production of "experimental neurosis" in the white rat. *Psychosom. Med.,* 1939, **1,** 293–308.
8. Denny, M. R., Koons, P. B., and Mason, J. E. Extinction of avoidance as a function of the escape situation. *J. Compar. Physiolog. Psychol.,* 1959, **52,** 212–214.
9. Dollard, J., & Miller, N. E. *Personality and psychotherapy.* New York: McGraw-Hill, 1950.
10. Grosz, H. J., & Zimmerman, J. Experimental analysis of hysterical blindness: a follow-up report and new experimental data. *Arch. Gen. Psychiat.,* 1965, **13,** 255–260.

11. Hogan, R. A. Implosive therapy in the short-term treatment of psychotics. *Psychother.: Theory, Res., Prac.,* 1966, **3**, 25–31.
12. Hogan, R. A., & Kirchner, J. H. Implosive, eclectic verbal, and bibliotherapy in the treatment of fears of snakes. *Behav. Res. Ther.,* 1968, **6**, 167–171.
13. Hogan, R. A., & Kirchner, J. H. A preliminary report of the extinction of learned fears via short-term implosive therapy. *J. Abnorm. Psychol.,* 1967, **72**, 106–111.
14. Kirchner, J. H., & Hogan, R. A. The therapist variable in the implosion of phobias. *Psychother.: Theory, Res., Prac.,* 1966, **3**, 102–104.
15. Knapp, R. K. Acquisition and extinction of avoidance with similar and different shock and escape situations. *J. Compar. Physiolog. Psychol.,* 1965, **60**, 272–273.
16. Levis, D. J. Effects of serial CS presentation and other characteristics of the CS on the conditioned avoidance response. *Psycholog. Rep.,* 1966, **18**, 755–766.
17. Levis, D. J. Implosive therapy, Part II: The subhuman analogue, the strategy, and the technique. In S. E. Armitage (Ed.), *Behavioral modification techniques in the treatment of emotional disorders.* Battle Creek, Michigan: Veterans Administration publication, 1966, pp. 22–37.
18. Levis, D. J. The case for performing research on nonpatient populations with fears of small animals: a reply to Cooper, Furst, and Bridger. *J. Abnorm. Psychol.,* 1970, **76**, 36–38.
19. Levis, D. J., & Carrera, R. N. Effects of 10 hours of implosive therapy in the treatment of outpatients: a preliminary report. *J. Abnorm. Psychol.,* 1967, **72**, 504–508.
20. Levis, D. J., & Stampfl, T. G. Implosive therapy: a bridge between Pavlov and Freud? *Assoc. Advan. Beh. Ther., Newsl.,* 1969, **4**(2), 8–10.
21. Liddell, H. S. The challenge of Pavlovian conditioning and experimental neuroses in animals. In J. Wolpe, A. Salter, & L. J. Reyna (Eds.), *The conditioning therapies.* New York: Holt, Rinehart & Winston, 1965.
22. London, P. *The modes and morals of psychotherapy.* New York: Holt, Rinehart & Winston, 1964.
23. Lowenfeld, J., Rubenfeld, S., & Guthrie, G. M. Verbal inhibition in subception. *J. Gen. Psychol.,* 1956, **54**, 171–176.
24. Masserman, J. H. *Behavior and neurosis.* Chicago: University of Chicago Press, 1943.
25. Masserman, J. H., & Pechtel, C. Neuroses in monkeys: a preliminary report of experimental observation. *Ann. N.Y. Acad. Sci.,* 1953, **56** (2), 253–265.
26. Meehl, P. E. Schizotaxia, schizotypy, schizophrenia. *Amer. Psychol.,* 1962, **17**, 827–838.
27. Miller, N. E. Learnable drives and rewards. In S. S. Stevens (Ed.), *Handbook of experimental psychology.* New York: Wiley, 1951.

28. Mowrer, O. H. A stimulus-response analysis of anxiety and its role as as a reinforcing agent. *Psychol. Rev.,* 1939, **46,** 553–565.

29. Mowrer, O. H. Two-factor learning theory reconsidered with special reference to secondary reinforcement and the concept of habit. *Psychol. Rev.,* 1956, **63,** 114–128.

30. Mowrer, O. H. *Learning theory and behavior.* New York: Wiley, 1960.

31. Mowrer, O. H. *Learning theory and the symbolic processes.* New York: Wiley, 1960.

32. Mowrer, O. H. *Abnormal reactions or actions?* Dubuque, Iowa: Wm. C. Brown, 1966.

33. Shoben, E. J. Psychotherapy as a problem in learning theory. *Psychol. Bull.,* 1949, **46,** 366–392.

34. Solomon, R. L., & Wynne, L. C. Traumatic avoidance learning: The principles of anxiety conservation and partial irreversibility. *Psychol. Rev.,* 1954, **61,** 353–385.

35. Stampfl, T. G. Avoidance conditioning reconsidered: An extension of Mowrerian theory. Unpublished manuscript, 1960.

36. Stampfl, T. G. Acquisition and resistance to extinction of avoidance responses to simple, congruent, and serial-congruent conditioned stimuli. Unpublished manuscript, 1961.

37. Stampfl, T. G. Implosive therapy: a learning theory derived psychodynamic therapeutic technique. Unpublished manuscript, 1961.

38. Stampfl, T. G. Implosive therapy, Part I: the theory. In S. G. Armitage (Ed.), *Behavioral modification techniques in the treatment of emotional disorders.* Battle Creek, Michigan: Veterans Administration publication, 1966, 12–21.

39. Stampfl, T. G. Implosive therapy: an emphasis on covert stimulation. In D. J. Levis (Ed.), *Learning approaches to therapeutic behavior change.* Chicago: Aldine, 1970.

40. Stampfl, T. G., & Levis, D. J. The essentials of implosive therapy: a learning-theory-based psychodynamic behavioral therapy. *J. Abnorm. Psychol.,* 1967, **72,** 496–503.

41. Stampfl, T. G., & Levis, D. J. Phobic patients: treatment with the learning theory approach of implosive therapy. *Voices: The Art Sci. Psychother.,* 1967, **3,** 23–27.

42. Stampfl, T. G., & Levis, D. J. Implosive therapy—a behavioral therapy? *Behav. Res. Ther.,* 1968, **6,** 31–36.

43. Stampfl, T. G., & Levis, D. J. Learning theory: an aid to dynamic therapeutic practice. In L. D. Eron & R. Callahan (Eds.), *Relationship of theory to practice in psychotherapy.* Chicago: Aldine, 1969.

44. Wall, H. W., & Guthrie, G. M. Extinction of responses to subceived stimuli. *J. Gen. Psychol.,* 1959, **60,** 205–210.

45. Weinberger, N. M. Effects of detainment on extinction of avoidance responses. *J. Compar. Physiol. Psychol.,* 1965, **60,** 135–138.

46. Wolpe, J. *Psychotherapy by reciprocal inhibition.* Stanford: Stanford University Press, 1958.

Chapter 4

# Conditioned Reflex Therapy

ANDREW SALTER and
RATIBOR-RAY M. JURJEVICH

Andrew Salter: b. 1914, Waterbury, Connecticut.
B.S., in psychology, New York University, 1937.
Chairman, Membership Committee, Association for Advancement of the
Behavioral Therapies.
Books: *The Case Against Psychoanalysis* (1952; paperback 1963). *Conditioned Reflex Therapy* (1949; paperback 1961). *What is Hypnosis* (1944; paperback 1963). (Co-editor) *The Conditioning Therapies* (1964).
Articles: Three techniques of autohypnosis. *J. Gen. Psychol.*, 1941, **24**, 423–428.


Ratibor-Ray M. Jurjevich: b. 1915, Ristovac, Yugoslavia.
B.S., in forestry, University of Edinburgh, Scotland, 1938. M.S., in social group work, George Williams College, 1953. Ph.D., in clinical psychology, University of Denver, 1958.
Clinical Psychologist, Court Consultation Service, Model Cities, Denver, Colorado, 1970–date. Chief Psychologist, Psychiatric Clinic, 3415 Dispensary, Lowry Air Force Base, Denver, Colorado, 1961–1970. Clinical Psychologist, State Training School for Girls, Colorado, 1958–1960. Program Director and Executive Director, North Side Community Center, Denver, 1952–1958.
Books: (Editor) *Direct Psychotherapy: 28 American Originals,* 1972. *Direct Psychotherapy: Developments on Four Continents,* (in preparation). *No Water in My Cup: Experiences and a Controlled Study of Psychotherapy with Delinquent Girls* (1967). (Co-author) *Srpsko–Engleski Recnik* (Serbian-English Dictionary, 1948). *Pisma Hromog Dabe* (Serbian translation of C.S. Lewis: *Screwtape Letters, 1948). (Editor) Srpski Biseri* (An Anthology of Serbian poetry, 1947). *Englesko–Srpski Recnik* (English–Serbian Dictionary, 1947).
Articles: Changes in psychiatric symptoms without psychotherapy. In S. Lesse (Ed.), *The Evaluation of Results in Psychotherapy,* 1967. Personality changes concomitant with institutional training of delinquent girls. *J. Gen. Psychol.*, 1966, **74,** 207-216. Short interval test-retest stability of MMPI, California Psychological Inventory, Cornell Index, and Symptom Check List. *J. Gen. Psychol.*, 1966, **74,** 201-206. Normative data for the clinical and additional MMPI scales for a population of delinquent girls. *J. Gen. Psychol.*, 1963, **69,** 143-146. Interrelationships of anxiety indices of Wechsler Intelligence Scales and MMPI Scales. *J. Gen. Psychol.*, 1963, **69,** 135-142.

## THEORETICAL AND EXPERIMENTAL CONSIDERATIONS

### *Conditioning and Hypnosis*

Salter's psychotherapeutic approach is diametrically opposed to that of psychoanalysis.[1] His feeling is that psychoanalysis, like the elephant of the fable, should drag itself off into some distant jungle graveyard and die. It has outlived its usefulness: its methods are imprecise, the treatment drawn out, and results unimpressive. Salter disagrees that psychotherapy should be that inefficient. He proposes to build a psychotherapeutic model, not on "Freudian metaphysical quicksands," but on experimentally verified and verifiable Pavlovian principles of conditioning.

Salter suggests that a more appropriate term for "conditioned reflex" be used in the context of psychotherapy—the "associative reflex." Pavlov concentrated on physiological, primarily salivatory, reaction of dogs, disregarding other behavioral reactions accompanying the conditioning. The dog also pricked his ears, made anticipatory chewing movements, turned his head toward the source of food, etc. Obviously, the "psychological" behavior reactions were conditioned alongside the physiological.

Another theoretical consideration appears essential to Salter, namely, to establish identity of hypnosis and conditioning. He uses Hudgin's (7) experiment as an illustration of this point.

Hudgins started with associating the sound of a bell to the appearance of light, which was his unconditioned stimulus for contraction of the pupils. After a period of training, the pupils were contracting to the bell alone. Then he extended his experiment to letting the subject press a grip upon experimenter's command to start both the bell and the light. After further training, the grip could be eliminated, and contraction of pupil would occur upon the experimenter's saying "contract." In this way an involuntary reflex was brought under conscious control. Some subjects could be trained to bring about contraction by their own pronouncing of the word "contract" loudly or in a whispering tone, others could contract or dilate their pupils by thinking "contract" and "relax" to themselves. An aspect of the "unconscious"

---

[1] The first and third sections of this paper consist of a summary by Ratibor-Ray M. Jurjevich of Andrew Salter's ideas expressed in Andrew Salter. *Conditioned reflex therapy.* New York: Capricorn Books, 1966. The quotations, unless marked differently, are from Salter. The second portion is a reprinted chapter from his book.

mind, the pupillary reflex, was thus brought under control of the conscious mind.

"Words are bells of associative reflexes," Salter points out. We react with psychophysiological responses to words denoting delight or disgust, fear or anger. Hypnosis uses such associative reflexes, triggering the previously conditioned reactions in subjects. The auditory or visual hallucinations can in this way be produced by hypnosis. Ellson (4) produced auditory hallucinations in normal subjects, even in two of the psychologists who knew the nature of the experiment. He paired a light as conditioned stimulus to a sound gradually increasing to a high pitch and fading away again. After sixty trials, thirty-two of forty subjects heard the sound when only the light was turned on. They could not distinguish between the hallucinatory experience and sensory impressions. Such hallucinations can be set off internally. Luther, for instance, preoccupied with the devil, saw one so vividly that he threw the inkwell upon the wall. Erickson (5) produced color blindness by hypnotic suggestions to his subjects. Salter experimented together with a physician on three subjects who were trained to be insensitive to pain and the sound of guns. They could turn their anaesthesia on in ten seconds. Genuineness of insensitivity to guns was attested by no changes occurring in blood pressure when gun was fired, even though the subjects were in a waking state.

Diven (2) demonstrated the conditioning of emotion to words. The subjects were asked to give their associations to a list of words. The word "barn" was repeated six times on a list. It was always preceded by the word "red," and an electric shock was administered with this word. A galvanometer attached to the subject indicated that the shock evoked considerable emotional reaction. Then the word list was given again without electrical shock. The galvanometer indicated that an emotional reaction was established to words associated with shock. The conditioned disturbance also spread to other words with a rural connotation, e.g., cow, hay, pasture. The emotional reaction was spread to even words that were not on the conditioning list, e.g., farm. Whether the subjects could or could not recall the traumatic word did not matter; the conditioned reaction persisted even when the original circumstances were outside awareness. "Here is Pavlov's experiment again," writes Salter. "Instead of a bell, there is a word. Instead of the meat, there is an electric shock. And instead of the saliva at the sound of the bell, there is the emotion at the sound of the word. Here is the linkage between word conditioning and emotional conditioning. The 'subconscious' of hypnosis, and the so-called 'unconscious' of emotions, may therapeutically be considered aspects of conditioning."

Problems are born through distressing experiences and associatively spread upon other circumstances besides the traumatic one. Expectations of rejection or acceptance by others are established through favorable or unfavorable experiences.

Diven's experiment pointed also to one of the reasons of inefficacy of psychoanalytic therapy. Even when the subjects knew how they came to react to the word barn and associated words with emotional disturbance, their awareness did not reduce the conditioned affective response. "Many people have tediously learned that 'digging out' painful experiences from their 'unconscious' does not cure, any more than a man is healed when we determine that he was hit by a southbound freight, and not by one going north." What is necessary in most cases is not only passive review of traumas but an active training to overcome them. Here Salter introduces his basic concepts of excitation, inhibition, and disinhibition; they are taken directly from Pavlov.

*Inhibition and Excitation*

An infant's behavior is excitatory; he acts without restraint. The training acts in an inhibitory direction. Salter's main therapeutic goal is to move his patients from unnecessary inhibitions to what he calls "excitatory personality." "My cases want logic to guide their emotions. I want free, outgoing emotion to guide their logic. The happy person does not waste time thinking. . . . To be human is to be juvenile. . . . Excitation is a matter of emotional freedom . . . honesty of response. . . . The excitatory person is direct. . . . When he is confronted with a problem, he takes immediate constructive action. . . . Above all, the excitatory person is free of anxiety."

In contrast, the "inhibitory personality" is conceived as cautious, withdrawn, ill at ease, suffering from "constipation of emotions." "They keep roadblocks between the heart and the tongue. The code of the inhibitory personality is to suppress the gut and to inflate the brain." They try to please but remain friendless. "They express anything except what they feel." They are self-abusing, apologetic, indecisive, worried about the future and the past. They are overly dependent, "looking for the spine his mother, or father, or brother, stole from him . . . they are the neurasthenics and the perpetually psychoanalyzed. . . . Bluntly put, the inhibitory personality is a type. Therapy consists in making him an individual."

Salter enumerates six techniques of reconditioning his patients:

1. Feeling-talk. "It means the deliberate utterance of spontaneously felt emotions." He suggests to his patients to put emotion in their talk. "Our golden rule is emotional truth, even if it means risking expediency."

2. Facial-talk. "The inhibitory person need not snarl like a tiger, nor grin like a Cheshire cat that read Dale Carnegie. However, he should furrow his brow when he is vexed and wear a long face. Be emotionally Gallic is my counsel."

3. Contradicting and attacking rather than being amenable when you disagree with someone.

4. Deliberately using the word "I" frequently.

5. Agreeing with those who praise you and expressing your agreement. Self-praise is "excellent self-conditioning."

6. Improvising, instead of bogging down in indecision; acting spontaneously.

"I am advocating a return to excitation, because psychology deals not with the brain but with the heart. Thought is the smoke screen of emotions. . . . These emotional exercises may seem juvenile, boring, and unimportant, but they are the very things that build a cure. . . . The emotionally paralyzed say that such exhibitionism is in poor taste."

Salter is not worried that his patients could go too far in excitation; there is the counterweight of their lifelong conditioning in inhibition. He knows that they need a few stop lights, but not as many as to impede a healthy responsiveness to life. He wants them to overlearn their new habits in the beginning until these habits become second nature to them. The following section is from Chapter 8 of *Conditioned Reflex Therapy* by Andrew Salter.[2]

## RECONDITIONING AND DISINHIBITION THERAPY

The principles of excitation apply to every psychological problem no matter how remote they may first appear. It will be found that claustrophobia, for example, though presumably the imprint of a particular experience, is discarded when the individual develops greater excitation. This principle is important, and I shall use three cases of claustrophobia to illustrate it.

---

[2] Reprinted from *Conditioned reflex therapy* with permission of the author.

*Case 1*

Let us consider a stockbroker, aged forty, who has suffered from claustrophobia and fear of the dark since childhood. He is pleasant and somewhat dynamic and speaks impersonally and to the point. His parents were always formal with him, and I soon realize that he is the classical inhibitory type that always seems calm. Fortunately, he is happily married, so that presents no problem. He works easily with mental abstractions, and he is well informed about psychology.

I tell him that he may expect results quickly because he has the learning attitude. It is not one of contradiction or dull acquiescence but is rather that of a professional violinist, studying with a teacher, and trying to translate the instructions into muscular action with a violin. More cannot be expected of anybody.

I explain to him that his claustrophobia and fear of the dark are merely two aspects of this inability to liberate any emotion at all. "You're like flypaper. Every feeling sticks to you, and the more so when you try to shake it off. Don't be so agreeable. Tell people what you think at all times, regardless of whether it's polite or impolite. Down with Emily Post! Live with the shades up. Get the steam out! Be an emotional broadcaster, not a receiver. Don't degenerate into logic. Don't be so brainy in your work. Be more gutty. Practice these setting-up exercises for the emotions."

I showed him how to apply these principles with his wife, servants, office employees, and business associates, and after five hours of such therapy his claustrophobia and fear of the dark were gone. His sessions were helpful, but his psychological exercises outside of my office had been more important. He lost his phobia because he had become more emotionally free and had acquired greater ease with people.

The originally disturbing claustrophobic and darkness experiences were never elicited from him. To me, his symptoms were manifestations of his inability to shake off experiences of high emotional content. This is not symptom therapy, for it is the balance between inhibition and excitation that determines the extent to which an individual participates in life. The success of this approach to claustrophobia is probably not a coincidence, as shown in another case.

*Case 2*

The forty-five-year-old head of a huge advertising agency has had claustrophobia since childhood and has also suffered from stomach cramps and gasping breathing for the past dozen years. This feeling comes over him in his dealings with the men who decide whether or not to give their advertising to his agency, in short, with the men who have the power of life or death over his business.

As he sits before me, he is calmly puffing on a pipe, looking tweedy and like a young college professor. "My nervous ailment is getting so bad it is threatening to interfere with my work. I have been X-rayed and tested from head to toe, and nothing organically wrong has been found." These are the first steps that are usually taken upon the onset of a psychological disturbance. "My trouble seems to be a psychopathic disturbance of my breathing function. I seem to have a continual spasm of the muscles which control my breathing. About half the time I can't draw a deep breath, which is very frightening. I get severe headaches during which I pant and fight for my breath and gasp for hours. These attacks come on after meals, or when waiting in a theatre, or during important business conferences. It is hard for me to carry on a prolonged conversation because I seem to be unable to coordinate my breathing with my speaking."

He has seen "dozens" of psychiatrists, which is probably an exaggeration. Those who were psychoanalysts imply an Oedipus complex; the others counsel him not to "worry so much," and to "get a grip on yourself," and he bids them adieu and is a perambulating hypochondriac again.

He is unhappily married to a modern Xanthippe, and he has read much, but not wisely, in psychology. He has the learning attitude, and any "psychological diet list" I give him will be followed implicitly. He owns a racing stable, and it is easy for him to see the importance of training healthy emotional habits in humans as well as in horses.

"Yes," he says. "You make sense. You're right when you say my emotional percolator is always perking, and I never pour a cup. Everybody thinks I'm cool, but I'm bursting inside. I'm always the first to pick up a dinner check, even if it's not my turn. I want everybody to love me."

"I see you have been reading a book."

He continues without a smile. "I suppose you want me to become a 'louse'."

"I wouldn't put it that vigorously. Let us say that in this wicked world it is simply a question of fighting for your emotional rights. You never get your privileges anyway. You want nothing that isn't coming to you. The chances are," I continue, with superficial logic, "that if you do the opposite of what you have been doing all your life, you will probably feel the opposite of the way you do now."

He agrees that this seems plausible.

I speak to him much as I did to Case 1. "Never be reasonable about anything. Get rid of your irritations. I don't care what you feel. I only want to know what you express. Don't keep your real feelings corked up, any more than you would your stomach. Yelling gets the knot out of your gut. Remember they that spit shall inherit the earth."

We dispose of his childhood in a few minutes. This is the one with the overprotective mother, the uninterested father, the house full of children, and the selling of newspapers when he was ten. There is often no point in going into the background of the case. We see the mal-conditioned dog before us, and his problem tells us all that we need to know about the kennel from which he came.

At his next appointment, he told me that he had called at the office of one of his clients after leaving me last time and was the sole passenger in an elevator operated by a young woman. The elevator stuck between floors, the nightmare of a claustrophobiac. He said that he had been practicing by chatting with my secretary after he left and with the cab driver riding to his "account."

"I was in a good mood when I entered the elevator."

"What happened when it jammed?"

"The girl was frightened and turned to me. She was pretty. 'What am I supposed to do now?' she said. 'How the hell do I know?' I told her. 'I'm not running this elevator.' She said, 'I just got the job this morning.' 'Well,' I said, 'damn it, let's see.' And we went over to the button panel and began pushing buttons. The elevator got going and after a few wrong stops reached my floor."

I asked him how long he remained agitated after he left the elevator. He said not more than five minutes.

"Come now."

"That's exactly right," he answered.

"How would you have acted in the elevator if you hadn't seen me?"

"I would have told the girl, 'Keep calm, Miss. There's no point in being excited,' but I would probably have been ready to faint. After I left the elevator, I would have been dead to the world for the rest of the day and most of the next one."

"You said the elevator operator was pretty. Don't you think you were showing off in front of her?"

"Maybe," he answered, "but I didn't give her the keep-cool routine. I exploded, like you told me."

He had a total of five hours of consultation, and now, two years later, his claustrophobia is still gone. He feels much freer, and his stomach symptoms occur rarely and with diminished severity. His business activity distresses him substantially less, and, in general, he is a much happier person. "I am greatly improved. I am advancing instead of going back."

Were the two cases of claustrophobia that I have so far presented really cured, or did they only get symptom relief? If the latter is true, was the relief temporary or permanent, or did the symptoms remain, but in a different form? Fundamental issues all, but answerable, I believe, to the satisfaction of persons with forbearance enough to follow the thread of my discussion.

Surely, these objections lose weight when they are voiced by those seldom able to provide their patients with temporary relief, to say nothing of permanent cure. But more fundamentally, the question of symptom relief versus root cure turns on what happens to be denominated as the roots of an individual's problem; and these will always reflect the school of psychology to which the critic or the therapist belongs.

"Know thyself," says the proverb, but with what? The individual has only himself to know himself with, so acquiring new knowledge is not easy. I realize it can only be difficult, for those whose conditioning in psychology is nonreflexological, to believe that claustrophobia can be solved as simply as I have explained. Nor should such persons be criticized when they find repugnant the thesis that the solution to personality difficulties lies in increasing the individual's level of excitation, whether the problem be claustrophobia, alcoholism, shyness, drug addiction, stuttering, homosexuality, or anything else.

To those of them who are endowed with the true scientific spirit, I commend Francis Bacon. "We find no new tools because we take some venerable but questionable proposition as an indubitable starting point. Now, if a man will begin with certainties, he shall end in doubts; but if he will be content to begin in doubts, he shall end in certainties."

## Case 3

One man's symptoms are another man's roots. An understanding of this, as shown in yet another case of claustrophobia, will lead us deeper into the techniques of conditioned reflex therapy.

Dr. T. is a fifty-five-year-old surgeon. He has suffered from claustrophobia since the age of seven or eight. His home looks like a medieval castle, and he has called in a procession of contractors to estimate the cost of putting windows through three feet of masonry because he wants to feel closer to the outside world. Every door, including the bathroom, is kept open or ajar. Sleeping in the house makes him uneasy, but he sleeps comfortably in the open air. In summer he spends most of his time camping so that he can sleep outdoors. He will not ride in an elevator; he cannot ride on trains except near the door, and then he is uncomfortable. He has no recollection of the onset of the claustrophobia, but he recalls that when he was ten he once slept in an attic at his aunt's house and felt oppressed by the confined space. The approach of cold weather always frightens him, but curiously, when winter comes, he rather enjoys it. He reports no other fears.

"Isn't this rather illogical?" he says.

I answer that by "illogical" we usually mean "emotional."

His marriage, I quickly see, is happy. Here, then, is a man with claustrophobia and fear of the onset of cold weather, who can recall neither of the original experiences, although he can think of times in his childhood when they disturbed him. I decide to consider the claustrophobia first, because it is probably a simpler problem than his fear of winter weather.

He has a strong scientific bent and, quite unsuccessfully, has often tried to recall his original experience with claustrophobia that his reading tells him must have occurred. He has read my "Three Techniques of Autohypnosis" and is hypnotic minded.

"Well," I say, "first I will teach you to recapture the feeling of claustrophobia at will. Then the stimuli which originated it will come surging back to you." I explain how moods carry memories in their wake, and I direct the conversation so that he becomes completely retrospective toward his childhood. That is where his attention is directed, and that is all that occupies him. Then, with dramatic emphasis, I read the following passage from W. H. R. Rivers (9, p. 176).

> The incident which he remembered was a visit to an old rag-and-bone merchant who lived near the house which his parents then occupied. This old man was in the habit of giving boys a halfpenny when they took to him anything of value. The child had found something and had taken it alone to the house of the old man. He had been admitted through a dark narrow passage from which he entered the house by turning about half-way along the passage. At the end of the passage was a brown spaniel. Having received his reward, the child came out alone to find the door shut. He was too small to open the door, and the dog at the other end of the passage began to growl. The child was terrified. His state of terror came back to him vividly as the incident returned to his mind after all the years of oblivion in which it had lain. The influence which the incident made on his mind is shown by his recollection that ever afterwards he was afraid to

pass the house of the old man, and if forced to do so, always kept to the opposite side of the street.

When I finished, he looked bewildered. "That's it! That trapped feeling." He repeated, "That trapped feeling! It's come back to me! When I was a child on my aunt's farm, they were building a link to a reservoir across the property. They had big six-foot pipes lying next to each other before they dug a trench and covered them. It used to be fun to get in at one end of the pipes and run through to the spot of light way down at the other end. One afternoon, I started to run through, and about halfway, something in the darkness grabbed me and held me. It was a man inside, fixing something. I was absolutely petrified, and I couldn't even scream. He let me go after a while, and I thought I'd never reach the other end. . . . Yes," he said, "it's odd how that thing comes back to me. I'm sure that's how I got the claustrophobia."

I said nothing. He continued, "Isn't it peculiar how I feel that frightened feeling right now? It's almost as if I'm back in the pipe again, but it's less than the original feeling. . . . You know; this is the first time I've thought of this in fifty years, and I have tried hard to recall it many times." Needless to say, knowing where a man got a bullet wound does not stop the bleeding.

I found that he had tried self-suggestion and had been able to induce feelings of lightness and heaviness in his limbs. This meant I would probably succeed in teaching him how to get his arms and legs warm or cold. I said, for example, "Your right arm is very light, extremely light, just as if there's a rope tied on your waist, pulling it up, pulling it up. Your arm's just floating in the air, floating in the air. . . ." I then gave him suggestions of cold—his hand is frozen in a cake of ice, winter is here, and it's very cold. And so on. I told him to seat himself in a comfortable chair in his living room at home and to practice these exercises in sensory recall.

At his second visit, he reported that he could turn on the sensations with ease. He listened with interest to my explanation of verbal conditioning, and next I told him to practice turning his feeling of claustrophobia on and off and conditioning relaxation to it. He was also to continue the sensory exercises, except that now they were to include vigorous statements that he was grown up and that his nonsensical childish fears no longer plagued him. He was also to tell himself that the pipe broke open when the man grabbed him.

My plan was for him to establish a link between controlling his senses and feeling good. I also told him to take care not to make his claustrophobia stronger than his feelings of well-being, or the conditioning would increase his discomfort.

Before his third session he wrote, "No mental suffering today. Just a weak pair of legs which I can stand or stand on." He continued the exercises. When I next saw him I asked him to try to recall any distressing associations he may have had with cold weather, but he could think of none. Since he was somewhat plump, I told him, with a smile, that his fear of the cold did not seem to be physiologically determined. Shortly thereafter, pursuant to my instructions, he made his body feel relaxed and heavy at a living room self-suggestion session. He built up his fear of the coming of winter and kept a retrospective attitude toward his childhood at the same time. He piled mood on mood, and another experience that he had completely forgotten returned to him.

On his aunt's farm was a lake, and in the winter ice was sawed from it and stored in a big icehouse. One summer afternoon, when he was no more than ten, he was accidentally locked in among the cakes of ice, and only after becoming cold and frightened and running hysterically back and forth in the icehouse was he able to open the door and get out. This experience followed the one in the reservoir pipes and no doubt reinforced his earlier claustrophobia. Without instructions from me, he worked on his experience in the icehouse as he had with his experience in the pipe. He told himself that such childish nonsense would not distress him any more, and besides, the doors of the icehouse had been wide open all the time. It was not possible to check the effect of these suggestions because he was seeing me during the winter.

By this time, he was going about the house, giving himself what he called, "those anticlaustrophobia vaccinations." On his fifth session, he reported a complete absence of any claustrophobic symptoms whatever, and he has remained free to this day, five years later. Gone also is his fear of the onset of winter. Further, although I gave him no direct therapy to facilitate relations with people, he reported a greater ease with them. We had one more session, in which we discussed the rationale of my therapy with him, and that is all there was to the case.

Please note that I devoted no attention to his basic personality, which was one of confidence in professional activity and polite inhibition in personal relations. Although I treated him purely as a victim of specific claustrophobic conditioning, repercussions nevertheless soon occurred in his social relations.

In the previous discussion, Cases 1 and 2 received no specific conditioning against claustrophobia, and they seem to have been cured through an increase in excitation. A similar approach, I have found, is also successful with agoraphobia (fear of open spaces).

Apparently, it makes no difference which part of a "vicious" circle we start with, as long as we get a firm grip on any of its many radii. Conditioned patterns are an intermeshed set of gears, and it is not too important where we apply motive power. If we apply some force anywhere in the system, all of the other wheels will turn together. If we keep our eye on emotions and their conditioning, that is all that will be necessary.

In the case of the claustrophobiac who feared the onset of winter, the amnesia surrounding the original experiences seemed to have been lifted, although I entertained some doubt as to the relevancy of the icehouse episode. In Cases 1 and 2, which were treated as problems in excitation, I made no effort to ascertain the original experiences, nor were they ever elicited. It is seldom the trauma that does it. It is the slow grind.

In terms of relief reported, there seems to be no difference. Both approaches to claustrophobia seem equally fundamental because substantial improvement occurred in areas that were neither probed nor treated. If it be contended that the relaxation techniques in Case 3 were also a form of excitation, it still would not affect my thesis. Let me recall my analogy of the gears. Turn one of them, and you turn them all.

## Case 4

But what shall be done with the persons who do not let you turn the wheels? Often they should be chased from the office with a broomstick, although they are not to be blamed for their personalities.

I explain to them that my appointment book is like a life raft. There is room for only a limited number of people, and I do not intend to waste my time trying to convince any of the bobbing heads around me to get on board. There are others drowning who are only too happy to cooperate in their rescue. Here, however, let us consider one of these recalcitrant cases and implement our principles some more.

J. R. is the tall, handsome son of a millionaire. He is twenty-five years old, a postgraduate student in sociology, and he talks vaguely of improving the welfare of humanity. He is convinced he is uninteresting. He is an alert, if too agreeable, young man, and acts somewhat mulelike when I disagree with him. Though he does not find his studies difficult, he cannot concentrate on them because his mind "wanders constantly." He tosses restlessly for hours before falling into a fitful sleep. He wants to learn how to hypnotize himself so that he may be rid of his insomnia. I test him for hypnosis, but his attention wanders as he compares my technique with what he has read about the subject and with what he thinks I should do. Needless to say, nothing happens.

I then become stern, and I tell him that I am utterly uninterested in the claptrap that clutters up his mind. I am the authority, and he has come to consult me. He will do exactly as I say if he wants to learn autohypnosis. All that he has to provide is the broken leg. I will decide the splints that are indicated. This approach is necessary with the spoiled-child type of adult, because our only means of communication with him (and with everybody else) is through his conditioned emotions.

He is interested in music and possesses absolute pitch. I decide to mold my technique accordingly and tell him to listen intently.

I snap my fingers. "Can you still hear that pitch in your head, now that I have stopped snapping my fingers?"

"Yes."

I tap my desk with my pen. "Can you hear this sound in your head?"

"Yes."

"That's fine. I see the procedure necessary, and we'll take it from there when I see you next."

"Aren't you going to hypnotize me today?" he asks.

I smile blandly. "If you want me to help you, it will have to be in my way. I can't be bothered having you tell me what to do."

It might appear that such insulting disinterest would frighten him away permanently, but experience demonstrates that this is the only efficacious technique with persons who try to guide the therapy. This technique has to be tempered with judgment, but it involves a difference in tactics, not principles. If messages to people are not enciphered in their own peculiar emotional code, there is no communication. To condition something new, we have to take advantage of something old.

Our young man is annoyed when he leaves, but he is very curious about what I have up my sleeve, which is precisely my intention.

When I next see him, I tell him that he simply has to listen to me and obey. He has my permission to waste his own time, but I resent his wasting mine, and unless he is completely and absolutely cooperative he might as well leave right now.

"What have I done to deserve this tirade?" he asks.

"You are guilty of being you. That's all. The fact that you bought a ticket doesn't give you a license to tell the actors what to say."

He smiles.

"Very well," I say. I point to the glistening thermos jug on my desk. "I want you to look at the spot made by the reflection of the light. Do you see that spot?"

"Yes."

"Now, each time I snap my fingers, I want you to close your eyes in a docile, browbeaten way. For your sake, please close them in a docile, browbeaten way. You will find this very interesting."

Many persons go through life in a constant flight from boredom, and their cooperation can be enlisted only by promising them relaxation and entertainment. Ringing these bells involves no hypocrisy. Our therapeutic duty to a human being in distress is all the validation we need.

He relaxes in the easy chair and stares at the jug. I snap my fingers. He closes his eyes. I wait about three seconds and then say quietly, "Open them." He opens his eyes and continues looking at the spot. I snap my fingers again, and he closes his eyes. I wait another three seconds and then say, "Open them." He does so. "That's fine," I say. "From now on I want you to think thoughts of blankness, relaxation, and quietness in a vague daydreaming way. At the same time, as I snap my fingers, close your eyes without thinking and keep them shut until I tell you to open them. Think 'relax', and try to feel blank in every part of your body. Do you understand?"

"Yes," he says. I see that I have his complete attention, and that now, at least, he has no negativism toward me.

I snap my fingers. His eyes close. I wait three seconds and say, "Open them," and I snap my fingers again. He closes his eyes. I permit them to remain closed for three seconds and say, "Open them," and I repeat this ritual once more. After about forty times I stop. "How are your thoughts now?"

He is somewhat surprised. "I feel relaxed."

"That's fine," I say. "Now I'll tell you what," and without ado I snap my fingers, although he is not fixating the jug. He blinks. "What happened?" I ask.

"I blinked when you snapped your fingers."

"That's fine," I say, for this means that now his lid closure has become somewhat conditioned.

We resume the finger-snapping eye-closing exercises for another forty times, and then I stop. "Can you imagine my fingers snapping when I'm not snapping them?"

"Yes," he says.

"Can you hear them clearly in your mind?"

He nods.

"I'll tell you what I want you to do," I say. "Practice this ten minutes at a time, in the morning when you get up, and at night before you go to sleep. Imagine yourself looking at the shiny spot on the jug. Imagine the mood you're in now, and make believe you hear my fingers snapping. Think that relaxed feeling lightly, and then close your eyes. It sounds more complicated than it really is."

"I think I know what you mean. I'll do it, but what if I still can't sleep?"

"Just do the exercises," I say, "and if you continue tossing around, stop them. I don't want you to hitch bad conditioning to them. You'll fall asleep eventually. Maybe it will take some time. I'm only asking you to do the exercises. If you do that, forgive me if I sound cruel, the rest doesn't matter. Just do as I say."

On his next visit he reports that the exercises at night make him feel increasingly relaxed. Also, that his concentration has improved when he reads. He volunteers that a tension he has had in social relationships seems to diminish if he practices the exercises before going among people. In fact, he has been practicing the exercises as much as eight and ten times a day. He seems to get relaxed more thoroughly and quickly each time.

"Fine," I say. "I am not surprised that you violated my instructions and practiced more than I told you to, but this is one time when your being an *enfant terrible* has worked out well." He smiles beatifically. "Keep practicing those exercises," I say, "and particularly before any social activity. You do not even have to open and shut your eyes. Just keep them closed and mentally go through the whole procedure."

"Yes," he says, "that's much the way I have been doing it."

My purpose in all this is to make life easier for him. He is a thoroughly spoiled, grown-up child, and any slight frustration of his wishes causes tension. I want to make him calmer, which will make him much more endurable, and in turn, will make him feel better. "The emotionally free animal has no trouble falling asleep, and as we get you more relaxed (that's what he wants, relaxation) you will be able to feel better through the day, and at night your tension will be less, so sleeping will come easier. Does this make any sense to you?"

"Yes," he answers. "I see what you mean."

I continued seeing him, and there was much chatter of pedagogy, hypnotism, and sociology, but now what intrigued him was that these relaxation exercises were making his relationships with women easier. At a night club, a seminude performer volunteered to dance with a member of the audience. Formerly, much as he wanted to, he would have lacked the courage to do so, but now, with very little prodding from his friends, he got up and rhumbaed, to the great acclaim of the audience. This he liked very much, and it made him a great believer in the importance of relaxation. He continued to pay little attention to excitation.

His interest in hypnosis became more marked, and he took great delight in demonstrating it upon such young women as he could snare. "Do you think you can hypnotize me now?" he asked one day.

"Let's try," I said. Nothing happened except that he felt more relaxed. His mind stopped wandering, and he became subdued. Meanwhile, I must add, he was tossing about in bed less and less. Instead of three hours each night, he now tossed around for about an hour and a half.

I then decided that the time was ripe for emphasis on the concept of excitation, which I tied up to greater social adequacy with women. I presented it as a laundry drier for social wet blankets, which indeed it is.

"Come to think of it," he said, "I have the same inadequacies with everybody. I'm just a boy of good family. You say I'm bright but that's about all. Really, I've never done anything of interest." This from someone who had spent a summer as an overseer on a rubber plantation in Africa and during another vacation had hunted tigers in India, *pour le sport*.

He continued the exercises in auditory imagination. Once I jokingly snapped my fingers for him to check the pitch, but he said it only confused him. Before long, he had become more excitatory, and he was sure that now people liked him. What is more, by thinking of the finger-snapping exercises, he was able to go to sleep at night *almost instantly*.

At the end of our fifteenth hour, I said, "That seems to be that. You are now a social lion without insomnia."

"Yes," he said, "but frankly I'm disappointed because I haven't learned how to hypnotize myself."

I answered, "We acknowledge the fact that you are much less of a bore socially." He nodded with a wry smile. "And tell me," I said. "Let us suppose that you had told a friend that you had come to see me, and that you had suffered from insomnia and would toss about for three or four hours before falling asleep. Now, after seeing me, by merely imagining that you're in my office, and that you hear me snapping my fingers, you fall asleep at night almost instantly. In fact, you almost go out like a light. You seem to have acquired a strange power over yourself. Don't you think that if your friend heard all this he would say that it was hypnotism?"

"Yes," he said, "but it still isn't hypnotism. It's just conditioning."

I was annoyed and amused. "Ho-hum. There isn't much else I can add. If you're not proud of the results, believe me, I am."

He left disgruntled, and that was the last I heard of him. Shakespeare could be rewritten to say, "Above all, only to thine own conditioning canst thou be true."

What is interesting about this case is that instead of tiptoeing around the young man's idiosyncrasies, I boldly took advantage of them. Since his language was emotional Greek, and it was the only one he understood, I spoke it.

Further, the therapy was successful, although his attitude showed that his basic recalcitrance had remained. Faith and belief are inadequate substitutes for science. As for gratitude, it is achievement enough to have helped such a person, without expecting the impossible. There will be others who will be grateful, and who will make therapy emotionally rewarding. Although I cannot expect to act without my nervous system, such things no longer disturb me—at least, for not more than a day.

## OTHER TREATMENT APPLICATIONS

The psychopathological scheme of Salter is simple: The diagnosis is *always* inhibition. Inhibition may be expressed in many ways, but Salter finds it as the basic component of every maladaptation. "My case histories are like Hollywood Westerns. The names are different, but the plot is always the same. The villains may be called alcoholism, shyness, or the lack of the work urge, but behind their mask they are always inhibition. And the hero is always the same—disinhibition, or excitation, if you will. This is an oversimplication, but it is the outline of all psychotherapy."

## Shyness and the Well-Bred Neurosis

Salter reports the treatment of a middle-aged manufacturer who suffered from dizziness, weakness of legs, and heart palpitation whenever he had to meet customers. He suffered from sweating and insomnia. He felt inferior to his customers because he had not even completed high school. He would blush in talking to people. While growing up, he had felt that his mother preferred his younger brother.

Salter used Dunlap's beta hypothesis in the beginning with this patient: he advised him to try blushing deliberately, both when alone and with others.[3] In the following session he reported that he could not blush, whether he tried to or not. The therapist directed him now to express his feelings to his brother, customers, other people, to stop being a "polite dishrag." He also asked him not to drink before going into these exercises of disinhibition. After seven sessions he felt better than ever before in his life. He came three times after that to confirm his progress with the therapist, to thank him, and to convey the thanks of his wife. He kept referring persons to the therapist.

## Anxiety

Anxiety follows inhibition like a shadow. It is a learned emotional response, based probably on an innate disposition. "We need not flog the dead Freudian horses of birth trauma and repressed early sexual experiences as the causes of anxiety." Pavlov created what looked like an anxiety neurosis in his dogs when he presented them with insoluble discriminatory problems. He first conditioned a dog to expect food after presentation of a circle and no food after an ellipse was shown. When the shape of the ellipse was made closer and closer to circular, the dog became restless, chewed at apparatus, and barked when brought to the laboratory room, all behaviors which he did not show before.

Salter was successful in treating anxiety in humans by disinhibition. His Case 35 was a man in his thirties who experienced a sharp pain in his left temple and felt dizzy one evening at work. He was straining himself to the limit: maintaining his top student performance in a course in biochemistry, working full time, courting a refined young lady to whom he was engaged. He had started medical studies

---

[3] Independently of American behavior therapy practices, Frankl had developed a similar method of "paradoxical intention" (6).

but had to drop out of the course for lack of money; other friends of his received medical degrees.

He went to a physician for consultation. He advised the patient to take a week's rest from the strenuous schedule. The symptoms grew worse and new ones appeared: periodical excitement, extreme fatigue, vague fears. He went to another physician who recommended bed rest, vitamins, sunray treatments. A month of treatment brought no improvement: besides former symptoms he became bothered by street noises, and the pressure in the temples persisted.

He then went to a psychiatrist. The doctor pronounced the case relatively mild, explaining it as dependence on parents and separation anxiety. He advised the patient to get married to ease his tensions. Six more interviews followed, and no improvement was shown. The psychiatrist decided to give him electric shock treatments. Three shock treatments and marriage did little to make his condition better. Three more shocks were given, vitamin tablets were tried for a few weeks, and, as the patient was not improving, six more shock treatments were administered with no benefit to the patient. When the patient persisted, the psychiatrist told him that he suffered from chronic neurosis and that nothing more could be done for him.

In despair he contacted Salter. He was told that he needed to stop trying to be a gentleman "with an amiable disposition and an asinine smile," and start expressing his neglected emotions. After eleven weekly sessions, the patient was less excitable, his self-confidence increased, the headaches did not appear as often, and the fatigue was less pronounced. The progress apparently continued after termination of regular interviews. Salter heard from him eight months later. This fearful young man had gotten the courage to leave his safe job of an office worker and take up the position of a pharmaceutical salesman abroad.

## Stuttering

What is wrong with the stutterer is not his speech but his inhibitory personality. Bender (1, p. 143), comparing 249 male stutterers with nonstutterers, found that the former were more neurotic, more introverted, less dominant, less confident, and less sociable. The stutterer is tensed up bodily and emotionally. If he takes phenobarbital, relaxes, or talks relaxation, to himself or to some person he considers to be inferior to him, his speech will improve. "The stuttering pattern is not a problem for the elocution teacher. Stuttering is a problem in the psychology of personality and should be treated accordingly. . . . The stutterer who insists on regarding his problem purely as a speech problem is doomed."

*"The stutterer must talk excitationally."*

A charming woman of forty visits Salter. She had tried some psychiatric treatment for stuttering without much benefit. She experiences fear of stuttering, and that makes her stutter. She moved away from mother, but she is kept under parental dominance by letter and telephone. In Salter's experience such severe dependence and immaturity are typical of stutterers. She has to break her leaning upon parents if she is to improve her speech. *"Disinhibit the inhibitory* remains our guiding principle at all times."

### Unlearning Homosexuality

Dunlap (3, p. 221) protested the preposterous psychoanalytic implications of homosexuality: "Two men, or two women, lunching together are literally engaged in a homosexual luncheon. In this literal (but spurious) sense of the term, homosexuality is indeed normal. It is, in fact, one of the finest features of human life. To become confused by verbal juggling and conclude, consequently, that homosexuality in every sense of the term is fine and normal is an appalling procedure, but it is a procedure, which camouflaged in vague phraseology, has become a social blight." It is entertaining to find Kinsey reporting that though Freudians might have confused others on the score, they are careful not to apply their teachings to themselves. Several dozen psychoanalysts who contributed their histories to the study "insisted that they . . . never identified homosexual experience or reactions in their own histories." (8, p. 627)

Another nonsense, solemnly announced by some behavior scientists, is that homosexuality is based on heredity and therefore practically incurable. "The sooner the glandular—constitutional—heredity approach to homosexuality goes into the garbage can of overripe hypotheses, the sooner the rational treatment of the homosexual can begin."

A thirty-year-old physician, in considerable mental distress, contacted Salter. (The report is based on the patient's own notes.) He had sexually normal development in childhood and early adolescence. From his sixteenth to twentieth year he noticed an unusual interest in male genitalia and male sexual functions. He dated girls as much as did his friends. A high school friend introduced him to masturbation, a girl seduced him to heterosexual experience when he was in college.

Passivity characterized him. His father was weak, mother overprotective. There was little male identification that he could acquire in the family.

He became concerned about his sexual excitement when a homosexual approached him, but he rejected the temptation. He moved later to a neighborhood where homosexuals were more numerous. He avoided contacts, but every two or three months he would let himself be drawn into a casual contact. For fear of infection, he limited the experiences to mutual masturbation. He was experiencing strong revulsion and self-disgust after these episodes. He avoided any repeated contacts, fearing that he would be finally exposed. People who knew him did not suspect him of homosexuality.

After several years of such clandestine living, he was becoming more careless and more worried on that score. He maintained some heterosexual experiences but could not decide to start a family, although he wished for a respectable social role. He noted several indications of a neurotic reaction in him: gastric pains, loss of weight, nausea; insomnia; depressive spells; easy crying in excitement; hyper-irritability; suspicion; and lack of confidence. He wished for help but did not seek it, being hesitant to reveal his condition even to a therapist; he rather thought of finding an escape in suicide.

Therapy lasted three months, in eight sessions. Instead of dealing with homosexuality, Salter directed him toward changing his inhibitory personality. He also suggested the practice of sexual reassociation. The improvement of eating and sleeping came in the beginning of therapy. The patient noticed establishment of normal emotional reactions in himself. His mood improved, and homosexual thoughts receded.

Six months and three additional interviews later he reported no homosexual difficulties. His co-workers were expressing recognition of his performance, he was busy socially, and he had started athletics. Three and a half years later he was still doing quite well.

The misdevelopment in the "mama's boy" is repeated in many thousands of cases. "We need no mysterious incest taboos to explain homosexuality. Some boys have no opportunity to learn to become men—they are castrated by their mother's apron strings." Homosexuality is primarily social maladjustment in inhibitory individuals. Excitation is the principal method of unlearning masochism, self-insufficiency, and immaturity, which are basic features of homosexuals. Disinhibition widens the horizon to include females, and reassociation of normal sexual interests leads to heterosexuality.

## REFERENCES

1. Bender, J. F. *The personality structure of stuttering.* New York: Pitman, 1939.
2. Diven, K. Certain determinants in the conditioning of anxiety reactions. *J. Psychol.*, 1937, **3**, 291–308.
3. Dunlap, K. *Habits: their making and unmaking.* New York: Liveright, 1932.
4. Ellson, D. G. Hallucinations produced by sensory conditioning. *J. Exp. Psychol.*, 1941, **28**, 1–20.
5. Erickson, M. H. The induction of color blindness by a technique of hypnotic suggestion. *J. Gen. Psychol.*, 1939, **20**, 61–89.
6. Gerz, H. O. The paradoxical intention technique. In R. M. Jurjevich (Ed.) *Direct Psychotherapy: Developments on four continents,* Coral Gables, Fla., University of Miami Press, in preparation.
7. Hudgins, C. V. Conditioning and the voluntary control of the pupillary light reflex. *J. Gen. Psychol.*, 1933, **8**, 3–51.
8. Kinsey, A. C., Pomeroy, W. B., and Martin, C. E. *Sexual behavior in the human male.* Philadelphia: Saunders, 1948.
9. Rivers, W. H. R. *Instinct and the unconscious.* New York: Cambridge University Press, 1920.

Chapter 5

# Therapy # 52 — The Truth (Operant Group Psychotherapy)

## WILLARD A. MAINORD

Willard A. Mainord: b. 1917, Denver, Colorado.
B.S., 1950, M.S., 1952, Washington State College. Ph.D., University of Washington, 1956.
Associate Professor of Psychology, University of Louisville, 1966–date. Assistant Professor of Psychology, University of Louisville, 1963–1966. Chief, Training and Education in Psychology, Western State Hospital, Ft. Steilacoom, Washington, 1961-1962. Psychologist, V.A. Neuropsychiatric Hospital, American Lake, Washington, 1956–1961.
Member, Advisory Board, Lilly Institute for Psychology and Religion. Consultant, Southern Indiana Mental Health and Guidance Center, Inc.
Articles: Sources of discomfort and uses of symptoms. In O. H. Mowrer (Ed.), *Morality and mental health*, 1966. Confrontation versus diversion in group therapy with chronic schizophrenics as measured by a "positive incident" criterion. *J. Clin. Psychol.*, 1965, **21** (2), 222-225. A therapy. *Res. Bull.*, Division of Mental Health, State of Washington, 1962, **5** 85-92. Some effects of sodium amytal on "deteriorated" schizophrenics. *J. Consult. Psychol.*, 1953, **17**, 54-57.

In recent years, O. H. Mowrer has often referred to what he believes to be the fact that we are in the midst of a psychotherapeutic revolution. This book comprehensively illustrates his point, and the reader may have wearily concluded that for each new therapist there is to be found a new therapy. Revolutions are all very well, but it is probably inevitable that many of the revolutionaries will proceed completely independently. As a result, many of our efforts are overlapping and largely redundant. In spite of this, as a function of the isolation of independence, each new therapist is likely to see himself as a lonely pioneer battling against nearly overwhelming odds in the attempt to purvey the truth to a smugly erroneous universe.

The process seems to begin with disillusion centered about the methods adopted while still in training. This is followed by a period of

129

casting around with other established approaches which, in turn, do not seem to be strikingly effective. At long last, perhaps out of a sense of desperation, the therapist starts acting in a way that, as far as he knows, is almost entirely a novel one. If these initial efforts seem productive, enthusiasm, energy, and dedication mount, and the increasing number of successes leads to the almost irresistible conclusion that the therapist has single-handedly created *the* valid therapy.

If one is lucky enough to be the discoverer of a new phenomenon, clearly his duty is to communicate his findings to a waiting world, and it is also his right to name his intellectual brainchild. So he may then label his psychotherapeutic system something like "Infallible Therapy," subtly damning previous approaches while simultaneously reifying the new ones. Then, if the new system attracts notice, it will also attract criticism, and it becomes necessary to refute the unbeliever. As the truth is being defended, creeping rigidity is likely to set in which may—as has been the case with psychoanalysis—demand another revolution.

The reader should be warned that I am not immune from the disease. I am going to present my baby, and to me it is without flaw. Nonetheless, it will be extremely surprising if the system turns out to need no revising, and it has already developed that many of my "original" discoveries were, at best, rediscoveries or concurrent findings. I prefer to ignore "at worst."

At this time, a general intellectual debt should be acknowledged. Ideas have been adopted from Mowrer (5, 6), Szasz (14), Glasser (3), London (4), Bandura (1), Skinner (13), and Pratt (10, 11). The trouble is that I am no longer able to specify what came from whom, in addition to whatever unconscious plagiarism may have occurred. Having acknowledged the debt, the remainder of the paper will be written as if every idea in it is exclusively my discovery.

London (4) states that behind every system of psychotherapy is a theory of personality that may be either implicit or explicit. Only if a general statement, such as "people can learn to be crazy," qualifies as a theory of personality is London necessarily correct. Rather, I would argue that any system of psychotherapy has behind it a definition of the disorder—again either implicit or explicit.

In analytic theory the tendency has been to move to more social contexts (7) as the crucial background for a disorder still defined much as before. For the Sullivanians the content of the therapy was greatly modified, but the operations changed comparatively little. By and large, this characteristic seems to be true of almost all of what London (4) calls the "insight" therapies.

Such behavior therapists as Wolpe, Stampfl, et al., did redefine the disorder as simply maladaptive learning. Such a term is so broad as to encompass any ineffective behavior by anybody at any time, and so typically the practice has been to allow the patient to decide what maladaptive behaviors shall be dealt with. The operational definition then becomes any maladaptive behavior that elicits a complaint from the behaver. Such a definition obviously does not need to be, although clearly it could be, related to any sort of social context.

Inasmuch as some disorders are clearly social in their implications, it would seem desirable to combine social factors with maladaptive behaviors to define the disorder. The definition then would assert that pathology of an emotional nature is maladaptive learning in social contexts, thus opening the door to complaints arising from the social environment as well as the complaints of the "patient." In the scientific approach, the use of operational definitions is well known; what is apparently less often recognized is that some operational definitions are to be found originating from society rather than from a scientist. The operations of a complaining society then might lead to a useful definition.

The extreme case is the clearest example along any continuum, so let us look at the extreme mental case for purposes of conceptualization. It will probably be accepted that the extreme case is the committed mental patient whose difficulties are seen as being important enough to justify legal but nonetheless coercive treatment. Literally, the committed patient is tried and convicted even though the euphemistic statement is that the patient has been discovered unable to be responsible because of mental illness. "Because of 'mental illness' . . ." is a redundancy inasmuch as the evidence of mental illness is an enumeration of unacceptable behaviors from which the abstract label of "sick" is drawn.

Examined dispassionately, commitment follows an accusation or complaint (usually by a relative) followed by trial and conviction and sentence to a mental hospital. If an individual has pneumonia and refuses treatment, he is not sentenced to a hospital if he is conscious and refuses to go, even if it is the opinion of the physician that lack of hospitalization will result in a fatality. He can, however, be quarantined if he has a communicable disease without regard to whether he likes it or not, because of the social consequences of allowing him his freedom. I would argue that the analogy is a fair one—coercive hospitalization is always a function of social consequences and never a function of the disease itself.

Thus, the operational definition of the committed mental patient as determined by society is: (1) The patient has been behaving in a socially unacceptable manner and (2) Because of certain mitigating circumstances, confinement will be in a mental hospital rather than in a correctional institution.

It is probably consensual to say that any complaint has as its basis some form of subjective threat. If the complaints are examined and put through a distillation process, it should be possible to start labeling the kinds of behaviors that lead to the complaint, and from there we can argue that the therapeutic task is one of eliminating old and building new behaviors that will erase the patient's threat properties.

In one way or another the social complaints about the committed patient fall into two classes: (1) The patient is frightening; (2) The patient is unproductive. By frightening all that is meant is that the complainer is apprehensive as to what will happen to him if he continues to be subjected to the patient's behavior. By unproductive all that is meant is that the complainer reports that the patient does not carry out the minimal demands of self-sufficiency in a social context.

The mental health propagandists have recognized that the patient is frightening by saying, in effect, that no one should feel threatened by a sick man. It is hardly surprising to discover that such propaganda efforts (12) have not been particularly effective, inasmuch as a deliriously berserk and undeniably sick person would be just as frightening as he would be if berserk and well. Further, it is impossible to read papers, magazines, etc., without learning of case after case in which violent behavior has been ascribed directly or indirectly to emotional difficulties. For an overwhelming majority of the population, the very words "mental patient" carry connotations of unpredictability and possible danger. The complaining member of society may feel more sympathy for the "ill" and may be slower in registering the complaint, but he does not find the disturbing behaviors any more comforting merely because they are described as symptoms.

Thus, family members report actual fear of physical damage, or fear that the patient may damage himself, or fear that the damage may be inflicted upon someone else. There is the fear that the patient's behavior patterns will demand so much care and so many concessions as to make the complaining individual's prospects extremely unappealing. The patient is described as not amenable to logic, or to out-patient treatment, or to any of the available mechanisms devised to solve problems of social living, and there is no reason to believe the improvement can be expected. One way or another the complainer states, "I have had all that I can take."

Productivity is important for two reasons. Egocentricity is much more tolerable if it is found in useful as opposed to nonuseful people, and bizarre behavior will be tolerated in someone who is socially valued. Productivity forestalls many complaints. But nonproductivity in itself becomes intolerable because few people are willing to support an individual who exhibits nothing but consumer behavior. The non-responsive patient is hardly frightening in the usual sense to those who know him well. He is a massive inconvenience, however, and will become intolerable to his family after some period of time. It should be remembered that only because the patient has a family and because the diagnosis of mental illness has been applied does he get sent to a mental hospital rather than to jail as a vagrant.

A few actual examples will perhaps sharpen up the argument. Suicidal patients are typified by the following example. The husband reported that he reluctantly agreed with his wife's psychiatrist that commitment should be obtained in order to protect his wife's life. He stated that he could not give her all of his time that was necessary to ensure her protection and keep his job at the same time. He worried about the possibility of doing the wrong thing and decided that he was not equipped to accept personally the responsibility of providing the proper care. And finally, he was almost sure that the children were being upset. The crucial part of the complaint is that the husband was in favor of his wife's survival in or out of the institution, but from his point of view her condition required from him things he could not and would not do if she remained in the home. He could protect her if he stayed by her side twenty-four hours a day or if he paid enough money for around-the-clock nursing care, but such prices were too high to pay from his point of view.

Then there was the young wife who insisted that her young child was a chicken. The husband did not feel it was difficult to deal with his wife and would have been willing to have her treated on an out-patient basis except that he could not afford it nor did he dare leave her with the child.

A mother had her son committed because he would do nothing but eat, sleep, and watch television. When she insisted that a twenty-three-year-old man should be out looking for a job, he slapped her. From that one slap, she had the blinding insight that her son was undoubtedly "mentally ill."

It must be emphasized that bizarreness in itself does not result in commitment. When one woman's infant child was found dead, she reported that she had killed it. Her supporting statements were rambling and garbled. Psychiatric examination resulted in a diagnosis of schizophrenia, and the murder story was considered delusional. A few years later the same thing occurred, but this time the evidence of murder seemed conclusive. At that point she was committed.

In a short, pungent phrase that is meant to be descriptive rather than judgmental, the committed mental patient is a social reject. Social acceptance and social rejection are functions of the social environment, and the affective tone and the symptomatic behaviors, while unpleasant and inefficient for the patient, do not in themselves ensure commitment.

If all or most emotional disorders are essentially different degrees of the same kinds of processes (obviously not necessarily true), we can assume that the apparently milder forms of psychopathology contain within them behaviors leading to unfavorable social judgments. The diagnostic consequence of such an assumption is to identify and modify the behaviors that have already or will lead to social rejection.

As social behaviors might be classified in any number of ways, it might be useful to examine what kinds of activities are most closely associated with social rejection of whatever kind. In our culture, happily, a variety of unusual activities are quite tolerable to most of the people most of the time. Idiosyncracies, per se, not only do not lead to rejection, but in an admired person, will be the basis for such adjectives as colorful, original, or creative. Unusual behaviors are considered to be adequate reason for rejection *only if the behaviors in question are judged to be immoral.* If someone claims to be the unrecognized hereditary king of North America and lets it go at that, few people will care, and the chief emotional response will be one of amusement. But, if that individual attempts to act on his claim—coerce others, appropriate property, act above the law—he will rapidly find his freedom curtailed. If the acts are carried out by anyone presumed to be "well," they would be called such things as bullying, stealing, and depriving others of their rights. Restated, if the act rather than the actor is subjected to a moral judgment, the behaviors of the committed mental patient are often immoral.

Because of the closeness of moral questions and social judgments, it seems necessary to deal with moral issues in psychotherapy (a conclusion already reached by others, Mowrer and Glasser in particular) but from a somewhat different framework. More often than not the immoral behaviors are rather subtle and well concealed, particularly in the out-patient. It is not necessary, then, to look for what would be ordinarily called gross immorality. Any conflict between the patient's behavior and his ethical code may be sufficient to set off avoidance or escape maneuvers which will often have the bizarre flavor that leads to their being called symptoms.

Mowrer has already spelled out his theory of the origins of psychopathology, which is largely the point of view of this paper. Our disagreements center around the prominence of guilt as the basic variable with the correlated concept of self-punishment. The assumption here is that socially punishing consequences in the patient's history have taught him a variety of escape and avoidance behaviors that are maintained because they still have utility at least part of the time. Only by blocking or extinguishing avoidance behaviors, is it possible to elicit or teach new and acceptable behaviors that will be socially reinforced.

Emphatically, this does not mean that the successful psychotherapeutic outcome will produce graduates who also have adopted the therapist's ethical code. (One of those whom I consider to be an outstanding success once asked me to write her a letter that would help her enlist in the Republican political cause. This was a bitter blow to a lifelong Democrat). The usual patient, when not in the institution, lives in a social environment that, on the whole, shares his ethical code. Thus, if moral judgments are made from the patient's own ethical code, it will be found that a similar judgment will be forthcoming from the patient's circle of intimates.

Most people—and patients are people—believe that it is morally imperative to maintain one's integrity, which can only be done by standing up against some consensus; otherwise, such behavior is no different from conformity. If his patients maintain integrity, the therapist will have no reason to worry about producing moral stereotypes.

As yet, little has been said about patient discomfort or unhappiness or anxiety or stress etc., because from a strictly social framework it is not necessary. One of the postulates or assumptions of most social learning approaches is that an individual raised in a social setting is going to derive both his joys and his pains as a consequence of his interpersonal activities. It is assumed that the behavior of others is reinforcing, positively or negatively, and that the patient is a social responder and a social stimulus simultaneously. If positive social reinforcement is the rule, an over-all sense of well-being would be expected; and the opposite, of course, with consistent negative reinforcement. If our patient's social skills are such that he customarily elicits no positive reinforcement, life is probably rather dull and tasteless for him. If he customarily elicits rejection or its threat, life must be rather miserable. But if he learns methods of extracting positive reinforcements from his particular social world, he should then find himself in a perfectly satisfactory affective state.

If the affect is viewed as a consequence of behavior, then control of affect resides in the choice of behaviors. This is fortunate as the therapist has no tools by which to manipulate affect directly, leaving him impotent to reduce discomfort if he is not to modify behavior. It is out of concern for patient well-being that psychotherapy is seen as a two-part process: (1) The patient must give up his socially objectionable behaviors, thereby eliminating negative consequences; and (2) The patient must acquire acceptable skills by which he can extract from others the behaviors that will be gratifying to him—this will culminate in positive, affective consequences.

I share others' concern with the patient's sense of self-esteem, but I argue that self-esteem is mostly a function of social validation. If what I say is true, any improvement in social functioning will automatically be a boost to self-esteem. The converse is perhaps for the patient even more importantly true: Shabby social behavior as judged by one's own standards must inevitably lead to loss of self-esteem.

One final preliminary point should be made in answer to a familiar question. Is not the voluntary patient at times an equally extreme case who has nonetheless not been socially rejected? Quite simply the answer is no. The voluntary patient differs chiefly from the committed patient in that his behaviors have not yet resulted in formal rejection but will if they are not modified. The voluntary patient who has reached the stage of honest reporting of his behaviors often makes it clear that he sought out the hospital in a way to make the word asylum more appropriate. Such patients, as the fugitives of other times, seek asylum in the face of impending social retaliation. In clinical practice the difference between the voluntary and involuntary patient is mostly a matter of how much legal power can be employed, whether or not the patient likes it. In terms of patient variables, very little difference can be found, with the possible exception that the voluntary patient may be a bit more sensitive to the social environment. In the same vein, the out-patient is more sensitive to those around him but nonetheless is engaging in behaviors that court rejection.

## THE STRATEGY AND ITS APPLICATION

### *The Context of Change*

For illustrative purposes in presenting the therapeutic strategy, the extreme example may be the easiest to apprehend quickly. As behavioral changes are conceptualized as a function of consequences, the most efficient process necessarily involves control of the consequences by the behavior change agent, usually called the therapist. Therefore the program will be described in terms of the mental hospital setting. It should not be inferred, however, that drastic changes in strategy will be necessary without institutional support. At the present stage of knowledge, it is still defensible to assume a continuity of degrees of pathology. The accompanying assumption is that the same variables are involved but that operations will be modified in order to have reasonable if less reliable control of consequences. Without the institution the therapist's burden is greater because he must be able to anticipate accurately the social consequences of the behaviors he chooses to manipulate.

Returning to the assumption that maladaptive behaviors are learned in a social context, elicited in a social context, and maintained by a social context, it would appear logical that corrective learning must occur in a social context. An effective social-learning approach would need what can be called a teaching community that accurately reflects the larger society in terms of the crucial problems, contingencies, and successful solutions. The teaching community will differ from the larger community by protecting the learner against disastrous consequences for maladaptive behavior and by modifying its curriculum for each patient as the patient exhibits the behavior patterns that need to be modified. The program must elicit the undesirable behaviors, as there is no other currently feasible method of identifying them other than direct observation. A group of people has the potential to apply almost every type of social pressure and response, thus theoretically providing the most accurate diagnosis and maximizing the power of social sources of change.

In the proposed framework group approaches will inevitably be preferred to individual approaches—not as a second-best expedient or as a stopgap measure for emergency need but, instead, as the approach of choice.

The teaching community can vary all the way from a total-institutional, twenty-four-hour-a-day approach (Synanon, Daytop Village) to a small group meeting together only intermittently. What must be present is a reacting social body that will respond with helpful reinforcements and feedback.

When functioning properly, the remedial community will demand adequate functioning and productivity while simultaneously demonstrating that such behaviors combined with developing skills will culminate in warm, affectionate, genuinely valuable human relationships.

## The Role of the Therapist

It is a pleasure to agree emphatically with the other therapists in these volumes who insist that the psychotherapist is not a healer. The usually preferred alternative, which happens to be the one most compatible with a social-learning approach, is to see the therapist as a teacher. It is necessary to find the most effective tools in the world of the pedagogue rather than the healer if the most effective program is to be implemented. As already stated, the crucial tool for controlled learning is the systematic manipulation of consequences. The therapist, then, necessarily should have the power to determine when, where, and what the consequences shall be. Unless the consequences are under either the direct or indirect control of the therapist, the patient's day will be filled with either irrelevant or contradictory teaching, which leads to total frustration for patient and therapist alike. (An incidental benefit to the patient is the elimination of the "omnipotent 'they'" who so anonymously and implacably impose unpleasant constrictions with immunity from attempted retaliation or reason. A patient knows with whom to deal if he asks, "Who says so?" and gets the answer, "I do.")

In the traditional mental hospital program anyone *but* the therapist is likely to make the most significant decisions for therapeutic change as part of his administrative duties. It is not at all unusual in such settings to see completely unacceptable behavior followed by pleasant consequences and vice versa. (For instance, one patient was apparently rewarded with a weekend pass for physically assaulting the ward psychologist.) It is not unknown for a psychotherapist to attempt to keep a psychotherapeutic appointment only to discover that the patient has been discharged since their last meeting. Under such an arrangement, nothing resembling systematic manipulation of reinforcements is possible. Or to state it differently, if you will find the manipulator of reinforcements you will also find the most effective therapist, even if the therapeutic lesson is destructive to the patient.

Skill training programs involve some combination of new knowledge along with acquisition of new skill. The therapist can look at his task in the same way. The patient needs new knowledge ("This is what my social world is all about") and new skills ("Here are the kinds of things that I can do about it.") The therapist exercises pedagogical function—a purveyor of knowledge and a trainer in skills—and he modifies his pedagogy in terms of feedback from related situations in which the trainee performs. The therapist's administrative power needs to be enough to establish and maintain accurate feedback from anyone who has the opportunity to observe the patient's progress. The mechanics of feedback require accurate and frequent reporting, and to the staff the whole process becomes a pain in some unspecified portion of the anatomy. Without effective precautions, reporting is likely to be dropped, done poorly, or done infrequently. The therapist then needs the power to ensure the adequacy of his feedback system.

Luckily, he does not need the power to enforce staff consistency. I say luckily because, practically speaking, it is impossible to get such consistency in any case. Inconsistency is actually needed if the patient is to learn to deal with the world as he will again find it.

Both Bandura's experimental work (1) and Mowrer's actual practices point up "modeling" as a method of eliciting new behaviors that are capable of being maintained by reinforcements just as any other newly acquired behavior. Among other things Bandura found that modeling effects were enhanced if the model was perceived to be in control of the pertinent reinforcers. The decision-making power of the therapist would then be correlated with his effectiveness as a model. As modeling effects are inevitable, the therapist might just as well capitalize on the process as much as possible by acquiring power to dictate consequences while exhibiting behaviors that will be useful to the patient if adopted. The principle would seem to hold in the face of disagreement as to what kinds of behaviors would be most useful for the patient to adopt.

With the exception of Mowrer (6), the conscious use of modeling as a remedial device has rarely been employed. The self-help groups, such as Alcoholics Anonymous, Synanon, Daytop Village, etc., have unconsciously placed great emphasis upon this variable by their extensive use of testimonials and the equally extensive use of improved patients as workers to help the new members of the program. Mowrer, who sees himself as an improved patient, logically regards his as another example of self-help programs. However, as he does have a professional degree with much public recognition, it may be questioned as to whether or not his improved patients believe that they have become his peer. While Mowrer attempts to model only what he asks of his patients—openness, self-disclosure, honesty—he may well be obtaining some of his modeling effects by his use of positive and negative verbal reinforcers. Further, Bandura found that peers who behaved and visibly received consequences were effective models. Thus, those of us who argue with Mowrer about the desirability of self-disclosure are probably arguing only about the necessity.

Frank (2), in an examination of the placebo effect, isolated several more or less intangible variables associated with what the therapist is rather than what he does. He did not specifically mention modeling. He did, however, find that a positive placebo effect would be enhanced by an aura of prestige and expertise. It can be assumed that the new behaviors elicited by the placebo effect will have to be maintained by reinforcements and that the therapist's ability to be an effective verbal reinforcer possibly may be correlated with the degree of prestige and apparent expertise. Peer status would then weaken reinforcement powers.

Agreement with Mowrer that therapist behaviors will be adopted still does not clearly indicate precisely what behaviors should be exhibited. Mowrer and I both seek for honesty, responsibility, and mutual concern in our programs, but I would argue that there are alternative methods available to be an effective model. The recommendation made in this framework is that the therapist exhibit honesty, responsibility, and concern as an integral part of problem-solving, but as the presenting problems are the patient's, self-disclosures by the therapist are often irrelevant. Therapist honesty and responsibility within the framework of a somewhat different therapeutic contract would then be part of the role. Open adoption of expert and superordinate status should add to the placebo effects. Visible control of reinforcers would add to the effectiveness of therapist modeling effects. Of course, it is an empirical question as to the relative efficiency of various therapist roles. Mowrer has the clinical impression that self-disclosure modeling is not very effective with sociopathic and/or chronic patients. In any case, I would agree that the therapist should be direct, nonevasive, socially reliable, and behaviorally seeking involvement with the patient.

The role of the therapist is really defined by the terms of the therapeutic contract. A description of the intake interview will help clarify therapist activities.

### Intake Criteria and the Therapeutic Contract

Intake criteria are necessarily determined by the nature of the projected program. The ones to be described here evolved in the development of a short-term intensive effort and could be modified for other approaches which cannot be covered for lack of space.

Control of learning is obtained by the manipulation of reinforcements contingent upon observed behaviors. Clearly the nonbehaving patient would be difficult to teach as he would do nothing that could be reinforced. For rapid change programs, then, it is necessary to have responsive subjects. It is not necessary that responsiveness be centered around pleasant stimuli; it will suffice if initially only verbally noxious stimuli induce responsiveness. If a therapist can get the appearance of anger or grief, he will find that the behavioral baseline is sufficiently rich for potentially rapid teaching.

The only other personality requirement is that the potential group member be of near average intelligence or better. As the group meetings are centered around verbal interchanges, some skill in abstraction is necessary. In practice, an IQ of 90 and up on most any standard intelligence test has worked out satisfactorily. More often than not, the IQ estimate has been obtained by interview rather than by test.

As a negative indicator, it was found that a history of much EST (electroshock therapy) seemed correlated with slow progress, but it was not possible to come up with a hard and fast rule.

The patient should be reached as soon as possible after admission. It seems reasonably clear that the typical mental hospital is very effective in teaching the new patient to be a "good" patient, which too often results in hospital invisibility. Thus, the therapist should have access to all new admissions and should recruit them for his program inside of a few days. Of course, he will also be responsive to referrals, diagnostic evaluations, etc., but if he relies on these entirely he will miss many patients who meet the criteria.

Previous hospitalizations are not particularly indicative. In most cases, previous treatment has been desultory at best and absolutely misleading at worst. Under such conditions, previous failures have little prognostic meaning. Using the suggested criteria, one can see that the overwhelming majority of the selected patients will have been previously hospitalized or have had out-patient treatment or both. There are very few psychiatric virgins to be found in a mental hospital.

The interview strategy has become rather routinized and can usually be completed within a half-hour. The patient is told that he is being considered for a rather intensive and rapid program designed to get him out of the hospital as quickly as possible. Most patients who meet the criteria of potential membership also express interest in leaving the institution. The therapist then lays the groundwork for building a set for the procedures to come. If the statement is made that whatever it was that got the patient in trouble it was undoubtedly not his assets, it is a rare patient indeed who will not agree. He will also agree that the therapy then should clearly be focused on his defects. With those initial agreements, the therapist then asks the patient for his own version of what brought him to the hospital.

The new patient, in spite of agreeing that he is not in the hospital because of his own assets, will usually explain his presence, not in terms of his own inadequacies but in terms of a misunderstanding or an actually hostile social environment. The therapist will have his first opportunity to point out that the patient's plight might be more profitably examined from the framework of the patient's inadequate handling of the situations. The effective argument is that neither the patient nor the therapist can hope to change the world to the patient's liking—but the patient might be able to force some desirable changes if he learns to behave more effectively. From that point, therapy has begun.

The therapist gives the first lesson in retranslating *everything as the patient's responsibility*. The patient in turn will probably exhibit one of his modes of disavowing responsibility. At this point the most likely excuse will be helplessness because of "sickness," and the second most likely excuse will be the patient's insistence that he has in some way been victimized.

If the excuse is sickness, the therapist can ask the patient to explain in what way he is sick. The patient will fumble around and eventually describe himself as sick because he feels bad, because he does not know "why" he behaves as he does, or because he cannot control behaviors that are seen as symptoms. The therapist, redefining everything in terms of patient responsibility, can reply by insisting that one does not have to feel well to behave adequately, that one does not have to know the why's of behavior in order to learn how to do better, or that helplessness is an excuse offered because behavior is not controlled even though it clearly can be. It is impossible to describe every eventuality; but, if the therapist is prepared to insist always upon patient responsibility, it is not difficult to answer any patient rationalization.

Further (and as a psychologist this is particularly helpful), the therapist can explain that he is not an expert in illness and would be incompetent to deal with one, but that he is an expert in helping people with emotional difficulties. Chipping away at the medical model is essential if personal responsibility is to become a dominant theme.

Many patients are somewhat startled at the denial of sickness and ask what they are if not ill. After experimenting with a variety of answers, the blunt reply, "You're not sick—you're crazy" seemed to have the most impact. When the patient indignantly demands to be excluded from the "crazy" group, he is informed that crazy means only that the patient has been indulging in foolish behaviors or making foolish decisions or both. (The Daytop Village program for drug addicts routinely uses the word "stupid" but with substantially the same aims and results.) If the patient needs evidence, he can be reminded where he is and how he got there. Startled or not, most patients can accept this framework rather quickly, many with an appearance of relief, apparently at the prospect of losing their craziness by making better choices and exhibiting better behaviors.

If the patient has apparently (and that is all that is necessary) gone along that far, the therapist can proceed with the recruitment. The patient is told that the program has three primary rules mandatory for all patients. Although the patient is unaware of it, the three rules are the principles that arm the therapist with the power to manipulate reinforcements effectively. The first requirement is that the patient must agree to be completely honest with the group and with the other group members. (Later, the patient will discover that he is also being asked to be honest with all the significant people in his life, but this demand is reserved until the patient has experienced the usefulness of the rule in the program.) In this culture practically everyone verbally agrees that he should be honest, and the patient automatically accepts the requirement. At this point the patient is told that meeting this obligation clearly implies that he no longer has the freedom to be silent. Honesty is defined as the making of all information accurately available to whomever it may be of concern. Anything of personal importance will be of concern to the group. Probably because of the lack of understanding of the revolutionary nature of such a set of behaviors, the patients still agree to the rule.

The second requirement is also automatically accepted with the same lack of understanding of the behavioral demands that will result. The patient must agree to accept total responsibility for all of his behavior twenty-four hours a day. Operationally, responsibility is defined as behaving in congruence with the patient's own ethical code. Another therapeutic step has now been taken: The patient has unwittingly agreed that he is capable of producing behaviors to meet the terms of a social contract—a capability in direct contradiction to any self-concept of helplessness.

The third requirement, assumption of responsibility for every other patient in the program, is often bewildering. The therapist explains that he is going to do whatever he believes to be best for the patient whether the patient likes it or not. The patient is to take whatever action he believes to be best for other patients whether they like it or not. This rule not only makes social responsibility a given in the total program, but it also provides the basis for a system of feedback that will be of much importance to the therapist.

Finally, the patient is told that all decisions are to be made by the therapist with the exception of those necessary to maintain physical health. The therapist states that it will be a violation of great seriousness to attempt to bypass the therapist for a nonmedical decision.

At the end of the intake interview the patient has committed himself to the basics of social living. It is impossible to uphold the concepts as defined and not engage in social activity, in problem solving, and in social interdependence. The mechanics of the programs vary tremendously, but the three rules have been found useful in every type of program with every type of patient, in or out of an institution.

Note that the therapist makes no promise of confidentiality. When the issue is brought up, usually in a group meeting, the therapist states that he is going to communicate with whomever and about whatever he thinks would be helpful. On the other hand, he pledges that he will not be either secretive or gossipy and will always keep the patient informed. Whenever possible, any conversations about the patient will be conducted in the presence of the patient; if this is not possible and if it is important, face to face confrontation will be arranged later. The families of patients, incidentally, are subjected to the same rules. For the therapist, information from the family that cannot be quoted to the patient is worse than no information at all; if the therapist agrees to a minor conspiracy, its exposure would destroy his credibility as an honest model. It does, however, reveal something about the nature of the family with which the patient must react.

Another empirical discovery has been that a reluctant new patient is much more likely to be recruited by challenge or judgmental statements than by placating behaviors. As an example, one patient joined the group out of anger at the therapist's statement that she did not have enough "guts" to go through a difficult program after saying she desperately wanted a solution to a hopeless problem. Her reason to prove the therapist wrong in no way interfered with her ability to profit from the program. If a reluctant patient is successfully bribed by making concessions to his objections, he has been taught to expect that the program can be modified to meet his, rather than the therapist's, terms. Operating on that principle, no system of psychotherapy can be effective, including those based upon permissiveness.

If a program is a good one, it will still be good if the patient has to be coerced into entering it. If the program is poor, all the voluntary enthusiasm in the world will unhappily be wasted and the patient disillusioned.


## IMPLEMENTATION

### The Social Milieu

The teaching community must respond to the patient's activities in such a way as to ensure that he must earn everything he gets. The contingencies by which that happy lesson will be taught have as common elements social acceptability and productivity.

When the patient joins the program, he has as yet earned nothing, so he gets nothing beyond the absolute minimum—bed, meals, clothing, and necessary medical treatment. (Again to illustrate a point: Daytop Village demands that even the first bed and the first meal be earned. However, they are dealing with what are presumed to be rational people. A mental hospital staff would probably rebel at such a rule for "sick" people, even if the therapist has been given administrative control.) Access to on-the-ward television, for instance, may be made available only if the patient makes his own bed, keeps his immediate living  area clean, and takes care of his own personal grooming. Any additional pleasures or opportunities should be made contingent upon increased output.

It is necessary to have easily accessible methods of demonstrating productivity for the patients to learn the lesson that earnings lead to privileges. Ideally, nothing will be done on the ward by the staff that can legally be done by the patients. Such an arrangement opens up tasks, such as the many housekeeping jobs on any ward, kitchen policing, and serving, manning and running linen and supply rooms, providing orientation for new patients, doling out cigarette allotments and controlling and providing lights, helping with clerical tasks, carrying messages, and cooperating in laundry, repair, and redecorating tasks. The number of things that have to be done are many, and it is only a matter of ingenuity to capitalize upon them.

It is, of course, not unusual for the patient to protest that he is not in the hospital to work but to be treated. The therapist points out that he has the responsibility for treatment and is better equipped than the patient to decide what is and what is not rehabilitative. In addition, the patient is reminded that in a publicly supported institution fees collected from him do not even cover room, board, and medication. The services of the psychotherapist on the outside would cost the patient an additional substantial fee. Consequently, the patient is costing the institution far more than he is paying. Under the circumstances, to be responsible the patient must take care of his indebtedness by doing work of genuine use to the institution and its inmates.

The therapist and the patient, in the group meeting, reach an understanding (not necessarily an agreement) of the patient's responsibilities to be met as a first step toward more privileges and freedom. Nonperformance or substandard performance will keep the patient at the bottom of the privilege ladder. Responsibilities should be individually appropriate when possible. For instance, one patient seemed to have managed to avoid all the grubby aspects of living by being so "upset" by tawdry, physical toil that she was unable to pursue her self-admitted creativity and intellectuality. Her average-income parents had succumbed to her anguish and hired a full-time domestic. The patient literally did not know how to make a bed or clean a floor adequately. The therapeutic step was an assignment of cleaning and then keeping clean the ward bathroom with emphasis upon the toilets. This procedure was dramatically effective. When escape from noxious stimulation depends upon adequate performance, performance improves rapidly.

If the patient behaves well with the assigned tasks that are designed to fill up an eight-hour day aside from meals, group meetings, etc., he can then ask for and get not only some of the smaller privileges but also more demanding assignments which are the route to more substantial benefits. Evaluation, far from incidentally, is made on the basis of standards applicable to a paid, nonpatient employee doing the same job. If a patient does not like a job and does it well, he can ask for and receive a change of assignments. If a patient does not like a job and does it poorly, he cannot get a transfer. If a patient argues that he is unfairly evaluated, the therapist has to be prepared to submit chapter and verse to document inadequate performance, and further, to spell out the criteria for adequacy. An off-the-ward assignment requires the patient to take his complaint of "unfair" to the staff person who is responsible for the initial evaluation and to find ways of obtaining an improved report. In other words, the therapist does not attempt to ensure "fairness" but instead reminds the patient that such treatment is a part of normal living and it is up to him to deal with it. Of course, if there is any sort of blatant mistreatment or clear underevaluation, it is up to the therapist to intervene. In actuality, other staff members are far more likely to ask too little than too much from "sick" people.

Once the patient reliably demonstrates good ward performance, he may then be given a privilege card that may be used to seek off-the-ward job activities, to go to movies, to the canteen, or to other special events without staff supervision but only with therapist approval. Once an off-the-ward assignment is found, the card may also be used to go to and from the now regular work site. No privileges are potentially unavailable. The work may be work as usually defined or it may be going to school or to on the job training activities. But whatever the assignment, the same standards should be employed: the patient is to meet the same criteria of performance that would be applied if he were a nonpatient, paid employee. Not until such standards are met is the patient allowed complete freedom of the grounds or weekend visits off the grounds with family or ultimately unaccompanied freedom. If a request for an off-grounds activity is denied, the explanation is often something like, "If you cannot behave responsibly here, you cannot behave responsibly anywhere. As long as that is the case, we must take the responsibility for you, and we can do that only in the hospital."

The therapist, as has already been briefly mentioned, must have an adequate feedback system so that he can be quickly responsive to patient performance. He must also work hard, for a while, to get most of the employees to take seriously the request that the patient be treated and evaluated as a responsible adult. Job opportunities have to be excluded from the program if it is found that the supervisors continually evade therapeutic requirements and are apparently unteachable by the methods available.

The step-by-step addition of increased freedom as a function of increased productivity continues until it culminates in a complete discharge. As progress is noticed, the patient is given the task of patching up family relationships, primarily by demanding and observing adult responsibilities. He is also given the responsibility for an adequate post-discharge plan and for implementing it as much as possible before discharge. If progress is slow, he is given responsibility for that, and he may lose privileges if the lagging continues. He is required to demonstrate not only adequate weekends off the grounds but also a trial period of ten days to two weeks before complete severance may be granted. Whenever possible, a feedback system is arranged with the patients' families, particularly with those who visit the hospital and can be interviewed in the presence of the patient.

It is difficult to overestimate the therapeutic benefits of such a regime. One patient with a long history of psychotherapeutic failures coupled with dependence upon drugs was given a very gloomy prognosis indeed. She finally worked herself up to being assigned to an ironing job in the laundry. She soon established a pattern of going to her detail, only to return in a short time with the explanation that she was too anxious or nervous to continue ironing. She was told that such a state was not an acceptable excuse. Nervousness could occur whether she was doing something or doing nothing. With those alternatives, she would have to be useful while nervous. Not really expecting that she would be impressed, she was nonetheless told that how she felt was a direct result of what she did; to feel better, she would find it necessary to do better. Her improvement dated from that incident, and four years later a letter stated that whenever she found herself "feeling bad" she immediately looked for some way of "doing better," and that it always worked.

Another patient refused an assignment because "I am schizophrenic." She learned that she could be as schizophrenic as she pleased as long as she did not show it and turned out the typing she had been trained to do. A few weeks later, when asked about the state of her schizophrenia, she reported, "It's gone, I guess."

The ubiquitous medical model makes it necessary to state the following: It is impossible to teach a patient how to be a first class citizen if, by the implication of the demands put upon him, it is clear that he is seen as either unable or unlikely to perform up to the social level of the nonpatient. Many therapists argue that it is important to demonstrate respect for the patient. I would agree if it is remembered that there is no profounder way to demonstrate disrespect than to act as if the patient has no available assets. The patient who is continually advised to baby himself in one way or another can only conclude that he is, at that time at least, incapable of functioning as a peer of the nonpatient.

The demand that the patient find methods for dealing with unreasonable people is one of the few direct training devices to counteract the already usually well-learned lesson that to be accepted as sick is also to have a special set of rules which are less demanding than those for well persons.

If the patient has been gradually elevated to the point that he has been given an adult's load of responsibility, has been evaluated by adult standards, and has consistently demonstrated adult performance, clearly he is not behaving in a mode that courts social rejection. If, in addition, his social performances have become more successful in eliciting approval rather than, at best, toleration, he has found ways of operating upon his social environment to receive enough reinforcement to maintain his new behaviors. If the therapist has been skillful enough to teach the appropriate flexible skills, recidivism should be greatly curtailed. In any case, the criteria for termination must be in terms of good functioning outside the group meeting, never by good verbal participation alone.

The group meetings are to be sources of new information and an avenue for feedback, for manipulation of consequences, and even a place to learn skills in new modes of interaction, but the truly important social environment will never be some group sharing a similar plight with reinforcements manipulated for the patient's benefit. The appropriate social skills can never be completely demonstrated in the therapeutic group, and only a rigid adherence to the use of an external criterion makes it possible to expect much generalization.

The group meetings should result in extracting new behaviors, but the crucial reinforcements can come only from the environment.

## THE GROUP AS A GROUP AND ITS OPERATIONS

### Starting the Group

Initiating a group into a verbal problem-solving kind of conversation is not too difficult if the therapist will take advantage of his previously extracted agreements. The members have agreed to be completely honest, totally responsible, and mutually responsible.

Each patient is asked to introduce himself to the group along with a brief explanation of the circumstances leading to hospitalization. The purpose is not necessarily to get all the group members to "know" each other, but instead the therapist needs an opportunity to demonstrate how the group will work. The basic strategy, which will never be abandoned, is to detect discrepancies between the stated ethical code and the actual behavior. The discrepancy must be made obvious to the patient, and once the incongruency is clear, the remedial step— usually blatantly obvious—must be taken. The therapist attentively listens for signs of such discrepancy, and as interaction is beginning to occur, he watches for signs of discrepant behavior in the visible social behavior.

It does not take long for one of the group members to exhibit clearcut violations of the commitment to honesty or responsibility. A few selected examples will illustrate the point. (The examples, although real, are often paraphrased and condensed. The strategy in execution is rarely as smooth as the statement of working principles.)

Patient (P.) B: How did you get along sexually?
P. A: Not very well.
P. B: What do you mean?
P. A: I'd rather not talk about that—it gives me this terrible feeling just to think about it.
Therapist (T.): Your agreement was to be completely honest, and it was explained to you that withholding information is dishonest. You did not explain that you were going to be honest only when it felt good.

P. My husband is just trying to humiliate me. He would do almost anything to make me look bad.
T. How do you know that is what he's trying to do?
P. Why else would anyone treat me like he does?
T. I don't know. Have you asked him?
P. There is no reason to ask him. He'd just deny it.
T. You've just told us that without even asking your husband about it, you know both what his motives are and what he enjoys. How in God's name can you do that? Are you asking us to believe that you're a mindreader?
P. No, I'm not a mindreader.
T. Then what is your evidence that your husband wants to humiliate you so much that he would go to almost any lengths?
P. Because he's always doing things to make me humiliated, and. . . .
T. Look, I'm not questioning the fact that you are always finding yourself humiliated, but I ask again, "How do you know that that is what he *wants* to do?"
P. Well, I can't be sure, but. . . .
T. If you are going to report to other people that you are married to a stinker, don't you think that as a responsible person you first have to be sure of your evidence? You seem to be quite willing for us to believe that you are married to a very deliberately mean man.
P. No, I don't mean that.
T. Then isn't it up to you to mean what you say, to stick to facts especially about someone who is not here to defend himself if you are to behave honestly and responsibly?

T. Well, I don't know much about you yet except that you are occasionally rude.
P. That's uncalled for. What do you mean by that?
T. Several times Mrs. _____ tried to say something, and in every case, you went on as if she didn't exist.
P. Well, I'm sorry about that, but I didn't see her.

T. The point remains that several times you treated her as if she didn't have any right to speak.

P. I told you I didn't see her, and I think you've got no right to go around accusing me of things I don't do.

T. You are only accused of not letting Mrs. _____. . . .

P. There you go again. It seems to me that you want to make mountains of molehills, and I wonder what kind of a therapist you think you are to stir up trouble for no cause.

T. Mrs. _____. . . .

P. I don't want to hear any more about Mrs. _____. I want to know where do you get the right to go around accusing people of things they don't do.

T. But look at what you did do.

P. (literally shouting and red in the face) You make me so mad I would like to throw this ash tray at you. You must have a lot of fun picking on people if you have to stoop so low as that. (The pattern continued for several more interactions.)

T. Mrs. _____, I have been tabulating the number of times that you have not (completing the sentence only by outshouting the patient) let me finish a sentence. Nine times in a row you did not let me speak. Refusing to let someone else talk is clearly rather rude. And if you have any doubts, let's ask the group members. (The group was polled.)

P. I don't like this group. I don't know why I should sit around listening to a bunch of people when I couldn't care less about them or their problems.

T. I thought that you just told us that the most important thing in your life was being a good Christian.

P. I certainly did, and these patients would be a lot better off if they did the same.

T. In addition to noting that you managed to reach the same nuthouse, I'd like to point out that claiming to be a galloping Christian while simultaneously indicating that you don't give a damn for these other human beings is the phoniest thing I've heard all day. Christianity is supposed to stand for, among other things, love of your neighbor. These people you couldn't care less about are, currently, literally your neighbors. If you are an example of good Christianity at work, turn me over to the infidels.

The variations on the theme are endless, but the therapist will have no trouble identifying discrepancies either in terms of the group's three basic rules or in terms of some other moral claim of the patient. The therapist must be willing to stick to his point until the evidence is so overwhelming that its significance cannot be missed. Once accepted by the patient, the discrepancy noted will then be thrown back to the patient with some form of the question, "What are you going to do about it?" Whatever it is that the patient replies can lead either to more exposure or to a plan for change in behavior, which can often be implemented right in the group. For instance, the patient who interrupted sentences decided that she was not going to continue in that way. The therapist tabulated interruptions ostentatiously which then rapidly diminished in both frequence and persistence.

No matter which patient is being dealt with, all the patients are learning. Therefore, it is important that the therapist stick to his point until he makes it (unless he is wrong, when he must quickly apologize and move on.) If the therapist does not persist, the group members are going to learn that one way to evade issues is to keep resisting until the therapist gives up and moves on to something else. If, instead, the group learns that the therapist will settle for nothing short of an honest recognition of the behavioral discrepancy between what should be and what is, the members will tend to drop that particular device, and it will ultimately become the kind of demand that the group members put upon each other.

It is much easier to demonstrate convincingly the gap between the stated morality and the actual morality if the questioned behavior is observed as part of the group's interaction. The patient almost has to be impressed whenever a group of witnesses all report a mistreatment of some other group member in terms of the offending patient's own standards. As the patient gets feedback from his fellow members, he will become defensive in his verbalizations (who knows about his feelings?), and the sustained pressure yields more and more examples of dishonesty and irresponsibility until the pile of evidence becomes too large to resist. If the evidence is subtle at first, the continued demand for better behavior draws forth more and more blatant examples that become unmistakable in time. This kind of recognition, generalized to parallel encounters with nongroup people, is the only kind of "insight" pursued. The recognition of relationships between current behavioral modes and current interpersonal problems is valuable rather than the recognition of relationships between current behavioral modes and their historical antecedents. The patients often bring with them the conviction that their salvation lies in teasing out the historical why's, and this pursuit must be blocked if progress to to be made. Reinterpretation of the patient's proffered historical insights as assigning responsibility for one's own behavior to some scapegoat (typically a parent or two) will soon eliminate much of that type of verbalizing.

The points already presented, if pursued consistently, will take more time than is probably available in the first meeting, particularly when it is necessary to use part of the group time to spell out the group rules and to explain procedures and assignments. By the end of the first meeting, each patient should have a full schedule and a clear idea that being held responsible for all behavior will be both consistent and the key to more autonomy. It is also in the first session that the patients learn that no one will be discharged from the hospital while still on any sort of tranquilizer and psychic energizer. They are given the assignment of convincing the physician in charge of medication that the pills can either be reduced or eliminated. Prior agreement with the physicians will make them responsive to such requests if the patient is presenting no management problems.

Immediately then, all goals are made contingent upon satisfactory progress with the ultimate arbiter—the therapist. Challenges of decisions are always permissible, but no decisions will be changed on the basis of anything but evidence or overriding emergency.

*The Working Group*

As the group continues to meet (the scheduling is arbitrary; in my programs it has usually been every day, two hours per day), its members will begin to adopt the strategy of the therapist, and gradually much of the initial work of the leader will be assumed by group members. In the early stages, there will be many instances in which a patient successfully pleads lack of responsibility in terms of fellow group members' responses, and the therapist must eliminate this kind of destructive reinforcement. This is most easily done by pointing out to the reinforcing patient that he is approving behavior beyond the group's rules—the reason, perhaps, being that if he can get the rules changed for some other patient they will necessarily be changed for him too. In any case, approving unacceptable behavior is another example of irresponsibility.

The most ubiquitous form of unwitting sabotage will be found in the patients' attempts to explain themselves and each other in terms of motivations. Inasmuch as there is never anything inherently wrong in a motivation, any talk of this kind leads to no identification of a behavior that should be changed. The problem comes up so often that a fairly standard method has been gradually built up that will usually take care of the situation. The patients are told flatly that their motivations are being used as an excuse. The fact that they "mean well" is small comfort to anyone who has been hurt by them. Further, if they mean well, then they will do well in the kinds of situations that repeat themselves, and until they do, it is impossible to believe in the honesty of the claim. Again they are reminded of their inability to read each other's minds. These kinds of interchanges tend eventually to lead to statements that are very much like group slogans. For instance, "There are no good reasons for bad behavior," and "If reasons are important, you don't tell someone what his reasons are—you ask him."

With the pseudosophistication which will be part of every group, it is inevitable that the group will attempt to dwell on materials that are usually found in the more traditional approaches. Thus, the question of being misunderstood will be commonplace. The patient will complain that the therapist, the group, the family, and the world do not understand him, and this complaint is always clearly stated as an indictment. If the therapist does not deal with such complaints adequately, the group will reinforce the conviction by agreeing that being misunderstood is a terrible cross to bear and by almost pleading to be given another chance to understand.

There are at least two effective ways of dealing with such a complaint. The first and more brutal is usually used when the behavior the patient is discussing is clearly socially destructive. At such times, the therapist insists that he understands the patient very well and the asking for understanding of an explanation of unacceptable behavior in terms of social operations is really a demand for license. A verbatim response to a homosexual patient was, "What's to understand? You like to seduce little boys, you agree that it's wrong, and you do it anyhow. You're not asking for understanding. You're asking us to tell you what a nice guy you are no matter how many kids you foul up. Well, the hell with that; you're going to get no *Good Housekeeping* seal of approval from this group."

The other mode of response usually follows any kind of complaint that implies that the patient is a victim of other people misunderstanding his needs and sensitivities. By now the answer is succinct and almost stereotyped: "If you want understanding, then it's up to you to make yourself understood." No matter how the patient approaches his difficulties, the therapist must put the responsibility back on the patient.

The experienced group, bound by evidence, learns to follow the admonition to provide "enough rope" and gets a certain amount of ironic amusement from any claims of an excess of virtue. The most common assertion of this kind has repeatedly been, "One of my troubles is that I'm too perfectionistic." The group asks for concrete examples which invariably turn out to be either fictitious or trivial. One housewife gave as her example her never-ending attempt to keep her house meticulously clean for an unappreciative family. In spite of the fact that she forced them to take their shoes off at the door, demanded that they do their smoking outside, confine their reading, studying, television watching, etc., to the den, and had them following a list of household rules covering almost all daily activities, they continued to mess up the place so that it was never as good as her perfectionistic traits demanded, and they did not appreciate her besides. She was asked if she had a duty to be a good wife and a good mother, and she responded with the automatic endorsement. We asked more questions and learned that she spent almost no time with any of her children about matters of concern to them, that her wifely activities were confined to housekeeping, and that she had reports from the school that her children were having adjustment difficulties. In various ways, she was told that it was hard to accept a woman as perfectionistic who saw houses as more valuable than people, who completely abdicated her responsibilities to all the people around her, and who could not be bothered to investigate and do something about the reports of her children's difficulties. Under the circumstances, it was agreed that minimal performance would be a great improvement and any claims of perfectionism were wildly dishonest as well as feeble excuses.

Examples of this kind lead to another often used statement: "You'll have to explain that further; we've yet to find anyone suffering from excessive nobility."

The therapist and the group gradually develop increasing skill in translating virtuous statements into demonstrations of culpability. One of the commoner categories is the explanation of some behavior as an effort to avoid hurting someone. One patient reported that she avoided intercourse because her husband had once had an affair with another woman and even though he had broken it off and had been "faithful" ever since, she was unable to forget it. As her husband had reformed, she did not want to "hurt" him by reminding him of his former mistress. The group, to get even more rope, asked if she would be willing for her husband to get his sexual gratification somewhere else. The question elicited an emphatic negative on the grounds (among others) that such behavior would be sinful. The group, knowing her stated religious convictions in greater detail than they wished to, convicted her of sinning by evading her religiously imposed wifely obligations, by refusing to forgive, and by going back on her word. It was suggested that her husband would get more Christian treatment from any handy prostitute, and that her treatment of her husband was so callous that her stated desire to avoid hurting him was simply unbelievable. Her entire pattern of behavior was subsumed as a massive and childish bit of sulking.

Not wishing to hurt someone is offered as a reason almost always to explain what has not been done rather than what has been done, with the exception of lying. The number of patients who lie for someone else's benefit is truly impressive. However, most patients find it somewhat difficult to explain how the self-protective properties of the lie—and there are always some—are to someone else's advantage. Thus the group was inclined to be skeptical of the wife who reported amassing and hiding a number of unpaid bills in order to spare her husband worry. For illustrative purposes, the examples have been blatant ones, but the more subtle explanations are subjected to the same strategy.

One woman was in the habit of concealing from her husband much of what she knew about their teen-aged daughter's difficulties. Her reason was that her husband had a quick temper, would say the wrong things, and make matters worse by treating the daughter unfairly. As always, the group asked for some concrete examples, and the first few which were offered asserted what the husband would have done had he known the true state of things. The group pressured for some examples of what the husband's behavior was like when he was not kept in ignorance. The examples then offered revolved around disagreement about disciplinary measures to be taken if the daughter had misbehaved, her husband advocating "unfair" practices. When asked to give the evidence that her husband's recommendations were unfair, she offered the group a series of conclusions based upon "I believe." The group demanded more evidence than strongly held opinions after extracting the broad-minded admission that "I could be wrong." She was then brought to the point where logically she had no choice but to agree that she was not talking about fairness at all, that she did not know what her husband would do if he had been given a chance to react. The pressure was increased, and she ultimately found herself agreeing that it was close to libel to describe her husband as impossible in the absence of evidence and that she was giving her daughter an object lesson in selective lying, a possibly useful lesson but one that was alleged to be morally offensive except, of course, as a means of doing the right thing.

The group insisted that the patient was quite bright enough to have known all of these things already and that there had to be a payoff. What was our self-sacrificing mother getting out of all of this? It then turned out that her husband was also impossible about money; and, after a long excursion through this set of husbandly inadequacies, the patient admitted that she and her daughter, in collaboration, presented the father with financial requests allegedly to meet the daughter's financial and social needs. These went far beyond the actual requirements, and the profits were then available to them both—the split of the funds not always being amicable. As is so often the case, there was some truth to the complaints about money and about the quick temper, although both were greatly exaggerated. In the final analysis, the group insisted and the patient agreed that the basic problem was that she "didn't have enough guts" to do what she should do, namely, insist that her husband temper his temper and make reasonable financial arrangements that would obviate any need for her own series of misbehaviors. The operating principle is that once such an analysis has been reached and accepted by patient and group, something must then be done. In this case, the wife's weekend assignment was to get an agreement from her husband, both about his temper and his money, but only after she had first communicated to him what she and her daughter had been doing. With much apprehension, she agreed to carry out the assignment and returned to the hospital rather euphoric. Her husband had unhesitatingly agreed to work on his anger behaviors and to make more money available for family needs, but more importantly, he gave her more warm attention and behavioral signs of appreciation than she could remember for some years. It was, she said, an eye-opening and wonderful weekend. As long as she remained in the hospital, she was the group's chief advocate of setting the record straight with anyone important to any of the patients.

Everything else being equal, it is usually more effective to label behaviors with strong rather than with emotionally diluted words. One patient forced this insight upon the therapist. The patient had a long history of unsuccessful exposures to therapies that were "symptomatically" expressed by repeated and destructive drinking bouts. As she described her plight and her behaviors to the group, her account was restated by the group as examples of lying, emotional blackmail, evasion of responsibility in the name of love, and being a parasite. She summed up the feedback by saying, "You're telling me I'm not sick. You're telling me I'm a slob." To which the reply was, "Yes, but *you* are providing us with the evidence." Insofar as any single incident can be said to be a turning point, this one was. The patient stated that whatever she might be, she was not going to be a slob, and her progress became both visible and speedy.

The capacity for people to evade recognition of shoddy behavior by the use of pleasant language is apparently unlimited. Lying in bed all day with no physical disorder will be explained as being a function of "too depressed to do anything" with no apparent signs of guilt or remorse. The same behaviors recast as dumping all responsibility on others with sadness as the excuse are not so casually dealt with.

Asocial behavioral modes are often possible within the institution in almost the same form as they are in society. Any clever patient with minimal effort can arrange for a supply of drugs or alcohol, for instance. Typically, the patients band together against the institution to protect the patient or to join him and participate in joint methods of indulgence and concealment. The demand that the patients carry responsibility for each other is probably the easiest way to stop such activities before any great damage is done and to aid in the educative process. One group member, with the knowledge of several of her peers, took an assortment of pills for several days until she reached a point that it was impossible to conceal her condition any longer. When exposure resulted in the loss of all privileges, extreme physical distress, and a husband's vow not to visit again until the hospital could assure him that his wife would be coherent, the group members decided that they had done their fellow patient no favor by covering up for her. They also conceded that their commitment to honesty and responsibility had been flagrantly violated.

It was from this kind of situation that another repeated slogan evolved: "It's your duty to snitch." Once this atmosphere has been established, much more useful as well as extensive feedback begins to appear. Further, the group then moves in the direction of remaining a group twenty-four hours a day. The group members seek each other out, have informal and sometimes formal meetings, and often work on issues that have not been satisfactorily handled at the regular meeting. It is not an unusual occurrence for the therapist to return to a meeting prepared to struggle with difficult and unresolved business only to discover that the work has been completed in his absence. Clearly, physical access is necessary for much work of this kind to be done, so the group should be housed in the same dormitory or room complex.

To enhance the cohesiveness of the group, the therapist should have an almost invariant policy of insisting that he will deal with individual problems only in the group, labeling anything else as a conspiracy to withhold information from fellow members committed to revealing equally difficult materials.

A common response to this requirement is for the patient to insist "but I'm different." The patient is asked to prove to the group that the difference is a real one, and the group invariably provides convincing evidence that the difference is asserted rather than real. The therapist will probably point out that the insistence upon being special actually turns out to be an attempt to extract exemption from some common rule. With the therapist's ever-ready insistence that no behaviors will be shown in the group that will not also be employed elsewhere, the suggestion can be that a plea of being different has probably been successful in extracting permission to ignore rules in the home situation, and chapter and verse are cited whenever possible. It is interesting to note that in the very process of resisting such an interpretation the patient typically provides verbal examples which, when restated, buttress the therapist's point. Thus, one wife insisted that it was obvious that she got no special favors as she had to work so hard that she was too exhausted and nervous to get up until after her husband had fed himself and the children, gotten them off to school, and himself off to work.

The reader may be somewhat uneasy at the lack of discussion of the "really" psychotic symptoms, but little discussion is appropriate because the symptoms as symptoms are simply not dealt with. If delusional statements are made, supporting evidence is demanded; if that is deemed unreasonable, an assignment is made to get evidence. And it is repeatedly pointed out that without the evidence, verbal statements are misleading, libelous, and a handy excuse, all of which gives the group unmistakable evidence of dishonesty and irresponsibility.

Psychotic behaviors can be expressed to an observer in only two ways: Peculiar verbal statements and peculiar motor activities. If the patient is held responsible for productivity and for accurate communication, the "crazy" behavior will have no pay-off value and will disappear, sometimes dramatically. The resisting patient will often ascribe his crazy behaviors to chaotic thought processes, but he will be told that the group does not require tidy thinking, merely acceptable performance.

Such a strategy has been successfully employed in dealing with hoarding, compulsions, hallucinations, delusions (as noted), ideas of reference, religiosity, withdrawal, and almost any other repetitive behavior that is usually considered symptomatic.

As the therapist is in control of all administrative decisions, the patients quite naturally tend to center much talk around their requests if the therapist permits it. One satisfactory control of the problem was to schedule a half hour or less, one meeting per week, to consider and answer requests. If the therapist is to do this efficiently, it must be clear that his feedback system must be both prompt and accurate.

As the patient learns that good behavior reliably leads to desired consequences, he is likely to start asking for credit for not drinking, not sulking, not starting fights, not breaking sexual rules—the examples could be extended indefinitely. The therapist should never reward positively the absence of unacceptable behavior; at most he should merely remove negative reinforcers. Humor often seems helpful at such times, and many patients laugh when reminded that at any given moment he is not doing several million things and the therapist has no way of knowing which of them is not being done at the time. A more cutting response is often employed, and the patient is reminded that the world rarely gives much credit to anyone for stopping what should never have begun in the first place. It might be pointed out that the patient is asking maximal credit for minimally acceptable output.

Variations of the theme are infinite because of varying verbal styles of both patients and therapists. But as long as the patient is held responsible for his own behavior he is going to learn, since being held responsible always means being differentially treated as a function of adequacy of behavior. This is just one more way of saying that the law of effect still applies.

Conceptually, termination is also simple. When the patient reports that he is handling things to his satisfaction, and when the external reports concur, discharge should be imminent. If the patient's family adds its opinion of improvement and if the patient has worked out and begun to implement an adequate posthospital plan, the therapist has gone just about as far as he can go. Patients have suggested that it might be desirable to keep an out-patient group going using the same principles to maintain progress in the initial postdischarge phases. We have been unable to follow through, so have nothing in the way of supporting opinion, even of a clinical nature.

## CLINICAL RESULTS AND COMMENT

Unfortunately, I am left with the weak report that the system is effective and that I have no control groups. For institutional patients selected by the criteria noted with adequate administrative control and feedback, the discharge rate has been satisfactory. The best of the program in terms of the therapist's needs involved two women's groups, one of which ran for roughly a year, the other for four months. Of 130 selected patients, 5 were dropped for one reason or another, 25 were still in the hospital when the therapist left the institution, and 100 had been discharged. There is no reason to think that the 25 remaining would not have done as well as their predecessors, but because they did not complete the program, they will be excluded from any further figures. Then, of the 105 cases whose outcomes are known, 100 were discharged from the hospital. With an average follow-up of one year, there were twelve returnees of whom ten were quickly re-discharged, leaving two of the returnees still hospitalized. There were some subsequent returnees although the exact number is not known.

Other programs set up by people trained by me have averaged an 80% discharge rate, even though in every case, the administrative control deemed so necessary was incomplete. No follow-up figures are available to me.

About 50% of the patients had been diagnosed schizophrenic and the other 50% were spread among most of the functional labels, es-pecially depressives and drug and alcohol users. Only about 20% had never been either previously hospitalized or received out-patient treat-ment. The average time in the program from the initial interview to discharge was slightly less than two and one-half months. The age average was in the early thirties—with a range from 16 to 58. The original group averaged 12 patients at any one time and typically dis-charged 6 to 7 patients per month. This group met every day for two hours, which often seemed too little.

The judgmental attitude so often assumed to be fatal to group ac-tivity did not constrict patient activity but, if anything, enhanced it. Waskow (15) found a similar phenomenon in a controlled study, and repeated use of the approach has rather conclusively demonstrated that critical judgments elicit responses rather than depress them. Nor does a group treated in this way suffer from poor morale or lack of cohesive-ness. Instead, close and intense relationships became the rule, and the group, the program, and the therapist were supported with gratifying intensity.

Although the "moralistic" atmosphere was maintained, there was nonetheless much humor, controversy, and diversity. The usual prob-lem of absentees was practically nonexistent, and the patients became such ardent proselyters that it was difficult to keep the group down to a manageable size. Confidence in the approach became intense enough that we had the unusual experience of discharging a patient on the same day that we accepted her mother who checked into the hospital specifically to join the group at her daughter's urging.

The group's commitment to total honesty made it possible to dis-cover two hospital employees who were involved in drug traffic with the patients and to discover the whereabouts of a still which had been successfully concealed in spite of mammoth search efforts by the nurs-ing staff.

Attempts to understand the factors involved in the case of the returnees suggested that many of the failures could have been headed off had the program been more, rather than less, demanding. In every case in which it was discovered that the patient had been allowed to leave the hospital while still taking tranquilizers, the patient had to return. Sloppy administrative habits on the part of the therapist account for the discharges in violation of the stated policy.

A co-therapist was necessary to maintain continuity if the therapist had to be absent. As there were several over a period of time, it was possible to get some idea of the teachability of the approach. Nursing aides, nurses, social workers, psychological trainees, and psychologists were all indoctrinated with the approach. They were able to learn and to carry out the strategy, although, as would be expected, with marked personal variation in verbal styles.

My attacking style is distasteful to many, but a more diluted version accomplishes the same ends although not as efficiently. Vigorous therapist behaviors ensure quicker involvement and, usually, more rapid progress. My conclusion is that the therapist should be more concerned with the job to be done than with his "image" as a nice person. The gratifying result, ultimately, is that warm, affectionate relationships become the rule, and that they are based upon mutual respect and achievement rather than upon the more abstract factors of empathy and acceptance.

Much concern about "dependency" is often expressed if the therapist is seen as "directive." Again, such worries are unnecessary if the program demands evidence of independent functioning in order to get therapist approval. In other words, if dependency is likely to be a problem, an accepted and implemented directive to be independent takes care of it.

It was interesting to discover the power of the verbal commitment to a cohesive group. If a remedial step is left implicit, even though completely unambiguous, it is much less likely to be taken than if it is stated explicitly in the form of an agreement with the group. Pratt's (10, 11) "transactional" approach, and Parlour's (8, 9) use of literal contracts demonstrate the same principle from somewhat different frameworks. Further, the use of commitments is a concrete way for the patient to demonstrate social responsibility or its absence. No patient attempts for long to maintain a stance of honesty and responsibility in the face of broken commitments, and a therapist can have confidence in the strength of patient change if difficult promises are reliably kept.

Any need for concepts, such as the "unconscious," transference, and countertransference, repression, etc., disappear completely with the consistent emphasis upon the here and now with responsibility as the key concept in the manipulation of consequences. By this device, I find that I can escape the Mowrer–Freud argument as to whether or not the basic difficulty is a matter of too little or too much superego. In this framework, the patient is asked to make his behavior and his standards congruent and either no standards or impossible standards would be dealt with as examples of irresponsibility. A completely un-socialized patient would have to be taught some sort of ethical code in order to profit from the approach, but the mental hospital patient without a potentially adequate code is hard to find. It is easy to find, however, patients in or out of the hospital who have yet to learn the behavioral implications of the moral planks they insist they value. As moral directives are also prescriptions for social living, it is rather easy to direct the patient toward an examination and implementation of behavioral modes demanded by the patient's own stated values. We find, actually, that there is an occasional change in the moral code (for instance, one wife left the Catholic church rather than continue to take birth control pills and then deceive her priest), but whether such changes are strengthening or weakening the moral code depends upon the framework of the observer.

In conclusion, my patients have taught me to believe that no one ever goes crazy because he has insisted upon doing the "right thing."

## REFERENCES

1. Bandura, A., & Walters, R. H. *Social learning and personality develop-ment.* New York: Holt, Rinehart & Winston, 1963.
2. Frank, J. *Persuasion and healing: A comparative study of psychother-apy.* Baltimore: Johns Hopkins Press, 1963.
3. Glasser, W. *Reality therapy.* New York: Harper & Row, 1965.
4. London, P. *The modes and morals of psychotherapy.* New York: Holt, Rinehart & Winston, 1964.
5. Mowrer, O. H. *The crisis in psychiatry and religion.* Princeton: Van Nostrand, 1961.
6. Mowrer, O. H. Integrity therapy: a self-help approach. *Psychotherapy: Theory, Research, and Practice,* 1966, **3,** 114–119.
7. Mullahy, P. *Study of interpersonal relations: New contributions to psy-chiatry.* New York: Hermitage Press, 1949.
8. Parlour, R. R., & Van Vorst, R. B. Permissiveness and structuring in

modern psychiatry. Paper prepared for 120th Annual Meeting of the APA, Los Angeles, 1964.

9. Parlour, R. R., & Van Vorst, R. B. Structuring the psychotherapy. Unpublished manuscript.

10. Pratt, S., & Tooley, J. How differing concepts of the nature of psychological disorders lead to differing practices in the hospital, the clinic, and the community. Paper prepared for 70th Annual Convention of APA, St. Louis, 1962.

11. Pratt, S., & Tooley, J. Psychology and social action. Unpublished manuscript.

12. Seeley, J. R., Sim, R. A., & Loosley, E. W. *Crestwood Heights.* New York: Basic Books, 1956.

13. Skinner, B. F. *Science and human behavior.* New York: Macmillan, 1953.

14. Szasz, T. S. *The myth of mental illness.* New York: Paul B. Hoeber, 1961.

15. Waskow, I. E. Counselor attitudes and client behavior. *J. Consult. Psychol.,* 1963, **25,** 405–412.

Chapter 6

# Attitude Therapy:
# A Behavior Therapy Approach

## EARL S. TAULBEE and JAMES C. FOLSOM

Earl S. Taulbee: b. 1923, Lee City, Kentucky.
B.A., in psychology, Georgetown College, Kentucky, 1948. Ph.D., in clinical
psychology, University of Nebraska, 1953.
Chief, Psychology Service, V.A. Center, Bay Pines, Florida, 1968–date; V.A.
Hospital, Tuscaloosa, Alabama, 1963–1968; V.A. Hospital, Lincoln,
Nebraska, 1959–1963; Norfolk State Hospital and Out-patient Clinic,
1958–1959; V.A. Mental Hygiene Clinic, Omaha, Nebraska, 1955–1958.
Adjunct Professor at both Florida State University and University of
Miami, 1968–date. Lecturer, University of Alabama, 1966–1968.
Associate Clinical Psychologist, University of Nebraska, 1957–1963.
Instructor, Medical Psychology, University of Nebraska College of
Medicine, 1954–1959.
Fellow: American Psychological Association; Society for Projective Tech-
niques and Personality Assessment. Member of Editorial Board and
Staff Editor, *Journal of Projective Techniques and Personality Assess-
ment.*
Articles: Relationship between certain personality variables and continuation in psychotherapy. *J. Consult. Psychol.*, 1958, **22**, 83-89. The
relationship between Rorschach flexor and extensor M responses and
the MMPI and psychotherapy. *J. Proj. Tech.*, 1961, **25**, 477-479. (Co-
author). The role of psychology in an Attitude Therapy treatment
program. *Newsletter for Research in Psychology*, 1965, **7** (3), 45-57.
Veterans Administration Center, Hampton, Virginia. A behavioral
approach to therapeutic structuring for acute and chronic patients.
Paper presented at the Central Office Conference of V.A. Psychologists, May 25-27, 1965, Chicago, Illinois. A psychodynamic-behavioral
model of therapeutic structuring. Paper presented at the Conference
on V.A. Psychiatry-Psychology Program, May 23-24, 1966, Chicago,
Illinois.

James C. Folsom: b. 1921, Sweetwater, Alabama.
M.D., Washington University, School of Medicine, St. Louis, Missouri, 1946.
Diplomate, American Board of Neurology and Psychiatry, 1954.
Director, V.A. Hospital, Tuscaloosa, Alabama, 1966–date, and Chief of Staff,
1962–1966. Assistant Professor of Psychiatry, Medical College of
Alabama, 1963–date. Clinical Director, Mental Health Institute, Mt.
Pleasant, Iowa, 1960–1962. Chief, Physical Medicine and Rehabilita-
tion Service, V.A. Hospital, Topeka, Kansas, 1955–1960; Admitting

**165**

Physician, 1953–1955. Faculty Member, Menninger School of Psychiatry, Topeka, Kansas, 1953–1960.

Fellow, American Psychiatric Association. Former Editor: *Alumni Bulletin* of the Menninger School of Psychiatry Alumni Association, *Newsletter* of the Kansas District Branch of the American Psychiatric Association. Former Editor: *Newsletter* of the Alabama District Branch of the APA. Resident, the Alumni Association of the Menninger School of Psychiatry, 1958. Member, Editorial Board of *Staff Magazine* of the APA.

Articles: Attitude therapy and the team approach. *Mental Hospitals,* November 1965, 31–47. Geriatric medical patients pose growing problem. *U.S. Medicine,* 1966, **2,** 56–58. Attitude therapy has marked effect, *U.S. Medicine,* 1966, **2,** 1-8. The psychiatric team. *Official Journal of the American Association for Rehabilitation Therapy, Inc.,* October 1966, 1-8. Attitude Therapy workshop. *American Archives of Rehabilitation Therapy,* June 1966.

**A**ttitude Therapy may be defined as a procedure or process utilizing psychological principles to effect desired behavioral changes by structuring an environment in which a variety of consistently and systematically applied attitudes and techniques will reinforce adaptive behavior and extinguish maladaptive behavior. Admittedly, this is an inadequate and oversimplified definition, but it will serve as an introduction.[1]

This concept of a special therapeutic environment, where the underlying philosophy is that the maladaptive behavior we wish to change has been learned and can be modified through the application of learning theory principles of reward and punishment, is not new. As can be seen in the discussion of Attitude Therapy which follows, its historical roots are found in some well-known theories of personality and behavior modification—milieu therapy, moral treatment, conditioning, and psychoanalysis, to name a few. It is for this reason that Taulbee (10) has referred to this treatment approach as a "psychodynamic-behavioral model of therapeutic structuring."

Since an individual's behavior, whether adaptive or maladaptive, is acquired in a social setting, then logically, the place to modify it is in a social setting. As early as 1845 Pliny Earle (2), describing moral treatment, said, "The primary object is to treat the patients, so far as their condition will possibly admit, as if they were still in the enjoyment of the healthy exercise of their mental faculties. . . . Nor is it

[1] The authors are greatly indebted to H. Wilkes Wright, Ph.D., for his invaluable assistance in the preparation of this paper.

less essential to extend them the privilege, or the right, of as much liberty, as much freedom from personal restraint as is compatible with their safety, the safety of others, and the judicious administration of other branches of curative treatment. The courtesies of civilized and social life are not to be forgotten, extending, as they do, to the promotion of the first great object already mentioned, and operating, to no inconsiderable extent, as a means of effecting restoration to mental health." Bockoven (1), in defining moral treatment, stated, "Moral treatment might be defined as organized group-living in which the integration and continuity of work, play and social activities produce a meaningful total life experience in which growth of individual capacity to enjoy life has maximum opportunity." A more recent description of "Milieu Therapy" by Karl A. Menninger is very similar to that described as practiced around 1850. To quote Menninger (5), "The essence of milieu therapy lies in the definite therapeutic structuring of the special environment provided. We have spoken as if this were always a hospital; of course it can be a school, a colony, or even certain kinds of places of legal detention which might categorically be called prisons. But the important aspect is not the confinement or restraint, but the structure."

While Attitude Therapy does not strictly follow any of these quotations, it does utilize principles and techniques derived from all. This psychological model, with the underlying assumption that maladaptive behaviors are learned behaviors, leads to the categorization of patients for treatment purposes in terms of behavior patterns (e.g., patterns of social withdrawal, depression, and manipulation), rather than groupings according to the current standard nosologies. All behavior, then, both adaptive and maladaptive, becomes the focus of treatment within a fairly definite structural framework. Through a variety of consistently and systematically applied attitudes and techniques, it might be said that adaptive behavior is reinforced, new behavior learned, and maladaptive behavior extinguished. The key people in the patient's life (e.g., the nursing assistant, members of the family, employer, and significant others), become what have been referred to, in the behavior therapy literature, as social reinforcers. Thus, Attitude Therapy provides for, and facilitates the use of, reinforcing techniques.

The following is a quote from a paper by Taulbee (9),

"Basic to Attitude Therapy is the philosophy that there is no such thing as a hopelessly ill mental patient. Also, that regardless of age, intelligence, chronicity, diagnosis (functional or organic), level of anxiety, etc., there are maladaptive or troublesome behavior patterns for a particular patient which can be identified and modified, at least to some extent, in order to effect a better adjustment—providing the proper therapeutic situation is established. The first step in doing this is to identify such a behavior pattern, not an isolated symptom, note how it works, and then select the treatment attitude which is appropriate (e.g., Active Friendliness, Passive Friendliness, Kind Firmness, Matter-of-Fact, or No Demand). After an attitude is prescribed, it must be applied consistently around the clock by all personnel having contact with the patient. The particularly disturbing pattern of behavior is pointed out to the patient, and it is explained to him how we will help him modify it. Members of the family are very frequently involved in the treatment plans and become members of the treatment team. Through this rather direct and structured manner the patient gets the feeling that the team knows what it is doing and that he can be helped. Anxiety is reduced, the interfering behavior pattern is modified, and new responses acquired."

Two special treatment programs which illustrate the use of the model described are the Anti-Depressive Program and the Geriatric Reality Orientation Program. These have been described in earlier works (Refs. 3, 7, 8, 11–13), and they will be discussed later in the paper.

In 1952, Folsom modified the fairly lengthy and detailed "Attitudes" originally delineated by Menninger and introduced them into the Physical Medicine and Rehabilitation Service of the Veterans Administration Hospital, Topeka, Kansas. From this experience he concluded that consistency of attitudes in dealing with patients is highly desirable, if not necessary, in successful treatment. Folsom then formulated five basic attitudes which he used at the Topeka VAH and later at the Mental Health Institute, Mount Pleasant, Iowa, prior to his coming to the VA Hospital in Tuscaloosa, Alabama. It was at Tuscaloosa that Attitude Therapy received theoretical modification, refinement, and hospital-wide application.

The Tuscaloosa VA Hospital is a 964-bed, neuropsychiatric hospital, with approximately 250 beds for the psychiatric medically infirm patients. When Folsom arrived to assume his duties as Chief of Staff in 1962 (later appointed Director), he was faced with a difficult problem. The majority of the patients were chronic, the treatment program was limited and traditional, and the staff less than enthusiastic. A shift to the unit system was being encouraged. There were 680 psychiatric patients so distributed that although a natural goal might seem to be four treatment units, each containing 140 patients, lack of personnel made the organization of more than two psychiatric units impossible.

Thus, with the adoption of the treatment philosophy and concepts mentioned above, and set forth in previous articles by the authors, an Attitude Therapy program was developed. Since treatment was defined as the creation of a special environment tailored to the needs of the patient, and since primary therapeutic impact was the reactions of those in the environment toward the patient, and since the effects of these reactions could be taught and understood in at least their basic form, there was no reason why an effective program could not be achieved.

It was recognized, in organizing a treatment team, that such a group of individuals could work together in many different ways. The team could be controlled and governed by rules and regulations and administer these; or, it could be organized around one dominant leader, and implement treatment as he directed. It was believed, however, that under either of these two conditions, the development of treatment and the growth of the individuals on the team would be entirely dependent on either those who wrote the regulations or those who directed the teams. On the other hand, if the individuals were of sufficient stature, a third possibility existed; to provide the group with certain basic ideas about the effectiveness of environmental treatment, suggest that they organize themselves into a team-centered team (rather than leader-centered) where each has an equal voice in decisions, give the team full and unqualified responsibility for the treatment care of all patients under their control, give them support and education as needed, but let them do the job. This third alternative was viewed as being necessary in an Attitude Therapy program where the decentralization of treatment must be assured. Also, it was seen as the one alternative under which team growth would more likely reflect the insights that it gained in the course of its experience in successfully meeting the treatment needs of the patients entrusted to its care. The more varied the past experience and training of those who comprised the team, the less likely that team growth would reflect the perceptions and ideas of but a single professional individual or group.

With the initiation of the team-centered team and the adoption of the treatment philosophy described, the team members moved to a point where they no longer thought of illness in the traditional or medical sense. Instead, they saw patients as ordinary individuals who had learned techniques of coping with reality in ineffective, self-limiting, and self-defeating ways. They understood that there was nothing abnormal about the learning process per se that had taken place. The patient had learned and was exhibiting behaviors which were meaningful and rewarding in the context in which these behaviors were learned, in the social context of his family, and his particular interpersonal environment. Once the habit of trying to understand the behavior of the patient in learning and adjustment terms was established, it was reinforced by every treatment success. On no wards was this more dramatically in evidence than on our geriatric and medically infirm wards. Personnel on these wards in many hospitals are strongly oriented to think in terms of organic deficit, deterioration, and failing faculties as the etiological factors in the development of patients' symptoms. In our hospital, senility is viewed as being very much like a psychosis. What the patient is trying to communicate, to achieve by his mutism, anger, regression and memory loss, and his confusion, are the questions that are raised. Once the team members can answer these, they ask, "What can we do to make it unnecessary for the patient to communicate in this way?" or, "How can we go about removing the gratification the patient is gaining by these forms of behavior?"

The growth involved in the understanding and development of a basic treatment philosophy by our personnel has, like all learning, not been a matter of smooth, orderly progression. For a time, it seems, a plateau is evident, during which experiences are being consolidated. Then a major change takes place. It took a visiting lecturer (Muriel F. Oberleder, Ph.D., Bronx State Hospital), especially selected for her point of view, to give acceptance to a growing conviction that senility in many ways is like a psychosis and should be treated as such. And then, wise person that she is, she went one step further by suggesting that we drop the label "psychosis," because of its frequent connotation of irreversible illness, and replace it with "adjustment problems of the aged."

It has been the task of Taulbee to keep formulating our program and establishing the theoretical implications involved. This he has done on several occasions. His most recent writing uses the concept of a psychosocial behavioral approach to therapeutic structuring. That Taulbee is a psychologist no doubt has contributed to our move toward a learning paradigm, utilizing many of the principles and techniques contributed by both learning and dynamic theorists.

It is necessary, at this point, to pause and reflect on the unusual and most significant aspect of this hospital: the continuous development of its treatment philosophy, which emerges from the hospital personnel and is not imposed from the top. It is our firm conviction that this has been made possible by the willingness of the Director and the Chief of Staff to delegate treatment responsibility. A basic ingredient is, of course, having enough dedicated and concerned personnel in all the various services to make possible a common group objective—modifying the patient's maladaptive behavior to the point where he can adjust satisfactorily in society. But the second requirement, without which no such growth would be likely, is the delegation to that group of the complete authority and responsibility for patient treatment and care. Authority delegated to but one individual may promote growth in that individual, but since his can be an awesome responsibility, probably it will not. An evolving treatment philosophy like ours will move more and more in the direction of an open hospital, where patients are encouraged to assume responsibility for their own behavior. Unpleasant consequences may ensue, but our personnel prefer to run these risks rather than keep patients on locked wards and operate a custodial institution. Such treatment responsibilities and decisions are an intolerable burden for one person, and when one person attempts to assume these, he will certainly be more conservative in his treatment and more inclined to see the locked ward as the way to be safe rather than sorry. Although these experiences can be, and are, crushing and immobilizing to any person who has full responsibility for these decisions, they are maturing experiences for the team.

The roles of the Hospital Director and Chief of Staff in such a program evolution are not always comfortable. Although they have the ultimate responsibility for patient care and related community welfare, and for the public image of the hospital, they must be willing to see their treatment teams make decisions that may not appear to them to be the soundest or most desirable. There are times when either of them must become involved with the deliberations and decisions of a treatment team. This is most likely to occur when a crucial decision must be made concerning the direct welfare of the patient, a member of his family, or someone else, or affecting the institution directly. If the busy Hospital Director or his Chief of Staff issues an ultimatum that the team must, or must not, take a given action, his ultimatum is certain to have a seriously undermining effect on team morale or its sense of mission. Our experience has been, perhaps contrary to expectations, that such intervention is rarely needed and most frequently will occur in the early months of a team's growth, when the members are most accepting of help and direction.

## THE TREATMENT PROGRAM

### The Hospital As An Environment

It is clear from the previous discussion that the treatment program that has evolved is an expression of what the personnel have come to understand about patients. They believe that the patients have learned maladaptive behavior and that treatment is largely a relearning process; that it becomes a matter of creating an environment for the patient where his maladaptive behavior is no longer adaptive, no longer rewarded, no longer expected, and in certain instances, no longer tolerated. The hospital environment must be a learning environment, but that is not all. If it is to be a place where the patient is to learn to live effectively in society, then it must be a real environment, not an artificial one.

This last point merits attention. If one labels the environment from which the patient comes and in which he learned his maladaptive behaviors as "unrealistic," what precisely do we mean? We mean that what the individual has learned is contrary to the covenant binding the individual to the society in which he exists. Much has been written about the social origin of the meaning of the word "normal." Much less has been written concerning the implications of this for a hospital community striving to represent and clarify the expectations of society. If a hospital staff is to communicate that it is imperative to conform to social expectations in order to survive, the hospital staff itself must have no doubts on this matter. If a hospital environment is to teach self-responsibility, it must be composed of individuals who practice self-responsibility. The hospital staff itself must have a distinct character. It must reflect a value system that is truly reality oriented.

If a hospital group accepts the responsibility of reflecting reality to the patient, thereby helping the patient to experience this basis for rapport with the rest of his fellowmen, it cannot easily depart from this stance. If it is the fate of the average citizen to be subjected to unpleasant consequences for being drunk and disorderly, making threats, or passing bad checks, so it should be the position of the hospital personnel that the patient must likewise be subjected to such consequences. This is not always an easy position to maintain. There are many, in addition to the patient's family, who would pressure that the patient should be assisted in every way to avoid the unpleasant consequences of his behavior. We have become increasingly convinced of the damage that accrues from permitting these sentiments to distort reality. We have found, as have others, that this sentiment and others closely akin are basic to the perceptual distortions of reality which characterize so many patients.

### The Treatment Team

Earlier in the paper we discussed the relationship between treatment team growth and team autonomy. In the immediately preceding paragraphs, we considered our view of the treatment environment. Now we need only to point out who and what the treatment team is.

An environment might be defined as the surrounding conditions, influences, or forces that influence, modify, or determine an individual's behavior. In the sense in which we use it, it is composed of people, and all people who come into contact with the individual concerned become a part of that environment. It follows, then, that in the structuring of a therapeutic environment, all those having significant contact with the patient are important to him and must be considered as part of his treatment team. This idea is cumbersome in some ways and involves a tremendous amount of communication among hospital personnel, but there is no alternative. That this amount of interpersonal consistency in treatment is at all possible arises as a consequence of (1) there being a relatively limited number of maladaptive behavioral patterns on which the team must focus its efforts; and, (2) the application of Attitude Therapy, which is a psychiatric shorthand technique for conveying throughout the hospital the manner in which all must interact with the patient.

Remembering that the treatment team has full and unqualified responsibility for the treatment of all patients assigned to it, the team must have the skills of many disciplines available in establishing a treatment goal: physician, psychologist, social worker, nurse, and nursing assistant, representing a minimal group. All of these use their special talents and information to answer the questions: (1) What is happening to the patient? (2) How did he get to be as he is? (3) How is his behavior to be interpreted? and (4) What changes can be brought about by the treatment modalities at our disposal? Once a decision can be reached on these points, then all hospital personnel become involved directly or indirectly in treatment. Interdisciplinary roles tend to become merged and identities lost in the process. Whoever can contribute what needs to be done to create the desired environmental press does so. Changes in patient behavior are immediately communicated, suggesting the possible need for revision of his program. As he becomes more responsible and tractable, his horizons are expanded, and not only all hospital personnel, but other patients, his family, and even the patient himself become involved in his treatment.

It is characteristic of many of our patients, like patients elsewhere, to yield their symptoms quite readily in this setting, only to take them up again upon return to their home environment. This phenomenon is seen as further evidence that maladaptive behaviors arise as a consequence of particular patterns of interpersonal interactions and not as a disease process that is rendered "in remission" in the hospital. It is clearly apparent, therefore, that families must become involved in the treatment process and that the hospital must become involved with the patient and his family in the community whenever this is possible.

Although the "moral" and "humane" treatment of these types of patients has a long history, it would be a mistake to conclude that the program being described is just another application of the philosophy of tender, loving care. For a very limited number of patients and for a limited time, this may be true. But, as will be seen in the descriptions of the specific treatment environments, the goal is to reflect reality to the patient, or help him find reality himself. In all instances the dignity of the individual is preserved, and his worth as an individual is assured. But it is not our understanding that we can make learning always pleasant and never painless. It is not pleasant for a patient to be confronted at every turn with the futility of his misrepresentations of the facts of his behavior. No patient enjoys having his image as a respectable and loving husband and father, an image he wants the staff and others to accept, destroyed by having his wife report openly and in front of him his cruelty, inadequacy, and almost total irresponsibility. It is not easy for a neurotic, who finds comfort in the conviction that all his failures are the consequence of poor health, to accept that no physical basis has been found for his complaints, or at least not to the disabling degree he believes.

The ability to structure a learning environment makes another demand upon the treatment personnel. They must be seasoned and experienced. They must have witnessed, for example, the tremendous changes that can be produced by Kind Firmness before they can be effective in treating depressed patients with this treatment modality. Some hospital personnel, seemingly, can be effective only in a loving and supporting relationship.

## Treatment Modalities

In what is to follow, five distinct treatment environments will be described and case material presented to illustrate how the program works and with what results. It would be incorrect to assume, however, that a patient is assigned to one or the other treatment program, and that is that. Patients will be treated with the staff attitude that is believed provides the best corrective counter pressure. For example, when the Kind-Firm environment has produced a lifting of depression, the patient will immediately be provided with the environment most suitable to help him consolidate his gains and strengthen his reality testing techniques.

One question can be raised profitably at this point in the discussion, prior to a description of the treatment situations. Is it essential to the effectiveness of this type of program for the patient to gain insight into his own dynamics?

The answer to the question is in the negative. To be sure, many do gain insight, some into their own needs and the ineffective techniques they have employed to satisfy them. Some become more and more conscious of the difference between family expectations and societal expectations. It is believed that a considerable number come to see that they themselves, by their own behavior, have elicited the negative behavior in others that they so resent. But the treatment does not aim directly to produce insight. The goal is behavioral change, and this can be accomplished without insight.

## TREATMENT ENVIRONMENT: ATTITUDES PRESCRIBED

Attitudes prescribed are summarized in the following paragraphs. They are prescribed according to the needs of the patient, but it should be noted that understanding and acceptance are basic to all of them.

### Active Friendliness

The basic principle in Active Friendliness (AF) is giving attention before the patient is able or willing to request it. The initiative is taken in showing a consistent, genuine interest in the patient and his activities. He is given sincere praise for accomplishments that show progress. Other descriptive terms for this approach are "tender loving care" and "giving love unsolicited." The AF treatment is prescribed for the withdrawn, regressed, apathetic, failure-prone individual who seemingly has lost all interest in life. A team member practicing AF might sit beside the patient, slowly leaf through a magazine and comment on certain pictures. Or, he might go with him to occupational therapy, on walks, or engage him in other activities.

#### Example

Mr. A was a frightened, withdrawn, severely regressed (incontinent, would not keep his clothes on) catatonic who was delusional and hallucinating. It was recognized that he was making a flight from reality, that he needed to be motivated to develop interest in, and concern with, his environment, and that his fear of rejection and failure would have to be overcome. A Unit Nurse Supervisor and a Nursing Assistant were assigned major responsibilities for carrying out the prescribed attitude. They spoke to him whenever they passed where he was sitting, invited him to go places with them, introduced him to others. Alert to his most hesitant evidences of interest and response, he was quickly rewarded for each. Whatever request he made was granted, and he was not permitted to fail in things he attempted to do. His own worthwhileness as a person was conveyed to him. Progress was rapid. In a matter of a few days, he was smiling, then talking, then initiating conversation and practicing Active Friendliness himself. Incontinence, disrobing, delusions, and hallucinatory behavior disappeared. When he was functioning satisfactorily, he was assigned to the Dietctic Service where he worked in unison with others and did well. Soon he was going on weekend passes by himself. The team was successful in helping him to modify his self-concept and to regain confidence in his ability to relate to others. He was discharged from the hospital three years ago, encouraged not to return to his home environment. Subsequent reports indicate that he is doing well and has not been rehospitalized.

## Passive Friendliness

This attitude is similar to AF except that team members' attentions are not focused on the patient. The basic principle underlying Passive Friendliness (PF) is being available and alert but not pushing. Wait for the patient to take the initiative and then respond accordingly. At times, it may be necessary to be firm, but friendliness must still prevail. In prescribing such an attitude, the team might say to the patient, "We are here to help you; we know you are frightened of others. You are suspicious. You find it difficult to relate yourself to other people, therefore, we will not move in too close. We will be here to help you; you may ask us anything you want, but we will not offer things to you because you might misinterpret our intentions." Passive Friendliness is prescribed for distrustful and suspicious persons, many of whom have problems of a sexual nature.

### Example

Mr. B was received as a transfer from a Navy hospital. According to the records which accompanied him, he had made an initially adequate adjustment to Navy life, worked conscientiously, but seemed something of a "loner." He began to act strangely about six months after he was inducted. He became suspicious of the motives of others, and he refused to eat some foods because he suspected that they were doctored with saltpeter. He became more outspoken in his accusations of a companion, which led to a fight and his hospitalization. At that time he was found to be hearing voices, with well-developed ideas of reference and delusions of persecution. He did not improve and was transferred to us with a diagnosis of schizophrenic reaction, paranoid type.

The reaction of our treatment staff to this type of patient is based on our belief that in such cases the usually adequate psychological defenses against unconscious conflict have been breached, and that the individual is in a state of confused panic as he tries to reorganize his defenses, incorporating what has so recently happened. Since this is an internal reorganization, it will be accomplished by the patient himself, and our task is to furnish a stable environment in which the individual can re-establish his psychological defenses. The environment should not contain pressure, too close contact with either males or females; but, it should contain some techniques of conveying to the patient that the team members understand he is uncomfortable and tense, and that they are available to help him if he desires it. These are the essentials of Passive Friendliness. Psychological examination had revealed a deep-seated sex role ambivalence, somewhat feminine vocational interest pattern, and good intelligence. Assignments were made to recreational therapy (tennis and bowling), educational therapy, and the manual arts therapy printing clinic.

The consolidation of the patient's defenses could be perceived through his behavior. He became more relaxed, more comfortable, and more self-assured. The counseling psychologist worked with him concerning his educational goals. He left the hospital, completed his university program, got married, and is reported to be doing well.

## Kind Firmness

This attitude is basic to our treatment program for depression and is prescribed for patients whose major pattern of behavior is characterized by depression, guilt, feelings of inadequacy, and worthlessness, and who usually internalize their hostility. Kind Firmness (KF) will be described more fully in connection with a description of the Anti-Depressive (AD) Program.

## Matter-of-Fact

This attitude is very similar to that used by people to deal with each other in day-to-day relationships. The Matter-of-Fact (MOF) attitude is the most commonly used one and is prescribed for the acting-out, manipulative, somatically preoccupied, passive-dependent, passive-aggressive, alcoholic, or organic individuals who need a well-structured environment. Patients for whom this attitude is necessary often complain about such things as hospital routine and somatic ailments in order to gain sympathy and attention, and many deny that there is anything wrong with them. The team members respond to the patient's pleas, apparent distress, or maneuvers, in a consistently casual, calm manner. In essence, the team says to the patient (and may literally say it), "You have loused things up to a rather remarkable degree. We have no magic to offer you, but we will offer you an environment in which you may learn to modify your behavior to the extent that you can live comfortably in the world with people."

### Example

Mr. D was brought to the hospital from jail at the insistence of his parents. He was married and the father of three children. He had a long history of alcoholic overindulgence, marital discord, and poor work habits. He was deeply in debt. Being a friendly and ingratiating person, he quickly made a good adjustment to the hospital, and became friendly with both staff and patients.

When brought before the treatment team, he presented himself as a loving and devoted father and husband, whose main concern was the welfare of all about him. He admitted to drinking but denied that it was a problem. He admitted indebtedness but stated he had to borrow money to maintain his family as they deserved. He acknowledged a poor work history but attributed this to his never finding work that really interested him.

The staff had already been informed by the wife that the situation was far different from this. She was brought into the conference where she reported that the veteran was frequently drunk, abusive, and hostile when drinking, spent most of his income on liquor, and borrowed to meet the demands of creditors. The picture she painted of him was that of an immature, narcissistic, self-centered individual who was completely untrustworthy and unreliable. These personality characteristics were quite evident in the psychological test findings.

The patient was confronted with this information in the wife's presence. His initial reaction was to minimize the account given by his wife. This was pointed out to him. He then stated that he believed family problems should not be aired in public, but he was reminded that the problems had resulted in his being here. He then stated that his wife was lying, and he was confronted with his previous statement that he loved his wife and, therefore, why should she lie? He then stated that his parents were on his side and would defend him against the wife's report, and this playing of wife against parents was pointed out. He was informed that we were going to counsel the wife and parents not to tolerate his behavior further, and in subsequent sessions they were helped to see how their tolerance had played a role in the patient's behavior. He was informed that we would keep him here while he came to a realization of his problems and saw what had caused them.

As anticipated, his behavior here was quite similar to his previous behavior. He attempted to have one staff member agree that the wife should not see the social worker for help. He was confronted with this behavior. He made an unauthorized call to his wife, telling her not to come for her appointment, but she informed the staff, and he was faced with this. He became intensely angry, and he was faced with this. In each of these situations, the immaturity and inadequacy of his behavior was pointed to as the cause of his past and present problems.

Progress with the patient has not been rapid. He has been re-admitted twice. In general, however, he is functioning better. The family see their need to surround him with inflexible expectations. He is learning to live better with these controls. He is a more serious, perhaps more worried man than he once was. He seems to be establishing, for himself, a concept of a future which has relevance for his present. He is working regularly.

## No Demand

The No Demand (ND) attitude means that no demands whatsoever, with the exception of four to be mentioned later, are placed upon the patient. This treatment approach is used with the violent, threatening, angry, and literally "striking out" individual who is in a state of panic and is trying to destroy everything around him. This is sort of a global suicide with the patient wanting to be the last to go. He is the person who is always picking a fight with you—and the world. He is attempting to overcome his state of fear by frightening the world away, by threatening it with destruction. The patient is told that there are four rules he must follow. These are: (1) He may not leave the treatment program without permission, (2) he may not hurt himself, (3) he may not hurt anyone else, and (4) he must take medications, if prescribed. It has been observed that no matter how destructive the patient's behavior is, if it is not reinforced by counter-aggression, he will rapidly settle down. Personnel do not get into a verbal or physical power struggle with this type of patient. He is told that no one is going to fight with him but that the team members want to help him.

### Example

Mr. E, a small thin man, was brought to the hospital handcuffed and heavily guarded by two state troopers. They reported that he had been living alone for many months on a small farm and had been having a running feud with his neighbors. For the past several days, he had been carrying a gun and threatening everyone, firing the gun frequently but without clear intent to injure. He was arrested and taken to jail and then brought to the hospital.

It was recognized that the patient was terrified and fearful, that he expected abuse and punishment, and that he was trying to make others afraid of him to check this. The admitting staff immediately removed his restraints, and repeated over and over that here, in this hospital, he would be safe. He was informed of the four restrictions he must observe. Although never assaultive and violently destructive, for the next two days he was verbally abusive, taunting, hostile, tore his clothing and, on occasion, was obscene. It was the staff's task to convey (1) that they recognized his fear, (2) that they were aware that he would have to test the limits of the situation, but that (3) they were confident he would eventually see how concerned they were about his welfare.

It was many hours before the patient gave any indication that he was responding to treatment. Gradually, however, his behavior began to change. Recognizing his need for interpersonal contact, the staff stayed close to him, even though this seemed to trigger more anger. Within five days, however, the veteran was quiet, friendly, cooperative, and yet seemingly not quite able to accept the reality that fighting was not necessary.

He was in the hospital several months, not because he was still manifesting symptoms, but because he was so frightened at the prospect of having to return to his home community. He was transferred to a domiciliary where he is making a useful and productive adjustment.

## SPECIAL TREATMENT PROGRAMS

While the usual treatment modalities, such as activity therapy, individual psychotherapy, group psychotherapy, etc., are included in the Attitude Therapy program, there are two special programs which appear to have been very effective in the treatment of depression and of confusion resulting from the aging process and brain injuries. They are the Anti-Depressive (AD) program and the Geriatric Reality Orientation (GRO) program.

### Antidepressive Program

The purpose of the Anti-Depressive (AD) program is to provide the depressed patient with a highly-structured environment where everyone coming in contact with him will apply the Kind Firmness (KF) attitude. The depressed patient is placed in a small, rather drab room, furnished with chairs, table, and a few shelves, where he is assigned to work on monotonous tasks. The tasks assigned may consist of sanding a small block of wood, bouncing a ball, counting little seashells into a cigar box and starting over again when he is distracted and loses count, and other such menial tasks. The work gives him some muscle action and something else to focus on besides his own misery. He is never given anything to do that will bring him gratification. The KF attitude indicates that all personnel working with the patient are to insist that he carry out all tasks assigned no matter how much he may complain. They are not to give in to his pleadings to be left alone to suffer, nor try to cheer him up, nor offer sympathy and encouragement. The patient is kept on a closed ward and during the day he is with a small group of other depressed patients. The patient performs all assigned tasks under the extremely close supervision of nursing assistants. They assume a level of expectancy approaching perfection and do not fail to point out to the patient any shortcomings in his performance. In the case of the patient who is severely depressed, it may be necessary for a nursing assistant to take him by the hand and "help" him sand or mop. Patients on this program are kept busy during all their working hours except during meals and for very brief hourly breaks. It should be emphasized that while a patient is treated impersonally and is given criticism, he is never ridiculed nor belittled. The purpose of this program is to provide an opportunity and cause for the expression of hostility. After there has been an appropriate externalization of his anger, the patient is taken off the program. The prescribed attitude is then changed, of course, usually to a Matter-of-Fact attitude. The Attitude Therapy program at the Tuscaloosa, Alabama, Veterans Hospital was begun in the fall of 1962 with the prescription of KF for a depressed suicidal patient. The rather dramatic improvement in that first patient convinced many of the hospital personnel that the consistency of attitude had much to recommend it.

*Example*

Mr. C was admitted to the hospital in an acute state of suicidal depression. He was in his late 50's and an executive for a large corporation. His children were grown and had left home. His wife, an obviously overprotective and mothering person, reported that he had been going downhill for several months, becoming increasingly sad, eating little, not sleeping, and frequently on the verge of tears. About a month prior to admission, he had requested sick leave from his employer, and this had been granted. The evening prior to admission he had purchased a gun and ammunition, and his wife discovered him preparing to take his own life.

On admission to the hospital, his psychological examination revealed him to be very severely depressed, confused, experiencing feelings of depersonalization, and ideas of reference. He spoke in an inaudible whisper. Psychomotor retardation was very marked. He was placed on the AD program without any delay.

For the first several hours, he worked slowly, seeming not to hear the requests that he work harder and faster. The first positive sign was when he began to respond to these requests. During the second day, he attempted to involve the staff in a discussion of his feelings. He was told that he was there to work, not talk. Evidence of confusion became markedly less as he seemed to focus more on his work, feeling somewhat rejected by the staff. He became more obviously upset and frustrated when he was interrupted and asked to begin again. During the third afternoon, he lost control of his anger, stood up, and dared anyone to attempt to make him do more. He was immediately escorted to a room where a few of the staff were in conference.

He was asked if he were depressed. He replied that he was not, but that he was angry. He was asked how often, previously, he had gotten this angry. He replied, "Never," that he had "swallowed" his anger all his life. He was asked how it felt to be angry and he replied, "Good."

The behavioral changes in the patient were dramatic. Before treatment he shuffled slowly, head down, oblivious to what was happening around him. After treatment he walked erect, head up, alert and very clearly in control.

Much remained yet to be accomplished. He needed to see how his excessive dependency needs had structured for him a subservient role at the office and at home. His good ability and prior good health had, until the last year, permitted him to meet what he believed to be the expectations of others with remarkable success. He had evolved a role for his wife resembling a mother–son relationship in which he felt obligated to more than satisfy her every request. The anger, which was mobilized by what he recognized as excessive demands, had nowhere to go but inward. He dared not express it overtly and alienate those he needed. The result was depression.

Staff work with the family was needed to prevent them from casting him into a sick and helpless role. He was encouraged to do some self-evaluations with our help.

The veteran remains anxious when he ventilates hostility and anger, but he does so in socially acceptable ways. There has not been a recurrence of his incapacitating depression.

In 1964, an unpublished pilot study was carried out by Dr. Earl S. Taulbee and Mr. Truman Crowder comparing the effectiveness of the AD program to one in which the more usual type of treatment was provided for depressed patients. In the latter program the patient was given ego-building tasks, had AF prescribed, and the team members encouraged, reassured, and complimented him. The two groups consisted of six patients each, randomly assigned, and they were evaluated on the basis of test scores on the various scales of the Minnesota Multiphasic Personality Inventory (MMPI), the Tennessee Self-Concept Scale, and the Depression Inventory. Patients were tested at three points in the treatment program: first, before treatment was begun; secondly, at the time that the experimental patients were removed from the AD program; and again at the end of three weeks following admission to the hospital. The significant differences and trends that were found supported the theoretical contention that depression is associated with the internalization of hostility and that a program designed to help the patient in externalizing his hostility is superior to "tender loving care" in the alleviation of depressive symptoms. The posttreatment testing revealed that the AD patients had a much more positive self-concept, were significantly less depressed, anxious, ruminating, and repressed; also, they were more able to admit to psychological problems and had a more positive picture of their physical condition. The authors recommended that an extended replication of the study be done. Such a project is underway currently by the authors and Drs. W. E. Patterson, R. F. Horner, and H. W. Wright. Newly admitted patients whose major symptom was depression were randomly assigned to one of six groups: (1) AD program only, (2) AD with placebo, (3) AD with antidepressant drugs, (4) AF only, (5) AF with placebo, or (6) AF with antidepressant drugs. Before assignment to one of the groups, the patients were given the MMPI, Time Reference Inventory, Interpersonal Check List, and the Tennessee Self-Concept Scale, as part of their initial work-up. All subjects were retested with the same battery of tests at intervals of two weeks, six weeks (or at time of discharge, whichever came first), and a follow-up testing six months from the initial testing session. Although the results are still in the process of being analyzed, a preliminary report was presented at the Thirteenth Annual Conference, Veterans Administration Cooperative Studies in Psychiatry (8). In brief, the tentative findings were:

1. Depressed patients improved with both forms of milieu therapy studied.

2. Patients treated on the AD program continued to improve or hold their gains up to the six-months follow-up, whereas patients treated on the AF program tended to regress. This is what one would expect since the AF program merely supported the individual while the AD program attempted to modify behavioral patterns.

3. Following treatment on the AD program, patients were less depressed, less somatically preoccupied, and less self-deceiving. In addition, they were less confused, anxious, ruminative, and repressed. They had a more positive self-concept and manifested improved interpersonal relationships with family members and others.

4. The groups treated on the AD program without medication made greater gains than any other groups, and their mean test profiles were significantly more normal in appearance at the six-months evaluation.

5. The addition of antidepressant medications as prescribed in this study did not improve the effectiveness of the two forms of milieu therapy in relieving depression.

6. Similar results obtained by the two independent treatment units cross-validated, with some limitations, the findings of this study.

7. The AD program is a safe and effective treatment technique that can be learned and carried out by different treatment teams.

A number of clinical observations also support the previous conclusions. Patients on the AD program spent an average of 14 days less time in the hospital during this study than did the patients on the AF program. One patient on AF remained depressed throughout the six months of the study but quickly responded to treatment on the AD program. Five patients assigned to AF had to be removed because of a dangerous increase of psychological disturbance, but no patients were removed from the AD program for that reason. Many patients on the AD program spontaneously commented to the effect that the problems they had prior to hospitalization still existed but that they had personally changed so that they would be able to face and deal with them. The results of this study offer support for the greater effectiveness of a specific type of milieu therapy utilizing some learning theory principles. Further research is anticipated to follow up this study.

*Geriatric Reality Orientation Program*

The confused geriatric patient represents a significant and growing problem. As far back as the earliest work of Freud, the limitations of the applicability of psychoanalytic techniques to older individuals were recognized. Freud (4) wrote: "near or above the fifties the elasticity of the mental processes, on which treatment depends, is, as a rule, lacking. . . ." Unfortunately, perhaps, this attitude, reinforced by the belief held by many that the confusion and poor social adjustment of the geriatric patient is due to brain damage and therefore irreversible, have resulted in feelings of futility in applying the traditional therapeutic techniques. However, more recognition is being given to the fact that their confusion is not always due to brain damage but can be caused by emotional factors exclusively. In either case, brain damage or emotional factors, much can be done in a short period of time to help the confused elderly patient with his feelings of being lost and bewildered. Some new treatment programs throughout the country use a variety of techniques based largely on learning theory to effect a better adjustment in the elderly and other brain-damaged individuals. One such program is the Geriatric Reality Orientation (GRO) program developed at the Tuscaloosa VA Hospital. The program uses reality orientation classes, operant conditioning procedures, and the prescription of MOF and AF attitudes. Classroom materials include individual calendars, word-letter games, blackboard, felt board, mock-up clock, unit building blocks for coordination and color matching, plastic numbers, and large piece puzzles. A prominent classroom feature is the reality-orientation board. The board lists the name of the hospital and its location; the current year, month, and day of the week; the name of the next meal; the weather; and other details. The teaching process goes on continually, in the classroom, individually on the unit, and in reality-orientation groups.

Reality orientation is ideally suited for the patient with a moderate to severe degree of organic cerebral deficit, usually the result of arteriosclerosis. His first symptom may have been absent-mindedness. His friends began to avoid him. His family began to show anxiety and became worried about his loss of recent memory and his aimless wanderings. Frequently, partial or complete loss of vision, hearing, or speech accelerated the downhill process. The treatment objective is to reverse this process.

After a psychological evaluation has been completed, the members of the treatment team interview each patient, and the reality orientation program is prescribed if it is felt the patient can benefit from it. An attempt is made to correct as far as possible any defects, loss of hearing, sight, or speech. The patient's re-education is begun by helping him use the part of his cerebral functioning that is still intact. The team approach is the most effective, because a consistent attitude can be maintained by everyone dealing with a particular patient. The attitude most frequently adopted is one of Active or Passive friendliness; it is supportive and makes the patient feel that he is worth something after all, that he can still accomplish something, that life has not passed him by, and that there are still people in the world who care about him. However, at times, other attitudes are prescribed. The therapeutic atmosphere is quiet and calm. The demands are minimal; the patient progresses slowly in the treatment program. When he masters one simple task, his accomplishment is made known to the entire team. This is important, because nursing personnel on the day, evening, and night shifts may see the patient in different ways. Detailed records are kept on each patient. These records have occasionally shown that a patient has regressed, and on review it was found that either his medication had been changed or the dosage adjusted. Short home visits are planned if the patient progresses; family members also take the patients outside the hospital to restaurants, clothing stores, or the barber shop, provided the family members remember how much anxiety the patients can tolerate.

The following two patients will demonstrate our approach to the treatment of different types of confused geriatric and organic disorders.

Mr. M is a 67-year-old brain-damaged patient due to a CVA [cerebro-vascular accident]. He was a very successful businessman until he suffered a stroke on September 1964, which left him confused, disoriented, and paralyzed on the right side. The team reported that he was very hostile, yelled and screamed when he didn't get his way, was disoriented most of the time, and seldom said anything that was relevant or coherent. When the patient was brought to the Treatment Planning Conference (TCP) he was slouched down in his wheelchair and was drooling. He did not know the year of his birth, his age, or the current date. Dr. Folsom asked him if he could swallow and he replied, "Not very good," so he was encouraged to swallow and shown how to wipe his mouth. The patient was told, "You can get well enough to go home if you try. Every day all of us are going to remind you what day it is, not to be yelling and screaming, to sit up in your chair, and not to be drooling. We are going to count with you and give you a calendar. We are going to expect you to remember your age, the date, your birthdate, and where your wife is. You have stayed in bed too much, and we are going to get you up and back home. We are going to get pictures of your family to put by your bed. We are going to get football and baseball schedules and watch the games on TV with you." (Social history information revealed that his two main interests had been baseball and TV.) Further aspects of the program were explained to him, and then he was asked, "How does that sound to you?" The patient replied, "It sounds good to me." The nursing supervisor remarked that that was the most alert and lucid she had ever seen the patient. The personnel were told to get him to walk, to watch TV with him, to remind him to stop screaming and drooling, to get him on graduated exercises, to wear his dentures, etc. By the end of the interview, the patient was quiet, had stopped drooling, was sitting erect in his chair, and he made relevant comments about his condition and the planned treatment program. A Matter-of-Fact attitude was prescribed, he was started on the GRO program, and all personnel were instructed to follow through round-the-clock. Since the patient's treatment planning staff, he has almost stopped drooling and responds well to verbal reinforcement. However, whenever the reinforcement is not consistently administered, some regressive tendencies appear in his behavior. The patient is very messy in his eating habits, and a behavior therapy program is being planned to modify this behavior.

Dr. X, a severely regressed, confused, disoriented, 41-year-old physician, was admitted in 1962 as a transfer from a private hospital. He had attempted suicide by shooting himself in the right temple. Immediately after the incident, surgery was performed in the right temporal region, and left hemiplegia resulted. From the time he was admitted until he was presented at a Treatment Planning Conference for review and placement on a more effective treatment program two years later, he remained confused, disoriented, hostile, profane, and almost totally uncooperative. During the conference he was loud, profane, verbally abusive, and he threatened the interviewer. A MOF attitude was used in dealing with him. It was pointed out to him that he had shot himself, that he is mentally ill, and that he is in a mental hospital. His anger was pointed out to him, and his demands and attempts to prescribe his own treatment were met by the reply that although he is a physician he is now a patient and the team will decide his treatment. The patient was allowed to express his rage, but the team steadfastly refused to reject him and informed him that he could not frighten them away by his threats. During the following months he was seen once a week by the treatment team and his progress reviewed with him. At times he appeared confused, but at other times he was quite clear in his thinking. The team felt that he was capable of doing much more for himself than he had been willing to do previously. This problem was handled in a MOF manner. He was given an electric razor and told that he not only could but would be expected to start shaving himself. He was told that he should push his own wheelchair from the dayroom to his bed, instead of expecting the nursing assistant to do it for him. This at first took one hour, but during the next few weeks was cut to fifteen minutes. For the first time since his injury, he was able to and interested in reading medical journals. His successes were pointed out to him in order to cut through his protests of inability to perform. Attention and approval were given to him by the team for his achievements. Outbursts of anger decreased in frequency. As he progressed, arrangements were made for him to make brief visits to the home of a friend who had maintained contact with him. Before the treatment program was initiated, no one believed there was any future for Dr. X. The MOF Attitude has cut through his depression, his complaints of inability to do anything for himself, and much of his demandingness. It has helped him to use his anger in a healthy manner and has helped him to face reality, which he finds rather painful at times. The ultimate goal is to return this patient to live with his family. [Milby, Stenmark, and Horner (6) set up an operant conditioning paradigm to see if social reinforcement would be an effective agent in modifying this patient's wheelchair-wheeling behavior. They found that he increased his rate of self-wheeling more than 100% over the baseline of the operant.]

Many patients who are similar to these cases and who have been suffering from acute and chronic brain syndromes, CNS syphilis, and geriatric patients suffering from neurological disorders of various kinds, have improved to the point where they are leaving the hospital, some after as many as 20 years, to return home or go into nursing or foster homes. Whether their poor memory, regressed, confused, or disturbed adjustment is a result of emotional factors, brain damage, or both, they can learn, their behavior can be modified, and they can live again outside of the hospital.

## SUMMARY AND CONCLUSIONS

A treatment program called "Attitude Therapy" and defined as "a procedure or process utilizing psychological principles to effect desired behavioral changes by structuring an environment in which a variety of consistently and systematically applied attitudes and techniques will reinforce adaptive behavior and extinguish maladaptive behavior," has been described. Underlying assumptions are that the maladaptive behavior to be changed has been learned and that it can be modified through understanding the underlying dynamics and the application of learning theory principles of reward and punishment. Maladaptive behavioral patterns are identified; and special, but as societylike as possible, therapeutic environments are structured in which new learning can be facilitated.

The crucial question is, "Is this psychodynamic-behavioral model an effective treatment model?" Extensive research must be done to answer this question. The present evidence for its efficacy, other than subjective evaluations by the staff, patients, families, and a few hundred professional visitors who have observed the program, and the preliminary findings from the research on the AD program, are the following changes that have occurred since this program was begun formally approximately five years ago: (1) The number of patients discharged increased from 577 in fiscal year (FY) 1962 to 970 in FY 1963 and to 1226 in FY 1964, representing an increase of 68% and 112%, respectively. This was accomplished without a significant increase in the readmission rate or the number of employees; (2) the number of patients awaiting admission decreased from a high of approximately 130 to essentially none at present; (3) the use of drugs has significantly decreased during this period: during FY 1967 the cost of drugs per patient was only 82% of what it had been three years earlier; and (4) the mean length of hospitalization was reduced from 91 months in FY 1962 to 57 months in FY 1968. Initially 47% of our patients had been hospitalized five years or longer; that percentage now has dropped to 25%.

One might argue that these measures are not adequate criteria for testing the effectiveness of any treatment program. Although this statement may be true, one cannot ignore the obvious economic benefits to the patient, his family, and society, much less the obviation of psychological trauma to the patient and his family produced by long-term custodial hospitalization.

## REFERENCES

1. Bockoven, J. S. *Moral treatment in American psychiatry.* New York: Springer, 1963.
2. Earle, P. History, description, and statistics of the Bloomingdale Asylum of the Insane. New York: Egberg, Hovey & King, Printers, 1849. In J. S. Bockoven, *Moral treatment in American psychiatry.* New York: Springer, 1963.
3. Folsom, J. C. Intensive hospital therapy of geriatric patients. In J. Masserman (Ed.), *Current psychiatric therapies.* Vol. 7. New York: Grune & Stratton, 1967.
4. Freud, S. (Collected papers on psychotherapy) In E. Jones (Ed.), *Collected papers.* Vol. 1. *Sigmund Freud.* London: The Hogarth Press and the Institute of Psycho-analysis, 1948. Pp. 249–263.
5. Menninger, K. A., Pruyser, P. W., & Mayman, M. *Manual for psychiatric case study.* (2nd ed.) New York: Grune & Stratton, 1962. P. 108.
6. Milby, J. B., Jr.; Stenmark, D. E.; & Horner, R. F. Modification of locomotive behavior in a severely disturbed psychotic. *Perceptual & Motor Skills,* 1967, **25,** 359–360.
7. Mitchell, R. A. Reality orientation for brain-damaged patients. *Staff Magazine,* May-June 1966.
8. Patterson, W. E., Jr.; Taulbee, E. S.; Folsom, J. C.; Horner, R. F.; & Wright, H. W. Comparison of two forms of milieu therapy in the treatment of depression, preliminary report. Paper presented at the meeting of the Thirteenth Annual Conference, Veterans Administration Cooperative Studies in Psychiatry, Denver, April 1968.
9. Taulbee, E. S. A behavioral approach to therapeutic structuring for acute and chronic patients. Paper presented at the meeting of the Central Office Conference of VA Psychologists, Chicago, May 1965.
10. Taulbee, E. S. A psychodynamic-behavioral model of therapeutic structuring. Paper presented at the meeting of the VA Psychiatry-Psychology Program, Chicago, May 1966.
11. Taulbee, Lucille. Nursing intervention for confusion of the elderly. *The Alabama Nurse,* 1968, **22,** 1–3.
12. Taulbee, Lucille R., & Folsom, J. C. Reality orientation for geriatric patients. *Hospital & Community Psychiatry,* May 1966, 133–135.
13. (The) Treatment Team. Attitude therapy and the team approach. *Mental Hospitals,* November 1965, 307–323.

Chapter 7

# Group Behavior Therapy
# with Offenders

## FREDERICK C. THORNE

Frederick C. Thorne: b. 1909, New York, New York.
A.B., 1930, A.M., 1931, Ph.D., 1934, in psychology, Columbia University.
M.D., Cornell University, 1938.
Adjunct Professor of Psychology, University of Miami, 1965–date. Assistant
Professor of Psychiatry, University of Vermont, 1939–1953. Director
Brandon (Vermont) State School, 1939–1947. Editor and Publisher,
*Journal of Clinical Psychology*, 1945–date.
Books: *Psychological Case Handling*, 2 vols. (1968). *Integrative Psychology*
(1967). *Tutorial Counseling (How to be Psychologically Healthy)*
(1965). *Clinical Judgement* (1961). *Personality* (1961). *Principles of
Psychological Examining* (1961). *Principles of Personality Counseling*
(1950).
Articles: Over one hundred articles on clinical psychology. The following
articles represent the latest development of the system of integrative
psychology and the nature of psychological states: The structure of integrative psychology. *J. Clin. Psychol.*, 1967, **23**, 3-11. Theory of the
psychological state. *J. Clin. Psychol.*, 1966, **22**, 127–135. The etiological
equation. *J. Clin. Psychol.*, 1967, **23.** Diagnosis and nomenclature of
psychological states. *J. Clin. Psychol.*, 1964, **20**, 3-60. An operational
approach to the diagnosis of levels of personality integration or
psychopathology. *J. Clin. Psychol.* 1959, **15**, 255–259.

## PROBLEM

To conduct behavior therapy with large groups on different wards of
the Dannemora State Hospital (DSH), Dannemora, New York, in relation to specific aspects of criminality and adjustment to prison life.
Selected problems of the modification of criminal attitudes and adjustment to prison life will be made the topic of group behavior therapy
sessions directed toward reconditioning large groups of inmates simultaneously.

190

## PILOT STUDY

The therapeutic community of Ward 10 at DSH was selected for pilot experiments with group behavior therapy which was begun on September 1, 1967. Ward 10 had been organized as a therapeutic community in April 1967. In addition to an intensive program of recreational and occupational therapy, the basic pattern of the therapeutic community consisted of two group meetings held daily five days per week.

The morning conference (9:30 to 10:30 A.M.) was devoted to discussions limited to personal problems led by the president of the therapeutic community. Individual members of the group were encouraged to discuss any personal problems relating to mental health, community adjustment, and prison life. The other patient members of the therapeutic community discussed the matters at question with minimal participation of DSH staff members, who replied only to direct questions.

The afternoon conference on Ward 10 was limited to discussing matters of ward administration and inmate government. The patients were encouraged to regulate their own affairs by the democratic process within the limits of prison regulations and security.

## DESIGN OF GROUP BEHAVIOR THERAPY

The behavior therapist attended as many of the Ward 10 morning conferences as possible in order to (a) discover the nature of problems currently bothering the patients and (b) diagnose pathological or erroneous ideas and attitudes leading to personal or social maladjustment. Although the Ward 10 inmate group contained individuals with sufficient psychological knowledge to make sound contributions to the group discussions of personal problems, abundant evidence of misinformation, unhealthy attitudes, and personal maladjustments continued to become apparent during successive morning conferences.

Observations of individual patients and of typical patient interactions provided a rich source of psychiatric diagnostic information to supplement the mental status examinations of patients. In many instances, the actual dynamics of personal and interpersonal maladjustments were enacted vividly during the ward conferences, and this information was utilized to plan the topics for the afternoon behavior therapy sessions.

The general plan was developed to utilize the afternoon behavior therapy sessions to deal with clinically important problems uncovered in the Ward 10 morning conferences. The interrelatedness of the topics of the afternoon sessions with the problems uncovered during the morning sessions provided not only a natural continuity but also an immediate modification of unhealthy attitudes and states.

## RATIONALE OF BEHAVIOR THERAPY PLAN

Following the standard pattern of behavior therapy, the general program is to reinforce healthy responses while extinguishing unhealthy responses. Typically, this is accomplished in a series of steps as follows:

1. Identification of healthy and unhealthy response patterns. This may be accomplished (a) theoretically by outlining positive or negative behaviors in lecture form or (b) practically by commenting on various behaviors as they are emitted.

2. Operant conditioning. Positive responses are reinforced as they are emitted by patients, whereas negative responses are ignored or discouraged.

3. Reciprocal inhibition. A progressive desensitization of entire hierarchies of anxiety- or anger-producing stimuli is accomplished by progressively introducing and approaching central problems. Attention is given to approaching critical issues gradually under conditions of relaxation and decreased threat.

4. Selective positive reinforcement or negative punishment. The therapist establishes the pattern which presumably is adopted by the group of the selective reinforcement or punishment of positive and negative behaviors. This involves maximizing the positive and minimizing the negative. In all instances, the therapist indicates the guidelines and limits for what is to be considered acceptable and healthy.

5. Reality-oriented therapy. The general goal is to bring the patients into closer contact with reality by (a) indicating what reality is, (b) indentifying and rejecting unrealistic attitudes, and (c) indicating the realistic solution of all problems.

6. Alternative solutions to problems. Alternative new responses not formerly included in the inmates' experiences are suggested by the therapist who indicates their advantages and disadvantages.

7. Task-oriented therapy. Inmates are encouraged to solve former problems in new ways. Specific assignments are made to practice new solutions.

The full elaboration of the theoretical rationale for the directive counseling involved in group behavior therapy is outlined in the text-book of tutorial counseling by Thorne (1). This system is based on an extensive review of the entire mental hygiene literature, and it reflects the most up-to-date psychological knowledge available at the time of publication. This viewpoint of group behavior therapy is offered tenta-tively and permissively, with the admonition that it may not be valid or indicated in any particular case even though it represents the con-sensus of scientific opinion available at this time.

The research design calls for validating the method of group be-havior therapy by the use of (a) standard psychological testing includ-ing the Minnesota Multiphasic Personality Inventory (MMPI) and projective tests, (b) direct observations of ward behavior and other indices of community adjustment, and (c) a battery of special tests involving the Integration Level Test Series designed to evaluate spe-cifically many of the topics dealt with in this approach to behavior therapy.

## GROUP BEHAVIOR THERAPY SESSION #1

*Problem:* To identify and modify criminalistic self-concepts.

Many felons openly admit and subscribe to criminalistic self-concepts. The opportunity to discuss this idea came up in a ward meet-ing where one patient openly referred to himself as a "killer" and several other inmates identified themselves as habitual criminals.

*Strategy and Tactics:* To elicit overt statements about self-concepts so that their nature can be identified, defined, and discussed. The role of the self-concept in organizing integration is explained, along with the differences between the actual, objective, and ideal self-concepts.

The importance of the self-concept as the central "core" of the self is explained. Discrepancies between the actual and ideal self-concepts are explained and illustrated. The difference between "authenticity" and "phoniness" is illustrated.

| *Tasks* | *Rationale* |
|---|---|
| 1. "Who are You?" test. Patient is asked to answer this question three times. | 1. Often this question elicits ad-missions of criminalistic self-con-cepts. Some openly admit regarding themselves as convicts, felons, "killers", etc. |

2. The members of the ward meeting were asked how many regarded themselves as criminals.

2. Several admitted regarding themselves as criminals, and this admission gave evidence concerning the reality of the problem.

3. The members of the ward meeting were asked how many regarded themselves as "good citizens."

3. Many felons at least give lip service to being good citizens. This is an entering wedge.

4. The group members were asked how many of them ideally would like to be good citizens even admitting that they had been less than this in the past.

4. An attempt was made to call attention to the goal of achieving something closer to ideal self-status via more positive self-concepts.

5. The group was asked how many members thought some rehabilitation was actually possible, i.e., how many thought there was any possibility of changing behavior in more healthy directions.

5. An attempt is made to establish at least the possibility that change for the better can be accomplished.

## Group Behavior Therapy Session #2

*Problem:* To operationally define and catalyze more-realistic self-concepts and evaluations.

Many felons seem to have no understanding of the nature of positive self-concepts or of the nature of mental health. They constantly express criminalistic credos and openly adhere to the "prison ethic." Such overt verbal expressions can be utilized to illustrate the issues involved. For example, one inmate openly boasted about and advocated a life of crime.

*Strategy and Tactics:* To identify and expose criminalistic concepts whenever they are expressed, so that their nature and implications can be openly discussed and negatively reinforced.

### Tasks

1. Explain the nature and differences between "strong" and "weak" self-concepts.

2. Compare strong and weak self-concepts:

### Rationale

1. Explain the self-concept as the "backbone" of the mind, as the supporting structure of mental life.

2. State the basic cornerstones of mental health in simple operational

| *Strong* | *Weak* |
|---|---|
| Intelligent | Stupid, dumb |
| Healthy | Sick |
| Mature | Immature |
| Strong | Weak |
| Attractive | Unattractive |
| Well-liked | Disliked |
| Sexually attractive | Sexually unattractive |
| Good role player | Poor role player |
| Popular | Unpopular |

terms that every patient can understand. Examples can be given as to what constitutes intelligent, healthy, mature, strong behavior in any situation.

3. Ask each patient what he would really like to be, i.e., strong or weak, etc.

3. Emphasize that every person has a basic choice concerning what he can be.

4. Confront each patient with the importance of deciding what kind of a person he wants to be in relation to the ideal self.

4. The patient is confronted with the direct choice of to be or not to be healthy, mature, strong, etc. To be or not to be a good citizen as compared to being a criminal.

5. Emphasize that mental health depends upon the strength of the self-concept and ego structure.

5. An attempt is made to motivate the patient to want to be a strong person.

6. Emphasize the relation between self liking or dislike and like or dislike for others.

6. Patient must understand relation between self attitudes and social adjustment.

GROUP BEHAVIOR THERAPY SESSION #3

*Problem:* The search for self-consistency.

Most criminals constantly show great inconsistency between professed intentions of good behavior and actual delinquent behaviors. In the ward meetings, patients frequently relate life experiences illustrating the breakdown of good intentions and the patients cannot explain these lapses from grace. Our practice is to stimulate detailed investigation of what happened and what went wrong in such episodes.

*Strategy and Tactics:* Self-consistency is defined in terms of basic needs for unification and integration. Self-consistency is a positive concept underlying conflict-avoidance and resolution. Loss of self-consistency results in conflict and disablement. The person must decide what he wants to be (ideal self) and then strive self-consistently to attain it. The basic goal is to maximize self-consistency and avoid conflict.

| *Tasks* | *Rationale* |
|---|---|
| 1. Identify instances of lack of self-consistency. Cite examples. | 1. Make patients aware of areas of inconsistency. |
|   a. Cite discrepancy between professed intentions and actions. |   a. Give actual, realistic operational examples of how to get into trouble. |
|   b. Cite inconsistency between affect and reason. |   b. Illustrate incompatibility of love and hate. |
| 2. Confront patient with examples of lack of consistency. | 2. Select suitable examples for therapeutic tasks. |
| 3. Demonstrate inconsistency as the cause of conflicts. | 3. Analyze actual ward happenings to illustrate the dynamics of inconsistency. |
|   a. Cite the "prison ethic" as a cause of conflict. | |
|   b. Illustrate the conflictual results of the "we–they" dichotomy between inmates and officers. | |
| 4. Differentiate the various alternatives in specific situations. | 4. Confront the inmates with "to be or not to be" consistent in specific situations. |
| 5. Assign tasks of being self-consistent. | 5. "Fish or cut bait." Either be true to what is professed or drop it. |
| 6. Attempt constantly to upgrade self-concepts in the direction of higher consistency. | 6. The endless struggle for higher self-consistency. |

GROUP BEHAVIOR THERAPY SESSION #4

*Problem:* In presenting their personal problems, felons admit recurrently their inability to do what they know is right. In the daily ward sessions devoted to personal problems, the patients produce countless illustrations of inability to control the self. Our practice is to analyse and discuss these examples in detail to discover the reasons for failure.

*Strategy and Tactics:* To encourage the progressive acquisition of higher levels of controls. Self-control is operationally defined in terms of the learning of specific control skills. Controls are not innate but must be learned.

The level of integration which man can achieve is a function of the levels of controls acquired. Positive mental health depends upon acquiring increasingly complex levels of control throughout life.

All mental illness involves some type of loss of control. Disintegrations involve progressive breakdown of controls. Loss of control is the one common symptom of all mental disorders.

| *Tasks* | *Rationale* |
|---|---|
| 1. Evaluate and identify areas of effective control vs. loss of control. | 1. Each person must understand the magnitude of problems of control, and particularly his own control status. |
| a. Cite examples of loss of control from ward behaviors. | |
| b. Differentiate areas of absent or defective control. | Everyday ward events such as too much noise, lack of grooming, uncleanliness, cursing and swearing, etc. are cited as examples of loss of control. |
| 2. Describe operationally the acquisition of controls: | 2. Control cannot be achieved through exhortation but only through detailed operational analysis of the steps necessary to master any type of control and following through until controls are attained. |
| a. Discriminate areas where controls are to be learned. | |
| b. Perceive various alternatives of possible actions and controls. | |
| c. Achieve adequate verbal representation of control steps. | |
| d. Teach adequate self-prompting. | |
| e. Provide practice opportunities. | |
| f. Achieve overlearning. | |
| g. Provide feedback and incentive. | |
| 3. Assign specific tasks in learning controls. | 3. This program can be adapted to fit the needs of individual wards and patients, starting with the most obvious deficiencies and gradually working through until desired goals are achieved. |
| a. Program the steps of acquiring controls. | |
| b. Institute training sessions one at a time until controls are achieved. | |

## Group Behavior Therapy Session #5

*Problem:* To influence attitudes toward work and the self-concept of being a good worker.

Many felons report a completely ineffectual work history, never having held a job and never having learned to work. Many felons refuse to accept work assignments, complaining that the State sent them to prison and why should they work? Such cases disrupt institutional work programs and exert an undesirable influence on others.

*Strategy and Tactics:* To stimulate interest and motivation for work. Work ability is one of the most important criteria of mental health. The poor worker is the last to be hired and the first to be fired.

Breakdown of work habits may be one of the first signs of mental disorder. Conversely, one of the first signs of returning mental health is the ability to work well. Productivity is an index of mental health.

| *Tasks* | *Rationale* |
|---|---|
| 1. Evaluate self-concepts relating to worker roles, i.e., "What role does work play in your life?" | 1. Motivation for work usually depends upon what the person expects to get out of it. |
| a. Discuss prisoner disinclination to work, e.g., "The State put me here; now it can take care of me." | Strong self-concepts usually include the goal of being a good worker. |
| b. Investigate and analyze specific examples of refusal to work. Question nonworkers in the meetings as to why they do not work. | The inadequate person avoids work as a possible source of further failure and this avoidance leads to further dependency states. |
| 2. Discuss work and self-actualization. | 2. Self-actualization depends basically upon productivity. |
| a. Interpret vegetative living as living death. | Reward must be earned. |
| b. To work is to feel alive and worthy. | Anything but truly earned status is phony. |
| 3. Differentiate unhealthy attitudes towards work, i.e., | 3. Most vocationally disabled persons express unhealthy work attitudes. The first step in rehabilitation is to instill more positive work attitudes. |
| a. The work rut is unhealthy. | |
| b. Work is boring. | |
| c. Only the stupid work. | |
| d. The bosses oppress workers. | |

4. Assign tasks to do unpleasant or menial work without protest.

    a. All inmates to do all kinds of work without protesting.
    b. Provide rewards for work well done.

4. Even the most menial work is considered constructive in leaving the world a better place.

### GROUP BEHAVIOR THERAPY SESSION #6

*Problem:* To desensitize anxiety and panic reactions incident to imprisonment.

Many convicted felons react to their first contacts with a maximum security prison or hospital for the criminally insane with extreme anxiety or even psychotic decompensation. For example, an inmate reported in ward meetings that he felt he would become violently insane if he were confined under such conditions any longer. He demanded to be released to preserve his mental health.

*Strategy and Tactics:* Conditioning and desensitization to extreme anxiety and panic. (a) To condition the patient to tolerate anxiety without panicking. (b) To uncover causes of fear and anxiety, i.e., homosexual threat. (c) To reduce anxiety by reducing threats to integration and personal security. (d) To utilize success experiences as the natural antidotes to anxiety.

| *Tasks* | *Rationale* |
|---|---|
| 1. To catalyze the verbal expressions of fears and anxieties. | 1. Get fears and anxieties out in the open. |
|     a. Accept, reflect, and clarify fears and anxieties as normal. |     a. Desensitization. |
|     b. Stimulate catharsis and abreaction. |     b. Bleed off tensions. |
| 2. Analyze causes of anxiety, preferably by getting the patients to expose their own reactions. | 2. Attacking etiologic causes. |
|     a. The prison situation. Fears of the institution, custodial officers, or other inmates. | |
|     b. Fears of rejection and censure. | |
|     c. Worries about home, loved ones, separation, etc. | |

d. Imminent breakdown of defenses.

3. Diagnose interpersonal causes of anxiety.

3. Break up neurotic circular interpersonal reactions.

4. Assign tasks to modify neurotic reactions.

4. Systematic reconditioning.

    a. Removing neurotic secondary gains.
    b. Reciprocal inhibition therapy.
    c. Learning to tolerate anxiety without panicking.
    d. Actively confronting anxiety-stimulating situations.

## GROUP BEHAVIOR THERAPY SESSION #7

*Problem:* Understanding and coping with hostility and violence.

Ward rules require that all episodes of quarreling, fighting, or violence be brought before the ward meetings for full discussion of events and causes. This discussion provides a mechanism whereby disagreements and resentments may be brought out into the open and resolved amicably by the ward government without need for recourse to the officer staff.

*Strategy and Tactics:* The psychology of anger, hate, and aggression is explained in detail, particularly the frustration-hostility-aggression hypothesis which postulates thwarting or restriction of bodily movement as the unconditioned stimulus to anger.

The epidemiology of hate is interpreted in terms of hate as a psychological virus involving all who come in contact with it. Hate usually involves primitive, affectively determined thinking, i.e., the either-or dichotomy. Distrust and suspicion are usually due to lack of acquaintance and understanding.

| *Tasks* | *Rationale* |
|---|---|
| 1. Accept and reflect verbal expressions of anger and hate. | 1. Get hate into the open where it can be modified therapeutically. |
|     a. Anger toward the self.<br>    b. Toward other inmates.<br>    c. Toward authority. |     Much hostility stems from self-hate. |

2. Attempt to find some resolution for legitimate causes of frustration.

    a. Allow legitimate griping.
    b. Remove needless irritations.

3. Interpret and clarify the causes of frustration and anger. Analyze specific examples in ward life.

    a. Suicide as self-hate.
    b. Study causes of fights.

4. Explain the psychology of ambivalence.

    a. Situational examples.
    b. How to handle ambivalence.

5. Tasks to modify anger and hostility.

    a. Arguing without injuring.
    b. Accepting limits.
    c. The Yablonsky technique.

2. Minimize inevitable causes of frustration in the prison environment.

3. Interpret anger as a natural reaction to frustration in life. Clarify its dynamics to provide better insight.

4. Explain the natural polarity of emotions, that no one can expect to be universally liked.

## GROUP BEHAVIOR THERAPY SESSION #8

*Problem:* Coping with teasing and verbal aggression.

    Hostility and aggression exist at high levels in every correctional institution. Each new inmate is tested out at the time of his admission to determine his vulnerability and position in the "pecking order."

    Verbal aggression involves name-calling, derogatory comments, and other psychological attacks upon the ego. Physical aggression includes assault and invitations to fight.

    Institutional troublemakers keep the pot boiling by stirring up controversy, inciting rebellion, taunting, and otherwise seeking to "get the goat" of vulnerable persons.

*Strategy and Tactics:* To teach inmates how to cope with aggression by ignoring it or channeling it into harmless channels.

| *Tasks* | *Rationale* |
| --- | --- |
| 1. Discuss the psychology of name-calling. | 1. Interpret as the child in the person stimulating the child in his victim. |

a. Problems of being called a "fag," "pervert," "queer," etc.
b. Problems of being called a "punk," "fink," etc.
c. Problems of being called a "stoolie," "squealer," etc.

Childish taunting: "Yah, yah, Yah. I'm better than you."

2. Ignoring name-calling or aggression.

2. No defense is often the best defense.

a. "So what?" Refusing to react.
b. "Pick on somebody your own size." Deflecting.
c. Avoid such situations. Isolation.

3. Get the aggressor talking instead of fighting.

3. Bleed off aggression non-directively.

a. "Why pick on me?"
b. "What have you got against me?"
c. "What have I done to you?"

4. Appeal to peers for protection.

5. Appeal to authorities for protection.

4. and 5. Under normal social conditions, peers and authorities do not permit continued aggression.

6. Joke and take it good naturedly.


## GROUP BEHAVIOR THERAPY SESSION #9

*Problem:* The control and sublimation of sexual drives.

Research studies indicate that only the drives of thirst and hunger involve unalterable instinctual needs which can be satisfied only by water and food.

Cross-cultural research indicates (a) that the sex drive may be successfully sublimated under many conditions, such as the priesthood, and (b) that patterns of sexual expression are not instinctive but are acquired through learning.

Great individual differences exist in levels of control over sexuality and in the patterns of its expression. Mental health does not inevitably depend upon full expression of sexuality but rather depends upon the patterns of its channeling.

*Strategy and Tactics:* To provide insight into the nature of sexuality and the methods for controlling it.

| *Tasks* | *Rationale* |
|---|---|
| 1. Facilitating more frank verbal expression of sexual problems. | 1. Total repression tends to be unhealthy and blocks insight. |
| 2. Correcting misconceptions and invalid ideas about sexuality.<br><br>3. Structuring valid concepts and expectations concerning sex. | 2 & 3. The possibility of controlling sexuality depends largely upon acquiring self-concepts of moderation and that some control is possible. |
| 4. Indicating the limits of what is socially permissible and acceptable.<br><br>  a. Channeling auto-eroticism.<br>  b. Limiting homo-eroticism. | 4. The prime limitations are against becoming a social nuisance or pathologically seductive.<br>    Masturbation in private considered acceptable. |
| 5. Correcting misperceptions of sexual realities. | 5. Sexuality usually healthy and satisfying only when properly accomplished with due regard for realities of the situation. |
| 6. Clinical analysis of episodes of sexual delinquency. | 6. Operational analysis of etiology. |
| 7. Intensive training in observing social proprieties relating to sexuality. | |

## GROUP BEHAVIOR THERAPY SESSION #10

*Problem:* To clarify problems of developmental sexual adjustments.

Among felons with a high incidence of sex offenses, it is inevitable that many unresolved sexual problems exist. This is evidenced by the number of questions about sex which come up in ward conferences.

Much misinformation and error exists in the area of sex behavior and this needs to be brought out into the open and clarified.

Clinically, it is important to stimulate healthy discussions of sexuality under controlled conditions.

*Strategy and Tactics:* To provide continuing sex education in relation to questions and issues brought out by inmates.

| *Tasks* | *Rationale* |
|---|---|
| 1. To clarify the normality of sex behaviors. | 1. Many patients are very anxious over deviant impulses and require reassurance as to normality. |
| a. Explanation of incest dreams.<br>b. Normality of masturbation.<br>c. Changing attitudes toward homosexuality. | A common patient question concerns the normality of deviant impulses such as incest. |
| 2. Explanation of mechanisms of normal psychosexual development.<br><br>a. Auto-erotic stage.<br>b. Homo-erotic stage.<br>c. Heterosexual stage. | 2. Explanation of aberrations of psychosexual development in terms of the mechanisms of regression and fixation. |
| 3. Explanation of the neural mechanisms of sex drive.<br><br>a. The rise of sexual excitement with seminal vesicle tension.<br>b. Nocturnal emissions. | 3. Explanation as a normal physiological function which must secure outlet for tension. |
| 4. Explanation of control mechanisms to cope with sexual impulses. | 4. Control mechanisms must be learned and practiced until functional. |
| 5. Discussion of normal modes of outlet. | |

## GROUP BEHAVIOR THERAPY SESSION #11

*Problem:* Indoctrination with nondirective methods of human relations.

Authoritarianism and judgmentalism tend to stimulate resentment and hostility. Hostile-aggressive persons stimulate reactions of frustration and counteraggression. The problem is how to break up vicious circles of hostility and aggression.

Nondirective methods provide powerful tactics in avoiding unproductive arguments and strife.

*Strategy and Tactics:* To improve human relations and avoid needless strife by utilizing nondirective methods to circumvent neurotic chain reactions involving hostility and aggression. This provides a new pattern of psychological defense mechanisms.

| *Tasks* | *Rationale* |
|---|---|
| 1. Define and illustrate the non-directive methods of acceptance, reflection, and clarification. | 1. Recognize and react primarily to the affective content of interpersonal communications. |
| 2. Identify and bleed off the emotional charge underlying hostile reactions. | 2. Recognize that it is impossible to win emotionally charged arguments. |
| a. "You feel . . . angry over what I did."<br>b. "You feel . . . that I did wrong." | React to the affective content of what is said. |
| 3. Redirect or shunt aside all hostile attacks. | 3. Interpersonal conflict may be avoided by refusing to become involved. |
| a. "Thank you for telling me how you feel."<br>b. "You feel I should have done differently?" | Refuse to react seriously. |
| 4. Recognize the validity of factors on both sides of the argument. | 4. Acknowledging the possibility that different viewpoints and more than one solution may satisfy the opponent and avoid conflict. |
| a. "You may be right."<br>b. "Thank you for calling this to my attention." | |
| 5. Prevent or break up neurotic affective interactions by refusing to become involved. | 5. Recognize that the other person is just looking for trouble and do not cooperate by joining in a quarrel. |
| a. The stronger person must refuse to become involved.<br>b. The stronger person can terminate a potential argument by refusing to get involved. | |

## GROUP BEHAVIOR THERAPY SESSION #12

*Problem:* To modify and undercut paranoid ideation and projection mechanisms.

Paranoid behavior constitutes one of the most common problems uncovered in ward meetings, which provide a laboratory situation for manipulating paranoid ideation and actions directly as they appear. Paranoid ideation characterizes many delinquents and must be dealt with effectively to effect rehabilitation.

*Strategy and Tactics:* Paranoid ideation and projections are never healthy. They may be undercut by improving the patient's contacts with reality and by interpreting the insecurities and guilts underlying projections of suspiciousness, hostility, and negative emotions.

All delusional ideas should be promptly identified, analyzed, and interpreted as to their projective significance.

| *Tasks* | *Rationale* |
|---|---|
| 1. Encourage frank, open expression of emotional conflicts, anxiety, and guilt. | 1. The best defense is no defense. Admit error and guilt immediately, and strive to make up for it. |
|   a. Admit inadequacies frankly.<br>  b. Do not rationalize or defend.<br>  c. Accept emotions and conflicts. | |
| 2. Cite examples of projection mechanisms, preferably as they become evident in ward life. | 2. Insight into the operation of projective mechanisms tends to undercut their effectiveness. |
|   a. Interpret suspiciousness.<br>  b. Identify paranoid ideation whenever it occurs. | |
| 3. Assign tasks of never taking paranoid ideas seriously. | 3. Corrective handling and neutralization of paranoid ideas at their inception tends to prevent the development and spread of systematized delusions. |
|   a. Correct all paranoid ideation as it occurs.<br>  b. Never act out the implications of paranoid ideas. Forget it!<br>  c. Reject considerations of sibling rivalry, favoritism, jealousy, feeling sorry for one's self, etc., whenever they appear. | |
| 4. Institute ward rule that paranoid patients should not expect consideration for discharge as long as such ideation is active. | |

GROUP BEHAVIOR THERAPY SESSION #13

*Problem:* To explain the usages of basic medications to inmates and to discuss the applications of individual medications to inmates who ask for information.

In the private practice of medicine, the usual practice is to outline the usages of medication to patients who request such information.

In the private practice of medication, continuing attention is given to adjusting individual medications to maximum advantage. This includes listening to patient complaints about medication, with the modification of dosages to maximum indications.

*Strategy and Tactics:* To clarify and quiet down patient dissatisfaction with medication programs. The patients believe that no one can be discharged from DSH while on medication. They have been told that Clinton Prison refuses to accept patients who are on medication, hence they are all trying to get off medication in order to be considered for staff.

| *Tasks* | *Rationale* |
|---|---|
| 1. To explain basic usages of psychiatric drugs.<br><br>   a. Stimulants.<br>   b. Sedatives and depressants.<br>   c. Ataractics.<br>   d. Specific drugs. | 1. Patient cooperation and insight into the purposes of medication is necessary for maximum effects.<br><br>Many patients admittedly are refusing or destroying drugs. |
| 2. To individualize drug prescription by giving daily opportunity to patients to report their reactions. | 2. Daily attention to medication requirements reassures patients of continuing attention and concern for individual problems. |
| 3. To provide opportunity for patients to make complaints and recommendations concerning medication. | 3. Repeated catharsis concerning patient anxieties about medication should bleed off conflict and resentment. |
| 4. To clarify misinformation and policies concerning medication in relation to discharge. | 4. If patients believe that medication hinders discharge, their cooperation with medication programs cannot be obtained. This issue should be clarified. |

## GROUP BEHAVIOR THERAPY SESSION #14

*Problem:* To establish reasonable goals and limits for self-regulation in the ward therapeutic community. Some working agreements are necessary to compromise inmate needs for self-regulation and freedom with institutional needs for maintenance of security and authority.

Mutual misunderstandings have arisen between staff and inmates in part because clear statements of policy and objectives have not been understood by all concerned.

The general goal is to encourage attitudes of hope and constructive change within the limits of what is possible and practical.

*Strategy:* To establish priorities of all factors that need to be considered from the viewpoints of both institution and inmates.

*General Principles:*

1. Hospital administration is now organized in the team approach in which the professional and security staff work in cooperation. Successful hospital operation depends on the complete cooperation of all concerned.

2. In any maximum security prison, factors of security command the highest priority. Nothing can be allowed to threaten security.

3. Complete authority for general security administration must reside at all times in the chain of command in the hospital officer staff under the supervision of the security office.

   a. The charge officer is at all times responsible for the maintenance of security and authority on the ward, and his decisions as relayed through hospital officers must be respected at all times.

   b. Within the general supervision of the charge officer and his staff, the general goal of the ward community is to regulate inmate behavior, observing the limits of the ward rules. It is understood that hospital officers may intervene at any time in administering the ward, and particularly when law and order are threatened.

   c. Forcible restraint of violent inmates should be a last resort after both the inmate government and verbal persuasion have failed.

4. Once complete security has been achieved, then regular psychiatric, psychological, social work, occupational, and recreational activities will proceed under staff supervision. In all professional matters, the ward physician is the responsible authority.

5. All inmate requests, problems, recommendations, and gripes should be referred upward through the proper channels. These channels should be clearly understood.

6. In general, the level of inmate freedom will depend upon the degrees of good behavior and responsible conduct achieved.

## GROUP BEHAVIOR THERAPY SESSION #15

*Problem:* To clarify the proper dynamics of the democratic form of government utilizing a human relations workshop based on the events taking place in a disorderly and contentious ward conference.

One inmate pinned an insulting note disparaging the occupational therapy painting of another inmate. Inmate 2 became insulted and tore off the note, whereupon Inmate 1 replaced the note. After Inmate 2 tore off the note once more, Inmate 1 smeared the painting with fresh paint, ruining it. A physical altercation occurred for which both inmates were punished by the ward president who assigned work details. Inmate 2 did not accept the assignment, and a group of the inmates friendly to Inmate 2 challenged the president's application of ward rules, insisting upon a group vote. The ward conference became disorderly and contentious.

*Strategy and Tactics:* To review what took place in order to analyze it dynamically, indicating the psychology of the developing situation, and indicating other solutions whereby a more orderly solution could be reached.

| *Tasks* | *Rationale* |
|---|---|
| 1. Question the motivations whereby Inmate 1 disparaged and mutilated the picture. | 1. Inmate 1 interpreted as an attention-seeking paranoid who constantly needles people to stimulate controversy. |
| 2. Inmate 2 should have referred the episode to the ward government for solution. | 2. Inmate 2 reacted to the bait and lost his temper, taking the law into his own hands. |
| 3. Indicate how Inmate 2 became involved in illegal and unhealthy reactions. | 3. Inmate 1 deliberately started out to "get the goat" of Inmate 2. Inmate 2 should have avoided the bait. |
| 4. Inmates advised that they must respect the president's decisions within the duly adopted ward rules. | 4. Inmates who debate every decision or command, by attempting to vote new rules in every situation or to impeach the president are out of order according to accepted parliamentary tactics. |
| 5. Inmate 2 must accept the disciplinary action of the ward president since he became involved in an altercation prior to referring the issue to the ward governmnt. | 5. Inmate 2 must accept some guilt for not referring the incident to the proper authorities but instead attempting to take the law in his own hands. He also must submit to decisions of the ward president. |

## GROUP BEHAVIOR THERAPY SESSION #16

*Problem:* To structure the necessary conditions whereby an inmate may establish eligibility for a discharge conference. One of the central problems of prison life is to regain freedom at the earliest possible moment.

Unfortunately, many inmates plead to be given freedom without establishing their mental normality and psychological rehabilitation to the point where they could be considered eligible for a discharge conference.

Too many inmates use the regular ward conferences as devices for gaining more privileges rather than as a means to their own rehabilitation. Although the improvement of conditions of inmate living is an important consideration, psychological rehabilitation must remain the primary objective.

*Strategy and Tactics:* To establish a priority system for establishing the fact of psychological normality and readiness for discharge.

| *Tasks* | *Rationale* |
|---|---|
| 1. Cooperativeness with the therapeutic and rehabilitational program. | 1. Cooperation and rapport must be attained before therapy and rehabilitation can occur. |
| 2. Self-study. Each inmate should assume responsibility for trying to understand his own behavior and motivations. | 2. Each patient must drop his defenses and expose his deepest reactions and motivations to study. |
| 3. Insight is the important goal. | 3. Maximally effective contact with reality depends upon insight. |
| 4. Learning higher controls on all types of behaviors. | 4. Loss of control characterizes all mental disorders. |
| 5. Minimal social conformance. Group adjustment depends upon a minimum of cooperation with the limits established by society. | 5. Without the relinquishing of individuality, a realistic cooperation with law and order is necessary. |
| 6. Symptom removal. | 6. This step is usually a secondary gain after insight and controls are acquired. |

### GROUP BEHAVIOR THERAPY SESSION #17

*Problem:* Reinforcement of positive attitudes toward sobriety in relation to alcohol and drugs, and the explication of aversive therapy for addictive habits and attitudes.

The issue was raised in ward meeting by younger group members who questioned why they should not smoke marihuana and take "dope" in order to experience the alleged gratifications of psychedelic drug effects.

*Strategy and Tactics:* To replace the usual moralistic and judgmental exhortations against drug-taking by a realistic evaluation of the dangers and costs of ingesting potentially poisonous drugs even though these drugs have transient psychedelic effects. The basic argument is that the brain is man's most valuable asset which must be protected against the damaging effects of intoxicating drugs. All psychedelic drugs are defined as being potentially damaging and dangerous to health and personality development.

The basic appeal is to being consistent with a strong healthy self-concept.

| *Tasks* | *Rationale* |
|---|---|
| 1. Unimpaired mental functioning as the highest value. | 1. The very real dangers of brain damage and resulting incapacitation. |
| 2. Rational self-interest demands that a person not damage himself. | 2. Appeals to being "smart" enough to stay out of trouble. |
| 3. Authentic ego strength must be built upon positive self-actualization, i.e., to be real and not phony. | 3. Drug-induced euphoria is unreal, phony, not authentic, a snare and a delusion. |
| 4. The healthy person secures sensual gratification in healthy ways. | 4. Drug-induced emotional arousal is phony and transient. |
| 5. Eliciting personal testimonials of the costs of drinking and addiction. | 5. Progressive sociopathic character disintegration to pay for the habit. |
| 6. Challenge to the self-concept and self-consistency to achieve success the right way. | |

### GROUP BEHAVIOR THERAPY SESSION #18

*Problem:* Counteracting and undercutting the influence of the "prison ethic."

The question arose in group meeting as to how to maintain "honor" and self-respect when confronted with peer pressures to conform to the prison ethic. This is brought up frequently by new inmates who are challenged by the prison ethic to conform or be ostracized. The prison ethic is that every prisoner must be faithful to his peers. Every man has to prove himself or face retaliation by established inmate cliques who defend the prison ethic and require allegiance.

*Strategy and Tactics:* To break the hold of the prison ethic by challenging its logic and by removing its secondary gains. The general principle is that the jungle-rule ethic of "an eye for an eye" reflects personal immaturity and that conformance to the prison ethic only reinforces immaturity and criminality.

Conversely, the mature person is depicted as refusing to conform to jungle-rule games by developing resources for evading challenges and patiently developing higher level adaptive techniques.

| *Tasks* | *Rationale* |
|---|---|
| 1. Teach new techniques for avoiding jungle-rule interactions. | 1. Emphasize that higher adjustment techniques exist. |
| 2. Establish ward government rules rejecting the prison ethic and insisting upon democratic government. | 2. Create an atmosphere whereby the prison ethic is rejected and democratic government is accepted. |
| 3. Describe and identify the various games and tactics supporting the prison ethic and jungle rule. | 3. This may be approached in terms of the games people play. |
| a. "Eye-for-an-eye" tactics are rejected as mutually self-defeating. | a. Structure jungle rule as socially and personally immature and unrewarding. |
| b. The psychology of getting another person's "goat". | b. Ignore or bypass challenges as to being "chicken," etc. |
| c. Stress ways of maintaining noninvolvement in unhealthy games. | c. Do not react defensively; the best defense is no defense. |
| 4. Structure the "strong" solution as resisting the prison ethic rather than going along with it. | 4. The "strong" person does not submit to the prison ethic but thinks things out for himself. |
| 5. Deflect threatened aggression by laughing it off, reacting good-humoredly, avoiding displays of timidity and fear. | 5. The strong man backs off would-be aggressors by nonaggressive methods. |

## GROUP BEHAVIOR THERAPY SESSION #19

*Problem:* Inmate complaints of occasional harsh treatment and lack of understanding on part of hospital officers. Patient complains of not being treated like a human, of being cursed at, and of being denied privileges.

*Strategy and Tactics:* All patient complaints to be taken seriously, and patients allowed to ventilate resentments. The situation structured as a game, the objectives of which are to refrain from losing one's temper and fighting back and to increase frustration tolerance.

The patient is encouraged to view life realistically, to try not to be over-perfectionistic, to expect to encounter a certain amount of hostility and frustration, and to develop techniques for riding out the hostility rather than going to pieces.

| *Tasks* | *Rationale* |
|---|---|
| 1. Patient complains that he has the feeling that no one really cares about him, that the staff officers really think he is a dog, and that he senses the smell of death hanging over the infirmary. | 1. The reality of these existential feelings is accepted. Does the patient expect that everyone will like him? Does the patient expect all officers to be perfect? Should not the patient anticipate some hostility and lack of understanding? |
| 2. Patient complains of being given inconsistent orders from doctor and nurse. | 2. How to cope with inconsistent orders? Make the best of it? Go along with what cannot be changed. |
| 3. Patient expresses frustration that life is not perfect. Protests that things should not be run the way they are. | 3. Patient allowed to ventilate protests and complaints. Does he really think the world is ever perfect? |
| 4. Patient expresses hostilities and states that he feels like fighting back, to get back at the "scummy" officers who are after him. | 4. Alternative solutions to the problem are explored. The patient is encouraged to anticipate some hostility and not to let it panic him, to accept what cannot be changed, to joke and kid instead of fighting back. |
| 5. Patient expresses the idea that the only way he can keep his self-respect is to fight back. | 5. The best way to maintain self-respect is to maintain personal dignity at all times no matter what anyone else does. Act like a man and you will be treated like a man. |

## GROUP BEHAVIOR THERAPY SESSION #20

*Problem:* To increase understanding and communication between prisoners and hospital officers. One principle of the prison ethic is that criminals and authorities constitute two distinct classes who are natural enemies that must fight for survival.

One patient brought up the idea that the only way to get along in prison is to go along with the prison ethic and to identify at all times with the prisoners against authority represented by the guards. Another inmate expressed the idea that the only way to defend honor in prison was to support the other prisoners at all times, otherwise one would be called "yellow" and a "stoolie."

*Strategy and Tactics:* To install a new set of rules under the democratic system of ward government to supplant the prison ethic. Under the democratic system, prisoners and guards interact cooperatively rather than competitively, all working for the smooth operation of the system. Inmates are encouraged to defend and support self-government authority by reporting potential difficulties ahead of time.

| *Tasks* | *Rationale* |
|---|---|
| 1. During a ward meeting, an inmate spoke of the ward officers as being "rats" who should not be allowed to hold such jobs. Several other inmates applauded this statement. | 1. This outburst accepted and reflected nondirectively. Inmates asked to give reasons for such feelings which were gradually bled off. |
| 2. A patient contended that one could not get along in prison without accepting and following the prison ethic. | 2. The inmate was asked whether he thought the prison ethic was the only way to get along in the ward community. The group disagreed with him violently. |
| 3. A prisoner expressed the idea that his life was ruined anyway so he might just as well go along with the criminal class. | 3. This idea was reacted to nondirectively. However, it was suggested that if he wished parole, he should reconsider. |
| 4. A prisoner said he did not feel comfortable with the officers who he felt were keeping him in the hospital by spreading bad rumors about him. | 4. The inmate was asked which officers he objected to and what they had done to him. |

5. One ward member had the courage to go against the prison ethic and report other men engaged in homosexual activities by writing a note to the charge officer. When the other men discovered what he had done, they attempted to vote him off the ward, calling him a stoolie and threatening to beat him up.

5. The whole episode was brought up in ward meeting, discussed objectively as an example of how the situation should be handled democratically by free citizens. After angry protests had been ventilated against the informer, he was allowed to continue on the ward and his action approved.

## GROUP BEHAVIOR THERAPY SESSION #21

*Problem:* In ward meeting, a patient accused the medical staff and hospital officers with conspiring to keep him in the hospital by keeping him on medication, which "makes me sick" and otherwise making him look bad so he will not be eligible for discharge. He went on to explain his ideas that the staff was keeping patients in the hospital so that they could keep their jobs. Several other patients applauded this statement and indicated their agreement.

*Strategy and Tactics:* To identify paranoid ideation as such; to isolate the paranoid person from the rest of the group by demonstrating the pathologic nature of such thinking; to bring out the unhealthy nature of paranoid thinking at all times.

| *Tasks* | *Rationale* |
|---|---|
| 1. Patient is allowed to ventilate feelings of being persecuted and abused. | 1. Such ventilation is indicated to bleed off resentful feelings and to bring the exact nature of complaints out into the open. |
| 2. Patient asked to bring out specific complaints rather than make general charges. Patient claims that he is being kept on medication to keep him in the hospital ineligible for discharge. | 2. Vague or overgeneralized complaints are rejected and disregarded. Once specific issues are raised, their validity can be examined in detail. |
| 3. Patient is asked why he is on medication. This issue is also presented to the group as a whole. | 3. The group as a whole usually recognizes why the person is on medication, particularly when specific evidences of disturbances are brought up. |

4. Patient goes on to express resentment against the hospital as a whole, expressing blanket distrust of the staff.

4. Patient further demonstrating his delusional systems and general irrationality to the group. At this point, group pressures begin to peel away his supporters.

5. Patient asked frankly to tell what he holds against the therapist, to make specific complaints.

5. The rest of the group begins to perceive how unrealistic the paranoid attitudes are.

6. Therapist assumes a non-directive attitude, turning the initiative over to the group to straighten out one of their peers.

6. Several members of the group now state openly that the patient is "off the beam" and not thinking realistically. Group support for the delusional system is removed.

## GROUP BEHAVIOR THERAPY SESSION #22

*Problem:* To curtail and counteract the influence on the group of a sexually disturbed patient who constantly talks in the most obscene and perverted manner, attempting to influence younger patients in lewd manner, and otherwise disrupting group meetings with foul language and talk.

*Strategy and Tactics:* To neutralize the influence of the sexually disturbed patient, emphasizing the "sick" nature of his verbalizations, deflating the shock value of his asocial verbalizations, defusing his outrageous proposals to other patients, and generally reducing all secondary gains for such behavior by lack of reinforcement.

*Tasks*

*Rationale*

1. The patient spoke out loudly in the meeting, stating that all his troubles were caused by women, that all women were nothing but "cunts" good for nothing but "fucking."

1. No attempt made by the therapist to stem this outburst. The rest of the group was at first shocked, then curious to see what the therapist would do; when the therapist reacted passively, the group leader called the patient out of order.

2. The patient continued to talk in the most foul, obscene language. Described perverted acts which he claimed to have observed on the ward. Several of his followers were observed to be stimulated by and enjoying this performance.

2. The group as a whole manifested much ambivalence. The more healthy members rejected the whole performance as unhealthy while others cheered and whistled.

3. Therapist did not react to the content of what the patient was saying but instead opened the question to the group of why any one would talk in such a way in public. What is the motive?

3. The group quickly perceived the exhibitionistic and attention-gaining elements. The group decision was that such behavior transcended the limits of what is socially acceptable. Such behavior is ruled unacceptable in this group.

4. Therapist raised the question as to why the patient is in the hospital, and how he expects to be considered for discharge with such unresolved problems.

4. The group recognizes the existence of intense sexual conflicts and unresolved frustrations. Behavior labeled as "sick" by the group.

5. Group gradually ceases to react to this patient's verbalizations.

5. Removal of positive reinforcements gradually desensitizes the situation until the group ignores such outbursts.

## GROUP BEHAVIOR THERAPY SESSION #23

*Problem:* Handling protests against authority.

On an occasion when the ward was being observed by a group of visiting dignitaries, several members of the therapeutic community took this occasion to criticize the program and several staff members severely. The ward physician was criticized for never being available, and other staff was criticized for not carrying out promises.

*Strategy and Tactics:* To accept, reflect, and clarify frustration, resentment, and angry protests, and thereby to provide catharsis and abreaction on a systematic basis.

All patient protests are to be accepted at face value and taken seriously. All staff are advised to react passively and nondefensively. After working communication channels between staff and patients are functioning smoothly, the details of disagreements can be worked out by negotiation.

### Tasks

1. The staff is directed to react passively to direct criticism.

### Rationale

1. Recognizing high levels of patient insecurity and tendency to overreact.

2. Anger and hostility are accepted and reflected nondirectively until adequately bled off.

2. It may require relatively long periods of catharsis to bleed off long-sustained resentments.

3. The staff is instructed not to over-react to the patient's griping by "all-or-none" reactions of disgust and rejection.

3. Untrained staff members tend to overreact to vicissitudes of the therapeutic community program.

4. Temporary regressions or plateaus reflecting transient lack of progress of the program are to be disregarded.

4. Continuous sustained progress in the therapeutic community cannot be expected.

5. Normal griping is to be regarded as a healthy development and facilitated.

5. The program would not be working if no griping occurred.

## CLINICAL EXPERIENCE WITH GROUP BEHAVIOR THERAPY

Now in its third year of operation in intensive treatment therapeutic communities, the advantages and limitations of group behavior therapy have become established. Experience indicates the necessity for providing expert leadership for community therapeutic meetings, since with few exceptions, the patient population has not contained sufficient leadership potential to keep the meetings going. In the absence of professional leadership, which not only provides therapeutic guidance but also seems to reassure the community members to the effect that the hospital staff supports the activity from which more practical developments can be expected to derive, the meetings tend to bog down, community members do not feel sufficient trust and confidence to bring up personal problems, and the most frequent outcome is early adjournment because nothing productive develops.

This population of the criminally insane in many ways expresses needs for directive case handling. In contrast with college and upper class populations with higher resources of ability and experience, lower class, mentally disturbed felons rarely demonstrate the psychological insights and skills necessary to resolve serious psychiatric problems. If left relatively unsupervised, ward meetings frequently become dominated by more unstable and unhealthy community members who can quickly disintegrate group cohesion and structure by supporting undesirable goals and advocating destructive actions. Longer established therapeutic communities may have developed sufficient stability to withstand unhealthy developments by limiting or isolating the influence of disrupting members, but less well organized and less stable communities tend to disintegrate rapidly in the absence of firm professional leadership.

Perhaps the main contribution of professional leadership is to develop constructive goals and group interactions and to keep the program on the track in its purposes of behavior modification in healthy directions.

## PROGRAM INVOLVEMENT WITH ACTUAL GROUP PROBLEMS

Over three years of experience, a definite shift has occurred in the modus of planning the group behavior therapy session topics. At the start of the program, the group therapist developed a list of topics for discussion based on general mental hygiene principles utilizing a more formal presentation of lecture type. Some of these topics proved relevant, but too often they did not relate practically to actual community problems.

In the search for greater relevance, the group therapist developed a more spontaneous approach based on the solution of everyday problems of community living and ward management. The technique was developed of reviewing actual occurrences on the ward during the past week, devoting particular attention to interpersonal and situational problems stemming usually from the personal problems of individual ward members. This technique of relating the group behavior therapy topics to actual recent community problems tends to generate immediate interest and personal involvement of ward members who are now dealing with their own relevant affairs.

In actual practice, the ward personal problems meetings become workshops that contribute much to urgent issues of community management. In a hospital for the criminally insane, it is vitally necessary for inmate self-government to proceed consistently within the limits of institutional policy, i.e., inmate self-government must be kept constructive and positive in its operations and objectives. Inmate self-government cannot be allowed to become the locus of rebellion against authority or for the nefarious antisocial goals of individual felons. Only a trusted and effective professional leader can provide the subtle guidance and balance necessary for constructive operations.

Every therapeutic community eventually becomes involved with problems and issues concerning institutional management and common grievances. If kept in hand, cooperative relations can be maintained between the staff, which is under attack and therefore stimulated to defensiveness, and the inmates who are insatiable in advancing their status. The group therapist must have sufficient institutional status and personal stability to walk the tight rope in maintaining rapport both with institutional management and the patients. This balance usually can be accomplished if the therapist achieves a reputation for sincerity and meticulous fairness in mediating the best outcomes for all concerned.

## REFERENCE

1. Thorne, F. C. *Tutorial counseling (How to be psychologically healthy).* Brandon, Vt.: Clinical Psychology Publishing Co., 1965.

Chapter 8

# Therapy for Scrupulosity

## V. M. O'FLAHERTY, S.J.

V. M. O'Flaherty, S.J.: b. 1901, Dixon, Nebraska.
A.B., in philosophy, 1926, M.A., in cosmology, 1927, St. Louis University.
S.T.L., in theology, St. Mary's College, 1934. Ph.D., in canon law,
Gregoriana, Rome, Italy, 1937.
Lecturer, Marquette University: in medical ethics, School of Medicine,
1957–1968; in philosophy, 1936–1941, 1945–1957; in mathematics in
the College of Engineering, 1943–1944; in theology, College of Liberal
Arts, 1936–1956.
Member: Executive Boards of Medicine, Nursing, Liberal Arts; Curriculum
Committee of Medicine, Medical Technology, Physical Therapy, Nurs-
ing; Admissions Board, School of Medicine, Marquette University.
Student Counselor and Premedical Advisor. Representative,
Marquette University School of Medicine in the Academy of Religion
and Mental Health. Retreat Master, Missouri and Wisconsin Provinces.
Books: *Imagine That: A Handbook on Contemplation* (1971). *How to Make
Up Your Mind* (1969). *How to Cure Scruples* (1967).

## INTRODUCTION

Several remarks will orientate a reader to the relation of this article
to my book.[1] The book is directed to a counselor and his counselee. The
first chapters are concerned with the definition and description of a
scruple. The third chapter starts the directives for bringing about a
cure (p. 42). "First, the chief incidents about which the counselee is
scrupulous are listed. This corresponds to the list prepared in writing
by St. Ignatius for his three-day confession. Then, in Phase II, the
counselee becomes aware that, due to a disorderly emotion, he is
yielding to a temptation to engage in a futile argument with a doubt
about a sinless sin. When the counselee is convinced that a scruple is
a mental evil to be avoided, rather than the obligation he considered
it to be, the next phase will be to learn how to avoid the scruple by
turning attention to some distracting thought. This would be the last
phase, since refusal to pay attention to a scruple cures it; but, un-

---

[1] V. M. O'Flaherty, S. J. *How to cure scruples.* Milwaukee: Bruce, 1966.

**221**

fortunately, the counselee has formed the habit of scrupulosity. Habits are not usually broken by the first refusal to indulge them . . . there is a fourth phase during which the acquired appetite is gradually killed by starvation and the ability to turn to some distracting thought is strengthened."

The two "cases" studied in the book are St. Ignatius and Martin Luther. St. Ignatius has a descriptive definition of a scruple (p. 6). "After I have trodden upon a cross formed by two straws, or after I have thought, said, or done some other thing, there comes to me from 'without' a thought that I have sinned, and on the other hand it seems to me that I have not sinned; nevertheless I feel some uneasiness on the subject, inasmuch as I doubt and yet do not doubt. This is properly a scruple and temptation suggested by the enemy."

Martin Luther left no record of the incidents about which he was scrupulous, nor did he leave a formal definition of a scruple. The story of his struggle with scrupulosity centers around his failure to achieve a sense of justification by the use of indulgences, confession, and severe penances to atone for his doubtful sins. His heroic effort to assure himself of salvation by fervent acts of contrition serves as a witness to the futility of trying to remove a doubtful sin by accepting guilt and making atonement. If we were to frame a definition of scrupulosity from his experience it might be the following. A scruple is a situation in which doubt about sinfulness renders one helpless to avoid possible guilt and damnation to eternal punishment.

## THE ULTIMATE CAUSE OF A SCRUPLE

In the consideration of scrupulosity so far, we have asserted that it is caused by an errant emotion; we have described what happens during an attack; but we have not explained how the emotion is excited and why it is errant. Probing into the ultimate cause of a scruple can give a counselee the fundamental insight that will enable him to start a cure at the root of the difficulty.

St. Ignatius has an excellent explanation of the tendency to scrupulosity. We esteem his analysis highly because he had an astounding ability to acquire self-knowledge. He states simply that a scruple is due to an inclination found in devout people to go too far in the right direction, to be too cautious, too safe, too sure about pleasing God, too anxious to be certain that they have not sinned. The tendency is described as follows.

The second kind of scruple is for a time of no small advantage to a soul for it greatly purges and cleanses such a soul separating it far from all appearance of sin, according to that saying of St. Gregory, "It is the mark of good souls there to recognize fault where there is none."

The scrupulous reaction to avoid sin is best understood in its framework of a mean with two extremes. In the mean position, a person free of all deviant inclinations would see sin where sin exists and would not see sin where sin does not exist. The extremes are created because people have prejudices for and against sinning. To the left, one who wants to do something questionable will be reluctant to admit that what he wants to do is a sin. On the contrary, a person who dreads an offense against God will regard the mere appearance of sin as a possible offense against God. Moreover, these diverse tendencies are disposed to become stronger with indulgence each in its own direction. The two contrary tendencies and their mean are described by the Spiritual Exercises:

> The enemy observes very closely whether the conscience is dull or tender. If it is tender, he tries to make it more tender to an extreme degree, in order that he may the more easily trouble and overthrow it; e.g., if he sees that a soul does not consent to any sin either mortal or venial, nor even to the appearance of deliberate sin, then the enemy, since he cannot make it fall into what has the appearance of sin, contrives to make it judge that there is sin where there is not, as in some word or insignificant thought. If the conscience is dull, the enemy contrives to make it still more dull; e.g., if before it made no account of mortal sins; or if it did make some account of them, now he will contrive that it cares less or not at all about them.

## THE VERY BEGINNING OF A SCRUPLE

A person who is trying to avoid sin unwittingly sets up a necessary condition for a scruple by trying to decide that he did not sin in an incident. The effort to find proof that he did not sin is quite the opposite of trying to find proof that he did sin but, at first, he is not aware of the difference; much less does he realize that it is a temptation. Nevertheless a sincere soul prepares the way for a scruple if he tries to maintain a sense of justification by assuring himself that he did not sin in this incident, nor in that one, nor in the other. His method of clearing each item that comes before conscience of any taint of sin could be called a method of "elimination." No problem will occur if he can arrive at a conviction of certitude that each alleged sin was a false accusation. But, if his effort to prove that he did not sin in a particular incident ends in doubt, he can build the resulting, baffling situation into a scruple. The strength of the temptation to arouse a scruple will vary with the need he feels to remove the doubt about his guilt of sin in the incident.

The series of mental actions which occur during a scruple could be followed in slow motion with the following example. Suppose that a teenage girl became sexually aroused while reading a novel written for adults only. An account of an intimate amorous affair stays in her mind for several days after finishing the book. The scruple starts with the thought that she may have sinned in the incident. When she becomes defensive about her innocence, she cannot satisfy herself completely. If the attempt to "justify" herself is unsuccessful, she has a scruple. The intensity of the scruple will vary with the amount of time and effort she gives to finding arguments to prove her freedom from guilt.

An analysis of the ultimate cause of a scruple should start with a breakdown of the mental experience into the following successive parts.

A. There must be an incident; for instance, reading a racy novel.
B. The incident must have the appearance of sin. (Thus, if sin is not present in the lines, it might be found between the lines.)
C. An accusation that I sinned in the incident must come into the mind with enough emotional force to arouse alarming fright.
D. The accusation of sin must be followed by an effort to prove that no sin was committed.
E. The evidence that I did no sin in the incident must be unsatisfactory; argumentation must end in doubt.
F. On the other hand, reflection on the positive evidence of sinning is not convincing.
G. In the resultant ambiguity, I experience anxiety about my eternal salvation.
H. A false religious obligation, an emotional compulsion, arises to settle the doubt about my guilt.
I. The torturous thought that I cannot help sinning begins to haunt my mind.
J. An assurance from my confessor that no sin was committed fails to stifle my apprehension of guilt.
K. My duties and responsibilities start to be overlooked as I become more absorbed in settling my scruples.

L. Continuous examination of conscience brings me to a state of ex-
haustion which, in turn, is a handicap in settling my doubts about
sinning.

## TWO KINDS OF SCRUPLES

At this juncture, St. Ignatius distinguishes between two kinds of
scruples. This distinction clarifies still more the nature of a genuine
scruple. The distinction is made as follows. If one can find a proof
that an alleged sin was an error, the scruple was of the first type.
But if proof that the incident was not a sin ends in doubt, it was the
second type of scruple. The first type is described as follows.

> The name of scruple is frequently applied to what proceeds from
> our own judgment and liberty, that is to say, when I freely judge (an
> incident) to be a sin which is not a sin, as happens when anyone hav-
> ing accidently trodden upon a cross formed of straws decides of his
> own judgment that he has sinned. But this is strictly speaking, an er-
> roneous judgment and not a real scruple.

In particular, an indirect removal of a doubt must be classified as
a first-type scruple. Thus, if a counselee can settle his doubt with a
dictum, such as, a doubtful law does not bind; his scruple does not
end in doubt. To have a genuine scruple he should doubt about
whether the principle could be invoked. The genuine scruple has
doubts about doubts.

The occurrence of the second kind, the emotional type of scruple,
while using the method of elimination can be compared to the procedure of a mother who is trying to find out whether her seven sons have
been pilfering the cookie jar. She knows definitely that number five
is guilty; he did not get rid of the telltale crumbs. Numbers one, two,
and three are certainly innocent; since they were absent, they did
not have access. But numbers four, six, and seven offer only tenuous
evidence for either innocence or guilt. Considering these three, her
motherly solicitude is not aroused by numbers four and seven. But
number six is a born rascal; she cannot be sure that he is free of guilt;
she feels compelled to investigate his case; she would like to have clear
evidence that he did not steal cookies.

The nature of the emotion which causes the mother to be apprehensive about number six is brought out by the contrast to her indifference to numbers four and seven. Her reason for being anxious
about number six is not rational; she has no more intellectual evidence
against him than she has for numbers four and seven. The urge she

feels to pursue his case should be called a hunch, a feeling, a suspicion, or an apprehension. Such mental movements are blind emotional impulses as opposed to rational operations based on evidence. St. Ignatius distinguishes between the two distinct kinds of mental movements by saying that a rational conclusion is a "decision of his own judgment"; whereas, in an emotional urge "the thought comes to me from without that I have sinned."

While examining her own conscience for sins of thought, word, or deed, the mother finds the same four kinds of incidents. Some are clearly sinful, some are obviously free of sin, and some are doubtful. The majority of the doubtfully sinful incidents do not bother her. But she can become apprehensive about the matter of a rebellious appetite. Among the seven capital sins, number six, gluttony, her weakness for a snack now and then, somehow appeals to her inborn rascality. Hence, she can become emotionally disturbed about breaking her fast on the vigil of Ash Wednesday. The seed of the scruple is planted when the thought comes to her that she may have sinned in this incident. The scruple is obviously present when she begins to look for proofs that she did not sin. If she catches herself wondering why she procrastinated about observing the obligation and she cannot dismiss the thought from her mind, the scruple has arrived at the stage of vigorous growth. If she spends the day trying to find arguments to prove that she did not sin, she has a fully ripened scruple.

The mother's confused condition is brought out more clearly when she manifests her perplexity to her pastor. He is not suffering from emotional apprehension about a sin of gluttony. Moreover, when he listens to the mother's account of her problem, he will be looking for evidence that a sin was committed and will not assume the position of trying to prove that a sin was not committed. When the mother's arguments are presented to him, he will dismiss the incident about gluttony as easily as she passes over other doubtful incidents on her conscience. Only for the mother is the thought of breaking a fast emotionally toned. Consequently, when she reveals her temptation to her pastor, the conditions for an endless argument are present. Her pastor will insist that the evidence for guilt is doubtful; the mother will try to vindicate her apprehension that she sinned. Since the matter is doubtful, conclusive arguments for either position are impossible to find. The argument can go on indefinitely.

Hence, the basis of a scruple is twofold. There must be emotional apprehension about sinning in a certain type of incident; and, secondly, an incident must occur in which sinfulness is clouded in doubt.

These two conditions combine to furnish a situation for a scruple. Doubtful situations are bound to happen sooner or later. Hence, the ultimate cause of a scruple is an emotional apprehension of sinning. It is instructive to notice that this emotion of scrupulosity belongs to the same family of emotional quirks as the following.

1. A widow alone in the dark fears fire in her home. She will smell smoke in each unfamiliar whiff of any kind that is wafted into her chamber.
2. A man who fears that he is being followed will see a figure dash into cover from each shadow behind him.
3. An apprehensive wife will force her husband to prove his innocence for any stray strand of hair that attaches itself electrostatically to the lapel of his coat, even if the hair is the same color as her own.

## MAYHEM IN THE LOGICAL ORDER

The deceptive emotion that fears sin where there is no sin has its counterpart in the logical order that gives rise to the presumption of guilt where there is no guilt. If an unwary person tries to decide that he did not sin in a given incident, he makes a logical commitment which ensnares him in the fallacious conclusion that he has sinned. To point out the logical invalidity clearly, one must review a fundamental law of thought. Correct reasoning demands that a logical operation should proceed from premises to conclusions. A logical inversion of the syllogism of conscience takes place if a thinker assumes that a conclusion is true and then tries to find premises to prove that it is false. Thus, if my first thought is that I have sinned, I am asserting the truth of a conclusion. If, then, I try to prove that I have not sinned, I am trying to prove that the conclusion is false. When the conclusion comes first and the premises which determine its truth or falsity come second, reasoning is proceeding backward. Reasoning in reverse works out satisfactorily when it arrives at a decision with certitude, but, if the attempt to prove that the conclusion is false ends in doubt, the assumed truth of the conclusion stands as asserted because it cannot be proven to be false. It is profitable to study the logic of the syllogism of conscience in each of the three positions, the mean and its two extremes.

In the position of the mean, the premises are known before a conclusion is drawn, that is, evidence is consulted before a conviction is established. Thus, if a woman dropped into a church for a visit and discovered that she had done so with an uncovered head, she should ask herself whether the admonition of St. Paul bound under sin before she decided anything about her guilt. If this investigation ends in doubt, she does not know whether the incident could be a sin or not. It is important to observe that she simply does not know with certitude whether sin is involved. Neither can she conclude that the action is an indifferent action without morality. Her only conclusion should be that she does not know how to classify the incident with certitude. In this state of her conscience, liberty may or may not be in possession; how she finally forms her conscience is beside the point. A scruple can be started if she is tempted to raise a doubtfully sinful situation to a certitude. She will be inclined to scrupulosity if she has no place for doubtful situations in her method of forming her conscience.

A rightist can see his own mistake in the corresponding error of a leftist. The dull conscience wants to do something morally debatable and does not want the act to be prohibited. Without realizing clearly what takes place in the logical order, a leftist assumes that an action is not a sin unless the contrary is proven. He does so by asking the question, "What's wrong about it?" This question shifts the premises and conclusions of the syllogisms of conscience very subtly. A question in this form has been used by the promoters of evil from time immemorial. This is the question which the devil asked Eve when he wanted to break down her logical ramparts. Even today, posing the same question is the best way to start to seduce a person. Of course, the leftist position cannot be condemned outright. The assumption that a man is innocent until he is proven guilty is a necessary procedure at law. This presumption guarantees that an innocent man will not suffer injustice; but, it can also establish the fallacious conclusion that a criminal is innocent when the evidence to condemn him is doubtful. Presumptions work out nicely when they turn out to be true or false, but when they cannot be proven to be either and stand as truths without sufficient reason to support them, they can be destructive of both truth and justice in every order.

In the position to the right, the attitude of an apprehensive conscience, an accusation is made that an incident was a sin unless the contrary is proven. St. Ignatius explains this experience very carefully, "the thought comes to me from 'without' that I have sinned." Following this accusation is an effort to prove that I have not sinned. In this way an overcautious emotion of scrupulosity moves reason into the fallacious logical presumption that an incident was a sin unless the contrary is proven. The victim of the emotion is caught by an allegation that he must deny. If his attempt to prove that no sin was committed fails on account of doubt, he is left with the accusation of guilt. A counselee should study this deception until he can recognize the logical fallacy in his own scruple. He should ask himself whether he spends his time trying to prove that he did not sin in an incident. For practical purposes in therapy, he could take this definition of a scruple; a scruple is a futile effort to prove with certitude that one has not sinned in a doubtful incident. When he tries to refute this logical entrapment, he should reflect that it is also impossible to prove with certitude that he did sin. In this way, we are told by the Rules for Scruples, the contrary presumptions of the extremes bring one back to the mean.

The preceding analysis of a fallacy in a scruple was made from the point of view of categorical relations between contradictories and contraries in logical opposition. A like fallacy occurs if the victim of a scruple starts with the possibility of a sin and reasons with a "maybe," a "could be," a "must be," or a "cannot be," that is, with the moods of possibility, impossibility, necessity, and contingency. In this area of reasoning, the first thought in the mind is that the incident could be a sin. To deny this possibility only the assertion that no sin was committed is required; to refute possibility only the truth of the contradictory is demanded, not the truth of the contrary. However, a scrupulous person demands greater assurance of innocence; he would like to have convincing proof that sin was impossible. Thus, if a woman suffers blasphemous thoughts, she will not be satisfied to be told that they were not sinful; she wants proof that sin was impossible in the incidents. To satisfy this demand of a counselee, a counselor is easily trapped by the fallacy of trying to prove that a sin was impossible in the incident. Both the counselor and the counselee should meditate on this statement: It is impossible to prove that it is impossible to sin in an incident in which it was possible to sin. A still better procedure would be to rule out arguments about possible sins altogether.

## BAITING

Thus, the temptation to argue with a scruple could be called baiting. Baiting in its harmless form is a conversational skill acquired by crafty people. First, they survey the target individual for an area of sensitivity. Second, they make some stinging remark which goads him into an anticipated response, usually an act of self-defense. For instance, the baiter might know that his intended victim is touchy about using correct grammatical language. In a sneering way, the baiter might remark that his victim splits infinitives. If he springs to his own defense, the victim was baited successfully. A professional baiter does not care much whether the sensitive area is good or bad, nor is he concerned about whether the cutting remark is true or false. Baiting is rewarding if the chosen jibe gets a rise of self-justification out of the victim. Baiting for a scrupulous response finds a ready-made situation. A scrupulous person is touchy in the area of offenses against God. The thought that he has sinned is the greatest provocation he could be given. The reaction of self-defense to the possibility of losing eternal life stirs up the strongest motives of self-love. Scruple baiting requires less skill than any other form of baiting. A counselee who considers the temptation of a scruple as a form of self-baiting has a valuable insight into his emotional problem.

In review of what has been said about the ultimate cause of a scruple, the following point should be emphasized. The mental battle in the rational order which a scrupulous person wages against a false accusation of sin can be settled easily. Any counselor can tell the person that he is trying to raise a doubtful situation to a certitude. However, the more basic cause of a scruple lies outside the realm of reason somewhere in the emotional order. When everything dictated by common sense has been settled, the scrupulous person will suffer thoughts such as the following. "What if it was a sin?" "Are you asking me to throw myself on the mercy of God blindly?" "Must I leave my destiny in doubt?" "How can you prove that I am not in the state of sin?" When the counselee becomes aware that these thoughts are coming into his mind, he is in direct communication with the emotion that is the ultimate cause of scrupulosity. Here, at last, he is face to face with the elusive devil of scrupulosity in person. Fortunately, the devil of scrupulosity is easily exorcised; he can be driven out by ignoring him. In other words, dropping the personification, the counselee is whispering to himself, "You sinned." If he wants to be cured, he can also whisper, "No sin," in countermand. Neither whisper amounts to much in actuality, but mentally, they silence each other.

## RESORT TO PENANCE

Hence, when the argument to prove that the incident was not a sin ends in doubt, the counselee is left with guilt. His next impulse will be to try to get rid of his sinless sin by acts of contrition, confession, and penance. However, it is a mistake to try to correct a mistake with another mistake. Since the sin is sinless, sorrow is merely penitential shadowboxing; nothing existential happens. The victim intensifies his problem tenfold if he blames his failure on a "bad" confession. When his confessor denies that the incident was a sin, the victim will feel that he did not make himself understood, or, to make matters worse, that he deceived his confessor. Now the fear of damnation can start to assert itself in earnest. When the victim realizes that he cannot escape from mental torture even by artifice and strategy, he emits his first whimper of wounded self-love and drops his first tear of despair. By urging himself a bit he can break into the unrestrained cry of the damned. Moral torture hurts; but, worst of all, he begins to like the peculiar way in which it hurts. Now he is prepared for long days and nights of misery; he has learned to console himself with bittersweet sadness, sorrow, and self-pity.

Non-Catholics and Catholics who do not get satisfaction from a confessional may, or may not, resort to ceremonies of purification to rid themselves of scruples. To appreciate "washing" as a religious impulse we must consider the notion of the clean and the unclean.

Religious cleanness has several titles; it may be called legal, liturgical, or ceremonial purity. Religious cleanness demands much more than freedom from sin; anything impure or imperfect is included. Obviously, freedom from filth, contamination by disease, and the vulgar forms of defilement is demanded. However, of greatest interest to the scrupulous who find sin where there is no sin are the forms of uncleanness in which there seems to be no spot or wrinkle. For example, fasting is required to receive Holy Communion, and cleanness on Sunday demands abstinence from servile work. These forms of cleanness seem to imply that there is something unclean about eating or laboring. Moreover, a gesture of proper protocol signifies purity. Thus, to be ceremoniously clean when entering a church, a man removes his hat and a woman covers her head. Christians use the word, worthiness, to signify religious purity; the Jews use the word, kosher.

## THE CLEANSING POWER OF A SYMBOL

A rite of purification can remove much more "uncleanness" than the cleansing power of the rite itself may possess. A liturgically minded person can attribute tremendous purifying power to what seems to observers a routine rite. For instance, Pontius Pilate cleaned away his guilt in the crucifixion by washing his hands. A mother teaches her child that she can patch up almost anything by kissing it. A punctilious person can feel perfectly groomed by adjusting his tie. With a terrifically symbolic gesture of spotlessness, a wife flicks off the last imaginary speck of dust from her husband's sleeve and sends him forth into the waiting world immaculate. The Old Testament contains many purifying rites, and the Church has approved countless sacramentals, such as Holy Water, to purify tainted members. Thus, Scripture and Tradition offer many purifying rites; to these, individuals add a few of their own design. However, washing remains the ordinary rite of cleansing; it washes away the impurities of Pagans, Jews, and Christians alike.

A scrupulous person may be in one of four conditions with regard to ceremonial cleanness. First, he may not be much concerned about ritual purity. A scrupulous person is not necessarily kosher minded. For some people the whole world of symbolism is unexplored.

Second, a counselee may have a correct attitude toward rites of purification. A man strives to keep a clean image of himself. He has a duty to appear clean before God and man. The Church seriously intends the sacramentals to be used as remedies for the failures of human nature. Cleanliness has more than an ascribed title to be placed next to godliness.

But, thirdly, some people develop a nonreligious need for continuous purifications. Unfortunately, compulsive cleansing is called scrupulosity. This fourth meaning of the word has caused perennial harm to progress in therapy for scruples. As long as those involved think that a scrupulous person is one who washes his hands to get rid of imaginary dirt, the cause of therapy for religious scruples is stymied. If the counselee has a problem of compulsive cleansing, the counselor must carefully explain that the disorder may have no connection whatever with religious scrupulosity.

Fourth, the counselee may try to use a purifying rite to get rid of his scruples. If so, the use of a cleansing ceremony resembles the use of an act of contrition to become free of guilt. The counselee should be able to cure himself of making such attempts by realizing precisely what he is trying to do. His scruple concerns an incident about which he is carrying on a continuous argument between innocence and guilt. During the development of the scruple, many pros and cons for each side came into the struggle. To settle the battle, the counselee suddenly declared guilt the winner and branded it as uncleanness which could be washed away by a ceremony. But the forced decision did not resolve the argument; the urge to prove that no sin was committed is still very strong. In due time the ineffectiveness of soap and water to settle a doubt will become obvious, and hostilities will resume at the point at which a truce was declared. The net result of a frustrating attempt to settle a scruple with a purifying rite will be to advance the counselee into a deeper state of confusion and consternation. The thought that soap and water will not remove the doubt should be sufficient to enable the counselee to refrain from the inept gesture. At best, purification is a form of symptomatic treatment which does not reach the ultimate cause.

As scruples develop and the victim tries the alternatives of proving innocence or seeking forgiveness in vain, he will begin to look hopefully toward indirect methods of escape. By chance, a drug, a beverage, a temper tantrum, a tic, or some odd stratagem may bring relief. If so, he will quickly add the soothing quirk to his personality. Hypnotism has been tried by some; amnesia would solve the problem if one knew how to work it. When these forms of escape fail, desperation sets in and with it recourse to the fantastic and the weird.

However, by far the most crippling forms of maladjustment are the inhibitions, the loss of self-confidence; withdrawal from participation in social life; lack of interest in amusement; and, finally, total inability to carry on the daily routine of eating, sleeping, and performing the chores of personal cleanliness. Metastasis from mental distress to handicaps in social and economic life grows apace. Thus, the victim of scrupulosity gradually becomes a problem beyond the healing powers of the pastor. Now, physical therapy is required. When the victim cannot live a normal life, he qualifies for a clinic in which professional therapists restore the power of living to the disabled. In the complete program to conquer scrupulosity such clinics must be established at least as a department of an organized general clinic.

## "AGERE CONTRA"

Ultimately, therefore, a scruple is due to a "feeling" that a sin was committed in a doubtful incident; an emotion from "without" pressed the mind into a false conviction of guilt. If so, the cure of scruples must follow the method of curing irregularities in emotion. Emotions do not reason; they push and pull; they attract and repel; they excite with joy and paralyze with fear. Emotion must be fought on its own grounds, in its own way; push for push, pull for pull, attraction for attraction, pressure for pressure. St. Ignatius gives us his famous principle of "Do the opposite."

The soul which desires to advance in the spiritual life ought always to take just the contrary course to that which the enemy takes; that is to say, if the enemy wishes to make the conscience dull, let it try to make itself tender. In like manner, if the enemy is striving to make it tender to an extreme, let the soul try to establish itself solidly in the mean, so as to make itself altogether tranquil.

Hence,

1. If the scruple presumes that the incident was a sin the counselee should presume that it was not a sin.
2. If the scruple howls for attention, the counselee should give it the utmost contempt.
3. If the scruple puts out bait for an argument, he should refuse to become involved adamantly.
4. If the scruple makes him feel desperate, he should remain imperturbable.
5. If an emotion tricks him to an extreme, he should trick the emotion back to the mean.
6. If an emotion does anything at all, the counselee should do just the opposite.

## SELECTIVITY IN THE INCIDENTS

Having watched the emotion at work in its victim, a counselee is prepared to understand scrupulosity better by observing how the emotion selects its incidents. If there are ten categories of matter for scruples, a counselee will have scruples in one, two, three, or seven of the categories. Each scrupulous person picks out a combination to suit his own personality. Moreover, within a category, not every situation will be chosen. Thus, one counselee will be scrupulous about honesty in money matters but not about breaking a fast. Another will fear detraction but will not be bothered about blasphemous thoughts. Within a category, the selection of situations is still more puzzling to those who are not familiar with the workings of emotions. Thus, in the phobias, to use an undisputed emotional phenomenon, the same person will fear germs on doorknobs and on phones but will have no hesitation about coins, bus seat handles, chair arms, and other patent habitats of germs excelling the family doorknob in infestation many times over. All of the inconsistencies become intelligible if one remembers how emotion makes a choice. The incidents will be selected like a butterfly picks out a flower; like a bird chooses its mate from a flock of a thousand; like a dog chooses a spot to lie down; like a child selects a toy for play. When emotion, not reason, picks the incidents, they will be selected whimsically.

Since a genuine scruple is caused by failure to find convincing proof that an incident was not a sin, we can understand why counselees find scruples in the incidents that are popular with scrupulous people. We can also surmise the areas in which scruples are likely to occur. In general, they are found in the vague, in matters of opinion, in the gray area between black and white, in situations where there is a safe and a safer way of acting, along the shifting border between the deliberate and the indeliberate, among small details that happen on the fringe of awareness, in incidents that are half forgotten, and, subjectively, in any incident about which the question of consent is debatable. The following are typical examples.

1. If a woman decides that she has consented to blasphemous thoughts on the way to receive Holy Communion, no one can convince her that she did not consent to them.
2. If a son decides that he should have bought medicine that was rumored to be helpful to cancer during his father's terminal illness, no one can convince him that he had no obligation to do so.
3. If a girl permitted her fiancé to go further than she thought he should in signs of affection, who can prove to her that it was not a sin.
4. If a mother decides that it would have been safer to keep her medicine under lock and key before junior used a chair to climb up to the medicine cabinet, no one can convince her that she had no obligation to keep the medicine safely locked away.
5. If Susan meets her grandfather weaving his way home from a cocktail party in his honor and accuses herself of rash judgment, who can say that she went beyond the objective evidence.
6. If a wife decides that she coveted her neighbor's husband and goods, there is no convincing proof that the thoughts were indeliberate.
7. If a person who fears fire decides that he smells smoke, there is no way to convince him that the house is not on fire except to take him through the whole house, one room at a time, and to be prepared to make a second trip when he is not satisfied with the first.
8. If a scrupulous person decides that he has sinned in an incident which is doubtfully sinful, it is quite impossible to prove to him that no sin was committed for the obvious reason that a doubtful situation cannot be made a certitude.

## HOW MANY PEOPLE ARE SCRUPULOUS?

Statistics about the number of scrupulous people are difficult to find. In a sanitarium, even though the condition has been diagnosed and is known to the physicians and personnel, no one will write the word, scrupulous, on the chart. If a novice is sent home from a novitiate on account of scruples, some other reason will be used to explain the dismissal. The best source of information, the confessional, must be absolutely and unequivocally excluded as a basis of estimates. If an effort is made to count the number of scrupulous persons by asking individuals whether they are scrupulous, no one will stand up to be counted. Finally, scrupulosity varies in intensity from an occasional scruple permitted by God to arouse a tepid soul from complacency in sin to the case of continuous mental torture and complete loss of serviceability. Consequently, no survey could be attempted without defining the state to which the problem must advance before it would be called scrupulosity. Hence, it is not completely out of order to say in a jocose way that according to statistics no one is scrupulous. Nevertheless, it is profitable to speculate a priori in the light of the ultimate cause of scruples on the number of scrupulous persons a counselor expects to find.

Since scrupulosity is a temptation of the rightists, the tendency will be high among those striving to attain the perfection of the Christian life. A counselor should expect to find a comparatively higher number of scrupulous persons in a seminary, among the faithful who frequent churches, and, with or without religious motivation, among the cultured, the educated, and the refined. He should not expect to find scrupulous persons on the pads of beatniks or in the cellars of radicals. There is a saying among counselors that good people do not escape the temptation to scrupulosity. The majority of those tempted probably make a working adjustment that is more or less successful, but there will always be a few who do not. Without sufficient "scientific" data for doing so, we venture the following estimate of expectancy. If you counsel 100 select counselees, for example, 100 students in a Catholic college, expect more than one to be maladjusted to the temptation of scrupulosity. If the number begins to hover around seven, look for some factor other than the normal tendency to explain the high incidence. It is possible for an incompetent counselor to "cause" scruples.

Sooner or later every student of scrupulosity will be asked the question of whether scrupulosity is more frequent among women than among men. A reason will be offered for a difference, namely, that women are more delicate and more sensitive to emotion. In answer to the question, we have no reliable statistics; however, we can cite arguments against the affirmative answer. Our first observation is that the two cases cited in this book were Martin Luther and St. Ignatius; and, that our definition of a scruple was written by a man, moreover, a layman.[2] Yet we must concede that more women than men seek help from a pastor. But this statistic must be limited to exactly what it surveys, namely, that more women seek help. Men are more inclined to work out a solution for themselves. When reason fails to offer a satisfactory method of settling conscience, men are more inclined to use the indirect methods of relief. They abandon religion; they withdraw to cry their sorrow into a stein; they give up to become vagabonds; when local relief fails, they join the foreign legion. Whatever the number of scrupulous men compared to women may be, the number of scrupulous men is far greater than the number who seek help from the pastor. A special program of therapy must be designed to pursue male escapees.

## HOW MANY PROTESTANTS ARE SCRUPULOUS?

The incidence of scrupulosity among Protestants should be comparatively low for several reasons. First, many Protestant churches have remedies for scrupulosity in their doctrines. Lutheranism offers a solace for scrupulosity in the doctrine of justification by faith alone; any Protestant church following the teaching of predestination with Calvin is made up of members who are assured of salvation; again, any Protestant church which requires accepting Christ as the Savior receives only the "saved" into membership. Secondly, Protestantism is a religion for the liberal as opposed to the conservative and the authoritarian. As a protestor, a Protestant should be tempted toward ultraliberalism rather than toward scrupulosity.

But Protestantism in practice is not always identical with theoretical Protestantism. Moreover, not every descendant of a liberal inherits the propensity toward freedom. Some Protestants do not know the doctrine of the church in which they are registered. By way of exception the Puritans see sin in the appearance of dancing, entertainment, sports, and games of chance. Hence, a counselor should not reject a Protestant counselee on an a priori opinion that he cannot be tempted

---

[2] St. Ignatius wrote the Spiritual Exercises several years before he studied theology and was ordained.

to scrupulosity. Nor should therapy differ from that used on the ultra-orthodox. A Protestant should be told to list his incidents, recognize that they are scruples, and learn how to avoid these temptations by ignoring them.

## SUMMARY

In summary of the answer given by the Spiritual Exercises to the question of the ultimate cause of a scruple, we make the following statements. A scruple is the result of an inclination found in some good people to carry their fear of sin to an extreme. The scruple starts when the emotion of scrupulosity causes the thought that a sin was committed in an incident. The frightening guilt of sin is followed by an effort to find an argument that the act was not a sin. The genuine scruple begins when this attempt fails. The next impulse is to accept the incident as a sin and to try to have it forgiven by making acts of contrition. When this fails to quiet the emotion, various other methods of finding relief are tried out by individuals each according to his character. Scrupulosity grows each time one of the escapes fails.

## THERAPY

The following excerpts from the four phases of the cure for scruples should clarify the procedure. They are verbatim quotations from the book *How to Cure Scruples.*

### Phase I. "Booking" the Incidents

The outstanding incidents in the history of the development of scrupulosity in this individual case must be listed and identified with all of the precision used by the FBI in its description of the Ten Most Wanted Criminals. They have been able to persist as distorted decisions of conscience because they remained hidden and were able to conceal their vicious character; the more their harmful nature can be exposed and the easier they are recognized, the more therapy will be facilitated. Each one should be given a number; or, for greater emphasis, each one should be given a girl's name in alphabetical order after the manner of naming hurricanes. The counselee should be instructed to make out this list; the counselor should never commit these "most personal secrets" to writing. As therapy proceeds, the counselee may add a new member to the list, drop an old one, or change the qualifications of an incident for its First Ten rating, but these changes should not alter the value of the counselee's preferred incidents. The counselee could be told that he should draw up this list with the nicety with which St. Ignatius wrote out his doubtful sins for the three-day confession. When complete, it should appear as follows with topic sentences to identify each incident.

Alice. I stepped on two crossed straws.
Bernice. I broke my fast on the Vigil of Ash Wednesday.
Clare. I lied in confession.
Dolores. I am not sure that I said my penance.
Ethel. I short-changed a clerk.
Florence. . . . .

Above all, the counselor should look for an incident on the list drawn up by the counselee which is *free of all of the complications* of material sin, associated emotional problems, and complicated reasoning. For example, a mother might have a scruple about exposing her baby to malaria by not swatting a mosquito that entered the home. A student might have a scruple about keeping a rubber band which he found on the front steps of the school. The less of the appearance of sin and the greater the scrupulous response, the better will the incident be for purposes of recognizing the nature of a scruple. An ideal way of becoming aware of the nature of the temptation in a scruple is to start with a clear, uncomplicated incident and to transfer the insight to the complex. In fact, if the counselor uses an incident in which real guilt is mingled with scrupulous guilt, an insight into the nature of scrupulosity is almost impossible. St. Ignatius uses the example of stepping on two straws in the form of a cross. No doubt he realized that if he could make a scruple out of that, he could make a much more vicious one out of incidents involving sin.

*Phase II. Systematic Study of the Incidents*

It can happen that the mere consideration of the incidents suffices to bring the counselee to a determination to refuse to dwell on them anymore. If not, the following questions can be used as a guide to study. Although the most important questions concern the definition of a scruple given under number 10, the other circumstances in questions 1 to 9 can help immensely in understanding a scruple as it appears in this particular individual.

1. Do they concern thoughts, words, or deeds?
2. What subjects do they concern? Contamination? Sex? Disobedience? Stealing? Distractions in prayer?

3. When do they occur? Regularly? At night? On the job? On weekends? Monthly?
4. Under what conditions? When fatigued? Under tension? At one
   type of occupation? On vacation? With certain people?
5. Where do they occur? In church mostly? At school? In dangerous
   places? While watching TV? When alone?
6. With whom are they associated? My confessor? My mother? Po-
   liceman? Lovers? Employers?
7. Are they connected with the reception of sacraments? Have they
   caused me to avoid the sacraments?
8. What escapes do I attempt? Extraversion? Drugs? Alcohol? Severe penance? Acts of contrition? Travel?
9. Did they begin or stop with changes in my state of life? When I
   moved from one place to another?
10. Do they fit the definition of St. Ignatius?

   *a*) Are they concerned about incidents?
   *b*) Do I fear sin in them contrary to fact?
   *c*) Do I doubt and not doubt?
   *d*) Do I argue with myself about them?
   *e*) Is the argument continuous?
   *f*) Do I feel a compulsion to settle them?
   *g*) Do I consider them a temptation or a sort of duty? (pp. 60–61)

*Phase III. Rejection by Distraction*

During Phase III the counselee learns *how to free himself from
the tyranny of the emotion of scrupulosity.* The mental operation by
which he does this can be expressed in different words. A spiritual
director might say that one *overcomes a temptation.* A psychologist
might say that one *frees himself from the dominance of an emotion.*
A layman might say that the scrupulous person finally *got hold of
himself.* We might speak of ignoring a compulsion to settle a doubt
about sin. In whatever words the activity is expressed, the mental
operation can be explained as follows.

Control of the different activities of the mind is a matter of attention. When, for instance, we want to remember something, we direct
attention to the faculty of memory. Moreover, attention is like a spot-
light; if it is directed to one activity, it is not shining on another. Consequently, if I do not want to give attention to "A," I give attention to
"B." Thus, if I am urged to enter an argument about whether it is a
sin to step on two crossed straws, I can let this inclination come to

naught by giving attention to some other activity, for instance, to watching a football game on TV. It is quite impossible to give full attention to both the scruple and the game; the one will get less attention in proportion to the liveliness of my interest in the other. The chief point to be noticed is that I do not get rid of the unwanted thought by a positive act of rejection. It is not necessary to pound my head and say, I do not want it, I do not want it, I do not want it. To attempt positive rejection is, indeed, to curse darkness instead of lighting a light. Such adverse attention is just as effective in keeping a thought in the mind as is approval. A scruple is excluded by not being included. Anyone who has not been invited to a party knows that not being invited is just as exclusive as being told not to come. We call this method of rejection, "ignoring the scruple." (pp. 68–69)

### Phase IV. Breaking the Habit ("One for the Road")

Yielding to a temptation before a habit is formed occurs in the manner in which Eve consented to eat the forbidden apple. If a counselee yielded to the temptation of a scruple in this way, he would know that the proposed argument is a scruple and be drawn into it by some kind of an attraction or be driven into it by some sort of compulsion. But after the habit of scrupulosity has been acquired, the counselee is several minutes into the argument before he discovers what is going on. The mental syndrome of scrupulosity has become so much a part of the counselee's thought, is so natural to him, so obvious a way to think, that releasing it seems to be giving up himself. When the counselee discovers that he left the last promising conference only to return to the same old set of thought patterns, he will be terrifically discouraged. A novice in conducting mental affairs has so little self-knowledge that he thinks he can break a mental habit as easily as he learns how it is done. It will be difficult for him to find out how a scruple starts and still more difficult to resist it when he recognizes it. A counselee will do anything to avoid the effort of self-conquest required to give up a cherished habit; but, if a cure is to come about, he must study how his scruples start and train himself to reject them energetically right at the very beginning. The sooner he is alerted and the faster he diverts his attention to the distracting thought, the easier a victory becomes.

In the Ignatian system of acquiring self-mastery, *the method of the particular examination is used.* The following is a description of this method. If a person has the courage to follow it, no habit can resist it.

The particular examination is to be made three times daily. In the morning, immediately on rising, the man ought to resolve to guard himself against the particular defect which he desires to correct and amend. After the midday meal, he ought to ask grace to remember how often he has fallen into that particular defect. After this, let him demand an account from his soul of the particular matter which he desires to amend, reviewing the time elapsed hour by hour, or period by period, beginning from the time he arose till the moment of the present examination. Let him record the number of times he has fallen into the defect. After supper, a second examination is made in the same way going over the interval hour by hour from the noon examination to the present one, and marking in the second bracket the number of times he has fallen into the defect. . . .

The subject of this particular examination will be to mark the number of times that the counselee started to think about one of the incidents about which he is scrupulous.

 . . . every time a person falls into the defect, he should lay his hand on his breast and grieve that he has fallen (a thing that he can do even in the presence of many people without their perceiving it). In the evening, he should compare the morning with the afternoon; he should compare the first day with the second; one week is to be compared to another.

The fruit of this self-study will eventually be an astounding knowledge of the nature of a scruple, a clear perception that it is a temptation, an ever increasing strength to ignore its demands, and a decisive victory over the habit of scrupulosity. (pp. 77–79)

## GROUP THERAPY

*Fruits of a Group*

Although many fruits are to be derived from group therapy, three, in particular, are worthy of mention to serve as reasons for attending the sessions. First, another scrupulous person is a sort of *mirror* in which the counselee can see what he, himself, looks like. Susan, for instance, who has never been bothered by contamination, will not understand why Betsie should be so upset about washing the dishes in lukewarm water. Susan will be more surprised when she finds no one interested in the problem of breaking a fast on the vigil of Ash Wednesday. Children in school learn as much or more from each other as they do from the teacher. A school of scrupulosity for mature people will have the same effect on adults through mutual intercourse between its members.

Second, *group action builds up courage.* Although one small boy lacks enough courage to sleep out in the woods of the back yard, and a second small boy has the same shortage, taken together, they can brave the hootings of distant owls and the chirping of nearby crickets. The laws of group behavior defy mathematical calculation. If one scrupulous person has two ergs of will power and a second has two ergs of will power, the sum is more than four ergs when they group together. Here again, the counselor may be hard put to explain why two and two are ten in the emotional order; but the Alcoholics Anonymous have demonstrated that it is true. A counselee who did not have courage enough to ignore a scruple before a meeting may come home with enough will power to do so and have a few ergs left over.

Third, *no one really masters a subject until he teaches it.* Those who are not familiar with education imagine that the wisdom of a teacher accumulates over a period of time as a student. Such is not the case. The attempt to teach creates more understanding than is possible by any amount of student effort. If the scrupulous person attempts to cure another of scruples, he will cure himself in the effort. (pp. 92–93)

Chapter 9

# A Physiologic Therapy for the "Neuroses"

## GERHARD B. HAUGEN

Gerhard B. Haugen: b. 1905, Stoughton, Wisconsin.
B.A., University of Oregon, 1932. M.D., University of Oregon Medical School, 1935. M.P.H., Johns Hopkins School of Public Health, 1942.
Assistant Clinical Professor of Psychiatry, University of Oregon Medical School, 1950–date. Lecturer, University of Oregon Law School, Willamette University Law School, 1956–1958.
Past President, The North Pacific Society of Neurology and Psychiatry. President, The Portland Psychiatrists in Private Practice.
Books: (Co-author) *A Therapy for Anxiety Tension Reactions* (1958).

Current medical literature is replete with suggestions that the non-psychiatrist physician, primarily the general practitioner (GP), should take a greater role in dealing with mental illnesses. Most of the writers to that effect appear to be ignorant of how the average physician spends his time. A typical GP will see upwards of 20 patients a day in his office. In addition, he will have hospital calls, perhaps home calls, maybe an operation or a delivery to perform. He is supposed to take part in civic affairs. He has a family that deserves some of his time. He may feel the need for some hours of recreation. Still, he is expected to spend an hour or more with every patient who has a "problem," "listening to the patient's story." And a high percentage of his patients can qualify for this demand on time he does not have.

A search for some sort of psychotherapy that would be effective without being inordinately time consuming, so that it would be practical for the GP, was begun by the author and his colleagues about 30 years ago. Experiments leading to the development of concepts presented herein began in 1939. At first, the physiologic aspects were used adjunctively, subordinated to a Dejerinian type of psychotherapy. Gradually, as a new hypothesis began to develop and crystalize, the latter was abandoned.

244

The present model, in the hands of an experienced therapist, can be effectively used in the therapy of anxiety reactions, compulsive and phobic reactions, and in mild depressive reactions where tension is an obvious component. A first introductory session need not last over half an hour for the GP who already knows his patient. Following this, a quarter hour, perhaps twice a week at first, later once a week, can attain and maintain good progress. The average patient should attain efficiency and comfort in six months or less. They will also by then have learned basic principles that they can usefully apply for the rest of their lives.

The assumed hypothesis falls within the broad definitions of "Learning Theory." The symptoms, objective and subjective, which form the complaint, are considered as unadaptive conditioned responses. They are determined by individual differences in conditionability and autonomic lability, as well as accidental environmental circumstances. Historical development is considered largely irrelevant. The therapy is aimed at extinguishing improper conditioned responses and developing similar ones. The relation of the therapist to the patient is that of teacher to pupil. No metaphysical concepts, such as "transference," are involved.

Current psychiatric literature speaks frequently of the "mind," another metaphysical term. If the brain is mentioned, it is usually spoken of as if it were semiinsulated from the rest of the organism; mostly efferent activity is emphasized. (Presumably, like the captain of a ship, it gives orders but does not receive any.) However, neurophysiologists have demonstrated the constant interaction between the nervous system and the other organ systems—both through conventional transmissions and through "humeral" (endocrine) influences. Various areas are continually altering in activity as the result of afferent stimuli. Since the phenomena embraced by the term "mind" are conceded to be the results of neural action, it would seem only reasonable to try to construct hypotheses on the basis of what we know about nervous system physiology.

The chief difference between our concept and the conventional Learning Theory approach is that greater importance is given to the state of the animal as it is placed in the learning situation. It is postulated that if a state of fear exists, learning compatible with fear will be facilitated and other learning inhibited. The same would be true of a condition of sexual arousal, depression, satiety, etc. The state of interest for the hypothesis under discussion is that of chronic bracing, otherwise described as "increased neuromuscular tension."

The late Howard Liddell demonstrated that animals could be trained by conventional conditioning methods to be chronically, constantly braced or tense. He showed that after this state had been achieved the "personalities" of his animals (sheep) changed profoundly; from then on they tended to eat and sleep poorly, gave evidence of altered autonomic activity, and would in other ways act abnormally.

Dr. Edmund Jacobson has demonstrated that electromyographic examination reveals chronic and constant increased striate muscle activity in individuals suffering from "neuroses." This finding has been repeated and confirmed by others.

Every animal can, on appropriate occasions, experience a state of being braced—chiefly at times when fight or flight is considered. The situation is normally of brief duration. Homo sapiens shares this type of reaction, and for him also it is ordinarily only temporary.

Our hypothesis postulates that some persons, for various reasons, have attained a state similar to that of Dr. Liddell's sheep—the reaction is no longer brief and intermittent, but constant—morning, noon and night, week after week, month after month. These are the people in whom Dr. Jacobson has found electromyographic abnormalities.

It is further postulated that in such persons one would expect to find, continuously, more or less the same type of mental state that is normally found intermittently when any of us are braced for a fight-or-flight situation. Reaction to stimuli and consequent learned responses would therefore be affected and would often be different from those elicited in a person at rest.

The hypothesis considers the nervous system as simply a component part of the organism, no different from its status in an earthworm. In order to maintain homeostasis it must receive as well as send out stimuli. Its activity is continually modulated by the input. Just as pain can markedly modify the mental state, so can an increase in signals from braced muscles. The altered reactions of Dr. Liddell's sheep would seem most reasonably explained on that basis. It seems doubtful that man's nervous system is so different as to make him an exception.

Attempts to modify human behaviour by methods similar to those of the Skinner box are now familiar to all. If our theory is correct, difficulties will be encountered in conditioning the chronically tense individual if the behavior to be learned is contrary to preparation for fight-or-flight.

In 1958, Dr. Joseph Wolpe published "Psychotherapy by Reciprocal Inhibition" in which he described a regime somewhat parallel to that which the author and others have been developing the past 25 years. He first gave the patient some instructions in "relaxation," based largely on Dr. Jacobson's methods, and then proceeded with deconditioning procedures for specific complaints or adverse reactions. Later publications by Dr. Wolpe have indicated considerable permanence for his therapy.

Many papers have been written on other experiments based upon the Learning Theory, particularly under the term Behavior Therapy, but as a rule these have paid no heed to the basic physiologic state of the subject, neither assessing it nor trying to attain first a relatively neutral state, such as Wolpe described. Our chief contribution, if it turns out to be one, is emphasis on that point, which we stress to a much greater degree than Wolpe appears to.

If an animal is braced for fight-or-flight, it appears to us that homeostasis demands a certain type of mentation. The environment must be viewed with suspicion, apprehension, anxiety. Each change—noise, light, movement—must be judged as to whether it presents a threat. The decision may be difficult to make, and rumination would be natural. Augmented organ changes (heart palpitation, "stomach in a knot," etc.) can occur from what would ordinarily be relatively minor stimuli, now assuming great importance. The development of a lasting conditioned response appropriate to the state would seem to be facilitated.

As a possible example, a child sees its mother jump on a chair and shriek when a mouse runs across the floor. If the child is frightened, this one experience can set a pattern of considerable permanence. (Presumably most of us are handicapped by similar conditionings, the origin long forgotten.) After the child calms down, reassurance and explanation may effectively neutralize the effect of the trauma (psychotherapy), and there may be no adverse result. But attempts to do this while the child is still excited and frightened may have poor success and even accentuate the reaction.

What is described in the previous paragraph is fairly acceptable to psychiatric theorists, in general, since it falls within common experience. Throughout their lives most persons are occasionally tense, frightened, or blue. During those periods they are prone to overreact to stimuli in a way that is appropriate to the mood or state, and they are hard to reason with. If the state were constant, the reactions induced by it would be persistent.

Those persons who have, through assiduous practice (which they do unknowingly), developed a chronic bracing reaction operate continually as though facing an emergency. Homeostasis demands that thought patterns be appropriate, just as are the accompanying visceral changes. Consequently, there is "free floating anxiety"; irritability; impatience; distortion of judgment; retraction of interests, etc. All of these inhibit learning of anything not appropriate to the state and facilitate the development of phobias, compulsions, and obsessions.

The necessary laboratory experiments to establish the exact relationship of neuromuscular tension to this chronic reaction are incomplete. Liddell's work suggests that it be the prime, initiating factor. Regardless of how this finally turns out, the muscle bracing is a consistent part of the pattern.

Our therapy, like Wolpe's, begins with steps to reduce the muscle tension. The theory is that by reducing input, one reduces the modulating effect on important cortical areas. At least one alters the homeostatic pattern by promoting relaxation.

For a tense person to learn to relax voluntarily and completely all major striated muscle and finally to substitute a state of "chronic relaxation" for one of chronic tension will require time and attention on his part. Ideally, instruments (galvanometers) should be used, both to evaluate progress and as a teaching aid. Jacobson has written extensively about their use. Our experience is that unless the patient learns this process of relaxation thoroughly until it becomes automatic, he will tend to revert to the old pattern if later in life he encounters prolonged stress.

It is worth mentioning here that the methods of J. H. Schultz and followers reported in European literature have nothing in common with those of Jacobson, except some terminology. The former are basically autosuggestion. The latter are muscle training—analogous to learning swimming, or typing, or any similar sort of activity requiring precise muscle control.

When sufficient ability in relaxation has been achieved so that the patient can maintain it fairly well under nonstressful circumstances, he is started on a series of experiments similar to Wolpe's "hierarchies." This will be a graded series of situations which he is to approach, to discover how well he can control the bracing reaction in such an encounter. The tests will vary according to the patient, what his phobias are, the nature of his work, how much opportunity he has for practice, etc. Pains are taken to arrange it so that he will achieve many more successes than failures.

The previous paragraph applies chiefly to phobias. In dealing with obsessions and compulsions, we find a greater degree of mastery of tension control is necessary. The control must be sufficient to allow the patient to sit and contemplate his obsessions and compulsions at length and still remain relaxed.

As the patient becomes familiar with the subjective advantages of a relaxed state as compared to the previous chronically tense one, the latter becomes aversive. He becomes disgusted or angry with himself whenever he relapses, which at first is very frequently. Thus he serves as his own Skinner box. Part of the pay-off is the decrease in somatic discomforts—the knotted gut, postnuchal headaches, tachycardia, hyperventilation, etc., which accompanied the chronically tense state. The mental changes are also striking—the decrease in anxiety, improved interpersonal relations, loss of irritability, return of appetite, etc. In some cases where no fixed or severe phobias have developed, the patient will not need any special deconditioning once the tension is subdued; he is able to carry on like the "normal" individuals that he previously envied.

For basic principles to be used in assisting the patient to acquire control of his muscles, Jacobson's work is unequaled, and space will not be given to that issue here. There is and will continue to be experimentation in teaching these principles. An illustrated outline of fundamental steps can be found in chapter six of *Anxiety and Tension Control* by Edmund Jacobson, M.D., published by the J.B. Lippincott Co., Philadelphia, Pa., in 1964.

The author suggests the following variations in application of the technique:

1. Since it is the practice the patient does for himself that is important, no more time is spent with him than is necessary to demonstrate a procedure and be sure he understands it.

2. At each office session he is first checked on what he has been practicing to date. If he has not achieved his task, no new one is assigned. Mistakes in technique or approach are looked for, and if found, are re-explained. He must master each step before proceeding to the next.

3. If possible, frequent brief periods of practice instead of one or two long ones are used. Ten minutes out of every hour, for example.

4. No attempt is made to achieve anything more than basic relaxation until after the patient can consistently sit down and let go quite completely, in neutral surroundings, in a few minutes.

5. After the above steps are achieved, the patient begins to tackle simple tasks (peeling potatoes, sewing a button, etc.), learning to use only the muscles necessary, the remainder of them being at rest.

6. When the patient has achieved step 5, plans are made to expand this practice to work situations.

7. When definite progress is manifested in controlling tension in

work situations, he is asked to prepare a list of phobias, aversions, and similar uncomfortable situations in which he reacts excessively. From this list are chosen ones that can be brought about the most frequently and easily. One situation is chosen for the first experiment. The patient is to perform it under as favorable circumstances as possible the first few times.

8. Gradually the experiments are made more challenging. As a rule no new one is added until at least fair success has been achieved in those previously assigned. (A common one, toward the end of therapy, is to comfortably spend an hour in a crowded department store).

If possible, other members of the patient's family are asked to cooperate, first in understanding what the patient is trying to do and why, second in reminding him regarding practice. After the patient has learned to recognize tension and lack of it, he is directed to check on his state every few minutes, no matter where he is or what he is doing. Members of the family can be particularly helpful in the latter situation, in reminding him.

Probably every physician who deals with patients has intuitively recognized that often the complaints and symptoms would diminish if the patient would only "relax." Some persons will be able to do this; the bracing reaction has not become chronic. Others, with a low degree of tension, can let go fairly well with the aid of a sedative. There remains a group for whom even strong sedation is only a poor palliative. These latter two groups comprise the population for whom this type of therapy seems indicated. The tremendous number of prescriptions for "tranquilizers" indicates how large it is.

If the physician can conceive of the basic tension as a learned, unadaptive response, repeated until it is now a "habit," he will also recognize that possibly it can be "unlearned" if proper training methods are used.

It would appear possible, within our present knowledge and laboratory skills, to test the basic hypotheses described in this paper. "Psychologic" testing of animals is becoming fairly sophisticated. Liddell's techniques are well known. Suitable electromyographs are available. Animal experimentation would presumably eliminate most of the subjective factors that make it difficult to evaluate the currently conventional psychotherapies. Suggestion, for example, should interfere little if at all.

Eventually it will be the results of objective, unbiased evaluation of results, time involved, and ease of administration that will decide which psychotherapy can be recommended to the average physician.

He is always eagerly receptive if the technique offered him is on a solid basis—witness, for example, the present-day handling of gonorrhea and syphilis as compared to the era before the sulfas and antibiotics.

## A CASE ILLUSTRATION

The following is a brief case history. This patient was intelligent, cooperative, and strongly motivated; satisfactory results were obtained more quickly than usual.

The patient was a 26-year-old, married, white female, with two young children, and she was in good general health. Increasingly for the previous year she had been handicapped by fatigue, postnuchal headaches, gastric distress, tachycardia, anorexia, insomnia, irritability, and frequent brief depressions, along with other less threatening symptoms. She had lost ten pounds. She could not tolerate her children. She was brought in by her mother, who had been treated for an anxiety reaction ten years previous.

*First session.* She had some familiarity with tension control procedures through her mother. It was therefore possible to quickly outline to her the changes in body function that occur with excessive tension and to give her a general understanding of what had been and was taking place. (This may take several sessions with some patients.) She was instructed regarding relaxing the forearms and hands and sent home to practice.

*Second session.* It had been ascertained via telephone that she had succeeded fairly well with her first project. This time she was instructed regarding the neck, face, and shoulder muscles; this exercise to be done sitting in a chair. The head was to be held up by the back of the chair, not by her. The face muscles to be loosened until the jaw dropped. The shoulders to sag. If these are done successfully, breathing becomes quiet, even, and comfortable. This latter was her test as to her degree of success. She was to set aside ten minutes every hour for this practice.

*Third session.* She had now been on the previous routine for a week. She occasionally achieved fair success. She was asked to continue. In addition, when she did achieve her goal, she was to continue sitting and begin to do something with her hands (peeling potatoes, sewing on a button, etc.), trying to use only the essential muscles and to the extent necessary.

*Fourth session.* The past week she had managed to get fairly comfortably relaxed within a few minutes about half the times she set aside for practice. She was instructed regarding the abdominal muscles and legs.

*Fifth session.* Sleep was beginning to improve and occasionally food tasted good. She was continuing to practice conscientiously. This time she had specific questions regarding her heart and stomach, which had caused not only discomfort but much concern and worry the past year. The principles of homeostasis were explained to her. No new projects were added at this time.

*Sixth session.* She had been fairly comfortable the past week. Sleep and appetite continued to improve. The depressive periods were less intense. The project taken up this time was to try to remain relaxed in the presence of her children, who previously "drove her wild." She was instructed to let go as much as possible before trying the experiment, to stay with them as long as she was doing well, and to withdraw from the situation if she found herself losing control.

*Seventh session.* She reported progress with her project. Her appetite was good most of the time and sleep seldom a problem. There had been little depression. She was instructed to continue the same as the previous week.

*Eighth session.* Continued progress in all phases plus beginning weight gain. The next project was going shopping, first with someone and later alone. Again she was to choose a time when she could relax well, get started, and call a halt if she began to lose control. She was to work on this two weeks. All other projects to continue.

*Ninth session.* Weight was approaching normal. Fatigue was disappearing. She had managed to diminish her bracing for shopping sessions considerably. She was to continue with that project and also to begin visiting friends, following the same principles. To return in a week.

*Tenth session.* Being with the children was now enjoyable. She had no concern about the workings of her body. She was not yet entirely at ease in shopping or visiting friends but felt confidence that she would in time achieve it. Instructed to continue another week.

*Eleventh session.* She was now becoming lonesome for her husband, who had been attending summer school, and wished to join him. She was given final instructions regarding the need for continued consistent practice in tension control. She was told that for a while she would find herself tending to brace for every new situation and that each time it would take her a while to relax in it.

Word from her two months later indicated that everything was going well and that she was continuing to practice and to use the principles taught her.

## SUMMARY

A physiologic therapy for certain of the neuroses is described. The hypotheses behind it come within a broad definition of Learning Theory. It varies from the more widely known Behavior Therapy in its greater emphasis on the physiologic state of the subject in the learning situation. It would appear to be testable in the laboratory, at least sufficiently to indicate probability of the hypotheses being true or false. A case description is provided.

Part Two

# COGNITIVE
# RESTRUCTURING METHODS

This section demonstrates the wealth of direct approaches to mental aberration which have developed outside the Freudian traditions.

Anderson deals with prideful assumptions that result in troubled adjustments. Ellis works hard to disabuse his patients of irrational suppositions. Blake describes what seems a valiant effort of breaking through psychotic misconstructions. Garner nudges his patients to a larger self-awareness by posing to them the challenging confrontation formula. Weitz describes the therapeutic effects of problem-centered guidance. Ligon demonstrates another rational approach to psychopathological, perceptual, and emotional distortions. Incidentally, Ligon utilizes an approach diametrically opposed to the prevalent orientation in psychotherapy: instead of applying the norms of sick people upon the presumably mentally healthy population, he proposes the utilization of principles derived in working with nonsick people to those who need psychotherapeutic help. Simkin proposes a fresh point of view of

Gestalt psychology for interpreting and directing the events of the psychotherapeutic situation. Berne, Steiner, and Dusay depict an original development in Transactional Analysis. The late Professor Kelly asks the patients to assume in real life a role different from the one into which they have fallen.

The methods are manifold, but they all have one underlying feature: they help the patient to achieve a more efficient reaction to himself and others and lead him to a more accurate perspective of his reality.

Chapter 10

# Assumption-Centered Psychotherapy

## CAMILLA M. ANDERSON

Camilla M. Anderson: b. 1904, Sidney, Montana.
A.B., University of Oregon, 1925. M.D., University of Oregon Medical School, 1929. Psychoanalytic training in Philadelphia, 1939–1941, and at the Washington School of Psychiatry (William Allanson White Institute of Psychiatry), 1944–1946. Certified as Psychiatrist, American Board of Psychiatry and Neurology, 1938.
Chief Psychiatrist, California Institute for Women, Frontera, California, 1964–1969. Director, Outpatient Department, Oregon State Hospital, Salem, Oregon, 1958–1964. Chief Psychiatrist, Veterans Administration Mental Hygiene Clinic, Salt Lake City, Utah, 1948–1952. Psychiatrist, Washington (D.C.) Institute of Mental Hygiene, 1941–1945. Private psychiatric practice, 1938–1957. Lecturer: Willamette University Institute for Advanced Pastoral Studies, 1962-1964; University of Utah Graduate School of Social Work, 1952-1956; University of Utah College of Medicine, 1948–1957; Temple University Medical School, 1939–1941; University of Pennsylvania, 1937–1942; Duquesne University, 1935–1938. Consultant, Oregon Governor's Committee on Childhood and Youth, 1961–1964. Consultant in Psychiatry for Utah, Western Interstate Commission for Higher Education.
Charter Member, Academy of Religion and Mental Health, 1954. Fellow, American Psychiatric Association, 1944.
Books: *Society Pays: The High Cost of Minimal Brain-Damage in America* (1972). *Jan, My Brain Damaged Daughter* (1963). *Beyond Freud* (1957). *Saints, Sinners and Psychiatry* (1950, paperback ed. 1962). *Emotional Hygiene* (1937; 4th ed. 1948; Spanish ed. 1945).

> *The human being is and must remain inescapably grandiose, prideful, vain, and egotistical.*

This statement summarizes the essential nature of the human frame, the most characteristic of human attributes. From these characteristics we derive our acquired character traits, our road map for living, our stresses, and our symptoms. Understanding this fact is the foundation for functional and realistic psychotherapy.

257

## HISTORY

I came into psychiatry with no preconceived notions regarding behavior dynamics, probably because the year was 1931. I was taught the Freudian frame of reference by my significant authorities and, like any good child, I did not question because I had never doubted my parents; nor did I realize there might be anything else to believe.

I had been in psychiatry a dozen years before there was any conscious awareness that my current experiences seemed to have little relationship to what I had been taught and was trying to practice. Up to this time, I had assumed that any discrepancy between my findings and the details of the master plan were due to my own shortcomings in perceptual acuity, in ascertaining the facts, or in making proper connections.

Probably the precipitating factor in starting my growth and emancipation was the occurrence of dermatologic symptomatology in myself. Although I had had a Freudian training analysis, the tried and true answers seemed either invalid or insufficient when applied to myself.

My starting point was neurotic stress symptoms and an awareness of resentment. Whereas psychiatry had much to say about hostility, it had not said anything loudly and clearly enough about resentment to make any impression on me. I found that hostility was not a helpful term in my case; it did not move me on toward understanding the dynamics, so I used the term that fit.

Once I had labeled the feeling resentment, the next step followed logically: I had resentment because of another person's failure to give me what I believed (assumed) I was entitled to. I suffered from frustrated entitlement. Now I was dealing with interpersonal dynamics. Clearly, the basis of my own operations and consequent feelings and symptoms lay in my assumptions concerning what was right and proper behavior not only for me, but for another person.

The ironic factor was my failure to understand the universality of these simple details. Fortunately, I was involved with a variety of patients, and I discovered I had been blind to what really ailed them until I saw what ailed me. I, impeccable; I, deserving; I, worthy; I, special; I, better than; I, superior; I, virtuous, was entitled. In my case, it was entitlement to appreciation, to assistance, to cooperation equal to the measure that I gave, to fair play. Someone else might have felt (assumed) an entitlement to a variety of other things.

I learned that one never does anything unrelated to other people; one does not merely do something. *Whatever one does has interper-*

*sonal implications with respect to assumed entitlements and expectations*. Human action is always an assumed transaction rather than an interaction. The person himself is completely unaware of these dynamics. To build from this point to the development of the total theoretical framework took me another ten to fifteen years. Each new insight added to the total theoretical structure. In the beginning, there was no attempt to develop a system or a theory, to prove or disprove anything. There was merely the consciousness of a series of insights which gradually formed a totality.

The farther I went, the more I realized there were factors in common with those of many other theoretical systems, but it was identical to none of them, insofar as I was aware. After my earliest insights were published (3–6, 8), I received letters from people wanting to know whether Karen Horney (24–27) and I had ever worked together. This question made me curious, but I made it a point not to read Horney or to find out what she was saying, since I wanted to arrive at my own concepts. To be in considerable agreement does not necessarily denote that one has influenced the other. The more validity there is in our observations and conclusions, the more likely it is that others will find a measure of agreement with us through their independent work.

As I read the works of various people in subsequent years, I found myself in partial agreement with many: Adler (1), Freud (21), Fromm (22, 23), Korzybski (29), Pavlov (32), Rank (34, 35), Sullivan (37), and others. Probably I came closer to the concepts of Bernard Robbins (36), Walter Bonime (19), and Krishnamurti (30) than to others. I found the Learning Theory (31) of the psychologists compatible with my ideas, but it seemed to provide more mechanics than dynamics. Some who have known my work have called me an Existentialist (33), and this label may well have merit; however, I believe we are far from identical.

The last major insight, that of psychological self-preservation through maintaining one's grandiose self-image, is now about ten years old. I had written about it quite plainly for years before I realized fully what I was saying. My book, *Beyond Freud* (11), barely mentions grandiosity, even though it is now obvious to me that this is what I was talking about. Within my framework, grandiosity, the pride system, the value system, vanity, or the narcissistic self-image provide the real dynamics behind the mechanisms. These may be for development of the individual's character traits, for the consistency of his behavior, for the nature of psychological man, for the nature of stress experiences, and for the nature and goal of the therapeutic process. Grandiosity provides the dynamics of man's total behavior both in his usual state and in decompensation.

For the human being, it seems essential that he maintain his prideful self-image intact. He equates preserving and enhancing his vanity or his grandiosity with self-preservation because his psyche, or psychological self, and his pride system are identical. Thus, in the psychological realm, as in the physical, self-preservation is basic.

The theory which has evolved is a simple, unified concept, and seemingly universally applicable. In my experience, it serves the therapist far better than any eclectic approach. Although eclecticism frees one from being hamstrung by "a spurious theory," it provides no solid point of reference and does not show the direction in which to look or the way to go.

The more fully I comprehended the basic truths I had come upon (for so they still seem to me after these many years), the more I was impressed that these were no different from the teachings of the Judeo-Christian religion, which the behavioral scientists have singularly neglected as source material for understanding behavior dynamics.

Side by side with my involvement in understanding the psychodynamics of behavior has been my involvement in understanding human behavior that is the product of defective neurological equipment rather than of psychodynamics. Learning to be aware of the subclinical evidences of minimal cerebral deficit or dysfunction is as essential as learning to be aware of the multiple expressions of grandiosity. As clinicians, we have been largely blind to this total field, probably because we were taught that behavior is the product of internal or interpersonal psychological dynamics. This assumption is neither factual nor adequate. This presentation will not concern itself with spelling out the characteristics of organically determined behavior (7, 10, 13, 14, 20, 28). This does not imply that I regard psychodynamics as of primary importance in the total field of human behavior.

My intention was never to be in the uncomfortable position of belonging to the out-group, whether in relation to Freud, or to "organicity," or any other position I have taken. However, the stress was no greater for me than for the stream of others who have found themselves in similar predicaments.

I have come to view the behavior of people in the in-group toward those in the out-group as merely corroborative evidence of the validity of my theory: whatever an individual learns which relieves him of a sense of helplessness and loneliness in any specific area becomes one of his right beliefs and guiding lights. When this sense of right belief can be reinforced through consensual validation, then he belongs to the in-group. Holding the accepted right beliefs of the in-group entitles him to feel smugly superior to others who are in error, i.e., who do not see eye to eye with him, and to express a measure of contempt or benign tolerance toward them.

Many are the times I have smiled (with superior assurance) as I listened to young therapists who had been well taught by some other authority, as they invariably made the same repetitive response to the patient who had asked a question, "And what do you think?" Or I have noted their expressions of shocked superiority when they witnessed a therapist "being directive." It is not so much that we will not see as that we cannot.

## THEORY

Man is unique among animals by reason of his psychological nature. He develops this aspect or quality because of two determining factors: his nervous system organization and potential, and his long dependency period. The former makes development of his psyche possible, and the latter makes it necessary or inevitable. As a result of the interplay of these two factors, man has an identity which is more than physical. He is an "I," a being that functions within the framework of his physical capacities and limitations but according to a schema that is not determined solely by these physical characteristics, for he is as much psyche as he is soma.

Except for giving full measure of support to the natural neurologic potential of the individual (through introducing as little hazard or interference as possible, such as "poor heredity," genetic handicaps, marginal nutrition, metabolic problems, including anoxia, etc.), there probably is little that man can do to alter the basic phylogenetic nervous system which he brings to the scene. However, his long dependency period provides sufficient opportunity for variety in experiences so that the individual product is as unique as are fingerprints or voice prints. Each psyche is unique.

As with the soma, many similarities exist among people's psyches, but no two are identical. The similarities result from common or similar experiences. When these similarities are widespread, we may consider them to represent a culture, a more or less homogeneous set of values or orientations with regard to behavior patterns.

By reason of his long dependency period, both the developing infant and the ones on whom he is dependent for survival must make enough mutual accommodations to come through this long period without danger to either party. In fact, to achieve on-going stability the changes should be effective far beyond the period of dependency. Since there is a reciprocal relationship both parties are changed by the experience, but because the child is more helpless, he must make the major changes to conform with the adult patterns. The process of making the accommodations to the stronger world of people around him might be called maturation or socialization, but it is also properly seen as the period of development of psychological structure or psyche.

Psyche, thus, according to my schema, is developed after birth rather than being an innate aspect of man. It is developed out of the drive to survive physically in a world of people where one is helpless if left to himself. It is related to acquisition of mind sets or assumptions or beliefs concerning the way to behave—interpersonal functioning—and derives from personal experiences of security and insecurity in the particular world of people in which he experiences his dependency. That behavior which is harmonious with the mind sets of people on whom the child is dependent will be fostered whereas behavior that is incongruous will be discouraged or punished.

We may say that psyche not only is developed in an interpersonal context but that it functions in an interpersonal setting. That body of assumptions each individual has relates to interpersonal behavior. Every person knows through experience from very early in life what behavior is acceptable to his significant authority figures and what is not acceptable. As this knowledge accumulates, the reasons for having developed the detailed knowledge become blurred and finally lost, and merely the beliefs or assumptions concerning behavior and interpersonal processes remain, and these are accounted as right and correct.

These assumptions, born out of personal experience with significant people, are the substance of the psyche, that aspect of the person which is peculiarly unique and valuable and with which he identifies. It determines how he regards himself, how he behaves, and how he responds to others. It determines his attitudes, his feelings, and even determines what constitutes stress.

Once having developed a psyche, this body of assumptions concerning interpersonal behavior, it operates to make the person's behavior consistent and dependable. It is so dependable that it resembles obsessive behavior. It determines the moment by moment patterns of living. The whole of life is occupied by the security operations implicit in structuring, enhancing, and protecting the psyche. This means simply that survival is the basic law of life. Whether this survival be physical or psychological survival will depend on the circumstances, but survival of that aspect of the person with which he has major identification is the goal of living.

That with which the person identifies has great value to him; it is as though it is himself. Thus, his opinions, his beliefs, his assumptions, as well as more concrete details, are treasures to be properly regarded. The high esteem accorded the facets of one's self-image suggests that each person's self-concept is inflated. Likewise, it becomes evident when working with people that maintenance of their grandiose self-image is their constant endeavor, and stress is whatever threatens the continuity of their gradiosity.

Because anyone who wishes to work with people who feel troubled or disturbed needs to understand the dynamics of behavior, it is essential to comprehend everything that is implicit in the term grandiosity. Although a segment of disturbed behavior no doubt has organic neurologic failure basic to its occurrence, the overtones in these psychotic expressions run true to form in that grandiosity is the essential theme.

The basis of development of the grandiose self-image; how it expresses itself in everyday life; why the threat to one's pride system is synonymous with stress; what are the symptoms of stress; and what is the mechanism of reconstitution or healing will be presented now in greater detail.

## Bases of Grandiosity

Grandiosity or the prideful self system, the central dynamic characteristic of man, appears to derive from several sources. Because it is a universal, it appears to be the product of a universal experience. This could well be the fact of surviving, which in and of itself is evidence that there is innate strength. It may also derive from the fact that at a biologically critical point in the infant's existence, he was important enough to others to be in the center of someone's concerns and ministrations. Moreover, the self-image is in process of formation at the very time that the developing child occupies this central position in his cosmos—when his experiential world is still small enough so that his central position is difficult to challenge. Survival itself lends plausibility to one's sense of specialness. And, as though this were not sufficient, there is western civilization's religious tradition to explain man's special position in the cosmos by attributing to him divine sonship.

Universal primary grandiosity, or, as Freud called it, primary narcissism, is gradually reinforced through a secondary process, the incorporation (note the Garden of Eden story) or development of a value system that is made up of "right beliefs." Man ascribes to himself ultimate wisdom, with finality, on the basis of his limited experience, and he does this as a result of surviving despite his dependency. To be acceptable and therefore secure the child must come to see things as do the people on whom he is dependent, or he must suffer the threat of abandonment, which is tantamount to annihilation.

The matter of surviving gets shoved into the realm of the forgotten, as does its relation to the development of the assumptions about behavior which fill our lives, and the only thing that remains is the unquestioned certainty of the correctness of our beliefs. Having right beliefs is a universal, and each person and each culture regards itself as unquestionably better than others by reason of embodying these correct beliefs. Nobody holds a wrong belief; the moment he suspects one of his beliefs to be wrong, he drops it. Having right beliefs is a more potent source of self-esteem than is an action which is carried out, i.e., "I may eat peas with my knife, but at least I am superior to (better than) the poor misguided person who doesn't know that peas should not be eaten with a knife!" Everyone, without exception, finds a basis for believing or assuming he is superior or special.

### The Self-Image

Our beliefs concerning human behavior constitute our value system. They are also the material that makes up our self-image. Each individual identifies himself with his beliefs or assumptions, which are regarded as self-evident truths. He is the person who believes women should manage the money; or that men ought not to do any housework; or that children should obey without question; or that one must always tell the truth; or that girls should have first choice. Each person's life, his actions and his feelings, is made up of the patterning resulting from the hundreds of thousands of beliefs that he has acquired. Each belief about behavior is tagged with a value of more or less right or wrong so that there is a gradation or hierarchy from "must" through "may" to "must not." No value is assigned arbitrarily but derives from one's experience of having lived in the particular interpersonal world which was one's lot.

### Basis of Right–Wrong Judgments

Every belief or assumption about behavior concerns interpersonal behavior or interaction and derives its assigned value of right or wrong from the relative degree of security or insecurity having accrued to the individual as a dependent person through holding such a belief in his particular interpersonal world. Illustrative of this concept, it is still "wrong," not only for Jane herself to leave food on her plate, but for her guests to do so. This is because, in her formative years, her father demanded no food be wasted, and it would have been "dangerous" to defy him. Whereas it is liberating to recognize the source of this value, it still is not easy or automatic to disregard it. Even though the practice she carries out may make a measure of sense, the feeling attached to it belongs to her past.

The value system (assumptions concerning right and wrong) of the significant people (parents, teachers, and other surrogates) determines the attitudes, reactions, and pressures or lack of pressures which these people exert on the child. These are the culture-making and culture-binding influences. The assumptions of authorities will produce the sense of interpersonal security or danger which the child experiences. This feeling, in turn, will determine the values assigned by the child to the behavior and the underlying assumptions which he develops as he gradually and unconsciously sorts, organizes, and classifies his experiences. Going contrary to the values of his significant persons has some level of danger which he learns by experience; behaving harmoniously with their value system results in security. Generally speaking, whatever makes or permits the significant people feel at ease or gratified he classifies as right, because when they are at ease they promote the feeling of security in the child. Only that which brings about tension in the significant ones is accounted as wrong because anger is whatever generates their anger or tension.

As an illustration, we may refer to a situation familiar to many of us. This era being perhaps best designated as the era of rights or entitlements, it is understandable that Los Angeles should have experienced the Watts riots. A factor that seems to lie back of it is apropos, in that in this particular geographic area, there is a relative absence of the family as our culture knows it. Marriage and divorce are "the white man's racket," as a patient in Pennsylvania told me years ago, and the characteristic Watts family consists of mother and the children, usually fathered by many men. There is no authority figure because there is no male authority, and mother is the permissive one—the enduring lap and breast who holds things relatively together through her "love"— not her authority. Thus, these children grow up free of the firm hand of authority and develop the assumptions not only that they are entitled to do what they please, but that there should be no real interference with this license. On occasion, the mother, or more likely grandmother or aunt, may object, but never "with teeth"; therefore, the children growing up feel entitled to be left alone or not be interfered with. When one believes he is entitled to no interference, it is inevitable to regard the police as persecutors. Something comparable to this obtains, in general, in that parents who have long been concerned about being good-parents-who-make-their-children-happy, have succeeded in inculcating the assumption in their children that they are entitled to happiness.

Right–wrong concepts (11), or the person's value system, result from an individual having survived during relative dependency in his specific interpersonal world. Whatever was experienced as assisting in survival is regarded as right, and whatever was found to interfere with comfortable survival in his world of people is regarded as wrong. Doing right is generally equated with keeping mamma free from tension. In our culture, being happy makes mamma happy or teacher happy and is therefore right.

An important aspect of the value system is that it is chiefly laid down fairly early (because the greatest dependency period is early) and then it tends to operate as a more or less completed dynamism which ordinarily is neither clearly recognized nor greatly modified by the subsequent experiences of life. The effects in human behavior are that beliefs or assumptions remain stable, and consequently, the derived behavioral patterns are stable. The individual is minimally aware either of what he does or the dynamic force that determined his behavior and his feelings.

The implications are clear also that there is an unconscious element in all behavior, unconscious not because of being painful or traumatic and therefore repressed, but because the brain is constantly accumulating sensations and percepts that never come into awareness and because much that enters into formation of the value system occurs prior to use of word symbolization, an important aid to conscious awareness.

## Self-Identity

The basic entity of a given person is his ever-correct value system which has been accumulated through the experience of living in his specific interpersonal world. This value system with which he identifies is also his psychological self. This essential "I" or psyche is the "computerized reservoir" of beliefs or assumptions that one holds which relate to interpersonal functioning. Each detail is associated with right–wrong value judgments. It is always organized or programmed in terms of roles, such as men, women, children, boys, girls, in-group, out-group, older, younger, strong, weak, big, little, good, bad, employer, employee, family, outsiders, husband, wife, mother, father, and innumerable other categories. Because it developed in an interpersonal setting, every assumption invariably has two parts, namely, (1) what a person does in any role and (2) what the response of the person in any role should be to what one does. We may say that every psychological assumption includes the actor-reactor concept.

## Action-Reaction Concept

Because the basis of the two-pronged assumption usually is not in awareness, the habitual practice is for the person, A, to take for granted (assume) not only that he is doing what is right or what is justified, but that the other person, B, the reactor, is supposed to behave in response as A's assumptions or value system has predetermined that he should. The person's assumptions-concerning-responses are expressed through the felt entitlements which he holds. This makes difficulties because the reactor also has a system of values, assumptions, and attitudinal sets regarding interpersonal behavior on the basis of his own past experience. This system may not coincide with the anticipations or felt entitlements of the one to whom he is reacting. An additional difficulty arises because in any interaction the roles of actor and reactor are continually shifting. A person may conceive of himself as the actor at one moment and the reactor at the next moment. A further complicating factor is the disparity in the manner in which different people perceive a given situation. Semantics is also involved, both in this perception and in the expression of the concept to the other individual. It becomes obvious that human behavior is fraught with misunderstandings.

To untangle these details, to assist the individuals involved to perceive themselves in their interactions, and to recognize the beliefs or assumptions that are the dynamics behind these actions and feelings is the job of the psychotherapist.

## Primacy of Thought over Feeling

As I see it, feeling or emotion is secondary to or results from thought: it is the product of an assumption, an assigned meaning, a belief. One basis for confusion regarding what is primary is the loose use of the term "feeling." It stands for an emotion, a physical sensation, and a belief or an assumption. Perhaps we need to be more explicit. We say "I feel" when we actually mean "I think."

When a person behaves in accordance with his value system, he feels good about himself, smugly self-satisfied, virtuous, and comfortable. The belief has led to the feeling as well as the action. If, for some reason, he behaves contrary to his values and does what he believes to be wrong, he feels uncomfortable and guilty, unless he can bring to bear another value that alters the relative position of the first value on the hierarchy. In such a case, he will have mustered his forces and determined (thought out) that while he did do this thing that was wrong according to his value system, at least he did not do that thing. As long as one can keep his "at leasts" available, he has no feeling of guilt. He may also shift from the role of actor to reactor and thereby be spared any guilt. I may not, as the instigator (actor) insult another person, but if he insults me, I as the reactor am justified in retaliating. People use these mechanisms for self-justification or what is commonly termed rationalization, which is another way of saying that they thereby maintain their grandiose, prideful self-images intact. They have achieved psychological survival. Destruction of one's pride system or grandiosity is tantamount to psychological death. It is no wonder people protect their vanity or their value system so fiercely.

### Case

Laura, age 31, came complaining of anxiety symptoms of several weeks duration. She had been involved with the law since age 10 for a variety of crimes and delinquencies, including use of narcotics, prostitution, shoplifting, robbery, etc. Though she had been in two juvenile institutions and in prison most of the time for the past ten years, this was the first time she had experienced anxiety symptoms.

She had always been very close to her mother, who was a long-time narcotics dealer. All her life she had helped mother package the "stuff," and she would have "taken the rap" for mother any time had the police come, because the daughter was a known "user." Mother had been very clever and had "never been busted," i.e., found guilty. Mother always insisted that "stuff was to be sold, not used."

On the occasion of her last parole, the patient found her close relationship with mother usurped by mother's boy friend; furthermore, as all three were returning from across the border with a good supply of narcotics, and patient wanted a few hundred dollars to set up an apartment, it seemed to her that mother was more interested in having all the profits from the sale of the narcotics than she was in being helpful to her daughter, recently released from prison. Mother treated the request as though it were fantastic and implied she would not help if all the daughter expected to do was "use." Patient (reactor) felt "put down," belittled by mother (actor). She was angry (resentful), so she called the Federal Bureau of Investigation and informed on her mother, who was "busted for the first time."

Now both were in prison. The symptoms the patient experienced were due to guilt which she was experiencing for the first time in her life. Not only had she violated the criminal's basic code which says that one should not be an informer, she had done it against her own mother. The anger was gone; the justification was gone; the jealousy was gone; and there was left only the guilt of having broken her code (value system).

## The Masks of Grandiosity

As I use it, grandiosity has implications different from those generally understood. It is not typically a strutting, although it may assume this aspect. It is not an officiousness, nor does it necessarily have a blatant quality. It is usually not offensive or loud or insistent, although all these characteristics may express grandiosity. In fact, we have been quite literally led astray through being taught that when we see assertiveness or obvious grandiosity, it connotes just the opposite self-appraisal: that these characteristics signify overcompensation for a sense of inadequacy or self-devaluation. The belief that aggressive self-assertion implies poor self-esteem has been the basis of much of our failure as psychotherapists. Although grandiosity definitely does express itself assertively, more often it is apologetic, shy, timid, sensitive, or even "paralyzed-in-living."

Fear of competition or fear of not showing up well are present in most people. The person who cannot ask for a job or face strangers cannot tolerate the possibility of even partial rejection. He can tolerate nothing less than complete acceptance without reservations. People do not want anyone to suspect they are without all the answers or that they have any lacks or flaws.

One homosexual could not stand the possibility of being rejected or laughed at by someone who could hurt his pride, so he chose to be chosen rather than to be the seeker. Another homosexual derived gratification of his narcissism through frequenting the gay bars where everyone is openly recognized as a very special and superior person. The female homosexual is often weary of catering to the male egotism through making believe he has provided her something special when, as a matter of fact, she feels contempt for his disregard of her needs and capacities. She will not subject herself to the indignity of being taken for granted.

*Case*

After being rejected once by a young suitor whom she idolized, Sally developed "a terrible fear of men" and passed her days as a homosexual with very special homosexual partners. She made it a point of honor never to make the first overture but followed through when the desired one had given the invitation. Finally, in one long-term relationship, the partner to whom she had given her very valuable all was faced with making a choice. When she chose her husband, Sally killed him.

When we find any sensitiveness, we can be sure it derives from the need to be so special that no blemish or inadequacy is manifested. When a person says, "I don't want to be better than others, I just want to be as good as," it is safe to assume that what he really is saying is that he must be as good as this one—and this one—and then this one—until he is clearly as good as everyone with whom he compares himself. There is no one so paralyzed-in-living as the one who cannot stand to be found with an inadequacy. Not daring to expose oneself to any aspect of failure is the great stunter of growth. Chronic dependency frequently masks the grandiose assumption of entitlement to tender loving care.

Everyone in his secret heart sees himself as special and in some important way superior and "better than," or at least he believes that any other than the special role is intolerable or not befitting him. "I may be an abominable cook (but who cares about that?), but at least I'm a good conversationalist (and that is really important)." In our society, being openly grandiose or prideful is dangerous. It engenders rejection (it's in bad taste!) or leads to a mental hospital. We thus have the proper ingredients for conflict, since the person must simultaneously preserve his grandiosity yet appear appropriately meek, reticent, and retiring. The common solution is to hide even from ourselves the fact of our supercolossal vanity. It is ubiquitous, yet it is absolutely intolerable.

*Stress Feelings*

When a person lives out his "good" or "right" values, he feels good about himself. When he does not behave in accord with them, he must justify himself so that he comes out feeling good in his own eyes, or he will feel guilt. If he behaves in such a fashion as to accept his own behavior as right and justified, and the other person, his operational partner, responds in a manner compatible with his expectations or assumed entitlements, as determined by his earlier experiences, then his feelings are comfortable and he scarcely is aware that an interpersonal transaction has taken place. If, however, the reactor has not responded as he is "supposed" to and has, in effect, failed to give what the "actor" believes he is entitled to, then he feels resentment; or, if his value system precludes resentment in the situation, he will feel self-pity. He will invariably feel self-accepting and sinned against and see the other person as the offender, the sinner. "It is incredible that this should happen to me!" or "I, saint; you, sinner" (3).

There is, however, a situation in which the person, the actor, despite doing his best to achieve the level of performance either in himself or in the reactor that his value system dictates, fails; yet, he feels no guilt. Instead, he feels helplessness. Some have described it as "copeless"; I would say "helpless to cope with." Helplessness is experienced only when there is a sense of necessity, a sense of inner have-to, with regard to some objective. This goal may be to measure up to some conceived level of perfection in oneself, or it may be to bring about a supposedly necessary change in the other person. It is more common to feel helpless about effecting changes in the other person than in oneself, partly because changing the other person is the direction his efforts usually take, since the other person clearly needs changing; and partly because he sees himself as having already arrived at near perfection in these particular areas, or at least justified in imperfection. A change in himself could only entail a change for the worse; and, since no one can bear guilt, it is obvious that the change must be made by the other person.

The feeling of helplessness, always being associated with a feeling of inner have-to, is related to the value system since it clearly pertains to something that is regarded as important. Psychological homeostasis demands that his prideful self-image not be put in jeopardy, that his value system be maintained, that he measure up properly, and that the other person behave as he is supposed to. Since the self-concept is always a functioning concept, it is necessary that both activities, the action and the reaction, be maintained.

We may say that maintaining one's pride system or value system is the continuing goal of everyone throughout his life, and the dynamics of on-going life is simply this—no more, no less. We are all familiar with other cultures and how highly they regard *amour propre,* self-esteem, and saving face. Rather than regarding these as amusing foibles, I consider them as dynamisms central to psychological existence. This is the way of maintaining the culture without which physical survival would be impossible. When vanity or grandiosity is sensed to be threatened, anxiety results, exactly as when physical integrity is threatened.

Just as felt entitlements and resentments or self-pity are the result of assumptions, so helpless feelings are the product of assumptions, such as, "I have to improve myself in this or this manner," or "He must change for his own good and so that I can live with him." Helpless feelings often are expressed in the guise of rage or of depression. Rage represents a lesser degree of felt helplessness than does depression, and depression is often the way helplessness is expressed when rage is prohibited by the person's value system. One may also feel helpless to express rage or resentment, or even to admit its presence; in such a case, depression often provides a respectable, i.e., acceptable to the pride system, expression of helplessness. Depression signifies not repressed rage or hostility, but felt helplessness to accomplish something that is deemed essential for maintenance of one's self-image. If one is helpless to express rage or resentment, he may become depressed, but it is helplessness rather than repressed hostility which is etiologic.

Hostility, which psychiatry is wont to deal with, needs to be broken down into its component parts if we hope to perceive behavior more clearly and accurately or hope to deal with it more effectively. What ordinarily passes for hostility has at least three different aspects: (1) hostility or a long-standing character trait, (2) resentment which derives from frustrated entitlement, and (3) rage which derives from sensed helplessness.

Hostility, the character trait, is developed just as any other character trait is, early in life or during a dependent state, by necessity or by permission of a significant person. It is often copied from one's model and thus is more relevant to the past of the model than to the person's own present or past. Minority group attitudes in our current culture exemplify this mechanism. Hostility is quite different dynamically from either resentment or rage, though the expression of one is not unique or characteristic and may resemble the expression of the others.

It is customary to accept a person's self-devaluing statements as evidence of a low self-esteem. To make apologies for oneself is ordinarily regarded as evidence of the person's poor or worthless self-image. Nothing could be farther from the truth. Such people are expressing their grandiosity openly. They often are manipulating the listener into denying the truth of the statement and giving reassurance that they are indeed worth a great deal in all sorts of ways; or, they may not be trying to manipulate in this manner, but they deal with a black and white world: if they are not ultimate perfection, they are therefore poor, valueless wretches. Thus, their complaints about themselves derive from their perfectionism and their grandiosity. Their pride system cannot tolerate themselves as human beings, and they wail about not being "god." Wherever we find persisting self-devaluation or an inferiority complex, we may be assured that the person is grandiose and he takes himself so seriously that he is actually apologizing or castigating himself for having a blemish or two!

Average citizens brought up in our religious culture believe they mean what they say when they repeat certain accepted cliches, such as, "Of course I'm a sinner." If they are asked for clarifying evidence, with particulars, they are commonly totally unable to present anything meaningful, or if they finally do, it usually refers to something that happened a very long time ago. In the here and now they find nothing amiss, and their grandiosity has habitually gone unchallenged.

### Repetitive Patterns

Repetitive patterns come about in one of two ways: (1) because of organic neurologic limitations there is the tendency to be perseverative or stuck in some particular rut of action or feeling; or (2) because of his value system the person is dealing with certain inner feelings of necessity or have-to which bring about a compulsive type of behavior. People have-to do this or that lest they feel guilty or threatened in their pride system. The one type is about as common as the other, but the latter needs psychotherapy, whereas the former cannot make use of it.

Much has been said about the relation of guilt to compulsive behavior. The common assumption has been that the person was compulsive because he was guilty, or that he was rigid because of guilt. I see it as quite the opposite. The person is compulsive or rigid not because of experienced guilt but because he must prevent guilt at all costs. We deal here not with guilt but with maintained virtue. These are quite different psychodynamically.

Suicide occurs in a variety of situations, but it is never an expression of Thanatos or a self-destructive drive; in my experience, there is no such thing. Perhaps the commonest suicidal attempt or gesture occurs in people with minimal cerebral handicap or dysfunction. The most characteristic trait of this group being impulsivity, or poor higher center control over their actions, a suicidal gesture or attempt is just another expression of their impulsivity. The situation that has "driven" them to this would be regarded by any average person as so inconsequential that their act seems almost senseless or bizarre. They are also the ones who are easily rendered helpless, since they do not "add up" with any degree of adequacy, their integrative capacities are faulty, and they have trouble arriving at logical conclusions; therefore, they are especially vulnerable to the adaptational demands of living. These are the people who escape death by a whisker and then pick up and go on essentially untouched by the total experience. Trying to do psychotherapy with these individuals is a waste of time. Counseling may be in order, or the voice of authority, or reassurance or environmental manipulation, but not psychotherapy.

Suicide may represent a choice to die rather than to give up certain values that are important, e.g., love of country. Thus, suicide represents in some instances a preservation of the honored value system with which the person identifies, or a form of psychological self-preservation. It may also represent a "shucking" of a useless quality or appendage (the body), after the value has already been lost. After "I, wealthy" or "I, reliable" went down the drain in the 1929 stock market crash, there were many who committed suicide because what they regarded as valuable was already gone and seemingly not retrievable. Suicide may also represent a device for injuring another person without feeling any guilt. When the value system dictates suicide, it has its roots in grandiosity—perhaps even the grandiosity of playing god, through determining, through knowing the answers, or even through the power to haunt.

So-called masochistic behavior, which supposedly takes pleasure in the suffering invited or meted out by the choice that is made, represents not a self-destructive or self-punishing drive but a survival drive—psychological survival. The cherished value, the important pride or vanity is maintained even when the cost is physical destruction. "Rather lose your life than your honor." Who but a heathen would rush to take the last piece of bread, or cake, if it meant someone else did without? In the prisoner of war experiences, there is no doubt about the primacy of psychological values. A "civilized" man does not save his skin without regard to the welfare of others. On board a sinking ship, although there is no pleasure in the prospect of drowning, no self-respecting man would insist on getting into the lifeboat while women and children go down. There are some things that are worth preserving more than physical life, according to the nature of our assumptions.

Some instances of self-destructive or self-defeating behavior have little or nothing to do with preserving a value system, and superficially they appear to have only self-destruction as their goal and intent. Careful scrutiny of these instances will show destruction is purely fortuitous and the actions stem from their being poor at comprehending cause and effect relationships; or in other words, they are merely stumble-bums. One must be cautious when labeling something masochistic, that the intent of the person is actually self-defeat, and that this goal produces pleasure. Because I destroy or short-change myself does not imply that this is my goal. To understand a person, one must understand what his objective is, as well as what actually happened. It is like the old adage, "Meant well, did little, failed much."

I am frequently aware that in working with felons who are repeaters, counselors have been emphasizing the erroneous concept that they wanted to return to prison or wanted to destroy themselves. Although this is true in some cases, in general it is not. The fact is that they thought they were smart or clever enough to get away with it; or they had never accepted the idea that if they wanted something, they should not have it; or they believed they were justified in doing it; or their appraisal of the situation was totally inadequate; or they are habitually impulsive. Wanting to return to prison rarely enters the picture.

We see that the orientation which I present here goes contrary to the usual way of looking at things in that I do not see any person as having "a poor self-image" which needs bolstering; the therapist must look for the grandiosity of the assumptions which will tolerate nothing but conceived perfection or the ultimate in oneself—everything else is trash. Likewise, to interpret "masochism" as having the goal of self-destruction is to miss the total meaning of the behavior. Because it is usually true that the patient cannot move farther than the therapist, it is essential that the therapist perceive the situation accurately.

## PRACTICE

### Selection of Patients

The acceptance of a patient for psychotherapy is contingent upon my assessment of a number of factors. If he is suffering from a psychosis and therefore cannot think reasonably, I accept the fact of my limitations in having any appreciable psychotherapeutic effect on him. If it is due to a biochemical disturbance, as in alcoholic hallucinosis or thyroid toxicosis, psychotherapy is not the treatment of choice. If his problem is a basic chronic thinking disorder, founded in the association disturbance described by Bleuler (18), it is unlikely that through psychotherapy I can effect any essential change in his deficit, even though I may succeed in clearing up some confused detail that has come to attention at the moment. I regard these thinking disorders as lifelong deficits which interfere with the ability to appraise, to integrate, to abstract, and to make shifts from the general to the specific and vice versa. No matter how much I clarify or alter or educate or make free from the realm of unconscious material, the essential thought disorder remains, and there is little expectation on my part that there will be necessary transfer of learning, which is essential if psychotherapy is to be really effective.

Many people with normal or high I Q 's are handicapped with this type of deficit (7, 10, 13, 14). They might be described as "bright but dumb." Although they are not good subjects for psychotherapy, they can often utilize a ready-made clarification, or one handed to them, and the therapist ought not strain at providing this service if this is realistic and helpful. After all, therapy is not carried out for the benefit of the therapist's pretty self-image!

Not infrequently, a "directive" session or two accomplishes as much for these patients as protracted sessions geared toward insight or basic change in assumptions. An on-going, now-and-then relationship with a reasonably mature, objective, insightful, and nonexploitative therapist will usually accomplish more for these patients than endless analysis or psychotherapy as I am describing it in these pages.

I need further to determine whether the basis for seeking help is a concern about the regular and usual patterns of his life, the symptoms of a character disorder or personality trait disturbance, or whether there is little concern about life patterns but a great deal of concern about the uncomfortable symptoms that represent a decompensation from his usual relatively comfortable way of feeling. In this latter case, we are dealing with neurotic or psychotic symptomatology stemming from the person's inability to maintain his prideful self-image. This is what stress or anxiety means: that one's grandiosity or vanity or pride system is somehow threatened.

No matter what my appraisal may show with regard to diagnosis, whether psychosis, psychoneurosis, or character disorder, I must always be aware of any organic limitations that may be present. It is a fallacy to see a patient as psychotic, neurotic, *or* organic, for nothing is so likely to make a person stress prone and therefore decompensation prone as organic neurologic limitations. Minimal cerebral dysfunction, often congenital or incurred in early life, is probably the chief single etiologic factor in psychiatric decompensation as well as in the other areas where people are not making the grade, such as in delinquent and criminal behavior, chronic welfare cases, or school failures (7, 10,

13, 14). What I expect of a patient and what I expect from myself should bear an important relationship to the presence or absence of this organic factor. If there be any appreciable thinking deficit, there are better ways of helping him than through insisting he be put through the analytic or insight therapy mill.

I believe that a deficient awareness in the therapist of the characteristic symptomatology of minimal cerebral dysfunction is one of the reasons why psychotherapy has come into fairly general disrepute. It also may be a factor in the interminable analyses which are reported. One of the marks of an expert is that he knows his own limitations; also, he should have a fairly accurate judgment with regard to what can and what cannot be done; and he should be able to make a fairly accurate appraisal of what methods and tools are called for and not have to insist that one method be universally applicable, such as "play therapy for children," or "group therapy," "insight therapy," "therapeutic community," "corrective reconditioning," or even psychotherapy.

The more the patient suffers from a thought disorder (18) with its roots in an organic deficit, the less he needs insight therapy and the more he needs structure, external authority, guidance, assistance in the learning process, support, limited expectations of change, and perhaps modification of the environment. If the person is not handicapped in this manner, it is a disservice to him to attempt to manipulate or change his environment, since it is important that he be held responsible for making whatever changes come about.

Patients with another type of problem may come for help, but I have considerable reluctance in accepting them for therapy. These patients characteristically cannot give a straightforward account of their difficulties but nevertheless present endless material, with great detail, and tend to get lost or to lose me in the minutiae. The only thing that emerges clearly is my own confusion. At the end of the initial session, or even the second one, I am as far from a clear concept of the real problem or the real dynamics as I was before we started, despite a plethora of words and despite my sincere and undivided attention. I have learned that this type of individual probably is too paranoid to make use of psychotherapy, too defended against seeing himself, and too rigid to make any changes. He may also be a neurologically handicapped person who has difficulty in figure-ground determination, and thus value assignments are inappropriate. Spending time with such a patient often is an interesting experience and may assist the therapist in his own growth, but if one expects to make any change in the pattern in the foreseeable future, he is somewhat overoptimistic.

Motivation for therapy is a frail reed on which to rely. There are people who are "highly motivated" for therapy who could not possibly use it, usually because of their basic minimal cerebral dysfunction; and there are people who, though they had never considered whether they need psychotherapy, happen to come into contact with a therapist, and on the basis of this contact, get an insight that forever makes life different. Working among felons demonstrates how difficult it is to make cut and dried rules regarding motivation and suitability for treatment. Change sometimes is effected when there is no discernible motivation, and seeming motivation more often covers manipulation and search for secondary gain.

In a prison, where manipulation is the rule, I am especially reluctant to accept a patient for psychotherapy if I am reasonably sure he will be using therapy as just one more device for evading responsibility for his own actions and feelings and as a focal point for rationalizing his failure to change. If I believe that the patient is intellectually capable of making use of therapy, but I still do not wish to accept him in a treatment relationship, I tell him explicitly the reasons for my decision and terminate the session. I have learned that such candor often is therapeutic. It usually is true that if the therapist is not too available or if he is not "understanding personified," the contact, however brief, tends to be more meaningful and more provocative of reflective thought by the patient. It serves as a jolt.

The matter of fees as affecting treatment has been given much attention (12). It seems important that if a fee is not to be charged, the gift implicit in this feeless arrangement not come from the therapist but from an agency or institution that makes it a regular practice to provide this type of service. This eliminates the special arrangement implication.

## The Psychotherapist

It is dangerous for a nonsalaried therapist to "give away" his time and know-how without some clearly defined remuneration. Whatever the detail that is being bought with free service to patients, it should be clearly held in mind by the therapist, so as to avoid the grandiose notion that he is kind, generous, or put-upon.

I conceive of psychotherapy as a two-party relationship, the goal of which is to bring about in the one labeled patient changes in his beliefs or assumptions concerning himself and his interactions with people. It requires genuine involvement on the part of the therapist with the patient and his on-going life, but not in it. I have found it impossible to wear two hats. I cannot be a therapist and have a personal involvement with my patient as well. I cannot step in and out of the therapist role. Violation of this role on a single occasion usually means the therapist has forfeited not only his right but his ability to pick up the therapist role again. The psychiatrist, guided by the oath of Hippocrates to serve his patient faithfully, ought to count ten before he cheats his patient of his therapist. Sometimes the regard of the therapist for the patient is so genuine that dates, intimacies, or marriage are considered or entered into. Any chance of being professionally helpful to the patient is vitiated by such unwarranted, short-sighted, and greedy personal involvements.

Although life is constantly providing opportunities for growth, these are not likely to come about through further contact with such a spurious therapist, who has not learned that he must never manipulate the patient into fulfilling his own felt needs. The eyes of the therapist must be focused singly on being as good and effective a therapist as he can be. There can be no personal relationships of any kind lest he, in some planned or unplanned manner, use his patient. If the therapist has a variety of unmet needs (9), whether for companionship, for labor, for "helping" the patient, or something else, he must not permit his patient to become involved in fulfilling them, even when the patient's seeming needs appear to coincide precisely with those of the therapist. It is easy for the therapist to think so well of himself that he deludes himself into believing he can manage this tightrope performance, but it cannot be done without violating the responsibilities implicit in the role of therapist.

Being a therapist carries with it many hazards, chief of which is self-delusion. By reason of his vanity, he may fail to see he is playing into the hands of the patient's neurotic patterns, reinforcing both his own and the patient's narcissism. It is tempting to feel gratified by having been chosen, or to feel he is doing a better job than this or that previous therapist, or that "except for me" the patient would fall to pieces. When we cannot resist the temptation to feel special, it is time to take time out for a little therapy for ourselves. The task of the therapist is to assist the patient to see himself in his feelings, actions, attitudes, and beliefs now, here, in present tense, and then to help him recognize that his assumptions are not necessarily valid because he takes them for granted.

Awareness that the patient rarely moves faster or farther than his therapist does not mean that the therapist must strain every nerve and muscle lest he miss something and thereby fail his patient. He must be alert and attentive, to be sure, but fortunately for most of us, if a detail is of any consequence, it will recur time and again. The therapist must step into the frame of reference of the person to be understood, to be aware of his assumptions, and see that no matter how the patient violates another person's value system, the patient is operating by his own self-preserving code.

### Case

A 36-year-old woman with an IQ in the superior range had spent the greater part of 20 years in prison for a variety of crimes. When asked to sketch her self-image, she responded that though it sounded egotistical, she did not mean it to be, but she was the kind of person that would make the world better off if there were more people like her in it. Specifically, she saw herself as one who minded her own business and one who did what she said she would do; she was a person who kept her word. Although she saw herself as this very nice person, the record indicated something else. She thought nothing of burglarizing a place or carrying out a robbery with the help of a deadly weapon in order to have money to see a certain play she had promised herself she would see. The fact that her money was all gone because she got bored with her job and quit it was of little consequence. She never stole from individuals but only "from large establishments where no one is hurt by it because they carry insurance."

Although she was aware of the values which she presented freely, she was not quite so conscious of other values which she told about more indirectly, e.g., she believes egotism is wrong, inasmuch as she apologized for it and discounted its presence in her case; furthermore, her value system says it is not improper egotism if one does not flaunt it and if one says the appropriate propitiating words, or if one knows egotism is bad. Additionally, she devalues the importance of steady working, particularly when it does not require her to use her creative and superior capacities, and she feels superior as she chooses to go to certain plays that are "in" even if she must rob to get the price of the ticket. She also feels superior to those who steal from individuals who are not insured.

The way the patient behaves toward me is his usual and characteristic way of behaving. He brings me himself. Our situation is not unique except that in this circumscribed situation, we may actually see how he relates to people rather than rely solely on his retrospective descriptions, which are commonly distorted both by his need to preserve his self-image and by an actual failure in his perceptions.

*The Sessions*

Since I do not regard psychotherapy as a type of catharsis, and since I do not wish the patient to recover from his distresses by reason of finding in me a kind, understanding mother figure, I do not encourage the patient to use any session, even the initial one, as a dumping ground. Permitting a person to vent his spleen not only once, but repeatedly, can hardly pass for therapy. From the moment of contact, the relation with me is focused on the patient and his problem, with the goal of clarifying for both of us as much as possible of his behavior, his feelings, and his assumptions as quickly as possible. Since no one really sees himself, the picture that emerges is by inference or implication rather than by his direct presentation.

It is surprisingly difficult to be aware of whatever it is one takes for granted. In some instances, the therapist must assist the patient to understand the forces operating in his life which determined the laying down of these particular assumptions and values and not some others. Psychotherapy is at least in part an intellectual process and a learning experience.

I do not start the treatment program with the idea that "this will take a long time," or that we will have sessions once or twice a week indefinitely, or even for six to eight months. It is not unusual that I may see a patient once or twice and then not again for a month or two. When the patient returns, I find out what he derived from our session and how he is using it. The sicker the patient, the closer I space the initial two to three sessions, but I expect him to make use of our sessions from the very first, or I suspect he wants something other than psychotherapy. Appreciable movement may take some people a long time, but in such cases I still expect to spend minimal time with them. They must do work on their own.

Medicine has provided a general outline or guide for evaluating a patient, which serves me very well as psychotherapist. In our initial session, I start with Chief Complaint (CC), progress to History of Present Illness (HPI), follow with Personal History (PH) and Family History (FH). I want to know exactly why the patient comes for help now; what troubles him; where he hurts. I wish to know how and when the trouble started, under what circumstances, what has been its course, what has aggravated or alleviated the trouble. I want to reach some tentative impression concerning the nature of the illness or disability (diagnostic label), how disabling it is, how the patient has tried to cope with his problem in the past and with what results, what is the reaction of the environment to his illness. The next part of the evaluation will be a synopsis in chronological sequence of the person's total life—the broad panorama, including family and other relationships, health, education, work, financial and other achievements, and general goals and directions of striving.

In this first session, I also want to determine whether further clarifying procedures are indicated, such as psychological tests to check on my impressions of minimal cerebral dysfunction, an EEG test, or medical evaluation.

I need to appraise whether the information he gives me is reliable or whether I need to turn to other sources. There has been far too much attention paid to the garbled and distorted feelings of patients and too little to obtaining factual data. The very essence of the people with minimal cerebral dysfunction is a deficiency in capacity for appraisal, and therefore, seeing life through their eyes can lead the therapist only to compounded error. The therapist needs to know how the patient sees whatever it is he is looking at, but the therapist should be very cautious in accepting it as factual. Appraising the appraisal capacity of the patient is so essential it should be attempted in the very first session.

A case in point is the widespread tendency to regard rejection in childhood as the chief etiologic factor in much disturbed and delinquent behavior. The patient tells his story of rejection sincerely and repetitively, but he has probably failed to see that his own impossible behavior preceded the rejection or that his family has actually demonstrated an on-going sincere concern that no one but a misguided or limited person could misinterpret. He may also have failed to see that the real problem is due to his failure to come to terms with authority.

One of the great hazards in psychotherapy is failure to clarify. A patient makes a statement that sounds all right, but I have learned I must constantly remind myself to get the specific data and details that have led him to make the statement. I may say, "Such as?" or "Exactly what do you refer to?" or "Tell me how you arrive at that," or "Give me some specific examples." I need to know if he thinks and reasons the way I do or if he is mouthing meaningless cliches. I have to be the measuring rod of the adequacy of his thinking. The leader has to lead. Everything must "add up," and it cannot do this until his assumptions coincide with reality.

It is obvious that I take very great pains to structure the initial contact in such a manner as to provide me with a working skeleton drawing of the patient as a person in a continuum, in relationship with others, including me, and as one who brings to me the picture of himself and how he functions. Can he tell a progressive story? What are his repetitive patterns? Is he capable of listening and following directions? Does he see cause and effect relationships? Does he have the capacity to clarify or only to use generalities? Does he have trouble assigning values? Can he tell what is more important from what is less important? Is he capable of organizing? Is he capable of relationships? What are his dominant feeling patterns?

By the end of the first session, I wish to have a comprehensive picture of the person, and this I cannot get if I encourage the patient to take command or "just talk," or if I spend time with trivialities or try to "sell" him on what a fine doctor he has come to. I do not waste time establishing rapport; rapport will have to take care of itself in due time. Nor do I typically wait until I am sure to the point of being positive about some detail in behavior before I make a psychodynamic "interpretation." The very first session may have numbers of these interpretive comments, like on-going summarizing or clarifying commentary, but these comments are always in the form of recognizable questions or tentative statements: "Is this what you are saying to me?" "Are you telling me that so and so?" "I think I hear you telling me that so and so?" "Am I hearing you say that you always do so and so?"

I hope to accomplish several things with this approach: it shows I am listening to what he says; that I believe what he says is meant to be intelligible; that everything must "add up" or we must know why; that although I am not arbitrary, I listen to what he presents in what to him is an unaccustomed fashion; that we are partners and I need his cooperation every step of the way; that only he can validate or invalidate my tentative impressions. In taking a nondogmatic approach, we minimize resistance. We demonstrate through example that vulnerability (my vulnerability) is not lethal, that I could be hearing incorrectly or my tentative conclusion might be in error, but this does not prevent me from offering it. In other words, I must run the risk of being wrong or looking silly through not seeming profound or "psychic" if I am ever to get my patient to be willing to do the same thing. My comments must be presented simply, briefly, nonmoralistically, and in language familiar to my patient so that he is not placed at a disadvantage or with any need for defensiveness. The patient often is able to say at once, "I never thought of it that way, but I guess that is what I really said."

The task of transferring responsibility to the patient has begun as soon as I share with him the responsibility for clarifying and for validation. Furthermore, I usually find that rapport or acceptance of me begins at the point where I am genuinely meeting his needs.

It has been customary to give attention only to a person's evidences of discomfort, such as his rages, his guilt, his depressions, his "paralyses," his alcoholism, or his physical symptoms which often stem from his resentments. Although these are essential focal points in understanding a person, it is equally important to pay attention to those aspects of the patient which are not threatened, where he feels smugly secure and invulnerable. We need to be aware of these areas where he feels contempt, disdain, superiority, intolerance, or any other feeling that shows that he sees the other person as not up to his own superior standards or values. Awareness of his "have-to's" or his usual repetitive patterns is essential, since these are the earmarks of his neurotic patterns. The characteristic, though disguised, self-appraisal is "I, better than," and the attitude toward the other person can be summed up as, "I wouldn't be caught dead doing what he is doing." Any time we find the assumption that the other person is somehow beneath him, we are dealing with unadulterated grandiosity.

When the therapist is listening to distress signals, he listens to determine which of the three primary stress feelings the patient is experiencing: guilt, resentment, or helplessness. If it is helplessness feelings, are they expressed in rage, depression, physical symptoms, feelings of alienation or loss of identity, in confusion, or in hallucinatory experiencies? If it is helplessness that is present, what is it he feels helpless about? What is it he has to bring about? Why does this particular thing have to be accomplished? What would happen if he did not get it accomplished? Although the therapist does not ordinarily ask these specific direct questions, he listens and inquires with these questions in mind because the patient's assumptions must be made explicit and his grandiosity exposed.

Not infrequently, symptoms start in a comprehensible situation and then continue in what seems to be a haphazard manner. In such instances, the therapist needs to find out if it is the symptoms themselves that are terrifying and that he feels helpless to deal with, producing a vicious circle. It is often essential to deal in considerable detail with the original or initial circumstances and see how they relate to the present. He also needs to appraise whether the symptom is a conditioned response or an aspect of perseveration.

If the symptoms spell out resentment or self-pity, then who is it that has failed him and how? What makes him assume that the other person should behave differently toward him? What is it he feels entitled to receive from the other person, and what makes him entitled? Has this ever happened before? How has he gone about obtaining what he feels entitled to? In what situation did he learn that this particular detail in behavior merited or made him entitled to this particular response from the other person? Is the other person aware of the patient's strong feelings in the matter? Does he also feel disturbed? Is this the other person's usual and characteristic manner of behaving? If this be true, how can the patient expect him to behave out of character? Does the patient regard himself as such a unique experience for the other person that he has deluded himself to think, "For me he will be different"? And is this not the ultimate in grandiosity? What is there about him that makes it seem unreasonable that this should happen to him?

It is hard to accept that people behave according to their own well-established patterns. We often find that a patient actually feels guilty if he accepts another person as he obviously is; instead, the patient's code demands that he always expect the other person to be different from what past experience with him has given clear evidence he is and will be. The patient has to expect him to change "for the better," that is, as the patient thinks he should. But it usually turns out that the demanded change is "one for you and two for me."

If one does not know anything about the other person's patterns of response, then one can hope for anything. There is no reason not to hope for a completely gratifying and satisfying response. But if time, experience, and observation have shown that the person, the reactor, characteristically and habitually behaves in this other way, then it is time to use faith rather than hope: the patient should begin to have faith that the way the person has behaved in the past is the way he will behave now and in the future, since behavior is always a product of the stable and dependable operating structure of an individual. If the patient can cease expecting the other person to change, then he has already made a salutary change in himself.

There seems to be a never-ending procession of people coming for help. They have symptoms; they have unbearable distress; but the more carefully one listens, the clearer it becomes that the one they want help for is the other person, the one who ought, obviously, to do the changing. Sometimes the request is simple and direct, with no time wasted; in other instances, the therapist could listen hour after hour to the same complaint about the other person and how miserable he is making the patient, and how the therapist ought to be able to do what is necessary to change that person. I try to make clear the message I am receiving, namely, that he is telling me it is the other person who is in need of help, not himself. However, much as the other person may need help, he is not present, nor has he sought help. I cannot do therapy in absentia, and furthermore, it has been my experience that if a wheel squeaks—as I hear the patient loudly squeaking—it is that wheel that needs the grease. If we both accept the fact that the patient, the one present, is hurting, and that the only person one can change even slightly is oneself, then it would seem obvious that we need to concentrate on him, the patient, the one present, and see how he is failing to function appropriately in the given situation, how he is getting in his own way, and how he can begin to make necessary changes.

Sometimes when people are chronically preoccupied with their feelings, my expressed lack of interest in their feelings may be an unexpected and disturbing experience to them. When I determine that such preoccupation has aided in their habitual dramatization of themselves, I tend to give them the specific task of concentrating on "what needs to be done right now," hour after hour and day after day. This lessens the emphasis on vanity and emphasizes reality contact, with commensurate gains in self-acceptance.

When I was young in psychotherapy, I do not recall anybody telling me that disappearance of symptoms is not cure or change. It is very important to recognize that a patient may lose all his uncomfortable symptoms and yet be as sick as he was when he had them. This means that when we deal with decompensation symptoms, such as those of the psychoses and psychoneuroses, we still need to deal with the life patterns, the character disorder traits, the assumptions, and effect changes in them if there is to be any worthwhile or lasting improvement. It does not do any good to blow away the smoke; one must put out the fire.

### Case

A colleague described a patient he had been seeing, a Sister in a local convent, who was so depressed she was confined to bed and had been unable to function for a considerable period. She was attractive, intelligent, talented in many ways, and she had come from a privileged background. The problem, as the therapist saw it, was the stultifying experience in the convent, particularly because the Mother Superior seemed not to appreciate or make use of the fine talents which the Sister had to offer.

With the passing of the weeks of therapy, her symptoms improved, and she was able to be out of bed, partially functioning. One day my colleague asked me to see both the Sister and the Mother Superior. I saw the Sister first. She was as attractive as I had been led to expect.

She would not, however, talk with me; she let me know that if there was anything about her which I cared to know, I could ask the doctor who was her therapist. She hardly deigned to pass the time of day with me. Then came the Mother Superior, whom I perceived to be a big, rather broad-shouldered woman who spoke clearly and directly and had a sense of humor and a twinkle in her eye. She was well aware of the fine talents of the young Sister and she appreciated them. But, she explained, it was not her function as head of the convent to single out one Sister for special preference and responsibility, and much as she was aware of all the factors in the situation, she could not permit the Sister to manipulate her to the detriment of the total group.

In discussing the case with my colleague later, I suggested that he was not really doing psychotherapy with this patient; he was merely providing her with the appreciation she craved; he was siding with her against the Mother Superior and in this way was actually reinforcing her pathology. I could not say whether she was so rigid or brittle and paranoid that this was the only form of treatment she could use without decompensating into psychosis, but the therapist needed to quit deluding himself that he was doing psychotherapy. Only when there is a change in the patient's assumptions is there any actual healing. Only when the magnitude of one's grandiosity dawns on him, and then, after a moment of shock, it begins to appear hilarious, can the therapist say that he is helping to effect any genuine therapy.

This failure to see that the decompensation symptoms are not the patient's real problem is glaringly apparent in so many aspects of psychiatric practice, perhaps chiefly among the younger therapists, but also in mental hospitals. It is one of the reasons why drugs have been so acceptable to psychiatry. Patients tend to recover from their decompensation symptoms as a result of a variety of factors: removal from home, change in some part of the environment, the protection and security of such a structured environment as a hospital, freedom from the presence of a critical person, or finding a therapist who "really understands and appreciates me." This improvement is due to removal of stress and has nothing to do with true change or improvement in the patient's psychological being, which is the area of his assumptions concerning specific human interrelationships—what he should do and how he is entitled to have others treat him.

## RESOLUTION

The more realistically attuned an individual is, the easier it is for him to catch on to the relationship between his insistence on maintaining or enhancing his grandiose self-image and his on-going difficulties in life. He will not have so much invested in preserving the status quo or in not seeing his tendency to assume divine attributes. The more difficult it is for an individual to see his patterns as unrealistic and nonfunctional, the more important we may assume it must be for him to have this particular lens distortion.

Depending on the type of patient, ranging from fairly healthy to extremely "brittle" and sensitive, the therapist will use various techniques to help the patient see (1) what are his repetitive patterns and (2) what are the bases within himself for experiencing the behavior of others as stressful. The therapist may make direct observations and comments to the fairly healthy patient. For those with greater pathology, the pace is slower, the comments are more indirect, and much more support is offered in the sessions, though confrontation must take place sooner or later if the therapeutic relationship is to have any significance. Confrontation, however, is never an attack, nor is it condemnatory. It is a tentative statement.

It is anxiety-provoking to find oneself vulnerable by giving up or losing the basis for one's smug superiority, and the patient needs to be dealt with tenderly and with adequate support while he is in process of experiencing this anxiety. But while the therapist understands the threat the patient feels, he also calmly expects movement in the direction of experimenting with the unknown danger. It is the relationship with the therapist, the solid, stable, expectant one, that enables the patient to move into new and unexplored areas. The patient needs to discover that his world does not crumble when the old defenses are gone; that if preservation of his pride system is his only discernible goal, there had better be some reorientation and realistic changes.

One of the really difficult aspects of movement away from the pride system or value system as the guide for life is that any course of action other than the old one which brought distress (but it also brought assurance that one was "doing right" and therefore a smug, superior self-regard) is sure to bring about a new stress—the anxiety of guilt. Many people find this guilt too difficult, and they return forever to the old smug ways that are familiar but that bring only resentment, rage, or self-pity. There is no possibility of growing or maturing except by way of the path of guilt because any time we violate old established guiding codes, we feel guilt. This does not mean that guilt in and of itself signifies growth or maturing. But guilt, not retrospective guilt, but guilt produced in the here and now, is the inevitable consequence of a movement toward more realistic behavior. Healthy and necessary guilt is derived from present realistic choices and behavior and does not refer to guilt of the past.

*Case*

Mary, age 34, came complaining of physical symptoms that the doctor said had no physical basis. She seemed to be such a fine, capable person, doing a praiseworthy job of living and raising her family. However, her husband had recently been found to be having an amorous affair, and her symptoms had some relationship to this. Her tendency was to feel injured and to place the blame on her husband. Exploration, however, showed that for years he had had to play second fiddle, first to her father who was her chief confidant and advisor, and more recently, since father's death, to mother, who lived nearby. Mother's welfare, peace of mind, and contentment seemed always to come first. Mary had to telephone her every day at least twice. She had to take mother along shopping. When they had guests or special outings or events, mother was always invited to participate, and mother took it for granted she would be included. There seemed to be no stopping point, as the husband saw it. It was not within his code to wish mother-in-law would drop dead, so, in order to feed his own vanity and felt need to count, he was an easy prey to the female manipulators who look for a male whose wife does not understand him.

It would be simple to agree with Mary that the husband had failed her and that it is he who needs help. But he has not asked for help; it is Mary who has symptoms. It then becomes the therapist's task to help her look at how she lives her life and to see that it was she who got herself into this bind through her wonderful sense of duty toward mother, as well as her need to have nothing but the right answers in every decision, as evidenced by her reliance on father's superior judgment. When a person shifts conceptually from the role of victim (reactor) or injured one to being a participant culprit (actor), it is no longer possible for him to feel so resentful or have so much self-pity.

There is still more movement to be made with Mary, however, before the therapist's task is finished. It is clear that she has devalued the role of wife and elevated the role of daughter. If she behaves realistically, she will pay less attention to mother, who through necessity, may begin to shed some of her dependency and her enjoyment of being the corpse at every funeral. But whatever happens to mother's feelings, Mary needs first to try to develop the sense of appreciation for family and husband, with primary emphasis placed on her more mature roles rather than on her place in the childhood family constellation. This choice will be accepted as realistic if she is growing and maturing. However, guilt toward mother is not thereby obviated; it will plague her and make her anxious and uncertain, but if she persists in doing the realistic thing, the guilt will gradually diminish to liveable proportions, and she may anticipate that the symptoms will disappear eventually.

If she is unable to bring about the reality of "family" through her new emphasis, and she feels everything has been in vain, she will need to see that she is not honestly involved with her family but that she has made her changes as a manipulative device to get her husband to do what she wants him to do. She may not be permitted to regard her feeling for her husband as love as long as she is trying to manipulate him into giving her what she wants from him. Love never has self-seeking strings or stipulations attached. She will need to face her own dishonesty with herself and toward her husband whom she has been trying to convince of her love.

The next step in growing and maturing has to do with learning that she is responsible for her own welfare; that she cannot delegate this to anybody else. She needs to learn that she must do whatever she does, not so that she will get some desired response from the outside, for this is pure manipulation, but she must make choices moment by moment which call for appraisal and judgment with regard to her acceptance of her responsibility for her own total welfare, physical and psychological. To be healthy, one must be self-centered rather than other-centered. One's own welfare must be central rather than, "What must I do to get this or this reaction from people?"

This new way of thinking begins to eliminate the unrealistic dependency and the manipulation, the resentment and the entitlements which have been part of her life. It eliminates the necessity to make another person the center of her life so that she can manipulate him or her into giving the desired response and then feel angry or resentful when the other person is not manipulable. The healthy person gives priority to his own total welfare. When Mary is emotionally healthy, whatever she does will in her considered judgment be for her welfare rather than for manipulative purposes. Her decisions may show up errors in judgment of the factors involved, but there will be an honest attempt, and one can be sure there will be growth. She will be easier to live with the moment she gives up manipulation and dependency, because neurotic dependency is merely a flattering device for controlling, for demanding, and for imposing an unrealistic entitlement upon others.

Psychotherapy involves changing one's assumptions with regard to what is important both for oneself and for the other person. There may be a brief sadness if she cannot help bring about "family," as she drops her need to be the good, dutiful daughter, but she can no longer feel resentment or self-pity or smug virtue. Instead, she will be so involved in living each moment as realistically and responsibly as she has ability to see reality and responsibility that she will be grateful for the wider vistas that have opened for her. The focus as well as the goals have changed. The proper goal of psychotherapy is to help the patient to be, even momentarily, without the need to make feeding one's vanity his guide for living. To succeed completely is an impossibility, but with sincere desire, he can catch himself from time to time as he gets off the track and loses his way.

Once having seen himself in his ridiculous presumptuousness, the end is not yet achieved, for no one can keep his mind on living in the here and now and on his newly discovered insight at the same time. We have one-track minds. Since the great need is to be involved in the here and now, rather than with the past or the future, or with the great insight, or with oneself, then the "cure" for one's human predicament, which is his pride system and his grandiosity, is never complete; but as he catches himself more often, he may, with a true if momentary humility, realize, "Here I go again." If one truly sees himself in present tense, revealed in all his carefully disguised vanity, he will have perspective and he will be able to be nonmoralistically judgmental, which is tantamount to being kind. The shackles that obstruct growth will come off, and the gulf between himself and his brother will disappear, but only for a moment, and then he needs to be off again, living in the here and now, hoping sincerely to become aware of himself again when he sorely needs to do so.

"Salvation" is thus not through perfection and the ultimate. One is saved only for a fleeting moment; it is never an accomplished fact. But the great religious signpost also says that vulnerability is not so bad. We find that even a moment of glimpsing one's preposterous stance is sufficient to enable one to carry through this moment in healthy and creative relationship with others. Thus, relationship is possible only when one is vulnerable, that is, honest, rather than when he pretends to be or insists on being special and perfect, and only through relationship can there be growth. The whole orientation is one of maturing and growing rather than one of arriving. The process is the important thing. It is creating in the here and now through relationship.

## RECAPITULATION

Let us recapitulate a few of the assumptions or beliefs I have as I begin work with a patient. I believe I must keep the therapeutic relationship inviolate; I believe the dynamic of life of every person is self-preservation, both somatic and psychologic; I believe that symptoms of anxiety or stress occur when there is felt threat to the pride system; I believe that decompensation symptoms are not important except as they call attention to the assumptions on which they are based; I believe that any assumption of a patient which is important for understanding his disability will recur time and again; I believe that whether I wish it or not, my beliefs and assumptions that guide my attitudes and behavior will affect the patient; I believe that no person sees himself in action or fully knows himself; I believe that the great secret which man keeps from himself does not concern infantile sexuality but rather his own grandiosity; furthermore, I believe that it is man's vanity that gives him his difficulties in living, that paralyzes him and stunts him, that creates the interpersonal estrangements which exist; I believe his vanity prevents him from experiencing reality and from developing his own creative potential.

I see psychotherapy as an adventure in honesty. It is mediated through a relationship in which one person is designated the patient and the other the therapist. There is a constant utilization of all behavioral material at hand toward the goal of showing the patient to himself; "all is grist that comes to the mill." This self-revelation pertains to both the manifest behavior and to the beliefs or assumptions that give rise to the attitudes and behavior.

Another belief I hold is that once having seen ourselves, we can never again be quite the same. I believe it becomes easier and easier to catch ourselves in our unrealistic grandiosity once we have seen it. I also believe that no therapist can effectively help the patient to see himself until the therapist has seen himself. The more adept the therapist is in catching himself in his own grandiosities, the better he is able to recognize comparable patterns in the patient.

## SUMMARY

This brief report on Assumption-Centered Therapy is presented in three parts, the first of which deals with the historical background of the development of my theory of behavior dynamics. In the second section, a fresh concept of the nature of the psychological self is presented which provides a rationale for understanding and dealing with the broad spectrum of human behavior. This unitary, integrated, and simple conceptual framework is offered as applicable in the area of development of character traits, in the on-going patterns of living, in determining what constitutes psychological stress, in the development of symptoms, and in the healing process. The third section spells out (1) criteria for selection of patients for psychotherapy, (2) some of the special hazards for the therapist, (3) the specific patterning of therapeutic sessions, and (4) the nature of the goals of therapy.

## REFERENCES

1. Adler, A. *The practice and theory of individual psychology,* New York: Harcourt, Brace, 1929.
2. Adler, A. *Understanding human nature.* New York: Greenberg, 1946.
3. Anderson, C. M. All the world is queer but me and thee. *Ment. Hyg.,* 1950, **34** (2), 241–252.
4. Anderson, C. M. The anatomy, physiology and pathology of the psyche: a new concept of the dynamics of behavior. *Amer. Practit. Digest Treat.,* 1950, **1** (4), 400–405.
5. Anderson, C. M. The psychiatrist looks at saints and sinners. *J. Amer. Med. Women's Assn.,* 1950, **5,** (5), 186–189.
6. Anderson, C. M. *Saints, sinners and psychiatry.* Philadelphia: J. B. Lippincott, 1950. (Republished in paperback: Portland, Oreg. Durham Press, 1962.)
7. Anderson, C. M. Organic factors predisposing to schizophrenia. *The Nerv. Child,* 1952, **10** (1), 36–42.
8. Anderson, C. M. The self image: a theory of the dynamics of behavior. *Ment. Hyg.,* 1952, **36** (2), 227–244.
9. Anderson, C. M. The doctor–patient relationship in therapy. *Amer. J. Psychoanal.,* 1955, **15** (1), 13–16.
10. Anderson, C. M. Early brain injury and behavior. *J. Amer. Med. Women's Assn.,* 1956, **2** (4), 113–119.
11. Anderson, C. M. *Beyond Freud: a creative approach to mental health.* New York: Harper & Bros., 1957.
12. Anderson, C. M. Variations in the dynamics of the analytic relationship in the clinic and in private practice. *Amer. J. Psychoanal.,* 1960, **20** (1), 73–78.
13. Anderson, C. M. and Plymate, H. B. Management of the brain-damaged adolescent. *Amer. J. Orthopsychiat.,* 1962, **32** (3), 492–500.
14. Anderson, C. M. *Jan, my brain-damaged daughter.* Portland, Oreg.: Durham Press, 1963.
15. Anderson, C. M. The pot and the kettle. *J. Amer. Med. Women's Assn.,* 1963, **18** (4), 293–298.
16. Anderson, C. M. Depression and suicide reassessed. *J. Amer. Med. Women's Assn.,* 1964, **19** (6), 467–471.
17. Anderson, C. M. Guilt is not the problem. *Rational Living, 1966,* **1** (2), 31–36.

18. Bleuler, E. *Dementia praecox or the group of schizophrenias.* New York: International University Press, 1950.
19. Bonime, W. R. Paranoid psychodynamics. *Psychotherapy,* 1955, 1 (1), 61–71.
20. Clements, S. D. The child with minimal brain dysfunction—a profile. Paper presented at the Annual Conference of National Society for Crippled Children and Adults, Chicago, Nov. 23, 1963.
21. Freud, S. *The basic writings of Sigmund Freud.* The Modern Library. New York: Random House, 1938.
22. Fromm, E. *Escape from freedom.* New York: Rinehart, 1941.
23. Fromm, E. *Man for himself.* New York: Rinehart, 1947.
24. Horney, K. *The neurotic personality of our time.* New York: Norton, 1937.
25. Horney, K. *New ways in psychoanalysis.* New York: Norton, 1939.
26. Horney, K. *Our inner conflicts.* New York: Norton, 1945.
27. Horney, K. *Neurosis and human growth.* New York: Norton, 1950.
28. Kaliski, L. The brain-injured child: learning by living in a structured setting. *Amer. J. Ment. Def.,* 1959, **63** (4), 688–695.
29. Korzybski, A. *Science and sanity.* Garden City, N. Y.: Country Life Press, 1949.
30. Krishnamurti. *Krishnamurti writings.* Authentic report of ten talks. Ojai, Calif., 1944.
31. Mowrer, O. H. *Learning theory and behavior.* New York: Wiley, 1960.
32. Pavlov, I. P. *Conditioned reflexes.* London: Oxford University Press, 1927.
33. Plymate, H. B. Existentialism and its application in existential analysis: a descriptive summary. May 1960. Unpublished private communication.
34. Rank, O. *Beyond psychology.* New York: Dover, 1958.
35. Rank, O. *Will therapy and truth and reality.* New York: Knopf, 1945.
36. Robbins, B. S. The myth of latent emotions: a critique of the theory of repression. *Psychotherapy,* 1955, **1** (1), 3–29.
37. Sullivan, H. S. *The interpersonal theory of psychiatry.* New York: Norton, 1953.

# Chapter 11

# Rational-Emotive Therapy

## ALBERT ELLIS

Albert Ellis: b. 1913, Pittsburgh, Pennsylvania.

B.B.A., City College, New York, 1934. M.A., 1943, Ph.D., 1947, in clinical psychology, Columbia University.

Private practice in psychotherapy, 1952--date. Executive Director, Institute for Rational Living, 1959–date. Chief Psychologist, New Jersey Department of Institutions and Agencies, 1950–1952.

President, Division of Consulting Psychology, American Psychological Association. President, Society for Scientific Study of Sex. Vice-President, American Academy of Psychotherapists, Council of Representatives, APA.

Books: *Emotional Education* (1972). *Is Objectivism a Religion?* (1968). *The Case for Sexual Liberty* (1965). *Homosexuality—Its Causes and Cure* (1965). *Sex and the Single Man* (1964). *Reason and Emotion in Psychotherapy* (1962). *The Folklore of Sex* (1961). *How to Live with a Neurotic* (1961). *The Art and Science of Love* (1960). (Co-editor) *The Encyclopedia of Sexual Behavior* (1961). (Co-author) *The Search for Sexual Enjoyment* (1966); *Nymphomania: A Study of Oversexed Woman* (1964); *A Guide to Rational Living* (1961); *Creative Marriage* (1961).

Articles: Over 250 articles, including about 50 on psychotherapy.

**R**ational-emotive therapy (or RET) is the full name for a method of psychological treatment which is also called rational therapy (RT). I originated this form of treatment around the beginning of 1955, after I had been practicing classical psychoanalysis and psychoanalytically oriented psychotherapy for the previous half dozen years. Much to my surprise, I found psychoanalytic methods exceptionally shallow and ineffective, although I had believed, prior to my practicing them, that they were the deepest and most efficient therapies known to man.

The superficiality of psychoanalysis lies in that it practically never arrives at the fundamental cause of an individual's basic emotional disturbances; and, when it accidentally does so, it provides him with little information to help him change or eliminate this cause and thereby to become truly unanxious and unhostile and maximally self-actualizing (42). Although it claims to treat the individual's un-

295

derlying disturbance rather than merely his symptoms, psychoanalysis actually does the opposite: sometimes it enables him to ameliorate his symptomatology but rarely to understand and forcefully attack his deep-seated disturbance-creating tendencies. Worse yet, by inducing the client to focus upon great masses of irrelevant information about himself, by encouraging his prolonged dependency on the analyst, and by teaching him a number of highly questionable assumptions about the whys and wherefores of his behavior, psychoanalysis leads him to divert himself from doing exactly what he had better do to help himself, namely, to work at scientifically questioning and challenging his irrational philosophic premises about himself and the world and to work at training himself to behave differently from the indulgent, undisciplined manner in which he has allowed and conditioned himself to behave in the past and present.

Psychoanalysis does not greatly contribute to therapy because (together with naive behaviorism) it assumes that events and experiences are of paramount importance in a person's life, that he cannot help being traumatized by the unpleasant occurrences of his earliest years, and that if he fully understands the origins of these occurrences he will overcome their noxious influences. Actually, as Epictetus (57) demonstrated some two thousand years ago, humans are not bothered by the things that happen to them but by their view of these things. They bring to external stimuli a special kind of receiving apparatus that enables them to create joys or traumas in connection with the events they experience (33, 39). Their "experiences," in fact, include both stimuli and responses; and if they were, say, Martians or Venusians instead of Earthmen, they would doubtless have had much different "experiences" than they commonly would have had when they were toilet trained, rejected by their mothers, or threatened with disapproval by their fathers.

A human is primarily a responding or creative individual. He not only perceives external (and internal) stimuli, but he concomitantly thinks or conceptualizes about them. He also becomes so prejudiced by his own generalizations and philosophies that he perceives succeeding stimuli (or, if you will, "experiences") in a distorted and distinctly human way. So he continually makes his own responses, not, to be sure, entirely out of whole cloth (for he is also pushed or motivated to some degree by the nature of some stimuli themselves), but partly out of his own predispositions to be strongly biased (or to have what many psychologists vaguely refer to as his "emotions").

When, moreover, he experiences severe psychological upsets, man hardly feels disturbed because he is born with a blank mind that is then traumatized by the events in his early life. On the contrary, he appears to be born with many strong biosocial tendencies to think and act foolishly and thereby to make himself maladjusted. I list about forty of these innate predispositions in the last chapter of *Reason and Emotion in Psychotherapy* (33). They include tendencies toward short-range hedonism, oversuggestibility, grandiosity, overvigilance, extremism, overgeneralization, wishful thinking, inertia, ineffective focusing, discrimination difficulties, etc. Practically all humans, as far as I can see, are strongly burdened with these predilections; and therefore, no matter how they are reared, they can hardly help being somewhat self-sabotaging and disturbed. Although Freud vaguely noted this fact, especially in his views on the "pleasure principle," he somehow missed clearly connecting it with emotional malfunctioning— which he stubbornly kept relating to the individual's early experiences instead of to his early and later interpretations of these experiences (61).

Naive behaviorists make much the same error. They view a set of stimuli and the "conditioned" responses that follow the presentation of these stimuli, and they wrongly conclude that the stimuli "cause" the responses. Obviously, an even more basic "cause" is the conditionability of the responding person. For if he were not intrinsically the kind of individual who does respond to $S_1$, $S_2$, $S_3$, etc., even an infinite number of their presentations would hardly affect him. Even Pavlov's famous dog did not become conditioned to salivating when he heard the sound of a bell presented in connection with his being fed only because he had an inborn tendency to respond to food. He also, surely, had an inborn tendency to hear bells and to connect their sound with other stimuli that were presented to him. If he were born deaf or if he had no innate capacity to connect the hearing of the bell with the smelling of the food, he would hardly have served Pavlov very well!

Both humans and dogs, then, bring something important to their conditioning "experiences." Especially in regard to the most common forms of emotional disturbances, such as feelings of inadequacy, worthlessness, and overweening hostility, it is not merely rejection or brutal treatment by a child's parents that makes him feel upset. Rather, it is his own innate vulnerability to criticism and pain and his own inborn tendency to internalize others' negative attitudes toward him and to perpetuate self-criticism and damnation of others long after his original tormenters' barbs have ceased (33, 56).

Humans, in other words, are highly suggestible, impressionable, vulnerable, and gullible. And they are self-talking, self-indoctrinating, self-stimuli-ing creatures. They need, of course, some environmental influences to develop into suggestible and self-propagandizing individuals, just as they need external stimulation in order to develop at all. But with a wide variety of stimulation from outside people and events, they will still tend to be exceptionally vulnerable and self-indoctrinating.

If this is true, it follows that feelings of worthlessness do not stem from the attitudes that an individual's parents take toward him but from his own tendency to take these attitudes too seriously, to internalize them, and to perpetuate them through the years. And if he is to conquer such feelings, a therapist will hardly help him by showing him that his parents were castigating and by claiming that this is the cause of his present lack of ego strength. The insight that is thus given him through psychoanalytic therapy may be partially correct; but, it does not go far or deep enough. For he requires, to get better in an elegant and sustained way, the insight that, whatever his parents' behavior may have been, he no longer has to take them seriously, to agree with their criticisms of him, and to keep castigating himself.

To acquire a truly elegant solution to the problem of his own worth, the individual would better understand his own propensities to exaggerate the significance of others' attitudes toward him; and to see clearly that he can vigorously question, challenge, change, and minimize these tendencies to think crookedly about himself and others. Even more elegantly, he had better finally understand that all measures of self-worth are tautological, definitional, and essentially magical; that although he is born and reared with a strong tendency to rate or value himself, he does not have to give in to this tendency; and that he can rigorously and empirically rate only his traits and performances rather than his being or his self, and in that manner can truly stop deifying and devilifying himself (52, 54).

This is what I saw as I continued to use psychoanalytic methods: that they largely focus on past events rather than the human thinking that gives special meaning to these events; and that they indirectly, passively, and inefficiently teach the client how to work at changing his disturbance-creating meanings. I saw that the individual's anxieties, depressions, hostilities, and other symptoms of disturbance are not caused by his past misinterpretations of his parents' behavior and attitudes but by his present continuation of these interpretations and that unless these current residuals of his old crooked thinking are vigorously and persistently attacked, there is little chance of his modifying them significantly.

The more I worked on the premise that my clients were "emotionally" disturbed because they thought crookedly and that if I helped them to change their thinking they would also change their emotional reactions, the more effective my psychotherapy became. As I indicated in a paper published in 1957, in which I compared my results when I was using psychoanalytic and rational methods (although I had an improvement rate of about 60% with neurotic clients with whom I practiced classical analysis and a somewhat higher rate with those with whom I practiced analytically oriented therapy), I had an improvement rate of 90% of the same kind of clients with rational-emotive methods (31). Since that time, many of my associates have also found RET significantly increased their effectiveness over previously employed analytic, client-centered, and other models of therapy. Some of them have been converted to the rational approach because they obtained almost immediately better results when they tried it with several clients who were not responding to other approaches. It has likewise been found that whereas only a small number of clients can be reached with psychoanalytic techniques, all kinds of clients can be seen with the rational-emotive method, including disturbed individuals whose traits include fixed homosexuality, psychopathy, schizophrenic reactions, mental deficiency, and other syndromes that are usually unresponsive to most therapeutic methods.

It has also been found that the main essence of RET—the A-B-C theory of personality disturbance—can be used effectively by non-RET therapists who wish to incorporate it into their own systems. Thus, psychoanalytically oriented therapists, behavior therapists, existential therapists, marriage and family therapists, and various other kinds of therapists often show their clients, following RET principles, that whenever they get upset about an Activating Event (occurring at point A) by reacting with disturbed emotional Consequences (occurring at point C), their upset is not directly caused by A but by their Belief System (at point B). They can then (at point D) ideationally and actively Dispute their irrational Beliefs and thereby enormously change or eliminate their dysfunctional emotional Consequences.

Many therapists, of course, still vigorously oppose RET and insist that it is too simple, oververbalized, too intellectualized, authoritarian, and brain-washing. Actually, it is none of these, but it is complexly philosophic, quickly gets at unconscious and unverbalized material, deals with the individual's basic emotions, and helps him to act as well as to think in order to change them. It is authoritative rather than authoritarian and is aimed at inducing people to be less suggestible and more independent in their thinking. I have tried to answer the more serious objections to RET in my book, *Reason and Emotion in Psychotherapy,* and in several other writings (33, 36, 43, 45).

One of the most gratifying aspects of developing the theory and practice of rational-emotive therapy has been the concomitant discovery that many other psychotherapists, most of them originally psychoanalytic in their thinking, have independently divined and applied similar principles in their own work. Thus, Alfred Adler (1, 2), Aaron T. Beck (7), Eric Berne (13), John M. Dorsey (29), Victor Frankl (60), Haim Ginott (68, 69), William Glasser (71), Jay Haley (81), George Kelly (95), Arnold Lazarus (100), Prescott Lecky (102), E. Lakin Phillips (116, 117), Julian Rotter (122), Jurgen Ruesch (123), Virginia Satir (124), Wilhelm Stekel (132), Donald Stieper & Daniel Wiener (133), and Frederick Thorne (135) have all, often with little or no knowledge of my own work, developed overlapping theories and practices of psychotherapy.

Although when I first elucidated the principles of RET in a paper given at the American Psychological Association convention in Chicago in 1956 (31) there was relatively little experimental evidence to back its major hypotheses, there now is a vast amount of confirmatory data. For example, the fundamental thesis of RET, that human thinking is a basic cause of emotion and that healthy and unhealthy emotional reactions are significantly affected by changes in people's cognitions, has been experimentally validated by many psychological studies, including those by Beck and his associates (7–10); Becker (11); Becker, Spielberger, & Parker (12); Breznitz (15; Carlson, Travers, & Schwab (18); Davies (21); Davison (22–24); Deane (25); Frank (59); Fritz & Marks (62); Garfield, Gershon, Sletten, Sundland, & Ballou (63); Geer, Davison, & Gatchel (65); Glass, Singer, & Friedman (70); Jones (91); Jordan & Kempler (92); Lang, Sroufe, & Hastings (99); Nisbett & Schacter (113); Rimm & Litvak (119); Schacter & Singer (125); Taft (134); Valins (136); Valins & Ray (137); Velten (138); and Zingle (147).

Research studies which provide empirical evidence that rational-emotive therapy and similar cognitive therapies actually work have also been appearing with increasing frequency in the psychological literature. Successful studies in this respect have been done by Baker (6); Burkhead (16); Coons & McEachern (20); di Loreto (28);

Gewitz & Baer (67); Gliedman, Nash, Imber, Stone, & Frank (74); Gustave (80); Hartman (83); Kamiya (93); Karst & Trexler (94); Krippner (96); Lazarus (101); Maultsby (109); Nuthmann (114); O'Connell & Hanson (115); Shapiro & associates (126, 127); Sharma (128); and Steffy, Meichenbaum, & Best (131). Research studies that clearly support the efficacy of the type of *in vivo* desensitization, or homework assignments, which are constantly employed in rational-emotive therapy have also been consistently appearing in the literature, including those by Cooke (19); Garfield, Darwin, Singer, & McBrearty (64); Litvak (103, 104); Ritter (120); and Zajonc (146). All told, therefore, considerable objective data now support the main hypotheses of RET.

As for clinical findings, these have also been voluminous. Thus, successful reports of rational-emotive treatment have been published by Ard (3–5); Breen (14); Callahan (17); Diamond (27); Ellis (30, 33, 35, 37–39, 41, 44, 46, 47, 49–51, 54–56); Geis (66); Glicken (73); Greenberg (75); Grossack (76, 77); Gullo (78, 79); Harper (82); Hauck (84–87); Hudson (90); Lafferty (98); Lazarus (100); Maultsby (107, 108); Sherman (129); Wagner (139); and Weston (140, 141). For a relatively new form of treatment, therefore, there has been and continues to be considerable professional and research interest in RET.

Is RET a form of behavior therapy? In some ways, yes. Eysenck (58) includes it under "other methods" in his book, *Experiments in Behaviour Therapy*. Davison and Valins (24) include it among the techniques that are taught to the postdoctoral students in behavior modification at the State University of New York at Stony Brook. Lazarus, in his book, *Behavior Therapy and Beyond* (100), shows how he employs it in his own practice. Beck (8) indicates that it is one of the main cognitive therapies that are an important aspect of virtually all behavior therapies.

I quite agree with these views, since RET is based on the assumption that although humans are born with the tendency to learn one set of responses much easier than to learn another set, it also holds that specific patterns of disturbance are learned and that (albeit with some difficulty) they can be unlearned. It therefore not only shows the client what his maladjustment-creating philosophies are, but it directly and actively induces him to attack, challenge, and work against these philosophies and to retrain himself to think and behave more efficiently. It employs many of the time-honored educational and reeducational techniques, including didactic explanation, role playing, reinforcement, desensitization, persuasion, repetition, practice, modeling, and homework assignments. It also includes preventive teaching and may therefore be properly called, instead of by the medically toned term psychotherapy, by the education-centered terms, behavior modification or emotional education. Although it goes beyond the usual methods of Wolpe's reciprocal inhibition (143, 144) and Skinner's operant conditioning (130), and although it deals with global states of emotional disturbance rather than (as these methods often do) with limited symptoms, it legitimately includes many of the regular conditioning, deconditioning, and self-conditioning techniques, such as those proposed by Homme (88, 89) and Premack (118).

## THE TECHNIQUE OF RATIONAL-EMOTIVE THERAPY

The main technique of RET is for the therapist to use the A-B-C theory of personality theory and to start with point C, the Consequences (or disturbed symptoms or responses) which the client presents. Usually, these include inertia, procrastination, anxiety, feelings of worthlessness, phobias, compulsions, feelings of intense hostility, depression, inability to love, lack of commitment to anything, and various psychosomatic complaints. The therapist's main hypothesis is that whatever the client's dysfunctional emotional Consequences are, they are not really caused by A, the Activating Events, in his life, but by B, the Belief System, that he brings to these events.

At point B, the client almost always has two distinct Beliefs: rB, a rational Belief and iB, an irrational Belief. It is the rational-emotive therapist's intent to show the client exactly what his irrational Beliefs are and how to Dispute them—at point D—until he gives them up and thereby changes or eliminates his inefficient emotional Consequences at C.

If, for example, the client's main symptom or Consequence is anxiety, and if this occurs when the Activating Event is the likelihood of his being rejected by, say, his fiancée, the therapist quickly shows him that at point B he is probably convinced of a rational set of Beliefs—namely, "It would be highly unfortunate if she rejected me; how frustrating that would be!"—and an irrational set of Beliefs—namely, "It would be awful if she rejected me! I couldn't stand it! What a worthless person her rejection would make me!"

The therapist then tries to induce the client to Dispute, at point D, his irrational Beliefs by, first, vigorously challenging and questioning them: "Why would it be awful if she rejected me? Why couldn't I stand it? Where is the evidence that her rejection would make me a worthless person, to myself and to the rest of the world?" Second, the client is induced to perform, if possible, some activity homework assignment, such as staying with his fiancée (instead of defensively breaking off the engagement with her) and continuing to risk being rejected, in order to prove to himself that it would not be catastrophic if he actually were rejected. Or he is shown how to try other kinds of risks (such as applying for a new and better job) to help convince himself that he can stand being rejected.

Some of the main irrational ideas which the client tends to consciously or unconsciously believe, and which the therapist keeps showing him he holds and keeps logically and empirically refuting, include:

1. The idea that it is a dire necessity for an adult human to be loved or approved by virtually every significant other person in his life.

2. The idea that one should be thoroughly competent, adequate, and achieving in all possible respects to consider oneself worthwhile.

3. The idea that certain people are bad, wicked, or villainous and that they should be severely blamed and punished for their villainy.

4. The idea that it is awful and catastrophic when things are not the way one would like them to be.

5. The idea that human unhappiness is externally caused and that people have little or no ability to control their terrors and disturbances.

6. The idea that it is easier to avoid than to face life difficulties and self-responsibilities.

7. The idea that one's past history is an all-important determiner of one's present behavior and that because something once strongly affected one's life, it should indefinitely affect it (33, 54–56, 111).

Assuming that the client, in creating his own disturbance, dogmatically adheres to one or more of these irrational ideas, the rational-emotive therapist incisively inspects the client's feelings and response and looks for the specific notions with which he is indoctrinating himself to create his disordered Consequences. The therapist then shows the client how each and every one of his dysfunctional emotions or acts is preceded by such an unscientifically held and empirically unvalidatable hypothesis and how this unwarranted premise will inevitably cause his ineffective behavior.

Another way of stating this is to say that the therapist shows the client that whenever he becomes emotionally upset, he is invariably devoutly believing in some magical, unverifiable hypothesis: namely, that something is awful; that it should not exist; and that in order to be in the least happy he has to have it changed. There is no way of his ever validating (or invalidating) these mystical hypotheses, since awfulness is an indefinable term with surplus meaning (as opposed to inconvenience or misfortune, which can be defined in terms of empirical referents); since there are really no *shoulds* or *should nots* in the universe (though there are many desirables and undesirables); and since the only real reason one has to have anything in order to be in the least happy is because one thinks one has to have it.

A disturbed human response stems from the individual's illogically and irrationally escalating a desideratum into a necessity; from his hypothesizing that something is sacred rather than desirable; from his deifying or devilifying some aspect of himself, of others, or of the universe around him; from his departing from empirical reality and the logico-deductive method of scientific thinking and resorting to absolutistic, magical, dogmatic, entirely unprovable assumptions to which he then rigidly and uncritically holds. Rational-emotive theory and practice holds that if the individual, instead, stayed rigorously with the scientific method in his thinking about himself and the universe he would probably never have any emotional problems, though he would certainly have many reality problems. Or, stated differently, he would have life problems; however, he would not have problems about having problems but would interestedly and absorbedly tackle the issues of today and tomorrow and usually enjoy this kind of problem-solving.

The therapist, then, shows the client that his poor emotional Consequences, at point C, stem from his dreaming up and pigheadedly sticking to his own irrational Beliefs, at point B, and that it is highly likely that only by changing his own childish, whining, unempirical Beliefs will he obtain better Consequences. He also shows the client exactly how to find and to stoutly challenge his own irrational Beliefs. Thus, he demonstrates that these insane ideas are absolutistic demands or dictates on himself or others: that they consist of puerile insistences that he or they should, ought, or must act in a certain way, when the truth is that it would be nice if he and they did act this way, but that there is no law of the universe that says they must.

When the client is shown that his negative and inappropriate emotions at point C are caused by the irrational ideas he is positing at point B, he is also shown that he usually has generalized philosophies which create most of his misleading point B interpretations. Thus, if he comes to therapy because he is sexually impotent, at point C, whenever he has sex with a woman, at point A, and it becomes obvious that he is telling himself, at B, "I may fail at having sex relations with this woman and wouldn't that be awful! What a slob I would be!" he is shown that his point B Belief is silly since it would not be awful but merely inconvenient and frustrating if he failed, and he would not be a slob but merely a fallible human who had done poorly in this particular respect.

Equally to the point, the therapist actively tries to show him that he tends to have the same self-denigrating philosophy in other aspects of his life—such as in his vocational, social, and sports performances. He is helped to see that he generally catastrophizes about the possibility of his failing; and that, if he is to lose his symptom of sexual impotence and also to reduce his basic anxiety-creating proclivities, he had better change his whole philosophy of life by seeing that no failure is truly awful and that he can never be a totally worthless individual, no matter how many times he fails.

By inducing the client to generalize to the philosophic source of his present and future symptoms, RET becomes a holistic kind of psychotherapy which helps him to become minimally anxious and hostile in virtually all respects. It is, moreover, one of the most humanistic methods of emotional education ever created since it essentially teaches people to accept themselves and others as inevitably fallible humans and not to expect, in any way whatever, that they or any other person will be perfect, nonerrant, and superhuman. When I expect myself to be superhuman, I become anxious and depressed; when I expect you to be, I become hostile; when I expect the world to be superperfect, I become self-pitying and rebelliously inert. If I am truly human, and expect nothing but humanness from others, I will practically never upset myself about anything.

The generalized, holistic, humanistic aspect of RET is also prophylactic. For therapies that concentrate on symptom removal are limited because (a) the client's symptoms may gradually or suddenly return some time after his treatment ends and because (b) even if his particular symptom does not recur [as Wolpe (143, 144) claims that it usually does not in deconditioning therapy], it is likely that some other symptom, sometimes of a different order, will erupt later. Thus, an individual who is now relieved of his fear of riding in automobiles may subsequently become afraid of planes, new cities, meeting strangers, failing on his job, and a host of other things.

In successful RET, however, the client essentially learns that nothing is truly awful, terrible, or horrible; that he can never be rated as worthless (nor as being great); and that no human can legitimately be condemned for anything he does. Consequently, the "cured" RET client is not likely to experience a recurrence of his old symptoms or an outbreak of new ones that is so common among other "cured" individuals. Moreover, since he learns a scientific method of dealing with personal problems that he can use for the rest of his days, he will tend, if he keeps applying this method, to become still healthier and to experience more personality growth after he leaves therapy. This is not to say that relapses never occur with clients who are significantly helped by RET. But its basic goal is not merely to help people with their symptoms but with all possible emotional malfunctionings they may experience now or later—and to help them do so by showing them how they can radically alter their fundamental philosophies of life—which are their symptom-creating mechanisms.

Is RET an insight-producing form of therapy? Yes, it is; and on a level that goes deeper, I believe, than that of the usual dynamic psychotherapies. Where these techniques help the client to gain insight into the presumed antecedent causes of his behavior, and often induce him—wrongly!—to focus on the origins of these causes (if, indeed, these can ever truly be known), RET helps him gain three important kinds of insight.

Insight No. 1 consists of the client seeing that his present dysfunctional behavior not only has antecedent causes in the past but that these causes still exist and are presently observable. Thus, the person with an intense anxiety about bugs gains insight, during RET, into the fact that he is a human being who was born and reared with general catastrophizing tendencies, that because of these tendencies he easily acquired a fear of bugs (which, possibly, his bug-fearing mother may have abetted), and that he is still, in the present, foolishly devilifying bugs and sacredizing their absence and thereby retaining his original heredity-environmental-acquired overconcern.

Insight No. 2 consists of the client acknowledging that the main reason why his early tendencies to disturb himself continue to exist is because he is now actively instrumental in perpetuating them. That is to say, he keeps endlessly repeating to himself the same irrational beliefs with which he originally upset himself, such as, "Aren't bugs awful! I can't stand them! They shouldn't exist!"

Insight No. 3—which is in many respects the most important insight of all—consists of the client acknowledging that there probably is no other way for him to get better but by continually observing, questioning, and challenging his own belief system, and by working and practicing to change his own irrational beliefs by verbal and by motor counterconditioning activity. Thus, he had better admit, in order to overcome his fear of bugs, that he is keeping alive the beliefs that bugs are awful, that he cannot stand them, and that they should not exist; and that he preferably should keep forcing himself, on many occasions, to actively encounter bugs while he vigorously questions and challenges his exaggerated beliefs about them.

The three main insights derived through RET, then, involve the client seeing that he had better act against as well as understand the philosophic causes of his disordered behavior. Whereas most psychotherapies, including psychoanalysis and other "depth-centered" methods, give the client what has been wrongly called "intellectual insight" into his problems (or what I have more accurately called, I believe, his knowledge that he is acting badly and his wish to correct his behavior), RET, when it is successful, gives him so-called "emotional insight," meaning his determination to work hard at using his "intellectual insight" so that he finally and forcibly changes—that is, reconditions himself in regard to—that behavior (33).

To this end, RET not only tries to persuade the client to actively engage in some changed behavior in order to get better, it also offers him specific homework. Thus, the individual who is afraid to date members of the other sex may be given concrete assignments to approach and talk to, let us say, at least one new person every week. Or he may be given the assignment of doing a difficult and unpleasant task (such as talking to a strange girl) first before he is to allow himself to do an easy and pleasant task (such as listening to an opera he loves).

Are transference relationships importantly employed in rational-emotive therapy? Not usually—at least not in the sense that transference is generally analyzed in psychoanalytic therapy. The rational therapist is sometimes supportive when a client is exceptionally self-downing; and, he frequently serves as a good model for the client in that he tries to follow a sane philosophy of life and to remain minimally anxious and hostile himself, no matter what transpires during the therapy sessions. He also may show the client that if he is in dire need of the therapist's approval he also probably needs (or thinks he needs) others' acceptance; and that if he is exceptionally demanding of and hostile toward the therapist he probably makes the same childish demands of others in his outside life. The therapist thereby uses some of the experiences of the therapeutic relationship to help the client in his regular existence.

But the rational-emotive therapist does not believe that all the client's significant emotions are unconscious transfers from his early attitudes toward his parents, nor that everything he does during the session is indubitably a function of this kind of transference. He does not encourage the establishment of a transference neurosis, and he frequently sees a client for a good many sessions with few intense transference reactions developing. This is because the rational therapist talks sanely and directively to the client; he does not encourage undirected fantasies and free associations; and he does not use the sessions mainly for existential encounters (which he might well enter with his personal friends but which he deems largely inappropriate with a highly disturbed individual who has come to him for help). Moreover, RET is usually done on a once-a-week basis, in face-to-face settings, and in as efficient and rapid-fire manner as the client can handle, so that intense emotional relationships between therapist and client are less likely to occur than they are to arise in many other kinds of therapy.

When transference reactions do occur in RET, the therapist quickly shows the client not only that he is acting today as he tended to act years ago but that he still has the same irrational beliefs which caused him to act that way in the past, and he had better do something about changing, instead of merely acknowledging, these beliefs. Thus, a client who hates the therapist because he confuses him with his authoritarian father, whom he also may have (consciously or unconsciously) abhorred when he was a child, is shown that (a) his original hatred for his father was inappropriate, even if the latter had acted tyrannically, because although it was proper for the client to violently dislike his father's behavior it was irrational for him to conclude that his progenitor was condemnable as a person for displaying this behavior; that (b) all hostile reactions are the result of crooked, moralistic thinking; that (c) he does not have to condemn anyone, such as his father, for acting the way he does; and that (d) he is foolishly seeing the therapist as his father, when the two are obviously discrete individuals. In RET, in other words, not only transference reactions but their philosophic causes are brought to light, and the latter are vigorously attacked until the client changes them for more tenable attitudes toward past and present significant others.

How about unconscious material? Is this used in rational-emotive therapy? It very definitely is! Although I do not believe that most human motivations are deeply unconscious, in that they were once conscious and were then repressed by the individual who could not face them, I do acknowledge that many ideas which people tell themselves to create their disturbed reactions are preconscious, or just below the level of consciousness. When, for example, a client is afraid of dating, he may be fully conscious of his anxiety; but he may not be conscious of his creating this anxiety by telling himself, "Wouldn't it be awful if I tried to date a girl and she rejected me!" Because his preconscious or unconscious belief is usually not far below the level of awareness, the rational-emotive therapist can often quickly help him bring it to full consciousness. After a few sessions of RET, moreover, he can learn the A-B-C method that will help him bring into consciousness virtually all his disturbance-creating philosophies.

Thus, if he starts at point C (the emotional Consequence), acknowledges his feeling of anxiety, and realizes that this anxiety arose in connection with point A (the Activating Event), when he was about to call a girl for a date, he can realize (on the basis of RET theory) that A cannot possibly cause C and that therefore he should look for its real cause, his Belief System, at point B. This Belief system first includes rB, his rational Belief, which (by inference) can easily be seen as something like: "I don't like to get rejected by a girl; wouldn't it be unfortunate if I were!" Since his rational Belief could only, if he stuck rigorously to it, produce such appropriate feelings as sorrow, regret, frustration, and concern, it is fairly obvious that to produce his emotion of severe anxiety he has an additional, magical, irrational Belief (iB). And that irrational Belief, as noted previously, is probably something like: "Wouldn't it be awful if I tried to date a girl and she rejected me! How worthless I would then be!" By using the A-B-C (or C-A-B) system, clients frequently learn to ferret out their unconscious (or preconscious) irrational Beliefs very quickly, especially when they are aided by using the Homework Report, Figures 1 and 2.

Are the client's defenses and resistances revealed and analyzed in RET? Yes, they are revealed; but, they are attacked and uprooted, rather than merely "analyzed." He is shown that he rationalizes, denies, projects, represses, or uses other kinds of defenses. But he is also shown what irrational ideas he is convincing himself of in order to create this kind of defensiveness and how he can go about changing these ideas.

Suppose, for example, the client denies that he is afraid to go on

**HOMEWORK REPORT**

**Consultation Center**

Institute for Advanced Study in Rational Psychotherapy

45 East 65th Street, New York, N.Y. 10021 / (212) LEhigh 5-0822

Name ................................................................ Date ................ Therapist ................................

*Instructions*: Please draw a circle around the number in front of those feelings listed in the first column that troubled you *most* during the period since your last therapy session. Then, in the *second* column, indicate the amount of work you did on each circled item; and, in the *third* column, the results of the work you did.

| | Amount of Work Done | | | | Results of Work | | |
| --- | --- | --- | --- | --- | --- | --- | --- |
| | Much | Some | Little or none | | Good | Fair | Poor |
| **Undesirable Emotional Feelings** | | | | | | | |
| 1a Anger or great irritability | 1b ............. | ............. | ............. | 1c ............. | ............. | ............. |
| 2a Anxiety, severe worry, or fear | 2b ............. | ............. | ............. | 2c ............. | ............. | ............. |
| 3a Boredom or dullness | 3b ............. | ............. | ............. | 3c ............. | ............. | ............. |
| 4a Failure to achieve | 4b ............. | ............. | ............. | 4c ............. | ............. | ............. |
| 5a Frustration | 5b ............. | ............. | ............. | 5c ............. | ............. | ............. |
| 6a Guilt or self-condemnation | 6b ............. | ............. | ............. | 6c ............. | ............. | ............. |
| 7a Hopelessness or depression | 7b ............. | ............. | ............. | 7c ............. | ............. | ............. |
| 8a Great loneliness | 8b ............. | ............. | ............. | 8c ............. | ............. | ............. |
| 9a Helplessness | 9b ............. | ............. | ............. | 9c ............. | ............. | ............. |
| 10a Self-pity | 10b ............. | ............. | ............. | 10c ............. | ............. | ............. |
| 11a Uncontrollability | 11b ............. | ............. | ............. | 11c ............. | ............. | ............. |
| 12a Worthlessness or inferiority | 12b ............. | ............. | ............. | 12c ............. | ............. | ............. |
| 13a Other (specify) ...................... | 13b ............. | ............. | ............. | 13c ............. | ............. | ............. |
| ...................................... | ............. | ............. | ............. | ............. | ............. | ............. |
| ...................................... | ............. | ............. | ............. | ............. | ............. | ............. |
| **Undesirable Actions or Habits** | | | | | | | |
| 14a Avoiding responsibility | 14b ............. | ............. | ............. | 14c ............. | ............. | ............. |
| 15a Acting unfairly to others | 15b ............. | ............. | ............. | 15c ............. | ............. | ............. |
| 16a Being late to appointments | 16b ............. | ............. | ............. | 16c ............. | ............. | ............. |
| 17a Being undisciplined | 17b ............. | ............. | ............. | 17c ............. | ............. | ............. |
| 18a Demanding attention | 18b ............. | ............. | ............. | 18c ............. | ............. | ............. |
| 19a Physically attacking others | 19b ............. | ............. | ............. | 19c ............. | ............. | ............. |
| 20a Putting off important things | 20b ............. | ............. | ............. | 20c ............. | ............. | ............. |
| 21a Telling people off harshly | 21b ............. | ............. | ............. | 21c ............. | ............. | ............. |
| 22a Whining or crying | 22b ............. | ............. | ............. | 22c ............. | ............. | ............. |
| 23a Withdrawing from activity | 23b ............. | ............. | ............. | 23c ............. | ............. | ............. |
| 24a Overdrinking of alcohol | 24b ............. | ............. | ............. | 24c ............. | ............. | ............. |
| 25a Overeating | 25b ............. | ............. | ............. | 25c ............. | ............. | ............. |
| 26a Oversleeping | 26b ............. | ............. | ............. | 26c ............. | ............. | ............. |
| 27a Undersleeping | 27b ............. | ............. | ............. | 27c ............. | ............. | ............. |
| 28a Oversmoking | 28b ............. | ............. | ............. | 28c ............. | ............. | ............. |
| 29a Taking too many drugs or pills | 29b ............. | ............. | ............. | 29c ............. | ............. | ............. |
| 30a Other (specify) ...................... | 30b ............. | ............. | ............. | 30c ............. | ............. | ............. |
| ...................................... | ............. | ............. | ............. | ............. | ............. | ............. |
| ...................................... | ............. | ............. | ............. | ............. | ............. | ............. |
| **Irrational Ideas or Philosophies** | | | | | | | |
| 31a People must love or approve of me | 31b ............. | ............. | ............. | 31c ............. | ............. | ............. |
| 32a Making mistakes is terrible | 32b ............. | ............. | ............. | 32c ............. | ............. | ............. |
| 33a People should be condemned for their wrongdoings | 33b ............. | ............. | ............. | 33c ............. | ............. | ............. |
| 34a It's terrible when things go wrong | 34b ............. | ............. | ............. | 34c ............. | ............. | ............. |
| 35a My emotions can't be controlled | 35b ............. | ............. | ............. | 35c ............. | ............. | ............. |
| 36a Threatening situations have to keep me terribly worried | 36b ............. | ............. | ............. | 36c ............. | ............. | ............. |
| 37a Self-discipline is too hard to achieve | 37b ............. | ............. | ............. | 37c ............. | ............. | ............. |
| 38a Bad effects of my childhood still have to control my life | 38b ............. | ............. | ............. | 38c ............. | ............. | ............. |
| 39a I can't stand the way certain people act | 39b ............. | ............. | ............. | 39c ............. | ............. | ............. |
| 40a Other (specify) ...................... | 40b ............. | ............. | ............. | 40c ............. | ............. | ............. |
| ...................................... | ............. | ............. | ............. | ............. | ............. | ............. |
| ...................................... | ............. | ............. | ............. | ............. | ............. | ............. |

*(please complete other side)*

Figure 1.

PLEASE PRINT! BE BRIEF AND LEGIBLE! ANSWER QUESTION C FIRST; THEN ANSWER THE OTHER QUESTIONS.

A. ACTIVATING EVENT you recently experienced about which you became upset or disturbed. (Examples: *"I went for a job interview." "My mate screamed at me."*) ....................................................................................................................

rB. Rational BELIEF or idea you had about this Activating Event. (Examples: *"It would be unfortunate if I were rejected for the job." "How annoying to have my mate scream at me!"*) ....................................................................................................
....................................................................................................................................................................

iB. Irrational BELIEF or idea you had about this Activating Event. (Examples: *"It would be catastrophic if I were rejected for the job; I would be pretty worthless as a person." "I can't stand my mate's screaming; she is horrible for screaming at me!"*) ....................................................................................................................................................
....................................................................................................................................................................

C. CONSEQUENCES of your irrational BELIEF (iB) about the Activating Event listed in Question A. State here the one most disturbing emotion, behavior, or CONSEQUENCE you experienced recently. (Examples: *"I was anxious." "I was hostile." "I had stomach pains."*) ....................................................................................................................

D. DISPUTING, questioning, or challenging you can use to change your irrational BELIEF (iB). (Examples: *"Why would it be catastrophic and how would I become a worthless person if I were rejected for the job?" "Why can't I stand my mate's screaming and why is she horrible for screaming at me?"*) ..................................................................................................

cE. Cognitive EFFECT or answer you obtained from DISPUTING your irrational BELIEF (iB). Examples: *"It would not be catastrophic, but merely unfortunate, if I were rejected for the job; my giving a poor interview would not make me a worthless person." "Although I'll never like my mate's screaming, I can stand it; he or she is not horrible but merely a fallible person for screaming."*) ...........................................................

bE. Behavioral EFFECT or result of your DISPUTING your irrational BELIEF (iB). (Examples: *"I felt less anxious." "I felt less hostile to my mate." "My stomach pains vanished."*)...........................................................................

F. If you did not challenge your irrational BELIEF (iB), why did you not? .............................................................

G. Activities you would most like to *stop* that you are now doing....................................................................
....................................................................................................................................................................

H. Activities you would most like to *start* that you are not doing....................................................................

I. Emotions and ideas you would most like to change ........................................................................................
....................................................................................................................................................................

J. Specific homework assignment(s) given you by your therapist, your group, or yourself .................................

K. What did you actually do to carry out the assignment(s)? ...........................................................................
....................................................................................................................................................................

L. Check the item which describes how much you have worked at your last homework assignment(s): ...............(a) almost every day ...............(b) several times a week ...............(c) occasionally ...............(d) hardly ever.

M. How many times in the past week have you specifically worked at changing and DISPUTING your irrational BELIEFS (iBs)? ...............................................................................................................................................

N. What other things have you specifically done to change your irrational BELIEFS and your disturbed emotional CONSEQUENCES? ..............................................................................................................................................

O. Check the item which describes how much reading you have recently done of the material on rational-emotive therapy: ...............(a) a considerable amount ...............(b) a moderate amount ...............(c) little or none.

P. Things you would now like to discuss most with your therapist or group .......................................................
....................................................................................................................................................................

Figure 2.

dates, when it is fairly obvious from the material he discusses in individual or group sessions that he is actually afraid of such encounters. First, he is shown that he is telling himself some irrational idea, such as the idea that it would be awful and horrible if he were to admit his fears; and this defense-creating idea is attacked by inducing him to ask himself, "Why would it be awful to admit that I am afraid of dating?" "Why would I be a worthless individual even if I always remained afraid to go out with girls?"

Secondly, the client is shown that his specific fear of dating, and all other such fears, are groundless. As the therapist demonstrates that he never has to castigate himself if he fails on dates (or other similar encounters), and as the client internalizes the philosophy that it well may be inconvenient but never is horrible or catastrophic for him to be disapproved of by girls (or others), he begins to lose his basic fears of such encounters as well as his defensiveness about having such fears.

Is RET necessarily a short-term form of treatment? No, not necessarily. Usually, it takes from one to twenty sessions of individual and/or twenty to eighty sessions of group therapy. Consequently, many clients are seen for relatively brief periods of time. Ideally, however, I prefer to see my own clients for a total period of about two years, during which time they will have about twenty individual and about seventy-five group sessions, which is considerably less therapeutic time than I used to spend with clients whom I once saw for psychoanalytic therapy. Some of my associates, such as Dr. Maxim F. Young (145), are able to achieve unusually good results with exceptionally disturbed individuals whom they see from ten to twenty sessions.

## AN ILLUSTRATIVE CASE OF
## RATIONAL-EMOTIVE THERAPY

To show how RET works with a somewhat typical client, let me outline treatment procedures that were employed with Rhoda S., a thirty-five-year-old physician who came to therapy because she was unable to form any lasting attachments with males, although she said she was eager to be married. Previous to my seeing her, she had been in psychoanalytic treatment for four and a half years, had made little progress in her emotional relationships, and had mainly been told that she was overly attached to her father, sought males who resembled him, was afraid of having incestuouslike affairs with them, and was really a latent lesbian. Although she largely accepted these interpretations and had a warm relationship with her male analyst, she was still completely frigid with her boyfriends and frantically ran from them when her attachments seemed to be becoming fairly intense.

I first worked with Rhoda on her specific problem of frigidity and discovered that she seemed to have no interest in having sex with females but that she was terribly overanxious about succeeding with males. She kept indoctrinating herself with the ideas—which she had largely acquired from her college roommates—that (a) it was intolerably frustrating when she failed to reach an orgasm and that (b) there was something horribly wrong and shameful about her and her "femininity" when she did not climax.

During our first RET session, the dialogue between us went partially as follows:

> Therapist (T): Granted that it is frustrating when you come close to but do not quite achieve orgasm, why is there something intrinsically wrong with you for not achieving it?"
>
> Client (C): Because it is wrong—there is something malfunctioning about my sexual mechanism; and it is foolish and unrealistic of me not to acknowledge this.
>
> T: True. There is something wrong with one of the ways, the sexual way, that you function. But you are implying, much more holistically, that there is something essentially wrong with you. As you know, being a physician, it is impossible for you to have a malfunctioning limb or internal organ and not be generally ailing. Why, then, could you not be sexually inefficient and not be entirely dysfunctional?
>
> C: I guess you're right. I could be. But I still feel that there's something essentially wrong with me if I never come to orgasm. How come?
>
> T.: Well, first of all, you're doing the usual human thing of confusing the whole of you with the part that is not working too well. That is, you are overgeneralizing. But more importantly, perhaps, your overgeneralizing is aided by another confusion, namely, the idea that if you, as a whole, were behaving poorly, and if you were responsible for this behavior—because you theoretically had some choice in the matter and were not exerting it for your own good—you would also be reprehensible for being responsible.
>
> C: Wouldn't I be? If I could achieve sexual fulfillment by, say, really working hard to achieve it, and if I were just lazy or lax in this respect and therefore did not achieve what I could, wouldn't I then be reprehensible?
>
> T: No, of course not. You would be self-defeating and foolish. But you would hardly be a sinner or a blackguard for being foolish. You

would be a human being with failings. But that would not make you, except by arbitrary, moralistic definition, a Failure, with a capital F, who deserves to keep defeating herself and who could not possibly act in any nondefeating way in the future.

C: But wouldn't I deserve to keep failing if I didn't lift a finger to help myself succeed?

T: Yes, in the objective sense that not lifting a finger to succeed would normally cause you to reap the consequences of your inertia: namely, repeated failure. But not in the sense that the universe is so justly ordered that anyone who evades work must keep failing and ought to be punished by the powers-that-be for his iniquity.

C: You mean that, statistically speaking, there is a high probability that I would keep failing to achieve orgasm if I didn't try various methods of attaining it, but that nonstatistically and absolutistically there is no reason why I have to keep failing because some fate or God ordains that I must?

T: Yes, that's exactly what I mean. Realistically, the chances are high that you will fail, sexually or any other way, if you don't work and practice to succeed. But there is no necessity that you will. And, of course, we know that many of the women who hardly try at all to reach orgasm easily do so, while many other women who, like you, frantically try to do so often never achieve it. So there is no one-to-one correlation between trying and succeeding, although there is a correlation significantly above chance between these two variables. We are pretty sure, moreover, that there is no godly fate or presence looking over your (and others') conduct and making sure that the good workers get rewarded and the goofers do not. You may invent such a fate or presence in your head, but that does not prove its objective existence.

C: So even if I don't succeed at achieving an orgasm, you seem to be saying that I deserve to gain any happiness in life that I can obtain, and I don't have to punish myself.

T: Right! It would be far wiser if you worked, unfrantically and unfrenetically, to achieve sexual fulfillment. But even if you don't, and you therefore never achieve it, you are not a worthless individual, only a bright girl who is acting, in this respect, idiotically. And if you see this and don't condemn yourself as a person for acting in this manner, there then is a good chance that you will correct your future behavior, will focus properly on enjoying sex (instead of on proving what a great partner you can be), and will in fact enjoy it. If you never do, that's too bad—but not catastrophic and not self-demeaning.

C: You imply that I will actually succeed at sex if I don't condemn myself for not succeeding.

T: Yes, the chances are you will. Maybe you won't, but you certainly will give yourself a higher probability of doing so. For when you focus on, "What a louse I am for not trying properly to succeed!" you become as unsexual or antisexual as you can become. Whereas, if you forget this nonsense and concertedly focus on sex, on the possibility of your enjoying it, and on the best methods you can devise to increase that possibility, sooner or later you will probably succeed.

This is what actually happened. I induced Dr. S. to focus on sex enjoyment instead of her own lousehood, and she soon began to get closer to orgasm and within a few weeks reached it for the first time in her life. At first, she had to use somewhat bizarre, masochistic fantasies to bring on climax during intercourse; but after some further experience and practice, she was able to concentrate on her lover and on her own sensations and to fairly easily come to climax.

We then tackled her wider emotional problems with males. We soon determined that she was not getting deeply involved because she still felt traumatized by being rejected by her fiancé a decade prior to her therapy sessions. He had seemed to care for her greatly, but he became more and more anxious as their wedding day approached. He went into something of a panic a few days before the ceremony was to take place and went to see a psychiatrist who advised him not to marry anyone while he was so indecisive. She felt completely crushed by his agreeing to go along with the psychiatrist—with whose views she completely disagreed—and they never saw each other again. Since that time, she remained so afraid to get involved with anyone who might possibly reject her under similar circumstances, or who might even marry her and then withdraw from her emotionally, that she kept having a number of sex friendships but no deep emotional involvements with men.

During our sixth therapy session, this dialogue ensued:

T: What are you really afraid of in regard to marrying?

C: Of rejection, it would seem. Of being left alone once again, after I had built up high hopes of remaining together with a man forever, as I did with my ex-fiancé.

T: That's a surface explanation that really doesn't explain anything. First, you are constantly getting rejected, the way you are going on now, because you pick men who aren't marriageable or whom you refuse to wed. Therefore your hopes of a prolonged, intense involvement are perpetually being dashed—rejected. Secondly, you are really rejecting yourself all the time. For you are assuming that if you did get refused by some man, just as you once did, you couldn't possibly stand it, weakling that you are! This is a complete vote of nonconfidence in yourself. You are therefore truly refusing to accept your-self as you are. You are demanding that you be perfectly safe.

C: But isn't it better to be safe than hurt?

T: You mean, isn't it better to have never loved and never lost?

C: O.K. But if losing is so dreadful, isn't that better?

T: But why should losing be so dreadful?

C: Oh, loneliness. Not ever getting what you want.

T: But aren't you lonely this way? And do you now get what you want?

C: No, I don't. But I also don't get what I very much don't want.

T: Partly. But not as much as you think.

C: What do you mean?

T: I first of all mean what you mean: that you do not like to get rejected—and who the hell does?—and that you are avoiding this dis-likable event by not trying to get accepted. But I mean, secondly, that what you really dislike most about being rejected is not the re-fusal itself, since that merely gets you what you have when you do not try for acceptance: namely, being alone, but the belief that this kind of loneliness makes you a slob, a worthless person.

C: Oh, but I do dislike, and dislike very much, the refusal itself. I hate to be refused and then have to be by myself!

T: Partly. But suppose you won one of the males you desired and he died and you lost him that way. Would that make you feel as badly as if you won him, he were still alive, and he then rejected you?

C: No, I guess it wouldn't.

T: Ah! You see what I'm getting at?

C: That it's not really the loss of the man that I'm concerned about, but his rejection of me.

T: Exactly! It's not the loss of him—but the loss of you. That's what you're really worried about. If you lose a man by his dying or going away or something like that, you don't like it, for then you're not getting what you want, and you feel frustrated. But even if you lose a man by his being available, by his still rejecting you, then you're not only frustrated, but you wrongly conclude that if he rejects you, you must reject yourself. That is to say, you lose yourself as well as him. At least, that's the way you set things up in your mind, that's your conclusion, your hangup. And what you call "loneliness" is not merely your being alone (which I will grant is annoying and bother-some) but your being alone plus your falsely believing that you're no good for being in that state.

C: Looks like, in this area, I'm doing much the same thing as I did in the sex area. I'm condemning myself for not succeeding; and that makes things much worse than my merely not succeeding.

T: Right again! Just as you caused yourself, in large measure, to fail sexually, because you were overly concerned with succeeding and therefore focused on how you were doing instead of the pleasure of what you were doing, you are causing yourself to feel terribly rejected by defining yourself as a worthless individual in case you fail in your emotional relations. In fact, not only do you cause the feeling of rejection in this manner, but you also often may bring on the rejection itself. For if a man whom you find desirable finds that you are terribly anxious about your winning his approval, he may look upon you as being too crazy for him to become deeply involved with, and he may therefore leave you.

C: I'm afraid that that's just what does happen in many instances. The men, the good ones I mean, seem to be impressed with me at first. But then they seem to view me differently and to lose interest.

T: Yes. Probably because you view you so differently. At first, you are intent on them and their traits, since you are interested in finding what you consider to be a good man. But as soon as you find what you think you are looking for, you then focus on yourself: on how many failings you have, on what a phony you really are, on how he's sure to find you out soon. You then become so anxious and so little concentrated on him that he sees that something is wrong and finally rejects you. Then, of course, you take that rejection as "proof" that you really are no good, when actually it is only proof that you think you are and that rejections occur more frequently when you view yourself in this negative manner. And the vicious circle completes itself.

C: You seem to be describing my case with deadly accuracy. But what can I do about it?

T: Isn't it obvious? Your basic symptom is emotional inadequacy, just as, a few weeks ago, it also was sexual inadequacy. Your fundamental problem, however, is fear of rejection, just as it was fear of failure. Now, what did you do about that fear that you can again do about this one?

C: I guess I saw, mainly, that it was not terrible, although it was still highly undesirable, if I failed at sex. And I focused on doing my best to enjoy it, instead of severely criticizing myself in case I didn't succeed at it.

T: Right! Now, why can't you do the same kind of thing in regard to having deeper emotional relations with men?

C: Mmmm. You mean, concentrating on enjoying my relations with them, instead of knocking myself down if one of them, one of the good ones that is, rejects me?

T: Yes. And—as you said a moment ago in regard to the sex failure—convincing yourself that it is highly undesirable but not terrible
if you do get rejected. Convincing yourself, in other words, that you
will clearly be deprived but never be a worm if one of the good men
you choose indicates that he is not choosing you in return.

C: It's really the same thing, then, that I did before. Only bigger
and harder!

T: Yes, bigger and harder, but still the same basic thing and still far
from impossible to do. Why don't you try it and see?

Again, Dr. S. did try to work on her problem of defining herself as
worthless in case she was rejected by a desirable male. She had more
trouble doing this than she had had with the problem of sexual frigidity,
particularly because she could not too easily find suitable males with
whom to test herself. Within the next eight months, however, she did
find two fairly good candidates, and she boldly threw herself first into
an intense relationship with one of them and then with the second
when the first did not work out. Although neither of these relationships led to marriage, and one was an out and out rejection by the
man with whom she was involved and the other was a keen disap-
pointment because she chose the wrong sort of person, she for once
refused to castigate herself for her failures and managed to have
strong feelings of love for both these men. As a result of these experiences, she was looking forward hopefully, when she left therapy
after twenty-nine sessions, to a more successful love relationship in
the future. About three years later she did marry and has, to my
knowledge, been devoted to her husband and her work ever since.

## LIMITATIONS OF RATIONAL-EMOTIVE THERAPY

All psychotherapy, including RET, has its definite limitations. Human beings, as I show in detail in the last chapter of *Reason and Emotion in Psychotherapy* (33), are born as well as reared to think crookedly about themselves and others and therefore are practically never
completely uncondemning and tolerant. Even when they are helped
significantly by a psychotherapeutic process, they tend to slip back to
some degree into their old patterns of undisciplined and overemotional
behavior. To remain even reasonably rational and non-self-defeating,
they have to work hard and long; and they frequently fail to continue to
do this. Some of them, such as those who have serious mental deficiencies or exceptionally psychotic behaviors, do not seem to have

the capacity to help themselves too much. And though most of them do have considerable self-actualizing and regenerative capacities as Maslow (106) and Rogers (121) have shown, there is no guarantee that, even with the most effective forms of psychotherapy, they will permanently utilize their own abilities to grow and experience.

The RET method is unusually effective with clients who acknowledge that they have emotional problems and who are willing to work at understanding and changing their thinking and behavior. It often is useful with individuals with moderate to severe disturbance, with those afflicted with frigidity and impotence, with people with marital problems, and with those with vocational difficulties. Others, particularly those who will not face their problems or who refuse to work at therapy, such as individuals with character disorders and overt psychotic reactions, can be treated with RET and often considerably helped, but the rates of significant improvement are lower with these individuals than with more willing clients (31). Like most other psychotherapies, RET is more effective with younger and brighter clients; but, it also has been used with good results with those who are mentally retarded, with people over sixty, with those from lower-income brackets, with alcoholics and drug addicts, and with others with whom most forms of psychotherapy show poor rates of improvement (33).

Although originally designed for use with adults, RET has been successfully applied with young children (47, 48, 53, 56, 87, 97, 110, 139). The Institute for Advanced Study in Rational Psychotherapy in New York City, which trains therapists in the RET methods, also operates a private school for normal children, The Living School. At this school, rational-emotive principles are taught, by a variety of academic and other procedures, to grade-school children in an effort to prevent them from picking up as many of the emotional disturbances that children in our society so often acquire (142). Although this school is now in its formative phase, good results are already being obtained in this respect.

Usually, RET gets best results when employed by a vigorous active-directive, outgoing therapist who himself is willing to take risks and to be little concerned about winning his clients' approval. It can, however, be successfully applied by less outgoing therapists, as long as they are sufficiently active to keep challenging and questioning their clients' irrational ideas and as long as they persist at teaching these clients a more scientific method of looking at themselves and the world and of working against their own self-indoctrinations. A bright and well-motivated therapist (including a paraprofessional) can learn the fundamentals of RET in a relatively short length of time and can begin to practice it, on both himself and others, shortly after he becomes acquainted with its fundamental principles. Even disturbed clients who are undergoing RET can frequently help their friends and relatives by using some of its aspects with these others. The RET methods can also be used to a considerable degree through the use of bibliotherapy materials, written communications, tape recordings, programmed materials, etc., in addition to its regular uses in individual and group therapy sessions (40, 45, 53).

Eventually, when my associates and I at the Institute for Advanced Study in Rational Psychotherapy are able to obtain adequate research funds, we expect to test, with a large series of randomly selected clients, the efficacy of the rational-emotive approach compared to that of various other types of therapy, such as psychoanalytic, client-centered, and existential psychotherapy. Continued clinical experience by myself and my associates, however, leads me in the meantime to reaffirm the original two hypotheses that I stated in my first major talk on rational psychotherapy, which was given in 1956 (31): "(a) that psychotherapy which includes a high dosage of rational analysis and reconstruction . . . will prove to be more effective with more types of clients than any of the nonrational or semirational therapies now being widely employed; and (b) that a considerable amount of—or, at least, proportion of—rational psychotherapy will prove to be virtually the only type of treatment that helps to undermine the basic neuroses (as distinguished from the superficial neurotic symptoms) of many clients, and particularly of many with whom other types of therapy have already been shown to be ineffective."

## REFERENCES

1. Adler, A. *Understanding human nature.* New York: Greenberg, 1927.
2. Ansbacher, H. L., & Ansbacher, R. R. (Eds.). *The individual psychology of Alfred Adler.* New York: Basic Books, 1956.
3. Ard, B. N. A rational approach to marriage counseling. In Ard, B. N., Jr., & Ard, C. C. (Eds.), *Handbook of marriage counseling.* Palo Alto: Science and Behavior Books, 1969. pp. 115–119.
4. Ard, B. N., Jr. The A-B-C of marriage counseling. *Rational Living,* 1967, **2** (2), 10–12.
5. Ard, B. N., Jr. Rational therapy in rehabilitation counseling. *Rehabilit. Counsel. Bull.,* 1968, **12,** 84–88.
6. Baker, J. N. Reason versus reinforcement in behavior modification. Ph.D. Thesis, University of Illinois, 1966.

7. Beck, A. T. *Depression: clinical, experimental and theoretical aspects.* New York: Hoeber-Harper, 1967.

8. Beck, A. T. Cognitive therapy: nature and relation to behavior therapy. *Behav. Ther.,* 1970, **1,** 184–200.

9. Beck, A. T., & Hurvich, M.S. Psychological correlates of depression. *Psychosom. Med.,* 1959, **21,** 50–55.

10. Beck, A. T., & Stein, D. The self concept in depression. Unpublished study summarized in Beck, A. T., *Depression: clinical, experimental and theoretical aspects.* New York: Hoeber-Harper, 1967.

11. Becker, J. Achievement-related characteristics of manic-depressives. *J. Abnorm. Soc. Psychol.,* 1960, **60,** 334–339.

12. Becker, J., Spielberger, C. D., & Parker, J. B. Value achievement and authoritarian attitudes in psychiatric patients. *J. Clin. Psychol.,* 1963, **19,** 57–61.

13. Berne, E. *Games people play.* New York: Grove Press, 1964.

14. Breen, G. Active-directive counseling in an adult education center. *J. Coll. Student Personnel,* July 1970, 279–283.

15. Breznitz, S. Incubation of threat: duration of anticipation and false alarms as determinants of the fear reaction to an unavoidable frightening event. *J. Exp. Res. Pers.,* 1967, **2,** 173-179.

16. Burkhead, D. E. The reduction of negative affect in human subjects: a laboratory test of rational-emotive psychotherapy. Ph.D. Thesis, Western Michigan University, 1970.

17. Callahan, R. Overcoming religious faith. *Rational Living,* 1967, **2**(1), 16–21.

18. Carlson, W. A.., Travers, R. M. W., & Schwab, E. A., Jr. A laboratory approach to the cognitive control of anxiety. Paper presented at the American Personnel and Guidance Association Meetings, March 31, 1969.

19. Cooke, G. The efficacy of two desensitization procedures: an analogue study. *Behav. Res. & Ther.,* 1966, **4,** 17–24.

20. Coons, W. H., & McEachern, D. L. Verbal conditioning acceptance of self and acceptance of others. *Psychol. Rep.,* 1967, **20,** 715–722.

21. Davies, R. L. Relationship of irrational ideas to emotional disturbance. M. Ed. thesis, University of Alberta, 1970.

22. Davison, G. C. Relative contributions of differential relaxation and graded exposure to in vivo desensitization of a neurotic fear. *Proceedings of the 72nd Annual Convention of the American Psychological Association,* 1965. Pp. 209–210.

23. Davison, G. C. Anxiety under total curarization: implications for the role of muscular relaxation in the desensitization of neurotic fears. *J. Nerv. Ment. Dis.,* 1967, **143,** 443–448.

24. Davison, G. C., & Valins, S. Maintenance of self-attributed and drug-attributed behavior change. *J. Pers. Soc. Psychol.,* 1969, **11,** 25–33.

25. Deane, G. E. Human heart rate responses during experimentally induced anxiety: effects of instruction on acquisition. *J Exp. Psychol.,* 1966, **67,** 193–195.

26. Diamond, L. Defeating self-defeat: two case histories. *Rational Living,* 1967, **2**(1), 13–14.
27. Diamond, L. Restoring amputated ego. *Rational Living,* 1967, **2**(2), 15.
28. di Loreto, A. A comparison of the relative effectiveness of systematic desensitization, rational-emotive, and client-centered group psychotherapy in the reduction of interpersonal anxiety in introverts and extroverts. Ph.D. dissertation, Michigan State University, 1969.
29. Dorsey, J. M. *Illness or allness.* Detroit: Wayne State University, 1965.
30. Ellis, A. *How to live with a neurotic.* New York: Crown Publishers, 1957. (Republished: New York: Award Books, 1969.)
31. Ellis, A. Outcome of employing three techniques of psychotherapy. *J. Clin. Psychol.,* 1957, **13**, 334–350.
32. Ellis, A. Rational psychotherapy. *J. Gen. Psychol.,* 1958, **59**, 35–49.
33. Ellis, A. *Reason and emotion in psychotherapy.* New York: Lyle Stuart, 1962.
34. Ellis, A. Toward a more precise definition of "emotional" and "intellectual" insight. *Psychol. Rep.,* 1963, **13**, 125–126.
35. Ellis, A. *If this be sexual heresy . . .* New York: Lyle Stuart, 1963.
36. Ellis, A. An answer to some objections to rational-emotive psychotherapy. *Psychotherapy,* 1965, **2**, 108–111.
37. Ellis, A. *Homosexuality: its causes and cure.* New York: Lyle Stuart, 1965.
38. Ellis, A. *Suppressed: seven key essays publishers dared not print.* Chicago: New Classics House, 1965.
39. Ellis, A. The treatment of psychotic and borderline psychotic patients with rational-emotive psychotherapy. In *Symposium on therapeutic methods with schizophrenics.* Battle Creek, Michigan: Veterans Administration Hospital, 1965. (Republished:) New York, Institute for Rational Living, 1969.
40. Ellis, A. The use of printed, written, and recorded words in psychotherapy. In Pearson, L. (Ed.), *The use of written communications in psychotherapy.* Springfield, Illinois: Charles C. Thomas, 1965.
41. Ellis, A. Phobia treated with rational-emotive psychotherapy. *Voices,* 1967, **3**(3), 34–40.
42. Ellis, A. Is psychoanalysis harmful? *Psychiat. Opinion,* 1968, **5**(1), 16–24.
43. Ellis, A. *Is objectivism a religion?* New York: Lyle Stuart, 1968.
44. Ellis, A. Emotional problems of the young adult. In Forest Hospital Foundation (Ed.), *The young adult.* Des Plaines, Ill.: Forest Hospital Foundation, 1969, 83–102.
45. Ellis, A. A cognitive approach to behavior therapy. *Int. J. Psychiat.,* 1969, **8**, 896–900.
46. Ellis, A. Rational-emotive therapy in the private practice of psychotherapy. *J. Contemp. Psychother.,* 1969, **1**, 82–92.
47. Ellis, A. Tape recording of a psychotherapy session with an eight-year-old enuretic girl. New York: Institute for Advanced Study in Rational Psychotherapy, 1969.

48. Ellis, A. Teaching emotional education in the classroom. *School Health Review,* November, 1969, 10–14.
49. Ellis, A. The emerging counselor. *Canadian Counsellor, 1970,* **4**(2), 99–105.
50. Ellis, A. Rational-emotive therapy. In Hersher, L. (Ed.), *Four psychotherapies.* New York: Appleton-Century-Crofts, 1970. pp. 47–83.
51. Ellis, A. A weekend of rational encounter. In Burton, A. (Ed.), *Encounter.* San Francisco: Jossey-Bass, 1970.
52. Ellis, A. Psychotherapy and the value of a human being. In Davis, J. W. (Ed.), *Value and valuation: essays in honor of Robert S. Hartman.* Knoxville: University of Tennessee Press, 1971.
53. Ellis, A. *Emotional education.* New York: Julian Press, 1972.
54. Ellis, A., & Harper, R. A. *A guide to rational living.* Englewood Cliffs, N.J.: Prentice-Hall, 1961. (Republished: Hollywood, Wilshire Books, 1968.)
55. Ellis, A., & Harper, R. A. *Creative marriage.* New York: Lyle Stuart, 1961. (Republished: *A guide to successful marriage.* Hollywood: Wilshire Books, 1969.)
56. Ellis, A., Wolfe, J., & Moseley, S. *How to prevent your child from becoming a neurotic adult.* New York: Crown Publishers, 1966.
57. Epictetus. *The Works of Epictetus.* Boston: Little, Brown, 1899.
58. Eysenck, H. J. *Experiments in behaviour therapy.* New York: Macmillan, 1964.
59. Frank, J. The influence of patients' and therapists' expectations on the outcome of psychotherapy. *British J. Med. Psychol., 1968,* **41,** 349–356.
60. Frankl, V. *Man's search for meaning.* New York: Washington Square Press, 1966.
61. Freud, S. *Collected papers.* New York: Collier Books, 1963.
62. Fritz, C. E., & Marks, E. S. The NORC studies of human behavior in disaster. *J. Soc. Issues,* 1954, **10,** 26–41.
63. Garfield, S. L., Gershon, S., Sletten, I., Sundland, D. M., & Ballou, S. Chemically induced anxiety. *Int. J. Neuropsychiat.,* 1967, **3,** 426–433.
64. Garfield, Z. H., Darwin, P. L., Singer, B. A., & McBrearty, J. F. Effect of "in vivo" training on experimental desensitization of a phobia. *Psychol. Rep.,* 1967, **20,** 215–219.
65. Geer, J. H., Davison, G. C., & Gatchel, R. J. Reduction of stress in humans through nonveridical perceived control of aversion stimulation. *J. Pers. Soc. Psychol.,* 1971, in press.
66. Geis, H. J. Toward a comprehensive framework of unifying all systems of counseling. *Educational Technology,* 1969, **9**(3), 19–28.
67. Gewitz, J. L., & Baer, D. M. Deprivation and situation of social reinforcers as drive conditions. *J. Abnorm. Soc. Psychol.,* 1958, **57,** 165–172.
68. Ginott, H. G. *Between parent and child.* New York: Macmillan, 1965.
69. Ginott, H. G. *Between parent and teenager.* New York: Macmillan, 1969.
70. Glass, D. D., Singer, J. E., & Friedman, L. N. Psychic cost of adapta-

tion to an environment stressor. *J. Pers. Soc. Psychol.*, 1969, **12**, 200–210.

71. Glasser, W. *Reality therapy.* New York: Harper and Row, 1965.
72. Glicken, M. D. Counseling children. *Rational Living,* 1966, **1**(2), 27–30.
73. Glicken, M. D. Rational counseling: a new approach to children. *J. Elementary Guidance and Counsel.,* 1968, **2**(4), 261–267.
74. Gliedman, L. H., Nash, E. H., Imber, S. D., Stone, A. R., & Frank, J. D. Reduction of symptoms by pharmacologically inert substances and by short-term psychotherapy. *Arch. Neurol. Psychiat.,* 1958, **79**, 345–351.
75. Greenberg, I. Psychotherapy: learning and relearning. *Canada's Ment. Health,* Supplement No. 53, 1966.
76. Grossack, M. Why rational-emotive therapy works. *Psychol. Rep.,* 1965, **16**, 464.
77. Grossack, M. *You are not alone.* Boston: Christopher Publishing House, 1965.
78. Gullo, J. M. Useful variations on RET. *Rational Living,* 1966, **1**(1), 44–45.
79. Gullo, J. M. Counseling hospital patients. *Rational Living,* 1966, **1** (2), 11–15.
80. Gustave, Alice. "Success is—" Locating composite sanity. *Rational Living,* 1968, **3**(1), 1–6.
81. Haley, J. *Strategies of psychotherapy.* New York: Grune and Stratton, 1963.
82. Harper, R. A. Marriage counseling as rational process-oriented psychotherapy. *J. Indiv. Psychol.,* 1960, **16**, 192–207.
83. Hartman, B. J. Sixty revealing questions for 20 minutes. *Rational Living,* 1968, **3**(1), 7–8.
84. Hauck, P. The neurotic agreement in psychotherapy. *Rational Living,* 1966, **1**(1), 31–34.
85. Hauck, P. Challenge authority—for thy health's sake. *Rational Living,* 1967, **2**(1), 1–3.
86. Hauck, P. An open letter to us. *Rational Living.* 1968, **3**(1), 29–30.
87. Hauck, P. *The rational management of children.* New York: Libra Publishers, 1968.
88. Homme, L. E. Perspectives in psychology—control of coverants, the operants of the mind. *Psychol. Rec.,* 1965, **15**, 501–511.
89. Homme, L. E. Coverant control therapy: a special case of contingency management. Paper presented at the 1966 Convention of the Rocky Mountain Psychological Association, 1966.
90. Hudson, J. W. Value issues in marital counseling. In Silverman, H. L. (Ed.), *Marital counseling.* Springfield, Illinois: Charles C Thomas, 1967. Pp. 164–176.
91. Jones, R. G. A factorial measure of Ellis' irrational belief system with personality and maladjustment correlates. Ph.D. thesis, Texas Technological College, 1968.
92. Jordan, B. T., & Kempler, B. Hysterical personality: an experimental

investigation of sex-role conflict. *J. Abnorm. Psychol.*, 1970, **75**, 172–176.

93. Kamiya, J. Conscious control of brain waves. *Psychol. Today*, 1968, **1**(11), 57–61.

94. Karst, T. O., & Trexler, L. D. Initial study using fixed-role and rational-emotive therapy in treating public-speaking anxiety. *J. Consult. Psychol.*, 1970, **34**, 360–366.

95. Kelly, G. *The psychology of personal constructs.* New York: Norton, 1955.

96. Krippner, S. Relationship between reading improvement and ten selected variables. *Perceptual and Motor Skills*, 1964, **19**, 15–20.

97. Lafferty, J. C. Values that defeat learning. *Proceedings of the Eighth Inter-Institutional Seminar in Child Development.* Dearborn: Edison Institute, 1962.

98. Lafferty, J. C. *Proceedings of the Blue Cross Association seminars in leadership and management.* Detroit: Adams, Laffery, Madden and Moody, 1965.

99. Lang, P. J., Sroufe, L. A., & Hastings, J. E. Effects of feedback and instructional set on the control of cardiac variability. *J. Exp. Psychol.*, 1967, **75**, 425–431.

100. Lazarus, A. A. *Behavior Therapy and Beyond.* New York: McGraw-Hill, 1971.

101. Lazarus, R. S. *Psychological stress and the coping process.* New York: McGraw-Hill, 1966.

102. Lecky, P. *Self-consistency.* New York: Island Press, 1943.

103. Litvak, S. B. Attitude change by stimulus exposure. *Psychol. Rep.*, 1969, **25**, 391–396.

104. Litvak, S. B. A comparison of two brief group behavior therapy techniques on the reduction of avoidance behavior. *Psychol. Rec.*, 1969, **19**, 329–334.

105. Low, A. A. *Mental health through will-training.* Boston: Christopher Publishing Company, 1952.

106. Maslow, A. H. *Toward a psychology of being.* Princeton: Van Nostrand, 1962.

107. Maultsby, Maxie C., Jr. The pamphlet as a therapeutic aid. *Rational Living*, 1968, **3**(2), 31–35.

108. Maultsby, Maxie C., Jr. Routine tape recorder use in RET. *Rational Living*, 1970, **5**(1), 8–23.

109. Maultsby, Maxie C., Jr. Psychological and biochemical test change in patients who were paid to engage in psychotherapy. University of Wisconsin, 1970. Unpublished manuscript.

110. McGrory, J. E. Teaching introspection in the classroom. *Rational Living*, 1967, **2**(2), 25.

111. Meehl, P. E. Psychologists' opinions as to the effects of holding five of Ellis' "irrational ideas." Report of the Research Laboratories of the Department of Psychiatry, University of Minnesota, Dec. 15, 1966.

112. Miller, N. E. Learning of visceral and glandular responses. *Science*, 1969, **163**, 434–445.

113. Nisbett, R. E., & Schacter, S. Cognitive manipulation of pain. *J. Exp. Soc. Psychol.,* 1966, **2,** 227–236.
114. Nuthmann, Anne M. Conditioning of a response class on a personality test. *J. Abnorm. Soc. Psychol.,* 1957, **54,** 19–23.
115. O'Connell, W. E., & Hanson, P. G. Patients' cognitive changes in human relations training. *J. Indiv. Psychol.,* 1970, **26,** 57–63.
116. Phillips, E. L. *Psychotherapy.* Englewood Cliffs, N.J.: Prentice-Hall, 1956.
117. Phillips, E. L., & Wiener, D. N. *Short-term psychotherapy and structured personality change.* New York: McGraw-Hill, 1966.
118. Premack, D. Reinforcement theory. In Levine, D. (Ed.), *Nebraska Symposium on Motivation, 1965.* Lincoln: University of Nebraska Press, 1965.
119. Rimm, D. C., & Litvak, S. B. Self-verbalization and emotional arousal. *J. Abnorm. Psychol.,* 1969, **74,** 181–187.
120. Ritter, B., The group desensitization of children's snake phobias using vicarious and contact desensitization procedures. *Behav. Res. Ther.,* 1968, **6,** 1–6.
121. Rogers, C. R. *On becoming a person.* Boston: Houghton Mifflin, 1961.
122. Rotter, J. B. *Clinical psychology.* Englewood Cliffs, N. J.: Prentice-Hall, 1964.
123. Ruesch, J. *Disturbed communication.* New York: Norton, 1957.
124. Satir, V. *Conjoint family therapy.* Palo Alto, California: Science and Behavior Books, 1967.
125. Schacter, S., & Singer, J. R. Cognitive, social, and physiological determinants of emotional state. *Psychol. Rev.,* 1962, **69,** 379–399.
126. Shapiro, M. B., Neufield, I., & Post, T. Experimental study of depressive illness. *Psychol. Rep.,* 1962, **10,** 590.
127. Shapiro, M. B., & Ravenette, E. T. A. A preliminary experiment on paranoid delusions. *J. Ment. Sci.,* 1959, **103,** 295–312.
128. Sharma, K. L. A rational group therapy approach to counseling anxious underachievers. Ph.D. thesis, University of Alberta, 1970.
129. Sherman, S. Alcoholism and group therapy. *Rational Living,* 1967, **2** (2), 20–22.
130. Skinner, B. F. *Science and human behavior.* New York: Macmillan, 1953.
131. Steffy, R. A., Meichenbaum, D., & Best, J. A. Aversive and cognitive factors in the modification of smoking behavior. *Behav. Res. Ther.,* 1970, **8,** 115–125.
132. Stekel, W. *Technique of analytical psychotherapy.* New York: Liveright, 1950.
133. Stieper, D. R., & Wiener, D. N. *Dimensions of psychotherapy.* Chicago: Aldine, 1965.
134. Taft, G. L. A study of the relationship of anxiety and irrational ideas. Doctoral dissertation, University of Alberta, 1965.
135. Thorne, F. C. *Principles of personality counseling.* Brandon, Vermont: Journal of Clinical Psychology Press, 1950.

136. Valins, S. Cognitive effects of false heart-rate feedback. *J. Pers. Soc. Psychol.*, 1966, **4**, 400–408.

137. Valins, S., & Ray, A. A. Effects of cognitive desensitization on avoidance behavior. *J. Pers. Soc. Psychol.*, 1967, **7**, 345–350.

138. Velten, E. A laboratory task for induction of mood states. *Behav. Res. Ther.*, 1968, **6**, 473–482.

139. Wagner, E. Counseling children. *Rational Living*, 1966, **1**(2), 28–30.

140. Weston, D. *Guidebook for alcoholics.* New York: Exposition Press, 1964.

141. Weston, D. *Different approaches to alcoholism.* Cleveland: Better Health Center, 1970.

142. Wolfe, J. L., et al. Emotional education in the classroom: The Living School. *Rational Living*, 1970, **4**(2), 22–25.

143. Wolpe, J. *Psychotherapy of reciprocal inhibition.* Stanford: Stanford University Press, 1958.

144. Wolpe, J. The systematic desensitization of neuroses. *J. Nerv. Men. Dis.*, 1961, **132**, 189–203.

145. Young, M. F. The treatment of schizophrenics with rational-emotive psychotherapy. Talk presented at the workshop of the Institute for Rational Living, Philadelphia, Sept. 1, 1963.

146. Zajonc, R. B. Attitudinal effects of mere exposure. *J. Pers. Soc. Psychol.*, 1968, **9** (Part 2, Monograph Supplement).

147. Zingle, H. W. A rational therapy approach to counseling underachievers. Doctoral dissertation, University of Alberta, 1965.

Chapter 12

# Confrontation Problem-Solving Therapy

## HARRY H. GARNER

Harry H. Garner: b. 1910, Chicago, Illinois.
B.S., University of Illinois, 1932. M.D., University of Illinois College of Medicine, 1934. Residency in Chicago State Hospital and the Illinois Psychiatric Institute, 1936–1939; Chicago Institute for Psychoanalysis, 1947–1951.
Professor and Chairman, Department of Psychiatry and Neurology, The Chicago Medical School, 1948–date. Assistant Professor of Psychiatry, University of Illinois, 1945–1948. Chairman, Department of Psychiatry and Neurology, Mount Sinai Hospital, Chicago, 1953–date. Chief, Neuropsychiatric Service, Veterans Administration (Illinois, Indiana, Wisconsin), 1947–1948. Superintendent Community Clinics, State of Illinois, 1945–1947.
Fellow, American Psychiatric Association. Member: Academy of Psycho-analysis; Honorary Medical Society, Alpha Omega Alpha; Academy of Forensic Science; Academy of Psychosomatic Medicine. President, Illinois Psychiatric Society, 1954. Winner, First Gutheil von Domarrus Award, 1969. Chairman, Deans Subcommittee on Psychiatry, V.A. West Side Hospital, Chicago. Vice Chairman, Illinois Psychiatric Advisory Council.
Books: *Psychotherapy: Confrontation Problem-solving Technique* (1970). *Psychosomatic Management of the Patient with Malignancy* (1966). *Continuing Education* (1964).
Articles: Over 70 articles. Brief psychotherapy. *Internat. J. Neuropsychiat.*, 1966, **1**, 616-622. Psychotherapy for the non-specialist. *Psychosomatics, 1965, **6**, 32–38. Cardiac pseudo angina. *Psychosomatics*, 1966, **8**, 139–143. Battered child syndrome: treatment of a parent. *Amer. J. Psychiat.*, in press. The confrontation technique. In Jules Masserman (Ed.). *Current psychiatric therapies*. New York: Grune and Stratton. Vol. 3. 1963, pp. 57-67.

## INTRODUCTION

Psychotherapy fits within the definition of an ideology as expressed by Tompkins (48). Psychotherapy is presented as a set of organized ideas, and people are at once most articulate and passionate about it and also least certain. Whether an art or science, it will probably never be free of ideology and, as such, will have adherents and believers who are either right wing or left wing. For, as was further stated, "The ideologies of all Western thought tend to gather around two poles. This is true of sciences and mathematics as of art and politics. The issues are simply stated:

—On the left wing the emphasis is on the importance and independence of man. He is an active, thinking, desiring, loving, creating force in nature.

—On the right wing, the emphasis is on external authority basically outside of himself.

This left-right polarity can be traced to all fields of knowledge." (48)

A similar left-right polarity was found among psychiatrists who express ideas consonant with the value of the individual, his right to be helped, a nonjudgmental attitude and avoidance of condemnation, the desirability of being aware of the possibility of choice and problem-solving propensity in the patient. The opposite right polarity includes psychiatrists whose orientation is one of an objective, aloof, calculated, clinical evaluation. Moral judgment and condemnation are expressed in the interpretations, advice, and suggestions given rather freely (46).

It has further been suggested that a revolution is taking place in efforts at conceptualizing psychotherapy. Social reinforcement and behavior control have been described as key concepts in this new approach. Behavior control studies have been encouraging in that human behavior is recognized as modifiable. However, the danger of behavior being imposed on others is seen as a threat to our concepts of free thought and free speech. In psychoanalysis, the intended neutral position of the therapist supposedly made it possible for the patient to use him as a screen by which the patient could see his reflected attitudes and undergo a process of inner observation leading to change (15). Sullivan's (47) influence replaced that of the earlier "activity therapists" who had pushed the therapist into the treatment with their emphasis on active interventions and the interpersonal relationship. Operant reinforcement technique and such conditioning systems as those used by Wolpe (50) and Mowrer (38) center around the therapist's reinforcing and social-learning influences. The confrontation problem-solving technique directs attention to how the patient sees the influence of the therapist. The patient's behavior suggesting compliance, noncompliance, or problem-solving is his basic mode of relatedness. I have described (20–23) the successful utilization of a confrontation technique in psychiatric treatment. This technique has a problem-solving rather than a permissive or coercive approach. It has been used on hundreds of patients, with diverse psychiatric, medical, and surgical problems. The application of the confrontation technique as a tool to be used extensively and intensively throughout the therapeutic process is based on the difficulty with which old learned patterns, which once had adaptive value, are unlearned. In the learning process, motivational pressures and the subjective needs of the individual have created goal-seeking behavior directed at satisfying the needs of hunger, love, and urge toward mastery. The responses that brought satisfaction were repetitively carried out until they become automatic responses no longer requiring problem-solving. The person accepts his adaptations, when effectively repeated over a significant period, as unalterable. Indeed, he reacts with resistance to alteration even when the pattern of behavior becomes obviously maladaptive.

## THE CONFRONTATION PROBLEM-SOLVING TECHNIQUE

The techniques of therapy applied in confrontation problem-solving psychotherapy include the presentation of a statement and a question. A problem that is crucial but only vaguely recognized or not recognized may be used as a therapeutic focus. It is then stated succinctly and in a positive tone: "Stop believing that you lost your womanhood. What do you think or feel about what I told you?" An actual solution to a problem may be presented or expressed in an exaggerated manner to illuminate the possible action. An alternative is to express the end results of a continued maladaptive activity in so exaggerated an expression that the person would wish to discontinue such behavior: "Stop believing that you have committed the world's greatest sin. What do you think or feel about what I told you?" The frequent reiteration of the statement is intended to create atmosphere or feeling that the status quo is unacceptable and a solution is found by continuous searching. It is as if the therapist's repetitious question acts as a continuous pressure to force the acceptance of a need to explore and solve a problem.

The use of a confrontation by the therapist has value in that it creates a situation wherein the patient feels that if his ability to control the undesirable impulse or to function independently is impaired, such control will emanate from sources outside of himself. Further, in headlong flight from reality, controls, and object relations, the patient finds himself confronted by the therapist in such a way that his line of retreat is cut off. If he wishes to evade reality now, he has to think about why. But thinking about reasons for evading reality requires differentiating among reasons, evaluating them, and choosing how to behave. The patient's crumbling controls are reinforced. Anxiety is reduced. The patient is invited to explore what he is doing with the help and support of someone who has obviously done his part in bridging the communication barrier.

The confrontation technique has developed within the framework of uncovering psychotherapy in which interpretations and questions are intended to overcome resistances and bring about varying degrees of reconstruction of the past. An understanding of the nature of the pathological defenses and an awareness of the personality structure in concepts expressed by such terms as drives, needs, desires, anxiety, controls, social conformity, superego, conscience, adaptive functions, and reality testing is necessary. An awareness of the influence of the past and the present interpersonal phenomena and their importance for transference is essential. The basic psychotherapeutic framework in which the technique has evolved might, therefore, be described as psychodynamically oriented psychotherapy. When insight is not involved because of the technique used or because the goals for the treatment of the patient are limited, transference interpretations, or dealing with the relationship of past and present, may be totally avoided. The goal is then to bring about a change in symptoms or to improve social functioning rather than focusing on an alteration of personality structure.

Controlling a patient through methods which reestablish the authoritarian parent–child relationship may be considered, at best, a form of supportive psychotherapy. However, the control of the therapist reassures the patient that his own controls will be strengthened by an external control and thus helps relieve an acute panic state and anxiety. Authoritarian directives intensify transference phenomena and the tendency to repeat a behavior pattern previously executed without questions as to its significance. However, the patient is invited to work out a mutually satisfactory solution to conflicts rather than being simply instructed or left to wander on alone by the question, "What do you think or feel about what I told you?" The question creates a desire in the patient to test the significance of the controls and to evaluate these further on a realistic basis. In other words, it tends to foster reality-testing instead of fostering transference neurosis. The use of confrontations may also strengthen the patient's favorable feelings of hope for recovery and restoration to health. Since the patient has lost a great deal of faith in his ability to recover, the promise of health through authority increases his capacity to control his anxiety so that he can be more realistically aware of the conflicts creating it. The patient, freed from anxiety, can construct more wholesome and more effective adaptations. Also, the struggle of impulses seeking expression against internalized controls becomes partially transferred to a conflict between impulses and an external parental figure and leads to an awareness of the attitudes toward such impulses in the general sociocultural milieu of the patient. The suggestion was that, as a guide to therapy, attention should be constantly focused upon the "integrative task," the problem that the ego is trying to solve at each particular moment. The use of this technique tends to highlight the integrative task for the patient.

Choosing the statement with which the patient is confronted will vary in light of the clinical picture of the patient and the nature of the relationship at the initial use of the confrontation. The area of conflict selected will vary from case to case. It is a question of the therapist's acuity in ascertaining the area of core conflict or immediate struggle, whether it is sexual, sibling rivalry, or some other disequilibrium. The patient may be confronted with a prohibitive statement: "You must never, under any circumstances, masturbate!" or an expressive or permissive statement: "It would be better if your husband dies" or an adaptive statement involving a mature value orientation: "I want you to continue to work at your job." By and large, all of the confrontation statements may be classified in one of these three categories. The confrontation, once stated, is used continuously. The process of developing self-assurance through mastery and achievement is not inhibited by fear of punishment, shame, failure, or fear of loss of love because of the noncondemning nature of the relationship and the encouragement to seek a solution suggested by the repetitive question.

Statements in the confrontation problem-solving technique are made to the patient with the intent to work on a limited therapeutic focus or on the resolution of a core conflict suggested by the longitudinal life history of the individual. Some of the statements that are used in confrontation problem-solving therapy may be determined in the near future by a study which will attempt to classify the basic attitudes expressed in our culture toward the goal directed need fulfilling desires of the child. The attitudes which will include those of the mother, father, siblings, and their substitutes may be used as a therapeutic focus. For instance, Gardner (19) indicated that his studies and observations demonstrated that severe disabilities in the reading and speaking area are, for a large part, experientially induced. Emotional blocks and inhibitions in reading and speaking constitute a neurosis with fear of death, mutilation, or abandonment as its pseudopsychotic core. Likewise, words and word sounds may have positive meaning for children; the written and spoken word may be highly valued by individuals. They may be personalized, as in describing the difficulty in starting the words of something to be written as requiring blood letting. The word flow in and of itself may be valued. In the future development of the technique, the basic attitudes of the culture will need clarification and codification. Many factors must be determined as to which attitudes are more easily adapted to therapy. For instance, is prohibition of drives or attitudes directed at encouraging open expression of drives more significant in creating change? At present, my feeling is that prohibitions are probably the attitude of choice earlier in the treatment and statements suggesting expression of drives are more desirable in the later phases of care. When the goal of psychotherapy is to create a compliant response associated with a feeling of well-being, the use of words intended to influence by their valuable magical qualities would be selected, i.e., "I want you to believe everything will turn out for the best. What do you think or feel about what I told you?" Or words intended to have the ability to counteract or undo the magical influences which create fear of death, mutilation, or abandonment might be selected, i.e., "Stop believing that you are in danger from terrible things happening to you. What do you think or feel about what I told you?"

The confrontation statement may be focused on the traumatic situations of infancy and childhood. Traumatic experiences have usually been considered to be: deprivation, overindulgence, rejection, hostility, excessive domination, restriction to excess, overprotection, seductiveness, ambition, actual physical injury. For instance a businessman raised in a situation in which extreme overprotectiveness seemed to create the atmosphere for a traumatic situation in infancy and childhood gave up a significant position in a large manufacturing firm because of family quarrels. A strong sense of pride had until then made him deny to a large extent his extreme feeling of dependence and need for protections. On planning to and entering a business in which he felt he suffered a considerable loss of prestige, the patient experienced an acute panic reaction with symptoms of anxiety, a sense of helplessness and inadequacy, and a seeking for a protective position. The confrontation statement made to the patient was, "I want you to get down to doing what is necessary to make a go of this business. What do you think or feel about what I told you?" The therapeutic focus was on his extreme needs for protection and control.

One may choose as a focus to bring about a return to a previously stabilized psychic economy from which one may have the choice of proceeding with further supportive or uncovering psychotherapy. The establishment of a previous stable state may be all that the patient seeks or all that is realistically desirable as a goal for therapy. The confrontation statement is used to support the defenses when the reality-testing function has been so impaired as to create such distortions as wish-fulfilling illusions, projections, hallucinations, delusions, exaggerated overdetermined hostility, and aggressivity. A patient with delusional thinking centering around ideas of reference and feelings of special significance in events she was experiencing was felt to be projecting her own need for sexual gratification. She had to deny and project her own desires as coming from others toward her by means of television and radio. It was considered necessary to fortify repressive and suppressive influences in order to create a return to a previous stable state. The confrontation statement was expressed as: "I don't want you to have anything to do with sex. What do you think or feel about what I told you?"

The focus of the confrontation statement may be based on the urgency of a required environmental change. Environmental changes of such a nature as to create improvement has been suggested as a therapeutic device by many authors. Gordon (25), in studying groups, found a significant difference between those patients treated with emphasis on creating insight and those treated with environmental changes in addition to the treatment. Patients who were helped by improving the environmental situation had an effective psychotherapeutic result with fewer treatments than those treated primarily by therapy directed at gaining insight. The suggestion was that groups who responded better were composed of those persons in whose life the milieu could more easily be improved. The importance of the acceptance of a dependent position and other influences in the psychotherapeutic procedure as being primary to the sociodynamic changes is not apparent in Gordon's paper.

Because of strong influences during her upbringing, a student was expected to live up to a standard of A grades. A recent marriage conflict related to meeting the responsibilities of a housewife, fear of pregnancy, and other problems compounded the difficulties of scholastic achievements. Her grades suggested she would fail in two courses. A deep depression with indecision about whether she should drop the two courses to avoid a failing grade was outstanding at the time of the first visit. The statement made to the patient was, "You should drop the two courses now. What do you think or feel about what I told you?"

Confrontation statements may be chosen with the intent to undermine vicious cycle patterns, such as those which diminish the patient's feeling of personal value. As a result of exploration of life patterns, the person can obtain reassurance as proof of his worth and can recognize that the feelings of insignificance are related to earlier experiences in which the feelings were not warranted by the actual situation, were disproportionate to the situation, and were developed in an immature individual. The experiencing within the transference of acceptance and a noncondemning, nonjudgmental attitude toward verbalization of thought, feelings, and behavior which the patient had expected to be met with criticism, disdain, humiliation, rejection, anger, and annoyance is also important for elevating the lowered self-esteem of the patient.

A similar basis for the choice of a statement is found in many clinical syndromes. For instance, in many patients the overt expression of conflict is seen in jealousy of an inordinate nature, in ideas of infidelity, in ideas of reference, or in delusional and hallucinatory experiences in which vile and uncomplimentary expressions and other expressions of jealousy and paranoid thinking are characteristic. As Freud (14) indicated, there is a transition from normal jealousy to paranoid delusional thinking, and this range of affective responses offers a spectrum of clinical expressions of varying intensity and scope. Somewhat basic to the entire spectrum of the clinical disorders associated with jealousy, ideas of reference, projected feelings of worthlessness and lack of morality, and the development of delusional systems of being the object of persecution are strong feelings of insignificance, immorality, sinfulness, and perversity, of unfaithfulness and lack of reliability and sincerity. When these feelings are stimulated by experiences in the day-to-day living of the individual, they provoke feelings of anger and hostility of such strength that the person is faced with defending himself against homicidal desires and with the danger to himself from retaliatory assault. The defense of projection serves the purpose of a defense against being the aggressor. ("It is not that I hate him. He hates me. Therefore, my hatred or jealousy is understandable.") That homosexual love may be the fountainhead for a clinical condition in which projection is the major defensive pattern does not contradict the concept that feelings of insignificance and hatred predominate. It is when such love is felt as confirming the insignificance, the dirty perversity or unworthiness of the individual that the many seemingly personally directed hints, illusions, and innuendoes are taken as barbs which stimulate the hatred and feelings of insignificance that must be defended against by projection. The statement used in treating such patients could be one of the following: "Stop believing you are the most insignificant person in the world." "Stop believing you are the most mistreated person in the world." "You are the most mistreated person in the whole world." The statement would be followed by the usual question.

The confrontation may be chosen to focus on a maladaptive assumptive system and the question, "What do you think or feel about what I told you?" challenges the patient to explore, affirm, or disprove the assumptive set and to modify, correct, or replace it. Behavioral therapies are related to theories in which maladaptive thinking and behavior is a result of a bad learning process that can be rectified by deconditioning and relearning. An example of such theorizing is expressed by Frank (11). It is in the correction of errors in the patient's assumptions concerning himself and others and the resulting conflicts created thereby that Frank finds the work of psychotherapy. The assumptions are organized into systems at various levels of consciousness and in harmonious or conflictual relations with each other. They affect and are affected by emotions. Healthy assumptive systems permit a consistent internal adaptation and a verification of assumptions as being in keeping with the actual circumstances of the world. Interpersonal experiences in which assumptions are verified tend to create comfort and security and a sense of well-being which permits continuous learning and modification of behavior, provided such interpersonal experiences are not associated with threats to the security of the individual. Unhealthy assumptive systems are full of conflict, are associated with lack of verification of their reliability in actuality, and are responsible for producing frustration, vacillating inappropriate responses, and failure. The assumptive systems concept is one which has similarities to other descriptions of mental states, such as the determining tendencies of Ach (2), the mental set and organizational factor of Rashkis (41), and those descriptions which emphasize the importance of conditioning and learning experiences on cultural patterns. The repetitive, cyclic nature of any assumptive system and its relative unmodifiability, either because there is reinforcement of the particular assumptive system in the environmental experiences or because unconscious factors tend to continue the system, is relevant to the use of a confrontation problem-solving technique.

The confrontation interventions of the psychotherapeutic process can also be divided into statements which represent emphasis on the following: What the patient has been (a genetic reconstruction of the past); what he is doing (behavior in the day-to-day interactions and that interaction which represents transference phenomena); and what he wants to do (that which represents the anticipated actions and the resulting inner reaction or interpersonal experience). Confrontation interventions by the therapist may be directed at getting more information for reconstruction of the past so as to better understand the present and the goal-directed striving of the patient. How the past attitudes are influencing present and intended performance so that the repetition-compulsion nature of his behavior can be better understood by the patient may be the therapeutic focus of confrontation statements. The following is an example: "Stop believing you have to get everything you want, immediately. What do you think or feel about what I told you?"

In selecting statements in which the therapist, in effect, becomes among other things a "reinforcing machine," we must clearly see the goals of therapy. The role of the "reinforcing machine" is determined by the nature of the behavioral change, which it is reasonable to presuppose would be the most desirable for the patient under the existing circumstances, and those changes one can expect will be accomplished with a reasonable degree of certainty. The nature of the statement will depend upon whether the goal is "cure" (significant personality alteration), symptomatic improvement, removal of an environmental pressure, or rehabilitation. The confrontation problem-solving technique makes full use of the potential for verbal conditioning in the interpersonal relationship of psychotherapy. When therapeutic goals warrant a "social reinforcement" operation and problem-solving is not to be expected, the establishment of the therapeutic implant could be, for instance, based on some of the following considerations:

What the therapist sees as the nature of the problem and the therapeutic goal.

Restoration of a state of mental health existing prior to an acute dysfunction, recently precipitated.

A failure to continue a socially effective life; the desirability of establishing more effective interpersonal exchange.

Specific deprivations in living, creating emotional turmoil and the need to make full use of the unused assets of the patient.

A failure to have developed assets and resources that were available for an adaptive life process; the therapeutic goal may focus on the defensive inhibitions.

Avoidance of responsibility which was creating conflict and non-economic patterns of adaptation; the resolution of the dependency–independency conflict may be a specific goal.

Fear of destructive impulses creating serious problems in living and the need to develop controls or a more realistic appraisal of the ability to control.

Conflictual and faulty value systems being used to the detriment of the patient and possibly of his society; the goal may center around achieving a more wholesome value system.

The patient's concept of his conflicts, anxiety, and problems may direct the therapist toward a therapeutic focus. The patient may feel or say that he is physically disabled and needs help for the physical dangers; that he is hopelessly inadequate to meet the challenge of life; that he has no control over himself; that he lacks intellectual or physical adequacy; that mistreatment by others has been his lot; and that he is unable to enjoy his life. What the patient thinks is wrong with the therapist's analysis of the patient's problem at the time of the initial interview may offer the clue to a significant therapeutic focus.

The principle of not selecting material by the therapist through conscious effort and the use of hovering attention so that the unconscious of the therapist would be responsive to the unconscious of the patient was recommended by Freud (15). A recommendation for the therapist's position aligned with the patient's free association is seen in the concept of therapist as a radar device set to receive the appropriate wave lengths by scanning the incoming signals and picking up those that are important. This principle has been used rather loosely in the treatment of patients in clinics and hospitals by methods which attempt to simulate the basic model technique but are not considered psychoanalysis. However, the selective inattention which is obviously present could be seen as an operant conditioning situation in which the therapist is a "social reinforcing" agent, a person whose supportive help might be withdrawn unless one is compliant, and as someone who seems to feel that one should demonstrate that problems are solved from within. The element of the attention of the therapist in a selective manner has been applied freely by psychotherapists. Skinner (44) has described it as a general reinforcer in the operant conditioning therapy model.

The concepts of compliance and psychotherapy: A hypothetical framework for psychotherapy as an interpersonal interaction, in which the focus on the compliance of the patient is used to clarify the psychotherapeutic process, has been described by me (24).

### Compliance as an Innate Behavioral Tendency

In the animal organism an important element seems to be inherent similar to that of the tropism of the vegetable kingdom, which is probably significant for understanding the development of the phenomena of imprinting, operant conditioning, learning, psychotherapy, hypnosis, and the like. This phenomenon is one of moving toward and responding with compliance to stimuli in the environment which do not startle. In the human organism the movements toward the infant create a response of motor activity directed at responding to the mother with compliance. The movements are of the body and mouth of the infant directed toward contacting and feeding from the mother. This bodily and oral receptiveness represents the primary uncritical compliance of the infant. The responsiveness is apparently determined by an innate readiness in the central nervous system of the infant. It may be considered an instinctual tendency to respond by turning toward the mother because of kinesthetic stimuli and opening of the mouth on contact with the breast. A similar readiness to react to the offspring, varying in intensity in different organisms, is in all likelihood present in the mother. The establishment of this physical relatedness seems important for the further interaction necessary for the development of pleasurable contacts with others, courtship, mating, and motherliness, and for the stimulus to develop a responsiveness to other maturational demands for human contact as they develop.

A neurophysiologic confirmation of the concept of primary compliance is furnished in the studies by Denny Brown summarized by Langworthy (32). It is postulated that two opposing forces exist in the cerebral cortex: one is directed at reaching out, which leads to exploration of space, and is located in the parietal lobe; the other is located in the frontal and temporal lobes and leads to avoiding responses. Damage to the frontal lobe results in release of parietal lobe functions: a grasp response to tactile stimuli and reaching out responses to visual stimuli.

### Primary Compliance

The action of the organism in being instinctively compliant creates the possibility for interacting with the feeding mother through which the earliest differentiation of the individual from objects can proceed. It is as though primary compliance at first tends to continue the bonds that made mother and child one, but the experiences in feeding enable an awareness of self and object to develop as the separation from the breast occurs with each feeding. The early experiences in life are thus seen as developing out of the innate need for compliance and for satisfying physiologic needs and not from a pleasure-seeking drive. The experiencing of pleasure is secondary, and it comes from the gratification and relief of tension which follows compliant acceptance of the mother and breast. It is the basis for encouraging compliant behavior and the seeking of further pleasure. Fixation on the mother was explained by Freud (17) as being based on the sexual attraction toward the mother. One may understand fixation, initially, as an expression of the primary compliance of the child. The resulting immediate gratifications, and later influences, further condition the child, and secondary fixations are developed.

Primary compliance represents the innate unconditioned response of the organism to a nonfrightening stimulus in the environment (movement). Primary compliance may become associated with the expectation of limitless consideration and service based upon the extent of the mother's giving and altruistic behavior without which the totally helpless infant would perish. I believe that the earliest defenses which Masserman (37) describes are an outgrowth of the instinctual need for compliance modified through experiences, shortly after birth. The need is modified into expectations. The expectations are of being accepted (loved), protected, and made invulnerable, through the mother. This secondary compliance, however, soon becomes engrafted upon the child in a complex manner, depending upon the totality of the experiences of the organism which produce pleasure, decrease discomfort, or create fear of punishment or separation. The essence of biblical faith, it has been said, is the believer's certainty of standing in relation to an unprovable and irrefutable God. Compliant tendencies, in the absence of a realistic reason for such feelings, may be significantly related to the believer's certainty and to religious conversion experiences in which there is a transformation from doubting to devotion. The religious conversion experiences seen in the psychotic may have their origin in the arousal of primary compliance feelings.

*Secondary Compliance*

Uncritical secondary compliance is initiated by reinforcement through conditioning in which behavior associated with primary compliance is rewarded or punished. It promotes attitudes that bring about an organization factor or mental set in which compliant behavior is an automatic and readily induced response. Although the secondary type of compliance has some degree of flexibility not seen in primary compliance, nevertheless, secondary compliance produced through early conditioning is basically characterized by being uncritical compliance. "Attitudes developed through social experiences in a milieu characterized not merely by censorious and authoritarian controls but also through gregarious and protective tendencies" are described by Whitehorn (49) as important for maturity. Such attitudes become significant in maintaining that orientation toward other humans which is one of uncritical compliance. Both authoritarian controls and the excessive gregarious protective tendencies mitigate against problem-solving thinking and behavior. It follows that the inadequacy of the physical apparatus for independent functioning in the human species has made the instinctual need to comply and the secondary compliance developed soon after birth particularly significant for his survival.

Secondary compliance develops, out of the helplessness of the human organism, to a much greater degree than occurs in other animals. The state of helplessness or dependency, the fear of loss of love, and the threat of punishment involve the child in a complex interaction with family, people other than family, environmental situations, and events. Obedience and submission rather than exploration is characteristic. I do not expect to go into the theories of learning process, conditioned reflex concepts, transactional theory, psychoanalytic and other psychological theoretical constructs used in explaining human behavior. What seems evident in most of the theoretical frameworks is that there is in the child an acceptance of the direction, control, and methods of thinking and behaving which are characteristic for the family, social, and cultural milieu in which the child finds himself. Secondary compliance, therefore, comes about through the conditioning initiated around primary compliance and through all the experiences which encouraged a compliant attitude and were not strongly antithetic to the inherent developing need for mastery and to other maturational forces. The innate potential for growth and development, the drive for mastery of the environment, and the development of other autonomous ego functions of the infant and child can be conceptualized as factors which tend to disrupt but also foster early secondary compliance tendencies in which critical appraisal is absent or very limited. However, the new experiences of the child necessitate a mastery of self and environment which becomes more and more dependent upon the capacity for critical appraisal.

The development of the rules of the game as portrayed by Piaget

(40) is confirmatory of the developmental backgrounds for the uncritical secondary compliance and compliance with critical appraisal. During the second stage of game development, rules are regarded as sacred and untouchable emanating from adults and lasting forever. Every alteration suggested is responded to as a transgression. During the third stage of game evolution, every rule is looked upon as due to mutual consent and requires your loyalty and respect, but it is permissible to alter this rule by enlisting opinion on your side.

## Critical Appraisal

Critical appraisal covers such expressions as adaptive behavior, secondary process thinking, conscious reality oriented thought processes, and similar concepts. The coercive force of instinctual patterns of life is not as great for the human organism as it is for other species. The result of the process of socialization through the forces in the family, society, and culture is not characterized by the same inflexibility characteristic of instinctual patterns. A degree of freedom and choice is possible which must be nurtured so that uncritical secondary compliance does not develop into a deforming and retarding growth. In "Comments" S. C. (6) discusses the Eddington Lecture by Thorpe. He mentions the use of the term "mind" by Thorpe to mean "discriminative consciousness." It is a term that, I believe, expresses the state of mind necessary for critical appraisal. This state of discriminative consciousness is described by him as "the essential thing that man has in such great measure and other animals, even the highest, have in such small degree." Critical appraisal also refers to man's problem-solving explorations.

Critical appraisal requires open channels in a neuronal network. Early in life the open channels tend to be closed by complete fulfillment in gratifying experiences, by fear, frustration, and anxiety. Such factors discourage exploration of the environment and cause a decrease in use of discriminative processes. The decreasing use of discriminatory consciousness is associated with a corresponding tendency to uncritical compliance. However, as the child develops and the capacity for critical appraisal increases, he becomes capable of critical appraisal of his compliant tendencies. He also becomes cognizant of how his needs for nourishment, warmth, shelter, play, protection, etc., are fulfilled primarily through those around him and are to a major degree dependent upon his compliant behavior. He is then able to develop attitudes and behavior which might be designated as critical compliance (compliance is cognitively recognized as being in his best interests). Uncritical secondary compliance characterized by the automatic and repetitive tendency to respond by compliance without a critical evaluation of the experience develops concurrently because earlier experiences have encouraged the development of automatic behavior. Uncritical secondary compliance is recognized as establishing a set or pattern that is repeated on appropriate stimulus without the necessity for the type of work involved in a problem-solving venture. Critical compliance is based upon a problem-solving experience in which the solution of the problem was seen as best accomplished by a compliant attitude.

*Noncompliance*

The early symbiotic phase of mother–child relationship which precedes the separation-individualization phase, toward the end of the first year, is probably only associated with such noncompliance as stems from automatic noncompliant motor activity brought on by states of frustration, anger, and helplessness. Toward the end of the third year of life a somewhat stable differentiation of self–nonself, self–object, inside–outside, and animate–inanimate has taken place. The developing maturation of the child has fostered a desire to "Do it myself," "Explore it myself," "Say it myself," which will lead to varying experiences of hurt, frustration, and anger accompanied by threats of loss of love and punishment. Wishes, fantasies, and behavior which are noncompliant in nature are eventually repressed automatically if the dangers are great from individuals who unequivocally remove love or threaten with punishment, and secondary compliance is enhanced. If the climate for problem solving is favorable, noncompliance based on discriminative capacity will become available as a mode of operation in interpersonal relationships.

The interpersonal experience in psychotherapy may activate noncompliant attitudes of the earliest symbiotic relationships. Unequivocal threats of loss of love or punishment are seen as less formidable by the adolescent or adult, and noncompliance may replace what was expected to be a compliant attitude. Overly compliant behavior may lead to considerable change in the patient, suggesting better adaptive capacity when in reality the behavior is determined by the fear of the consequences of noncompliant attitudes.

Noncompliance is, of course, readily perceived as a mode of behavior related to frustrations, unwarranted expectations, inconsiderate treatment, unfair exploitation, unjust treatment, lack of love, and undue punishment. It is associated with self-assertion, annoyance, resentment, anger, hate, and destructive violence. Noncompliance taking place before effective understanding and the problem-solving capacity have developed is an uncritical noncompliance. As the individual develops, noncompliance may be associated with critical appraisal and the realistic conclusion that the noncompliance is warranted. However, uncritical noncompliance usually becomes a fixed pattern of reactivity not easily unlearned and readily reactivated in the psychotherapeutic venture. Much of what has been described as acting out represents uncritical noncompliance in the treatment relationship. The therapist is seen by the patient as requiring attitudes and behavior characterized by dependency, obedience, and submission and is reacted to with noncompliant behavior based upon reaction to significant figures of infancy and childhood.

## COMPLIANCE AND INHIBITION OF PROBLEM SOLVING

The question remains as to what extent the instinctual response of primary compliance and the early experience of conditioning of this instinctual pattern have created a tendency toward uncritical compliance which strongly interferes with the development of critical appraisal and problem solving and have created a lifelong overdetermined pattern of obedience. The same question may be asked about the influences that have created strong secondary compliance tendencies and have correspondingly interfered with the capacity for critical appraisal. It is suggested that primary compliance be considered an instinctual tendency which is soon superseded as the need for it is no longer urgent and as pleasure in feeding becomes well established. Much has been written about dependency and symbiotic relations of child and mother which demonstrates how secondary compliance can cripple the capacity for critical appraisal and problem solving.

Confidence and hope may have its origins in compliance. Benedek (3) writes, "Confidence and hope maintain the ego through a period of waiting." The inability to tolerate tension and deprivation is characteristic of the individual suffering with addiction and perversions, neuroses, psychoses, and psychosomatic disorders. It is this inability which frequently prevents the patient from making the necessary changes in behavior to decrease the ineffectiveness and ungratifying adaptations so crippling to his living. Confidence and hope can be restored by the belief that one has reestablished a relationship in which the gratifying experience that characterized the infant child–

mother symbiosis is present. If such a relationship then promotes problem-solving ventures, the confidence shifts from one of confidence in the responses of the other person to one of confidence in one's own capacity to understand, control, master, and create. Confidence which comes "through multiple repetition of the gratifying experience of symbiosis" (Benedek) has the quality of encouraging compliance. Frank (12), in studies on patient expectancy, describes two effects of psychotherapy, noted in a comparative study of three different psychotherapy approaches—symptom relief and attitude change. About attitude change he writes that among the variables are those aspects of the therapeutic situation which influence the patient at emotional and cognitive levels, leading him to modify his behavior in directions deemed desirable by the therapist. The orientation of one's psychotherapeutic work around the compliance-critical appraisal axis of the patient's relationship to the therapist is clearly described by Lesse (33). Expectancy of relief through accepting of certain treatments known in the social milieu to have curative powers is part of a phenomenon of accepting a compliant relationship with the therapist, institution, or social system that affords the treatment procedure. The therapists, at least in America, are shown to have a relationship with patients in which the therapist expects to dominate and the patient to be dominated. The positive placebo effect in psychotherapy is ascribed to the patient's expectancy of relief through establishing a compliant relationship. Those who feel they cannot establish a compliant relationship or those who feel that such a relationship will not be responded to with the expected unequivocal devotion to their needs do not develop a positive placebo effect. The importance of the compliant attitude of the patient for psychoanalysis is suggested by Freud (16) in explaining the difficulty in overcoming the id resistances of the patient.

> Does the uncovering of these resistances also guarantee that they will be overcome? Certainly not always, but our hope is to achieve this by exploiting the person's transference to the person of the physician so as to *induce* him to adopt our convictions of the impossibility of conducting life on the pleasure principle.

If the aim of the psychotherapeutic process is to increase the capacity of the patient to function with the greatest degree of effectiveness under the most economic conditions with a minimal use of energy for effective adaptive responses, there should be a relationship between the interventions in psychotherapy and the intended effect.

When interventions, intended or otherwise, are accepted without critical appraisal, they can be seen as creating influences by suggestion. There probably is a continuous chain of possibilities for any intervention to be seen as a suggestion and accepted without critical appraisal. At one end of a scale, interventions can be seen as being critically appraised for their reality based significance; at the other end of the scale, interventions can be scored for the degree to which they are accepted without critical appraisal. In any therapy in which a widening of the ego span, increased capacity to learn, changed attitudes, decrease in self-alienation, or similar achievements are sought, critical appraisal of the interventions in therapy must develop in the patient. What must be avoided is the acceptance of cues from the therapist, without appraisal for their meaning, to the person in relation to his past experience, present conflicts, and future goals. The suggestive influence of noncritical acceptance of interventions must be continually weighed in the psychotherapeutic process by the therapist. In a description of suggestion and autosuggestion, Ehrenwald (8) referred to doctrinal compliance by the patient with the therapist's preconscious wishes and expectations. For evaluating the therapeutic technique of using a confrontation statement followed by a question asking for problem solving, valid observational data in the field of psychotherapy may be fostered. To quote from Ehrenwald:

> On what grounds, if any, can we decide that a "Freudian," "Jungian," "Adlerian," or "Rankian" dream produced by a given patient is not merely the outcome of his doctrinal compliance? How can we be sure that it is not the effect of suggestion, empathic communication with his therapist, or operant reinforcement, of tele or telepathic leakage? In short, how are we able to rule out the basic methodological objection that his productions are not of the nature of genuine clinical data, but merely reflect the preconceived ideas of his therapist and, by indirection, of the school of thought to which he owes his allegiance?

The task required by the therapist as expressed in a statement given to the patient in the course of therapy using a confrontation technique may evoke less anxiety than the anxiety created by fear, loss of love, separation, and punishment. The intervention may immediately be rewarded by a decrease in symptoms or conflict and should be recognized as doctrinal compliance. When the therapeutic situation warrants compliance without a significant degree of discriminative consciousness, the therapist recognizes that the effects of his interventions include a compliant attitude on the part of the patient. The repetitive question, "What do you think or feel about what I told you?" enables the therapist, by following the responses and behavior of the patient, to evaluate the degree to which doctrinal compliance or problem solving is developing in the patient.

The cornerstone of therapeutic work in psychoanalysis is the working through of the transference neurosis which many analysts seem to feel develops spontaneously and is a repetition of the experience with significant persons in the past. The degree to which the transference is distorted by the patient is apparent in the following quote from Freud (31): "If the patient does not show compliance enough to respect the necessary conditions of the analysis, we can regularly succeed in giving all the symptoms of the neurosis a new transference-colouring and in replacing his whole ordinary neurosis by a transference neurosis of which he can be cured by therapeutic work." Studies are needed of the influence of interventions, verbal or otherwise, with the emphasis on the degree to which they can be accepted with a minimum of uncritical compliance. The use of the concepts expressed in this paper are found valuable in determining how, when, what, and for whom certain interventions can be made therapeutic.

The question "What do you think or feel about what I told you?" accompanies the confrontation statement, or it may be used by itself when its relevance to the statement can be expected to be recognized. In the confrontation problem-solving technique, this question is considered a most significant key to therapeutic effectiveness. It becomes a lever for exploring the patient's tendencies toward compliance and noncompliance. The question becomes a prod to the reluctance on the part of the patient to develop problem-solving attitudes. The question "What do you think or feel about what I told you?" can also be significant in thinking of the therapist as a "social-reinforcing machine." The therapist is seen by the patient as a powerful figure who subtly influences his behavior. To the observer, behavioral change coincides with that desired by the therapist, depending upon the goal set for the patient's treatment. However, the influence toward conforming behavior when considered to be through free choice ("What do you think or feel about what I told you?") is more acceptable since the reward for such conformity is felt to be self-earned. Where the patient feels a strong urge to comply and conform there may be little or no need on his part to feel that personal choice and free will were necessary. However, the repetitive request for exploration may, in the most desirable circumstance, lead to a progressive problem-solving approach to restoration of health.

The question "What do you think or feel about what I told you?" stimulates in the patient the awareness of the therapist's constant involvement in observing and interpreting reality, and the patient tends to identify partially with this aspect of the therapist. In analysis, Greenson (26) among others, stresses the importance of the work the therapist and the patient have to accomplish together. The use of such terms as "let us look at this" or "we can see" promotes this accomplishment. Loewald (35) was impressed with how the analyst's concern for the patient's potential is a stimulus to new growth and development. The repetitive question, in the patient who does not have an overriding desire to be compliant, is just such a stimulus.

## RELIEF OR EXPECTANCY OF RELIEF AS A REWARD

The teaching of confrontation problem-solving techniques to individuals familiar with or who can be taught to treat deviant behavior causing internal discomfort or social disharmony is enhanced by the use of the model of operant conditioning. The rate and intensity of a response can be expected to change as one consequence of influence of psychotherapist on behavior of the patient. Stimuli are generated in the interpersonal relationship of psychotherapy which can have feed-back consequences identified as similar to those in the learning process described as reward and punishment. The consequence of behavior which is rewarding or reinforcing is the increased probability of similar behavior. The converse of this statement is, of course, that any consequence of behavior which is painful decreases the possibility of like responses. In operant conditioning of animals, extinction occurs if a bit of behavior previously rewarded is no longer followed by reward. If the psychotherapeutic situation is studied from a limited and narrow viewpoint, several factors can be selected as somewhat fixed and then used for observing the therapist's activity and the patient's responses from the frame of reference used in operant conditioning. The dependent position, for instance, and need for compliance by the person seeking help are usually vital to the operation of the interaction. Responses by the patient are seen by him as leading to reward or to punishment. The need for approval, fear of loss of love, and all the other anticipated dangers to the relationship based upon the earlier experiences in a similar one-to-one relationship, i.e., parent–child, adult–child, teacher–child, authority–subordinate, are mobilized by the new situation in which a need for help from the therapist is expressed by the patient. The patient's reward is the relief of anxiety upon the expectancy that the therapist will be responsive to the plea or request of the patient. Reward will also come from those responses to confrontation statements that are personally satisfying, i.e., pride in accomplishing something considered difficult to accomplish, praise received from others for changed behavior, less anxiety than expected in performing a task, etc. These rewards are similar to the reinforcing agents used in operant conditioning. Instead of behavior being rewarded by the appearance of food, it is rewarded by interpersonal experiences that are satisfying or by a release from discomfort that serves to reinforce the desire for repetition of the psychotherapeutic experience.

An expectancy of relief potential results from the inferences drawn by the patient from verbalized stimuli. The confrontation statement is expressed as a command or a statement of fact which the patient expects has evident benefits if responded to appropriately. The inference is that since this is a situation involving a person seeking help from a person whose function is to help, heal, cure, etc., then the statement made has particular significance for helping me. It may also be seen as threatening with punishment. There is lessened anxiety in anticipation of help which in itself tends to reinforce the transference relationship, creating an increment of reinforcement for subsequent interventions. This occurs even though consequences to relationships which may be more important to the patient in reality are worsened. This is evident from the frequency with which I have seen patients respond to the therapist's implied sanction by behavior which is in accord with interventions directed at "getting the aggression out." The patient seeks approval through aggressive behavior despite what it does to worsen the relationship with others with whom he works and lives. Where the response to the confrontation statement is one in which coping or adaptive behavior creates reinforcement from better relations with others, diminished anxiety and generalization to new situations take place. The transference relationship is reinforced as improved adaptive functioning is recognized as following upon the behavioral change in response to the statement or as increased success in effective problem-solving occurs. It is further reinforced as symptom-free living becomes more rewarding than any secondary gain in illness. The question "What do you think or feel about what I told you?" used repetitively in confrontation problem-solving therapy creates a significant potential for converting a therapy in which compliance is the obvious result to one of problem-solving.

Generally, a statement intended to create a response in the patient directed at diminishing discomfort and improving adaptive or coping responses tends to act as an operant reinforcement and does so for the following reasons:

1. The patient expects the therapist to intervene and help. Expectancy of relief is followed by diminished anxiety. Reinforcement of the expectancy by the statement takes the place of the need for very frequent therapy sessions. The sick role and its secondary gain value is less suitable as a coping mechanism and would tend to diminish. The magical expectations may strongly reinforce the expectancy of relief. Behavior previously avoided, although effectively adaptive, becomes possible and is reinforced by its own rewards and the evident or inferred approval from the therapist.

2. The confrontation-question statement or intervention, when expressed, has several possible consequences for further relief:

a. The patient recognizes the rather positive, direct statements as lack of equivocation on the part of the therapist: "He knows what he wants to do with me."

b. "He is taking over and directing me as if he intends to help"; expectancy of relief is reinforced, anxiety is diminished, and coping behavior is improved.

c. "He is telling me what I and others felt I should do. Now there is support from an expert"; ambivalence is lessened, anxiety is diminished, unadaptive behavior is lessened, and compliance is increased. The statement may have meaning in that regulation of of "bad" impulses can be expected, directions for living, for marriage, for taking care of children, for sexual behavior, for on the job, etc., will be forthcoming; forgiveness and understanding and the relief of feeling of guilt is now possible.

d. Passive-dependent compliant tendencies are experienced with the decision to seek help. They are further reinforced by the statement. Passive-dependent tendencies in the past were often reinforced by the helpful responses from others. The statement may act as a reinforcer to compliant tendencies thereby bringing about less anxiety and reinforcement of coping behavior.

Among the influences created by the confrontation technique which can be studied during the course of contacts with the patient are responses such as the following: overt emotional reactions of anger; anxiety; passive acquiescence; fear, including evident pallor of the face; laughing; verbal acceptance or rejection; questioning of meaning, reversal of the meaning; blocking; complete failure to comprehend; alluding to and recognizing or not recognizing the import of the statement; behavioral changes suggesting acceptance or rejection of the statement; ambivalence, displacement of behavior to areas not specifically stated in confrontation; influences on dreams that will give cues to the nature of the transference reactions of the patient; and transference phenomena that make the patient's attitude to the therapist crystal clear. The confrontation-question intervention may represent a fixed variable around which predictions can be made with reasonable certainty.

In the natural sciences predictive hypotheses are made with the assurance that the matter being studied will not be influenced to change by the prediction of the investigator. In interpersonal relations one cannot be certain that the authority of the therapist will not overwhelm the patient. Patients will often do that which was predicted for them. The boundary line between prediction and suggestion, which is of no consequence in the natural sciences, is difficult to maintain in any of the social sciences. A psychotherapy that can enable the therapist to predict the outcome of an intervention and then check on the prediction would be one that might offer possibilities for creating a science of psychotherapy. The confrontation statements as used in psychotherapy and followed by the question "What do you think or feel about what I told you?" are repeated frequently. The patient's responses offer an opportunity of studying the degree to which suggestion, or problem solving, dominates the patient's attempt to understand the significance of the statement. By constant observation of the patient's verbal responses, behavior, and propensity for exploring alternatives, one can reach some conclusions with reasonable certainty. For example, one may conclude that the patient is being compliant (showing the responses expected to a suggestion); critically compliant (his behavior suggests that compliance was recognized as being in his best interest); noncompliant (his behavior, affect, thoughts are appropriate for rejecting a suggestion); or problem-solving in his behavior (attitudes, thoughts, and affect are appropriate for decision-making).

## OPERANT CONDITIONING CONCEPTS ARE APPLICABLE TO CONFRONTATION TECHNIQUE

In operant conditioning the therapist is seen as being in a position to manipulate the patient's behavior. The presence of the therapist is, in itself, a factor in controlling the nature of the verbal productions. Sex, prestige, socioeconomic factors, role expectancies transmitted to the patient, the role the patient feels he is to assume, and the conditioning situation when structured in a positive way all determine the significance of the therapist as a "social reinforcement machine" (9). Karno (29) questions psychotherapeutic effect as being the result of a patient's acceptance of a model of more mature or healthy behavior following upon logical and verbal rationale of insight. "The large part of such persuasion is the person of the therapist, whose skillful communications form an elaborate system of operant conditioning."

Operant conditioning methods as a basis for treatment have been used in a variety of psychiatric problems and settings. Operant conditioning as a concept was used by Skinner (44) to explain the whole range of the child's learned behavior. He has referred to the parental responses that indicate attention, affection, and approval as general reinforcers. It is this earlier behavior that determines the relationship of the patient to the therapist and makes the operant conditioning of psychotherapy possible. The extensive experimental work with animals needs no elaboration in this paper. This use of operant conditioning techniques in treatment was recently reviewed by Krasner (30). Krasner cites the work of Ayllon in using nurses as "behavioral engineers," of Thomas and Goldiamond to reinstate verbal behavior in psychotics, Saslow and Matarazzo to enhance generalization of newly learned behavior, Slack to reinforce desirable behavior in delinquents, and Richard Dignam and Horner in rewarding nondelusional thinking.

Mowrer's (39) description of two types of learning is pertinent to operant conditioning therapy. The first type, referred to as sign learning, is associated with the development of a predisposition or set. Through association or contiguity, conditioning leads to the development of secondary drives or emotions connected with new objects. Such learning is more apt to create problems. In treatment a similar type of learning, through association of the therapist with potential loss of love or punishment, creates a mental set characterized by compliance. In this state of predisposition, anxiety is lessened as the patient engages in experiences suggested by the therapist which were previously anxiety provoking; the fear of loss of love or of punishment acts as a spur to action. Concurrently, the compliant attitude is associated with the expectation of being protected against anxiety-provoking experiences. There is an extinction of the anxiety as each new experience is associated with diminished physiological and psychological response. The second type of learning is problem-solving learning. The rewards springing from the problem-solving action lead to reduction of drive and giving of pleasure.

In operant conditioning, the concepts of general and specific reinforcers in learning theory have a built-in acceptance of the implied compliant attitude of the patient. Behavioral change can be recognized by its compliant, noncompliant, and problem-solving significance, whether the therapist is seen as a "social reinforcement machine," a teacher, or a parent whose influencing action is directed at decreasing the maturational needs for being a problem solver. Operant conditioning experimenters seem influenced toward compliance; teachers may waiver between seeking compliance or problem-solving. The intent in confrontation problem-solving is to recognize and utilize problem-solving potential whenever the situation permits. Confirmatory evidence of the significance of compliance is found in abundance in the literature. The following evidence demonstrates this point but is far from an inclusive report of the literature. Dreams have been described frequently as showing the influence of compliant tendency and as helping to establish the evidence for compliance and the operant conditioning concepts to psychoanalysis. "Confirmatory dreams" come about according to Freud (18) during analytic sessions by the analyst suggesting repressed material to the patient based on symptoms, associations, and other signs, and shortly thereafter the patient reports a dream that contains the repressed material. The analyst interprets, constructs, and propounds, and the patient confirms the validity of the suggestion by the subsequent dream material. The analyst's suggestions are seen as successful because an unconscious force in the patient derived from a positive transference yields a "compliance toward the analyst" which, in turn, aids the treatment process. It follows that "if anyone wishes to maintain that most of the dreams that can be made use of in analysis are compliant dreams and owe their origin to suggestion, nothing can be said against that opinion from the point of view of analytic theory." Certainly, the approval sensed by the patient for producing dream material may be a general reinforcer. More specific reinforcement resulting from "successful" dream interpretation is obvious evidence of the operant conditioning element in psychoanalysis on dream interpretation. Using a form of indirect suggestion patterned after verbal conditioning, Ritter (42) was able to influence the ratio of male and female figures in dream material; and Zubin (51), in referring to the possible implication of verbal conditioning for psychotherapy, wrote "reinforcement may be the reason why Freudians get freudian dreams, Jungians get jungian dreams, Rogerians get no dreams at all." Fisher's (10) experimental work with dreams on patients in analysis is likewise confirmatory.

The experiments of Sloane, Davidson, and Payne (45) confirm the desirability of the use of a technique that would tend to act as a process for deconditioning. Their results indicate that psychoneurotic patients are more easily conditioned than normal subjects. Their results are also in keeping with what has been termed the greater responsiveness to suggestion of the psychoneurotic or the individual in a situation in which he seeks help. The importance of compliance as a basis for bringing about social improvement in chronically ill schizophrenic patients is verified by studies such as the following. Cohen (5) treated 28 chronically regressed schizophrenics by focusing on specific behavioral patterns, demanded improved behavior, exerted group pressure on recalcitrants, and rewarded improvement publicly. Of the patients whose average length of current hospitalization had been 12 years, only five failed to show some improvement. It seems self-evident in this study that behavioral change is brought about as a result of compliant attitudes out of fear of loss of love or punishment. The compliant attitude of the patient was recognized as important by Freud (13) and is expressed in the following quote: "If the patient does not show compliance enough to respect the necessary conditions of the analysis, we can regularly succeed in giving all the symptoms of the neurosis a new transference-colouring and in replacing his whole ordinary neurosis by a transference neurosis of which he can be cured by therapeutic work."

Studies of the influence of interventions with the emphasis on the degree to which they are accepted with uncritical compliance are needed. Compliant tendencies would be significant as a factor in any therapy where the therapist is seen as a "social reinforcement machine." Insofar as the patient was hindered from developing problem-solving propensities in situations where more mature thinking was possible, the patient has not been properly helped. The question, "What do you think or feel about what I told you?" is recognized as offering a technique for avoiding this pitfall. The therapist in the confrontation problem-solving therapy is, if you will, programming his patient to be maximally involved in decision-making. The "social reinforcement machine" concept is one in which programming is directed at improved capacity for obedience. The problem-solving benefits then follow from the relief of anxiety and the resulting enhanced freedom for thinking through of a problem.

## THEORETICAL CONSTRUCTS USED
## IN CONFRONTATION TECHNIQUE

With relatively few exceptions, the patient is motivated to seek psychotherapeutic help by two conflicting wishes or desires. On the one hand, he is usually seeking help from a magical healer to reinforce his strivings against impulses threatening him with danger. On the other hand, he also seeks restoration to health. In its deepest sense, this would mean to the patient the gratification of all his impulses, hopes, desires, and expectations. Possibly, what the patient is seeking is the reestablishment of that state in which his basic defenses are no longer threatened. Many of the patient's hopes, expectations, and desires are prevented from fulfillment, not because of any reality barrier, but rather because of his attitude and feelings about these wishes, needs, and desires. The infant and child develop patterns of reacting which are adaptively related to the situation he is experiencing. However, these patterns usually fail to have positive adaptive value in later life. The breakdown in psychological homeostasis occurs because the patient's methods of dealing habitually with internal and external stimuli, developed during infancy and childhood, prove to be insufficiently adequate methods for dealing with parents, peers, parent surrogates, marriage, sexuality, parenthood, economic self-sufficiency, and all the other multiplex facets of life that may tax functional efficiency to the maximum.

The following factors are suggested as responsible for the tenacity of these poor adaptive responses:

1. At the time they were developed, the patient's responses had some effective adaptive value. They were then the best possible solution to his problem.

2. These responses assured maximum gratification of wishes and desires along with a minimum threat of danger, in terms of loss of love and security. They also assured freedom from aggression or injury from others and maintained self-esteem.

3. When such behavior was found to be adaptively valuable, the distance between stimulus and response became shortened. Introjection took place. This led to automatic behavior when situations actually or symbolically suggested a relationship to earlier configura-

tions. This tendency has been labeled, "repetition compulsion." To a large extent, nonacceptable impulses are denied because of fear of loss of love or fear of aggression from others. By denying the need for action, the patient decreases the danger. Therefore, control of such desires would best be exercised most effectively at the source. The self-imposed "don't," "you should not," "you cannot," "you must not," "you ought not" represents the shortening of distance between the stimulus and response.

4. To each new situation, the response constitutes those adaptive patterns previously tested and found to be most effective, or new adaptive patterns most frequently used in comparable situations. The use of previously tested responses leads to the phenomena of transference, repetition-compulsion, and narrowing of the ego span. Such economy of activity may have its immediate value. However, it creates difficulties which are directly proportional to the length of time required for maturation in any organism. The longer the period of dependence and the more such patterns are developed, the greater the probability that such adaptations will become the basis for uneconomical and inadequately adaptive behavior in later life.

5. We must also consider that the patient has certain innate characteristics determined by heredity, which will significantly influence the nature of his development. These characteristics are subject to independent external influences as well as to "feed-back" influences from the environment on exploratory acts by the individual. As he experiences responses of objects in the environment to his behavior, the patient may modify, inhibit, or intensify his behavior.

The following might be considered factors contributing to better integration and adaptation of the individual when the confrontation technique is used.

1. The more distant stimuli situations and events are from the efficient response, the greater is the capacity for appraisal and for integration of perceptual, conceptual, affective, and response phenomena based on the general principles of reality-testing. An inner conflict does not enable the type of evaluation possible when the stimulus is outside (the therapist), rather than the result of a struggle within. If we assume that this premise is true or in the nature of an hypothesis, the further the stimulus situation is from the appropriate efficient response, the greater is the capacity for appraisal and reality-testing, then it would follow that corrective emotional experiences might be created and their effects hastened by maneuvers calculated to increase the distance between stimulus and response.

2. "Repetition of an experience is a very powerful force with respect to modification of behavior. It derives from the no less exceptional tendency for behavior to undergo modification in consequence of experience," writes Cameron (4). The confrontation technique includes the presentation of a statement to the patient and the frequent repetition of a question: "What do you feel or think about what I told you?" As in the psychic driving detailed by Cameron, one must identify a major problem in selecting the key statement for driving. It should be a short statement and should not contain a multiplicity of topics.

3. Suppression of conflict and anxiety may be one response to the confrontation approach to the patient. Suppression to bring about an alteration in thoughts and action is based on the shifting of attention from one set of stimuli to another. Thoughts and acts, according to Dollard and Miller (7), act as verbal cues to produce motivation which, in turn, prompts further thoughts and actions. Motivation to suppress one set of stimuli may come from an urgent task or problem requiring solution. The confrontation statement may create the atmosphere for suppression by shifting the attention to new stimuli and away from those that are creating symptoms, anxiety, and discomfort. Problems which are seemingly insoluble produce a ruminative tendency and vicious cycle that may be temporarily altered by suppression through a shift of attention. The confrontation technique offers the patient the opportunity to shift his attention from involvement in a ruminative, vicious cycle associated with an ineffective functioning to one of a compliant constructively active person. A supportive type of psychotherapy is possible with the goal of therapy being alteration of symptoms and improved living in the family and community. This goal can be altered at any time to one of further exploration by pointing out that his response to "What do you think or feel about what I told you?" was one of uncritical compliance and that further exploration of the problem was another possible response. In psychotherapeutic work with patients, there is frequently a change in the patient's behavior or a decrease in symptoms and improvement in affect. The therapist not infrequently sees such change as improved reality-testing whereas in actuality it is uncritical compliance to what the patient feels the therapist wishes.

4. The confrontation statement may act as a precipitating agent. Kubie (31) has expressed the opinion that when we understand the fluctuating transitional processes by which we move from one state

of psychological organization to another giant strides will have been taken in understanding the dynamics of normal and pathological processes. Among the remarkable features of such transitional states he noted the speed with which they can occur and that they can be precipitated sometimes by a single word or gesture. In a simile he compares the seeding of a supersaturated solution to precipitate fully formed crystals with the key word or gesture dropped into an organized preconscious set to instantly precipitate a fully developed concept or role.

5. Encouragement is given to flexibility as against automatic responses. The tendency for repetitive nonadaptive type of behavior is to take on some of the characteristics of the performed structural automatisms of instinctual behavior. Lichtenstein (34) suggests that Brun sees lower animals as equipped by such structural automatisms, not only with a general disposition to behave in view of a certain goal and in a certain direction, but also with the realization of the behavior as so-called "instinctive action." Such equipment gives to lower animals a fixed identity that man lacks because of the absence of fixed behavior patterns. It might be hypothesized that the desire for such an identity is significant for such tendencies in human behavior as repetition compulsions to carry out behavior which is poorly adaptive. Mature attempts at active mastery are not present in the psychotic, in the neurotic, or in persons with character disorders to the extent that archaic patterns of reacting, rigid defenses, and inability to deal with upsurges of anxiety, fear, shame, and other affects prevent the use of effective adaptive patterns in meeting new situations.

Ability to learn, to classify new experiences according to past experiences, to discriminate and evaluate differences, and to use reasonable judgment in modifying behavior and characteristics is restricted in the mentally ill person by a repetitive tendency to react on the basis of past adaptations. The question, "What do you think or feel about what I told you?" forces the patient to evaluate and discriminate and to classify his experiences and, in a sense, it demands reasonable judgment and learning responses. It produces a push toward surrender of neurotic behavior or disarranged thinking and behavior for a flexible pattern of functioning or for establishment of an automatism that is less frustrating, uneconomical, and otherwise poorly adaptive.

6. The nature of the statement and the repetition creates a situation suitable for a conditioning and learning experience. The experimental work of Luria (36) with infants and animals demonstrates

the methods by which verbal regulation of behavior can be established and the significance of developmental processes for such regulation. Concepts of conditioning, perception, and the organization factor receive confirmation from Luria's work. Experiments on verbal regulation behavior, learning, and conditioning have many features which support the concept of the confrontation technique as a conditioning, learning experience. The confrontation technique acts to influence both the perceptual aspects and the organizational factors so as to decrease the disorganization. The nature of the confrontation, its repetition, and the repetition of "What do you think or feel about what I told you?" gains the attention of the patient and brings a shift of attention. This technique may, therefore, help fill the need for an approach that will bring about a correction of incorrect perceptions. There is a tendency for incorrect perceptions not to be corrected on the basis of new experiences because, as Imboden (27) points out, the anxiety associated with the new experiences, or a person's chronic state of anxiety, tends to create an avoidance reaction to any appropriate reevaluation of the incorrect perception. The repetitive confrontation virtually demands a correction of incorrect perceptions, at the same time offering a supportive relationship which decreases anxiety and feeds back to the capacity to correct perceptions. The importance of perception and perceptual errors is attested to by the frequency with which the patient does not perceive what he has been told. Several sites for perceptual error are apparent: (1) a defective perceptual apparatus, (2) an error in transmission of impulse, (3) at higher integrative levels, the assumptive set of the recipient may lead to failure to accept the stimulus in terms consonant with the object or the intent of the sender, and (4) the message may be accepted correctly, but the recipient may reinterpret its implications and direct them into secondary channels; there may be an improper expression or verbal reply.

7. The confrontation statement and the repetitive factor in the technique forms a wedge in breaking down the wall of rigidity formed to protect against the anxiety created by an abstract attitude. Conscious and volitional acts, generalization of concepts, and thinking in terms of principles require the highest degree of abstract thinking. Blocking of the capacity for such abstract thought may be seen in schizophrenic syndromes. Scher (43) discusses the problem of perception in the schizophrenic patient and the significance of intrusions from without to the schizophrenic patient. By altering the accessibility to intrusion, the patient maintains his defensive pattern.

The initial task of the therapist, as he sees it, is to establish contact with the patient through the regularity and reliability of his intrusion. In the confrontation technique, such regularity and reliability may be established in a very specific and meaningful manner for the patient.

8. Role-taking can be used to explain some of the therapeutic movement in the confrontation technique. The patient is continuously confronted with the necessity of evaluating his unquestioned adherence to certain thoughts or actions which prevent the exploring of the possible roles of others so that a solution to the problem might be found. The repetitive question, "What do you think or feel about what I told you?" requires an exploration of the role of the therapist. The patient is required in a sense to explore the transference and to discover, through what constitutes a corrective emotional experience, the parataxic distortions in the interpersonal relationship. Don Jackson (28), in describing the interactional dynamics of a family interview, focuses on the individual's perception of the self (how I see me), the perception of the other (how I see you), and the perception of the other in relation to the self (how I see you seeing me). The confrontation technique constantly enables one to explore these interactional dynamics of the therapy situation. One might express the perceptions in the following ways: "You are asking me to tell you what I think of how I behave, distort, magnify, or minimize what I tell you about myself." "You are assuming the role of a parent, teacher, guide, boss, and telling me in a way which isn't clear to me but seems to imply that I should stop behaving, stop distorting, and give up wrong attitudes." "You expect me to accept the role I feel you are assuming in our relationship, reject it, or evaluate it, since you constantly ask me the question, 'What do you think or feel about what I told you?' The problem of how I see you seeing me might be further expressed as, 'You seem to see me as capable of finding the explanations of why I have become a patient in the facts I have disclosed of my thinking, interpersonal relations, and my relationship to you.' "

9. Confrontation statements tend to encourage the expansion of the discriminatory, reflective, reality-testing and socially oriented thought processes, and behavioral tendencies of the individual. They also make the patient aware of the obligatory, insatiable, stereotyped nature of his thoughts and behavior, and the desirability of an effort at explanation. They lead to the uncovering of that which has been preconscious or unconscious. They create positive and negative reactions related to transference phenomena, a tendency to stimulate

working through of conflictual areas, and hasten the corrective emotional experience. Any emerging state of consciousness, according to Ach (1), is dependent upon associative, perseverative-reproductive tendencies, and determining tendency. "Determining tendencies (the task) arise from the specific content of the goal presentation and define the state of consciousness so that it accords with the meaning of the goal presentation." The confrontation statement may be said to bring a determining tendency (task) to the situation, to invite association (another task), and to create an awareness of the previous perseveration tendencies. The tasks set forth are essentially those of carrying out the request as in the statement, "Get busy and do your job properly" and simultaneously setting up another task, that of reflecting on the task given, "What do you think or feel about what I told you?" The confrontation technique, through encouraging an awareness of alternatives of choice of freedom and individuality, furthers the extension of abilities and a tendency toward healthful living and release from illness.

## APPLICATION OF CONFRONTATION PROBLEM-SOLVING TECHNIQUE

The confrontation technique has been found applicable to a variety of clinical situations:

1. It may be used in the course of psychoanalytically oriented psychotherapy. When in the course of treatment, a rather clearly defined area is in conflict with another, a confrontation statement may be utilized. A young male patient was seen because of the difficulty he had in maintaining a scholastic standing compatible with his superior intelligence. A definite study inhibition associated with feelings of hopelessness and incapacity to concentrate was readily uncovered. A pattern of using masturbation as a means of obtaining gratification was soon related to the problem of study inhibition. The conflict situation could be expressed as follows: "If I don't study, I will become frustrated and feel a sense of hopelessness. If I am unhappy and frustrated, then I can justify masturbation, which ordinarily is a bad thing but is justified if one is so unhappy and has few sources of pleasure." A confrontation statement, "I don't want you to masturbate under any circumstances. What do you think or feel about what I told you?" was used. This statement was used repeatedly when the problem of masturbation was brought up or when verbalizations were related to derivative material. The patient improved

considerably in many areas. He was able to complete his college work.

2. The confrontation statement may be used to bring about an alteration in a repetitive pattern of thought used as a basis for solving a problem for the patient but in a maladaptive manner. It may be used in this manner where the goal of therapy is limited by such factors as the age of the patient, the desire to avoid any uncovering of defenses other than those necessary for working with the surface conflict, or to interfere with a self-perpetuating vicious cycle pattern. A 65-year-old, well-groomed business man was seen after a period of several months of rumination over the "mistake" he had made in selling his business and retiring. Outbursts of "temper tantrum" reactions and a moderate degree of depression were present. Several visits were used for repetitive dealing with the "mistake he had made." During the first few interviews, the surface conflict was seen as being best expressed as follows: "The state of being retired is not a completely desirable one and is quite boring compared with my previous active life, and I would like to remain active. But, if I do, it means making decisions and purchases and getting back into responsibilities. This, however, isn't really what I want. If I indicate what a terrible mistake I have made and how it has affected me, then I will not be expected to make decisions and get back into harness again. I will have the attention and sympathy of my wife and children. This will then be a substitution for their previous confidence in me and their former acceptance of my position in the home."

The confrontation statement was intended to break the vicious cycle and create a clearer view of what was taking place. He was told, "You made the biggest mistake of your whole life when you sold your business. What do you think of what I told you?" In essence, he responded with the statement that he agreed with the therapist. However, there was a change in the clinical picture for the better after a few visits. New experiences again created a ruminative cycle. Further treatment resulted in rapid improvement.

3. The confrontation technique may be used to reinforce or help create a defense for a patient for whom limited goal therapy solves a previously unsolved special problem. A patient suffering from definitely diagnosed cancer of the bowels, being aware of the condition, developed a feeling of complete helplessness and mobilized strong dependent desires. He repeatedly indicated that he knew that the bowel surgery had been done for a carcinoma and that in a short

time he was bound to suffer from the ravages of cancer. The problem was seen as one in which the patient's needs were such as to obscure completely the fact that recovery was possible and that one could believe that recovery would take place. He was told, "I know some people who always believe that everything will turn out for the best. What do you think or feel about what I told you?" During the next few visits, the patient showed progressive decrease of his belief that recovery could not take place, until he finally indicated that he had nothing to lose by adopting an optimistic attitude toward his illness. He left the hospital in a markedly improved mental state. Of course, there was considerable doubt that the improvement would continue for very long without the continuous reinforcement of the magical expectations from a significant figure. Such confrontation results are related to the basic defenses of all human beings, that an omniscient and omnipotent being will look after them. There is a saying, an expression of a wish, "From your mouth into God's ear," which best describes the basis for the patient's improvement.

4. Altering the vicious cycle in a two-party relationship is possible where the circumstances are such that the conflict, which can be changed, is clearly understood. A hospitalized patient (an elderly woman) with considerable need to receive attention from the nursing and other personnel was constantly creating difficulties by making excessive demands that invariably provoked irritation at and denial of the patient's demands by personnel. She would then complain about their attitudes. She denied any desire to make excessive demands on others. The statement with which the patient was confronted when she complained of being mistreated by the nurses was: "I think I should have the nurse fired immediately. What do you think or feel about what I told you?" The patient responded by indicating, with considerable feeling, that she would not want that to happen. The following day the nurse in charge asked, "What did you do with Mrs. O.? She has not come to the nursing station more than once or twice in the last 24 hours, and she is so pleasant." The nurses' attitude toward the patient, in turn, became less hostile, and a much better climate for the further care of the patient was created.

5. The interruption of a phobic reaction causing constriction of the person's life activities by telling the patient that he should do what he is afraid to do was the first parameter in psychoanalytic therapy. Unless such active interference with the patient's defenses is attempted, a marked alteration in the style of life of the patient accepted by him and the family may take place and establish a

set pattern of behavior which cannot be readily altered. The confrontation technique may be used just to deal with the symptoms or as a technical device in the course of psychoanalytically oriented psychotherapy. Our patient described a considerable constriction of activity and indicated that anxiety was aroused whenever she went places, with some lessening of anxiety on being accompanied by someone. The history revealed a background of overprotection of the patient because of a supposed heart condition and problems of anxiety over the loss of a protecting person. The onset symptoms were precipitated by the death of the father who, at a banquet, died from coronary heart disease. She came to the office accompanied by her mother. After a positive relationship had been established, she was told, "I want you to come to the office alone. What do you think or feel about what I told you?" The subsequent visits were associated with considerable anxiety because the patient expected to be censured for her failure to comply. She developed a tendency to explore the possibilities of overcoming the constrictions of her activities with considerable insight into her dependency needs. Each failure to comply with the statement was associated with less anxiety and with an increasing awareness of the importance of overcoming the phobia for her own sake rather than out of a desire to please the therapist or because of her fear of his disapproval. In this particular case, uncovering psychotherapy was attempted with the goal of altering the patient's personality structure. In other cases, a more limited goal of symptom removal alone, with the hope that new gratifications and less stressful situations might lead to the resumption of a more effective social life, may be considered desirable.

6. Bringing about the resolution of an acute psychotic episode as the principal goal of therapy with intention to do further uncovering psychotherapy. Many years ago the patient had been seen in psychotherapy. After a period of relative stability, he acutely developed symptoms including hearing people talk about him at work. In addition, there was anxiety and tension sufficient to warrant the label of an impending panic reaction. The history of recent disturbing circumstances, as told by the patient, indicated that he had felt that at work he had not been treated as well as he should have been. He had decided to supplement his work by selling real estate on weekends and had engaged in fantasies of how when he became successful in his new venture he would "tell the boss off." The venture had been a failure. He had continued in his job, chagrined, but the failure to get a good Christmas bonus intensified his anger. He

had to justify his own hostility toward his employer by experiencing himself as the object of a hostile attack and by feeling that it had not been he who desired to attack and destroy. It was evident that the symptoms might bring about the loss of his job within a few days if they continued. It was the only job that he had held fairly successfully throughout his life. Advantage was taken of a strong positive transference. The statement made was, "I don't want you to pay any attention to the things you feel are going on at work. What do you think or feel about what I told you?" The patient, in essence, indicated that he was not imagining all that was taking place and that it would not be the easiest thing to do, but if that was my advice, he would heed it. During the rest of the visit, obvious alleviation of anxiety was noticed. In subsequent visits, he at first indicated again that he was not imagining what was taking place, but if it was best to ignore it, he would. After a few visits, he indicated that what had been happening at work seemed all cleared up. He felt that there was no further need for visits.

7. Altering symptoms which interfere with the adjustment of the patient to family and environment, with otherwise limited goals for therapy, is exemplified by the following. A patient, age 65, with a tremor of head and right upper extremity, as in Parkinsonism, following a purse-snatching incident, had a marked accentuation of her tremors and a fear of being alone, and she developed many other symptoms of a diverse nature about which she complained constantly. The examination created doubt as to the organicity of the tremor and revealed a long-standing pattern of dependency, limited participation in life, and a habit of utilization of complaints to influence her somewhat oversolicitous and overconcerned children. A "resignation syndrome"—"I'm sick, I'm helpless, I can't help it, you must take care of me"—was the evident core of the problems on the surface. It created guilt in the children, led to dependent care in a hospital, kept her from being concerned about being alone by bringing the family to her, and, in general, solved many conflicts for her. The confrontation statement was intended to illuminate the use of complaining as a way of life and its effectiveness for creating solutions to problems. "I want you to stop complaining. What do you think of what I told you?" was the statement made. Repetition of the statement and asking the patient what she thought about what was said brought about numerous changes. She complained less frequently to the nursing personnel, who in turn became less hostile. She complained less frequently to the family, who in turn showed evi-

dence of their better acceptance of her. Throughout a series of interviews, because of her increasing ability to control expression of hostility about what was being said, the patient became less fearful of the therapist as well as more introspective. At the end of three weeks, she replied with a smile that she should not complain so much. She returned to living in her own apartment and adjusted at a better social level than in previous years.

8. Treating a psychoneurotic depression. A married woman in her forties was admitted to the hospital because of an obvious depressed state with suicidal thoughts. A marked change had occurred for several months in which feelings of hopelessness and a sense of incompetence and inadequacy prevailed. The history of the past and recent onset suggested the following: She saw herself as the deprived, unfairly treated daughter in a household with an older brother whose success as a student and later as a physician easily maintained this feeling. Her own success was in being an orderly, neat, effective housewife and mother. Her husband disregarded her desire not to move from another city to Chicago to smaller quarters and in a situation which produced a state of disorder, insufficient room for developing order, and an absence of friendliness in the people she encountered. She reacted to this disregard with the feeling that her husband loved his business more than he did her, that no order could ever be made out of the disorder, that there was nothing in life worth living for. During the first few days in the hospital, no change took place. She was then told, "I want you to stop believing you have nothing in life worth living for. What do you think or feel about what I told you?" Recovery from the depression was immediate and associated with an exploration of all the reasons why life was worthwhile. She recognized that her feelings represented a response to a narcissistic hurt which was excessive and unwarranted. She made the choice of reacting on the basis of her assets rather than on the wound to her pride.

The confrontation statement can be used in any clinical situation. Free association is the basis for communication to the extent to which it can be encouraged or used. Minimal activity by the therapist is considered desirable whenever possible. The question: "What do you think or feel about what I told you?" is used repetitively. In patients treated intensively, interpretation of defenses, of "id" material, and the transference may be used. The introduction of new statements at very infrequent intervals may be tried when a new therapeutic focus is recognized. The statement that is selected and developed may be one which deals with either surface or core conflict. If the goals of therapy are very limited, the patient advanced in years, and symptom relief the immediate aim, the statement will be related to a surface conflict. For intensive uncovering psychotherapy, the statement may deal with a core conflict. In short, this technique offers the clinician an opportunity to treat without resorting to the questionable practice of selecting between "treatable" and "untreatable" patients. The therapist, by using this technique, increases his awareness of what can help his patients and how he fails as a therapist and decreases the inclination to ascribe failure to the patient's "untreatable state" or lack of motivation.

## REFERENCES

1. Ach, N. Concerning determining tendencies. In D. Rapaport (Ed.), *Organization and pathology of thought.* New York: Columbia University Press, 1951.
2. Ach, N. Determining tendencies; awareness. In D. Rapaport (Ed.), *Organization and pathology of thought.* New York: Columbia University Press, 1951.
3. Benedek, T. F. Toward the biology of the depressive constellation. *J. Amer. Psychoan. Assn.,* 1956, **4,** 389–427.
4. Cameron, E. Psychic driving. *Amer. J. Psychiat.,* 1956, **112,** 502.
5. Cohen, L. How to reverse chronic behavior. *Ment. Hosp.,* 1964, **15,** 39.
6. Comments by S. C. *Amer. J. Psychiat.,* 1962, **119,** 274.
7. Dollard J., & Miller, N. *Personality and psychotherapy.* New York: McGraw-Hill, 1950.
8. Ehrenwald, J. Doctrinal compliance in psychotherapy and problems of scientific methodology. In J. H. Masserman & J. L. Moreno (Eds.), *Progress in psychotherapy.* Vol. 3. New York: Grune and Stratton, 1958.
9. Ekman, P., Krasner, L., & Ullman, L. P. The interaction of set and awareness as determinants of response to verbal conditioning. *J. Abnormal Soc. Psychol.,* 1963, **65,** 387–389.
10. Fisher, C. Studies on the nature of suggestion. Part 1. *J. Amer. Psychoan. Assoc.,* 1953, **1,** 222–255.
11. Frank, J. D. *Persuasion and healing.* Baltimore: Johns Hopkins Press, 1961.
12. Frank, J. Relief of distress and attitudinal change. In J. H. Masserman (Ed.), *Science and psychoanalysis.* New York: Grune and Stratton, 1961. Pp. 107–124.
13. Freud, S. Further recommendations in the technique of psychoanalysis; recollection, repetition and working through. *Collected papers.* Vol. 2. London: Hogarth Press, 1946. Pp. 366–376.
14. Freud, S. Neurotic mechanisms in jealousy, paranoia and homosexual-

ity. *Collected papers.* Vol. 2. London: Hogarth Press, 1946. Pp. 232–243.

15. Freud, S. Recommendations for physicians in the psychoanalytic method of treatment. *Collected Papers.* Vol. 2. London: Hogarth Press, 1946. Pp. 323–333.

16. Freud, S. Turning in the ways of psychoanalytic therapy. *Collected papers.* Vol. 2. London: Hogarth Press, 1946. Pp. 392–402.

17. Freud, S. *Outline of psychoanalysis.* New York: W. W. Norton and Company, 1949.

18. Freud, S. Remarks upon the theory and practice of dream interpretation. *Collected papers.* Vol. 5. London: Hogarth Press, 1950. Pp. 136–149.

19. Gardner, G. E., & Sperry, B. Basic word ambivalences and learning disabilities in childhood and adolescence. *Amer. J. Psychother.,* 1964, **18,** 377.

20. Garner, H. H. A confrontation technique used in psychotherapy. *Amer. J. Psychother.,* 1959, **8,** 18–34.

21. Garner, H. H. A nascent somatic delusion treated psychotherapeutically by a confrontation technique. *J. Clin. Exp. Psychopath.,* 1959, **20,** 135–143.

22. Garner, H. H. A confrontation technique used in psychotherapy. *Compr. Psychiat.,* 1960, **1,** 201–211.

23. Garner, H. H. A confrontation technique used in psychotherapy. In J. Masserman, J. L. Moreno (Eds.), *Progress in psychotherapy.* Vol. 5. New York: Grune and Stratton, 1960.

24. Garner, H. H. Compliance and problem-solving therapy. *Compr. Psychiat.,* 1966, **7,** 21–30.

25. Gordon, R. E. Sociodynamics and psychotherapy. *Arch. Neur. Psychiat.,* 1959, **81,** 486–503.

26. Greenson, R. The working alliance and the transference neuroses. *Psychoanal. Quart.,* 1965, **34,** 155–181.

27. Imboden, J. B. Brunswick's theory of perception. *Arch. Neurol. Psychiat.,* 1966, **77,** 187–192.

28. Jackson, D., Riskin, J., & Satir, V. A method of a family interview. *Arch. Gen. Psychiat.,* 1961, **5,** 321–339.

29. Karno, M. Communication, reinforcement and "insight," the problem of psychotherapeutic effect. *Amer. J. Psychother.,* 1956, **19,** 467–479.

30. Krasner, L. The therapist as a social reinforcement machine. In H. H. Strupp & L. Luborsky (Eds.), *Research in psychotherapy.* Vol. 2. Washington, D. C.: American Psychological Association, 1962. Pp. 61–94.

31. Kubie, L. Distinction between normality and neuroses. *Psychoan. Quart.,* 1959, **23,** 167–203.

32. Langworthy, O. Only half aware; a review. *Amer. J. Psychiat.,* 1964, **121,** 116–122.

33. Lesse, S. Placebo reactions and spontaneous rhythms in psychotherapy. *Arch. Gen. Psychiat.,* 1964, **10,** 497–505.

34. Lichtenstein, H. Identity and sexuality: a study of their interrelationship in man. *J. Amer. Psychoan. Assn.,* 1961, **9,** 179–250.

35. Loewald, H. On the therapeutic actions of psychoanalysis. *Int. J. Psychoanal.*, 1960, **41**, 16–33.
36. Luria, A. R. Verbal regulation of behavior. In M. Brazier (Ed.), *The central nervous system and behavior*. New York: Macy Foundation, 1960.
37. Masserman, J. H. Faith and delusion in psychotherapy: the *UR* defenses of man. *Amer. J. Psychiat.*, 1953, **11**, 324–333.
38. Mowrer, O. H. Changes in verbal behavior during psychotherapy. In O. H. Mowrer (Ed.), *Psychotherapy theory and research*. New York: Ronald Press, 1953.
39. Mowrer, O. H. *Learning theory and behavior*. New York: John Wiley and Sons, 1960.
40. Piaget, J. *The moral judgment of the child*. New York: Free Press, 1965.
41. Rashkis, H. A general theory of treatment in psychiatry. *Arch. Neur. Psychiat.*, 1957, **78**, 491–499.
42. Ritter, W. The susceptibility of dreams recall to indirect suggestion patterned after verbal conditioning. *Amer. J. Psychother.*, 1965, **19**, 87–98.
43. Scher, J. Perception, equivalence, avoidance and intrusion in schizophrenia. *Arch. Neurol. Psychiat.*, 1957, **77**, 210–217.
44. Skinner, B. F. *Science and human behavior*. New York: Macmillan, 1953.
45. Sloane, R. B., Davidson, P. O., & Payne, R. W. Anxiety and arousal in psychoneurotic patients. *Arch. Gen. Psychiat.*, 1965, **13**, 19–23.
46. Strupp, H. H. *Psychotherapists in action*. New York: Grune and Stratton, 1960.
47. Sullivan, H. D. *The interpersonal theory of psychiatry*. New York: W. W. Norton and Company, 1953.
48. Tompkins, S. *The psychology of right and left*. Transaction Community Leadership Project. Washington University, St. Louis, Missouri (Nov.-Dec.) 1965.
49. Whitehorn, J. C. A working concept of maturity of personality. *Amer. J. Psychiat.*, 1962, **119**, 197–202.
50. Wolpe, J. Reciprocal inhibition as the main basis of psychotherapeutic effect. *Arch. Neur. Psychiat.*, 1954, **72**, 205–226.
51. Zubin, J. Criteria for evaluation of results in psychotherapy. *Amer. J. Psychother.*, 1964, **18**, 138–144 (Supp. 1.)

Chapter 13

# Transactional Analysis

## ERIC BERNE, CLAUDE M. STEINER, and
## JOHN M. DUSAY

Eric Berne: b. 1910, Montreal, Canada. d. 1970, San Francisco, California.
B.A., 1931 and M.D., 1935, McGill University.
Lecturer in psychiatry, University of California Medical School. Consultant
    in group therapy, McAuley Neuropsychiatric Clinic, San Francisco,
    California.
Chairman of the Board, International Transactional Analysis Association.
Books: *What Do You Say after You Say Hello? The Psychology of
    Human Destiny* (1972). *Sex in Human Living* (1970). *Happy Valley*
    (1968). *Principles of Group Treatment* (1966). *Games People Play* (1964).
    *Structure and Dynamics of Organizations and Groups* (1963). *Trans-
    actional Analysis in Psychotherapy (1961).*

Claude M. Steiner: b. 1935, Paris, France.
B.A., in psychology, 1957, M.A., in child development, 1960, University of
    California, Berkeley. Ph.D., in clinical psychology, University of
    Michigan, 1965.
Clinical Psychologist and Group Therapy Coordinator, Center for Special
    Problems, San Francisco, California, 1965–date. Director, Berkeley
    Transactional Analysis Institute, Berkeley, 1966–date. Consultant,
    Group Treatment, Napa State Hospital, California, 1966–date.
Vice Chairman, International Transactional Analysis Association, 1965–
    1966.

John M. Dusay: b. 1935, Topeka, Kansas.
B.A., chemistry, 1957, M.D., 1961, University of Kansas. Psychiatric resi-
    dency at San Francisco Medical School, University of California,
    completed 1965.
Senior Resident in Psychiatry, University of California Medical School, and
    private psychiatric practice, 1965–date.
Member, Board of Directors, San Francisco Transactional Analysis Associa-
    tion, 1965; President, 1966–date.

This paper is in three sections: a historical introduction (Berne), a
theoretical outline (Steiner), and a discussion of clinical application
(Dusay).

## THE DEVELOPMENT OF TRANSACTIONAL ANALYSIS

Psychoanalysis owes its birth to Mrs. Emmy von N., who "gave permission" to Freud to listen to her by frequent admonitions of "Keep quiet—don't talk." This was a license to Freud to disregard his teachers and their injunctions to impose his will on his patients. If he had been unable to avail himself of this license, psychoanalysis would not have come into being at that time, and perhaps never. Similarly, I had been trained for almost twenty years to listen to my teachers and not to my patients. The clinical question was always, "What would my teachers say about what the patient is saying?" rather than "What is the patient telling me?" The theory and practice of transactional analysis began to develop after I received permission (to use a transactional expression) to reverse this trend and listen to patients rather than to teachers. Thus, when a patient remarked: "I feel as though I had a little boy inside of me," I was supposed to interpret the "little boy" to mean an introjected penis, as in the similar case cited by Otto Fenichel. But instead of saying to myself, "What would Otto Fenichel think about this?" I asked the patient: "What do you think about it?" It was thus established that at times the patient really did feel like a little boy (for whatever reason), and this feeling was the most convincing and significant clinical fact in determining the course of his life. The next step was to ask him at appropriate times: "Which part of you said that, the little boy or the grown-up man?" This question marked the birth of transactional analysis.

Of the many influences that gave me permission to be grateful to my teachers but to listen to my patients, only the external ones will be mentioned. For someone who was accustomed to the exigencies of medical practice from early childhood, an analogy existed between the treatment of coughs and the treatment of neurotics. Psychoanalysis was like listening to the patient cough, year after year, learning more and more about various kinds of coughs and becoming very skillful in discussing them and diagnosing them. Formal psychoanalysis was like treating all kinds of coughs, even the common cold, by prolonged sanitarium care; psychoanalytic therapy was like treating tuberculosis by a weekly auscultation and an occasional mustard plaster, without looking for more specific remedies. Although with these approaches one might learn an enormous amount about the natural history of coughs, and become very expert at auscultation, neither of them seem profitable therapeutic measures in the rough and tumble of ordinary practice if there is to be any expectation of cure within a reasonable time. An added difficulty was that the most thorough treatment, psychoanalysis, the prolonged equivalent of "sanitarium cure," was by Freud's own statement, supported by the experience of others, not applicable to the most serious cases and could only be used for the milder ones. These paradoxes indicated a need for something better, not merely better "sanitariums" or better auscultation but better therapeutic methods.

The progress from the first question, "Which of the two is talking now," arose from further observations communicated by the patients and made by the therapist. It soon appeared that not all feeling and behavior patterns fitted into the two entities little boy and grownup, now called "ego states" in honor of Dr. Paul Federn. There must be a third. What was it, and where did it come from? It soon became apparent that this was a Parental ego state. This conclusion gave rise to a tripartite framework which could now contain every manifestation of every patient studied. This new framework was quite independent of Freud's tripartite system and stood on its own merits; on the other hand, it did not contradict anything in Freud, and in fact, the two systems reinforced each other while each maintained its own inner consistency. One was based on free association, the other, dealing with the same kind of patient population, was based on introspection and observation, both of which had gone out of style when psychoanalysis became predominant. This aspect of the theory, the diagnosis of ego states, constitutes structural analysis.

The next question that came into focus was: "If each of these two people talking is three different people, who is talking to whom?" This question emerged very cogently one day in a therapy group, which is its natural matrix, and led to the evolution of the analysis of individual transactions: e.g., "His grownup (or Adult, as it was now called) is talking to her grownup, but it is her little girl (or Child) who is answering. Aha! Where does this lead us?"

The next step was the observation one day that a conversation in the group (or what was now called a series of transactions) seemed familiar. This *déja vu* quality was not due to the content, which was new, but to the way the conversation went, to the operations which the speakers were performing on one another, the way they were "manipulating" each other, to use the vulgar term. It thus appeared that there was a class of conversations which was independent of the overt content and depended on the transactions: a kind of algebraic classification, in which the specific $x$'s and $y$'s under discussion were irrelevant, but the functional relationships between the parties were the same. Further study of such phenomena resulted in the concept of games.

The question after that was, "Why did people want to go through such stereotyped sets of transactions, and what did they add up to in the long run?" To answer this question required a longitudinal view of the patient's whole life, with the gratifying result that it became possible to extrapolate and predict what the patient was going to do with his life in the future. This gave rise to the study of scripts. All this process took about four years from 1954 to 1958.

By 1958, so many other people had become interested in learning the new approach that more formal meetings became necessary. Hence the formation of the San Francisco Social Psychiatry Seminars, which met weekly. As people from other cities, states, and countries soon began to use the method, further organization was necessary, and the International Transactional Analysis Association was established about ten years from the time the crucial question was asked of the first patient.

There was also another kind of interest. Because all clinicians deal with the same kinds of psychopathology, many of the things that transactional analysts say have been said in somewhat similar fashion in other contexts. Thus a volume of mail and personal communications appeared which stated that transactional analysis was not new; it was only revised Adler, Jung, Freud, Krishnamurti, Rudolph Steiner, Horney, Grinker, Rank, Heidegger, Fairbairn, and so on. Thus, a criterion was necessary to distinguish transactional analysis from other approaches. This criterion may be succinctly stated as follows: transactional analysis is based on the personality theory of ego states; everything follows from that premise and cannot be clearly understood without that. Therefore whatever explains human behavior on the basis of Child, Parent, and Adult ego states is transactional analysis. Whatever does not explain human behavior in terms of these ego states is not transactional analysis, even though many statements from other fields may sound similar to true transactional statements. Thus, similar conclusions may be arrived at starting from a different theoretical standpoint and traveling a different route. But only those conclusions which are derived from the existence of three ego states constitute transactional analysis, and it is this starting point which is new. Even a "flirtation" with ego states, such as has been carried on by R. Ekstein and R. Fairbairn, is not enough. As Freud remarked, it is one thing to flirt with an idea and another to be married to it.

The International Transactional Analysis Association now has about 600 members scattered across 30 states and four countries, which is evidence of an awakening interest in the therapeutic use of the theory of ego states, transactions, games, and scripts, particularly in group treatment.

## THE TRANSACTIONAL THEORY OF PERSONALITY

As a theory of personality, Eric Berne's transactional analysis can be seen to be a branch, rather close to the roots, on the tree of psychoanalytic personality theory. Thus, transactional analysis is essentially sympathetic to psychoanalytic concepts of personality. As a theory and method of treatment, however, it differs from psychoanalytic theory in a number of significant ways which will be elaborated in the section on treatment.[1]

The building blocks of the theory of transactional analysis (TA) are three observable modalities of ego function, the Parent, the Adult, and the Child. Because of the apparent similarity between these and the three basic psychoanalytic concepts, the ego, the superego, and the id, the difference and relationship between them will be outlined forthwith.

Transactional analysis can be called an ego psychology, but it must be remembered that ego psychology is a name reserved, perhaps rightfully, for that body of theory developed by Hartmann, Kris, Loewenstein, and Rapaport, all of whom are dedicated to psychoanalytic concepts but desire to modify what they consider to be an excessively narrow view of the ego. According to these writers, Freud's description of the ego does not do justice to the much broader spectrum of functions which they see the ego performing. Ego psychology, an extension of Freud's theories, deals largely with considerations of psychic energy available to the ego and has not produced, as Ford and Urban (9), point out, any notable innovations in treatment. Thus, if TA is to be called an ego psychology, it must be remembered that TA departs from orthodox psychoanalytic theory not so much on the issue of psychic energies but on the issue of the scientific and practical value of observable ego variables rather than dynamic hypothetical constructs. In addition, it might be pointed out

---

[1] The material presented in this section is based on Berne's books (1–4), writings in the *Transactional Analysis Bulletin,* and discussions at scientific meetings of the San Francisco Transactional Analysis Seminars.

that while the ego psychologists divide the ego in terms of functions (synthetic, adaptive, defensive, perceptual, etc.), TA divides the ego into three modalities, every one of which incorporates the several ego functions.

## Structural Analysis

A person operates in one of three distinct ego states at any one time. These ego states are distinguishable by the observer on the basis of skeletal-muscular variables and the content of verbal utterances. Thus, certain gestures, postures, mannerisms, facial expressions, and intonations, as well as certain words, are typically associated with one of the three ego states. When the observer is examining his own behavior, he has, in addition, kinesthetic, perceptual, cognitive, and affective information that is part of the ego state being observed.

The Child. *The Child ego state is essentially preserved in its entirety from childhood.* Thus, for example, in this ego state the person behaves as he did when he was three years old. Current thinking holds that the Child is never more than about eight years old and can be as young as one hour old. Not only does the person sit, stand, walk, and speak as he did as a three-year-old, but he perceives, thinks, and feels as the three-year old did. Perception is syncretic (14), and thinking is at a prelogical or preoperational level of development (11). In psychoanalytic terms mental activity is dominated by the primary process, in which tension is discharged through wish fulfillment.

Response to stimulation is direct rather than mediated, and the person is stimulus-bound rather than able to delay response. Internal (proprioceptive and kinesthetic) stimulation is not distinguished from external, sensory stimulation, and the person responds to the primary aspects of stimuli—color (amplitude), intensity, and movement—rather than the "meaningful" aspects of them. In short, it can be said that all which is known about the psychology of children (motivation, perception, and thinking) applies to the person when he is in the Child ego state (12).

The Child is visible in a fixated form in schizophrenics and in certain kinds of superfeminine women or supermasculine men; it appears consistently and for varying periods of time in normal, well-functioning persons, and of course is the habitual ego state in three-year-old children. Colloquially, lest the value of the Child be misunderstood, it is said that "it is the best part of the person" and "the only part that can really enjoy itself."

The Adult. *The Adult ego state is essentially a computer,* an impassionate organ of the personality, the function of which is to gather and process data for the purpose of making predictions. Thus, the Adult gathers data about the world through the senses, processing them according to a logical program and making predictions when necessary. In its perceptual function it is diagrammatic; while the Child perceives in color, in space, and from one point of view at a time, the Adult perceives in black and white, usually on two dimensions, and from several points of view at the same time. The most detailed description of the operation of the Adult is the one by Piaget in *Logic and Psychology* (11) under the rubric of "formal operations." When in the Adult ego state, the person is isolated from his own affective and other internal processes, a condition that is indispensable for the proper observation and prediction of reality. Thus, in the Adult ego state the person "has no feelings," even though he may be capable of appraising his Child or Parent feelings. Often a rational Parent ego state is confused with the Adult ego state, the latter being not only rational but also without emotion.

In this context it should be noted that the Adult grows, according to Piaget, through a series of developmental steps stretching out through childhood. This development proceeds over time as a consequence of the interaction between the person and the external world. The Parent, on the other hand, is not a result of actual development but of a nondevelopmental process of direct acquisition rather than gradual change.

The Parent. *The Parent is essentially made up of behavior that is copied from parents or authority figures.* It has, therefore, the quality of being taken whole, as perceived, without modification. A person in the Parent ego state will behave as his parent or whoever was or is "*in loco parentis.*"

Thus, the Parent ego state is essentially nonperceptive or cognitive, being simply a parameter or arbitrary but constant basis for decisions and feelings. It is the repository of traditions and values and therefore vital to the survival of civilization. It operates validly when adequate information for Adult decision is not available, but in the case of certain pathologies it operates in spite of adequate Adult information.

Structural analysis, then, is organized around these fundamental concepts, the ego states. Some further concepts in structural analysis will be advanced. Ego states are seen to operate one at a time, that is, the person will always be in one and only one of the three ego states. This ego state is called the executive, or will be said to have executive power. It is possible, however, that while one ego state has the executive power, the person is aware of literally standing beside himself, observing his own behavior. This feeling, that the self is not the ego state in the executive, is usually associated with a situation in which the Child or Parent has the executive power, while the "real self," perhaps the Adult, observes without essentially being able to behave. Thus, while only one ego state is cathected—that is imbued with the psychic energy necessary to activate muscular complexes involved in behavior—it is possible for another ego state to be cathected sufficiently to become conscious to the person even though it is not able to activate the musculature.

A clinical observation that might be seen to militate against the postulate that ego states occur one at a time is the situation where two sets of muscles seem to be powered by two separate ego states. For instance, a lecturer's voice and facial muscles might seem to indicate an Adult ego state whereas an impatient toss of the hand might reveal a Parent ego state. In cases such as this it is likely that the behavior is Parent in Adult disguise and therefore Parent or that Parent and Adult are alternating rapidly.

The possibility for alternation between ego states is a function of the permeability of the ego state boundaries. This permeability is an important variable in psychopathology. Low permeability leads to exclusion of appropriate ego states. Exclusions of the Parent, Adult, and Child ego states are all pathological since they preclude the use of ego states that, in a given situation, may be more adaptive than the excluding ego state. For example, at a party the excluding Adult is less adaptive than the Child, whereas a father who has an excluding Adult is preventing the more adaptive Parent from properly raising his children.

On the other hand, extreme permeability represents another form of pathology often manifested in an incapacity to remain in the Adult ego state for a sufficiently enduring period of time.

The above discussion is based on the assumption that every ego state, being a substructure of the ego, is, in its own way, an adaptive organ. The manner in which the ego as a whole functions adaptively has been elucidated by Hartmann (10); all three ego states share in this adaptive function, each ego state being especially suited for certain specific situations. It might be said that the Parent is ideally suited where control is necessary: control of children, of unknown situations, of fears, of unwanted expression, and of the Child. The Adult is suited to situations in which accurate prediction is necessary. The Child is ideally suited where creation is desired: creation of new ideas, procreation, creation of experiences, and so on.

One more concept is of first-hand importance: contamination. This phenomenon is characterized by an Adult ego state holding as fact certain ideas stemming from the Parent or the Child. An idea, such as "excessive masturbation leads to insanity," could presumably be part of a person's Adult ego state. Decontamination of the Adult is an early therapeutic requirement in treatment and is accomplished through an accurately timed confrontation by the therapist's Adult with the inaccuracy of the ideas that are causing the contamination.

To recapitulate, every person has three ego states which manifest themselves in sequence and which adapt to three different kinds of situations. These ego states have boundaries which can, in the case of pathological states, prevent the shift of ego states or the enduring application of them. The Adult is capable of developing contaminations from the Parent or Child.

Thus, TA is a theory committed to verifiable and observable variables. This commitment implies that variables are seen as observable and verifiable by patients as well as therapists or theorists. The wish to include the patient in the understanding, observation, and verification of behavior theories generates the extensive use of colloquialisms, the preference for group treatment over individual treatment, and the insistence that most relevant variables in treatment are conscious and therefore available to the patient himself by the simple application of attention to certain areas of his behavior. Because of these preferences, TA falls clearly within the area of direct therapy which constitutes the scope of these volumes.

### Transactional Analysis

Just as the ego state is the unit of structural analysis, so the transaction is the unit of transactional analysis. The theory holds that the behavior of one person is best understood if it is examined in terms of ego states and that the behavior between two or more persons is best understood if examined in terms of transactions. A transaction consists of a transactional stimulus and a transactional response, and stimulus and response occur always between specific ego states. In a simple transaction, there are only two ego states. One example might be between two Adult ego states, "How much is 5 times 7?" "Thirty-five"; all other combinations of ego states may occur in a transaction. Transactions will follow one another smoothly as long as the stimulus and response are parallel or complementary.

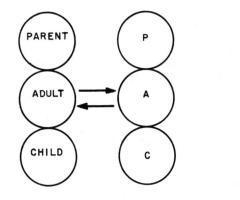

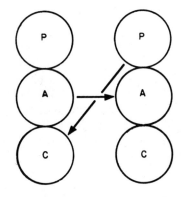

(A) Complementary Transaction          (B) Crossed Transaction

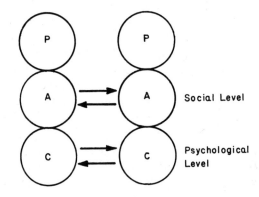

Social Level

Psychological Level

(C) Complex Ulterior Transaction

Figure 1. Three types of transactions.

In any given series of transactions, communication will proceed if the response to a previous stimulus is addressed to the ego state that was the source of the stimulus and is emitted from the ego state to which that source addressed itself. Any other form of response will create a crossed transaction and will interrupt communication. In Figure 1, transaction A is complementary and will lead to further communication whereas transaction B is crossed and will break off communication. Crossed transactions are of interest not only because they account for the interruption of communication but also because they are usually part of the transactions in games.

In addition to simple transactions, a very important form of transaction is the complex, ulterior transaction. This form of transaction has two levels: social and psychological. Each level involves two ego states. In Figure 1, transaction C is between A and A, "Come to my apartment and look at my blueprints," and between C and C, "Ever since I was a little girl I have loved blueprints." Usually, in the case of an ulterior transaction, the social level is a cover for the real (psychological) meaning of the transaction; thus, interpersonal behavior is not understandable until the ulterior level and ego states involved are understood.

*Games*

A game is a carefully defined event. To satisfy the definition of a game, a behavioral sequence has to: (1) consist of an orderly series of transactions with a beginning and an end; (2) contain an ulterior motive, that is, contain a psychological level different from the social level; and (3) result in a payoff for both players.

The payoff of games constitutes an important part of TA theory and can be seen as the motivational aspect of it. To use an analogy, structural analysis describes the relevant parts of the personality just as a parts list describes the parts of an engine. Transactional analysis describes the way in which the parts interact in the same manner in which a cutaway display engine operates and exemplifies the manner in which the engine parts relate to each other. But to understand *why* people transact with each other, some sort of motor power has to be postulated, and this explanation is found in the motivational concepts of stimulus hunger, structure hunger, and position hunger. Games derive satisfaction for all three of these hungers, and this satisfaction is referred to as the advantage or payoff of the game.

1. The satisfaction of stimulus hunger is the biological advantage of the game. There is considerable research in the literature indicating that stimulation is one of the primary needs of higher organisms. On the basis of these findings and clinical evidence, Berne (1) has evolved the concepts of stimulus hunger and stroking. Stimulus hunger is satisfied by stroking or recognition. Stroking is a more basic need than recognition, and it is said that a person needs stroking "lest his spinal cord shrivel up." Actual physical stroking can be replaced with symbolic stroking or recognition. Thus, the average adult is able to satisfy his hunger for stroking through, among other things, a ritual

that is essentially an exchange of recognition strokes. For example, the following is a six stroke ritual:

A: Hi.
B: Hi.
A: How are you?
B: Fine, and you?
A: Fine. Well, see you.
B: Yeah, see you around.

A game is transactionally more complex than the previous ritual but is basically still an exchange of strokes. It might be noted in passing that "Go to hell!" is as much a stroke as "Hi," and people will settle for the former form of stroking when they cannot obtain the latter.

2. The satisfaction of structure hunger is the social advantage of the game. Structure hunger is satisfied by the establishment of a social matrix within which the person can transact with others. Thus, to satisfy structure hunger, the individual seeks social situations within which time is structured and organized for the purpose of obtaining strokes. This need for structure can be seen as an elaboration of stimulus hunger and therefore as a more complex form of the basic need for stimulation. By virtue of being played, a game provides a series of ways in which time can be structured. For instance, a game of "If it Weren't for You" (IWFY), provides for considerable time structure with its endless face-to-face recriminations. It provides for additional time structure in that it makes possible the pastime of "If it Weren't for Him (Her)" played with neighbors and relatives and possibly "If it Weren't for Them" played at bars and bridge clubs.

3. The satisfaction of position hunger is the existential advantage of the game. Position hunger is satisfied by an internal transaction, within the player, in which a basic, lifelong, existential position is vindicated. This existential position, colloquially known as the patient's "racket," can be illustrated with a sentence, such as "I am no good," "They are no good," or "Nobody is any good." The internal transaction takes place between the player and another person, usually a parent, and it is a form of stroking or recognition in which the stroke is given internally.

Thus, after a game of RAPO[2], the players go home and White may say to herself, "That proves men are beasts; are you happy, Mom?" and her Parent will answer, "That's my good little girl." This trans-

---

[2] See RAPO, page 383.

action has stroking value, and at the same time it reinforces the existential position of the player. As will be elaborated later, every game has the added effect of advancing the script, or life plan of the person.

At the same time that a game provides strokes for the player, it also provides protection from intimacy. Intimacy, which is a social situation free of rituals, pastimes, and games, can also be seen as a situation in which strokes are given directly and therefore most powerfully. Intimacy, therefore, can be a threat to the person, essentially a threat of excessively intense stroking. Thus, a game is a carefully balanced procedure, the purpose of which is to obtain an optimal amount of stroking.

It should be noted, in addition, that strokes can be obtained without resorting to games which are basically subterfuges and that games are learned in childhood from parents as a preferred method of obtaining stimulation. Thus, a person giving up a game has to develop an alternate way of obtaining strokes and structuring time, and, until he does, he will be subject to despair, a condition parallel to marasmus in deprived children.

Two games will be described in detail. The first, a "soft" game called "Why Don't You Yes But" and the second, a "hard" version (second degree)[3] of RAPO.

*Why Don't You Yes But.* This is a common "soft" game played wherever people gather in groups, and it might proceed as follows. Black and White are mothers of grade school children.

> White: I sure would like to come to the PTA meeting, but I can't get a baby sitter. What should I do?
>
> Black: Why don't you call Mary? She'd be glad to sit for you.
>
> White: She is a darling girl, but she is too young.
>
> Black: Why don't you call the baby-sitting service? They have experienced ladies.
>
> White: Yes, but some of those old ladies look like they might be too strict.
>
> Black: Why don't you bring the kids along to the meeting?
>
> White: Yes, but I would be embarrassed to be the only one to come with her children.

---

[3] The softness or hardness of a game refers to the intensity with which it is played and the morbidity of its effects. First degree is the soft version, and third degree is the hard version of a game.

Finally, after several such transactions, there is silence followed possibly by a statement by Green, such as, "It's sure hard to get around when you have kids."

The above game, (YDYB), which incidentally was the first game to be analyzed by Berne, fulfills the three parts of the definition as follows. First, it is a series of transactions beginning with a question and ending with a silence. Second, at the social level it is a series of Adult questions and Adult answers; at the psychological level it involves a series of questions by a demanding, reluctant Child unable to solve a problem and a series of answers by increasingly irritated Parents anxious to help in a quandary.

The payoff of the game is as follows: It is a rich source of strokes; it provides a readily usable form of time structure wherever people congregate; and finally, it reinforces an existential position. The position, in this case, is exemplified by Green's statement, "It's sure hard to get around when you have kids." In the case of White, the game successfully proves that parents are no good and always want to dominate you, while at the same time it proves that children are no good and prevent you from doing things. In the case of Black, the game successfully proves that children are ungrateful and unwilling to cooperate. In the case of both Black and White, the existential advantage fits into their script. Both White and Black can come away from the game feeling angry or depressed according to what their favorite "feeling racket" is. After a long enough succession of such similar games, both White and Black may feel justified in getting a divorce, attempting suicide, or quitting.

*RAPO.* This game is played by a more specialized type of personality; that is to say, while YDYB can be played by almost anyone, RAPO's psychological content is such that it only attracts certain persons. It is a sexual game so it requires a man and a woman, although it may be played between homosexuals as well. It might proceed as follows.

At a party, after considerable flirtation White finds herself alone with Black reading aloud from the Decameron. Aroused by the inviting situation, Black makes an advance and attempts to kiss White. Indignant, White slaps Black's face and leaves in a huff.

Again we have a series of transactions, beginning with a sexual invitation and ending with a sexual rebuff. On the social level the game looks like a straightforward flirtation ended due to a breach in etiquette by Black, rightfully rebuffed by White. On the psychological level, between Child and Child, White has first enticed and then humiliated Black.

The payoff, again, consists of strokes, a way to structure time, and existentially, a ratification of the position holding that "Men (women) are no good" followed by feelings of anger or depression as the case may be, according to preference. Again the script is advanced since enough episodes of this game may justify a murder, rape, suicide, or depression for the players.

*Script Analysis*

When games are seen as parts of an on-going life course rather than isolated events, their existential meaning comes into relief. As previously mentioned, every game has an existential advantage. This advantage is the promotion of the script.

The script is a manifestation of the Child. The Child is the motor of the personality, not only in the biological sense, but also in a mental sense because ideas lodged in the Child have a pervasive influence upon the life course of the individual. Ideas in the Child will find expression and are not subject to correction by observation of their results.

The script is essentially a life course, decided upon by the person early in life, and therefore lodged in the Child. The decision is seen by the youngster who is making it as a valid solution or adaptation to the pressures under which he exists. The script is a product of the synthetic function of the ego, the Adult in the youngster (the professor)[4], who with all of the information at his disposal at the time decides that a certain position and life course are a reasonable resolution of his problems.

These pressures can be diagrammed in a script matrix. (See Figure 2.) It will be noted that the influences on the youngster are seen to be limited to influences by the parents. This essentially implies that culture has no effect on an individual other than as transmitted specifically by one of the parents or parent surrogates.

The most important influence or pressure impinging on the youngster originates from the parental Child. That is, the Child ego states in the parents of the person are seen as the determining factor in the formation of scripts. Present theory holds that in post-Oedipal scripts the contrasexual parent's Child is crucial or "calls the shots,"

---

[4] The professor is the colloquialism for the precocious Adult ego state in young children.

whereas in the pre-Oedipal scripts the crucial parent is the mother, no matter what the sex of the offspring (13).

As previously pointed out, games produce as part of their gains the existential payoff. With every repetition of a game, the script is advanced, because every game's last dramatic move is an acquiescence to the person's parental Child ($C_M$ or $C_F$), colloquially called the "witch mother" or "ogre." Acquiescence to $C_M$ or $C_F$, as discussed previously, results in stroking and recognition.

In the example of an alcoholic, the game begins with a sober individual whose predominant ego state is Parent and who ruthlessly

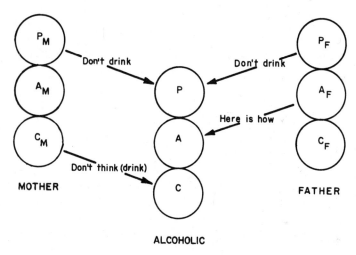

ALCOHOLIC

Figure 2. Script matrix. P, Parent; A, Adult; C, Child; M, Mother; F, Father.

restricts and castigates his Child. The end of the game or payoff takes place when the person is in a self-damaged Child ego state, essentially having done his parent's Child ($C_M$ or $C_F$) bidding. Figure 2 illustrates the alcoholic script. For this particular male alcoholic, the parent calling the shots is mother, and it is mother's Child (the witch mother) who says, "Don't think," "I will protect you when you are damaging yourself" (5). This statement, usually made nonverbally, may seem improbable at first blush. But it becomes more plausible when one considers that it originates from a three-year-old girl who enjoys caring for and forgiving people and who resents self-sufficiency (seen as rejection). This patient happens to have an alcoholic father who throughout shows him how being an alcoholic is a good adaptation to mother's Child's injunction. The patient decides that to obtain mother's protection and to avoid her Child's harassment, he must become self-destructive. As he does this, he observes that mother protects him; when he does not, he is subjected to subtle pressures to return to the self-destructive behavior. He might start playing such minor self-destructive games as delinquency, etc., but eventually he hits on alcohol and finds that it does exactly what his mother's Child wants him to do, namely not thinking, and damaging himself.[5] At this point he decides that he will become an alcoholic. This decision, made by the Adult in the young person, will seem reasonable and cogent and will continue to be seen as reasonable unless the script is changed. It should be noted that while, essentially, $C_M$ is saying, "Drink," $P_M$ and $P_F$, as well as the patient's Parent are saying, "Don't drink." The influence of the Parent is felt periodically during sober periods, but the witch mother ($C_M$) always wins out in the end.

The implications of this theory for the understanding of psychopathology are far-reaching. Diagnosis of psychopathology is far more meaningful in terms of TA, in which behavior is observed and pathology is described in terms of what the patient does, than in terms of psychoanalytic dynamics. "He is drinking himself to death" is a script diagnosis, in contrast to its psychoanalytic counterpart, "He is a passive, aggressive character with strong oral features." The script diagnosis implies (1) that the patient is carrying out an early life decision that is an adaptation to the pressures of the parental environment, specifically of the wishes of a parental child; (2) that the pathology is lodged in the Child ego state; and (3) that the elements of a cure are contained essentially in the psychology of persuasion of children.

## CLINICAL APPLICATIONS
## OF TRANSACTIONAL ANALYSIS

The goal of transactional analysis is to cure as many patients during the first treatment session as is possible. This means that the aim is 100% success and any failure to achieve this percentage is viewed as a challenge. "Cure" is not an ambiguous and vague term around which the patient and the therapist play mutually attractive games

---

[5] It is because of this that the hangover is seen to be the payoff of the alcoholic game.

but is clearly defined early in the course of treatment. The means of establishing criteria of "Cure" is by defining a clear, concise contract between the patient and therapist. The patient is asked a question, worded differently by different therapists, determining "How will you know and how will I know when you have achieved what you are consulting me for?" This is a variation of "What do you want?" which is avoided in some forms of psychotherapy. At times a clear Adult–Adult contract between the therapist and patient can be readily established. For example, "I will be able to make $100 a week in take-home pay" or "I will no longer be impotent with my wife," etc. When such a contract is established, treatment can proceed rapidly. Frequently other ego states will get involved in the formation of the contract; particularly noticeable is the Child of the patient and the Parent of the therapist. For example, "Doctor, I'm suffering, do something for me." "Of course, my dear, just relax and everything will be all right." Under some circumstances, the therapist may choose to enter into a Parent–Child type of contract. For example, when a very confused, disoriented, frightened, and contaminated Child ego state of a patient causes this individual to be hospitalized against his will, the therapist may, for some period of time, provide a protective and judicial position with which he will treat the patient. However, when the therapist is doing this in full awareness, he will soon be able to establish a more suitable contract with the patient, if it is indicated.

One distinct advantage of forming a clear, concise contract is that both the patient and the therapist, as well as other group members, will know when the patient is getting what he came to treatment for (6). The contract is not determined just by the patient but also by the therapist. If the goal in treatment is not acceptable to the therapist, he will not enter into a contract with the patient. The therapist himself, in forming a contract, will need to know what his Adult will be doing in the group, what his Parent will be doing, and what his Child will be doing. The training of therapists for transactional analysis has been discussed extensively in the book, *Principles of Group Treatment* (4). As frequently happens, group treatment is carried out in institutional settings. Therefore, another consideration is the goal of the institution. The therapist entering into some type of contract with the patient will clearly have in mind his contract with the institution in which he finds himself practicing. To facilitate this, the therapist outlines prior to the onset of group treatment a clear authority diagram including all of his supervisors and administrators, himself, and the patients. Without this diagram a conflict may arise; i.e., when a supervisor who holds some theoretical position that patients can be cured only after months and months of depth unconscious exploration is reluctant to allow a patient who has not "worked through his inner conflicts" to pass from the institution. A patient who has had considerable experience with the game "Let's you and him fight" may delightfully exploit the confused situation that results when the therapist does not have a clear-cut authority diagram in mind. Those persons familiar with institutional and hospital practices probably recall many instances in which the patient sat gleefully on the sidelines as the doctor and nurse had a nonproductive argument about his management. Games played between administrative supervisors, co-therapists, and other persons involved in a patient's treatment may affect the outcome of the patient's treatment. In the preceeding illustration, the patient may decide, "Why should I do anything around the hospital, I can go home and watch my mother and father fight."

Historically, transactional analysis evolved as a group treatment, and there are many advantages in this respect. There is a much larger variety of response to any individual patient in the group. When a patient and therapist are sitting together in a room, there is the Parent, the Adult, and the Child of the patient, and the Parent, the Adult, and the Child of the therapist. In this setting, actually six different people are in the room, and transactions will proceed from one ego state in one person to another ego state in the other person. A group of eight, then, has twenty-four primary ego states available to any one particular person in the group, and an increasingly large number of transactions are possible. (Refer to Figure 2.) A patient entering a group will stimulate other members in the group by one of his characteristic ego states and will in turn respond and be stimulated by others, whether he says anything or not. He can perhaps find a feeding mother, a punitive father, a gleeful child, and a logical adult, and because of the individual's characteristic background, he will be able to enter into transactions with the particular ego state of another individual in the group which appeals to him at that particular time. The therapist, by observing this carefully or by entering into the transactions, will soon be able to evaluate one person's characteristic ways of transacting with another person.

It has been found advantageous to select patients for group treatment at random without respect to age, sex, diagnosis, etc. This method is used because certain people with similarities in their background tend to pass the time with familiar topics that prevent more useful interaction. For example, a geriatric group may characteristically pass the time by saying "Ain't it awful that juvenile delinquency is on the rise, etc., etc." A group of juvenile delinquents, on the other hand, may pass time in saying things like "Ain't it awful, our parents are, etc., etc." There are also mutually compatible games that certain select groups tend to play. For example, a group of prisoners may play "How do you get out of here" and "Let's pull a fast one on Joey." A random selection saves a great deal of time and energy on the therapist's part in breaking up mutually compatible pastimes and games, and, where it is impossible to avoid this occurrence, such as in a penal institution, it becomes a subject for special consideration(8). Group attendance at a voluntary group can be used by the therapist as a gauge of the effectiveness of group treatment. When his attendance falls below approximately 70%, probably something is wrong with the treatment, and this is called an "ailing" group. On the other hand, with attendance at 100%, the therapist must realize that this percentage is beyond the bounds of normal group attendance at voluntary functions. Perhaps the therapist at this point needs to check his Parent aspects. When it is noted that there is an "ailing" group, the therapist needs to review the contract with the patient, the contract with the institution if he is practicing in an institutional setting, the authority diagram, and then question what his own Parent, his own Adult, and his own Child is doing in the group. Usually an "ailing" group means that an undiagnosed game is being played. Contract review with special attention to "Why aren't you getting what you want" promotes Adult–Adult assessment of expectations and limitations of the patient, therapist, and the institution. The authority diagram review will pinpoint the individuals between or among whom the game is being played, and ego-state review will further clarify what attitudes, beliefs, and feelings are involved. The transactional analyst does not spare examination of his own ego-state involvement and most prefer to use chalk and blackboard to insure direct examination. The therapist draws his own Parent, Adult, and Child ego state, including the actual transactions as diagrammed in Figure 1. In this position, the therapist is not passive or anonymous and the "ailing" group knows why it is ailing.

Procedures in transactional analysis are direct and active on the part of the therapist. As has been outlined previously, the very structure of the group implies that the therapist take an active role in determining how he is going to be in the group, in contradistinction to just getting a group of people together and seeing what happens. Different therapists have reported different sequences in undertaking group treatment. However, the usual course is to begin with a structural analysis. In this respect, each individual patient in the group, by confrontation or interpretation by the therapist or other group members, becomes aware of when he is thinking, feeling, and behaving as a Parent; when he is thinking feeling, and behaving as Adult; and when he is thinking, feeling, and behaving as a Child. The diagnosis of different ego states can be made from the behavior of the individual, his attitudes, and his gestures, etc. For example, when the therapist is confronted with the upright finger of the lecturing Parent in the group, he points it out immediately and does not let it be lost to posterity, unless he has decided there is some contraindication to confrontation at that point. The voice of the patient is also important. It is well known that an individual has two or three different voices that he uses in different circumstances, and awareness of this fact is readily made available to the patient. Vocabulary content, likewise, is indicative of the ego state that is predominant. For example, such words as "should, ought, must," etc., would be indicative of the Parent state. Adult ego-state content is characterized by such things as "probability, indications are, etc.", and Child ego-state words are usually spontaneous, terse, and well known to most readers. Frequently seen is the use of "Wow." An historical verification of an ego state is also important and strived for by the therapist. For example, the question, "When was the first time you placed your finger in the air like that?" might be met with the response, "I was six and my father did that when I said something naughtily to my mother." Another important verification of the ego state involved is the social response of others in the group. A Child attitude, gesture, and vocabulary will often elicit a Parent response from another individual, and the opposite, of course, is frequently seen. A prejudicial Parent statement will be met by rebellious comment from the Child of another patient. In a typical countertransference situation, the Adult of the patient may attempt to transact with the Adult of the therapist by asking the question, "Do you think I need further treatment?" and the therapist may respond from his Parent and say, "Don't ask that, be patient," and at that point the rebellious Child may appear. Final verification, sometimes attained only with difficulty, is the subjective phenomenological reexperiencing of the ego state. The sooner the patient is aware which particular ego state is functioning and operating in the group, the sooner he will be able to fulfill his contract successfully. This condition implies that the therapist observe and confront in an active manner.

A successful realigning of ego state and awareness on the part of the patient sometimes allows the patient to meet his contract. In two forms of psychopathology which are well known, a simple structural analysis may allow the patient to gain a social control. For example, in a manic depressive-type illness during the depressed stage, a strong, rigid, punitive Parent is the only ego state at that point which is in operation, and no laughter, sponstaneity, or creativity characteristic of the Child is in evidence at that point. This rigidity, as discussed previously, is known as exclusion. The therapist at this point, in addition to diagnosing the ego state, talks to the Child. In delusional states, it is seen that the boundary between the Adult ego state and the Child ego state has become fused. Ordinarily the Adult can clearly distinguish what is real and what is fantasy, but with contamination present, the child's fantasies and nightmares merge with the Adult to the extent that what appears like Adult functioning is actually programmed by the Child. Therefore, Child fantasies are experienced as Adult reality. The therapist gains access to the fantasies by entering the Child's world. It would be the Child of the therapist intuitively reacting in an active way with the Child of the patient who has a contaminated ego state. Once in the Child state with the patient, the therapist can suggest that there are other alternatives and discuss these with the Adult. This contamination must be clarified before going on to other therapy sequences, and in many cases a simple structural analysis will suffice to allow the patient to attain his treatment contract.

Therapy may proceed to analyzing transactions and the diagnosis of crossed transactions. Some therapists prefer to begin with these because they are so dramatically presented in groups, sometimes at the onset of group treatment. Occasionally games have little to do with treatment contracts which have been arrived at. However, it is usually found that the predominant game that an individual displays in the group is incompatible with what he wishes to attain as his goal in group treatment. When this is so, a detailed analysis of the game is undertaken. Having clearly in mind the structure of the Parent, Adult, and the Child ego states, the patient is in a good position to analyze what particular ego state is involved in any set of transactions with another individual. An awareness of the particular game an individual is playing then allows him to choose whether or not he wishes to continue this game. Knowing that there are advantages that a person gains by playing certain games, the therapist chooses the interventions to make. When the therapist recognizes that a game invitation has been extended to him, he has four types of choices open to him (6). He may respond by exposing the game. This action is taken when he feels that the patient has some alternative method available to him to make up for the loss that he will experience when giving up a certain game. The therapist at the point of exposure of the game stands ready to intervene actively if necessary. On some occasions the therapist may respond by going along with the game. This action would be taken only after carefully considering if continuing the game is beneficial to the patient's condition. Infrequently, but occasionally, the therapist will choose to ignore a particular game, usually for diagnostic purposes. It could also be utilized to acquaint the patient with the idea that perhaps he does not need to utilize his old patterns to achieve recognition with people. Alternative games are sometimes proposed by the therapist.

Games as an on-going part of the life course of an individual are not readily abandoned by the patient, and when given up the Child may experience a loss. Clinically there is usually a depression at this point in treatment. As seen in the script matrix, the life course, including the essential games, has been decided upon early in life and is determined by transactions from the biological parent to the Child. The therapist has intervened in the life of the patient and is distinguished from the biological parent. The Adult of the therapist clearly assesses the on-going treatment, the Parent of the therapist is available to the Child of the patient when a loss is present, and the Child of the therapist intuitively reacts with the Child of the patient. The laughter and humor common in transactional analysis groups is reminiscent of children playing together. With the loss of the script position, the Child is free to create new pleasures, find more acceptable games, and perhaps attain intimacy.

## REFERENCES

1. Berne, E. *Transactional analysis in psychotherapy*. New York: Grove Press, 1961.
2. Berne, E. *Games people play*. New York: Grove Press, 1963.
3. Berne, E. *The structure and dynamics of organizations and groups*. Philadelphia: J. B. Lippincott, 1963.
4. Berne, E. *Principles of group treatment*. New York: Oxford University Press, 1966.

5. Crossman, P. Permission and protection. *Transact. Anal. Bull.,* 1966, **5,** 9.
6. Dusay, J. M. Scientific proceedings (abstract). *Transact. Anal. Bull.,* 1965, **4,** 16.
7. Dusay, J. M. Response in therapy. *Transact. Anal. Bull.,* 1966, **5,** 18.
8. Ernst, F. H., & Keating, W. C. Psychiatric treatment of the California felon. *Amer. J. Psychiat.,* 1964, **120,** 10.
9. Ford, D. H., & Urban, H. B. *Systems of psychotherapy.* New York: John Wiley and Sons, 1963.
10. Hartmann, H. *Ego psychology and the problem of adaptation.* New York: International Universities Press, 1958.
11. Piaget, J. *Logic and psychology.* New York: Basic Books, 1957.
12. Steiner, C. Psychological functions of the child. *Transact. Anal. Bull.,* 1965, **4,** 16.
13. Steiner, C. Script and counterscript. *Transact. Anal. Bull.,* 1966, **5,** 18.
14. Werner, H. *Comparative psychology of mental development.* New York: Science Editions, 1961.

Chapter 14

# Fixed Role Therapy

## GEORGE A. KELLY

George A. Kelly: b. 1905, Perth, Kansas. d. Framingham, Massachusetts, 1968.

B.A., in physics and mathematics, Park College, 1926. M.A., in educational sociology, University of Kansas, 1928, B.Ed., University of Edinburgh, Scotland, 1930. Ph.D., in psychology, University of Iowa, 1931.

Riklis Professor of Behavioral Science, Brandeis University, 1965–1967. Professor of Psychology, University of Maryland, 1945–1946. Instructor, Associate Professor of Psychology, Fort Hayes Kansas State College, 1931–1943.

Former President: American Board of Examiners in Professional Psychology; Clinical Division, American Psychological Association; Consulting Division, APA.

Books: *The Psychology of Personal Constructs*, 2 vols., (1955).

Fixed role therapy is an experimental procedure that may be followed in cases where one wishes to activate psychotherapeutic processes without resorting to applied psychology. This is to say that it represents a form of inquiry designed to shed light on an urgent problem rather than a treatment warranted only by previous research. It is essentially experimental, not simply because it is novel, but because it involves the client in a calculated venture the extended outcome of which he must assess. In a strict sense it is not even a form of treatment but an investigative project in which the client is himself the principal investigator—and knows it!

### CONSTRUCTIVE ALTERNATIVISM

The form of the procedure is embedded in personal construct theory, which, in turn, is anchored in an epistemological position called constructive alternativism. Constructive alternativism holds that man understands himself, his surroundings, and his potentialities by devising constructions to place upon them and then testing the tentative utility of these constructions against such *ad interim* criteria as the successful prediction and control of events. It assumes that man's construction of events may ultimately converge upon reality, in the manner of non-Euclidian parallel lines, but that it is presumptuous to claim the convergence has already taken place. Any present construction is then open to an undetermined amount of reconsideration, no matter how obvious it may appear to be or how objective the evidence which supports it at the moment. Constructive alternativism stands in contrast to a view we may call accumulative fragmentalism, the notion that knowledge is a growing collection of substantiated facts—when we get all the facts we shall find ourselves arrived at the truth.

## PERSONAL CONSTRUCT THEORY

Personal construct theory starts with the postulate that a person's processes are psychologically channeled by the ways in which he anticipates events. It goes on to propose that one anticipates events by construing the manner in which future occurrences can be thought to replicate past ones. The unit of construction is the personal construct, which is defined as a way in which two or more events can be regarded as similar and in contrast to one or more other events. The personal construct is not a representation of an event or a group of events, as is sometimes said of a concept. It is, instead, a referent devised by the person upon which he may project events in order to cope with them. It need not be verbalized and it may be regarded as structuring smooth muscle and glandular processes, as well as skeletal muscle or verbal enactments.

The development of a personal construct system for the anticipation of events poses a "minimax" problem for the person—how to achieve maximum differentiation of events with a minimum of dichotomous discrimination units, or constructs. It also involves problems of ordinal relations between constructs, the employment of constructs in experience, commitment to behavioral inquiry, and the revision of constructs in the light of particular outcomes and the integrity of the system as a whole.

## THE SCIENCE PARADIGM

For purposes of understanding fixed role therapy there are two features of personal construct theory that must be kept clearly in mind. Both represent wide departures from the views of other personality theories. The first is the notion of the scientist as the paradigm of man. The second is the notion that one enacts a role, in the personal construct theoretical sense, only to the extent that he is guided by a construction of another person's outlook. Both notions require a little explaining.

A description of scientific method as it is practiced by scientists can quite properly be regarded as a personality theory—applied, of course, to persons who happen to be scientists. But the basic features of scientific method can be considered as basically human too. One can scarcely say the scientist does anything a human being cannot do, though he may do some things that not all his fellow humans do as well. But the behavior of the scientists is altogether human behavior, and a construction of his actions can provide guidelines for understanding all human behavior. Moreover, the tactics that scientists follow in pursuing their investigations are no less available to other men who have inquiries to pursue.

The thoughtful exploration of this line of theorizing suggests, then, that what a scientist does, man can do, and what a scientifically minded psychologist does, his client can do. It suggests, furthermore, that it may be as inept to try to get a client up on his feet by treating him or conditioning him as it would be to try to get a psychologist to make a monumental contribution by ordering him to do precisely what he is told. But if a client can begin to use the better methods of inquiry himself, if he can experiment appropriately, and if he can reformulate his hypotheses in the light of the relationships between his predictions and his observation of occurrences, he may be on his way to living his life in a manner that leads somewhere rather than going round and round in "healthy" orbits prescribed by his psychiatrist. Fixed role therapy casts the client in the role of a scientist intent on inquiring into his most perplexing problems. It casts his psychotherapist in the role of a colleague who has as much to learn as he does.

## ROLE

The other feature of personal construct theory that must be particularly well understood is its definition of role. The two conventional notions of role—a course of action articulated with the actions of others, and a set of behavioral expectations imposed upon a man— are both externalized definitions. That is to say their determinants are outside the person. Personal construct theory, however, makes every effort to employ terms which refer to the outlook of the person himself. The theory's definition of role represents such an effort.

If I attempt to understand another man mechanistically or behavioristically, it probably means that I am not concerned with the construction he is placing on me or the other events in his life, but only with those actions which I can observe and how I myself choose to construe them. For all I care, he could just as well be a combination of levers and wires. I may even refer to him as "an organism," rather than as "a person," in the manner of psychologists who think there is something unscientific about being a person. To be sure, I may be able to anticipate some of his behavior better by construing him in this way than if I listen to him too intently. This may turn out to be particularly true if I make the mistake of assuming that the words he uses have only the meanings attributed to them by the dictionary.

But however efficient may be this manner of construing my friend, personal construct theory would not call any of my ensuing behavior a role. On the other hand, if I make an attempt to see the world through his spectacles (through his constructs, I mean) and I structure my own actions in the light of what I think I see, what I do then is, for me, a role. This is not to say that my interpretation of his viewpoint is accurate, or even that I shall then choose to act in a manner compliant with his wishes. Indeed, my perception may be grossly inaccurate, which could result in considerable confusion, and I may even choose to use my version of his outlook to undo him, which also could have chaotic consequences. But in any case, my actions would constitute a role.

## IMPLICATIONS OF ROLE ENACTMENT

However badly I may choose to act, or some other individuals may choose to act, it should not be necessary to go into great argumentative detail to suggest that, notwithstanding, it is in role relationships that men may hope to combine their ingenuities as well as their labors. Thus they may advance mankind's cultural achievements beyond what can be accomplished simply by assembly line divisions of labor or by the imposition of regularized behavioral expectations upon the masses. On the other hand, a socialization of human institutions which is based on the two conventional notions of role is all too likely to lead to the suppression of human ingenuity, as, in the case of one of the notions, it did in the early stages of the industrial revolution, or as, in the case of the other, it has done in the headlong rush of ideological socialism.

The notion of role as a man's course of action articulated with the actions of others leads one to envision a society populated with a species of economic man. The notion of role as a set of expectations conjures up an image of a society of ideological man. I suppose we could add that, if the current notions of psychotherapy continue to catch on, we may look forward to a society of the self-conscious man. But personal construct theory envisions a different kind of society, a society of the inquiring man. Fixed role therapy depends greatly upon both client and therapist understanding the meaning of role in this personal construct sense, rather than in the sense of either of the conventional definitions, or in the implied sense that emerges out of present-day psychotherapeutics.

Having said only this much, we could easily break off the discussion and leave the reader with the impression that fixed role therapy is going to turn out to be no more than an epistemological pastime of gentle people. But this might be misleading. Fixed role therapy is as much an ontological venture as it is a perceptive psychoanalysis of one's neighbors. Personal construct theory is not a cognitive theory but a theory about how the human process flows, how it strives in new directions as well as in old, and how it may dare for the first time to reach into the depths of newly perceived dimensions of human life.

Personal construct theory's epistemology is an epistemology of creative action: Man understands his world by finding out what he can do with it. And he understands himself in the same way, by finding out what he can make of himself. Man is what he becomes. What he becomes is a product of what he undertakes—expected or by surprise. The peculiar genius of psychology, if it has one, is to see man in this perspective, as what the continuing effort of living can make of him. Here, beyond epistemology, lies the ontological rationale of fixed role therapy.

## OTHER FORMS OF PSYCHOTHERAPY
## WITHIN PERSONAL CONSTRUCT THEORY

Although fixed role therapy embodies the principles of personal construct theory, the reader should not be left with the impression that it is the only form of psychotherapy that may do so. It stands out as an example of the theory in action primarily because, on the face of it, it appears to disregard so much of what other systems hold to be essential. Psychoanalysis probes and strives for insight, yet fixed role therapy offers no necessary interpretations of the client's present problem. Behavior therapy prescribes a cure, yet fixed role therapy may propose an enactment no client or therapist would want to see continued. The client-centered therapist must offer his client "an unconditional positive regard" for the feelings he has so long experienced in dread, but fixed role therapy recognizes no such autonomy of feelings. Yet fixed role therapy is articulate about what it undertakes, it ventures to undertake unfamiliar modes of behavior, and it relies upon acute sensitivity to feelings arising out of one's own experimentation.

But however much at odds with better known approaches fixed role therapy appears to be, its rationale does not rest on any necessary conviction that they are wrong. The philosophical position, constructive alternativism, which underlies the theory and the method, does not require one to discredit one set of assumptions before daring to examine the implications of others. Indeed, this is, in effect, just what is proposed to the client: He need not invalidate his "neurotic" outlook before actively exploring what other outlooks have to offer. He has only to undertake psychotherapy as an ontological venture rather than as an epistemological exercise designed to convince himself of what he does not feel is so. All of this is a way of saying that one's personality is not altogether shaped by what he knows and what he accepts but emerges continuously through his modes of pursuing what he hopes to be and what he would like to find out.

Personal construct theory, more than any other system of psychotherapy I know, envisions an orchestration of techniques—perhaps as wide a variety of techniques as the human armamentarium stocks. Unlike psychoanalysis, in which Freud precisely combined the techniques of his mentor Charcot and his colleague Breuer, personal construct theory does not prescribe for the therapist a single orthodox procedure. Nor does it see the salivating dog as the prototype of the client, or an abiding faith in man as the climate in which all good things grow. Yet what the psychoanalyst does to help his client articulate what has remained estranged from language, the personal construct theorist may do also. He may, as well, see conditioning as an experiment the client performs rather than an operation performed on him, and he may offer his client the acceptance of feelings as a hypothesis worth experimenting with.

## APPROPRIATENESS OF FIXED ROLE THERAPY

One thing more: for my own part I do not employ fixed role therapy in the majority of cases I see, perhaps in no more than one out of fifteen. There are too many other orchestral possibilities for one to sit and hum the same therapeutic tune to his clients morning, noon, and night. Sometimes I employ the procedure when I can see the client for less than a month but can have him come in several times a week. I may resort to fixed role therapy when a client has become surfeited with other therapeutic efforts, including my own. It can be used to break through overintellectualization, and it can serve to direct the client to resources outside the therapy room which are not for hire. Now and then I use it to prepare the client for a protracted psychotherapeutic sequence and sometimes to finish off such a sequence. Occasionally it proves useful when a psychotherapist whom I am supervising becomes preoccupied with the "interesting material" that accumulates in session after session and starts "peeling his onion."

As for the appropriateness of fixed role therapy in various diagnostic categories, our experience so far does not permit us to put our finger precisely on the outer boundaries. My early apprehension about using it with "schizophrenics" has been allayed; it does not foster the delusions I was afraid it might. I am also less reluctant to employ it with mild "paranoid schizophrenics," now that I have had some experience with it. Handled properly, it seems to offer some stabilization for the aura of urgency that "manics" display. "Depressives," of course, experience difficulty mobilizing themselves for the continued enactment, but, since continued mobilization of their efforts is generally judged to be a good thing, this difficulty need not be taken as a contraindication for the method. I have even seen it work rather well in "conversion" cases and in cases of "immature personality." It has been tried with some success in cases of mental retardation, though not to "cure" the symptoms of mental deficiency itself, of course. Thus far I have not approached a "phobic case" through fixed role therapy; I must try that the next time a client comes in complaining of his inability to get along with snakes.

## THE SEQUENCE OF STEPS IN FIXED ROLE THERAPY

It would perhaps be helpful at this point to turn from rationale to technique, starting with a sketch of the process as a whole, and then following with a step-by-step account of the sequence of procedures.

The client, call him Q. M., is asked to write a character sketch of himself from a particular point of view. The therapist then studies this sketch in consultation with colleagues and, with their help, prepares an enactment sketch, one that might have been written by a hypothetical "E. S." in response to a similar request.

In the next therapy session Q. M. is shown the "E. S." sketch and his superficial reaction to it is tested. If the test is passed satisfactorily, he is asked to pretend that he, Q., "has gone to the mountains to enjoy himself," and that, in his stead, "E. S." materializes. The client is to enact as best he can, twenty-four hours a day, all that "E. S." might do, say, think, or even dream. At least three therapy sessions a week are scheduled, and in them client and therapist rehearse the enactment, plan critical tests of its effectiveness, and examine outcomes. At the end of the period Q. M. "comes back," whether he wants to or not, and is invited to appraise the experience in whatever ways make sense to him.

The undertaking is not as simple as it probably sounds. Our experience—the experience of my colleagues and myself—suggests many points at which variation in the procedure can lead to trouble, especially in the hands of a therapist who thinks of fixed role therapy as a form of "treatment." Although the method does not require one to make the usual psychoanalytic "interpretations," it is scarcely any the less vulnerable to the blunders of clinically insensitive therapists. It is neither easy nor routine. Clinical skill and perceptiveness are as crucial as they are known to be in a psychoanalytic relationship where volatile transference involvements are present. But, of course, the terms of reference are different.

## THE SELF-CHARACTERIZATION

At first glance it may appear that the self-characterization the client is asked to write is not essential to the experiment. I am convinced, however, that it is an important step in the process. The particular way in which the self-characterization is elicited is intended to imply that neither psychodiagnosis nor the ensuing psychotherapy is based on "confession." Moreover, having written the self-characterization, the client should be better prepared to see the "E. S." sketch as having both subjective and objective authenticity. "E. S." is a man, such as Q. himself is, who can see himself as a man, just as Q. has been asked to see himself, who faces human problems too and makes no pretense of psychological perfection. Furthermore, Q.

may begin to see that there is a sense in which one may credit a man with being what he represents himself to be, this being an application of the principle of the credulous approach, about which personal construct theory has a great deal to say.

As I write these sentences I recall that last night—by an actual count of candy bars—exactly seventy goblins, witches, and sundry suspicious characters of assorted sizes came to our door, some of them piping in small voices, "Trick or treat, trick or treat!" To be sure, you and I might be constrained to say that "they were not goblins, or witches, or even very suspicious," both of us being quite willing to assume that we know what real spooks look like. But if we agree to make such a denial, do we approach the psychological truth about these visitors, or do we retreat from it? Which, psychologically, is the real child: The child behind the mask, or the child "unmasked," standing barefaced in the bright light of the living room, surrounded by adults, and saying proper "pleases" and "thank yous?" Do I understand the child half as well if I refuse to see the part he is enacting? I think not!

A man becomes the President of the United States. But come now, between us psychologists, is he really the President? Or must we not diagnose him as the small time politician who has been playing "trick or treat" most of his life? No, I think that if he now undertakes to enact the part, he is, indeed, *The President.* If we are to understand psychologically a man who enacts such a commitment, we can do so only by empathizing the commitment, by being credulous to it. Of course, this does not mean that he will play the part the way we think we might or the way we think Abraham Lincoln or George Washington played it.

Psychological perceptiveness does not depend upon the precision with which we can fit our client into one of our own preconceived categories but upon our grasp of his construction of events and of the part his construction leads him to take in coping with them. The therapist, too, has a role to enact, a role in the personal construct theoretical sense, one that comes to life only after he puts the client's glasses on over his own and sees as best he can what the client sees.

## ELICITING THE SELF-CHARACTERIZATION

"I want you to write a character sketch of Q. M., just as if he were the principal character in a play. Write it as it might be written by a friend who knew him very intimately and very sympathetically, perhaps better than anyone ever really could know him. Be sure to write it in the third person. For example, start out by saying, 'Q. M. is . . . .' " This is the way Q. M. is asked to write a character sketch of himself.

The phrasing of this request has been carefully chosen and has gone through a good many revisions in the light of experience with it. The term, "character sketch," seems to work best in suggesting to the client that he is to present himself as a coherent whole rather than to catalogue his faults and virtues. The object is to see how he structures himself, and within what kind of framework, not to force him to diagnose himself within a psychologist's framework. He may find it difficult to present himself as an integral person. If so, it is worth knowing, and, furthermore, an appreciation of this fact should help the clinician structure his own role. A responsible therapist will seek to know something of how both Q.'s self and his outside world are seen through those glasses he wears.

It is easy to see that the therapist cannot suggest an outline for the sketch, though he may be asked to prescribe one. It is Q.'s outline, his own structural framework, however inadequate that may be, that is sought, not a burlesque of a man vainly juggling words to present himself in the alien language of a presumed expert. Nor is Q. expected to encapsulate himself in the terms of any particular friend, as the phrase, "perhaps better than anyone ever really could know him," is intended to suggest.

To be sure, Q. may find himself at a loss for words. If so, then that may be how it is with him—a self held together without the structure of language. Or he may say only, "I live at 35½ Commercial Street. I am five feet two inches tall. I am 32 years old, and I weigh 190 pounds." Can we then say he has offered us nothing of psychological importance? I think no sensitive clinician would say that! He may thus indeed have put his identity in the most poignant perspective.

Or suppose he says only, "I am of medium height and build, I live in an average community, and I have never been in trouble." Can we allow ourselves to think for one moment that this tells us nothing of his inner experience or of the illusive issues that plague his daily life?

There are occasions when a client will protest he is quite incapable of writing down anything about himself. Ordinarily one suggests then that he give it a try and come in next time with whatever he has managed to write. But the therapist can add, if he wishes, "Just suppose I have never seen Q. M. or talked to him. How would this friend, who knows him so much more intimately and sympathetically than anyone really does know him, write the character sketch? You and I need his help." It does not seem advisable to go further than this, if indeed to go even this far. After all, the success of therapy rarely hinges on the client's avoiding all confrontation with his own unproductiveness.

## PREPARING THE ENACTMENT SKETCH:
## AN EXPERIMENT

There is much more to be said about systematic methods of analyzing the self-characterization. But that is a whole chapter in itself, and the reader, if he plans to have a go at fixed role therapy, is urged to read what is written elsewhere about it (3). The analysis should be carried to the point where the therapist has some notions of the principal construct dimensions the client uses in identifying himself, of how he utilizes experience, and of the directions in which his sense of movement appears to carry him. One can begin to infer also what his words mean, although finding out precisely what a client's language means is an undertaking not likely to get very far in the brief course of a fixed role therapy sequence.

It may seem trite to say that "E. S." must, first of all, present himself as human. The image of mental health that most psychotherapists manage to project is not of a person that most of us would warm up to, much as we might admire his stark realism, his overpowering release of libidinal energy, and his unfailing competence in manipulating his associates. Such realism robs the world of mystery, the energy makes all obstacles trivial, and the competence eliminates any exciting risk of failure. Certainly personal construct theory does not for one moment paint such a picture of mental health.

There is no implicit guarantee of success in the character of "E. S." Like Q., he is a man of dreams, striving, and uncertainty. His answers turn out to be questions in another form, and his questions, if they are to lead him anywhere in his life, must be posed in judicious behavior, not merely in words. Any attempt to portray "E." as a walking solution to Q.'s problems makes him into a Madison Avenue advertiser's layout rather than an honest experiment. This portrayal would be as fraudulent as most applied psychology turns out to be, whether on Madison Avenue or in a practitioner's office.

## HYPOTHESES IMBEDDED IN "E. S."

The task one faces in writing the enactment sketch is, then, to design a genuine experiment in which both client and therapist are active participants and both are prepared to be surprised by the outcomes. That means there should be at least one hypothesis to be tested, and it should be stated explicitly in the "E. S." sketch. The hypothesis may be one Q. has already set up in his characterization of himself. Since, in human affairs, there is nothing that corresponds to the statistician's null hypothesis, we can examine Q.'s hypothesis only by testing its substantial alternatives. For example, if he has described himself as "meticulous," the alternative (from his point of view) might be to play the part of an "E." who was "casual," and then to see what would happen.

But more often than not the psychotherapist will want to cast the enactment in a new dimension, one that has never occurred to Q., and, indeed, one he may not initially be able to visualize. "E.," for example, may be characterized as "generous," and the implications of being so versus being "grasping," may be explored by actually playing the part. By structuring Q.'s behavior with respect to a new axis, the psychotherapist begins to make the whole of living take shape in a world Q. never suspected was there.

Contrast this kind of undertaking with one in which the client would simply play the part of a person who is "casual," as against Q.'s "meticulousness." He may even have tried it before; most clients have rattled back and forth in their slots. But to launch out in an altogether new dimension, through successive rehearsals and field trials, is to find a new kind of life space and to break out of the ruts that have too long channeled his life. The novel products of such a venture can, if properly recognized as outcomes of his initiative, be woven into the fabric of Q.'s life experience.

But without such sallies in new directions, life is no more than a series of accidental collisions with events, and the outcomes can be judged only as fortunes or misfortunes. The impact of an event, when no venture has been risked, leaves one's personality intact or bruised but, in either case, essentially unchanged. But a true commitment, the outcome of which is reflected back upon its design, recreates personality by carrying through the full cycle of human experience.

## "E. S." IS A ROLE

The reader may recall my early insistence that one must keep two features of personal construct theory in mind when he employs fixed role therapy—the science paradigm and the notion of role. Let us hope I have now said enough about the science paradigm to make it clear that fixed role therapy is a genuine experiment in which client and therapist are co-investigators and the major hypotheses are stated in the "E. S." sketch.

Now it will come as no surprise for me to say also that the enactment sketch must embody a role, a role in the personal construct sense. This is to say that "E. S." is to be depicted as a man who acts in the light of his continuing attempt to catch a glimpse of the way things seem to others. Not only, then, is he an anthropomorphized hypothesis for Q. to test, but he is such a man as would attempt to try on other men's glasses and to discover through experimentation if what he observed by looking through them was indeed what other men observe. Perhaps I had better say that "E." actively concerns himself with the outlooks of others not merely with their behaviors, and he is prepared to verify his perception of how the world looks to them. Whether his friends perceive accurately or not is another matter, and this he realizes too.

Sometimes I am asked if the client himself should not write, or at least take part in writing, the enactment sketch. This would seem to follow from the view of the client as a participating scientist. But when I have tried this approach I have noted that he does not often introduce a novel construct dimension. Probably it is not easy for him to express on the spur of the moment what has never before occurred to him. What he does then, if he tries anything new at all, is propose a reversal of his position on one of his prevailing construct axes. Although this reversal may eventually lead him to a new vantage point in construing his circumstances, it does not offer the dramatic possibilities that an experiment initially designed by an imaginative therapist might disclose. Nor is it likely to open up a world proportioned in new dimensions.

Nevertheless, there are stages and forms of therapy in which the client's design of his own experiments is not only valuable but essential. Indeed, we may hope that the design and calculated execution of experiments is something he will be doing for the rest of his life.

What I have mentioned here does not by any means exhaust the considerations that should be taken into account when one attempts

fixed role therapy in a particular case. A therapist should be prepared to consider not only the wealth of his own clinical experience
but also the skills, the perceptions, the weaknesses, the perplexities,
and the preoccupations of his client with "causes" and "circumstances." Moreover, he must respect the integrity of the Q. personality, lest, by invalidating particular neurotic approaches to life, he de-
stroys the man himself.

## ILLUSTRATIVE ENACTMENT SKETCHES

A few years ago the following enactment sketch was used in a
fixed role therapy sequence:

> K. M. is a man whose basic integrity governs all his daily acts. Never
> are his actions incompatible with his convictions. He has found from
> experience that this kind of integrity enables him to rise above life's
> vexing obstacles and personal handicaps. This quality in his personal
> make-up may not always be noted by others, yet it subtly flavors all
> his interpersonal relations.
>
> One of the conspicuous features of Mr. M.'s character is his obvious
> respect for the personalities of other people, even those who do not
> meet the standards he applies to himself. It is his basic integrity that
> makes him unique in this respect. While he is always free to express
> his own point of view, it would never occur to him that, by doing so,
> he would be trying to compel others to conform to his views. When
> he expresses himself, it is meant as a sincere invitation to others to
> express their own particular viewpoints also. Thus he interacts with
> people without feeling he must either teach or concede.
>
> When Mr. M. was an adolescent, his relations with his parents were
> sometimes strained because of their rigid insistence that he look at
> certain situations from their viewpoint. Out of this experience has de-
> veloped the point of view which now has become the characteristic
> feature of his personality.
>
> Sometimes his friends find him a stimulating companion—willing
> both to give and to take. At other times he falls silent to the company
> of others, perhaps because he is hesitant to stifle another's self-expres-
> sion. Although on these latter occasions he gives the impression of
> being withdrawn and reticent, actually he always remains an alert,
> though sometimes quiet, participant in any social situation.

The above sketch was prepared for enactment by a client who
was easily threatened by persons who did not subscribe to his "upright" virtues and often became disputatious. The initial "integrity"
theme in the sketch was designed to maintain this feature of his perception of himself, or his pose if you prefer, but to derive from it
a mode of action which lent itself to the development of rudimen-

tary role constructs. His experiences, as he remembered them, with his parents made the development of role constructs a tricky matter. It seemed best to incorporate somewhat similar "experiences" when writing the enactment sketch. It will be noted that the sketch also tried to provide grounds for his keeping his mouth shut while still "participating" in a group.

Following is a self-characterization written by a client for whom an enactment sketch was later prepared. The misspellings in her typewritten manuscript are reproduced.

> In my opinion C. N. is not a shy girl by no means. She mixes well with both sexes but is frequently moody and therefore is irritible to those surrounding her. Carrie lies quite often; knowing she is doing wrong, but continues to do so. She exaggerates about things concerning herself which she feels would like to be true but are not. I find she's becomes dissatisfied with herself and the things she is doing quite often. For example, she gets disgusted with school and wants to quit and has no desire to study. Also she feel as if she wants to go to a new environment to meet new people. I also feel she possess a selfish character at time and other times quite generous depending upon her so-called mood. She has a strong desire to be happy and satisfied with the things she has and therefore have peace of mind. She sometimes has the feeling that she wants everything to come her way without working for it and she would like to possess of feeling of wanting to give as much as receive. She would like very much to fall in love and not only look for what he could give her, now but first look for how ambitious he is and what he will have in the future. She is dead set against marry a doctor because of that life a doctor's wife leads. She feels she requires constant attention and love in order not to have that sence of insecurity she so frequently feels.

The following enactment sketch was prepared for this client and used in fixed role therapy.

> Julie Dornay is a good person to have for a friend. She is spontaneously and sympathetically interested in people. She is a good listener. She is sensitive to the ways other people feel. People value her friendship, not only because of the things she can give them or the favors she can do, but more because of the encouragement and strength her friendship gives them. Having had problems of her own, she is well equipped to play a sympathetically supporting role to the people who confide in her. While she does not feel that all her own problems are solved, when others come to her, she lays her own problems aside in order to be of help. Basically she believes that all people are worthwhile in their own right, regardless of their accomplishments or worldly successes. Because of this fundamental belief in people her own worthwhileness is simply and naturally taken for granted.
> There is an undercurrent of impatience in Julie's way of life. She

is quick to express her liking for her friends. She is always ready to speak up in their behalf. When she sees someone being pushed around she really stands up and lets her voice be heard. But this impatience never seems to come into conflict with her underlying feeling of kindliness and sensitivity for others. Indeed, one might almost say that her impatience is a result of this feeling.

Julie's capacity to be a good friend leads her into many new and interesting adventures. While some people pick and choose the friends who conform to their own narrow specifications, Julie selects a tremendous variety of friends, no two of whom fit precisely the same set of specifications. Thus her own life is enriched and widened and new horizons are continually opening up before her.

When you talk to Julie you soon become aware of the fact that she is interested in you because, first of all, she fundamentally accepts you as you are and wholeheartedly believes that you are genuinely a worthwhile person. She responds to you spontaneously and takes your acceptance of her for granted. But most of all you discover that she is ready and eager to know you as a unique and different personality among her many and varied friends.

In this enactment sketch the role construction is frankly stated, though in a concrete behavioral form. As can be seen, the enactment is designed to involve her in commitments, perhaps even premature ones. Her search for a Lochinvar is not invalidated, but she is to be kept busy attending to lesser characters along the way.

## PRESENTING THE ENACTMENT SKETCH
## TO THE CLIENT

The usual procedure is to present a copy of the enactment sketch to the client and ask him to follow as the therapist reads a copy of it. Then the therapist asks two questions: (1) "Has E. S. described himself in a manner that makes him seem genuine?" and (2) "Does he sound like a person you would like to know?" If the answer to both questions is "yes," the enactment can proceed.

If the answer to the first question is "no," the therapist should ask what there is about the sketch that makes "E. S." seem artificial. Sometimes this calls for rewriting a part of the sketch, but more often "an interpretation" will suffice. Sometimes the interpretation can be composed on the spot as an addendum to the sketch.

If the answer to the second question is negative, the therapist can seek to find out what feature of the sketch is threatening. Sometimes this difficulty, too, can be handled by "an interpretation" of "E." In any case, unless the sketch can be made acceptable in terms of both questions, it is better to start over by writing another characterization before attempting the enactment.

The enactment can be proposed somewhat in the following manner: "During the next two weeks, instead of dealing directly with your problems, I would like to suggest that we do something altogether different. Let us suppose that Q. M. is going to have a two week vacation in the mountains, and, in his place, you are going to be 'E. S.' You will act like 'E. S.,' talk like him, think like him, do the things you think he might do, eat the way you think he would eat, and, if you can, even have the dreams you think he might have.

"Here is another copy of 'E.'s' character sketch. Keep one copy with you all the time and read it at least four times a day—particularly at night when you go to bed, and again in the morning. Read it also whenever you have difficulty playing the part.

"During these two weeks I'll be seeing you every other day, so we can rehearse. We'll try to anticipate some of the situations that will arise so that you can be ready to be as much like 'E.' as possible.

"Don't worry about Q. We don't even need to think about him. Besides, he is going to be away enjoying himself, and we can assume he doesn't want to be bothered. In any case, he will be coming back two weeks from today and that will be time enough to see what he has on his mind.

"Now, let's see, your supervisor is who? Angus McGillicuddy? OK, let us suppose it will be 'E. S.' who shows up for work this afternoon. How would 'Mr. S.' greet Mr. McGillicuddy? I'll be Mr. McGillicuddy. Good afternoon, 'Mr. S.!' "

It is important to get the enactment under way immediately. Rather than attempting to persuade Q. that he should be "E.," the client is treated as if he actually was "E.," with the therapist expressing surprise or disbelief at any expression that is out of character. Even though Q. is speechless, or fails to play the part convincingly, his confrontation with a therapist who sees him as "E.," and as "E." only, cannot be ignored. Somehow he must cope with the novel situation in which he now finds himself. Though he may run the gamut of familiar manipulative devices to get out of it altogether, the most obvious pathways for movement are those staked out by the constructs "E." envisions.

During this stage of the enactment, the therapist may feel quite as strange as the client does. In fact, I find it generally more difficult to persuade therapists to commit themselves to the undertaking than to get clients to give it an honest experimental trial. I suppose that is because most clients expect to invest something in therapy, whereas all too many therapists, being applied psychologists rather than scientists, want little more than to be successful in the easiest possible manner. Perhaps we should remember that there is a great deal of difference between coming to a session to wager one's way of life and coming only to put in an hour of professional time.

Perhaps the most difficult thing for the therapist to realize is that, even when his client says nothing, a few moments of being perceived as "E." rather than Q. will stick in the troubled mind long after the session is ended. A man can scarcely fail to wonder, amidst all the tortured doubts about ever being anything other than his miserable self, what it would be like, what it really would be like, to walk out into the world and be recognized, not as Q., but as "E." Certainly, unless our observations have been quite misleading, the effectiveness of the therapeutic effort does not depend upon the glibness with which the part is played. Indeed, it seems to me that the reverse may be true; the client who finds the experience disruptively novel and his first words in the part labored and inept may be the one most deeply affected by the experience. He is the one who invests himself, who performs an experiment, not the skilled actor who makes a burlesque of the part and risks nothing.

## PROTECTING THE INTEGRITY OF Q.

Important as it is not to become embroiled in a debate with the client about whether he can or cannot enact the part of "E.," some questions should be answered. The one most likely to be asked first is what the purpose of the enactment is or how it "will help." It is a fair question and must be answered honestly, as I believe all questions must be in a psychotherapeutic relationship. Although I have not settled on any particular phraseology, as I have for some of the other steps in the sequence, something like the following is appropriate.

"We both need to know right off just how much you are prepared to invest in developing a new way of life for yourself. Sometimes people think they can simply close their eyes and have the therapist do something to them that will take all their troubles away without their having to take any risks themselves. But psychotherapy is not simply a matter of going to the doctor to be treated and then going back home to continue acting and thinking in the same old way. That won't work. Besides, life is an adventure from beginning to end, and right here is where we start. *I'm* ready; are *you*?"

Sometimes the client will persist: "But I don't see how this can help." The answer can be brief: "Of course not; you haven't tried it. Neither of us knows for sure what will happen. The only thing we know for sure is that nothing much is likely to happen until we start to experiment as thoughtfully as we can and keep our eyes open to what happens as a result. The first thing to find out is what happens this afternoon."

Now and then at this point the client may say, "But I'm afraid." The therapist may respond, "You mean, Q. is afraid. But 'E. S.' isn't. So let's send Q. to some place where he will have nothing to fear, and you simply be 'E.' I'll do everything I can to help. Now, 'E.,' at what time did you say you expect to arrive at work this afternoon?"

The second most common question is, "You mean 'E.' is the kind of person I should be?" Again, the answer must be candid. "No! At this point neither of us knows what kind of person you should be. That is something that will have to be developed as we go along, and let us hope it will continue to develop long after you stop seeing me. As far as you and I are concerned, 'E.' is simply an experiment, and the important thing for both of us to observe is exactly what happens when a man lives his life this way—what happens both inside his skin and what happens outside."

What is so important for the therapist to keep in mind, and so difficult for most of us brought up in the traditions of realism, determinism, and stimulus-response psychology, is that the object of therapy is not to eradicate Q. in order to replace him with some kind of "E." Q.'s integrity is neither criticized nor questioned. It is treated with respect and even reaffirmed. Certainly the client is never told that he is at odds with himself and thereby led to wonder what gremlins infest his psyche. The fact that "E.," by his contrast with Q., is so clearly make-believe rather than "real" is a key to the success of the venture, not a handicap.

And let us make no mistake about the basic methodology of science. For the genius of science is not its realism, but its calculated ventures into the world of make-believe—which scientists like to call "testing hypotheses." I doubt that an out-and-out realist could ever bring himself to test a hypothesis, any more than he could ever work himself out of a neurosis or a psychosis.

The "Q." the client has come to know is a hypothesis too. But how can a simple-minded realist know that? So he comes to the therapist for help. Since he can visualize no alternatives to the "Q." he knows, he cannot see that personality as hypothetical. All he can see are some of the outcomes of being "Q.," its "reinforcements," and he rarely needs a therapist to point out to him how unhappy those particular events are or that he is exhibiting a "neurotic paradox." Without constructive alternatives, without hypotheses, "reinforcements" can serve only as palliatives and irritants.

But "E." is so clearly a make-believe character, assuming the therapist is not too much of a realist himself to present him so or too much of an applied psychologist to risk an honest experiment, that he can be treated as a hypothesis indeed. From the moment the client experiences "E." as a hypothesis, science can have its day in the therapy room. And if "E." is a hypothesis the client finds he can test, the thought can scarcely escape him that there must be others too.

## INITIATING THE REHEARSALS

Let us turn back to where we left off—the beginning of the first rehearsal. The therapist can hardly expect that his own initial attempt to play the part of "E's" supervisor will portray that person accurately enough to provide strong support for the enactment of "E." After a few sentences the client is likely to say, "But old Gillie wouldn't say that." "All right," says the therapist, "let me play the part of 'E.' and you play the part of his supervisor. Good afternoon, Mr. McGillicuddy."

The exchange of parts which follows is important to the experiment. If the client does not say something that suggests it, the therapist should take the initiative and propose it himself. In any rehearsal the client is likely to see one part as dominant over the other, and, if he finds himself in an awkward position, he will wonder if the therapist is not taking unfair advantage of the inequity by casting himself in the dominant part. Exchanging parts is therefore a good practice in all psychotherapeutic enactments and especially so with children. Besides, being engaged in what must be both a true experiment and a true role enactment, the client reaching for the outlooks of others is almost as essential as is getting the knack of being "E." The exchange facilitates this attempt.

The effectiveness of the rehearsals probably depends as much upon the therapist's ingenuity as it does upon the client's cooperation.

If the therapist is inept it will be painfully obvious to both of them. He cannot hide behind esoteric terminology or owlish expressions of hidden wisdom. He, no less than the client, is caught up in an experiment, the outcomes of which cannot be accurately forecast. Both must take the risk that goes with being scientists. Fixed role therapy is a strenuous and demanding undertaking, as anyone who attempts it seriously will find out soon enough. It is not a job for dropouts who have taken up "psychotherapy" rather than continue to face the perplexities and frustrations of scientific inquiry.

## THE SEQUENCE OF SESSIONS

Generally we have planned the therapy sessions to emphasize, in succession, rehearsals for five kinds of interpersonal situations: (1) "E.'s" interaction with a supervisor on the job or with a teacher, (2) his interaction with his peers, (3) interaction with his spouse or with someone with whom he has an affectionate attachment, (4) interaction with parents or their surrogates, and (5) interaction in a situation involving religious experience. While the therapist must continually call attention to the need for playing the part at all times, and not merely in the situations which have been previously rehearsed, the ventures can be somewhat scaled to the depth and difficulty of the anticipated enactment.

Sessions should be frequent. It is particularly urgent to schedule the second session within one or two days of the first. A minimum of three sessions a week seems to be essential if the project is not to be abandoned by the client in the face of his first obstacles. He is usually discouraged during all the first week, and he will ordinarily come to the second session with a flat announcement that he cannot play the part. The therapist who thinks behavior is simply the pursuit of pleasant rewards will be easily "taken in." But he will have to remind himself that the client and he are scientists and that the object of the enterprise is to see precisely what happens under the conditions they have set up, not to scratch an itchy ego.

What is undertaken in fixed role therapy is a vigorous experiment, not a hit-and-miss search for the elixir of painless existence. Nothing short of persistent and ingenious effort is effective. This means frequent and arduous sessions that will tax the resources both of client and therapist.

Although many clients will maintain that their relations with their supervisors are more uncomfortable than with others, it seems best to point the first rehearsals specifically at this kind of enactment situation. Supervisory relations, even when strained, tend to be simple. This is to say they involve relatively few personal construct dimensions, and those that are necessarily involved tend to be ones which can be more easily put into words, or, as some might say, are more "cognitive." Personal construct theory is not, of course, a cognitive theory, as anyone who senses the depth of its personal involvements must surely realize. But as "cognition" goes, the relatively articulate and structured relationship between a work supervisor and an employee, or between a teacher and a pupil, can be considered to fit the category better than do most other important relationships.

There is another advantage in starting with this relationship. Playing out the first specific situation for which a rehearsal has been held usually proves to be a strenuous experience. It is just as well to make it one from which the client can withdraw before he becomes overwhelmed. Supervisory or student–teacher relationships usually lend themselves to this kind of touch-and-go dialogue.

The relations with one's peers, which usually mean with a group of persons of the same age and often of the same sex, are not so highly and articulately structured. To be sure, one may not feel himself under as much restraint in dealing with friends, but the complexities of interaction and the subtle invitations to impulse are greater, making one's unfamiliar enactment of a new role considerably harder to keep under precisely structured control. Moreover, it is in this particular enactment that the client is most likely to be told for the first time that he is "behaving strangely." For this reason the specific rehearsal for a peer enactment is scheduled after the one pointing toward a supervisory enactment rather than before.

## INITIATING ENACTMENTS

The client is often at a loss to think of some way he can precipitate a situation in which he can play the part of "E." In rehearsing the supervisory situation, the therapist may suggest that the enactment could start with some form of "shop talk." Usually that will be a question or a comment dealing with a matter of common concern between them. If the interaction is to be with a teacher, a brief after-class conversation on a topic recently discussed by the teacher is appropriate. Moreover, in this kind of situation it is quite reasonable for the client to play a role—in the personal construct sense. That is to say the interaction can be directed toward grasping the other person's point of view. Moreover, the feedback is immediate, thus lending itself to the purposes of a truly experimental venture.

As the first rehearsal gets under way, the therapist can begin to show the client how hypotheses can be used as a basis of interaction. What does the client think the supervisor will say? How will he say it? Can the client play the part, during the exchange, in the way he suspects the supervisor will play it? What variations might occur, and what clues should be particularly observed? What will his own feelings be at each stage of the enactment? Having raised such questions, the client may be urged to look for all deviations from the hypothesized responses of the supervisor and to make note of them, perhaps in writing as soon after the interaction as possible. He can, at the same time, make notes describing his own feelings.

When the second session is held, the client and therapist will want to go over the results of this particular enactment as well as what may have happened in others. The results may be reflected upon the hypotheses formulated in the previous session, though usually the therapist will not be as rigorous in comparing hypotheses with outcomes at this stage of therapy as later. When it comes to reporting feelings, it will be necessary to have the client make clear whether those feelings were ones that might be attributed to "E." or whether Q. is sneaking back from his vacation. Therapists who are used to exploring the "true feelings" of their clients are likely to get into trouble at this point, and I have seen some of them let the session deteriorate into an exploration of Q. rather than of "E."

Usually a replay of the supervisor enactment is in order during the second session. It can be played as it happened and again as it might have happened if the part of "E." were played to the hilt. Exchanges of parts between the client and the therapist are again in order. Subtle variations in feeling tone and in the trend of the dialogue can now be noted during the replays. The therapy session itself is part of the experiment, and its outcomes can be noted on the spot. What happens in the therapy room is a test tube experiment; what happens outside is a field trial. Both are component parts of the experimental undertaking.

But the second session must not bog down in postmortems. The next two days of enactment must be planned, and the peer interaction rehearsed. Here the problem is not likely to be so much a matter of initiating a conversation as contributing to it in the role of "E." The client will have to be alert to how the conversation is going and say what he has to say before it has gone off and left him. The rehearsal should prepare him for the quickened pace of the exchanges he may expect among a group of friends.

As I have already suggested, the enactment that follows the second session may confront the client with the reaction that he is acting strangely. It is just as well to prepare him for it. Rather than being disconcerted by his friends' surprise, he should take it as evidence that he has portrayed "E." as a person unlike Q. It is "E." with whom his friends must cope, and it will be important to him to note the various ways in which they attempt to do it. He may even ask them what they regard as "strange." Certainly it is an important part of any experiment to observe closely relevant changes in the dependent variables.

## SUPPORT FOR THE ENACTMENT

Often a client will ask if he should not tell some of his friends that he is enacting a role. He may particularly want to tell his wife. What this request usually means is that he is anxious—in personal construct terms, confused—and he is willing to sacrifice some of the realistic feedback that he might obtain from the enactment in order to acquire support. If others know that he is "only playing a part," what he does may appear to have more structure. He wants to say, "Look, I am not really this incoherent. Disregard what I am doing, and continue to see me as Q. Q. may not be the most effectual person in the world, but at least he makes a kind of sense."

But there is little to be gained by the enactment if one's friends are invited to ignore the experiment's independent variable—"E." The enactment becomes an exercise rather than an experiment. As an exercise it does little more than put the client through the motions prescribed by the enactment sketch. And only the most insensitive of "learning" theories would attribute much of psychological importance to that!

In personal construct theory, support has a specific meaning, and it is distinguished from reassurance. Support is a broad response pattern on the part of the therapist which permits the client to experiment widely and successfully. Successful experimentation, in terms of the theory's basic assumptions, is that which leads to clear-cut answers to the questions he poses behaviorally, thus tending to dispel anxiety. Success is thus not defined in any of the usual ways of reward, drive reduction, satiation, feeling tone, need fulfillment, etc.

In fixed role therapy the therapist does supply support, and it is important that he do so. He offers candid comments on the client's enactment. He joins the client in predicting what may happen and shares the client's surprise when unexpected results arise. He lends himself to the enactment by playing, as best he can, the wide variety of parts required by the rehearsals. He joins the client in seeking ways to put enactment experiences into words or in clarifying them through reenactment in the therapy room. If the therapist performs his part of the task well, he will minimize the client's urge to divulge the "E. S." role prematurely, as the poor fellow may in an effort to find elsewhere the support he craves.

After all, the client should soon discover that he can experiment much more successfully, that is to say, elicit more definitive answers to his behaviorally posed questions, if he lets the enactment of "E." speak for itself rather than asking his friends what they think of the enactment sketch. The object of "being E." for two weeks is not to amuse his friends or to see if he has at last "found himself" but to realize here and now that his innermost personality is something he creates as he goes along rather than something he discovers lurking in his insides or has imposed upon him from without. What others may say about the "E." sketch is of much less therapeutic concern than what they think and do when confronted with "E." in the flesh. Besides, the client is committed to "being E" for no more than the brief period of the enactment, and he needs to get the most out of the experience.

## THE DEEPER ENACTMENTS

When it comes to confronting his wife with "E.," the client has a more difficult task on his hands. Marriages can fall into rigid patterns, and often the partners, having struck a balance after years of painful interaction, are reluctant to risk breaking the uneasy truce. Yet each of them may wish he could refresh the relationship, and each may doubt the other's willingness to take chances.

It has been my experience that a client is often eager enough to have a different role relation to his wife but dreads what she may say when he attempts it. She may ridicule his fumbling efforts or tell him that he is doing only what he should have started a long time ago. But it has also been my experience that wives (or husbands) find the enactments of their spouses as exciting as they may be disconcerting. Susie M. may be a little nervous about living with

"E. S." for two weeks while her husband is "away on a holiday," but that is not the same as saying she would not like to give it a whirl. Making love as "E. S." can make one feel like a different man, but being made love to by "E. S." can make one feel like a different woman. It is a dull client indeed who, having plunged into this phase of the enactment, does not sense that his life could be very, very different.

For his enactments with a supervisor or with peers, the client can prepare himself thoroughly for a limited series of relatively brief encounters. But keeping up the enactment with his experienced spouse requires sustained attention. Moreover, theirs is a relationship that may long since have settled into a routine. Now he must innovate continually, often violating the unwritten rules by which he and his wife have been unwittingly playing the marriage game. The third rehearsal is designed to meet this condition of sustained role enactment.

There is another matter to be confronted in this rehearsal and in the two which follow it. Many of the constructs in terms of which a client has structured his marriage may be preverbal. He cannot represent them as precisely by symbols as he can the more intellectualized dimensions of his life. He therefore cannot point to them and say, "There, that is a dimension in which I shall discontinue making distinctions;" or, "This is a notion I shall now apply to my daily circumstances in a different way." It is expecting too much of fixed role therapy to hope that the use of preverbal constructions can be so deliberately altered.

But it is not expecting too much to hope that the events produced by the enactment will be different. And when events are different, there is occasion to reflect them upon the reference axes of one's construct system in positions where previous events have not been plotted. Gradually the construct system, verbal and preverbal, adapts itself in some manner to that with which it must cope, and the intentionality of a personal construct slowly aligns itself to the shifts in its extensionality. Changes in operational definitions erode and enrich essential definitions, and one's definition of his marriage or of his spouse is no exception.

Extending the enactment to a situation involving one's parents often runs into a practical difficulty. The parents may be deceased or may live too far away for a day's visit. Sometimes a letter embodying the enactment can be sent to the parents. And, indeed, if it is written, it must be sent, else we shall have indulged in an intellectual exercise without venturing the commitment which makes it into an enactment.

It is all too easy, both for client and therapist, to let fixed role therapy degenerate into intellectualism on the one hand or dissolve into expressionism on the other. The method does not strive for "insight," nor does it invite "self-expression." Personal construct theory, by the way, generally takes a dim view of "insight," observing that this term is more appropriate to naive realism than to a constructive outreach to the world. The theory is a little more tolerant of "self-expression," though that, too, seems often to be predicated on the notion of an inescapable "real self" rather than a self one creates through the process of experimenting with his life.

As with one's spouse, relations with parents involve preverbal constructions and often stalemated interactions. The fourth rehearsal, which is directed particularly at this arena of enactment, must make maximum use of the temporary disengagement of the Q. personality from the situation and the commitment, instead, to an enactment of "E." My experience suggests that a great deal of the value of the parental enactment accrues from the rehearsal in which the client exchanges parts and undertakes to feel and act as one or both of his parents would experience their relationship with him. The therapist can make a great deal of this opportunity by speeding up the tempo of this rehearsal and by playing it out in a number of presumed settings. Since role in the personal construct theoretical sense is based on a construction of another person's outlook, here in this particular rehearsal is an opportunity to take a long delayed second look through the parental spectacles. The client is likely to be surprised by what he sees even before he has confronted his parents in the experimental role of "E."

The final situation, for which a specific enactment is rehearsed, is the one involving religion. Now and then someone who has had little or no experience with fixed role therapy protests that this is much too intimate a matter to be approached as an enactment of any part other than that of the vacationing Q. himself. But the therapist need not prescribe any particular religious doctrine. He and his client can work out together the inferred religious outlook that would characterize such a man as "E. S." is. And why not? Must religion be a reluctant concession to the inevitable, or might it not be a commitment to an undertaking reaching far beyond the present self?

Just how the role is enacted through its religious implications will depend somewhat upon the situation available for its trial. At a minimum this will amount to holding a discussion of religious and ethical matters with others who have similar areas of concern. But I think the therapy works out best if the client takes the pains to search deeply for the implications of the part he has been playing. If he has had an incipient tendency to burlesque the part of "E. S." the man, the religious enactment should bring the client to the point of realizing that any man's commitment to behavior carries with it the profoundest of implications for the meaning his life will have and the deepest of obligations to take account of what happens as a result of his acts.

## TERMINATING THE ENACTMENT

In the end, of course, Q. must come home. The therapist should see that he does and that he takes responsibility for appraising what has happened and for what he himself will choose to undertake. We hope Q. will see his life open to fresh undertakings, and that he will not be unwilling to take candid account of what happens when he embarks upon them. It will be just as well if he decides to discontinue acting the part of "E.," valuable as he may feel the experience turned out to be. His next urgent task is to create the new Q., and that will take a little time, say, a lifetime. But if there was once an "E." who, in the course of a mere two weeks, took on the flesh and vision of a man, there can be a "Q.," and after him a " 'Q.,' " and a " 'Q.!' "

Perhaps it is not necessary to remark at the end of this discussion that there is much more to be said. The reader who is impatient to get on to other matters may think I have tried to say too much. The therapist who undertakes fixed role therapy will certainly wish I had said more.

Let us hope that I have not focused so sharply upon fixed role therapy as to leave the impression that it is the only therapeutic method to be derived from personal construct theory. There are so many other implications of the theory it would be a pity if this particular method I happen to have used in no more than ten per cent of my therapeutic efforts over the years were to be regarded as the definitive explication of personal construct psychotherapeutics.

It would also be a misfortune if I were to leave the impression that the steps I have outlined are the only ones that can profitably be followed. I have reported simply a part of what my experience seems to show, omitting, I fear, some of the interesting variants, such as fixed role therapy with groups of three to a hundred persons. But what experience I have reported I hope has been described in such a way as to make clear underlying assumptions about the nature of man and how he goes about making himself into what he is.

## REFERENCES

1. Bannister, D. A new theory of personality. In B. M. Foss (Ed.), *New horizons in psychology*. Baltimore: Penguin, 1966.
2. Bonarius, J. C. J. Research in the personal construct theory of George A. Kelly. In B. A. Maher (Ed.), *Progress in experimental personality research*. Vol. 2. New York: Academic Press, 1965.
3. Kelly, G. A. *The psychology of personal constructs*. Vols. 1 and 2. New York: Norton, 1955.
4. Kelly, G. A. Theory and therapy in suicide: the personal construct point of view. In E. Shneidman and N. Farberow (Eds.), *The cry for help*. New York: McGraw-Hill, 1961.
5. Kelly, G. A. The language of hypothesis: man's psychological instrument. *J. Indiv. Psychol.*, 1964, **20**, 137–152.
6. Kelly, G. A. The strategy of psychological research. *Bull. Brit. Psychol. Soc.*, 1965, **18**, 1–15.
7. Kelly, G. A. A psychology of the optimal man. In A. Mahrer (Ed.), *Goals of psychotherapy*. New York: Appleton-Century-Crofts, 1966.
8. Kelly, G. A. Sin and psychotherapy. In O. H. Mowrer (Ed.), *Morality and mental health*. Chicago: Rand-McNally, 1966.
9. Patterson, C. H. *Theories of counseling and psychotherapy*. New York: Harper and Row, 1966.
10. Sechrest, L. The psychology of personal constructs: George Kelly. In J. M. Wepman and R. W. Heine (Eds.), *Concepts of personality*. Chicago: Aldine, 1963.

# Chapter 15

# An Introduction to
# Gestalt Therapy

## JAMES S. SIMKIN

James S. Simkin: b. 1919, Winnipeg, Manitoba, Canada.

A.B., in psychology, Central Y.M.C.A. College, 1942. M.A., 1948, Ph.D., 1951, in clinical psychology, University of Michigan.

Lecturer in psychology, University of California at Los Angeles, Extension, 1965-1966. Visiting Associate Professor, Los Angeles State College, 1960-1965. Lecturer, University College, Rutgers University, 1954-1956. Clinical Psychologist in private practice, 1955-date. Chief Clinical Psychologist, V.A. Regional Office, Newark Mental Hygiene Clinic, 1952-1958.

Diplomate in Clinical Psychology, American Board of Examiners in Professional Psychology. Fellow, American Psychological Association, Division of Clinical Psychology. Editor, *Newsletter* of Los Angeles County Psychological Association. Chairman, Southern California Center for Research and Training in Gestalt Therapy. Former member, Executive Board, Gestalt Therapy Institute, New York City. Former member, Board of Examiners, New Jersey Psychological Association.

Articles: Two cases. In Charlotte Buhler, *Values in psychotherapy,* 1962.

Gestalt is a German word meaning whole or configuration. As one psychological dictionary put it: "an *integration* of members as contrasted with a summation of parts" (19). The term also implies a unique kind of patterning. Gestalt therapy is a term applied to a unique kind of psychotherapy formulated by Frederick S. Perls and his followers.

Dr. Perls began, as did many of his colleagues in those days, as a psychoanalyst, having first been trained as a physician in post-World War I Germany. In 1926 he worked under Professor Kurt Goldstein at the Frankfurt Neurological Institute where he was first exposed to the tenets of gestalt psychology but, as he puts it, "was still too preoccupied with the orthodox psychoanalytical approach to assimilate more than a fraction of what was offered [to me]" (5, p. 5). Later Dr. Perls was exposed to the theories and practice of

Wilhelm Reich and incorporated some of the concepts and techniques of Character Analysis into his work.

While serving as a captain in the South African Medical Corps, Perls wrote his first manuscript outlining the emerging theory and technique of personality integration (during 1941–1942), which ultimately appeared as a book, *Ego, Hunger and Aggression,* subtitled, *A Revision of Freud's Theory and Method.* The term Gestalt Therapy was first used as the title of a book on Perls' methods written by him with two co-authors, Professor Ralph Hefferline of Columbia University and Dr. Paul Goodman of New York City.

A thumbnail sketch of the aim of psychoanalysis has sometimes been given as Freud's dictum: "Where Id was shall Ego be," or in other words, to replace the instinctual striving with self-control as mediated by the ego. A capsule comment describing Gestalt Therapy might be Perls': "I and Thou; Here and Now." (With a bow to the late Professor Buber.) In Gestalt Therapy the emphasis is on the present, ongoing situation—which, of course, involves the interaction of at least two people, (in individual therapy) the patient and the therapist.

According to the theory underlying Gestalt Therapy, man is a total organism functioning as a whole rather than an entity split into dichotomies such as mind and body. With the philosophical backing of the brand of humanism represented by Otto Rank, the organism is seen as born with the capacity to cope with life rather than (what I call) the original-sin theory of human development: that the organism must learn to repress or suppress its instinctual (bad) strivings in order to become "civilized." Recently the emergence of existential philosophy appears to be so compatible with the development of Gestalt Therapy that Dr. Wilson Van Dusen in an article on "Existential Analytic Psychotherapy" (18, p. 35) claims that only one psychotherapeutic approach unites the phenomenological approach with existential theory and that is Gestalt Therapy.

Before examining some of the main concepts of Gestalt Therapy and describing actual situations that will give the experiential flavor necessary to an understanding of the approach, I need to do a little more "talking about" the approach (which is really a taboo approach to Gestalt Therapy) in order to supply an adequate context or background.

The theoretical model of the psychodynamic schools of personality, chiefly the Freudian school, envisions the personality as an onion consisting of layers, and each time a layer is peeled away there is still another layer until one finally comes to the core. (Incidentally, in the process of "analysis" of the onion, very little or nothing may be left by the time one comes to the core!) I envision the personality more like a large rubber ball that has only a thick outer layer and is empty inside. The ball floats or swims in an environment, so that at any given moment only a certain portion is exposed to the outside and the rest is submerged in the water. Thus, rather than inventing an unconscious or preconscious to account for behavior that we are unaware of, I would suggest that the unaware behavior is a result of the organism not being in touch with, not sensing, what is out there because the organism is submerged in its own background (environment) or is in contact with (usually preoccupied with) fantasies.

In his recent paper, "A Review of the Practice of Gestalt Therapy," Yontef summarizes the theory of Gestalt Therapy. Organismic needs lead to sensory motor behavior. Once a configuration is formed which has the qualities of a good gestalt, the organismic need which has become foreground is met and a balance or state of satiation or no-need is achieved. "When a need is met, the gestalt it organized becomes complete, and it no longer exerts an influence—the organism is free to form new gestalten. When this gestalt formation and destruction are blocked or rigidified at any stage, when needs are not recognized and expressed, the flexible harmony and flow of the organism/environment field is disturbed. Unmet needs form incomplete gestalten that clamor for attention and, therefore, interfere with the formation of new gestalten" (20, p. 3).

According to Perls, "the most important fact about the figure-background formation is that if a need is genuinely satisfied, the situation changes" (4, p. 571). Thus, in order to bring about change, patients are taught to focus their awareness, which is the primary tool for effecting change in Gestalt Therapy. Frequently, undirected awareness alone is sufficient to ensure change. At other times a person needs to experiment with directing awareness, as in some of the exercises in Perls, Hefferline, and Goodman (8, pp. 116ff.)

Gestalt Therapy emphasizes organismic self-regulation. The organism, in order to survive, needs to mobilize itself and its environment for support. The means whereby the organism contacts its environment is through the mobilization of aggression. If we successfully survive the attempts of others to civilize or enslave us, we pick and choose what we need from our environment to support ourselves. Picking and choosing, however, is not enough. We need also to chew

up and swallow those parts of what is out there that we find edible
and to our liking and thus make it (food or idea or whatever) part
of ourselves. What we do not need, we discard either as waste
products or garbage, etc. Thus, if we are able to mobilize sufficient
aggression to not only pick and choose but also chew up and swallow, we are able to get the support necessary for our survival. It
is important to note that the organism itself picks and chooses, chews
and swallows, etc., and not the significant other out there who determines for us what is palatable, nourishing, etc.

In Gestalt Therapy the therapist is frequently "active" in attempting to have the patient once again learn to use his sensory-motor
equipment. At one time Dr. Perls described the process as a sort of
"losing your mind to come to your senses" activity. This phrase
means that the patient is taught how to direct his awareness via the
resensitization of his primary sensory modalities: to look rather
than stare, to listen rather than overhear, or to play deaf and dumb,
and the like. Directed awareness experiments help the patient get off
what I call the "Why merry-go-round." Many patients trust only
their capacity to intellectualize, think, have fantasies. So when they
become aware of a bit of their own behavior that is incongruous
with their ideal self-image or role, they jump on the "Why merry-
go-round" only to repeat the same unacceptable behavior and then
again go chasing after reasons and explanations. Frequently, learning
*how* by directing his awareness, the patient is able to undo the unacceptable behavior. At least, the patient does not remain an intellectual cripple.

In working with my patients in the "here and now," using the
technique of directed awareness—"Where are you now?" or "What
are you aware of now?" etc., I have discovered that usually verbal
communication is indeed misleading or misdirecting and that body
language is not. Thus, both the patient and I take his symptoms
seriously in that these symptoms—I call them truth buttons or truth
signals—communicate how a patient really feels. If he is in conflict,
experimenting with first taking one side of the conflict in fantasy
and then the other, he will inevitably bring on the body language,
the truth signals, when he takes sides with that aspect of the conflict which is antiself.

Recently a patient was describing a conflict between continuing a
project on his own that he had begun with a partner or dropping the
project. His truth button was a hard, rocklike feeling in the pit of
his stomach. He worked through his conflict by imagining first that

he would continue the project without his partner and would see it through the acquiring of property, erecting a building, and manufacturing the article in the new plant. As he fantasied these various steps, he experienced increasing discomfort in his stomach; his "rock" was getting more and more unbearable. He then proceeded to fantasy dropping the project, abandoning the plans that had already been made plus his investment of time and money. At this point he reported feeling more and more relaxed and comfortable, especially in the pit of his stomach. Experimenting several times (reversing so that at times he fantasied giving up the project first and at other times continuing the project first) brought the same results. The patient became convinced that he knew via his truth button which was the appropriate decision for him.

Being able to self-validate what is the "correct" solution through one's own body language is a tremendous help in the economy of psychotherapy. Many of the transference, countertransference difficulties can be avoided, as well as the pitfalls of interpretation, through teaching oneself and one's patients how to use their symptoms—how to listen to their own body language (14, p. 4).

One of man's most basic experiences is excitement. If you become aware of your excitement and attempt to suppress its overt expression, you inevitably will wind up squeezing or tensing yourself. In addition, you will stop breathing. Perls formulated that excitement minus sufficient support of oxygen equals anxiety. And, as we know, anxiety is the experience least tolerated by the human organism.

In all the cases that I have seen so far, people seeking psychotherapy show an imbalance among their three primary modes of experiencing. Most patients that I see, and this seems to be also true of the bulk of the patients seen by my colleagues, are very dependent on and have overly stressed their development of the intellectual or the "thinking-about" mode of experience. Most of the time, these people are in touch with their thought processes, and their experience is with a fantasy (memory) of the past or a fantasy (wish, prediction) of the future. Infrequently are they able to make contact with their feelings and many are also sensory cripples—not seeing or hearing or tasting, etc.

In the organismically balanced person, there is the capacity to experience intellectually and emotionally and sensorially. The therapeutic task therefore is to help the patient regain the use of his own equipment which has been desensitized at some earlier time and which now desensitized is no longer appropriately at his disposal.

Contrary to the approaches of some schools which stress "insight" or learning "why we behave the way we do," Gestalt Therapy stresses learning "how" and "what" we do. Gestalt therapists are convinced that the only possibility for changing behavior is through an awareness of what we are doing, that is, using our sensory and motor equipment as well as our intellectual equipment and knowing how well we are doing whatever it is we are engaged in.

In Gestalt Therapy we begin with the obvious, with what is ongoing at the moment, recognizing that patients can and do quickly learn to tell us dreams if we stress dreams as the "'royal road to unconscious"! Or, that patients will spend session after session dredging the past (telling us stories about their previous experiences) if we are convinced that cures are dependent on the recall of genetic material. Thus, my question to the patient; "Where are you now?" or "What are you experiencing now?" may lead to the past or a dream, but the patient may just as easily not be in fantasy; he may be experiencing in the "here and now" feelings of expectancy or joy or anger or whatever. He may be concentrating his awareness on sensory experiences, seeing the room we are in or listening to sounds or experiencing his body against the chair he is sitting in or the like.

Many patients are quite startled to discover that they filter every experience through their "thinking machine," that it is almost impossible for them to trust their feelings or senses without first getting approval, so to speak, from their intellect. Frequently, when a patient becomes aware that he is overly dependent on his intellectual equipment, he will try to manipulate me into telling him that he should not be so dependent. He is very fearful of exploring other modes of experience without some support—approval from me—if he cannot experience support within himself. All people need support from within and from without. Each person finds a suitable balance (for him) of self and environmental supports. Most patients have very little or very inadequate self-supports and tend to lean heavily on environmental supports. Then they become very hurt or disappointed or shattered when the other to whom they gave this power (the shifting of self-support to someone out there) fails to live up to their expectations.

During Freud's time, repression appeared to be the most frequently used defense. My own clinical experience leads me to conjecture that projection is now by far the most commonly encountered defense. We project onto another person those attributes or traits that we find unacceptable in ourselves. Then we point our finger at him and castigate him for being whatever it is we do not like in our-selves. This act permits us to maintain a fantasy or fiction of how we imagine we are rather than realizing and accepting how we are. The problem here is the problem of the introject: Swallowing some-thing whole without first adequately chewing it up.

My primary psychotherapeutic task, as I see it, is to help the per-son I am working with accept himself. My patients say to me, in effect, "I want to change how I am." "I don't like myself when I act this way." "I'm so stupid." Yet, they expect to change how they are, not by fully experiencing their behavior and thus their discom-fort, embarrassment, joy, humiliation, excitement, pleasure, shame (feeling) but by judging their behavior as bad, stupid, unacceptable, and the like (intellectual judgments) and thus talking about rather than fully coming in contact with what they do and how they do it. And, paradoxically, these people will be the first to claim the or-ganismic truism that "we learn from experience." They confuse "thinking about" with experiencing.

I trust that if I fully experience what I do and how I behave, I will successfully finish (complete) a particular bit of behavior and learn from this experience. The crux is how I learn. Do I learn by fully experiencing organismically (sensing and feeling as well as judging), or must I restrict my experience to "thinking about?" When my patient says: "I did it again. I got angry at my wife and beat her," my patient is telling me a story (a memory of an event that has already taken place). I may ask, "What are you aware of now?" If his response is, "See how stupid I am; I never learn. I repeat the same idiotic behavior!" I may ask, "In telling me stories?" Once he understands what he is doing now, telling me a story and thus keeping two situations unfinished—the beating of his wife by recalling the memory of the event and the using of this memory with me now, playing the good patient perhaps by telling me how "bad" or "stupid" he is—he has the possibility of learning how he remains stupid. He can only learn by being fully aware of what he is experiencing. The other way he is split into the two (some-times more) aspects of himself.

Dr. Perls referred to these two selves as the top dog and under-dog who are constantly carrying on an internal (infernal might be a better term!) dialogue. "You stupid idiot, why did you beat her again?" "Gee, I'm sorry, I promise I won't do it again." Or, "How many times do I have to tell you not to repeat that silly mistake?" "I'm going to do better next time, I promise." Perls claimed that the underdog self—the promiser—usually wins: he defeats the top dog through unkept promises, sabotage, etc. I believe that the underdog always wins.

The integration of these selves, the full acceptance of how one is rather than how one should be, leads to the possibility of change. As long as people persist in remaining split and not fully acknowledging (taking sides with and experiencing) what and how they are, real change, I believe, is not possible.


## RESOURCES

There has been a sharp increase in interest and the practice of Gestalt Therapy during the past decade. At the time this article is being written in 1971 there are several Gestalt Therapy Institutes throughout the United States with at least three offering systematic training (Cleveland, San Francisco, and Los Angeles).

Several books have appeared in the last three years, ranging from a collection of ten older articles collected by Pursglove (12) and twelve original articles in Perls' *Festschrift* (13) to the excellent collection of twenty-five articles in their book on theory, technique, and application by Fagan and Shepherd (1).

Kogan (2), unhappy with the (then) absence of a systematic bibliography of source material in Gestalt Therapy, collected and published a pamphlet that lists books, articles, papers, films, tapes, institutes, and the gestalt therapist directory. He has some ninety references. Fagan and Shepherd list over sixty. Yontef cites forty-five in his paper.

Perls' autobiographical book, *In and Out of the Garbage Pail* (7) and Simkin's interview with him in 1966 (15) give much of the historical background of the development of Gestalt Therapy. Also of historical interest are the two excellent papers written by Perls' widow, Laura Perls (9, 10).

Practically none of the Gestalt Therapy literature has been channeled through conventional sources during the three decades of its existence. Major exceptions are Fritz Perls' article in 1948 in the *American Journal of Psychotherapy* (4) and Polster's more recent article in *Psychotherapy* (11).

Until 1969 the only films depicting Gestalt Therapy were all by Perls. His are still the primary source (over 30 varied films) with the addition of Simkin's training film (16).

An illustrative excerpt from a training film follows:

Jim:      What do you experience at this moment?

Colman:    A feeling of sadness . . . I don't know why. Because I said that they were in, I said I wanted them in.

Jim:      Yeah. Colman, would you be willing to say now that you are sad.

Colman:    I am sad.

Jim:      Again.

Colman:    I'm sad. I'm sad. And I'm angry.

Jim:      Yeah.

Colman:    Crazy.

Jim:      Okay, add that. "I'm sad, I'm angry, I'm crazy."

Colman:    I'm sad, I'm angry, I'm crazy.

Jim:      And now?

Colman:    Now I feel good again.

Jim:      Yeah. Now I think you're beginning to catch on. Any time that you acknowledge, really go with how you are, you finish . . . let go. You are sad, you are angry, you are crazy, you are happy, and so on. If you stay with . . . all your me's.

Colman:    My sad, angry, crazy me.

Jim:      Yeah. Okay, I'd like to stop at this point.

This excerpt illustrates how, by Colman being aware (responsible), his sadness changes first to anger and then his anger changes to perplexity and then he experiences the humor of his situation and then feels "good again." Much of the impact of this transaction, however, is not conveyed through the arid medium of the printed word. The best way to fully experience Gestalt Therapy is obviously through the experiential mode.

As Fagan and Shepherd say in their preface: "in Gestalt Therapy, much importance is attached to tone of voice, posture, gestures, facial expression, etc., with much of the import and excitement coming from work with changes in these nonverbal communications. . . . Fortunately the increasing availability of Gestalt films and tapes helps in making the nonverbal communications more accessible" (1, p. viii). Or, in the words of the late Fritz Perls, "To suffer one's own death and to be reborn is not easy" (6).

## REFERENCES

1. Fagan, J. & Shepherd, I. L. *Gestalt therapy now.* Palo Alto, Calif.: Science & Behavior Books, 1970.
2. Kogan, J. *Gestalt therapy resources.* San Francisco: Lode Star Press, 1970.
3. Lederman, J. *Anger and the rocking chair: Gestalt awareness with children.* New York: McGraw Hill, 1969.
4. Perls, F. S. Theory and technique of personality integration. *Amer. J. Psychother.*, 1948, **2**, 565–586.
5. Perls, F. S. *Ego, hunger and aggression.* London: Allen & Unwin, 1947. (Republished: New York: Random House, 1969.)
6. Perls, F. S. *Gestalt therapy verbatim.* Lafayette, Calif.: Real People Press, 1969.
7. Perls, F. S. *In and out of the garbage pail.* Lafayette, Calif.: Real People Press, 1969.
8. Perls, F. S., Hefferline, R. F., & Goodman, P. *Gestalt therapy.* New York: Julian Press, 1951. (Republished: New York: Dell, 1965.)
9. Perls, L. Notes on the psychology of give and take. *Complex*, 1953, **9**, 24–30.
10. Perls, L. Two instances of Gestalt therapy. *Case reports in clinical psychology.* Brooklyn: Kings County Hospital, 1956.
11. Polster, E. A contemporary psychotherapy. *Psychother.: Theory, Res. Prac.*, 1966, **3**, 1–6.
12. Pursglove, P. D. (Ed.) *Recognitions in gestalt therapy.* New York: Funk & Wagnalls, 1968.
13. Simkin, J. S. (Ed.) *Festschrift for Fritz Perls.* Los Angeles: Author, 1968.
14. Simkin, J. S. Innovations in Gestalt therapy techniques. Unpublished manuscript, 1968.
15. Simkin, J. S. *Individual gestalt therapy: interview with Dr. Frederick Perls.* Audio-tape recording, A. A. P. Tape Library, No. 31. Philadelphia, Pa., 1967.
16. Simkin, J. S. *In the now.* A training film. Beverly Hills, 1969.
17. Simkin, J. S. *An introduction to the theory of Gestalt therapy.* Cleveland: Gestalt Institute of Cleveland, No. 6., 1966.
18. Van Dusen, W. Existential analytic psychotherapy. *Amer. J. Psychoanal.*, 1960, **20**, 35–40.
19. Warren, H. C. *Dictionary of psychology.* New York: Houghton Mifflin, 1934.
20. Yontef, G. M. *A review of the practice of gestalt therapy.* Los Angeles: Trident Shop, California State College, 1969.

# Chapter 16

# Some Powerful Tools and Techniques for Positive Psychotherapy

## ERNEST M. LIGON

Ernest M. Ligon: b. 1897, Iowa Park, Texas.
A.B., M.A., in psychology, Texas Christian University, 1921. B.D., Yale Divinity School, 1924. Ph.D., in psychology, Yale University, 1927. LL.D., Texas Christian University, 1948.
Founder and Director of Union College Character Research Project, 1935–date. Professor and Chairman, Department of Psychology, Union College, 1929–1962.
Books: *Dimensions of Character* (1956). *A Greater Generation* (1948). *Their Future is Now* (1939). *The Psychology of Christian Personality* (1935). (Co-author) *The Marriage Climate* (1963).

There is no such thing as a 'mental illness' in any significantly meaningful sense." (1) The major inspiration for this paper is the conviction that many of the clients who seek guidance from the psychotherapist can best be helped by giving them positive things to do, with little or no emphasis on their negative problems. In other words, this idea implies a frequent disregard of the symptoms and a concentration on the development of positive reactions and attitudes that can supplant the maladapted responses. Occupational therapy is the classical forerunner of this principle. I am not a practicing psychotherapist, but in my lifelong exploration of human potential, basic principles have emerged. I am bold enough to hope that many psychotherapists will test these principles in their practices with those clients who, as their intuitive judgment suggests, are likely to respond to such an approach.[1]

It may well be that the reader will wish to know where he is going and what he will see along the way before he starts on such a journey

---

[1] I very much hope that those who do so will share their successes and failures with me.

as this paper represents. The research in our laboratory has disclosed to us three dimensions of character. The degree to which an individual is able to grow in these three dimensions not only measures his ability to achieve his own unique maximum potential but is also significant evidence of his mental health. The first half of the paper is devoted to these three dimensions. One strives toward his potential in the first dimension when he finds a dominating purpose toward which his life is directed. The second dimension is measured by the degree to which a body of integrated basic convictions determines the courageous quality of his behavior. The third is measured by the breadth of his social convictions.

The second half of the paper is concerned with the skills for growing in strength of character. The first two skills are less commonly recognized as such. These are skills for using one's patterns of uniqueness and skills for using the scientific method which the individual can employ in his daily life. The other three are more commonly recognized. They are learning skills that can be used in psychotherapy. Many of the basic skills of scientific decision-making are equally valuable in positive psychotherapy. Finally, there are the social influence skills that give strength to personality, so much needed by many who seek the aid of the psychotherapist. The role of these five areas of skills will be foreseen in the discussion of each of the three dimensions of strength of character.

With this brief road map, we are now ready to start our journey through positive psychotherapy.

Man is born as a unique individual. He is identical with no one else who ever lived or who ever will live. For him, therefore, there is a maximum potential, which if he discovers it and achieves it, will give life its deepest meaning. Anyone who helps him find it is doing psychotherapy in a most profound way.

The degree to which a man achieves his own maximum potential can be considered the best evaluation of his character. For example, early in life a girl envisioned her maximum potential destiny in becoming a nurse. She allowed nothing, not even the urge for marriage, to change her determination in the slightest. She achieved high success, and now, in her sixties, finds life full and, for her, complete. It is probable that another course would have produced frustration and conflict which could have caused her much unhappiness and weakened the strength of her personality.

What is the role of ethics and morals in character? Our research (11) leads us to believe that the sum total of one's basic convictions constitutes his working philosophy of life. To whatever extent they guide him toward his maximum potential unique destiny, they become a powerful force in his mental health.

Human personality can be regarded as the ongoing investment of one's energies. Among these are his emotional energies. It seems probable that each person has, as a part of his basic endowment, a fairly constant amount of emotional energy to invest, just as he does physical or intellectual energy. One does not ask, then, whether someone is emotional, but how he invests his emotional energy. He can invest it in such negative forms as anger, fear, depression, and so on. But he can also invest it in such positive forms as love, courage, high vision, curiosity, and the like. An important role for positive psychotherapy, therefore, is to guide the client toward investing his emotional energy toward achieving his maximum potential.

## CHARACTER, MAXIMUM POTENTIAL, AND MENTAL HEALTH

It will be obvious that character development is the central core of positive psychotherapy.

Character, as has already been pointed out, can be described as a force having three dimensions. It can be strengthened by the development of skills relevant to these dimensions. Purposiveness, the first of these dimensions, is probably the most integrating single force in personality. If, therefore, one examines the strength of his inherited aptitudes and trains them toward achieving his maximum potential life purpose (his destiny), this strengthens his character in this dimension.

The term character has often been used to refer only to morals and ethics. Our research indicates that such a concept of character is not likely often to be very effective in psychotherapy. Indeed, a sense of guilt, especially if it becomes too strong, is more likely to produce maladjustment than mental health. A deep sense of shame is indeed characteristic of much mental disease.

Our research leads us to measure character in terms of strength. This is certainly a far more useful concept for psychotherapy. Fear, anger, hate, suspicion—these are symptoms of mental illness. But the man of strong character is likely to show courage rather than fear, social confidence and breadth rather than hate or suspicion, a sense of purpose rather than inferiority. His ethics grow mainly out of his convictions about these healthy character aspects.

A large proportion of people who are in need of psychotherapy exhibit feelings of inferiority as one of their basic symptoms. How, then, do we apply positive psychotherapy? Developing strength in this area of character, just as is true for achieving progress in athletics or in intellectual fields, requires the mastery of skills. Positive psychotherapy, then, consists essentially in the mastery of appropriate skills of the types already named.

## DIMENSIONS OF STRENGTH OF CHARACTER

### Purpose, Unique Maximum Potential Destiny

The first dimension has to do with the degree to which a sense of purpose—in its highest form, a vision for one's unique destiny—guides a person's behavior. Much mental maladjustment has as one contributing factor lack of sufficient purpose in life. In such cases the psychotherapist will do well to begin his therapy by helping his client to find a deeper purpose for life. This recognition of the importance of purpose in mental health is not new in psychotherapy. Occupational therapy has been used for many years. It is generally recognized by psychologists that purpose is probably the most integrating single force in personality.

But now let us see how this "personality purpose" can be influenced by the concept of uniqueness. A biologist recently pointed out that the simple fruit fly has five thousand genes. Therefore, he said, it can be stated with confidence that no two fruit flies were ever completely identical. Every fruit fly is unique. If this is true of so simple an organism as a fruit fly, how much more true it is for human beings. Each human being has ten thousand million cells in his brain alone, give or take a few hundred thousand. In our own laboratory we have tested several thousand children, endeavoring to measure them in fifty-nine different traits (10). We have never found any two identical profiles. This is evidence that every person is unique.

What has been even more astonishing to us is that the correlation between an individual's endowment in any particular trait (such as IQ, for example) and the quality of his performance is remarkably low. The correlation between IQ and college marks, for example, is seldom higher than 0.40. This accounts for only 16% of the variance, which means that, in general, only 16% of college performance can be attributed to intelligence. Is it not reasonable to assume that if the student can find the maximum potential which is the potential of his unique endowment resources, his resultant achievement could be of such magnitude as to be almost infinite. For the psychotherapist, then, convincing the client, first, that he is unique is an important step toward challenging him to search for his unique maximum potential purpose. The personality integration that can be brought about by this is surely effective positive psychotherapy.

Many will ask whether high achievement is possible by all. "Can a feebleminded person achieve as much as a genius, if he can find his maximum potential destiny?" This is a pertinent question for which, at present at least, the realistic answer must be "no." Nevertheless, the range of intelligence in which we have found this principle of potential, even with our present knowledge, probably includes at least two thirds of people. At the risk of being considered unrealistic, I would point out that the maximum potential of the brain, even of the feebleminded, is still far from having been fully explored.

If this faith in one's maximum potential destiny is based upon a deep religious faith, the end result is still more effective. I have often presented this concept to religiously oriented youth in this way: "What did the Lord have in mind when He made you?" Obviously, this over-simplified expression is another way to express the assumption that the forces of the universe are so organized that any large coordinated group of them, such as human personality, must have some unique potential role, more powerful than any other possible role for that person to play.

Here are two brothers, high school age, one brilliant and headed toward an academic career; the other less bright, but physically superior. The latter was very jealous of his brighter, more spectacular brother. He had a strong religious faith. I suggested to him, "What right have you to question the Lord's will? If He had wanted you to do what he wants your brother to do, He would have made you that way." This statement solved the problem for him, and both men, today, are strong influences in their community.

Here is a boy, IQ 95, small, not well coordinated. He was caught stealing from the choir loft of his church while the choir was in church. His father had been a great football player. His mother was brilliant and wished him to become a lawyer. Obviously, he could do neither. His tests revealed that he had outstanding art aptitude. His course in school was changed to emphasize this talent. He is today a competent commercial artist. Nothing was ever said to him about his stealing. This case is a prototype of positive psychotherapy.

Make sure that you distinguish clearly between the concept of individual differences and the concept of uniqueness. Individual differences are due to the fact that for any given characteristic of human nature, such as height, weight, intelligence, musical aptitude, and so on, men differ over a wide range. All too often a person may choose his vocation on the basis of just one of these. One who is very bright becomes a college professor; the very tall athlete, a basketball player; the highly endowed in music, a musician.

The concept of uniqueness, on the other hand, is based upon the patterns among these individual differences which, in reality, constitute the personality. Many people, for example, have approximately average IQ. Many are of average height. But no two individuals have all characteristics at the same level. In other words, there is no such person as "an average man." It is in the pattern of characteristics that one finds his destiny.

Here is a man with striking physical characteristics who is well above average in intelligence, has remarkable mathematics ability, is high in characteristics important for administration, and has high social vision. This man has found his destiny in administering a research organization dedicated to social vision. For each of the listed traits he might have chosen a different vocation, but in the total pattern he found his maximum potential destiny.

The psychotherapist who uses only one or two outstanding characteristics as a guide for helping the client to find strong purpose is proceeding less effectively than if he seeks for the maximum potential destiny of the client growing out of the client's unique pattern of characteristics.

Achieving one's maximum potential destiny requires much learning. Even for the lower animals, learning is health-producing. Pribram (12) has shown that rats living in a learning-rich environment develop larger brains than those brought up in an environment in which learning is impossible.

Furthermore, when one has an ultimate purpose for his learning, he goes about the process with greater enthusiasm and greater effectiveness than when the learning is done for its own sake.

Here is a young woman working in a research laboratory all summer, learning and applying many research skills to assigned problems. Her father, a distinguished scientist, reported afterward that she could have passed any first-year research design course in a large university. She probably was not aware that she was learning research design at all. She was dealing with problems, mastering, in each case, the tools necessary for doing so effectively. The human mind is at its best when it is learning skills with which to achieve a purpose. This principle can certainly be used frequently in psychotherapy.

Let us note another characteristic of this concept of uniqueness which will interest the psychotherapist. A sense of inferiority is obviously a social phenomenon. One can feel inferior only when he compares himself with someone else. If he can acquire social skills by which he can carry social influence, this inferiority often disappears. The mastering of social influence skills, then, becomes another useful form of positive psychotherapy.

A young woman who was quite seclusive and unhappy was physically unattractive and had poor taste in clothes. But she did have a very good memory. She was a member of a large, rapidly changing youth group. She was urged by her counselor to get an attractive hairdo and some becoming clothes, in each case securing the advice of a competent professional. The first result was that she was made chairman of the social committee in the youth group and easily acquired skills of integrating new members into the group effectively. Not only could she remember their names, but she was able to bring together people with common interests. The ultimate results were equally spectacular, leading to presidency of the youth group and, eventually, to happy marriage. Today she is one of the social leaders in her city.

Achieving dominating purpose is strengthened by the mastery of lay-scientist skills. The skills of systematic observation are among these. Even so simple a technique as organizing observed performances into successes and failures usually makes it possible to evaluate them more accurately. It is valuable to teach the client how to look at all of his skills and abilities and how to see them as an organized whole; in other words, to see his unique personality. This can prevent overworry about incidental failures. It also prevents such experiences as showing deep despondency at one moment because of a minor failure only to follow it in the next by attempting a performance in an area in which his low competence almost guarantees another failure. A careful objective evaluation of his abilities can often prevent either from happening by challenging him to attempt performances in which he is likely to succeed.

A man's striving toward his life purposes consists, for the most part, of a succession of decisions. If one makes these decisions on the basis of fear, anger, ignorance, hearsay, or prejudice, he is likely to find life a continual succession of maladjustments. This may reach the level of requiring psychotherapy. If, however, he can be taught objective methods of decision-making and can acquire skill in using them, he is far more likely not only to achieve his purposes but is also more likely to make healthy-minded decisions.

Here, then, is the first dimension of strength of character and an introduction to some of the skills toward achieving growth in it. The skills themselves will be described more fully in the second half of this paper.

## Convictions Based upon One's Philosophy of Life

In a recent research project in which high school youth were major participants, the purpose was to discover social influence skills which enable one to stand by his convictions against social pressure to the contrary. The first and strongest skill that emerged, surprisingly enough, is that one must have some basic convictions to stand by. In other words, he must develop a sound philosophy of life and, upon the basis of it, create an integrated set of convictions growing out of it. This fact is characteristic of the body of evidence that has led us to set forth basic convictions as the second dimension of strength of character. A sense of guilt underlies much mental illness requiring psychotherapy. This sense of guilt is often quite irrational. Its solution often lies in finding a rational basis for making moral judgments.

Psychotherapists will agree that individual differences play an important role in one's convictions and in his sense of guilt. What is not so commonly recognized is that a systematic examination of the individual differences of a client and of the resultant pattern of uniqueness can become a powerful factor in creating a body of convictions for the individual which, in turn, contribute to mental health. Even moral principles are not general but, in part at least, unique to the individual.

Here is a young man who plays a leading role in many of our civic organizations from the Chamber of Commerce to the Rotary Club. His individual endowments are such that it would be quite wrong for him not to do so. For me, however, since I am research-minded, the same program would be quite wrong as well as disastrous for the community.

A healthy philosophy of life and well-thought-out basic convictions growing out of it are important in mental health. To be sure, one can express a great deal of piety and religiosity and be mentally unhealthy in the process. Nor is it possible to say that mental health cannot be achieved without adherence to a formal religion. It is, nevertheless, true that a deep faith can be a powerful asset in the search for mental health.

Everyone faces pain and suffering, frustration, and failure. If he sees this as evidence of a heartless, mechanical universe in which "omnipotent matter rolls on in its relentless way," as Bertrand Russell (5) put it, then depression and fear are common results. If, on the other hand, one has faith that there is order and purpose in the universe which give meaning to love and faith, then the worst that life deals out for him does not shake his basic convictions nor his mental soundness. Who has not seen a deep religious faith carry a man through almost incredible pain and disaster?

Here are sixty young people in a conference. They have been brought up in Christian churches but now wish to decide for themselves whether they can accept and endeavor to live by some of the major concepts set forth in the *Sermon on the Mount*. First, they study the evidence to make sure that they know what each teaching means; then they try to discover what purpose it can serve in their lives; then what skills need to be mastered to apply it effectively; next, what learning methods they will need in order to be able to master these skills; and, finally, what learning goals they can set to practice the principles involved. This schedule for learning can serve as a master pattern for positive psychotherapy where the needs of the client make it relevant.

It is clear that learning skills play a major role in the building of convictions into personality. It is not likely that religion will produce either powerful leadership or mental health unless the convictions implied in it are carefully defined and the skills fully mastered which are essential to living them. A young minister once said facetiously that a part of his regular Saturday night prayer was that one of his most ardent and devout parishioners would not be able to come to church the following morning. His reason was that she was so deficient in social skills that she usually antagonized a sizable portion of his congregation, especially the youth. In this process, she became increasingly unhappy because of her obvious unpopularity. The psychotherapy that she most needed was training in social influence skills. It should be obvious, then, that mastery of basic social influence skills will contribute substantially to one's social adjustment and, thus, to the elimination of many of the most important causes of the maladjustments in need of psychotherapy.

In our modern complex world, a decision as to which course of action to take, in matters involving one's convictions, is rarely so clear-cut as not to require a choice between at least two alternative courses of action; and, often, a choice not easily made. Such difficult decisions can easily lead to serious mental conflicts within the individual which, in turn, cause him to exhibit behavior calling for psychotherapy. The therapist should carefully consider the possibility that the problem lies in the client's lack of skills to make decisions rather than in what decision to make in any particular situation.

Teaching him some of the basic skills of scientific decision-making may add greatly to his confidence in his decisions, as well as to his skill in making wise ones. Some of these skills will be described later in this paper. They range from very simple ones to highly complex ones. How many of them a given client can learn must be left to the judgment of the therapist.

The sense of inadequacy that underlies so much mental difficulty grows out of the assumption that some people are better than others and that the client is inferior. The concept of uniqueness makes this assumption meaningless. If one is uniquely fitted for one unique destiny, there is no one else with whom he must compete in relation to it. To achieve this unique destiny, however, one must master the skills needed both to discover the nature of his uniqueness and to apply that uniqueness to the decisions and tasks to be faced each day, involving his convictions and his vision.

Here is a man who joins a city church. When asked what he could do, he replied that he could shake hands and, in this way, exhibit the quality of his faith. For three decades he did just this, standing each week in the doorway and shaking hands. He was given much credit for building that church into one of the largest in the city. He could, indeed, shake hands; but in the doing, he could congratulate the sucessful, comfort the sorrowing, encourage the discouraged—indeed, give to each man what he most needed.

There are few areas in which people make more unfounded generalizations than in this area of convictions. "Young people are going to the dogs," has been a commonly held conviction for many generations. It is a rare individual who is able to look objectively at the facts before making such a judgment. Then, too, some of our convictions, however rational or irrational, are likely to be among our most ego-involved attitudes.

Here is a man who holds a number of ill-defined convictions about how people ought to behave. His resultant antagonisms toward his associates when he believes them to be guilty of what he considers to be wrong is often so great that it disturbs his whole personality. If he could learn objective skills of evaluation, his judgments would be far more rational and his decisions about action far more creative.

Here, then, is the second dimension of strength of character. The degree to which a man has a well-rounded, consistent philosophy of life, has spelled out the convictions necessary to live it effectively, and has mastered the skills for doing so, the stronger his character and the greater the level of his mental health.

## Breadth of Effective Social Vision

The third dimension of strength of character we entitle breadth of effective social vision. Certainly, the force of a man's character is bounded, in part, at least, by the number of people whom he serves or influences. Psychotherapists will agree that social isolation is not conducive to mental health. If, therefore, their clients can be given the vision for broader social service and taught the skills for achieving it, this concept is conducive to mental health.

The fact that every individual is unique means that he ought to be dealt with uniquely. Some of our most useless social conflicts come about when we make judgments about our fellows on the basis of generalized principles, which, in the very nature of the case, overlook the principle of uniqueness. Learning to expect one's husband to think like a man and one's wife to think like a woman is necessary for successful marriage. If then a psychotherapist can teach his client to master the skills for perceiving the nature of the uniqueness of each person with whom he deals, and to make his judgments on the basis of it, he will contribute to the client's mental health, as well as to his social effectiveness.

Here are two people whom every psychotherapist will recognize. Both frequently experience, as does everyone, disappointments in their social contacts. The one makes these an excuse for maladjustive reactions. The other accepts them as inevitable and holds to his faith in mankind in spite of them. A firm faith in the basic goodness of others will add to any man's strength of character and to his social effectiveness. This statement presupposes, however, his ability to assess the minor strengths and weaknesses of others, so that the latter especially, do not prevent his seeing the former, or even blind him to them.

It will sound like a truism and, indeed, it is one, to suggest that the quality of one's social influence skills contributes not only to his success in carrying out the social dimension of his life purposes but, also, greatly decreases his social frustrations and thus contributes to his mental health. Psychotherapists, then, who train their clients in social influence skills add strength to their potential for mental health, as well as breadth to the social vision of which they are capable.

As is true of the other skill areas, learning skills must be a function of the individual himself, of the social groups whom he would influence, and of the types of influence he hopes to exert. Training in complex learning skills is clearly effective psychotherapy.

For example, if a young man were joining the sales force of a large company, he would be subjected to extensive training in social skills, such as Dale Carnegie training. It would be assumed that extensive learning would be essential to the social skills necessary for success.

It is highly probable that much mental disease comes from the inability of the individual to exhibit the social skills essential to carrying out his social responsibilities. It follows that the ability to learn in the mastery of such skills is an effective tool in psychotherapy.

There are few areas of behavior in which the uniqueness patterns of the behaver and the uniqueness characteristics of those with whom he is communicating are more important than in the success or failure of one's social vision.

Here is a committee of five who must work closely together. Each is different temperamentally, as well as in training, from the other four. Their "tolerance" of one another, indeed, their appreciation and respect for one another, make it a most effective committee.

In working with other people, countless decisions must be made as to the most effective way to deal with them. Certainly, a succession of social frustrations, with resultant feelings of social failure, can easily be a contributing factor to serious maladjustment. On the other hand, here is a young woman who was hired temporarily for clerical work on a large staff. She was retained permanently, in part at least, because of the social radiance that her personality added to the staff morale. If a group of people were ranked in terms of social skill—and these terms often require wise decision-making—this ranking would correlate highly with their ranking in terms of mental health.

Here is a group of fathers searching for their most effective roles as fathers. They applied some relatively simple lay-scientist skills to the problem and produced such remarkable findings that a book was published describing them (9). These lay-scientist skills, to be described later, are also essential in carrying out one's social vision.

For example, in our social relationships we are likely to put far too much emphasis on the negative experiences and to observe so haphazardly that any judgments based upon what we have seen are certain to be biased and inaccurate. There are some relatively simple lay-scientist skills that a psychotherapist can teach to most of his clients which will lead them to accurate and creative insights of great value to their social effectiveness and, in turn, to their mental health.

Here, then, is a bird's-eye view of the third dimension of strength of character. It is now time to turn to the skills themselves with which to grow in such strength and, in the process, to achieve good mental health.

## SKILLS FOR GROWTH IN STRENGTH OF CHARACTER

Now, let us look at the inverse of this concept of positive psychotherapy. In the first part of the paper, the three dimensions of strength of character have been described, with special emphasis on the role various kinds of skills can contribute to gaining strength in each dimension.

Five areas of these skills have been referred to in the discussion of the three dimensions. They are: (1) skills for the use of one's unique characteristics, (2) lay-scientist skills, (3) learning skills, (4) decision-making skills, and (5) skills of social influence. The potential of these skills has been derived from action research, which means that they have been developed by lay people and are being continually refined by scientific observation and evaluation.

The mastery of these skills can play a positive role in the personality of the client in many ways. These skills also play a role in the work of the psychotherapist himself. They provide effective tools, if he masters them, by which he can more effectively influence his client. They also constitute a set of skills with which he can train his clients. Let us now examine them in more detail.

### Skills of Uniqueness

First, there are skills for the objective evaluation of, and effective use of, one's uniqueness. If every individual is unique and has a maximum potential destiny for which he is uniquely fitted—if he can discover and achieve it—then such negative attitudes as professional jealousy and feelings of inferiority have no meaning. "The kingdom of heaven is within you," becomes more and more meaningful. One's only competition is with his own potential destiny. Achieving it is a significant role in the very nature of the universe. To whatever extent, then, the client can be taught the skills of drawing an accurate picture of his own uniqueness, and thus can discover the maximum potential usefulness to which his uniqueness can be directed, it becomes a powerful force for positive psychotherapy.

Here is a staff scientist who is experiencing a considerable amount of depression and feelings of inadequacy. The outside observer would find this difficult to understand. She successfully directs a sizeable staff into high achievement in a most important area of research. She herself has gained national renown as outstanding among those doing research in this area. Indeed, even this catalogue of her achievements could be much further extended. Why, then, is she depressed? Her own answer is that she, at present, does not feel a sense of making progress. Part of this, she says, is that there are a few attitudes which, while not unique to her, are, for her, a part of the picture which is her uniqueness. One of those is that she must have deadlines to meet. To tell her that such attitudes are irrational serves no useful purpose. A meaningful solution must respect and satisfy the unique drives indicated. This personality habit is, of course, a part of her strength, as well as a source of occasional unhappiness.

Let me describe a few of the tools that we have found useful in this process of exploring uniqueness.

First of all, there is the Character Research Project (CRP) *Personality Profile* (8), which includes fifty-nine traits. This particular set of traits has been developed over many years for popular use. There are physical traits, mental variables, the special aptitudes, social traits, and emotional attitudes. We have tested hundreds of children, youths, and adults over a period of thirty years. We have never found any two profiles alike. We have used such instruments as the Strong Interest Inventory (14) extensively. Again, no two were ever filled out exactly alike. We have used many other instruments, such as the Bernreuter Scale (2), and still the uniqueness pattern persists.

Note, however, that it is one thing to show that people are all different. It is quite another to identify their uniqueness patterns, which are configurations growing out of the many traits that characterize the individual.

In order to demonstrate dramatically this concept of uniqueness, let us try a simple experiment. Here are six hypothetical people. We will list just three of their key traits and oversimplify the measurement of these.

Two, "A" and "B," are of modest intelligence, far below college level potential. "A" has outstanding physical endowments and only average social-emotional strength. "B" is just the opposite in these last two traits with strong social and emotional strength but much more modest physical endowment.

Would it surprise you if "A" (with his only average social-emotional strength) should exhibit a sense of easygoingness to life, with no great expectation of himself as being even able to do anything of importance? Yet, here is a distinguished gardener, well known in his community and highly respected by all, who pretty much fits these three characteristics.

As for "B" (with strong social-emotional strength and only avererage physical endowment), you can well imagine such a person showing a strong fear of failure and experiencing feelings of jealousy and inferiority. Yet, here is a department store floorwalker in one community who shows just these characteristics. He does his job well and is a highly respected man in the city. Can you imagine that if each had come to a psychotherapist—"A" about his feeling of indifference and surrender, "B" concerning his fear of failure and feelings of jealousy and inferiority—the best psychotherapy would be to find for each his unique maximum potential destiny?

Let us picture two other men, "C" and "D," both with average college level IQ: "C" with high physical endowment and low social-emotional strength; but "D" with low physical endowment and high social-emotional strength.

Again, it would not surprise you that "C" (with his high physical endowment and low social-emotional strength) shows a surrender reaction to almost everything except athletics, even then with not much real enthusiasm for it. Yet, here is a department store manager of whom these three characteristics are quite descriptive.

As for "D" (low physical endowment and high social-emotional strength), one might not be surprised at a rather strutting approach to life, boasting and strutting to the disgust of all and, of course, experiencing strong feelings of social conflict. Yet, one of the most successful salesmen I know can be described with these three characteristics.

In these two cases as before, the search for their maximum potential destinies might be the best kind of psychotherapy for each.

Our final two hypothetical personalities, "E" and "F," both have very high IQ's. "E" has rather low physical endowment and modest social and emotional strength. "F," equally brilliant, has modest physical endowment and low social-emotional strength.

One might expect "E" (with low physical endowment and average social-emotional strength) to have rather strong feelings of inferiority because of his self-perception of lack of physical strength, especially believing that others think of him as being effeminate. It would be easy, however, to find many an outstanding college professor whose learning is remarkable and whose influence with his students is a significant factor in the lives of many of them for whom this configuration of traits would be fairly descriptive.

As for "F" (average physical endowment and low social-emotional strength), can you see him experiencing frustration in an administrative position that has been given to him because of his academic achievements? Imagine the same man in pure research. He is far more likely to experience great success and deep satisfaction.

Here, then, is the basic principle of uniqueness. Note that its strength does not lie primarily in the psychotherapist's ability to recognize individual differences, or to measure them with scientific tools, or even to avoid the use of stereotype solutions to problems. The concept of uniqueness becomes a force in personality when the client comes to believe that he is unique with a unique destiny; that he can draw an accurate picture of his uniqueness; and that his major task is to decide, at least tentatively, what is his unique maximum potential destiny and to set out toward mastering the skills and taking the steps necessary to achieve it.

There are many tools available by which this goal can be achieved. Among our CRP publications, *The Personality Profile* has been most widely used with success, with the client himself taking the major role in creating it. The CRP Publication, *In Search of a Vision for Your Life* (6) can be of real value in deciding on a unique destiny. *The Marriage Climate* (13) will open up new and positive approaches to achieving a unique and highly effective marriage.

This concept of potential has great potential in itself. For example, it may prove to be the solution of the perennial teen-age problem. For the most part, undesirable teen-age movements are characterized by attempting to dress and act alike. The concept of uniqueness is quite the opposite. The real leaders among the teen-agers are rarely conformists in the sense of the undesirable teen-age groups. I recently spoke to the student councils of ten of our area high schools.

Not one boy had fallen for the long-hair craze. None spent undue time watching television. Not one smoked. All were searching for their maximum potential destinies.

*Lay-Scientist Skills*

The lay-scientist principle is probably the most revolutionary one in the concept of positive psychotherapy. Stated succinctly, it is that if the layman can learn to utilize some of the powerful tools of science in his daily life and in his social actions, he can contribute toward bringing the power of the scientific method into our social institutions and exhibit creative mental health for himself. The use of such tools, however, must become an integral part of his personality if they are to achieve the high level of mental health of which they are capable. This aspect is more difficult than mastering the skills. Even distinguished scientists can be as opinionated and stubborn as anyone else when they approach problems outside their laboratories.

The last half-century of scientific achievement, however, has convinced everyone both of the effectiveness of the scientific method for seeking truth and of the miracles that are possible when it is mastered. The great achievements of science in the physical world, however, have done little or nothing to improve man's interpersonal relations. Politics is as emotional and irrational as ever. International relations, with the help of the physical sciences, bids fair to destroy the human race. Democracy in our day can work only if its citizens can learn scientific methods for making their political decisions. Psychotherapy may well make its greatest contribution to mankind when its clients learn to seek the truth and to master scientific tools for doing so successfully.

First, let us observe a few of the irrational methods by which most of us not only find a distorted truth, but often develop personal maladjustments and social conflict in the process.

In the first place, there is the innate tendency, common to us all, that has been referred to as present-mindedness, which gives the present a far greater role in our actions than any objective evaluation could possibly justify. Here is a teenager who is not invited to a coveted social event. At the moment, he is sure that "the bottom has dropped out of the universe." Without the use of scientific tools, a degree of present-mindedness is almost inevitable, even if we try to be objective in our thinking. For one thing, the present is what we remember best and what our emotional energies usually emphasize.

Then there is the equally strong tendency for many of us to over-emphasize the negative. Just as we pay more attention to one finger that pains than to all the rest of the body that is healthy, so we pay far more attention to one social injustice than to a hundred social experiences that are just. Who has not seen a friendship, or even a marriage, destroyed by one experience regarded by one or the other as "unforgivable" and generalized far beyond any justifiable inter-pretation.

There are, of course, our ego-involved attitudes. Everyone has some self-image, even if often ill-defined, from which emerges a number of attitudes. Here is a college professor who gains his great-est satisfaction out of being hated by his fellows. Here is another who will go to any extremes to be elected to a "prestige" post in any organization to which he belongs. Here is a man who gains his greatest satisfaction from having others subservient to him. Here is another whose shyness drives him to a miserable aloneness.

Any psychotherapist will recognize these common areas of malad-justment and can add to them endlessly. The point is: What to do about them? Simply "reasoning" with the individual, whether in seek-ing agreement or in extended psychoanalysis, is costly and often in-effective. The proposal here is that we teach the client a few power-ful scientific methods and help him to build them into his personality. If they are thoroughly learned, many of the maladjustive forms of reasoning will simply be displaced.

The first of these can be called systematic observation. This has two major dimensions, time and range of events. The time dimen-sion, which includes present-mindedness, can be connected by two forms of systematic observations. One is to make sure that a rep-resentative sample of events is recorded for a given period of time or is recorded at specified intervals over a longer period of time. Here is a woman who is sure another dislikes her and tends to observe only those acts on the part of the other that support this hypothesis. Using a lay-scientist, systematic observation procedure, she records every interpersonal experience with the other woman for a week, or she records the behavior of the other toward her for a given period of time each day.

The other dimension has to do with events. It consists of listing a wide range of events in which certain interpersonal experiences are probable and then recording what happens in each of them. How one behaves at a house party is a poor predictor of the total picture of his over-all behavior, as many a married couple discovers when the decision to marry has been based upon the house-party sample of behavior. If one wishes to use the method of systematic observation, he can list most of the common areas of behavior in which the person being observed acts and record a sample of behavior in each. The observed person can, of course, be himself.

A very effective technique, which the layman can use, was invented by Benjamin Franklin. It is known as the pro–con technique. It is used most often in decision-making but can also be used in such conflict-producing problems as interpersonal relations with others, the recurrence of favorable and unfavorable events, and the systematic recording of successes and failures. Owing to our natural tendency to emphasize the negative, this technique makes us much less susceptible to this kind of distortion in our judgments.

A little more difficult procedure that gives greater meaning to the pro–con technique consists of a search for characteristic differences between the two groups. The pro–con procedure prevents overemphasis on undesirable characteristics, very common in many forms of maladjustment. The technique of characteristic differences will often reveal characteristic or underlying trends which would never be observed in a haphazard or prejudiced recording of events. Both should be highly effective in positive psychotherapy. Here are two people who find it difficult to work together professionally. A systematic recording of their compatible experiences and their conflict experiences was examined with this technique of characteristic differences. It was quickly discovered that one worked better with deadline, whereas the other found deadlines to be a form of oppressive pressure. One did better with short-term goals, the other with long-term goals. One was given to frequent discussion of progress, the other found these to be irritating interruptions. An awareness of their persistent personal attitudes made them able to achieve a high level of teamwork.

A similar lay-scientist skill is that of ranking. To rank a set of observed events in terms of their desirability to the client is not unlike the pro–con technique. The pro–con technique puts items into categories. Ranking orders them from one extreme to the other. The method of characteristic differences can be used effectively between the top and bottom portions of the ranking. Ranking has another advantage over the pro–con technique in achieving objectivity. For example, friends can be asked to rank independently a list of items. Their independent rankings can then be summed and the sums reranked to give a more reliable ranking. Many clients will be attracted by the objectivity of this procedure and its usefulness in seeing how others see things. With experience, they will gain confidence in it and find it more attractive than the more common maladjustive types of reaction so often requiring psychotherapy.

In many social conflict problems, the sociogram is an effective tool that most clients can learn to use with a fair degree of competence. In its most common form, it consists of a large circle of small circles. Each of the small circles is assigned the name of one member of the group. Then on lines connecting the various circles with one another can be recorded the nature of interpersonal contacts between them. A study of these is almost certain to reveal to the client a more objective picture of the true facts in the characteristic interpersonal relations among the members of the group. When the psychotherapist observes, in the client's difficulties, a distorted view of the interpersonal relations within the groups of which he is a part, this technique can provide a highly effective procedure for positive psychotherapy. This tool is very commonly used in Group Dynamics.

Some forms of cluster analysis (7) can be mastered by the more intelligent client. This method reveals principles with which one can discover underlying principles in a body of observed data. To describe such a technique is beyond the scope of this paper, but the technique is one that the psychotherapist may well set out to master and to use in appropriate situations.

It should be noted that all of the methods described in this section on lay-scientist skills involve the use of what is commonly referred to as open-ended data. Questionnaires, with a choice required among three to five possible answers, and rating scales are among the closed-ended techniques commonly used. In many kinds of personality problems commonly encountered by the psychotherapist, open-ended data is likely to be more fruitful. In this technique, if a client is asked to write a brief description of his concerns, this description offers much richer data for studying personality. If its presentation to the client is accompanied by appropriate questions designed to bring about exploration of all the major facets of the problem, the open-ended data is especially valuable. The analysis of open-ended data is usually begun with some coding procedure in which various areas of behavior relevant to the problem are identified by appropriate coding classifications. Codes may often include such topics as: emotional behavior, learning behavior, ego-involved items, self-image items, interpersonal relations, and so on. These are then analyzed by using the lay-scientist techniques that have already been described.

*Learning Skills in Psychotherapy*

Probably of all the kinds of skills needed in today's world, learning takes first place. What there is to learn reportedly doubles every three years. Our decisions, especially as citizens in a democracy, become increasingly important and increasingly difficult to make wisely.

Not long ago, a friend resigning from an administrative post in a national adult education organization, said, "I am resigning because, although adults want to know, in general, they are quite unwilling to learn." This, of course, is not completely true. Adult education courses in high schools or colleges have packed parking lots every night. Popular books on mathematics, physics, art, music, and history sell very well indeed. The common expression, "I wish I knew," becomes a more sincere, as well as a more common, statement every day.

What have learning skills to do with psychotherapy? In psychotherapy, such skills provide many forms of increased potential.

In the first place, learning—or, at least, knowing—has a major role to play in feelings of security as against insecurity. It has been shown, for example, that at the high-school age ninth and tenth graders, on the whole, are not nearly as interested in "saving the world" as eleventh and twelfth graders. The reason is that the younger teenagers need first to gain a sense of security for themselves. Only then are they willing to give their energies to more self-denying objectives. Surely, one of the best ways to gain these feelings of security is to become well informed in the areas relevant to their life purposes.

It is also true that the more insecure a person feels, the less likely he is to be able to take criticism easily, or to be skilled in objective self-criticism. If the feelings of insecurity are there, either outside criticism or self-criticism can produce maladjustive reactions calling for psychotherapy.

In this matter of security and insecurity, the concept of uniqueness can play a powerful role. As has been pointed out, the idea that everyone is unique is not difficult to believe. Even to realize that no one else in the past or in the future can be exactly like the client is also readily accepted. But to believe that each person, because of this uniqueness, has in the very nature of this uniqueness a maximum potential destiny which, if he achieves it, will contribute something of importance to the future—this is not so easy to believe. Yet this concept is probably the strongest potential force in positive psychotherapy related to the whole area of learning. In other words, to have chosen (at least tentatively) one's maximum potential destiny gives fruitful purpose to one's learning as well as to life in general.

In one presentation of this concept of uniqueness, a teacher presented this personal problem. She has a son, twenty years of age. He is partially deaf and has a history of continual failure and frustration. All efforts to gain help from guidance counselors or psychotherapists have only convinced him of what he cannot do. This has given him a defeatist attitude, resulting even in threats of suicide. He became much impressed with the uniqueness concept, namely, that there is some area of unique achievement open to him. The task of the psychotherapist is to help him find this unique area of achievement and to point out the skills he will need in order to achieve it, and how to learn them. In other words, the mastery of learning skills plays a central role in effective psychotherapy for him.

Another concept that both stimulates learning and prevents some of the conflicts due to excessive dogmatism is the infinity principle. In common parlance, it is stated this way. No matter how good an answer you have, there is always a better one.

It is clear that such a principle is logically sound in theory. Applying it in daily life is quite a different matter. For example, most of us give undue weight to ideas that we ourselves have developed. Indeed, we often feel threatened when others reject or are skeptical of them. If the infinity principle can become a real part of our inner personalities, then, at least, its implication will usually temper our dogmatism and prevent much of the inner conflict that arises when we confuse our own ideas with ultimate truth.

Here are two men. "A" is a slow thinker and reaches conclusions only after careful thought. But once having reached a conclusion, he is dogmatic as to its infallibility. "B," on the other hand, jumps to conclusions much too quickly, but he is quite open to reason when their errors are pointed out. "B," in the long run, will appear far less frequently at the office of the psychotherapist than "A." The best positive psychotherapy for "A" is a consistent faith in the infinity principle.

A very large percentage of our fears and prejudices are due to varying degrees of ignorance. Learning, when it is accurate and relevant, eliminates many of them. Someone has said that "what we know is good." "What we know that we do not know, is equally good." Often, however, "what we do not know that we do not know, gets us into trouble." But worst of all, "what we do not know that we do not know, but think that we do know, commonly produces conflict and frustration, as well as contributing to the weakness of democracy."

Let us relate learning to the concept of maximum potential destiny. Consider the young man, partially deaf, who was challenged by the uniqueness concept. Let us suppose that the psychotherapist, using the positive approach implied in the uniqueness concept, gives him a high vision for his maximum potential destiny. This new outlook will certainly inspire him, at least for a time. But future failures may bring him back to an even greater depth of his defeatist attitude. The psychotherapist's task is to lay out with him a practical blueprint of how he is to achieve his unique maximum potential destiny. This destiny vision must be something that is inspiring to him but, also, something that is possible for him to achieve. This particular young man can carry out the trivial tasks assigned to him now, but they do not inspire him. He gets from them only a feeling of uselessness. Nevertheless, the alternative of building a vision in which he must ultimately fail is even worse. The vision must be both inspiring and possible to achieve.

Note, then, how this blueprint is to be drawn. The client, with the help of the psychotherapist, must first get an accurate picture of his strengths and weaknesses. In CRP we use our *Personality Profile,* upon which such a picture can be drawn. A careful examination of it, especially the various patterns of traits to be found in it, will always result in potentials not previously seen.

Let us recall the first dimension of character, purpose. The client asks several questions. What purposes does this pattern of traits of personality suggest as possible? What skills must be learned to carry them out? Finally, what learning skills, which the client can master, does he need to master in order, in turn, to master the skills necessary for achieving these purposes? Many a student has raised his marks substantially when inspired by the "vision concept of vocational guidance."

One principle in the dimension which has proved very useful, as demonstrated in our research, is the learning goal. When a person reaches a decision of a purpose to be achieved, a skill to be mastered, or something to be learned, the client is urged to set a learning goal that he can carry out at once, which will, on the one hand, give him confidence and, on the other, help him make progress toward his objective.

The second dimension of character, you will recall, has to do with one's basic convictions growing out of his philosophy of life. Many of us do not live our convictions with skill. It will be obvious that such skills involve learning. Having basic philosophy in which we have no real understanding, nor skills for living it, is not likely to be either a source of strong convictions or a way to live at the level of one's maximum potential destiny. Let the psychotherapist consider, however, the potential strength of a program in which the client is able to develop such a philosophy and to work out its convictions for living. The key step, then, is to plan a program of learning by which it can be developed, as well as the skills for living it effectively.

Finally, the third dimension of character is social vision. It requires no proving to the psychotherapist that the less a client centers his attention on himself and the more his major concerns involve others, the healthier his personality and the more effective his life. The learning involved in broadening effectively one's social vision is almost infinite. The client will need to learn many things about those whom he hopes to serve. He may even need to learn a new language in order to communicate with them. Here, again, the task of the psychotherapist, according to this theory of positive psychotherapy, is to guide the client in working out the social vision dimension of his destiny blueprint and in helping him to master the learning skills prerequisite for achieving it.

The learning skills especially chosen for this approach to psychotherapy are too many for inclusion in this discussion. We have prepared a booklet that will serve this purpose (3). The learning skills described in it are applicable in all types of learning. Their special application in the field of religion, however, makes them especially useful for the development of the second and third dimensions of character: a basic philosophy of life and social vision. This booklet illustrates to the psychotherapist the role of learning in positive psychotherapy.

*Decision-Making Skills in Positive Psychotherapy*

It is, indeed, appropriate to discuss decision-making skills after the discussion of lay-scientist skills and learning skills. Actually, good decision-making is an application of the scientific method and almost always involves learning. Both the scientific method and decision-making are powerful ways to search rigorously and unflinch-ingly for the truth. The scientist in his laboratory searches for the truth with all of the skill and force of his being. But even the scientist usually does not do so outside his laboratory.

If this is true for scientists, what hope have we that clients com-ing to the psychotherapist will have faith in the value of the truth? In many of our daily-life problems, we have no interest whatever in the wisest decision. We are concerned only in satisfying our per-sonal wishes. A youth in love is not concerned with an objective evaluation of the probable outcome of the envisioned marriage. He only wants to marry the girl. A mother cannot be objective about her son. She defends him against all comers, and she is usually blind to any undesirable truth about him.

Here are a few types of bad decision-making which every psy-chotherapist will recognize at once as being characteristic of much maladjustment. They can be best described as pairs of opposite extremes.

It is all too common to make decisions too quickly. This haste is usually due to looking at only one alternative, an everyday practice of most of us. It may be exhibited as the outcome of good impulses. It can also grow from fears or outbursts of anger or from just plain habit. Its opposite, of course, is indecision. Usually, in such cases, the person vacillates between two alternatives, unable to reject or accept either. Or there may be many alternatives. Indecision can also come from fear of doing the wrong thing. Such a person would rather do nothing than do something wrong. This situation is quite different from the fear of not doing the right thing. In the latter case, the person would rather chance doing the wrong thing than miss the possibility of doing the right thing.

Then there are those who have such a body of dogmatic opinions that they make decisions according to these opinions with no further consideration at all. Or there are those whose deliberations are so drawn out that they invest far more time in even a minor decision than it can possibly be worth.

There are those who are so obstinate that once having set forth a judgment they defend it against all comers. There are others so easily swayed that they cannot make firm decisions about anything.

There are those who are too strongly influenced by people with whom they fear to disagree. There are others who reject an alter-native because of their antagonism to the one who proposes it.

There are those who consider only the worst that may come from a course of action. Others jump quickly into something because they have seen only the best that can come from it.

Akin to this last group are those who put the worst possible interpretation on the data available as evidence. Others put the best possible interpretation on it. Either habit results in many wrong decisions.

Perhaps the first step in convincing the client of the value of decision-making skills in the search for truth is to point out the risk of wrong decisions, and set forth gradual training in the steps of making right decisions. These steps are not numerous or difficult to learn.

The basic skills in scientific decision-making can be described in terms of five steps. Even if only the first step is taken, decision-making is vastly improved. Indeed, the first step may well be the most important one, because it represents a healthy as well as an objective attitude. This objective attitude allows consideration of alternative courses of action. It is seldom that only one course of action is possible. If only one is considered, the resultant action cannot properly be called a decision at all. A very common type of decision, for which we seldom consider the alternative, is illustrated in this example. "Would you like to go to the game?" How often does one consider what he would do with that time if he did not go to the game? "Would you like to help me with this project of mine?" asks a friend. How often do we consider the alternative use of the time required? "Will you make this speech for our club?" writes a program-maker. Such a speech may take hours to prepare and to make. How often do we consider alternative courses of action? This one habit of always examining alternatives would vastly improve our effective living.

The second step is to consider the pros and cons of each alternative. These lists must include, of course, the objective evidence but, also, the pros and cons resulting from self-interest and from the elements of desirability or undesirability. These factors certainly constitute significant evidence. To leave out self-interest or desirability is as unrealistic as to make decisions based only upon them.

The next step is to consider what is the best and the worst that can come from each alternative. It is all too common for the optimist to consider only the best and the pessimist to think only of the worst.

The fourth step is to estimate the probability of these bests and worsts actually occurring. Here is a young woman in love. The man is recognized by everyone as a weakling and as useless. She is sure she can reform him. What is the probability that this will happen? It is very low. She almost guarantees for herself an unhappy future on a very poor probability. Pointing out this low probability may not change her decision, but it has made her think a little more realistically.

When these four steps have been taken, one is far better prepared to make a decision. The more significant the decision, the further along this series of steps one should go. Perhaps more difficult than convincing the client of the value of this process, and giving him faith in the desirability of truth, is making the process a part of the actual daily-life personality of the client. Many of us who are well versed in the skills of the decision-making process forget to use them. One teacher who was teaching these skills to a group of youths discovered that he himself had made five impulsive decisions in the three-hour period, forgetting to practice what he was teaching.

## *Social Influence Skills in Positive Psychotherapy*

It is an almost universal fact that all of us would like to have positive influence on all with whom we deal. But even the best adjusted among us experience some of our most common frustrations when we fail to do so. It follows that the psychotherapist can usually contribute greatly to the mental health of his client if he can teach him effective social influence skills. The problem is in how this teaching is to be done. To be sure, much research has been done on the subject. In CRP we have just published a book on the subject for youth (4). If all one needed to do was to look up a prescription in such a book, as we might recipes in a cookbook, our task would be much simpler than it is. Unfortunately, it is not that easy.

In the first place, we are talking about social influence skills, not just social skills. It is one thing to know how to behave properly at a formal dinner; it is quite another to have the skill to influence other people, especially if we want them to act contrary to their habitual form of behavior or to a plan of action upon which they have already decided. Such influences are functions not only of the individual, who is unique, and of the social groups he wishes to influence, all of whom are unique, but even of the purpose involved, which is likely also to be unique. Consider a fairly typical end of the week in my life. On Wednesday I speak to the members of my staff. On Thursday I address a group of school teachers. On Friday I teach fifty teenagers, all members of student councils of the area high schools. How different, indeed, are the types of skills required for the three groups, not to mention the highly unique individuals in each group.

Among the more common ineffective—or at least undesirable—efforts to achieve social influence which, in the extreme, constitute serious maladjustments, the following are a few. Sometimes one will use anger to overcome noncompliance or even exhibit so much fear at noncompliance that the other person may do what is wanted because of a sense of pure sympathy. In one college, a student regularly threatened suicide if he should be failed in any course. He received good marks in spite of almost no work because each professor was afraid he might be the cause of the suicide. Then here is another who makes actual or veiled threats to compel someone to carry out his bidding, and still another whose attitude, consisting of a demanding type of authority, is so aggressive that he either gets compliance, faces rebellion, or both. This leads to frustration and social conflict.

To begin with, the therapist, if he suspects that this area of social influence skills is crucial in his client's problems, should estimate the level of the client's innate social sensitivity. The lower this level is, the more skills are needed by the client and the more generous must be the tolerance of those he wishes to influence. Indeed, working only with those who can tolerate his social clumsiness may be the only practical way to solve his problem. Otherwise, he will constantly "be doing the right thing at the wrong time" or "the wrong thing at the right time." This tolerance may be the more important of the two.

Very few normal adults set out purposely to irritate others. It is this lack of sufficient social sensitivity that is usually the cause of socially irritating behavior. Not much can be done about this, for social sensitivity is an innate trait. Tolerance, however, can be learned. Developing such tolerance is quite as important to the mentally healthy as to those needing psychotherapy.

It has been pointed out that having basic convictions to stand by is one's best basis for social influence skill. If such convictions involve dominating purpose and broad social vision, they result in still greater influence. However, one must accept the fact that on any team or in any social group the uniquenesses of its members are certain to lead to frequent frustrations and conflicts. Tolerance and respect, expressed in forms of appreciation, help enormously. There is no other area, for example, in which "returning good for evil" carries greater social influence than for the socially insensitive individual in his efforts to be socially effective without betraying his convictions.

Some skills that the client can learn will increase his influence with those with whom he deals, no matter what the level of his social sensitivity. One of these is a variation of the pro–con technique. One keeps a record of the things that produce positive reactions on the part of another person, on the one hand, and of things that are reacted to negatively, on the other. In and of themselves, these observations are helpful in knowing some things to do and some things not to do. If, in addition to this, one examines these two lists in a search for characteristic differences, he may also discover principles that can be of real value in strengthening future relations.

As one might imagine, some kinds of convictions carry more social influence than others. In our own research, several interesting things have been observed. For one thing, the more difficult the conviction is to stand by, the more influential is the individual who stands by it. Then, too, convictions carrying a long-range point of view have more effect on others than those concerned only with immediate concerns. Convictions based upon broad moral principle are more influential than those consisting of miscellaneous beliefs about right and wrong. I imagine that most psychotherapists, when they consider maladjustments in which lack of or excess of conviction is a major factor, will find these same characteristic weaknesses commonly present. To whatever extent, then, the client can be guided into the deeper, more far-reaching convictions to fight for, the more these convictions will contribute to mental health.

Many of us who are among the less gifted in degree of social sensitivity will do well to adopt good social coaches. Here is a man whose wife and secretary are continually giving him clues to social influence possibilities that he would never see himself. Doing positive things for people usually makes them more amenable to social influence and more tolerant of social clumsiness.

This all-too-brief account of the value of social influence skills as good psychotherapy points out an important force in our efforts to deal with many of man's maladjustments. To be sure, the fact that each of us has a unique set of social attitudes, habits, and aspirations which differs in part, at least, from those of anyone else, makes complete social adjustment difficult to achieve. Because of this difficulty, acquiring skill in "putting ourselves in another's shoes" has great value if one can master these skills. The important principle emphasized here is that it be a positive approach. Instead of trying only to eliminate social maladjustments helping the client develop skills for effective social influence may often be more effective.

## CONCLUSION

"The best defense is a good offense" could well be the golden text for this paper. It is based upon this hypothesis: personality integration is a positive achievement. Essentially, most maladjustment is failure to achieve such integration.

It is also being proposed that personality achieves complete integration to the extent that one discovers his unique maximum potential. This potential can be measured in terms of three dimensions. The first consists of developing a philosophy of life and spelling out and standing for the convictions for living that grow out of it. The second is measured by the breadth of one's social vision and by the mastery of the skills necessary to achieve it. The third is the purpose dimension. Since a man is unique, there must be in the nature of his unique pattern of traits some maximum potential destiny that sets the direction for the highest achievement possible for him.

Achieving growth in these three dimensions is brought about by the mastery of five kinds of skills. The first such group of skills can be called skills of uniqueness. They consist in techniques by which one explores the potentials of his uniquenesses. The second set is the lay-scientist skills. They are skills by which one can use the powerful tools of science in the solution of his personal and social problems. The third is the learning skills. Since the mastery of skills consists in learning, it follows that the skills of learning are essential to such growth. The fourth group is decision-making skills. Since every day presents decisions with different degrees of importance, it follows that the scientific skills of decision-making are essential to the maximum integration of personality. The fifth group is the social influence skills. Almost all destinies require social interaction. Much maladjustment is, in essence, social maladjustment. Acquiring skills of social influence, therefore, is of great importance to achieving one's maximum potential destiny.

The thesis of this paper is that challenging and guiding one's clients in this kind of growth results in powerful psychotherapy.

## REFERENCES

1. Adams, H. B. 'Mental illness' or interpersonal behavior? *Amer. Psychol.,* 1964, **19,** 191–196.

2. Bernreuter, R. G. *The personality inventory.* Stanford, California: Stanford University Press, 1935.
3. Character Research Project Staff. *Powerful learning tools in religion.* Schenectady, New York: Union College Character Research Project, 1958.
4. Detweiler, H. J. *How to stand up for what you believe.* New York: Association Press, 1966.
5. Fosdick, H. E. *The meaning of faith.* New York: Association Press, 1921.
6. Hovey, E. H. *In search of a vision for your life.* Schenectady, New York: Union College Character Research Project, 1959.
7. Koppe, W. A. A theoretical framework for curriculum development. *Character Potential,* 1963, **1**(4), 159–174.
8. Ligon, E. M. *Personality profile.* Schenectady, New York: Union College Character Research Project, 1958.
9. Ligon, E. M. *Parent roles—his and hers.* Schenectady, New York: Union College Character Research Project, 1959.
10. Ligon, E. M. *Their future is now.* New York: Macmillan, 1959.
11. Ligon, E. M. Blueprint for a research design. *Character Potential,* 1964, **2**, 94–177.
12. Pribram, K. H. Theories of learning and instruction, neurological notes on the art of education. *The sixty-third yearbook of the National Society for the Study of Education.* Part I. Washington: National Society for the Study of Education, 1964.
13. Smith, L. J., & Ligon, E. M. *The marriage climate.* St. Louis: Bethany Press, 1963.
14. Strong, E. K. *Vocational interest blank.* Stanford, California: Stanford University Press, 1948.

Chapter 17

# The Illumination Method:
# A Specialized Type
# of Psychotherapy

## JOHN A. BLAKE

John A. Blake: b. 1904, North Augusta, South Carolina.
A.B., in biology, Presbyterian College, South Carolina, 1926. A.M., in psychology, Johns Hopkins University, 1933. Trainee, Psychiatry Department, Johns Hopkins University Medical School, 1933–1934.
Associate Professor, Virginia Commonwealth University, 1949–date. Chief Psychologist, Central State Hospital, Petersburg, Virginia, 1951–1956. Assistant Professor, University of Richmond, Virginia, 1946–1949.
Fellow, American Association for the Advancement of Science.
Articles: About thirty articles, both popular and professional.

$A$s is generally known, the natures of many kinds of psychotherapy place them in such descriptive categories as directive, nondirective, and various combinations of these extremes. These individual therapeutic systems vary widely in length, quality, and formality. Some require many sessions with the patient; others serve as so-called short-cut methods for attaining localized specific goals. Some are very formal in their procedures and highly refined in their techniques; others tend to be more or less informal, almost "personalized," and easily varied in their application to adapt to the individual patient's condition.

The present method of psychotherapy, which involves a number of special techniques, is specifically applied to psychoses. It was devised and employed in a mental hospital situation for nearly four years before I returned to full-time teaching. Although the method incorporates and occasionally employs a few recognized techniques of the "directive" category as variants,[1] it is generally considered a rather new, dis-

---

[1] See the reference section for certain other systems of psychotherapy which employ some techniques fairly similar, directly or indirectly, to the variant techniques mentioned above.

464

tinctive procedure in its own right. This general claim is based upon certain inherent characteristics of the method and, incidentally, these characteristics will also show how the method differs essentially from current therapies that deal with the neuroses, juvenile delinquencies, and similar atypical human phenomena.

## SPECIFIC CLAIM

The method attempts to accelerate the return of insight primarily, and secondarily and consequently to improve general mentation by reorganizing the thinking and reasoning, including judgment. Following improvement in these areas a stabilization will usually be found of emotionality and gradual waning of psychotic phenomena. As is well known, irrespective of the type of psychosis, whether due to organic or psychogenic factors, no recovery is possible unless and until the patient has gained insight into his condition. Briefly, the lack of insight is held to constitute an insurmountable and rigid "barrier" to recovery. It is therefore necessary to destroy this obstruction, and such is the main function of the Illumination Method.

With the appearance of true insight, there will almost inevitably soon follow gradual improvement in the patient's judgment and general mentation, as well as more evenly balanced emotionality. For instance, even if the physical ravages of paresis are arrested, insight does not necessarily return early, nor may it in some cases ever return. But, until insight does return, the patient will continue to retain his delusional and other psychotic traits and thus remain ill.

## SCOPE OF APPLICATION

The method is applicable to all psychoses of psychogenic origin and to certain ones having organic etiology. Such degenerative organic disorders as cerebral arteriosclerosis, senile dementia, and other progressively deteriorating disorders are rejected, although some of these occasionally do have temporary periods of remission, as is well known. The alcoholic psychoses are treated and often with much success, depending naturally upon the degree of cerebral damage done. Although the method has been found usually more effective with the purely functional disorders than with the limited organics, much overlapping of results has been found with these two groups since, for instance, some schizophrenic cases are far more inaccessible to return of insight than some organic ones, as would be expected. The determining factors naturally differ in all cases, and they will be dealt with in the section entitled "Limitations to Effectiveness."

It should be mentioned that although the method has been found to succeed independently of other therapies in a fair number of cases of functional types it is perhaps more often successful in supplementing others, such as electroshock, tranquilizers, antidepressants, and others in the functional cases, and antibiotic therapies in some organics. In such supplementation it is mainly successful in reorganizing the thought processes following the use of such drugs as reserpine, chlorpromazine, and other newer chemical agents, since clear mentation does not always follow their use immediately. Yet another reason for Illumination Therapy to be used to supplement other therapies is because of the condition of many cases. For instance, electroshock is often first necessary to bring the manic, or an excited catatonic schizophrenic patient, under control; or to restore dissociated patients to reality awareness; or to clarify a confused patient for, obviously, some degree of voluntary attention must be gained before any type of psychotherapy can be attempted. In the case of certain organics, such as the paretic, the method is used toward the end of the antibiotic treatments to hasten the return of insight. Finally, if it be said that eventually insight would return in most of these cases without supplementation by Illumination Therapy, it must be remembered that such supplementation is meant to accelerate such recovery with improvement in other spheres; and such time-saving may be in terms of days, weeks, or even of months in rare cases.

## LIMITATIONS TO EFFECTIVENESS

Despite confining the use of the method to functional psychoses and certain of the organic in origin, there are yet some factors or conditions which can and do preclude success. First, the most immediate and obvious were alluded to before, such as states of excitement, confusion, dissociation, et cetera, which prevent the gaining of the patient's attention and subsequent rapport. In most such cases there is merely the need for at least one preliminary electroshock treatment, after which the patient is usually amenable to rapport. Second, even when good rapport is established, success may be further precluded by two more serious conditions: first in functional cases, when there has been a too lengthy period of disturbed ideational and emotional behavior patterns in the patient's life before therapy is begun, and such distorted personality habit patterns are consequently too firmly fixed. (Some such cases are so firmly fixed that even one or more entire series of electroshock treatments cannot effect recovery, as is well known.) Second, in the organic psychoses, success will be lacking when there is too great amount of brain deterioration found, due to the ravages of organic agents, whether they be the spirochete, alcohol, or any other living or nonliving pernicious agent. Finally, any lack of success beyond these will usually be due to either outright erroneous practice or to some type of ineptitude on the part of the therapist in executing the general or specific techniques later to be described.

## RATIONALE

In physical medicine it is well known that the body has not only great resistive capacity to life's insults but also tremendous recuperative powers which enable it to return to normal health after harmful, disabling agents are destroyed. Similarly, the psychological functions of personality seem to possess similar resistive power through life and great recuperative resiliency when their distorting and deteriorating antagonists are removed. However, in the case of organic psychoses, the degree of such recovery will necessarily be within the limits of undamaged neural tissue. As in the case of the physical processes, likewise in the psychological, both will have long previously been functioning in a normal, balanced manner; then, when such processes are eventually relieved of the strain of pernicious psychogenic or organic influences, these personality processes will more readily tend to swing back to sound judgment, normal thinking and reasoning, and balanced emotional functioning, rather than remain distorted and off-balanced in their respective spheres. Such recuperation—by Nature, so to speak—within undamaged limits, will usually be gradual even if no specific therapeutic measures are taken, which may explain many slow remissions most likely. At this stage, therefore, the proposed method, which employs a more or less rigorous, direct, aggressive attack on the psychoses, begins to accelerate the recuperative activity by reinforcing nature's efforts. It has been thought that the method makes use of techniques somewhat similar to those of "brainwashing," but for constructive, therapeutic purposes.

Certain drastic measures, which would doubtless be contraindicated in the neuroses, are often successfully used here because of very definite differences inherent in the two groups of disorders. One of the major differences is that the neurotics, although ignorant of the etiology of their illness, do have sufficient insight to know that they are unwell, or at least that something is wrong with them. (Incidentally, in many cases they subconsciously do not really want to recover for various reasons, which we shall not elaborate upon here.) The psychotics, on the other hand, are usually totally lacking in insight, are hard to convince that anything is wrong with them, and consequently must recover such insight before further therapy can show them the etiology, development, significance, and other aspects of their pathological condition. Although this is considered the main difference, there is yet another important reason why the drastic techniques of the Illumination Method should not be used with the neurotics. For instance, since many neurotics are overly preoccupied with their subjective feelings, including hostility, anxiety, guilt, et cetera, they have to be shielded from such in therapy applied to them. On the other hand, most psychotics of certain categories, lacking insight completely, have definitely been helped by the use of strong, positive measures arousing them to a realization, i.e., insight, into their morbid condition. This is especially true of the simple and hebephrenic schizophrenias, both of which end in differing degrees of deterioration. These exceptional types for which such procedures are most strongly recommended, when successfully stimulated, have been definitely benefited, i.e., being brought to a stark realization of what is slowly happening to them, mentally and emotionally. That therapist is most fortunate who is able to reach such patients before deterioration has advanced too far. It is suspected that advocates of other types of psychotherapy may have advocated and used such measures as a last resort, as if to "startle the patient awake," so to speak.

Some shock-type therapies function somewhat similarly to the Illumination Method. Many confine their attack much more strictly to the emotional sphere of the distorted personality, as illustrated by the method developed by Fisher (2). Other methods deal with the ideational sphere as well but carry the "shock" procedures to a much more extreme point than does the Illumination Method, as illustrated by the methods of Rosen (3), Walder (5), and Synanon (6). As will be noted, the Illumination Method deals almost exclusively with the ideational sphere, concentrating by the use of special techniques on eradicating delusional material.

Furthermore, the lack of insight, combined with even slight degrees of confusion, excitement, apathy, preoccupation, mutism, and various other abnormal symptoms, make the method's overt "directive" type of attack on psychoses necessary; whereas the more or less "passive" nondirective method, used quite often successfully with neurotic disorders, and which tends to "allow" solution to the patient's problem to arrive if, as, and when it may, is not only haphazard but actually ineffectual and usually entirely impossible with the psychoses. Finally, whereas the neuroses, having some insight, are, so to speak, attacked from "below" in the region of the morbid desires, et cetera, the psychoses, lacking insight entirely, are attacked from "above" to "let in the light of insight" before anything more can be accomplished. When this barrier has been destroyed, however, any type of legitimate, effective therapy may be employed. On the other hand, in many cases little more need be done than to apply the method's techniques, and these can gradually reorient and reorganize the patient's ideational and emotional patterns toward more normal personality functioning.

## GENERAL NATURE AND PRELIMINARY STEPS OF ILLUMINATION METHOD

The general method, which involves strenuous efforts to create new insight in the psychotic patient, employs a number of specific techniques soon to be described. First, one should realize that, just as each profession has its own techniques, it also requires certain essential personality traits in its practitioners in order to be most effective. So the psychotherapist, dealing with psychotics, not only must use special techniques and be alert and ingenious to devise variations for emergencies, but he must clearly manifest certain essential personality characteristics in himself to the patient. Preferably, the therapist should be either rather strongly extroverted in personality or he should develop a close facsimile of this extrovertedness in his attack on the disorder, thus showing a rigorous but quiet persistence in attack, as will be discussed later. The introverted therapist may often succeed in the nondirective therapy with the neuroses, but he is not well suited to this method which carries the attack to the patient almost continuously.

### Rapport

In gaining rapport, the therapist must impress the patient with his friendliness, sincerity, calmness, and ability. There are no substitutes for these traits; and they must be genuine, for, if feigned, the patient will soon detect their falsity. In contrast, a coldly impersonal "professional" display of feelings and attitudes toward the patient, however skillfully presented, is quickly seen as superficial and insincere and will often prevent good rapport. It is especially necessary that the patient feel that the therapist speaks and acts with the authority of a fully competent expert and that respect and consideration are shown the patient in return.

The personal characteristics of the successful therapist, some of which have been thought to have developed largely as a result of profoundly satisfying experience in administering therapy per se, have been noted by other investigators (1).

After gaining the patient's attention, one can use various opening topics for gaining rapport, and a selection may be made casually on the basis of the patient's general condition and specific behavior at the time, as well as any personal interests that may be discovered. From here on the therapist checks orientation for time, place, and person. This naturally and quite smoothly leads to an investigation of insight present, which, as shown later, may be checked in three ways.

### Checking Degree of Insight

The patient is first asked if he knows why he was brought to this kind of hospital. Most patients will say something like "No, but I wish you'd tell me," which indicates complete lack of insight. The patient is then asked whether he remembers coming to this hospital and how long he has been here. True insight and its development as involving memory are ascertained, using from one to three temporal "points of reference" that, in turn, depend obviously upon how long the patient has actually been hospitalized. In the case of the fairly long-term or chronic ward patient, these points are checked as follows: he is told to think back to when he first arrived and is asked, first, if he thought then that he had anything wrong with his "nerves" or mind; second, he is asked to look back now on his arrival in the past and is asked if he can begin to see that he has really had something wrong; and, third, he is asked how he feels about his condition now. This procedure, which is executed in slightly different ways to adapt to the intelligence levels of the patients, as are all future techniques, naturally makes it possible not only to check the initial insight (in retrospect), but also to ascertain whether such insight has increased or decreased during the patient's period of hospitalization. Furthermore, this method also gives an indirect evaluation of some phases of the patient's memory at the present time. Such information can supplement later memory testing.

### Systematic Check on Major Psychotic Symptoms

Next, a concise and careful check is made on the major psychotic symptoms that were mentioned in the commitment papers and found by the admitting psychiatrist. (The adequately trained psychologist should also make his own psychiatric examination in order to supplement his psychological investigations.) In rechecking previous findings the therapist confronts the patient and asks him about such symptoms in either of two ways, depending upon his condition: first, one symptom at a time may be investigated, and appropriate discursive therapy be given it; or the therapist may investigate the presence and strength of all symptoms and then return to each for appropriate discussion. In dealing with each symptom, the therapist is quietly firm in assuring the patient that each statement read to him is completely true, and the therapist asks whether the patient sees anything not normal about each. I prefer the first procedure.

### Search for, or Implementation of, Doubt

Simultaneously while checking each symptom, the therapist must be alert to note in the patient's responses the slightest signs of doubt about his condition. To use a metaphorical analogy, doubt is the seed which gives rise to the blossom of insight which, in turn, produces the fruit of recovery. Therefore, it is most important to search for the slightest hint of doubt in the patient's mind, which, if found, must be carefully nurtured by the techniques to be later described. If no doubt can be noted, then it is necessary to deliberately instill such doubt—the stronger the better—and cultivate it steadily.

### Development of Insight Based upon Maturing Doubt

Here the therapist makes further use of some of the various special techniques, depending upon the diagnosis and the characteristics of the patient. However, as mentioned before, the therapist must be alert and resourceful to modify these techniques or, as in rare emergencies, even quickly devise a new one at the moment, since almost anything is thought justifiable which will initiate insight. By this time during the therapist's first session with the patient, insight may often have begun to appear to a fair degree. However, on the other hand, some cases do not show the slightest glimmer of insight until the second, or even the third, session. It is also very often possible for the therapist, by certain of the techniques, to note quite reliable indications that the case is chronic and hopeless. Such indicative signs may occasionally be noted during the first session, although it is safer to give another session to confirm one's suspicion. I have found almost invariably that the second session confirmed the unfortunate indications shown by the techniques.

### Dynamic "Educative and Reeducative" Procedures

When the patient has achieved a fair degree of insight, he will then be able with increasing ability to discuss, or at least have discussed for him (depending upon certain conditions), the most significant aspects of his present and past functioning. When such a careful discussion of an educative, or reeducative, nature is rather intensively done, the first session is usually concluded. This then leaves the patient with a fairly adequate amount of clearly, concisely, strongly, and persuasively presented material about himself to think over until the next session; and, he is strongly urged to do this, with the added reminder that he will be seen again soon to get his ideas about himself.

### Desirable Follow-up Procedures

During the second, or if necessary, the third session, there are begun and developed a few special follow-up procedures of psychotherapeutic and mental hygenic types for future use. (These will be briefly described in the final section.) It should also be realized that, once the insightless "barrier" has been destroyed, and the patient can discuss his condition with increasing ease and clarity, the therapist may employ any of the various pertinent types of recognized therapy for fathoming the depths of the personality, if this should be desired, as well as employ my educative, synthesizing techniques. Various existing factors should determine what combinations may be advantageously used in any particular case.

## SPECIFIC TECHNIQUES

Although I have already developed quite a number of specific techniques, the potential number is much greater and would depend upon the ingenuity of the therapist. Those given here vary widely in usefulness, depending upon such factors as diagnosis, the particular traits present, length of hospitalization, intelligence level of the patient, et cetera. Because of the variety of the Techniques, as well as their numerous possible modification to fit any particular condition, it will be possible to enumerate and briefly discuss only the main ones. It is also to be expected that new skills will be created in the method from time to time, for I do not believe that the potentialities are nearly exhausted. Furthermore, each of the following representative techniques is intended to indicate merely the area of mental content to be investigated, and then the patient is to be given the appropriate directive or educative type of therapy. The particular wording of each directive is not at all fixed but must be varied and adapted to the situation dealt with, both quantitatively and qualitatively.

Since there is a great variety of differentiating factors involved, not only among individual patients but also within each patient in terms of basic personality compositions, diagnosis and present symptoms, degree of rapport gained, adeptness of the therapist, et cetera, the following main techniques can serve merely as representative models. Consequently, each can be and, indeed, may be expected to be, modified in application by the therapist to adapt it to the particular patient and situation. These main representative techniques arc, as originally stated, intended to create degrees of doubt in the patient regarding his psychotic traits and gradually to elicit increasing true insight.

Technique 1. Convincing patient. In the preliminary check on orientation the therapist will have already determined whether the patient is correctly oriented for place. If disoriented in this area, he is told in a matter-of-fact way that he is in a hospital. (Patient: "Mr. S.") "But, Mr. S., do you know what kind of hospital this is?" If he does not recognize it, he is told that it is a mental hospital. "Do you remember being brought here, Mr. S.?" (Answer is usually yes.) "Did you agree to come here?" (Answer is usually no.) "Then, Mr. S., why do you think they brought you here without your consent?" Many patients at this point will, in effect, say "I don't know; I wish you'd tell me"; and this will often be followed by a brief account of how he was doing nothing out of the way but was merely minding his own business, and how he was picked up (usually by an officer) and brought along despite protests. Here we see the first main indication of lack of insight which is, and will continue to be, the heart of our problem.

At the start of the first technique, the therapist must read one after another of the symptoms as shown in the commitment papers and ask the patient if he remembers each. If he does not, he is assured that each is true. If he does recall them, he is asked what he thinks of their normality. (At this time, having no insight, he will usually see nothing wrong with them.) "Now, Mr. S., you say nothing is wrong with your 'nerves' or mind, and yet you were brought here without your consent. How do you explain this?" (Right here the insightless patient will often express some paranoidal ideas, which, under the circumstances, is rather to be expected.) When he admits he does not know, one after another of the most serious of his symptoms is mentioned, and he is asked what he thinks of each. If he thinks each is normal, the fact is pointed out to him that the other patients do not show these behaviors. Or, if they happen to be commonly found symptoms, the patient should be strongly reminded that he never used to show these behaviors at home and on his job some years ago. "Mr. S., why do you think or do such things now? Furthermore, your family does not think or do such things, but only you! Why?" After further and more detailed discussion of his peculiar ideas and other behaviors, he is firmly assured that such behaviors are not normal but indicate that his "nerves" or mind is sick right now. Furthermore, he is strongly assured that he may not be able to recognize this yet, but that he will later begin to see how "different" he is now from his usual self.

Technique 2. Contrasting patient's traits with others. In another technique the therapist makes a brief, clear distinction to the patient between two "classes" of "nervous" people: one class in which the patient knows his "nerves" are upset and will seek medical aid voluntarily. Regarding this group, the therapist might say, "In this case, Mr. S., since the person can see his condition, he will often recover fairly soon because he will cooperate with the psychiatrist." (At this point it is well to get the patient's reaction to what has been said as, indeed, should also be done frequently during the application of each technique.) "But the other class, Mr. S., consists of those patients who think, talk, feel, and act abnormally, but they do not and, for most of the time, they even cannot know that their behaviors are not normal! And, until they can see how different their thinking and other behaviors are, they actually cannot recover."

The therapist should illustrate the second group by pointing out other patients on the ward. "Now, Mr. S., you have seen others on the ward doing peculiar things and have heard them expressing queer ideas, and you know such things are not normal. But you also have found that they don't realize this in themselves." It may be well at this point to remind the patient that other patients can see his behavior as not normal also. "As for these patients, Mr. S., I can assure you that they cannot recover and begin to think and act normally until they can see themselves as they really are. Now, why do you think they cannot realize their condition, as you and others see them?" This question should lead to the patient's giving his own explanations or surmises. If the patient's condition permits, an exchange of ideas may be carried on to stimulate in the patient some glimmer of doubt about his own condition.

A variant on this technique would be for the therapist to discuss briefly certain peculiar traits of a hypothetical patient, i.e., a few traits that our patient himself shows, then ask what he thinks of these. If he should consider such traits abnormal, then he should be pointedly informed that his admission papers list these as precisely what he himself has shown just before he arrived at the hospital. He can be reassured impressively, however, that although he cannot now realize his condition fully, the truth about himself may come in a "flash" at any time or, in other words, he may at any time suddenly "see the light" about himself. He is urged to think closely about his "new" ideas and other behaviors and compare them with such in his past life. "Are there any differences, Mr. S.?"

Technique 3. Contrasting present with past behaviors. The next technique contrasts sharply the difference between the patient's present behaviors just before arriving and during his time in the hospital, on the one hand, with his mental, emotional, and physical behaviors during the long years back home. Strong efforts should now be made, if the patient's condition permits, to lead him to reminisce on his past life and to describe his home life, his kind of work, his social activities, etc. In order to elicit such "nostalgic" retrospections, the therapist might become a bit personal and mention some such facts about his own life. However, he should be prompt to turn the conversation toward the patient's experiences as soon as he has aroused his interest in talking about himself. Now he can ask adroit questions while showing much genuine interest in what the patient says.

In order to gain sufficient rapport to start this procedure, the therapist might say the following: "Mr. S., I would be much interested in knowing something about your life back home, and I know you must remember most of it, just as I can remember mine. Now, where were you five years ago, for instance, and what kind of work were you doing then?" The patient can usually answer this. "Now, Mr. S., let's think back five years, and discuss some things about that time. Let's imagine that you right now are living and working at your job back home; in short, imagine right now you are there. What would you be doing each day on the job and at home after work? Now, imagine you are on that job right now!" When the patient now seems to be "living and experiencing" in memory events of that period as if it were the present, such as telling about home, work, friends, etc., the therapist might suddenly broach one or two of the patient's most extreme ideas and say, for instance, "Mr. S., what would you think if I should tell you this?" (Therapist mentions a particular abnormal idea.) The patient may be a bit startled, since a definitely abnormal idea is suddenly planted in the midst of normal thinking in retrospect, that is, if he has been strongly "reliving" the earlier period. He may say, "Doc, that sounds crazy!" Then the therapist can say, "Yes, it is a 'crazy' idea which you never used to have before. Why have you been thinking this peculiar thing only recently?" Other peculiar behaviors should similarly be contrasted between the two periods of the patient's life. When the "reliving" is indulged in quite strongly, and the confrontation with the psychotic phenomena is made sharply and clearly, real doubt and some true insight may often be elicited.

Technique 4. Forcing a quandary. In discussing each symptom it is often possible and very effective to juxtapose strongly conflicting elements, which may be in the form of either concrete evidence, with which the patient is familiar, or even strong logical points, which are within the patient's ability to entertain. By such means the therapist often can and should put the patient into a quandary and thereby force him to think about just juxtaposed conflicting concrete evidence and ideas. Once in such a quandary, the patient is naturally given sufficient time to think and express himself, but the therapist should otherwise keep up the pressure firmly and persistently.

Although almost any type of delusional topic may be chosen to illustrate the quandary technique in essence, I will use one representing a few cases that I have dealt with in the past. For instance, the patient believes he has an impossible number of legitimate offspring, although having been married only a reasonable length of time and, in some cases, to only one woman.

First, it is well to have the patient firmly admit his belief in order to definitely establish the erroneous idea against which later arguments and evidence will be strongly pressed. Without commenting on the idea at this time, the therapist, as if leaving this topic completely in order to take the patient "off his guard," so to speak, should begin to show personal interest in the patient's ordinary affairs in life. Gradually, however, the questions begin to turn toward the much more delusionally pertinent topics regarding his marriage, his real children by this wife, their names, ages, and present whereabouts, et cetera.

In the case of this particular delusional topic, in order to increase the build up of counter arguments soon to be used, it is well for the therapist to remind the patient of certain ordinary biological facts as the duration of pregnancy, the limited number of possible offspring of a marriage, et cetera. Then, when the patient is thinking fully in terms of concrete facts about his life and family, the therapist should mention the real children specifically which have been described before. While still keeping this concrete topic fully before the patient, the therapist should suddenly and abruptly confront him with his delusion of the abstract offspring, perhaps in terms of "all those hundreds of imaginary children you've dreamed up!" At this point, and without waiting for the patient to "'marshal his ideas," so to speak, the therapist should press him for answers to such questions as the children's names, their ages, their present whereabouts, their occupations, and any other specific and overwhelming questions that will force the patient to begin to struggle mentally to account for his "hundreds" of imaginary children.

Such a sudden, pressing contrast of ideas will often cause the patient to begin experiencing some doubt about his belief, and this doubt should be reinforced by further intense questioning and pressuring for answers. After the patient begins to show that he is in an ideational impasse, the therapist should abruptly charge the patient's belief as being "clearly erroneous" and "a figment of wild imagination," assuring him that "obviously such an idea is utterly impossible to ever be true." The patient is then strongly urged, on the other hand, to concentrate his attention and interest on his wife and his real sons and daughters, as well as on other concrete, practical matters, and to guard against drifting into uncontrolled imagination.

Incidentally, this technique of conflict of opposing elements is a critical one for determining whether the delusional material is fixed and the case is permanent and hopeless. Very rarely have I found this technique to fail to indicate permanent delusion, and never has it failed in those cases otherwise thought to be chronic because of other accepted indications, both functional and organic. This technique is a two-step one in which the patient, holding Belief No. 1 (delusional), is first attempted to be "sold" conflicting Belief No. 2 (normal in ideation or evidence). This can frequently be done. The second step is where, when he now rather strongly accepts the opposing belief, he must be made to see that it and the former oppose each other, being mutually exclusive, and that he cannot hold both. If, after the strongest efforts, the patient accepts both but cannot relinquish one as impossible in such circumstances, it is strongly conclusive evidence that the case is chronic and hopeless.

Technique 5. "Challenging" the patient. There are situations when the therapist may effectively employ a "challenging" technique. (This is similar to the age-old propagandist's method of not even admitting for a moment that there is "another" side to a topic.) This requires an extreme degree of unabashed confidence in one's own opinion which, in dealing with a similar condition in the patient for his own (abnormal) belief, means that there is a powerful conflict created. This may, in the patient's thinking, begin to arouse some doubt about his belief leading to a glimmer of insight. The therapist, therefore, should use a calm, but firmly direct, attack. He discounts the validity of the psychotic phenomena, and he may speak in a matter-of-fact way to disparage and minimize—not the patient—the belief in the delusional material and other phenomena; he discounts such phenomena themselves as merely errors that upset nerves cause people to show, merely well-known "tricks of the mind" when one's "nerves" are upset. However, such disparagement and discounting of the symptoms must be done with much persuasiveness in voice and manner. Also, the therapist must be ever ready to revert to the use of comparisons, contrasts, et cetera, to support his discussion if they should be needed. Such comparisons and contrasts are made with the patient's normal behaviors at earlier times in his life or with the behavior of other patients, friends, et cetera, as described before.

In order to illustrate the challenging technique, let us assume the grandiose delusion of being a certain great personage now dead. However, many delusional topics might be chosen to illustrate this, since the "propagandist's" method of admitting only one side of a problem to exist can serve in each case. Perhaps the patient states his "identity" even casually to the therapist. The therapist, just as casually and matter-of-factly, might say something along this line: "No, Mr. S., I can't buy that idea of your being So-and-so at all!" The patient naturally continues to believe his false identity, so the therapist should suggest other particular "identities," such as questioning whether he could possibly be his (the patient's) own brother or his own father, et cetera. As the subject of the patient's "identity" is now deceased, the therapist should stress this fact, confirming it by stating that public notice was made of this in the past or even that the death occurred "before you were born." Here the therapist should pointedly ask just how the patient can explain his belief.

When the patient is allowed to state his reason for holding such a belief, the therapist should become more positive and challenge him by asserting, "Not only can I not accept your idea, which is clearly impossible, but I just know no one else can believe it. Suppose we ask a few people whether they agree with you or me." Without asking the patient's "permission," the therapist might draw aside, one by one, the next few individuals who happen to come past and, by way of avoiding embarrassment to the patient, casually ask such a "hypothetical" question as, for instance, "Could anyone now living be So-and-so?" (known to be deceased), or, "Could So-and-so, who died in (date), return to life and be another person today?"

After receiving a few inevitably negative replies, the therapist should say to the patient in a pointedly uncompromising manner something like: "Now, Mr. S., you see each of these people fully agreed with me that such an idea is not only definitely false but most peculiar besides.

Nobody accepts your idea. The great So-and-so died even before you were born, and no two people can be the same person, even if they are living at the same time. You cannot be your own brother, and you know this very well; so, neither can you be anyone else than yourself." After permitting a brief time for the patient to think about all this, the therapist might say very positively, implying that there are no grounds for even further discussion at all, something like: "Come now, Mr. S., you must see that your peculiar belief about being So-and-so, long dead, is not only false and even impossible, but shows plainly that your mind has merely tricked you into believing such a thing. When you can begin to see and accept the plain fact that your identification with the great So-and-so is utterly false, you will begin to recover from your present condition which brought you to this kind of hospital." The therapist has ample opportunity to note the emergence of doubt, at least, and perhaps some degree of true insight during this session. If so, he should strenuously press his advantage in this and later sessions, if necessary.

In many cases the patient can be benefited here by getting some educative information ahead of time. This is done by explaining in simple, clear language just what each symptom really means scientifically. (I have worked out a quick, simple scientific explanation for each of the major symptoms found. See Technique No. 7, "Discussing 'Tricks of the Mind.'") In this and the other techniques, the therapist must continue to demonstrate the aforementioned essential personality traits, especially impressing the patient with his sincere desire to help him to return to his former healthy state.

Technique 6. "Needling" the patient. A final special technique may be used in those cases in which the patient holds a delusion that seems so ideationally "compact" or self-contained that there are no apparent openings in which the therapist can get a hold or come to grips with the patient's thinking. In such cases, with or without logic-tight systematization, I use a technique in which I "needle" the patient with simple questions of the "Why," "How," "When," et cetera types, forcing him to explain each point in his answers in as minute detail as possible. Although many patients, depending upon the amount of schizophrenic material present, can often produce increasingly bizarre replies, other patients eventually come to the "I-really-don't-know" point. It is here that the therapist is quick to kindly, but strongly emphasize the patient's "helplessness" and apply the appropriate brief, clear explanation, but always with strong persuasiveness. In such a way the otherwise "solid" delusion, whether simple or complex, can occasionally be "perforated" and injected with doubts, which consequently begins to initiate improvement.

Occasionally a patient can be found with the delusion of having lived an earlier life, perhaps in an earlier age. Although this idea is rather rare in our Western culture, it is a type of delusion in which there is difficulty for the therapist to get a hold. In such a delusion little concrete evidence either proves or disproves the claim, and only logic argues against it; and these arguments are based upon ordinary materialistic facts mainly of a biological nature. Since this is so, the patient can often hold out against such arguments, as if challenging the therapist to prove him wrong. [Incidentally, it is known that there have been alleged cases, mainly in the Near East and India, in which rare individuals not only claimed a former existence but could clearly describe persons, places, and things pertinent to the claim which, according to reports of several investigating Western scientists, did corroborate such claims to a very high degree. Needless to say, such often accepted claims by natives of the East are more or less peremptorily discounted as delusional in the West (4).]

The therapist should first lead the patient to state his claim of a former life clearly and invite some specific details. Since it is impossible, or nearly so, to collect concrete information about the specific individuals and region alluded to by the patient—such meticulous checking was done by the previously mentioned investigators in the East—the therapist must resort to very specific, pointed questions, and also cross-questioning when possible, in order to elicit contradictions in the patient's answers. Such questioning must force very detailed explanations and may start almost casually with questions about the present life, including the inquiry about how far back he can remember. To his own conception? To his own birth? If he cannot remember either of these two events, why can he not do so? If he claims he can, in either case, then force him to describe each in detail and point out all discrepancies possible to be found in the account.

The therapist's inquiry should soon lead back into the patient's "former" life period and, needless to say, the possible number and varieties of specific questions are vast, limited only by the therapist's ingenuity and available time. Specific questions are in order from now on, about the patient's earlier "'death" and its details about his "reconception" following bodily disintegration, and numerous facts about such ordinary topical areas as education, occupational training and work experience, marriage, family, friends, interests, et cetera, of the "former" life. The possibilities are endless. Incidentally, in regard to educational and occupational preparation in the previous life, why was it necessary for the patient to undergo reeducation and retraining for work in the present life?

If the questions are very specific, detailed, and numerous and the answers are forcefully elicited, the patient can eventually be expected to arrive at a stage of bewilderment amidst a maze of contradictions, inadequate explanations, with inability to extricate himself until, finally, he reaches a veritable "I-just-don't-know" dead end. It is here and now that the therapist, in order to inject strong doubt in the patient about his delusion, should take full and emphatic advantage of the situation by bluntly pointing out the patient's helplessness and the weaknesses and downright errors in the thinking, stressing the faulty role of his wild imagination. The demonstration of the negative aspects of the case should then be followed by the more positive, therapeutic "indoctrination" of healthy, correct, realistic thinking, such as is familiar to the average therapist.

After these and other techniques have been used with occasional repetition in some cases, some insight will usually appear. At the first signs of insight, the therapist may in many instances inject some humor into the discussions, taking care not to let the patient think that it is done at his expense, however. Especially must caution be used in those patients who have paranoidal trends. As insight begins to appear, the patient will show some improvement in ability to discuss his condition, and the therapist should continue with more educative procedures by taking up one major symptom at a time (assuming that this has not previously been done in special situations), and explain it simply from various standpoints, such as its significance; how it occurs (if possible); how it is abnormal (which can usually be seen by now), and how it differs so radically from what had ever happened to him before; what he would have thought of it before he became ill, whether found in himself or another person; how impossible it would be for such phenomena to be real; what his attitude should be toward these "tricks of the mind when sick" now and in the future if they should ever occur again. Such discursive procedures are believed to have high rehabilitative value in that they tend to strengthen the newly gained insight and reorient the patient's thinking and feeling about himself and his condition as well as his relation to others; it is essentially an educative procedure once the insightless barrier is destroyed.

By maintaining throughout the discussion an undertone of unyielding assurance that, so long as one still has such traits as the patient has, one's mind is not well, the therapist should enable the patient's insight to continue to strengthen and his interest to improve. When insight has become quite complete, then the therapist may lessen his attack and begin to discuss the illness in as casual a manner as he would discuss any physical ailment, thus preventing the now insightful patient from becoming too anxious or preoccupied with his "past" condition, for he will by this time be well on the way toward recovery; any possibility of regression is naturally to be avoided. From here on the therapist and the patient will be able to delve freely into the origins and causes of his now-admitted abnormal mentation, emotionality, and general behavior so recently displayed. Therefore, it is here that the therapist may wish to use other types of therapy, including some depth therapy (if pertinent in the case) as is so often successful with neurotics, with or without more educative and reeducative supplementation.

Technique 7. Discussing "Tricks of the Mind." Assure the patient pointedly and sincerely from time to time that his symptoms, which are definite signs of "upset nerves," are also the results of "tricks of the mind; that the mind can and does often play such tricks on a person when the nerves are sick." In regard to explanations to the patient of the real significance of various psychotic phenomena, e.g., hallucinations, the therapist points out the similarity of dreaming while asleep, on the one hand, and the projection of visual, auditory, and other pseudosensory experiences while awake, on the other hand. Both are shown as involving the functioning of mental and emotional processes on the subconscious levels, with the waking experiences of vision and audition being projected outwardly.

Such explanations of the projecting of what one is thinking and feeling below consciousness, which is being projected outwardly—usually such "dream material" is quite different from what one may be thinking and feeling at that very time on the conscious level—must be put to the patient on his own level of comprehension, naturally. These explanations of how the conscious and subconscious levels can deal with different topics simultaneously, and the subconscious can without warning project its material into the subject's consciousness, should further confirm to the patient the fact that the mind can "play tricks on one." Furthermore, the therapist might also differentiate between the functioning of the dream state and the tricky projections of the unhealthy mind in the waking state, on the one hand, as being the result of the wild imagination of an uncontrolled mind, from the well-ordered, controlled imagination and thinking of the healthy mind, on the other hand.

Not only hallucinatory experience, but also delusional thinking and other psychotic phenomena, can be explained in terms of deficiencies, peculiar associations, distortions, projections, and the like, of conscious and subconscious levels of functioning. In dealing with such ideas, the therapist should maintain his advantage by pointedly relating such abnormal functionings with the idea of "mental tricks" being imposed on the patient. The close associations made frequently of such ideas will usually stimulate a healthy doubt in the patient's thinking, especially as he begins to see some rational explanations for his present peculiar and disturbing experiences (which, he should also be reminded, he had never experienced before in his early life—an observation which also has been found to have some doubt-elicitation value). It is felt that the therapist, by using his ingenuity, can both modify his procedures and devise others in innumerable ways as the variety of situations may require.

At this point the patient may be apt to say with some mild surprise, "Doc, I never thought of that before," or "I think you've got something there, Doc," or a similar statement indicating some degree of insight, as I have often heard during therapy sessions. Be sure to correlate such false mentation and other psychotic phenomena with his "lack of insight" also. The therapist should also play up the idea from time to time of the patient's present lack of insight, and how his own mind has now been tricking him into actually believing, feeling, and doing such things (mentioning them briefly), which he never in all his past life believed, felt, and did! The therapist should firmly urge the patient to concentrate on such contrasts for a while.

## DESIRABLE FOLLOW-UP PROCEDURES

Not only may the therapist make use of other techniques to ferret out deeper etiological factors in the recent illness, but he may be able to indicate to the patient, for future information and possible use, certain incipient signs denoting possible recurrence of the illness. These vary considerably with the disorder, naturally, but a knowledge of them could be of value to the patient in some exceptional cases. Finally, the therapist should give occasional helpful mental hygienic suggestions, wherever possible, for aiding the patient to avoid a recurrence of the illness. This obviously would depend upon the type of disorder for, although many illnesses come on imperceptibly with gradual loss of insight, there are some types in which the first signs can be easily noticed by the person, and he may take necessary precautionary measures before insight leaves.

I believe such sound information to be quite valuable in many cases, if for no more useful reason than that the patient will be forewarned to visit his physician at the approach of the first signs, since prevention is obviously of inestimably more value than doubtful cure.

In conclusion, we believe that the Illumination Method, as applied to psychoses, is a relatively new psychotherapeutic procedure for not only accelerating the return of insight to the patient and thereby initiating recovery but, in some cases with or without assistance from other therapies, ultimately completely effecting full recovery from certain functional and organic psychotic disorders in much shorter time by employing a direct, aggressive attack on them, rather than by depending upon passive, indirect, and necessarily slow, ponderous techniques. Furthermore, even in cases where other psychotherapeutic methods have been started originally, the Illumination Method may be successfully employed to supplement these by reorienting and reorganizing the patient's mentational and emotional patterns of behavior toward healthy personality functioning.

We also believe that the Illumination Method, for best results, requires a more or less extroverted, dynamic type of personality to administer it effectively and one who possesses and exhibits certain cardinal personality traits in himself, which stimulate confidence, respect, and even at times affection in the patient.

## REFERENCES

1. Bugental, J. F. T. The person who is the psychotherapist. *J. Consulting Psychol.*, 1964, **28** (3), 272–277.
2. Fisher, V. E. Psychic shock treatment in early schizophrenia. *Amer. J. Orthopsychiat.*, 1949, **14**, 358–367.
3. Rosen, J. Direct psychoanalysis. *Trans. N. Y. Acad. Sci.*, 1962, **25** (2), 201–221.
4. Stevenson, I. Twenty cases suggestive of reincarnation. *Proceedings of the American Society for Psychical Research*, 1966, **26**.
5. Walder, E. Synanon and the learning process—a critique of attack therapy. *Corr. Psychiat. J. Soc. Ther.* 1965, **11** (6), 299–304.
6. Yablonski, L. *The tunnel back: Synanon.* New York: Macmillan, 1965.

Chapter 18

# Problem-Centered Guidance

## HENRY WEITZ

Henry Weitz: b. 1911, New York, New York.
A.B., in economics, Dartmouth College, 1933. Ed.M., 1936, Ed.D., 1942, in psychology and guidance, Rutgers University.
Director, Duke University Counseling Center and Associate Professor of Education, 1950–date. Fulbright Professor, University of Ceylon, 1963–1964. Director, University of Delaware Psychological Service Center, 1946–1950.
Diplomate in Counseling, American Board of Examiners in Professional Psychology. Fellow, Division of American Psychological Association. Former President, North Carolina Personnel and Guidance Association.
Books: *Behavior Change Through Guidance* (1964).
Articles: (Co-author) Improving the academic performance of anxious college freshmen. *Psych. Monographs*, No. 590, 1964.

### PURPOSE OF PROBLEM-CENTERED GUIDANCE

Problem-centered guidance[1] is based on the general view that human experience is most likely to be personally satisfying and socially creative when it achieves a state of serenity, a state of dynamic peace that flows forward to achieve meaningful, distant goals, all the while spontaneously and effortlessly held on course by internal reference signals that in themselves have an internal consistency and order permitting them to check conflict before it arises. Thus problem-centered guidance is seen as a means of providing a set of internal reference signals, generalized problem-solving behavior, which will enable the inexperienced, the psychically enfeebled, or the troubled person to find serenity.

From the outset, the guidance movement has been concerned with the solution of human problems and with the general adjustment of individuals who have encountered difficulties in meeting the educa-

---

[1] A major part of the content of this paper is drawn from H. Weitz, *Behavior Change Through Guidance*, John Wiley and Sons, Inc., 1964, with the special permission of the publishers.

tional, vocational, personal, social, and emotional demands of their environment. (See References 2, 3, 9, 16.) The principal difference—if there is one—between the purposes of these earlier formulations of guidance and the purposes of the present formulation is that problem-centered guidance is centrally concerned with a generalized problem-solving process rather than, except incidentally, with the solution of specific problems.

## GUIDANCE, COUNSELING, AND PSYCHOTHERAPY

This process of developing generalized problem-solving behavior is more appropriately labeled guidance than, say, counseling or psychotherapy. The latter term, psychotherapy, carries with it the notion of illness and medical practice, despite efforts to color the term with a contrary connotation (11). Persons undertaking a program of guidance need not be sick, in the medical sense, although they are, for the most part, inexperienced in the solution of their personal problems and often troubled. The more generally used term counseling also seems inappropriate for the process being considered here, for it represents only one technique of guidance. Guidance, as viewed in this discussion, encompasses in addition to individual and group counseling, assessment through testing and direct behavior observation, information services, and direct intervention in the client's behavior. We have chosen, therefore, to return to the old term guidance. Not vocational guidance, just plain guidance. And we mean by it what it used to mean: professional assistance in solving problems and in acquiring generalized problem-solving behavior.

## THEORETICAL FOUNDATIONS

Problem-centered guidance is derived from the Behavior Product model of human behavior (15, pp. 1–43) which provides a theoretical basis for the techniques suggested. This formulation includes three basic considerations that are essential to the practice of guidance.

1. Human experience operates in two domains: (a) objective reality and (b) symbolic reality. The behavior performed in these two domains, objective behavior and symbolic behavior, interest and modify each other. Guidance depends, in a large measure, on this interaction and on the capacity of human beings to translate the behavior of one domain into the behavior of the other.

2. Human behavior is continuous and unsegmented. Each be-

havioral event is intimately united with and derived from every earlier act, and each act as it is performed establishes itself as an essential element of some future experience. Through the process of learning, past behavior modifies present behavior and present behavior modifies the behavior of some future event. Future behavior—symbolic, of course—can and does modify present behavior, both objective and symbolic. Moreover, present behavior can modify past behavior or at least the perception of it. Guidance can utilize this interaction of past, present, and future behavior to accomplish changes in both present and future behavior.

3. Although it is impossible in objective reality to segment the continuous flow of human experience, it is possible to do this symbolically in order to analyze the structure of behavior. The simplest analyzable unit of human behavior may be identified as the behavior product. This unit is composed of two basic elements, the reactional biography and the environmental context. Interactions of these basic elements produce a derived element, the stimulus function, which represents the meaning of objects and events to the individual. Interactions between this derived element, the stimulus function, and elements of the individual's response repertory (a part of the reactional biography) result in the behavior product. The dynamic structure of these components of the behavior product suggest ways in which intervention by means of guidance can be applied to effect behavior modifications.

## THE BEHAVIOR PRODUCT

Some elaboration of the behavior product model may help to clarify the discussion of problem-centered guidance which follows. As indicated previously, two primary elements are in each behavior product: the environmental context, which provides the stimulus objects and events, and the individual's reactional biography from which the response repertory is drawn.

The reactional biography (5, 15) may be defined as the total historical experience of the individual, both objective and symbolic, up to and including the immediate behavioral event under consideration. These experiences operating on the physiological mechanisms of the individual produce learned responses. These learned responses make up the individual's response repertory through which he interacts with his environment.

At least four types of responses make up the response repertory:

awareness, manipulative, communication, and feeling. Awareness responses interacting with stimulus objects and events produce stimulus functions by giving these objects and events meaning derived from the individual's historical experience. Manipulative, communication, and feeling responses, as well as awareness responses, interact then with these stimulus functions to form behavior products. It is important to note that within the response repertory the various categories of response can interact with each other. Thus the response itself becomes a part of the next stimulus function.

The environmental context is made up of the cultural matrix, the psychosocial climate, the time–space continuum of the physical world, and the individual himself. It is important to note that the individual (the reactional biography) is a part of the environmental context and all of its components, and simultaneously an independent element in the behavior product. From the environmental context element, stimulus objects and events emerge. These objects and events themselves, however, participate directly only in the preliminary interactions of the behavior product and not in the final interactions. This preliminary interaction between the stimulus objects and events and the awareness response produces the stimulus function.

The stimulus function of a stimulus object or event is the meaning extracted from the object or event through its interaction with the awareness responses in the response repertory (5, 15). Once the object or event has assumed meaning, once it has become a stimulus function, it can evoke manipulative, communication, and feeling responses to form behavior products.

Each behavior product as it is performed produces response-correlated stimuli (7, 8). These serve, among other things, as feedback signals to interact with feeling responses and inform the individual about the way in which the behavior is being performed. These response-correlated stimuli participate actively as part of the stimulus function of subsequent behavior products.

The behavior product, then, is composed of two primary elements, a derived element, and three interactions:

1. Primary elements: the environmental context and the reactional biography.
2. Derived element: the stimulus function.
3. Interactions:
   a. stimulus objects and events with awareness responses to form stimulus functions.

 b. stimulus functions with the response repertory to form behavior products.

 c. response-correlated stimuli with feeling responses to form feedback stimuli.

The guidance process is primarily a part of the environmental context. It functions especially as part of the cultural matrix and the psychosocial climate. Although it can do little to modify the reactional biography directly, it can achieve changes in behavior by manipulating the environmental context in such a way as to modify stimulus functions with which the individual's behavior repertory interacts. In this way the behavior products are modified through the external intervention of the guidance process, and, thus, future behavior is made more effective.

## GOALS OF PROBLEM-CENTERED GUIDANCE

Problem-centered guidance seeks to achieve three objectives:

1. To aid the troubled individual in overcoming the immediate obstacle to his on-going, goal-directed behavior;

2. To utilize this experience as a means of establishing in the individual a system of generalized problem-solving behavior;

3. To apply this generalized problem-solving behavior in such a way as to aid the individual in achieving a high level of serenity.

The third objective, of course, encompasses the other two. It is the most general and represents the over-all goal of problem-centered guidance. Behavior systems, however conceptualized, operate to create energy and to maintain it at a high level of readiness within the local system. This involves the reduction of entropy (locally), the decrease in confusion, disorder, and randomness in the interrelationships of the elements of the system. Thus, the individual who is functioning effectively is the one whose behavior is characterized by a high energy level and hence by a highly systematized and ordered structure of behavioral elements. Under these conditions order exists, energy for action is available, and the organism operates serenely. Here serenity is viewed as orderly, energetic, conflict-free, goal-directed activity, and not simply static stability.

The other two objectives—the solution of immediate problems and the establishment of generalized problem-solving behavior—are simply immediate means of achieving the ultimate objective of assisting the individual in finding ways to lead a productive, satisfying, serene life.

Within recent years there appears to have been a growing emphasis on the role of the interpersonal relationship between the practitioner and his client as a primary goal of guidance (12, 1). This mutually accepting relationship, involving unconditional regard of the counselor for his client, is presented as a central purpose of guidance. Such difficulties as those which drove the client to seek the aid of a counselor, such problems as those he faces, are resolved by the client himself through the strength he draws from the relationship. The present formulation of the goals of guidance takes the position that the client has a right to expect some professional intervention when he seeks the aid of a counselor. Although unconditional regard and acceptance may serve as a desirable frame of reference when they emerge spontaneously, as they do more often than not in the case of the dedicated practitioner, they are inadequate as goals of guidance and may not even be necessary means for achieving the goals suggested earlier.

Another recent concern of guidance practitioners has been the development of freedom as a goal. This is particularly evident in the work of practitioners who view themselves as existentialists. A. van Kamm, for example, states: "Counseling is essentially a process of making-free, a humanizing of the person who has lost his freedom in sectors of his existence where he can no longer transcend his life situation by freely giving meaning to it." (14, p. 403). And Arbuckle combines the goals of freedom and relationship when he says:

> A definition of counseling that I have attempted to work toward is one of human relationship—a warm relationship in which the counselor, fully and completely, without any ifs or buts, accepts the client as a worthy person. In this relationship of complete acceptance, the client can grow and develop, and come to use the strengths and capacities that are his and to make decisions and choices that will be satisfactory to him, and thus to his fellows. (1, p. 70)

Arbuckle, however, makes some concessions to reason and order when he concludes the preceding statement with "Such decisions will be rational and logical in that they will bear some relationship to the assets and liabilities that are possessed by the individual." (1, p. 70).

One is inclined to suspect that the freedom and free choice of the existentialists in guidance fails to take into account the objective reality of the society to which human beings are bound and from which man draws his humanness.

> Man has been shown to be a social being, nourished and shaped by the culture of the society in which he lives. Far from being endowed by nature, apart from society, with intelligence, personality, and inalienable rights, he is, without benefit of the culture built by the cooperative efforts of countless generations of men, little more than a mere brute, devoid alike of language, reason, conscious selfhood, or any sense of moral right. (13, p. 192)

Basically, then, it is the society that determines much of the general structure of man's behavior. Although the individual, in concert with his co-members, can and often does modify elements of the social structure, and although, over time, the cumulative effect of these minor changes may become a social revolution, during short periods of time—say, during an individual's life—the social structure governs, within fairly flexible tolerances to be sure, the structure of an individual's behavior.

From this general notion of the relationship between social forces and the individual's behavior we can derive one means of describing what is meant by ordered, systematic behavior, which, as suggested, yields available productive behavioral energy. Behavior may be ordered in such a way as to be consistent with the structure of the society in which the individual holds membership. Such a conception of order in human behavior often raises the goblin of "deadly conformity." This ghost, as in the case of most ghosts, is fantasy, that is, intentionally created unreality, for social behavioral norms, even in highly primitive and rigid societies, permit and even encourage wide variations. Ordered behavior can be developed within these tolerances and serenity achieved.

These, then, are the goals of problem-centered guidance: serenity, the development of generalized problem-solving behavior which facilitates the achievement of serenity, and the incidental solution of the immediate problem which can serve as an exercise in the acquisition of generalized problem-solving behavior.

## PRECONDITIONS FOR GUIDANCE

Problem-centered guidance requires certain preconditions before the enterprise can be initiated. These involve the individual before he seeks the aid of the counselor.

At the outset we have an individual going about his every-day business. His response repertory appears adequate to the demands placed on it. He performs the tasks required of him, and he meets his personal and social obligations with a minimum of stress and conflict. The feedback from his behavior is satisfying, and it informs him that he is meeting his own criteria for self-maintenance and development. As long as events continue in this style, there is no need for guidance.

At some point in this serene sequence of behavior some obstacle intervenes. The smooth behavioral flow is interrupted. His affective responses (feedback mechanisms) tell him that his behavior is not consistent with the tolerances permitted either by the social structure or by his own internal reference signals (value system).

The obstacle may be any event that interferes with the serene behavioral flow or that threatens to effect radical or unknown changes in his behavior. Obstacles to on-going behavior may be loosely categorized in the following ways: (1) new or unexpected demands of an institution, such as school or work; (2) demands of interpersonal relationships with members of the family, authority figures, friends, or associates; (3) demands of sexual pressures involving love, affection, or affiliation; and (4) demands of a personal or social value system involving religious, moral, or ethical conflicts. More often than not the obstacle involves some combination of these factors. The individual's inability to overcome these obstacles by meeting these new or unexpected demands effectively may be the consequence of limited talent or experience or it may result from some unfortunate or untimely configuration of events in the environmental context. In general, however, the individual's failure to meet the demands he encounters results from some combination of personal inadequacy interacting with an impersonal and seemingly hostile social environment.

More often than not, the individual is able—given time—to overcome the obstacles he encounters in a lifetime by utilizing the response repertory at his disposal, effecting on his own such minor modifications as the occasion may demand. Most people, most of the time solve their own problems in their own way.

Occasionally, however, an individual finds that no combination or modification of the behavior products at his disposal appears to provide a solution to his dilemma. Repeated attempts to overcome the obstacle with familiar behavior yields only repeated failure, which in turn evokes a sense of fearful urgency. Frantic, frequently irrelevant, efforts to surmount or circumvent the obstacle emerge. As these random endeavors yield additional failures, a state of malaise, stress, frustration, and anxiety permeates the behavior.

When the pressures of the situation become sufficiently great, the frustrated, anxious individual may seek professional assistance. The act of seeking professional help in solving the problem may be part of the random activity of the individual, a kind of last resort. In more highly structured and institutionalized situations, the process of seeking professional assistance may be a regular part of the individual's response repertory. When the individual seeks the aid of a professional counselor, his role changes. He becomes what Rogers (11) first called a client. In this new role he begins to accept the inadequacies of his own isolated attempts to solve his problem and to recognize his need to enlist the collaboration of another in finding solutions to his difficulties.

These, then, are the preexisting conditions that obtain at the time guidance begins. Some obstacle disrupts the on-going behavior of an individual. His own efforts to overcome the obstacle lead to failure and produce frustration and anxiety. As a further or last attempt to solve his problem, he seeks the collaboration of a counselor and becomes the client-participant in guidance.

A further consideration needs to be mentioned at this point. The client seeking guidance need not know the nature of the obstacle to his goals, nor even of the goals themselves. He need not know what is troubling him, only that he is troubled. The lurking sense that "things don't seem to be going right" accompanied by a feeling of anxiety is an adequate basis for guidance. Basic to the guidance process before it starts is an obstacle to the client's on-going behavior and the sense of frustration and anxiety evoked by the client's inability to resolve the issue on his own.

This basic state of affairs represents a problem. The resolution of the problem, the removal of the impediment to his on-going behavior should permit the client to rediscover serenity, to move forward productively toward satisfying distant goals. Furthermore, if guidance is effective, it not only identifies and resolves the immediate problem but also aids the client in acquiring generalized problem-solving behavior. Unless this latter step is accomplished, the client is faced with the long-run frustration of having to attack each new problem as it arises with no more effective behavior than he had previously. Thus the problem-centered counselor views the client as raising the question, "How do I solve problems like this one?" and not, "How do I solve this problem?"

## THE PROBLEM-SOLVING PROCESS

The problem-centered approach to guidance suggests the necessarily collaborative nature of the guidance relationship. The client and counselor, together, combine their resources and skills to solve the problem. The client uses the counselor as a device for solving his problem. In doing this, the client controls the process in such a way that he may extract from the collaborative relationship an understanding of how the counselor manipulated events to achieve a solution. Thus, if the counselor is a true collaborator and has been open, revealing, and instructive about what has been going on in the problem-solving process, he is able to facilitate the client's acquisition of new problem-solving behavior.

How, then, does the process operate? The solution of the day-to-day problems of human beings requires, at the outset, a clear, manageable statement of what the problems are. This statement involves not only the identification of the obstacles but also some clarification of the course which they obstruct. Thus, in securing an accurate and tractable description of the problem, it becomes necessary to know the client's goals, values, and objectives and his capacities for achieving them, as well as the social and personal limitations that serve as obstructions to achievement. This description of behavior products involving goals, means, and limitations constitutes the diagnosis or, as we shall call it here, problem identification. The problem-identification step in problem solving includes the observation of behavior, the structured description of it, and the identification of the many interrelated facets of the multiordinal problem.

Problem identification involves the coding of events that have occurred in objective reality in such a way that the symbols used in the guidance interaction, which is primarily a symbolic interaction, are closely related to the objective events they are intended to represent.

Problem identification, involving as it does the manipulation of symbols representing objective events and the formation of symbolic structures based upon higher-order abstractions, is a connected series of semantic reactions performed by client and counselor. Problem identification requires that the right (i.e., the realistic) symbols be found to describe events in the client's life and that they be organized into structures which clearly represent the relationship of events as they occur in objective reality.

Just as guidance cannot be segmented from the rest of the life of the client, so problem identification cannot be separated from the rest of the guidance process. We cannot think of problem identification as some discrete segment of the guidance process, for as symbols are manipulated in the total problem-solving process, new symbols and labels are called for to complete new patterns. The new symbols are generated from the application of new diagnostic procedures and techniques—tests, interviews, and the like—or are abstracted from the symbolic configurations already at hand. It is important to note, however, that the identification process is in operation throughout the entire course of the guidance undertaking.

This process of discovering appropriate symbols and realistic structures in the course of helping a client solve a problem takes place in somewhat the following manner:

1. The client participates in some event.
2. Out of all the elements in the event, the client selects some; these he perceives and responds to.
3. Out of all the responses made by the client in the situation, he selects some; these he reports to the counselor.
4. The counselor listens to the client, and while he is listening, he symbolically projects some of his own similar experiences into the client's description.
5. Out of this total description—including the counselor's projections—the counselor selects some elements; these he perceives and responds to by drawing inferences and formulating structures.
6. Out of all of these inferences and structures, the counselor selects some; these he reports. This report by the counselor, involving high-order abstractions in some cases far removed from the original event, is his tentative problem identification or diagnosis.

This description of the identified problem is made up of verbal symbols representing objects, events, conditions, and so on, of which some exist in the objective reality of the client, some in the objective reality of the counselor, and still others only in the symbolic reality of both. This description also represents the symbolic interrelationships of the events. The tentative identification of the problem is composed of the symbols that the counselor and the client will collaboratively manipulate in the problem-solving process. As can be seen from the above description of the problem-identification step in guidance, it is essentially a process of abstraction. As the diagnosis proceeds, the level of abstraction becomes more general and farther removed from the objective events as they occurred. In the process of abstracting from one level to the next in problem identification, the danger is always present of mistaking one level for another. For example, when a client in an effort to justify his present fear of animals reports a painful experience, let us say, of having been bitten by a dog when he was a child, and the counselor responds to this emotionally delivered report by saying, "You were frightened by that dog," the counselor must not delude himself into thinking that he is, or even can be, reflecting the same fear being described by the client. He is merely providing the diagnostic label *frightened by a dog*, which can subsequently be manipulated in the problem-solving process. This confusion of level of abstraction has led a generation of nondirective counselors to a fanciful view of their counseling behavior, their function, and their responsibility.

Thus far we have been discussing the process of abstracting diagnostic labels from the client's own reports of his experiences. The same semantic principles apply, however, to other diagnostic machinery. For example, counselors find tests extremely helpful as diagnostic tools in observing human behavior. This is especially true in that class of events that has been called educational guidance. Let us suppose that the client is a college sophomore seeking assistance in securing better grades in school. In such a situation the counselor and the client may collaboratively decide that it would be helpful in this problem-solving situation to know something about the client's ability to earn better grades. Thus they decide to make an estimate of the client's academic talents by using a test of ability labeled scholastic aptitude test. Just what does this mean on the objective level of behavior?

The client has a repertory of responses, acquired through a great variety of experiences, that makes it possible for him to behave, under certain circumstances, in ways which seem to please college professors. This mode of behavior we may call scholastic aptitude. Out of this rather vast store of responses, the client is stimulated by the test to produce a few. This sample taken from the client's response repertory is measured and assigned a numerical label. The counselor knows that this numerical label represents some combination of appropriate and inappropriate responses interacting with the test items. This label, he also knows, is subject to a variety of sampling and administrative errors. The test score, this numerical symbol, represents an error-loaded abstraction from the client's response repertory that the counselor calls scholastic aptitude of $X$ magnitude. In terms of what the counselor knows and feels about such a diagnostic label, he is prepared to draw inferences and manipulate the symbol in an attempt to help the student solve his problem and receive better grades. Note, however, that the scholastic aptitude test score is not the student's academic response repertory. Here, then, in using tests as diagnostic tools, we employ the process of abstraction in much the same way as we do when we attempt to generalize from the client's own description of his experiences. Both are symbolic structures representing but not duplicating objective reality. Both are subject to the same errors of confusing the level of abstraction. The counselor must keep constantly in mind that the symbol is not the objective event.

What has been said about abstraction in problem identification may be summarized in a general principle which holds that each object, event, condition, etc., occurring in nature or in symbolic reality is unique, having no exact counterpart. Thus, not only are labels different from the events they symbolize, but no two objects, events, conditions, etc., are the same. Similarly, no object or event is exactly like itself from moment to moment. This principle of nonidentity has important implications for problem identification. If we accept the principle that no two objects, events, conditions, etc., are exactly alike and that the diagnostic label is merely a considerably removed abstraction from the event it is intended to symbolize, we must employ our diagnostic terms in new ways. Old, familiar terms as anxiety, reinforcement, scholastic aptitude, aggression, rejection, and the like do not have the same operational meanings we used to think they had. This notion may become clearer when we examine the following illustration.

Take the diagnostic statement *25th percentile on a test of scholastic aptitude.* Suppose that it represents part of the problem identification in the case of the college sophomore mentioned previously. Even if great care is exercised in manipulating this symbol to ensure that it is not mistaken for the event it is intended to symbolize, it does not provide an adequate enough description of the objective event to permit meaningful inferences. In the case of the particular student in question, the diagnostic term may symbolize some of the following: This student performed better than 25% of the students at University X on a test involving samples of rather specialized verbal and quantitative reasoning administered on the day he arrived at the university from a small, rural community. This performance happened after one of the student's friends warned him that if he did too well on the test he would be assigned to an advanced section of the freshman English course where his chances of earning a grade better than a "C" were mighty slim indeed. All of this is quite different from saying that the student has low scholastic aptitude. The more extended diagnostic description provides more meaningful symbols to manipulate, whereas the shorthand higher-order abstraction may be misleading.

The situation is much the same in dealing with other diagnostic labels. Consider, for example, the notion of the rejected child. In the process of seeking guidance on a problem involving interpersonal relationships, a client presents the view that his parents did not want him when he was born and now hate him. If the counselor accepts this statement as given and abstracts from it the diagnostic label rejected child, he finds himself with a symbol that can be manipulated in certain ways in the problem-solving situation. If, on the other hand, the counselor encourages the client to explore the parent–child relationship further, he may and probably will find that there are situations in which the parents, in fact, did reject him, but there were also situations in which the parents displayed love and affection toward him, and there were still other situations in which they treated him in a neutral manner. Such extended descriptions of the objective-level relationships provide the counselor and the client with different diagnostic terms that operate in the problem-solving situation quite differently from the symbol rejected child.

Problem identification, then, depends in a large measure on the ability of the counselor to differentiate between events in objective reality and the symbols intended to represent them, between several orders of abstraction, and between individual events both objective and symbolic.

This situation suggests an important general principle of problem identification which may be stated somewhat as follows: *Problem identification in guidance should avoid the use of shorthand labels insofar as possible and should instead provide extensive descriptions of the objects, events, conditions, etc.* Extensive descriptions of life experiences require the identification and labeling of the unique behavior of a unique individual under a unique set of circumstances at a specific time in history. In theory, description by extension requires the identification of all elements in the situation, for only in this way can the uniqueness of a particular object, event, condition, etc., be understood and manipulated realistically within its particular structure. Since the time limitations in a human life make such complete descriptions impossible, it becomes necessary to resort to a notation device that permits us to limit the extent of our diagnostic labeling and simultaneously suggest its extensibility. The device operates as follows: A number of labels are selected for use in describing a situation. There should be a number of such terms, say, three or four for each important situation. These terms are then followed by the term etc. This term suggests that although the description is incomplete the event is capable of evoking additional symbols. Care must be exercised, however, to ensure that the use of the term etc. implies additional terms actually known to the client and counselor and does not serve simply as a means of avoiding further consideration of the matter.

Care needs to be exercised also in this extensive approach to problem identification to differentiate between those symbols that represent the client's experience and those that represent the counselor's projections of his own experiences. A certain amount of the counselor's experience will, of necessity, find its way into the diagnosis. Some of the events in the client's life can best be described in terms of normative information known to the counselor. Test performance is one example of this kind of event. Some client experiences having a heavy overlay of feeling can be described by the counselor, in the beginning at least, only in terms of the symbols he has used to describe his own similar emotions. As guidance progresses, however, the symbols provided by the client will be substituted for the counselor's original labels. The greatest danger, of course, occurs when the counselor mistakes his own idiosyncratic labels for those of the client and tries to draw inferences about the structure of the event without being aware of the difference.

Extensive labeling in problem identification provides certain safeguards against frequently committed diagnostic errors. It provides a safeguard against the possibility of treating the symbol as if it were the event it symbolizes. It reduces the chances of faulty labeling, for if the labels used are extensive enough and if the conditions of each event are adequately specified, terms that are inconsistent with the general outline of the situation soon become evident. Finally, extensive labeling will aid in preventing the client from developing erroneous perceptions or stimulus functions for events and thus facilitate his clarification of objective events as they occur.

The process of problem identification is designed to provide a structure of events and client behavior that can be manipulated in the later stages of the problem-solving process. As indicated earlier, this structure is composed not of the objective events but of symbols representing these events. It is essential, therefore, that the symbols provide an accurate representation of objective reality. The ways in which these symbols are abstracted from the events will, in part, determine their degree of congruence with objective reality.

Among the methods of securing problem identification data, the following are the most common: the diagnostic interview in which the client provides labels for events as he perceives them; testing which can provide indirect observations of the behavior under consideration—cognitive functioning, interests, personality structure, and the like; records of performance, as for example, cumulative school records, employment records, medical records, and the like, which can provide information on the nature and level of past performance; and direct observation of the client's behavior both in and outside the guidance situation. Each of these methods can provide data essential to identifying some problem faced by the client. Although all may not be relevant to a particular problem, each can serve the important function of extensive labeling, thus acting as a check on the internal consistency of the identified structure.

Once the problem has been identified, or at least partially identified, the counselor and his client collaboratively initiate the second phase of the problem-solving process, structural planning.

This step in the process involves making some estimate of the kinds of solutions that might be reached. Here the client's values are examined in the light of social values. His long-term goals and immediate behavioral objectives are tested against his values and the values and objectives of his society. The degree of reality of each of these is assessed; and, finally, alternative solutions to the problem are considered, and the probability of their being achieved is estimated. This assessment of possible solutions to the problem is, of course, carried on in a collaborative manner. The counselor, out of his considerable experience and understanding, suggests general courses of action. The client particularizes these to his own situation.

This seeking of possible solutions is, necessarily, carried on at the symbolic level of behavior. As these symbols are manipulated to form possible solutions, they take shape as components of a symbolic context element. The client reacts symbolically to stimulus functions that emerge from this symbolic environmental context and produces, among other things, feeling responses. Some of the feeling reaction to these collaboratively developed solutions will take the form of anxiety reduction. When the possible solution "feels good" to the client, that is, when one of the solutions tends to reduce the anxiety brought on by the problem, that solution becomes one of the alternatives to be given serious consideration in subsequent steps in the guidance process.

Problem identification provides the client and the counselor with an understanding of the behavioral events in the problem situation. The general nature of the difficulty and its sources are disclosed through extensive description. Inconsistencies, disorder, and overgeneralizations in the client's behavior are uncovered. Effective problem identification can lead to insight.

But insight is not enough; it is no substitute for structural planning. To know that behavior is ineffective and leads to confusion, frustration, and anxiety, even to know why it is so, does not lead inevitably to remediation. To be sure, in many if not most of life's day-to-day problem situations, the detection of behavior deviations from certain prescribed limits is usually adequate stimulation for the initiation of the necessary corrective action. The student who becomes aware that he is about to fail a course because he is not studying enough prepares a study schedule and follows it until he achieves the level of proficiency he has set for himself. This student is able to undertake corrective behavior because it is already an intimate element of his behavior repertory, having been learned previously.

A client seeking guidance, however, has generally tried those behavior products at his disposal, only to find them ineffective. Often, before he seeks help, he knows what his problem is, and frequently he is aware of many of the sources of his difficulty. These insights do not automatically evoke corrective behavior, because the behavior just is not available to him. Similarly, it would appear to be unreasonable to expect any additional insights derived from the process of problem identification to activate corrective behavior for the same reason. The troubled individual cannot be expected to initiate corrective action if the required behavior products are not a part of his immediate operating behavior repertory. *Insight into the nature and causes of noxious behavioral events can activate corrective behavior only when the appropriate behavior has previously been acquired and is available for release.*

This suggests that there may be several possible impediments to the activation of corrective behavior in the face of some obstruction to on-going activity. On the one hand, the individual may never have acquired the behavior, so that no amount of insight, however derived, can release it. On the other hand, appropriate corrective behavior may be a part of the client's behavior repertory, but it may be momentarily inoperative because it has not been sufficiently well mastered to be effective on call or because it was learned in a context different from the present one and hence does not seem appropriate to the present problem; or, it may be made ineffective (suppressed or repressed) because of some special conditions in the present environmental context. If the necessary behavior products have been acquired previously but are not immediately available for one of these reasons, it is possible that the insights acquired through problem identification may be adequate to activate them.

Since most individuals have developed a fairly extensive behavior repertory by the time they have reached adolescence, and since most studies of guidance, counseling, and psychotherapy have been conducted with adolescents and adults, it is not surprising that practitioners and students of these processes have given so much emphasis to the role of insight in problem solving. To be sure, insight is frequently followed by corrective action with little apparent further intervention by the counselor. More often, however, the behavior that has been ineffective in coping with the problem seems resistant to change even when both cognitive and affective insight appear to have been achieved.

The reasons for this factor seem quite obvious when the needed behavior has never been acquired by the client. They are less obvious when the behavior seems to be available or ought to be available but does not seem to be evoked by the insights. The case of inadequately mastered behavior can be explained and treated in much the same way as behavior that has never been acquired. Some form of remediation training or reconditioning seems called for rather than simple insight. When insight fails to evoke previously acquired behavior in situations in which the environmental context differs from that in which the responses were previously learned, or when events in the present situation acquire stimulus functions that are repressive rather than facilitative to the previously learned responses, it becomes necessary to provide a new set of structural relationships between stimulus functions and responses within which the previously acquired corrective behavior can be performed.

Since the new behavior or the new structural relationships for previously acquired behavior are not already available to the client in guidance, the counselor must intervene.

In essence, structural planning involves generalizing from the behavior performed in the problem situation to new behavior that is likely to resolve the problem. The structural-planning process produces a set of alternative courses of action that promise to provide relief in the client's present situation. These courses of action are given symbolic reality and are projected into the client's future. The client responds symbolically to these future events. Some seem to "feel right"; others do not; and some evoke ambiguous feeling responses. As possible solutions to the problem are collaboratively developed, the client projects them into the future and "tries each one on for size." From what he knows about his own past satisfactions and frustrations, he is able to make some estimates of the kinds of feeling responses that are likely to be evoked by these events projected into the future. This anticipation of future reinforcements is what Mowrer (8) calls hope and fear. By estimating the affective consequences of future events in terms of his own past experiences, the client is able to accept some solutions, reject others, and retain still others for later reexamination as events unfold in objective reality.

Effective structural planning yields a set of fairly clearly defined yet flexible symbolic behavior products that, in terms of the client's previously acquired behavior and the environmental context in which he will be functioning, have a high probability of occurring. This plan is a symbolic map of the client's psychological terrain, which permits him to chart a course between his present disordered state and his psychological destination, characterized by productivity, self-actualization, and serenity. We should more properly speak of maps than map, for structural planning yields not a single best course to satisfaction but rather a series of alternate routes, any one of which can be expected to lead to satisfaction. Human behavior and satisfactions being as flexible and multidimensional as they are, it is highly improbable that any single stream of events is the only appropriate channel for an individual. Williamson and Darley (16) emphasize multipotentiality as a crucial factor in the guidance process.

The structural-planning phase of guidance is used to map out a set of alternatives that have a reasonably high probability of aiding the client in moving forward and overcoming the obstacles in his path. This mapping is accomplished by utilizing those elements available in the client's behavior repertory as revealed in the problem-identification phase and adding to them alternatives drawn from the counselor's own experience. Selection of alternatives is governed by an overriding value, which has here been viewed as order, leading to available energy in the client's behavior structure. The client selects from among the alternatives considered those that, in terms of his past experience, give promise of having satisfying consequences. He also accomplishes this selection in terms of the degree to which each alternative contributes to his sense of order. Those alternatives he selects are organized into the client's structural plan for resolving his present difficulty.

Throughout the structural planning, care is taken to ensure that the client is made aware of the operation of the process, so that he is able not only to solve his current problem but also to acquire more effective problem-solving behavior.

The selection of possible alternative outcomes to a problem does not, however, solve the problem. Now comes the difficult and often tedious process of selecting and implementing the means of executing the solution to the problem. Again, the counselor suggests general means by which the alternative solutions may be achieved. Depending on his appraisal of the situation, the counselor may make these as direct suggestions, or he may manipulate the situation in such a way as to call forth the suggestion from the client himself. In carrying on this phase of the guidance process, the counselor may manipulate objects and events symbolically, as in face-to-face counseling; he may manipulate events by providing information, as in group guidance; he may manipulate events by direct personal intervention, as when he writes an employment recommendation or arranges for necessary remedial instruction; or he may manipulate events subtly, as when he reinforces certain client responses by saying merely "Uh-huh," and extinguishes others by saying nothing. Whatever his method, the counselor at this stage in the guidance process assumes a basic responsibility, which he cannot successfully abdicate, for manipulating events either symbolically or directly. This manipulation of objects and events in the client's objective or symbolic environment gives them new structure and clothes them in new meaning so that they will serve as new stimulus functions for the evocation of new patterns of response. As the client performs some of these new responses, he finds that the anxiety brought on by the obstacles to his fulfillment is reduced. Since the anxiety provided the energy necessary to the random, irrelevant behavior that was inappropriate to the solution of the problem, its reduction serves to reduce the number and frequency of random behavior products as well as to reduce the probability of their occurrence. Hence, with the number of inappropriate behavior products diminished, the behavior products that are appropriate to the solution of the problem have a higher probability of occurring in the newly structured situation. Goal-seeking energy appropriate to the corrective behavior is installed by the collaborative manipulation of the context element. Thus, when the context-element configuration reappears, the previously performed appropriate responses will be evoked again. If these responses are merely the symbolic responses that occur in the verbal interchange of the guidance situation, they must subsequently be translated into objective behavior. This phase of the guidance process, involving the selection and implementation of means of achieving possible solutions to the problem, may be called therapy or, perhaps more appropriately in the present context, structural activation.

What takes place in structural activation is something like this: Structural planning provides symbolic alternatives that appear to be appropriate in solving the client's problem. These symbols are now associated with symbols already a part of the client's repertory of symbolic behavior in such a way as to provide new meaning for these symbols. This permits (requires?) the client to begin responding in new ways. At first these responses will be the symbolic responses involved in the client-counselor interchange.

As these symbolic responses are reinforced by the counselor, they will become reference signals for subsequent behavior. Some of this subsequent behavior, of course, will still be verbal exchanges with others outside the counselor's office. If the feedback on these occasions demonstrates that the client tends to achieve the equilibrium of Miller (6) or the serenity previously considered, the state of affairs symbolized by the new word meanings learned in counseling will become established as effective reference signals for maintaining the desired state. Thus, as conditions develop over time to the state where the appropriate stimuli are available, the client will translate the talk of the consultation room and the social gathering into action. The meanings of the words will move to the events the words symbolize.

Since structural activation takes place by having new meanings—stimulus functions or reference signals—associated with events that, therefore, evoke new and more appropriate responses from the individual, and since these new meanings depend upon the organism's having these signs already available in his repertory, it must be clear that no behavior change could occur unless the required signs were already available to the client. Expecting to reorganize meanings or to give new meanings when the signs are not available would be like expecting a computer to perform the squaring operation without ensuring first that it had been wired to perform the process of multiplication.

The counselor must, therefore, proceed in a gradual step-by-step manner to build up the semantic generalizations appropriate to the kind of structural activation essential to the solution of the client's problem. This concept means that when new meanings not previously available in the client's repertory are required, these must be built up. This buildup may be accomplished either by reorganizing meanings already available and associating them with the new sign or by associating the new sign with closely related satisfying behavior presently being performed by the client. The first of these methods involves manipulation of symbols alone, and it is common in the guidance consultation. The second, however, involves manipulation of the environmental input in such a way as to produce the essential conditions for the acquisition of the necessary understandings.

Guidance has achieved its first goal when the client translates his plan into action and thus overcomes the obstacles to his on-going behavior. The immediate problem that drove the client to seek guidance begins to be solved when the client learns new modes of attack not previously available to him. The process by which the counselor and client collaboratively achieve this translation of plan into action relies heavily on language.

In the process of structural activation new meanings are first associated with symbols already available to the client. These new meanings are then moved forward to the events they symbolize, so that the client can now respond to these new meanings (stimulus functions) of objective events in new ways. These new meanings associated with external events and internal responses become the reference signals required by the individual to guide his behavior toward effective, active organization—that is, toward serenity.

If the entire guidance experience is to take on any meaning beyond that of solving the immediate problem, the counselor must see to it that the client's original question, "How do I solve problems like this?" is answered. The methods by which the immediate problem was solved must be generalized to other similar problems. Depending upon the maturity of the client and hence his ability to abstract principles, this process of generalization involves several modes of attack. In almost any general problem presented by the client there are several subordinate problems. As solutions to the latter are reached, the counselor may point out the methods by which they were solved, or he may manipulate the client's behavior in such a way—as is done with the nondirective techniques—as to draw from him the essential generalizations. Often when a client has received assistance in solving one problem, he will return to the counselor for help with another matter if he has not already learned how to apply the general problem-solving procedures. Under such circumstances, the counselor can use the earlier problem-solving experience as a source from which generalizations can be drawn.

In guidance we wish the client to apply the principles of problem solving learned in one situation to new situations as they arise. If he has acquired the responses necessary to solve one problem and has mastered them adequately to perform them with skill, we need to ensure that new problems as they arise produce stimuli that are similar to those found in the original problem so that they will evoke these previously learned problem-solving responses. It must be obvious, however, that the stimuli from one human problem to the next rarely have even a superficial similarity. In real life, even in the real life of a monkey outside Dr. Harlow's (4) laboratory, generalization of stimuli must be subtly mediated, generally by means of symbolic stimuli. The student who has learned to make satisfactory decisions about the courses he takes in high school may find himself in a relatively similar context when it comes time to choose his college major. Many of the stimuli—the body of courses from which he may choose, the administrative demands of the curricula, his own academic strengths and weaknesses, and his ultimate vocational goals—have a kind of generality that can call up stimulus functions similar to the ones evoked by the high school situation and thus result in satisfying interactions with the responses acquired in the former situation and applied to the present one. What appears to happen is that stimulus generalization is established from a single encounter with a somewhat similar stimulus configuration in the past. In the main, and even when we include the impact of the mediating influence of language, stimulus generalization is not such a one-shot affair.

In human experience what appears to be the application of generalizations derived from a limited number of encounters with similar stimuli turns out to be the abstraction, by means of symbolic processes, of principles drawn from a wide variety of experiences that have embedded in their contexts a few similar elements. Unless this were the case, we would be unable to account for a student learning something about choosing courses from his high school experience and then applying this information to the new problem of selecting a major field of study in college, meanwhile acquiring additional problem-solving skill that he can later apply to the problem of vocational selection or social orientation; the stimuli, on the surface at least, show little evidence of similarity. In a lifetime an individual encounters many problems and faces many decisions, no two of which ever appear to have the same external elements. Even such similarities as they may have are rarely obvious or clearly identifiable on the objective level. Yet man manages to survive these crises, in the main, and to maintain a serene progress toward his chosen objectives. How does he manage to do this when the stimuli he encounters in each new situation appear to be so uniquely dissimilar?

In part, he is able to make the shifts from one situation to another by reason of his ability to abstract and symbolize. His main aid, however, is his ability to generalize about behavior generalization. He learns that certain basic principles appear to function effectively in a variety of situations. In short, the stimuli that generalize from one situation to the next are not the events of objective reality but, rather, symbolic events of a high order of abstraction, organized into a structure that conforms to the individual's generalizations about generalizations. This process is, in effect, a two-step one. Elements in a situation are given a more general form through the processes of symbolization and abstraction; they are, then, reorganized in terms of the generalizing principles appropriate to problem solving. The organizing principles that permit stimuli to generalize from one decision problem to the next are those that we have been considering thus far: problem identification, structural planning, and structural activation. In this way the total problem-solving behavior product becomes the stimulus, which is first abstracted, given meaning, and then generalized to new situations.

The final step in the process of problem-centered guidance is evaluation. This step tells the counselor whether or not his goals for guidance were achieved. Evaluation permits him to answer two major questions, "Was the behavior of the client redirected into more productive channels?" and "Did the client acquire the necessary problem-solving behavior that will permit him to meet new emergencies as they arise?" Secondarily, the counselor needs to know which of his approaches and techniques were most effective and which turned out to be inadequate in achieving these goals of guidance. The practice of guidance is a learning process for the counselor as well as for the client. He must, therefore, be able to make some reasonable appraisal of his present effectiveness in order to revise and improve his performance in the future.

Evaluation of guidance requires the careful observation of client behavior during and subsequent to his participation in guidance, as well as a clearly defined value structure against which the observed behavior can be measured. Simply asking the client how he feels about his guidance experience is an inadequate and often misleading measure of its effectiveness.

What appears to be required is a standard of behavior. This standard is derivable from the application of energy concepts to the behavior product model. Using a somewhat different model of behavior, Powers, Clark, and McFarland indicate a similar conclusion when they state:

> In the optimum system, no significant conflict exists, so that all systems important to behavior are free to operate over their full range without internal opposition. . . . It is capable of modifying its systems as rapidly as changes in the environment may require.
>
> If the organism is in this state, it is performing properly; there is nothing wrong with it. The person perfectly organized in this respect can still fall into conflict with himself, but the . . . system is capable of finding solutions if they exist. The person is still subject to the limitations of his environment, to distortion of false information and the illusions inherent in the geometry of perception. The person may be a saint or a sinner, but he will not be mentally incapacitated.
>
> There is no morality inherent in our theoretical structure, although the phenomenon of moralizing can be easily described in its framework. The definition of an optimum FBCS (feedback control system) hierarchy reflects our personal preferences—we prefer to see people performing "up to specs," regardless of what they choose to do, and it is toward this end that we choose to work. (10, p. 322)

## GUIDANCE: AN INTERACTING PROCESS

The foregoing outline of guidance practice may leave the reader with the false notion that the steps discussed are sequential. To be sure, the problem situation is a precondition to guidance. This is to say that an obstacle to current behavior must intervene and anxiety must result from the unsuccessful attempts to overcome the obstacle. Beyond this, the steps in the guidance process follow no formal sequence. Although problem identification will usually precede structural planning, and it, in turn, will be followed by structural activation, generalization, and evaluation in that order, several of these phases are often carried on simultaneously. As a partial identification of the problem is made, it leads to some hypotheses about possible courses of action and the means for carrying them out. This development, in turn, often forces the process back to further diagnosis, which will help sharpen the structural plan and provide estimates of the client's capabilities for executing the steps leading to the solution. Throughout the processes of identification, structural planning, and structural activation, generalizations will be abstracted as they become evident. Intermediate evaluations are being made as the whole enterprise proceeds.

Since guidance is a collaborative behavioral effort, each set of responses as they are performed becomes a part of the reactional biographies and hence a component of the context elements in the next behavior products of both counselor and client. The stimulus functions that may arise from these context elements may evoke identification, structural planning, structural activation, generalization, or evaluative responses, depending on the total configuration of the context elements.

All this suggests that the mode of attack in guidance is not a step-by-step, formal approach to problem solving. All strategies are brought to bear at once. The practice of guidance demands a high degree of flexibility on the part of the counselor. Guidance requires of its practitioners that they be highly skilled in the use of these strategies, that they be sensitive to the appropriateness of a particular strategy at each stage in guidance, and that they exercise this sensitivity and skill with a high sense of responsible purpose.

## REFERENCES

1. Arbuckle, D. S. *Counseling: philosophy, theory and practice.* Boston: Allyn and Bacon, 1965.
2. Brewer, J. M. *Education as guidance.* New York: Macmillan Co., 1938.
3. Davis, J. B. *Vocational and moral guidance.* Boston: Ginn and Co., 1914.
4. Harlow, H. F. The formation of learning sets. *Psychol. Rev.,* 1949, **56,** 51–65.
5. Kantor, J. R. *A survey of the science of psychology.* Bloomington, Ind.: Principia Press, 1933.
6. Miller, J. G. General behavior systems theory and summary. In E. J. Shoben, Behavior theories and a counseling case: a symposium. *J. Counsel. Psychol.,* 1956, **3,** 120–124.
7. Mowrer, O. H. *Learning theory and behavior.* New York: John Wiley and Sons, 1960. (a)

8. Mowrer, O. H. *Learning theory and the symbolic process.* New York: John Wiley and Sons, 1960. (b)

9. Parsons, F. *Choosing a vocation.* Boston: Houghton Mifflin, 1909.

10. Powers, W. T., Clark, R. K., & McFarland, R. L. A general feedback theory of human behavior, *Part II. Perceptual and motor skills,* 1960, **11,** 309–323 (Monogr. Suppl. 3, No. 7).

11. Rogers, C. R. *Counseling and psychotherapy.* Boston: Houghton Mifflin, 1942.

12. Rogers, C. R. The interpersonal relationship, the core of guidance. *Harvard Educ. Rev.,* 1962, **32,** 416–429.

13. Stanley, W. O. The collapse of automatic adjustment. *Education and social integration.* New York: Bureau of Publications, Teachers College, Columbia University, 1953, pp. 192–206.

14. van Kamm, A. Counseling from the viewpoint of existential psychology. *Harvard Educ. Rev.,* 1962, **32,** 402–415.

15. Weitz, H. *Behavior change through guidance.* New York: John Wiley and Sons, 1964.

16. Williamson, E. G., & Darley, J. G. *Student personnel work.* New York: McGraw-Hill, 1937.